Lecture Notes in Computer Science 7809

Commenced Publication in 1973
Founding and Former Series Editors:
Gerhard Goos, Juris Hartmanis, and Jan van Leeuwen

Yun Q. Shi   Hyoung-Joong Kim
Fernando Pérez-González (Eds.)

Digital Forensics and Watermaking

11th International Workshop, IWDW 2012
Shanghai, China, October 31 – November 3, 2012
Revised Selected Papers

 Springer

Volume Editors

Yun Q. Shi
New Jersey Institute of Technology
323 M. L. King Blvd., Newark, NJ 07102, USA
E-mail: shi@njit.edu

Hyoung-Joong Kim
Korea University
Science Campus, Anam-dong Seongbuk-Gu
136-701 Seoul, South Korea
E-mail: khj@korea.ac.kr

Fernando Pérez-González
University of Vigo
EE Telecomunicacion, 36310 Vigo, Spain
E-mail: fperez@gts.uvigo.es

ISSN 0302-9743   e-ISSN 1611-3349
ISBN 978-3-642-40098-8   e-ISBN 978-3-642-40099-5
DOI 10.1007/978-3-642-40099-5
Springer Heidelberg Dordrecht London New York

Library of Congress Control Number: 2013944323

CR Subject Classification (1998): E.3, K.4.1, K.6.5, I.3, I.4, E.4, H.4, H.2.8

LNCS Sublibrary: SL 4 – Security and Cryptology

Typesetting: Camera-ready by author, data conversion by Scientific Publishing Services, Chennai, India

Printed on acid-free paper

Springer is part of Springer Science+Business Media (www.springer.com)

Preface

The International Workshop on Digital Forensics and Watermarking 2012 (IWDW12), hosted by Shanghai Jiao Tong University, was held in Shanghai, China, from October 31 to November 3, 2012.

Following the tradition of IWDW, IWDW12 aimed to provide a strong technical program to cover advanced theoretical and practical developments in the field of digital watermarking, steganography and steganalysis, forensics and anti-forensics, and other multimedia-related security topics. With 70 submissions from 20 different countries and areas, the Technical Committee selected 42 (27 oral and 15 poster) papers for presentation at IWDW12, one paper for the best student paper award, and one for the best paper award. Jianhua Li, the Dean of School of Information Security Engineering at Shanghai Jiao Tong University, in his welcome speech introduced the rapid development of Zhang Jiang Hi-Tech Park, where IWDW12 was held. There were three invited lectures. The first was entitled "Advanced Research in JPEG Steganography" given by Vasilii Sachnev; the second entitled "Counter-Forensics: The Art of Misleading" delivered by Rainer Böhme; the third entitled "Reversible Data Hiding in Encrypted Images" presented by Xinpeng Zhang. In addition, there was a 90-minute open discussion in the late afternoon of November 2.

First of all, we would like to thank all the authors, lecturers, and participants for their valuable contributions to the success of IWDW12. Our sincere gratitude also goes to all the members of the Technical Program Committee and several volunteer reviewers whose names have been included in the proceedings. Appreciation also goes to the International Publicity Liaisons. We appreciate the nice local arrangements and tremendous organizing work that were done by the Organizing Committee consisting of Shenghong Li (Co-chair), Shilin Wang (Co-chair), Aixin Zhang, Xiuzhen Chen, Xinghao Jiang, Lu Tang, and Weijun Huang.

Finally, we hope that the readers will enjoy reading this volume and that it will provide inspiration and opportunities for their future research.

March 2012

Yun Qing Shi
Hyoung Joong Kim
Fernando Perez-Gonzalez

Organization

General Chairs

Jian Hua Li   Shanghai Jiaotong University, China
Heung Youl Youm   KIISC, Korea

Technical Program Chairs

Yun Q. Shi   NJIT, USA
Hyoung Joong Kim   Korea University, Korea
Fernando Perez-Gonzalez   University Vigo, Spain

International Publicity Liaisons

Ton Kalker   Huawei, USA
Nasir Memon   NYU-Poly, USA
Anthony TS Ho   University of Surrey, UK
Stefan Katzenbeisser   TUD, Germany
Heung-Kyu Lee   University KAIST, Korea
Jiwu Huang   Sun Yat-sen University, China

Technical Program Committee

Lee-Ming Cheng   City University, Hong Kong, China
Jana Dittmann   University of Magdeburg, Germany
Jean-Luc Dugelay   Eurecom, France
Dongdong Fu   Intel, USA
Miroslav Goljan   SUNY, Binghamton, USA
Xiangui Kang   Sun Yat-sen University, China
Mohan Kankanhalli   National University, Singapore
Darko Kirovski   MS, USA
Alex Kot   NTU, Singapore
C.-C. Jay Kuo   USC, USA
Chang-Tsun Li   University Warwick, UK
Shenghong Li   Shanghai Jiaotong University, China
Jiang Qun Ni   Sun Yat-sen University, China
Alessandro Piva   University of Florence, Italy
Yong-Man Ro   KAIST, Korea
Kouichi Sakurai   Kyushu University, Japan
Hans Georg Schaathun   Ålesund University College, Norway
Ashwin Swaminathan   Qualcomm, USA
Shilin Wang   Shanghai Jiaotong University, China

Andreas Westfeld	HTW Dresden, Germany
Weiqi Yan	AUT, New Zealand
Hongbin Zhang	Beijing University Tech., China
Xinpeng Zhang	Shanghai University, China
Yao Zhao	Beijing Jiao Tung University, China
Dekun Zou	Amazon, California, USA
Abdelrahman Desoky	Academia Planet, USA

Volunteer Reviewers

Anthony Ts Ho	University of Surrey
Dawen Xu	Ningbo University of Technology, China
Feng Liu	Institute of Information Engineering, Chinese Academy of Sciences, Beijing, China
Guorong Xuan	Tongji University
Hao-Tian Wu	Sun Yat-sen University
Heung Kyu Lee	Dept. of Computer Science, KAIST, South Korea
Hong Zhao	Fairleigh Dickinson University
Jingyu Ye	New Jersey Institute of Technology
Jiwu Huang	Sun Yat-sen University
Nasir Memon	NYU Poly
Patchara Sutthiwan	New Jersey Institute of Technology
Peng Meng	Intel Asia-Pacific Research and Development Ltd., Shanghai, China
Rui Yang	Sun Yat-sen University
Takaaki Yamada	Hitachi, Japan
Tanfeng Sun	Shanghai Jiaotong University
Vasiliy Sachnev	Korea University
Wen Chen	New Jersey Institute of Technology, USA
Xinghao Jiang	Shanghai Jiaotong University
Yasushi Yamaguchi	The University of Tokyo, Graduate School of Arts and Sciences
Yiu-Ming Cheung	Hong Kong Baptist University
Zhaohong Li	Beijing Jiaotong University
Zhili Chen	University of Science and Technology of China

Organizing Committee

Shenghong Li (Co-chair)	Shanghai Jiaotong University, China
Shilin Wang (Co-chair)	Shanghai Jiaotong University, China
Aixin Zhang	Shanghai Jiaotong University, China
Xiuzhen Chen	Shanghai Jiaotong University, China
Xinghao Jiang	Shanghai Jiaotong University, China
Lu Tang	Shanghai Jiaotong University, China
Weijun Huang	Shanghai Jiaotong University, China

Advanced Research in JPEG Steganography

Vasiliy Sachnev

Catholic University of Korea
bassvasys@hotmail.com

The extreme growth of the communication technologies (i.e., internet, mobile communication) keeps attention on many aspects of information security. Important pieces of information have to be protected from threats and malicious actions. Hence, the steganography can be a very efficient tool for achieving high level of security. One of the most important purposes of information security is to hide existence of the secret information. Here, the secret message has to be hidden to a cover signal (i.e., image, sound, or text). The modified image with hidden data has to be statistically undetectable from unmodified images. Such approach enables an undetectable communication by sending both unmodified and modified images. Recent advantages in steganography keep interest among researchers to design new steganographic schemes with better performances.

Counter-Forensics: The Art of Misleading
Extended Abstract

Rainer Böhme

Department of Information Systems, University of Münster, Germany
rainer.boehme@uni-muenster.de

1 Keynote Summary

Counter-forensics is the art and science of impeding or misleading forensic analyses of digital images. Research on counter-forensics is motivated by the need to assess and improve the reliability of forensic methods in situations where intelligent opponents make efforts to falsify evidence. Another, less recognized but arguably equally important motivation is the use of counter-forensics to protect the privacy of sources of media data, for example to protect witnesses and whistleblowers. If a witness captures a crime scene with her mobile phone camera and the police includes this image in a "wanted" circular, she would not like the criminal's accomplices to link this picture to her Facebook profile using, for instance, the inherent sensor noise fingerprint.

The keynote speaker presented digital forensics as a decision problem threatened by attempts to induce false decisions using counter-forensics. He surveyed the state of the art of counter-forensics against image forensics, subsuming techniques to suppress traces of image processing and techniques to synthesize traces of authenticity. The keynote concluded with a broader discussion of relations to other domains in multimedia security, such as steganography and watermarking.

The arguments and examples presented were largely drawn from [1], so interested reader are referred to this source. Two points of the keynote are still unpublished to date and therefore outlined in the following sections. Section 2 briefly presents the "Shanghai Conjecture" on the relation between counter-forensic techniques based on adding randomness and steganographic security. In a more entertaining tone, Section 3 documents the speaker's interpretation of selected Chinese stratagems, taken from Sun Tzu's (544–496 BC) famous book "The Art of War", for applications in counter-forensics, the "Art of Misleading".

2 On the Difficulty of Undetectable Counter-Forensics

Conjecture 1 (Shanghai Conjecture). Counter-forensics by introducing random noise is at least as difficult as secure steganography.

Proof (Sketch). Replace the noise source with an encrypted and appropriately encoded message. Then the counter-forensic method becomes an embedding function. As a result, any steganalysis method that can distinguish between cover and stego object can also distinguish post-processed from authentic images. Conversely, if the counter-forensic method is secure and the encrypted message indistinguishable from random bits, then no algorithm can distinguish between post-processed (i. e., stego object) and unprocessed (i. e., cover) images. Hence we can construct a secure steganographic channel from this counter-forensic method and any encryption system that produces pseudo-random ciphertext.

Remark 1. Reasoning about the capacity of this steganographic channel is intentionally beyond the scope of this proof sketch. This aspects needs further attention when developing the conjecture into a theorem. Also the treatment of encoding remains superficial in this proof sketch. It is therefore an interesting open problem whether the conjecture or a weaker variant can actually be proven. Clearly, any such proof needs more specific assumptions on the nature of covers.

Remark 2. The conjecture only concerns the subset of counter-forensic methods that try to hide traces in random noise. The implication does not generalize to all counter-forensic methods. This raises the question whether adding random noise is a good idea at all. In fact, it might be suboptimal in general. So secure counter-forensics *not* relying on adding randomness might well exist even if constructing secure steganographic channels (for empirical covers) remains a hard problem.

3   Sun Tzu's View on Image Forensics

Our understanding of forensics and counter-forensics is a cat-and-mouse game between two opponents who try to strategically outsmart each other. When talking about it in China, it stands to reason to frame selected aspects with ancient stratagems bequeathed by Sun Tzu, an influential Chinese military strategist from the Zhou Dynasty.

For example, the creator of the forgery in Fig. 1 followed this stratagem:

Stratagem 1. 树 上 开 花 — *"Deck the tree with false blossoms."*

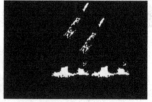

Fig. 1. Left: image depicting a missile test as published by the Iranian Revolutionary Guards in 2008; center: alleged original image; right: detector output. Source: [2]

The speaker recalled that successful counter-forensics requires two skills, first avoiding or removing suspicious traces of image processing, and second restoring plausible device characteristics. In Sun Tzu's words:

Stratagem 2. 连 环 计 — *"Combine stratagems."*

The success of forensic analyses crucially depends on the amount of information in the suspect image, that is the available image quality. A common strategy to thwart forensic investigations is to provide photographic evidence in very low resolution and with high compression rates. Again, Sun Tzu anticipated this:

Stratagem 3. 浑 水 摸 鱼 — *"Disturb the water and catch a fish."*

Resampling detection algorithms exploit a periodic grid of interpolation weights. Geometric distortion is the method of choice to impede this analysis, or:

Stratagem 4. 偷 梁 换 柱 — *"Replace the beams with rotten timbers."*

Image processing destroys the typical color filter array (CFA) interpolation pattern present in most authentic images. CFA synthesis helps to insert a plausible pattern into arbitrary images.

Stratagem 5. 无 中 生 有 — *"Creating something out of nothing."*

How to falsify an input device fingerprint? Well, just ...

Stratagem 6. 借 尸 还 魂 — *"Borrow a corpse to resurrect a soul."*

Most recently, researchers started to investigate counter-techniques against counter-forensics. Some methods presented are borrowed from the field of steganalysis, such as calibration of JPEG histograms. Sun Tzu knew this trick:

Stratagem 7. 借 刀 杀 人 — *"Kill with a borrowed knife."*

Finally, after a lively discussion, the speaker had to resort to a final stratagem and left the stage:

Stratagem 8. 走 为 上 — *"If all else fails, retreat."*

Acknowledgements. I thank Yun-Qing Shi and the IWDW 2012 organizers for their invitation and hospitality, and Shi-Yue Lai for her advice on the right interpretation and spelling of Sun Tzu's stratagems. All errors and omissions are my own.

References

1. Böhme, R., Kirchner, M.: Counter-forensics: Attacking image forensics. In: Sencar, H.T., Memon, N.D. (eds.) Digital Image Forensics: There is More to a Picture Than Meets the Eye, pp. 327–366. Springer, NY (2012)
2. Böhme, R., Freiling, F.C., Gloe, T., Kirchner, M.: Multimedia Forensics Is Not Computer Forensics. In: Geradts, Z.J.M.H., Franke, K.Y., Veenman, C.J. (eds.) IWCF 2009. LNCS, vol. 5718, pp. 90–103. Springer, Heidelberg (2009)

Reversible Data Hiding in Encrypted Images

Xinpeng Zhang

School of Communication and Information Engineering, Shanghai University
xzhang@shu.edu.cn

In some scenarios, when a content owner encrypts original images as unintelligible data for privacy protection, an inferior assistant or a channel administrator may hope to append some additional data, such as the origin information, image notation or authentication data, within the cipher-text images though he does not know the plaintext content. And it is also desired that the original plaintext content can be recovered without any error after image decryption and data extraction at receiver side. This talk will survey the concepts, principles and methods of reversible data hiding in encrypted images. For the cipher-text images produced by selective encryption methods, it is straightforward to use conventional techniques to perform reversible data hiding in the un-encrypted part. For the completely encrypted images by stream cipher, by exploiting the spatial correlation in natural image and the lossless compression of encrypted data, the embedded data can be successfully extracted in either the plain or encrypted domain, while the original plaintext content can be perfectly recovered after data decryption. When the additional data are embedded using a pseudorandom sequence modulation mechanism, the data extraction can be implemented in both the plain and encrypted domains. We will also discuss the potential directions of further investigations.

Table of Contents

Invited Lectures (Abstracts)

Session 1: Steganography and Steganalysis

Session 2: Watermarking and Copyright Protection

Session 3: Forensics and Anti-Forensics

Session 4: Reversible Data Hiding

Session 5: Fingerprinting and Authentication

Session 6: Visual Cryptography

Session 7: Others

New Channel Selection Criterion
for Spatial Domain Steganography

Yane Zhong, Fangjun Huang, and Dong Zhang

School of Information Science and Technology
Sun Yat-Sen University, Guangzhou, China, 510006

Abstract. In this paper, we propose a new channel selection criterion for spatial domain steganography. Via choosing those pixels in edge regions that may introduce minimal detectable distortion for modification, the proposed channel selection criterion can improve the security performance of the widespread block codes based matrix embedding schemes. Various experimental results tested on 5,000 grayscale images demonstrate the efficiency of our new channel selection criterion.

Keywords: steganography, block codes, matrix embedding, channel selection.

1   Introduction

Digital steganography is a new approach to transmit the secret message without arousing suspicion of the potential attackers. The carriers of steganography can be various kinds of digital media, such as image, video, and audio.

Due to the common use of images on the internet nowadays, image steganography has attracted more and more attention recently. In order to enhance the capability of resisting the steganalysis, two kinds of approaches have been proposed to improve the security performance of steganography. The first one is to improve embedding efficiency via using the error correction codes, generally called matrix embedding strategy [1–5], which can be utilized to decrease the modifications to the cover image while embedding the same number of information bits. The second one is channel selection strategy [6–8]. Through using it, the elements that may introduce minimal detectable distortion are selected for data hiding, thus the security performance of steganography can be greatly improved.

The idea of importing matrix embedding into steganography was firstly proposed by Crandall [1]. Westfeld [2] implemented it in F5 scheme, which resorts to the $(1, n, n\text{-}k)$ binary Hamming codes to embed k message bits into a discrete cosine transform (DCT) coefficient block with the length of $2^k - 1$ within at most one embedding change. A limitation for F5 scheme is that in each coefficient block, only one coefficient determined by matrix embedding can be modified. If this embedding change will introduce much distortion, the security performance of F5 scheme may greatly degrade with more and more such modifications.

Y.Q. Shi, H.J. Kim, and F. Pérez-González (Eds.): IWDW 2012, LNCS 7809, pp. 1–7, 2013.
© Springer-Verlag Berlin Heidelberg 2013

In [4], Kim et al. provided a simple and practical scheme to apply the perturbed quantization (PQ) channel selection criterion [6] to JPEG steganography, which is based on the $(t, n, n\text{-}k)$ $(t \geq 1)$ modified binary Hamming codes and allows more than one embedding changes in each coefficient block. This new embedding algorithm is called modified matrix encoding (MME). Since in each coefficient block, two or more coefficients that may introduce minimal distortion can be selected for modification, MME scheme can obtain a desirable security performance in general. According to the numbers of allowable changing bits in each coefficient block, the MME schemes are called MME2, MME3, etc. In addition to PQ criterion [6], some other channel selection criterions [7] [8] can also be employed on MME scheme to improve the security performance of JPEG steganography. As seen, compared with those schemes with one modification in each coefficient block, modifying two or more coefficients in DCT domain may introduce minimal distortion, and thus improve the security performance of JPEG steganography. This philosophy can be extended in spatial domain directly. As pointed out in [9–11], the statistical characteristics of smooth/flat regions in the cover image are rather simple, and embedding the secret message into these regions will inevitably contaminate the statistical characteristics of the cover image even at a low embedding rate. Whereas for the edge regions, since the statistical characteristics are more complicated, it will be preserved much better after data hiding. Thus the secret message should be embedded into the edge regions as much as possible.

In this paper, we propose a new channel selection criterion for spatial domain steganography. The main idea of our channel selection criterion is to find those pixels in the edge regions that may introduce minimal detectable distortion for data hiding. It is a general channel selection criterion for spatial domain steganography, and can be applied to widespread block codes based matrix embedding schemes.

The rest of this paper is organized as follows. In Section 2, the new channel selection criterion and its applications are introduced. Experimental results are illustrated in Section 3 and the conclusions are made in Section 4.

2   Proposed Channel Selection Criterion and Its Application

2.1   New Channel Selection Criterion

Generally, in block codes based matrix embedding scheme (e.g., the Hamming codes based matrix embedding scheme), the secret message bits are divided into sub-blocks of length k, and the elements (such as the pixels or DCT coefficients) of the cover image are divided into sub-blocks with the length of $2^k - 1$. The k message bits can be embedded into $2^k - 1$ elements of the carrier through modifying the LSB (least significant bit) of one pixel or coefficient in each sub-block. In order to minimize the introduced distortion, the steganographer may also select to modify the LSBs of the other two or more elements according to some channel selection criterion. For example, in [4], Kim et al. applied the PQ channel selection criterion [6] to JPEG steganography. With the utilization of modified binary Hamming codes, the steganographer can select to modify the LSBs of two or three DCT coefficients in each sub-block that may introduce minimal detectable distortion, and thus improve the security performance of the proposed JPEG steganography.

Different from that in [6], our proposed channel selection criterion is a spatial domain rule. Via using it, the steganographer can determine how to modify the pixels when the embedding is conducted with block codes based matrix embedding schemes. Without loss of generality, we assume that the dimension of the cover image $\mathbf{A}$ is $H \times W$. The gray values of the pixels in the cover image are represented as $a_{i,j}$ ($1 \leq i \leq H, 1 \leq j \leq W$), which is shown in Fig. 1. Each pixel in the cover image may be associated with a gradient value $G_{i,j}$, which is used to measure the gradient value between the current pixel and its neighbors (note that two different ways for computing the gradient value will be exemplified next in this section). In general, the pixels associated with big values of $G_{i,j}$ belong to the edge regions, and those associated with small values of $G_{i,j}$ may belong to the flat/smooth regions. According to the analysis in Section 1, in order to reduce the detectable distortion that may be introduced by data hiding, we need to embed the secret message into those edge areas which are associated with high gradient values. Thus the detectable distortion in our channel selection criterion is defined as

$$E_{i,j} = \frac{1}{G_{i,j}} \tag{1}$$

For simplicity, suppose that one of the secret message sub-blocks with k bits is $(s_1, s_2, ..., s_k)$, and the corresponding pixel sub-block with the length of $n = 2^k - 1$ for data hiding is $(p_1, p_2, ..., p_n)$. The detectable distortion values associated with the pixels are represented as $(E_1, E_2, ..., E_n)$. While conducting matrix embedding, we assume that the k secret message bits can be embedded into the pixel sub-block with two modification selections: 1) modifying the LSB of one pixel p_α; 2) modifying the LSBs of the other two pixels (p_β, p_γ). Note that $1 \leq (\alpha, \beta, \gamma) \leq n$ and the corresponding detectable distortion values associated with p_α, p_β and p_γ are represented as E_α, E_β and E_γ, respectively. Our new channel selection criterion is as follows. If inequality (2) holds, we modify the LSBs of the two pixels p_β and p_γ, otherwise we modify the LSB of the pixel p_α.

$$E_\alpha > E_\beta + E_\gamma \tag{2}$$

Note that while embedding the k secret message bits with block codes based matrix embedding strategy, we may also have some other modification selections, e.g., modifying the LSBs of three or more pixels. Our channel selection criterion can be extended easily in such a case. For simplicity, suppose the steganographer can select to modify the three pixels p_x, p_y and p_z in the aforementioned pixel sub-block (the associated detectable distortion values are represented as E_x, E_y and E_z) while embedding the k message bits. The channel selection criterion can be extended as follows. Compare the three values E_α, $(E_\beta + E_\gamma)$, and $(E_x + E_y + E_z)$. If E_α is the least among the three values, the LSB of pixel p_α is modified. If $(E_\beta + E_\gamma)$ is the least among the three values, we will modify the LSBs of pixels p_β and p_γ. Otherwise the LSBs of pixels p_x, p_y and p_z will be modified.

As mentioned above, we will introduce two ways for computing the gradient value $G_{i,j}$ at the end of this section, which are called average gradient (AG) strategy and maximum gradient (MG) strategy, respectively. As shown in Fig. 1, $a_{i,j}$ is one of pixels. According to AG strategy, the gradient value associated with $a_{i,j}$ is computed as in Eq.(3), and according to MG strategy, the gradient value associated with $a_{i,j}$ is computed as in Eq.(4).

$$G_{i,j} = (|a_{i,j} - a_{i,j-1}| + |a_{i,j} - a_{i,j+1}| + |a_{i,j} - a_{i-1,j}| + |a_{i,j} - a_{i+1,j}|) \div 4 \quad (3)$$

$$G_{i,j} = max(|a_{i,j} - a_{i,j-1}|, |a_{i,j} - a_{i,j+1}|, |a_{i,j} - a_{i-1,j}|, |a_{i,j} - a_{i+1,j}|) \quad (4)$$

Note that if $G_{i,j}$ is equal to zero, it will be set with a small value such as 10^{-3}. Some other pixels in the image may have only two or three adjacent pixels, e.g., the pixels in the first column on the left, or the pixel on the top left corner. When computing the gradient values of those pixels, only three or two neighbors will be considered in equations (3) and (4) in the light of actual conditions.

$a_{1,1}$	$\cdots$	$a_{1,j-1}$	$a_{1,j}$	$a_{1,j+1}$	$\cdots$	$a_{1,W}$
$\cdots$	$\cdots$	$\cdots$	$\cdots$	$\cdots$	$\cdots$	$\cdots$
$a_{i-1,1}$	$\cdots$	$a_{i-1,j-1}$	$a_{i-1,j}$	$a_{i-1,j+1}$	$\cdots$	$a_{i-1,W}$
$a_{i,1}$	$\cdots$	$a_{i,j-1}$	$a_{i,j}$	$a_{i,j+1}$	$\cdots$	$a_{i,W}$
$a_{i+1,1}$	$\cdots$	$a_{i+1,j-1}$	$a_{i+1,j}$	$a_{i+1,j+1}$	$\cdots$	$a_{i+1,W}$
$\cdots$	$\cdots$	$\cdots$	$\cdots$	$\cdots$	$\cdots$	$\cdots$
$a_{H,1}$	$\cdots$	$a_{H,j-1}$	$a_{H,j}$	$a_{H,j+1}$	$\cdots$	$a_{H,W}$

Fig. 1. The illustration of pixels in an image

2.2   Application of Our Channel Selection Criterion

The proposed channel selection criterion can be applied to all matrix embedding schemes based on block codes, such as Hamming codes, BCH codes. For simplicity, we will exemplify the application of our proposed channel selection criterion with MME2 embedding strategy [4], which is based on the modified binary Hamming codes.

As stated above, one of the secret message blocks with k bits is $S = (s_1, s_2, ..., s_k)$, and the corresponding pixel sub-block with the length of $n = 2^k - 1$ for data hiding is $B = (p_1, p_2, ..., p_n)$. The gradient values associated with the pixels in sub-block B are represented as $(G_1, G_2, ..., G_n)$. The message bits

$(s_1, s_2, ..., s_k)$ are embedded into the pixel sub-block $(p_1, p_2, ..., p_n)$ according to the following three steps.

Step 1: Conduct matrix embedding with $(1, n, n\text{-}k)$ binary Hamming codes to find the pixel that need to be modified in block B. Suppose the pixel that needs to be changed in block B is p_α $(1 \leq \alpha \leq n)$. Then we compute the distortion E_α according to Eq.(1). Note that if no pixel needs to be modified while embedding the k message bits, the next two steps can be neglected.

Step 2: Find the pairs of numbers (β, γ) in pixel sub-block B such that $dec2binve(\alpha) = (dec2binvec(\beta) \oplus dec2binvec(\gamma))$, where dec2binvec($\cdot$) is a function that converts decimal value to binary vector, and $\oplus$ represents the Exclusive-Or operation. Note that for any α, there are $(n\text{-}1)/2$ such pairs $(\beta_1, \gamma_1), (\beta_2, \gamma_2)...,$ $(\beta_{(n-1)/2}, \gamma_{(n-1)/2})$,which can be enumerated easily. For each pair, E_{β_i} and E_{γ_i} $(1 \leq i \leq (n-1)/2)$ are computed respectively according to Eq.(1) to find the distortion that will be introduced. Suppose that among all these pairs of pixels, modifying the pixel pair $(p_{\beta_j}, p_{\gamma_j})$ may introduce the least distortion (please note that the corresponding distortion is $E_{\beta_j} + E_{\gamma_j}$).

Step 3: compare $(E_{\beta_j} + E_{\gamma_j})$ with E_α, if $E_\alpha > (E_{\beta_j} + E_{\gamma_j})$, the LSBs of the two pixels p_{β_j} and p_{γ_j} in sub-block B will be modified (i.e., plus-minus one randomly); otherwise only the LSB of one pixel p_α in sub-block B is modified.

In the same way, all the message bits in different sub-blocks can be embedded into their corresponding pixel sub-blocks. Our channel selection criterion can also be applied with MME3 embedding strategy in the same way except it allows at most three embedding changes in each pixel block.

3   Experimental Results

In this section, some experimental results will be given to demonstrate the efficiency of our proposed criterion. Note that the proposed criterion can be applicable to any block codes (e.g., Hamming codes, BCH codes, etc.) based matrix embedding strategy. In our experiments, we will apply it with MME embedding strategy based on modified binary Hamming codes. According to the number of allowable changing bits in each pixel sub-block and the way for computing the gradient value, the obtained steganographic algorithms are called AG_MME2, AG_MME3, MG_MME2, and MG_MME3, respectively. For comparison, we also conduct matrix embedding based on $(1, n, n\text{-}k)$ binary Hamming codes directly without utilizing any channel selection criterion, which is called original matrix embedding (OME) scheme in this paper.

The Ensemble Classifier [12] is employed in our experiments and the features are extracted according to [13]. In our testing, the second-order subtractive pixel adjacency model (SPAM) features are extracted and the dimension of the feature vector is 686. The testing error given by the Ensemble Classifier is known as out-of-bag estimate (E_{OOB}). The larger the E_{OOB}, the better security performance of the steganography is. When the cover and stego images cannot be discriminated, the value of E_{OOB} is near 0.5. The test image database in our experiments consists of 5,000 grayscale images, which are randomly selected from BOWS-2 [14].

The embedding rates for the aforementioned embedding algorithms, i.e., OME, AG_MME2, AG_MME3, MG_MME2 and MG_MME3 are represented as bits per pixel (bpp). In Table 1, the E_{OOB} values corresponding to different embedding algorithms with different embedding rates are illustrated. It is observed from Table 1 that with the utilization of the proposed channel selection criterion, AG_MME2, AG_MME3, MG_MME2 and MG_MME3 have much better security performance than OME scheme. The experimental results have demonstrated the efficiency of our proposed channel selection criterion.

Table 1. Testing error results over 5,000 images with different steganographic algorithms

Embedding Rate (bpp)	Steganography Algorithms	Testing error (E_{OOB})
	OME	0.3624
	AG_MME2	0.4597
0.05	AG_MME3	0.4664
	MG_MME2	0.4783
	MG_MME3	0.4856
	OME	0.2201
	AG_MME2	0.3540
0.10	AG_MME3	0.3734
	MG_MME2	0.4168
	MG_MME3	0.4360
	OME	0.1669
	AG_MME2	0.3180
0.15	AG_MME3	0.3400
	MG_MME2	0.3965
	MG_MME3	0.4153
	OME	0.1189
	AG_MME2	0.2172
0.20	AG_MME3	0.2320
	MG_MME2	0.3050
	MG_MME3	0.3327

4   Conclusions

In this paper, a new channel selection criterion for spatial domain steganography is presented. It can be utilized to find the pixels that may introduce minimal detectable distortion for data hiding, and thus improve the security performance of the corresponding steganographic scheme. For simplicity, we have applied it with MME embedding strategy for a demonstration. The experimental results demonstrate that with the utilization of our proposed channel selection criterion, the security performance of the steganographic algorithms can be improved significantly. Furthermore, our proposed channel selection criterion is a general channel selection criterion for spatial domain steganography. It can be suitable for any block codes based matrix embedding strategy.

Acknowledgments. This work was supported by the National Natural Science Foundation of China (61173147, 61100170), the Fundamental Research Funds for Central Universities (12lgpy31,12lgpy37), and the State Key Laboratory of Information Security (Institute of Software, Chinese Academy of Science).

References

1. Crandall, R.: Some notes on steganography, http://www.dia.unisa.it/~ads/corso-security/www/CORSO-0203/steganografia/LINKS%20LOCALI/matrix-encoding.pdf
2. Westfeld, A.: F5–A steganographic algorithm: High capacity despite better steganalysis. In: Moskowitz, I.S. (ed.) IH 2001. LNCS, vol. 2137, pp. 289–302. Springer, Heidelberg (2001)
3. Zhang, W., Zhang, X., Wang, S.: Maximizing steganographic embedding efficiency by combining hamming codes and wet paper codes. In: Solanki, K., Sullivan, K., Madhow, U. (eds.) IH 2008. LNCS, vol. 5284, pp. 60–71. Springer, Heidelberg (2008)
4. Kim, Y.H., Duric, Z., Richards, D.: Modified matrix encoding technique for minimal distortion steganography. In: Camenisch, J.L., Collberg, C.S., Johnson, N.F., Sallee, P. (eds.) IH 2006. LNCS, vol. 4437, pp. 314–327. Springer, Heidelberg (2007)
5. Schonfeld, D., Winkler, A.: Embedding with syndrome coding based on BCH codes. In: Proc. The ACM Workshop on Multimedia and Security, pp. 214–223 (2006)
6. Fridrich, J., Goljan, M., Soukal, D.: Perturbed quantization steganography with wet paper codes. In: Proc. The ACM Workshop on Multimedia and Security, Magdeburg, Germay, pp. 4–15 (2004)
7. Fridrich, J., Pevny, T., Kodovsky, J.: Statistically undetectable JPEG steganography: dead ends, challenges, and opportunities. In: Proc. The ACM Workshop on Multimedia and Security, Dallas, TX, pp. 3–14 (2007)
8. Huang, F., Huang, J., Shi, Y.Q.: New channel selection rule for JPEG steganography. IEEE Trans. Inf. Forensics and Security 7(4), 1181–1191 (2012)
9. Yang, C.H., Weng, C.Y., Wang, S.J., et al.: Adaptive data hiding in edge areas of images with spatial LSB domain systems. IEEE Trans. Inf. Forenisics Security 3(3), 488–497 (2008)
10. Singh, K.M., Singh, L.S., Singh, A.B., et al.: Hiding secret message in edges of the image. In: Proc. Int. Conf. Information and Communication Technology, pp. 238–241 (2007)
11. Luo, W., Huang, F., Huang, J.: Edge adaptive image steganography based on LSB matching revisited. IEEE Trans. Inf. Forensics and Security 5(2), 201–214 (2010)
12. Kodovsky, J., Fridrich, J.: Ensemble classifiers for steganaylsis of digital media. IEEE Trans. Inf. Forensics and Security 7(2), 432–444 (2012)
13. Pevny, T., Bas, P., Fridrich, J.: Steganalysis by subtractive pixel adjacency matrix. IEEE Trans. Inf. Forensics and Security 5(2), 215–224 (2010)
14. Bas, P., Furon, T.: BOWS-2, http://bows2.gipsa-lab.inpg.fr

A Study of Optimal Matrix for Efficient Matrix Embedding in $\mathbb{F}_3$

Yuanzhi Qi, Xiaolong Li, Bin Wang, and Bin Yang

Institute of Computer Science and Technology, Peking University
Beijing 100871, China
yuanzhi920502@yahoo.com.cn, {lixiaolong,wangbin0903,yang_bin}@pku.edu.cn

Abstract. Matrix embedding (ME) is an effective way to reduce the distortion of steganography. In ME, the sender and recipient agree on a matrix in advance, and the message will be embedded into the cover data according to the matrix. By this means, matrices with the same dimension can provide the same capacity but may introduce quite different distortions. Thus the choice of matrices is crucial to the performance of ME and it is meaningful to determine the optimal matrix which can introduce the least distortion. In this paper, we study the optimal-matrix-determination problem for ME in $\mathbb{F}_3 = \{0, \pm 1\}$. Some initial results are obtained.

Keywords: Steganography, matrix embedding, optimal matrix.

1 Introduction

Steganography studies secure secret communication [1, 2]. By this means, a hidden message is embedded into the cover data by slightly modifying the cover content. The most important requirement of a steganographic scheme is its security, i.e., the perceptual and statistical undetectability of the hidden message. In general, there are mainly three ways to enhance stego-security: decreasing the embedding distortion [3–5], keeping statistical quantities of the cover data unchanged [6–8], and realizing content adaptive embedding [9–11]. In this work, following the first way, we study the technique to enhance stego-security.

If the cover data is a digital image, the embedding rate is defined as the average number of data bits embedded per pixel. Generally speaking, when two schemes have the same embedding rate, the one that creates fewer embedding changes is less detectable since it decreases the chance that others discover the existence of the hidden message. As another important attribute of steganography, embedding efficiency is defined as the average number of data bits embedded per embedding change. This concept is first introduced by Westfeld [12] and has since been accepted as a metric of stego-security [13]. Based on these definitions, a goal of steganography is to minimize the embedding distortion for a given embedding rate, or equivalently, to maximize the embedding efficiency.

Matrix embedding (ME) is an effective way to increase the embedding efficiency. This method is first proposed by Crandall [14] and systematically studied

Y.Q. Shi, H.J. Kim, and F. Pérez-González (Eds.): IWDW 2012, LNCS 7809, pp. 8–18, 2013.
© Springer-Verlag Berlin Heidelberg 2013

later by Fridrich *et al.* [13, 15]. In ME, the sender and recipient agree on a matrix in advance, and the message will be embedded into the cover data utilizing the matrix. By this means, matrices with the same dimension can provide the same embedding rate but may introduce quite different embedding efficiencies (see examples in Section 2). Thus the choice of matrices is crucial to the performance of ME and it is meaningful to determine the optimal matrix which can introduce the highest embedding efficiency. Some recent works [16, 17] focus on the optimal matrix for ME in $\mathbb{F}_2$. Here, ME in $\mathbb{F}_2$ means that the matrix elements are taken from the finite filed $\mathbb{F}_2 = \{0, 1\}$. Until now, the optimal-matrix-determination problem is only solved for some special cases for ME in $\mathbb{F}_2$.

In this paper, instead of $\mathbb{F}_2$, we study the optimal matrix for ME in $\mathbb{F}_3 = \{0, \pm 1\}$. We argue that it is valuable to extend ME from $\mathbb{F}_2$ to $\mathbb{F}_3$. On one hand, similar to the case of $\mathbb{F}_2$, ME in $\mathbb{F}_3$ can guarantee that each cover pixel value is changed at most by 1 in data embedding. On the other hand, compared with ME in $\mathbb{F}_2$, ME in $\mathbb{F}_3$ can provide a higher embedding efficiency at the same embedding rate. In addition, ME in $\mathbb{F}_3$ can give a maximum embedding rate of $\log_2 3$ bit per pixel (bpp), while that for ME in $\mathbb{F}_2$ is only 1.0 bpp. Based on these considerations, we propose to study ME in $\mathbb{F}_3$.

The rest of the paper is organized as follows. In Section 2, the data embedding and extraction procedures of ME in $\mathbb{F}_3$ are described in details. In Section 3, some general results about optimal matrix are given at first. Then the optimal matrices for the cases of $n - m = 1$ and 2 are investigated, where $m \times n$ is the matrix dimension. Finally, this work is concluded in Section 4.

2   Matrix Embedding in $\mathbb{F}_3$

Let $0 < m \leq n$ be two positive integers. Consider an $m \times n$ matrix $\mathbf{A}$ whose elements are taken from $\mathbb{F}_3 = \{0, \pm 1\}$. If $\text{rank}(\mathbf{A}) = m$, or in other words, if $\mathbf{A}$ satisfies,

$$\forall \mathbf{u} \in \mathbb{F}_3^m, \quad \exists \mathbf{v} \in \mathbb{F}_3^n \quad \text{s.t.} \quad \mathbf{A}\mathbf{v} = \mathbf{u} \tag{1}$$

ME can be defined utilizing $\mathbf{A}$. Notice that the addition and multiplication in (1) are operations in $\mathbb{F}_3$, e.g., $1 + 1 = -1$. Moreover, for convenience, we will use in the context either row or column vectors depending on the choice.

The data embedding procedure of ME in $\mathbb{F}_3$ is as follows. Let $\mathbf{c} \in \mathbb{Z}^n$ be a cover vector and $\mathbf{m} \in \mathbb{F}_3^m$ be a secret message. To embed $\mathbf{m}$ into $\mathbf{c}$, we first find $\mathbf{v}^* \in \mathbb{F}_3^n$ such that

$$\mathbf{v}^* = \underset{\{\mathbf{v} \in \mathbb{F}_3^n : \mathbf{A}\mathbf{v} = \mathbf{u}\}}{\arg\min} \; w(\mathbf{v}) \tag{2}$$

where $w(\mathbf{x})$ is the Hamming weight of a vector $\mathbf{x} = (x_1, ..., x_n)$, and $\mathbf{u} = \mathbf{m} - \mathbf{A}\mathbf{c}$. The stego vector is then taken as $\mathbf{s} = \mathbf{c} + \mathbf{v}^*$. In this procedure, $\mathbf{v}^*$ corresponds to the modification to $\mathbf{c}$. Therefore, to minimize the distortion, the minimizing condition in (2) is essential. Moreover, since $\|\mathbf{s} - \mathbf{c}\|_{l\infty} = \|\mathbf{v}^*\|_{l\infty} \leq 1$, the maximum modification to each cover pixel value is guaranteed to be at most 1.

To extract the embedded message, one only needs to compute $\mathbf{A}\mathbf{s}$.

Clearly, with the above scheme, $\log_2(3^m) = m \log_2 3$ bits are embedded into n pixels, and the embedding rate noted as $\mathrm{ER}(\mathbf{A})$ is $\frac{m}{n} \log_2 3$.

Let $f_\mathbf{A}(\mathbf{u})$ be a solution to (2) (notice that (2) may have more than one solution whereas each solution has the same Hamming weight). The average embedding distortion noted as $\mathrm{ED}(\mathbf{A})$, i.e., the expected value of l^2 error, $\|\mathbf{s} - \mathbf{c}\|_{l^2}^2/n$, can be then formulated as

$$\mathrm{ED}(\mathbf{A}) = \frac{\sum_{\mathbf{m} \in \mathbb{F}_3^m} w(f_\mathbf{A}(\mathbf{m} - \mathbf{Ac}))}{n3^m}. \tag{3}$$

Since $\mathbf{Ac}$ is fixed, the average embedding distortion can be simply rewritten in the following form

$$\mathrm{ED}(\mathbf{A}) = \frac{\sum_{\mathbf{u} \in \mathbb{F}_3^m} d_\mathbf{A}(\mathbf{u})}{n3^m} \tag{4}$$

where $d_\mathbf{A}(\mathbf{u}) = w(f_\mathbf{A}(\mathbf{u}))$. According to (4), the average embedding distortion is independent on the cover $\mathbf{c}$, and can be computed using only the matrix $\mathbf{A}$.

We remark that, the matrix $\mathbf{A}$ in ME can be viewed as the parity check matrix (PCM) of a linear code $\mathcal{C}$ with length n and dimension $n - m$. In this means, (2) is equivalent to finding a coset leader, i.e., the vector in the coset which has the minimal Hamming weight. Moreover, one can prove that $\mathrm{ED}(\mathbf{A}) = R_a(\mathcal{C})/n$, where $R_a(\mathcal{C})$ is the average distance to code:

$$R_a(\mathcal{C}) = \frac{\sum_{\mathbf{v} \in \mathbb{F}_3^n} dis(\mathbf{v}, \mathcal{C})}{3^n} \tag{5}$$

with $dis(\mathbf{v}, \mathcal{C}) = \min_{\mathbf{c} \in \mathcal{C}} w(\mathbf{v} - \mathbf{c})$ which is the distance from $\mathbf{v}$ to $\mathcal{C}$.

We now give some examples of ME.

Example 1: Consider here the simplest case that $n = m = 1$ and $\mathbf{A}$ is the 1×1 identity matrix. The embedding rate is $\mathrm{ER}(\mathbf{A}) = \log_2 3$. By definition, we know that for each $\mathbf{u} \in \mathbb{F}_3$, $f_\mathbf{A}(\mathbf{u}) = \mathbf{u}$. Thus the average embedding distortion is $\mathrm{ED}(\mathbf{A}) = \frac{2}{3}$. Clearly, for this scalar case of ME, its embedding procedure is in fact:

$$\mathbf{s} = \begin{cases} \mathbf{c}, & \text{if } \mathbf{m} \equiv \mathbf{c} \ (\mathrm{mod}\ 3) \\ \mathbf{c} + 1, & \text{if } \mathbf{m} \equiv \mathbf{c} + 1 \ (\mathrm{mod}\ 3) \\ \mathbf{c} - 1, & \text{if } \mathbf{m} \equiv \mathbf{c} - 1 \ (\mathrm{mod}\ 3) \end{cases} \tag{6}$$

where $\mathbf{c}$ and $\mathbf{s}$ are respectively cover and stego pixel value, and $\mathbf{m} \in \{0, \pm 1\}$ is the data to be embedded.

Example 2: We use the following 2×3 matrix in this example:

$$\mathbf{A} = \begin{pmatrix} 1 & 1 & -1 \\ 1 & 0 & 1 \end{pmatrix}. \tag{7}$$

The embedding rate is $\mathrm{ER}(\mathbf{A}) = \frac{2}{3} \log_2 3$. For $\mathbf{u} \in \mathbb{F}_3^2$, we can verify that $w(f_\mathbf{A}(\mathbf{u})) = 1$ if $\mathbf{u}$ or $-\mathbf{u}$ is a column vector of $\mathbf{A}$, and $w(f_\mathbf{A}(\mathbf{u})) = 2$ if $\mathbf{u} = (0, \pm 1)$. So, $\mathrm{ED}(\mathbf{A}) = \frac{1 \cdot 0 + 6 \cdot 1 + 2 \cdot 2}{27} = \frac{10}{27}$.

Example 3: Consider the ternary Hamming code in this example, i.e., we take PCM $\mathbf{H}_m$ of the $[(3^m - 1)/2, (3^m - 1)/2 - m, 3]_3$ ternary Hamming code. For instance, the matrix $\mathbf{H}_m$ for $m = 3$ is shown in (8). As the dimension of $\mathbf{H}_m$ is $m \times n$ with $n = \frac{3^m - 1}{2}$, the embedding rate is $\text{ER}(\mathbf{H}_m) = \frac{2m}{3^m - 1} \log_2 3$. Notice that for any non-zero $\mathbf{u} \in \mathbb{F}_3^m$, $\mathbf{u}$ or $-\mathbf{u}$ is a column vector of $\mathbf{H}_m$, so $w(f_{\mathbf{H}_m}(\mathbf{u})) = 1$. Thus $\text{ED}(\mathbf{H}_m) = \frac{2}{3^m}$.

$$\mathbf{H}_3 = \begin{pmatrix} 0 & 0\,0\,0 & 1 & 1 & 1 & 1\,1\,1 & 1\,1\,1 \\ 0 & 1\,1\,1 & -1 & -1 & -1 & 0\,0\,0 & 1\,1\,1 \\ 1 & -1\,0\,1 & -1 & 0 & 1 & -1\,0\,1 & -1\,0\,1 \end{pmatrix}. \tag{8}$$

Example 4: This example is derived from $[11, 6, 5]_3$ ternary Golay code whose PCM $\mathbf{G}$ is a 5×11 matrix (see (9)). The embedding rate is $\text{ER}(\mathbf{G}) = \frac{5}{11} \log_2 3$. Since this code is a perfect code, any non-zero $\mathbf{u} \in \mathbb{F}_3^m$ can be expressed as a linear combination of either one or two column vectors of $\mathbf{G}$ in a unique way. Then we have $\text{ED}(\mathbf{G}) = \frac{\binom{11}{0}\cdot 0 + 2\cdot\binom{11}{1}\cdot 1 + 2^2\cdot\binom{11}{2}\cdot 2}{11\cdot 3^5} = 0.1728$.

$$\mathbf{G} = \begin{pmatrix} 1 & 1 & 1 & -1 & -1 & 0\,1\,0\,0\,0\,0 \\ 1 & 1 & -1 & 1 & 0 & -1\,0\,1\,0\,0\,0 \\ 1 & -1 & 1 & 0 & 1 & -1\,0\,0\,1\,0\,0 \\ 1 & -1 & 0 & 1 & -1 & 1\,0\,0\,0\,1\,0 \\ 1 & 0 & -1 & -1 & 1 & 1\,0\,0\,0\,0\,1 \end{pmatrix}. \tag{9}$$

Example 5: Consider another 5×11 matrix $\mathbf{A}$ shown in (10). One can verify that $\text{ER}(\mathbf{A}) = \frac{5}{11} \log_2 3$ and $\text{ED}(\mathbf{A}) = 0.2028$.

$$\mathbf{A} = \begin{pmatrix} 1\,0\,0\,0\,0\,1 & -1 & -1 & 0 & 1 & 0 \\ 0\,1\,0\,0\,0\,0 & 1 & 0 & 0 & 1 & -1 \\ 0\,0\,1\,0\,0\,1 & 0 & 0 & 1 & -1 & 0 \\ 0\,0\,0\,1\,0\,0 & 1 & 0 & -1 & -1 & -1 \\ 0\,0\,0\,0\,1\,0 & 0 & 1 & -1 & 0 & 0 \end{pmatrix}. \tag{10}$$

From the last two examples, it can be observed that different matrices with the same dimension may introduce quite different distortions even though they have the same embedding rate. Therefore, it is meaningful to find the optimal matrix which can provide the minimal distortion. Specifically, for fixed m and n, an optimal matrix $\mathbf{A}^*$ is defined as the one that introduces the least embedding distortion:

$$\mathbf{A}^* = \underset{\mathbf{A} \in \mathbb{F}_3^{m \times n}}{\arg\min}\ \text{ED}(\mathbf{A}). \tag{11}$$

It should be mentioned that the optimal-matrix-determination problem is different from the covering radius problem extensively studied in coding theory [18]. The latter aims at minimizing the covering radius $R(\mathcal{C})$ of a code $\mathcal{C}$, where the covering radius is defined as the maximum distance of any vector in $\mathbb{F}_3^n$ to $\mathcal{C}$:

$$R(\mathcal{C}) = \max_{\mathbf{v} \in \mathbb{F}_3^n} dis(\mathbf{v}, \mathcal{C}). \tag{12}$$

As we know (see [13]), for the binary case, the code which has the minimal covering radius $R(\mathcal{C})$ among all $[n, n - m]_2$ linear codes might not minimize the average distance to code $R_a(\mathcal{C})$ defined in (5). So, finding the optimal matrix, i.e., finding the code which has the least average distance to code, is a new problem.

3   Study on Optimal Matrix

For two full-rank matrices $\mathbf{A}, \mathbf{B} \in \mathbb{F}_3^{m \times n}$, we say that they are equivalent in the sense of ME if $ED(\mathbf{A}) = ED(\mathbf{B})$. All equivalent matrices form an equivalence class, and any element in an equivalence class can be taken as a representative element of this class. Then we may only consider the representative element in a specific form. Now we give the following theorem.

Theorem 1. *For each full-rank matrix $\mathbf{A} \in \mathbb{F}_3^{m \times n}$, there exists a matrix $\mathbf{B}$ in the form of $(\mathbf{I}_m, \mathbf{P})$ such that it is equivalent to $\mathbf{A}$. Here, $\mathbf{I}_m$ denotes the $m \times m$ identity matrix, and $\mathbf{P}$ is an $m \times (n-m)$ matrix in $\mathbb{F}_3$.*

Proof. Consider two matrices $\mathbf{A}_1, \mathbf{A}_2 \in \mathbb{F}_3^{m \times n}$ satisfying $\mathbf{A}_2 = \mathbf{W}\mathbf{A}_1$, where $\mathbf{W}$ is a full-rank $m \times m$ matrix. We first prove that $\mathbf{A}_1$ is equivalent to $\mathbf{A}_2$. Actually, as $\mathbf{W}$ is full ranked, then for any $\mathbf{u} \in \mathbb{F}_3^m$, we have $\mathbf{A}_1\mathbf{v} = \mathbf{u} \Leftrightarrow \mathbf{A}_2\mathbf{v} = \mathbf{W}\mathbf{u}$. Thus we can derive $d_{\mathbf{A}_1}(\mathbf{u}) = d_{\mathbf{A}_2}(\mathbf{W}\mathbf{u})$. Notice that $\mathbf{W}$ can be viewed as an one-to-one mapping of $\mathbb{F}_3^m$, we then have $ED(\mathbf{A}_1) = ED(\mathbf{A}_2)$. We now prove the theorem. Clearly, by using elementary row transformations (interchanging two rows, multiplying a row with -1, or adding a row to another one multiplied by ± 1), the matrix $\mathbf{A}$ can be transformed into the form of $(\mathbf{I}_m, \mathbf{P})$. As elementary row transformations equal multiplying a full-rank matrix on the left, the theorem is proved.

According to Theorem 1, we may only consider optimal matrix in the form of $(\mathbf{I}_m, \mathbf{P})$. Moreover, we can prove that the optimal matrix in this specific form has an important property (see the theorem below): there is no zero row vector in $\mathbf{P}$.

Theorem 2. *Consider a matrix $\mathbf{A} = (\mathbf{I}_m, \mathbf{P})$, where $\mathbf{P}$ is an $m \times (n-m)$ matrix whose row vectors are $\mathbf{p}_1, ..., \mathbf{p}_m \in \mathbb{F}_3^{n-m}$. Suppose that there exists an index j such that $\mathbf{p}_j$ is a zero vector. Then, if we replace $\mathbf{p}_j$ by an arbitrary vector of $\mathbb{F}_3^{n-m}$ to form a new matrix $\mathbf{B}$, we have $ED(\mathbf{B}) \leq ED(\mathbf{A})$.*

Proof. Without loss of generality, we assume here $j = 1$.

For any $\mathbf{u} = (u_1, u_2, ..., u_m) \in \mathbb{F}_3^m$, we define two vectors $\mathbf{u}^+, \mathbf{u}^- \in \mathbb{F}_3^m$ as $\mathbf{u}^{\pm} = (u_1 \pm 1, u_2, ..., u_m)$. We first prove that, if $u_1 = 0$,

$$d_{\mathbf{A}}(\mathbf{u}) + d_{\mathbf{A}}(\mathbf{u}^+) + d_{\mathbf{A}}(\mathbf{u}^-) \geq d_{\mathbf{B}}(\mathbf{u}) + d_{\mathbf{B}}(\mathbf{u}^+) + d_{\mathbf{B}}(\mathbf{u}^-). \qquad (13)$$

Actually, for a solution $\mathbf{v} = (v_1, ..., v_n)$ to $\mathbf{A}\mathbf{v} = \mathbf{u}$, we have $v_1 = u_1$. Then, by taking $\mathbf{v}^{\pm} = (v_1 \pm 1, v_2, ..., v_n)$, one can verify that, if $u_1 = 0$, the solution sets to $\mathbf{A}\mathbf{v} = \mathbf{u}^{\pm}$ are respectively $\{\mathbf{v}^{\pm} : \mathbf{v} \in \mathbf{S}\}$, where $\mathbf{S}$ is the set of solutions to $\mathbf{A}\mathbf{v} = \mathbf{u}$. As a result, we can take $f_{\mathbf{A}}(\mathbf{u}^{\pm}) = (f_{\mathbf{A}}(\mathbf{u}))^{\pm}$. Moreover, it is obvious that there exists a vector $\mathbf{w} \in \{f_{\mathbf{A}}(\mathbf{u}), (f_{\mathbf{A}}(\mathbf{u}))^{\pm}\}$ such that $\mathbf{Bw} = \mathbf{u}$ holds. Then, $\mathbf{B}(\mathbf{w}^{\pm}) = \mathbf{u}^{\pm}$, and thus

$$
\begin{aligned}
d_{\mathbf{B}}(\mathbf{u}) + d_{\mathbf{B}}(\mathbf{u}^+) + d_{\mathbf{B}}(\mathbf{u}^-) &\leq w(\mathbf{w}) + w(\mathbf{w}^+) + w(\mathbf{w}^-) \\
&= w(f_{\mathbf{A}}(\mathbf{u})) + w((f_{\mathbf{A}}(\mathbf{u}))^+) + w((f_{\mathbf{A}}(\mathbf{u}))^-) \\
&= w(f_{\mathbf{A}}(\mathbf{u})) + w(f_{\mathbf{A}}(\mathbf{u}^+)) + w(f_{\mathbf{A}}(\mathbf{u}^-)) \\
&= d_{\mathbf{A}}(\mathbf{u}) + d_{\mathbf{A}}(\mathbf{u}^+) + d_{\mathbf{A}}(\mathbf{u}^-)
\end{aligned}
$$

Finally, (13) is proved and the theorem is a direct result of (13).

3.1   Optimal Matrix for the Case of $n - m = 1$

By Theorem 2, when $n - m = 1$, we may suppose that the optimal matrix is in the form of $(\mathbf{I}_{n-1}, \mathbf{P})$ where $\mathbf{P} = (p_1, ..., p_{n-1})$ is a column vector whose element p_i is either 1 or -1, for each $i \in \{1, ..., n-1\}$. Moreover, notice that multiplying a row or a column with -1 will not change the average embedding distortion, we may take $p_i = 1$ for every $i \in \{1, ..., n-1\}$. That is, $(\mathbf{I}_{n-1}, \mathbf{P})$ is an optimal matrix if $\mathbf{P}$ is an all '1' vector. In fact, this matrix is the unique optimal matrix when $n > 2$. We give the following theorem.

Theorem 3. *Let $\mathbf{A}_s = (\mathbf{I}_{n-1}, \mathbf{P}_s)$ be an $(n - 1) \times n$ matrix, where $\mathbf{P}_s = (p_1, ..., p_{n-1})$ satisfies $p_i = 1$ if $1 \leq i \leq s$ and $p_i = 0$ if $s < i \leq n - 1$. Then $\mathrm{ED}(\mathbf{A}_s)$ is a strictly decreasing function for $s \geq 1$. In addition, $\mathrm{ED}(\mathbf{A}_1) = \mathrm{ED}(\mathbf{A}_0)$.*

Proof. Take for convenience $m = n - 1$.
 For every $\mathbf{u} = (u_1, ..., u_m) \in \mathbb{F}_3^m$, it is obvious that

$$
d_{\mathbf{A}_s}(\mathbf{u}) = m - s - c + \min\{a + b, s + 1 - a, s + 1 - b\} \tag{14}
$$

where $a = |\{1 \leq i \leq s : u_i = 1\}|$, $b = |\{1 \leq i \leq s : u_i = -1\}|$ and $c = |\{s < i \leq m : u_i = 0\}|$. Then, we have

$$
n3^m \mathrm{ED}(\mathbf{A}_s) = \sum_{a+b \leq s} \sum_{c=0}^{m-s} \binom{s}{a} \binom{s-a}{b} \binom{m-s}{c} 2^{m-s-c} d_{\mathbf{A}_s}(\mathbf{u}). \tag{15}
$$

By a routine deduction, we can derive

$$
n3^m \mathrm{ED}(\mathbf{A}_s) = 2(m - s)3^{m-1}
$$

$$
+ 3^{m-s} \sum_{a+b \leq s} \binom{s}{a+b} \binom{a+b}{a} \min\{a + b, s + 1 - a, s + 1 - b\}. \tag{16}
$$

So, $\mathrm{ED}(\mathbf{A}_1) = \mathrm{ED}(\mathbf{A}_0)$.

Furthermore, to prove $\mathrm{ED}(\mathbf{A}_s) > \mathrm{ED}(\mathbf{A}_{s+1})$, it is sufficient to prove

$$\sum_{a+b \leq s+1} \binom{s+1}{a+b}\binom{a+b}{a} \min\{a+b, s+2-a, s+2-b\}$$

$$< 2 \cdot 3^s + 3 \sum_{a+b \leq s} \binom{s}{a+b}\binom{a+b}{a} \min\{a+b, s+1-a, s+1-b\}. \quad (17)$$

Notice that

$$\binom{s+1}{a+b}\binom{a+b}{a} =$$

$$\binom{s}{a+b}\binom{a+b}{a} + \binom{s}{a+b-1}\binom{a+b-1}{a} + \binom{s}{a+b-1}\binom{a+b-1}{a-1}. \quad (18)$$

Therefore, (17) is equivalent to

$$2 \cdot 3^s > \sum_{a+b \leq s} \binom{s}{a+b}\binom{a+b}{a} \delta(x, y, z) \quad (19)$$

where $\delta(x, y, z)$ is defined as

$$\min\{x, y+1, z+1\} + \min\{x+1, y, z+1\} + \min\{x+1, y+1, z\} - 3\min\{x, y, z\} \quad (20)$$

with $(x, y, z) = (a + b, s + 1 - a, s + 1 - b)$. One can verify that $\delta(x, y, z) \leq 2$ holds for all (x, y, z). Moreover, for special values of a, b such as $a = \lfloor \frac{s+1}{2} \rfloor$ and $b = s + 1 - 2a$, we have $x = y \leq z$, and thus $\delta(x, y, z) \leq 1$. As a result, the right side of (19) is strictly less than $2\sum_{a+b \leq s} \binom{s}{a+b}\binom{a+b}{a} = 2 \cdot 3^s$. Therefore, (19) holds and the theorem is proved.

By Theorem 3, for $\mathbf{P} = (1, ..., 1)$, we conclude that $(\mathbf{I}_{n-1}, \mathbf{P})$ is the unique $(n-1) \times n$ optimal matrix if $n > 2$, in the equivalence sense.

3.2   Optimal Matrix for the Case of $n - m = 2$

We consider the case of $n - m = 2$ for the matrix $\mathbf{A}$ in the form of $(\mathbf{I}_{n-m}, \mathbf{P})$. This case is much more difficult than that of $n - m = 1$. We can only provide some experimental observations.

According to Theorem 2, we assume that every row vector $\mathbf{p}_j$ of $\mathbf{P}$ is non-zero. Moreover, as multiplying a row or a column with -1 will not change the average embedding distortion, we can further assume that

$$\mathbf{p}_j \in \{\mathbf{v}_1 = (0, 1), \mathbf{v}_2 = (1, -1), \mathbf{v}_3 = (1, 0), \mathbf{v}_4 = (1, 1)\} \quad (21)$$

Then we define $\lambda(\mathbf{A}) = (\lambda_1, \lambda_2, \lambda_3, \lambda_4)$ with $\lambda_i = |\{1 \leq j \leq n-2 : \mathbf{p}_j = \mathbf{v}_i\}|$, for every $i \in \{1, 2, 3, 4\}$. For example, for the following matrix, we have $\lambda_1 = \lambda_2 = 1$, $\lambda_3 = 2$, and $\lambda_4 = 0$:

$$\begin{pmatrix} 1 & 0 & 0 & 0 & 1 & 0 \\ 0 & 1 & 0 & 0 & 0 & 1 \\ 0 & 0 & 1 & 0 & 1 & -1 \\ 0 & 0 & 0 & 1 & 1 & 0 \end{pmatrix}. \tag{22}$$

Clearly, two matrices $\mathbf{A}$ and $\mathbf{B}$ are equivalent if $\lambda(\mathbf{A}) = \lambda(\mathbf{B})$. As a result, $\mathbf{A}$ can be simply represented by $\lambda(\mathbf{A})$ in the sense of equivalence. Moreover, notice that multiplying the first column of $\mathbf{P}$ and some rows of $\mathbf{A}$ by -1, we can get an equivalent matrix $\mathbf{B}$ with $\lambda(\mathbf{B}) = (\lambda_1, \lambda_4, \lambda_3, \lambda_2)$; or, interchanging two columns of $\mathbf{P}$ and multiplying some rows of $\mathbf{A}$ by -1, we can get another equivalent matrix $\mathbf{C}$ with $\lambda(\mathbf{C}) = (\lambda_3, \lambda_2, \lambda_1, \lambda_4)$. We then may assume that $\lambda_1 \leq \lambda_3$ and $\lambda_2 \leq \lambda_4$.

To summarize, any matrix $\mathbf{A}$ is equivalent to a matrix $\mathbf{B}$ that $\lambda(\mathbf{B}) = (\lambda_1, \lambda_2, \lambda_3, \lambda_4)$ satisfies

$$\lambda_1 + \lambda_2 + \lambda_3 + \lambda_4 = n - 2, \ \lambda_1 \leq \lambda_3, \ \lambda_2 \leq \lambda_4. \tag{23}$$

We then search exhaustively all optimal matrices for small n. The result is shown in Table 1, where a matrix is represented by $(\lambda_1, \lambda_2, \lambda_3, \lambda_4)$ satisfying (23). One can see that when n increases, the optimal matrix tends to follow some laws, and we conjecture that optimal matrices are in the following forms when $n \geq 11$.

$$\begin{cases} (k-2, k-1, k-1, k+1), (k-2, k-1, k, k), & \\ \quad (k-2, k, k-2, k+1), (k-1, k-1, k, k-1) & \text{if } n = 4k-1 \\ (k-1, k, k-1, k) & \text{if } n = 4k \\ (k-1, k, k-1, k+1), (k-1, k, k, k) & \text{if } n = 4k+1 \\ (k-1, k, k, k+1), (k-1, k+1, k-1, k+1), (k, k, k, k) & \text{if } n = 4k+2 \end{cases} \tag{24}$$

Its proof is still an open problem.

Finally, we show in Fig. 1 the embedding efficiency for the following matrices: $(n-1) \times n$ optimal matrix for $n \geq 3$; $(n-2) \times n$ optimal matrix for $n \geq 6$; $(n-2) \times n$ random matrix $\mathbf{A} = (\mathbf{I}_{n-2}, \mathbf{P})$ for $n \geq 6$, where $\mathbf{P}$ is randomly selected from $\mathbb{F}_3^{(n-2) \times 2}$. For $(n-2) \times n$ optimal matrix, we use the matrix in Table 1 when $n < 11$, and the matrix in (24) when $n \geq 11$. For $(n-2) \times n$ random matrix, 100 matrices are randomly selected for each n, and the embedding efficiencies of those matrices are averaged as the final result. From this figure, we may conclude: first, $(n-2) \times n$ optimal matrix is better than randomly selected matrix and this result experimentally verifies our conjecture; second, optimal matrix with $n - m = 2$ is better than that of $n - m = 1$ and this observation encourages us to further study the case of larger $n - m$; finally, for fixed $n - m$, the study of optimal matrix is more profitable for high payload steganography since the embedding rate $\frac{m}{n} \log_2 3$ tends to the maximum $\log_2 3$ when n increases.

Table 1. All optimal matrices for $n - m = 2$ $(3 \leq n \leq 22)$

n	optimal matrix
3	$(0\ 0\ 1\ 0),(0\ 0\ 0\ 1)$
4	$(0\ 1\ 0\ 1)$
5	$(0\ 0\ 1\ 2),(0\ 1\ 0\ 2),(0\ 1\ 1\ 1),(1\ 0\ 1\ 1)$
6	$(0\ 1\ 0\ 3),(0\ 1\ 2\ 1)$
7	$(0\ 1\ 0\ 4),(0\ 1\ 3\ 1),(0\ 2\ 1\ 2),(1\ 1\ 1\ 2)$
8	$(0\ 2\ 1\ 3),(0\ 2\ 2\ 2),(1\ 1\ 1\ 3),(1\ 1\ 2\ 2)$
9	$(1\ 2\ 1\ 3),(1\ 2\ 2\ 2)$
10	$(0\ 3\ 2\ 3),(1\ 2\ 2\ 3),(1\ 3\ 1\ 3),(2\ 1\ 2\ 3),(2\ 2\ 2\ 2)$
11	$(1\ 2\ 2\ 4),(1\ 2\ 3\ 3),(1\ 3\ 1\ 4),(2\ 2\ 3\ 2)$
12	$(2\ 3\ 2\ 3)$
13	$(2\ 3\ 2\ 4),(2\ 3\ 3\ 3)$
14	$(2\ 3\ 3\ 4),(2\ 4\ 2\ 4),(3\ 3\ 3\ 3)$
15	$(2\ 3\ 3\ 5),(2\ 3\ 4\ 4),(2\ 4\ 2\ 5),(3\ 3\ 4\ 3)$
16	$(3\ 4\ 3\ 4)$
17	$(3\ 4\ 3\ 5),(3\ 4\ 4\ 4)$
18	$(3\ 4\ 4\ 5),(3\ 5\ 3\ 5),(4\ 4\ 4\ 4)$
19	$(3\ 4\ 4\ 6),(3\ 4\ 5\ 5),(3\ 5\ 3\ 6),(4\ 4\ 5\ 4)$
20	$(4\ 5\ 4\ 5)$
21	$(4\ 5\ 4\ 6),(4\ 5\ 5\ 5)$
22	$(4\ 5\ 5\ 6),(4\ 6\ 4\ 6),(5\ 5\ 5\ 5)$

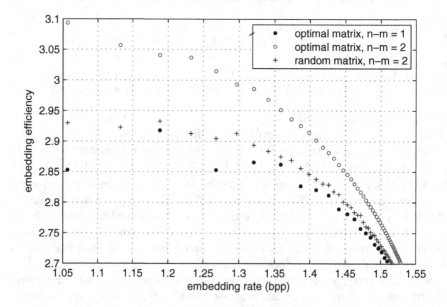

Fig. 1. Embedding efficiency of ME for different matrices

4 Conclusion

This paper is a beginning work of the optimal-matrix-determination problem for ME in $\mathbb{F}_3$. For $m \times n$ matrix, this problem is completely solved when $n - m = 1$, and, based on experimental observations, a matrix form conjecture is given for the case of $n - m = 2$.

References

1. Fridrich, J.: Steganography in Digital Media: Principles, Algorithms, and Applications. Cambridge University Press, Cambridge (2010)
2. Li, B., He, J., Huang, J., Shi, Y.Q.: A survey on image steganography and steganalysis. Journal of Information Hiding and Multimedia Signal Processing 2(2), 142–172 (2011)
3. Fridrich, J.: Minimizing the embedding impact in steganography. In: Proc. 8th ACM Workshop on Multimedia & Security, pp. 2–10 (2006)
4. Zhang, W., Zhang, X., Wang, S.: Maximizing steganographic embedding efficiency by combining Hamming codes and wet paper codes. In: Solanki, K., Sullivan, K., Madhow, U. (eds.) IH 2008. LNCS, vol. 5284, pp. 60–71. Springer, Heidelberg (2008)
5. Li, X., Yang, B., Cheng, D., Zeng, T.: A generalization of LSB matching. IEEE Signal Process. Lett. 16(2), 69–72 (2009)
6. Sallee, P.: Model-based steganography. In: Kalker, T., Cox, I., Ro, Y.M. (eds.) IWDW 2003. LNCS, vol. 2939, pp. 154–167. Springer, Heidelberg (2004)
7. Cachin, C.: An information-theoretic model for steganography. Information and Computation 192(1), 41–56 (2004)
8. Pevný, T., Filler, T., Bas, P.: Using high-dimensional image models to perform highly undetectable steganography. In: Böhme, R., Fong, P.W.L., Safavi-Naini, R. (eds.) IH 2010. LNCS, vol. 6387, pp. 161–177. Springer, Heidelberg (2010)
9. Yang, C.H., Weng, C.Y., Wang, S.J., Sun, H.M.: Adaptive data hiding in edge areas of images with spatial LSB domain systems. IEEE Trans. Inf. Forens. Security 3(3), 488–497 (2008)
10. Luo, W., Huang, F., Huang, J.: Edge adaptive image steganography based on LSB matching revisited. IEEE Trans. Inf. Forens. Security 5(2), 201–214 (2010)
11. Gui, X., Li, X., Yang, B.: A content-adaptive ±1-based steganography by minimizing the distortion of first order statistics. In: Proc. IEEE ICASSP, pp. 1781–1784 (2012)
12. Westfeld, A.: F5–A steganographic algorithm: High capacity despite better steganalysis. In: Moskowitz, I.S. (ed.) IH 2001. LNCS, vol. 2137, pp. 289–302. Springer, Heidelberg (2001)
13. Fridrich, J., Lisoněk, P., Soukal, D.: On steganographic embedding efficiency. In: Camenisch, J.L., Collberg, C.S., Johnson, N.F., Sallee, P. (eds.) IH 2006. LNCS, vol. 4437, pp. 282–296. Springer, Heidelberg (2007)
14. Crandall, R.: Some notes on steganography (1998), http://www.dia.unisa.it/ads/corso-security/www/CORSO-0203/steganografia/LINKSLOCALI/matrix-encoding.pdf

15. Fridrich, J., Soukal, D.: Matrix embedding for large payloads. IEEE Trans. Inf. Forens. Security 1(3), 390–395 (2006)
16. Khatirinejad, M., Lisoněk, P.: Linear codes for high patload steganography. Discrete Applied Mathematics 157(5), 971–981 (2009)
17. Gao, Y., Li, X., Yang, B.: Employing optimal matrix for efficient matrix embedding. In: Proc. IIH-MSP, pp. 161–165 (2009)
18. Cohen, G., Honkala, I., Litsyn, S., Lobstein, A.: Covering Codes. Elsevier, Amsterdam (1997)

A Novel Mapping Scheme for Steganalysis

Licong Chen[1,2,3], Yun Q. Shi[2], Patchara Sutthiwan[2], and Xinxin Niu[1]

[1] Information Security Center, Beijing University of Posts and Telecommunications,
Beijing 100876, P.R. China
[2] New Jersey Institute of Technology, Newark, NJ 07102, USA
[3] Fujian Normal University, Fujian 350007, P.R. China
{lcchen,shi,ps249}@njit.edu, xxniu@bupt.edu.cn

Abstract. Recently the research on steganalysis for breaking HUGO has been further moved ahead. A novel mapping scheme is reported in this paper. Through a Huffman coding like procedure, this scheme can lower the feature dimensionality from 625 to 120 generated from one residual image as a 4th order co-occurrence matrix is considered. Two experiments have been reported to demonstrate its effectiveness. In breaking the HUGO, the proposed mapping scheme has been applied to the frame work of the state-of-the-art [13] with some minor modification. With a total number of 15,840 features the new method can achieve 87.17% accuracy in BOSSbase ver. 0.92 at 0.4 bpp, outperforming the state-of-the-art.

Keywords: Steganalysis, steganography, co-occurrence matrix, Markov process, transition probability matrix, HUGO (Highly Undetectable Stegonagraphy), mapping scheme, local binary patterns.

1 Introduction

Steganography and steganalysis are a pair of modern technologies in the field of information security that have been moving ahead swiftly in the last decade. The conflicting between the two sides is a driving force for the rapid development of the field. That is, each side learns from its counterpart. From the modern steganalysis point of view, the machine learning framework, consisting of statistical features and classifier, has been first utilized in [1]. In [2], the first four statistical moments of wavelet coefficients and their prediction errors of nine high frequency subbands from three-level decomposition are used to form a 72-dimensional (72-D) feature vector with the modern classifier SVM(Support Vector Machine) for steganalysis. The steganalysis method based on the mass center of histogram characteristic function has shown improved effectiveness in steganalysis [3]. A framework combining wavelet decomposition and moments of characteristic functions is reported in [4]. To break steganographic schemes using popularly utilized JPEG images as carriers, such as OutGuess, F5 and model-based steganographic schemes, a group of 23 features, including both the first and second order statistics, have been used together with a calibrate technique in [5]. Markov process has first been used in [6] for steganalysis. How to

Y.Q. Shi, H.J. Kim, and F. Pérez-González (Eds.): IWDW 2012, LNCS 7809, pp. 19–33, 2013.
© Springer-Verlag Berlin Heidelberg 2013

handle the high dimensionality of elements in the transition probability matrix resultant from the application of Markov process has been studied [7] in the spatial-domain. In [8], a scheme called SPAM using both the first and the second order Markov models has been established to detect the more advanced steganographic scheme known as LSB matching. As expected, the competition between steganography and steganalysis always exists and moves our knowledge ahead. Consequently, a modern steganographic scheme, named HUGO (Highly Undetectable Stegonagraphy) [9], has been developed so as to fail the SPAM by taking high order difference into consideration in its data embedding. Steganalytic methods [10,11,12,13] have been reported to break HUGO. In [11], the difference arrays from the first-order up to the sixth-order are all used to generate residual images for feature extraction in addition to other newly designed features, resulting in a total number of features as high as 33,963. Because of the high feature dimensionality, an ensemble classifier using Fishers Linear Discriminant (FLD) has been developed and utilized. These novel measures result in a detection rate of 83.9% on BOSSbase ver. 0.92 [14,15] at the embedding rate of 0.4 bits per pixel (bpp). In [12] the local binary pattern technology, developed for texture analysis, has been applied to steganalysis for the first time. With 22,153 features, a detection rate of 83.92% has been achieved on BOSSbase 0.92 at 0.4 bpp. Based on [11], the detection rate has been further increased to almost 87% with 34,671 features, and 86.45% with 12,753 features (i.e.Top39 feature-set) at 0.4 bpp in [13].

In this paper, a novel mapping technology is presented. Using this mapping technique, the detection rate on the BOSSbase 0.92 at 0.4 bpp reaches 87.17% with only 15,840 features, most of which have been used in [13]. The rest of this paper is organized as follows. In Section 2, the proposed mapping technology is presented. The set of features used in this work is presented in Section 3. The experimental procedure and results are presented in Section 4. The discussion and conclusions are made in Section 5.

2   Proposed Mapping Technique

In this section we first provide some background on residual image and co-occurrence matrix. Then, the proposed mapping technique is presented.

2.1   Background and Residual Image

Co-occurrence matrix was proposed as textural features for image classification in 1973 [16]. Since then it has been widely utilized for image classification (as of 2012, having been cited about 7,000 times according to Google). In steganalysis, a special type of image classification, the co-occurrence matrix has been widely used as well [17,11,13]. The simplest and most frequent usage of co-occurrence matrixes involves pairs of two elements in an image, or more general, a 2-D array. As a result, it is a second order statistics in nature. This explains why it is more effective than using histogram in image classification, which is of the first order

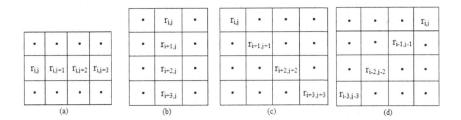

Fig. 1. Four different ways to generate co-occurrence matrix; a portion of residual image: 4 elements along (a) horizontal direction, (b) vertical direction, (c) diagonal direction, (d) minor diagonal direction

statistics. (Note that Markov transitional matrix has also been frequently used in steganalysis, e.g., in [7,18,8], which can be shown under certain conditions (that is often satisfied in reality) are equivalent to the co-occurrence matrices.)

In steganalysis, e.g., in breaking HUGO, the higher order co-occurrence matrixes are widely used. An example is that the order of co-occurrence matrix utilized is as high as the 4th order in [13]. There the symmetry property of some co-occurrence matrix is identified and utilized to reduce the feature dimensionality, hence making the algorithm more efficient and more powerful. Specifically, let us take a look at the co-occurrence matrix used in [13]. There four consecutive elements in horizontal and vertical directions of the so-called residual image are considered and utilized for steganalysis. Note that the residual images are obtained by applying some high-pass filters to the images followed by some other procedures. The model of residual image, R, is as follows:

$$R = Trunc_T(round(Filter(X, h)/q)) \qquad (1)$$

where h is a high-pass filter, $Filter(X, h)$ means the image X has been filtered by the filter h; followed by quantization with step q; and then rounded to integer; finally truncated with a threshold T. Here, the filter can be linear or non-linear. The purpose is to remove the image content and boost stego information for steganalysis. The filtered image is often referred to as residual image. The quantization is used to reduce the dynamic range of the residual image, thus reducing the feature dimensionality.

Note that the residual image can also be denoted as $R = \{r_{i,j}\}_{m \times n}$ where m, n are the size of residual image, and $r_{i,j} \in [-T : T]$, with T is the threshold as discussed above. The sign of [-T:T] means a integer set from -T to T.

2.2   Co-occurrence Matrices along Four Directions

The following four notations, i.e. C^h, C^v, C^d and C^m, denote the fourth order co-occurrence matrixes along the horizontal, vertical, diagonal and minor diagonal directions respectively. They are shown in Fig.'s 1(a),(b),(c) and (d),respectively.

Now the co-occurrence matrix generated by considering four horizontally consecutive elements of a residual image can be represented as follows.

$$C^h = |\{(r_{i,j}, r_{i,j+1}, r_{i,j+2}, r_{i,j+3}) \,|\, r_{i,j}, r_{i,j+1}, r_{i,j+2}, r_{i,j+3} \in [-T : T]\}| \quad (2)$$

where i and j are coordinates in vertical and horizontal two directions, respectively, and T is the threshold. Other three types of co-occurrence C^v, C^d and C^m are defined analogously.

As in [13] the T is selected as $T = 2$. Hence the total number of features generated from each residual image is $(2T+1)^4 = 625$. Some symmetry properties have been identified and used to further reduce the feature dimensionality.

2.3   A Novel Mapping Technique

Instead of employing the symmetry property to reduce feature dimensionality as done in [13], we present a new technique called mapping. It will be shown that this novelty makes the proposed algorithm work more efficient and effective than the above-mentioned state-of-the-art.

First, we utilize a large number of training images as samples from which we obtain useful information to guide the feature number reduction. That is, from a sufficiently large number of training samples we can randomly select certain number of images, say, N sample images. From these N sample images, we compute the corresponding residual images by applying some selected high-frequency masks. Working on these residual images we can then calculate the average probability of the number of elements, $r_{i,j}$, of the residual images that assume the values in the range of $[-T : T]$. Specifically we can obtain the statistics as follows.

$$P_k(t) = |\{(i,j) | t = r_{i,j}, r_{i,j} \in R_{mn}, t \in [-T : T]\}| / (m \times n) \quad (3)$$

where k represents the kth image among N sample images, m and n are the size of the residual images. For the kth given training sample, we can determine its $P_k(t)$. Since we have N samples available, we can then obtain $P_1(t)$, $P_2(t)$,...,$P_N(t)$.

$$P(t) = |\{P_1(t) + P_2(t) + ... + P_N(t)\}| / N \quad (4)$$

for $t \in [-T : T]$. In other words, we can find in this way all of the following probabilities: $P(-T), P(-T+1),...,P(T)$ from the N training samples. It will be shown that this novelty, i.e., working on the available training samples to estimate the probabilities of $P(t)$ can enhance our steganalysis capability effectively.

After we have obtained the $P(t = r_{i,j})$ for all of (i,j) pairs, we conduct the following processing.

1. Arrange all of $P(t)$ values according to their magnitude in the non-increasing order.
2. Then, we merge two items with the least probabilities into one item.

3. For the newly updated set of probabilities, we rearrange the probabilities in the non-increasing order.
4. We then repeat what we do in Step 2 and Step 3.
5. The process stops when only M probabilities remain as $M \in [2 : 2T + 1]$.

Hence at the end of this process, we can convert $(2T + 1)$ probabilities to M probabilities, where the M is an integer and $M \in [2 : 2T + 1]$.

One illustrative example is provided below. Assume T is equal to 2 as used in [13]. Further assume from the training image samples, the following five probabilities have been obtained. That is, the probabilities that $r_{i,j}$ assumes -2,-1,0,1,2 are, respectively, $P(-2) = 0.12$, $P(-1) = 0.23$, $P(0) = 0.28$, $P(1) = 0.24$, $P(2) = 0.13$. Our proposed mapping technology may go as follows. We start with arranging all of five probabilities in a non-increasing order, and then renumber them as 0, 1, 2, 3, 4, as show in Eq. 5. The procedures go as follows. The 1st mapping:

$$mapping(t = r_{i,j}) = \begin{cases} 0 & t(= r_{i,j}) = 0 & P(0) = 0.28 \\ 1 & t(= r_{i,j}) = 1 & P(1) = 0.24 \\ 2 & t(= r_{i,j}) = -1 & P(-1) = 0.23 \\ 3 & t(= r_{i,j}) = 2 & P(2) = 0.13 \\ 4 & t(= r_{i,j}) = -2 & P(-2) = 0.12 \end{cases} \qquad (5)$$

The 2nd mapping

$$mapping(t = r_{i,j}) = \begin{cases} 0 & t(= r_{i,j}) = 0 & P(0) = 0.28 \\ 1 & t(= r_{i,j}) = -2 \text{ or } 2 & P(-2 \text{ or } 2) = 0.25 \\ 2 & t(= r_{i,j}) = 1 & P(1) = 0.24 \\ 3 & t(= r_{i,j}) = -1 & P(-1) = 0.23 \end{cases} \qquad (6)$$

The 3rd mapping:

$$mapping(t = r_{i,j}) = \begin{cases} 0 & t(= r_{i,j}) = -1 \text{ or } 1 & P(-1 \text{ or } 1) = 0.47 \\ 1 & t(= r_{i,j}) = 0 & P(0) = 0.28 \\ 2 & t(= r_{i,j}) = -2 \text{ or } 2 & P(-2 \text{ or } 2) = 0.25 \end{cases} \qquad (7)$$

The 4th mapping

$$mapping(t = r_{i,j}) = \begin{cases} 0 & t(= r_{i,j}) = -2 \text{ or } 2 \text{ or } 0 & P(-2 \text{ or } 2 \text{ or } 0) = 0.53 \\ 1 & t(= r_{i,j}) = -1 \text{ or } 1 & P(-1 \text{ or } 1) = 0.47 \end{cases} \qquad (8)$$

It is noted that this mapping process does look like Huffman coding [19], in which one always first lists all items with their associated probabilities in a non-increasing order, then aggregates the last two items associated with the two least probabilities into a new item, this process repeats until only two items remain. However, in our context here, the process may stop as only M probabilities remain with $M \in [2 : 2T + 1]$. That is, the procedure can end up with any one of the four cases, as defined in Eq.s 5-8.

In using Eq. (2) to calculate the co-occurrence matrix, C^h, we have the following four consecutive residual values: $r_{i,j}, r_{i,j+1}, r_{i,j+2}$ and $r_{i,j+3}$, each can assume $(2T + 1)$ possible different values. In this work, we consider $T = 2$ which has been used in [13] because this assumption can facilitate the performance comparison late in this paper. Hence, the value M can only assume the following four possible values, i.e., $[2 : 5]$, which have been denoted by M_1, M_2, M_3 and M_4.

The mapping applied to $r_{i,j}, r_{i,j+1}, r_{i,j+2}$ and $r_{i,j+3}$ sequentially will result in a corresponding four-digit number, denoted by $d_4d_3d_2d_1$, where $d_i \in [0 : M_i - 1]$ with $i = 1, 2, 3, 4$. Furthermore, from the right to the left, the weight of d_1, d_2, d_3 and d_4 are, respectively, 1, M_1, $M_1 \times M_2$ and $M_1 \times M_2 \times M_3$. The number represented by $d_4d_3d_2d_1$ can be represented as a decimal number as follows.

$$(d_4d_3d_2d_1) = d_1 + M_1 \times d_2 + M_1 \times M_2 \times d_3 + M_1 \times M_2 \times M_3 \times d_4 \quad (9)$$

where $d_4d_3d_2d_1$ is a decimal number. In this way, the computation of all of the 4th order co-occurrences becomes equivalent to calculate the histogram of the decimal numbers, denoted by $d_4d_3d_2d_1$ from the residual image, i.e., $R_{i,j} = \{r_{i,j}\}_{m \times n}$ (which has been defined at the end of Section 2.1).

This type of histogram is referred to as HMCooc (here H stands for Huffman-coding-like, M stands for mapping, and Cooc stands for co-occurrence matrix) in this paper. Its dimensionality is $M_1 \times M_2 \times M_3 \times M_4$. If the values of M_1, M_2, M_3 and M_4 are all allowed to assume $(2T + 1)$ possible values, the HMCooc is equivalent to co-occurrence matrix. In this sense, the co-occurrence matrix is a special case of the proposed HMCooc technique. It is shown in Section 4 experimentation that we use $M_1 = 5, M_2 = 4, M_3 = 3$ and $M_4 = 2$, i.e., $T = 2$ as discussed above. Hence the 4th order HMCooc results in 120 dimensions because of $5 \times 4 \times 3 \times 2 = 120$. What discussed here is the 4th order HMCooc along the horizontal direction. Other order and other directions can be pursued similarly.

In summary, instead of the 4th order co-occurrence matrixes used in [13], we use the 4th order HMCooc technique presented here. The threshold used is the same as in [13], i.e., $T = 2$. According to our experimental works, considering the achieved performance and the number of features utilized, we choose to use 4th order HMCooc, where M_1, M_2, M_3, M_4 assume values of 5,4,3,2, respectively. How to achieve the optimal M values (equivalently for the 4th order, the optimal values of M_1, M_2, M_3 and M_4) remains for the future research.

3   Feature Set Construction

We have presented above a Huffman-coding like Mapping Co-occurrence matrix based strategy, HMCooc, in Section 2. As mentioned in Section 1, the pattern classification based steganalysis relies on statistical features. Experience has taught us a single type of feature set could hardly achieve a high steganalysis rate. Hence, multiple-type of statistical features are often used in steganalysis, e.g., in [11,13]. In this paper, the statistical features used in [13] are considered. In order to examine the performance of the proposed mapping scheme, the experimental works have been planned and conducted. What we have done is to

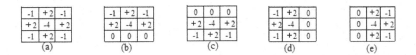

Fig. 2. $f_{3\times3}$ filters, from (a) to (e): $f_{3\times3spam}$, $f_{3\times3eu}$, $f_{3\times3eb}$, $f_{3\times3el}$, $f_{3\times3er}$

(a)

-1	+2	-2	+2	-1
+2	-6	+8	-6	+2
-2	+8	-12	+8	-2
+2	-6	+8	-6	+2
-1	+2	-2	+2	-1

(b)

-1	+2	-2	+2	-1
+2	-6	+8	-6	+2
-2	+8	-12	+8	-2
0	0	0	0	0
0	0	0	0	0

(c)

0	0	0	0	0
0	0	0	0	0
-2	+8	-12	+8	-2
+2	-6	+8	-6	+2
-1	+2	-2	+2	-1

(d).

-1	+2	-2	0	0
+2	-6	+8	0	0
-2	+8	-12	0	0
+2	-6	+8	0	0
-1	+2	-2	0	0

(e)

0	0	-2	+2	-1
0	0	+8	-6	+2
0	0	-12	+8	-2
0	0	+8	-6	+2
0	0	-2	+2	-1

Fig. 3. $f_{5\times5}$ filters, from (a) to (e): $f_{5\times5spam}$, $f_{5\times5eu}$, $f_{5\times5eb}$, $f_{5\times5el}$, $f_{5\times5er}$

apply the proposed mapping scheme to the framework of the state-of-the-art [13], then examine if the steganalysis capability is enhanced or not. Since our mapping can reduce the feature numbers from 625 to 120, we therefore add some features so as to make the total number of features of these two schemes similar to each other.

3.1   General Description

In Section 2, the residual images presented in [13] have been expressed in Eq.(1). All of co-occurrence matrixes have been calculated from the residual images. To facilitate the discussion we classify the residual images used in [13] into the following four types, called R_{1st}, R_{2nd}, R_{3rd} and $R_{\{h_{n\times n}\}}$. The subscripts: 1st, 2nd, and 3rd indicate the order of the filter used to generate the residual image. For instance, R_{1st} indicates such a kind of residual image which have been generated via applying a 1st- order filters. The subscript $h_{n\times n}$ represents a different kind of residual images, which are generated via applying a square filter, denoted by $h_{n\times n}$. The four types of filters in this category, i.e., $R_{\{h_{n\times n}\}}$, have been shown in Fig.'s 2,3,4 and 5 with notations of $f_{3\times3}$, $f_{5\times5}$, $g_{5\times5}$ and $h_{5\times5}$. Each kind of $h_{n\times n}$ filters has one spam filter and the corresponding four edge filters (i.e., $n \times neu$, $n \times neb$, $n \times nel$ and $n \times ner$). The naming of these edge filters is illustrated via an example shown below. For instance, the $f_{3\times3eu}$ indicates that this is a 3×3 filter, 'e' means an edge filter, 'u' means upper. The subscript 'b' means bottom, 'l' left, 'r' right.

In [13], two groups of filters, i.e., $f_{3\times3}$ and $f_{5\times5}$ are used. In our method, all of these four types of filters as shown in Fig.'s 2,3,4 and 5 have been used in our method. The $f_{3\times3}$ filters are defined as follows.

$$\{f_{3\times3}\} = \{f_{3\times3spam}, f_{3\times3eu}, f_{3\times3eb}, f_{3\times3el}, f_{3\times3er}\} \tag{10}$$

The $f_{5\times5}$, $g_{5\times5}$ and $h_{5\times5}$ filter-set are defined analogously.

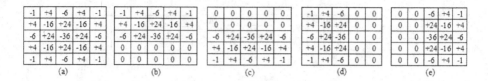

Fig. 4. $g_{5\times5}$ filters, from (a) to (e): $g_{5\times5spam}$, $g_{5\times5eu}$, $g_{5\times5eb}$, $g_{5\times5el}$, $g_{5\times5er}$

0	0	0	0	0
0	1	-3	3	-1
0	-3	9	-9	3
0	3	-9	9	-3
0	-1	3	-3	1

(a)

0	1	-3	3	-1
0	-3	9	-9	3
0	3	-9	9	-3
0	0	0	0	0
0	0	0	0	0

(b)

0	0	0	0	0
0	0	0	0	0
0	-3	9	-9	3
0	3	-9	9	-3
0	-1	3	-3	1

(c)

0	0	0	0	0
0	0	0	0	0
1	-3	3	0	0
-3	9	-9	0	0
3	-9	9	0	0
-1	3	-3	0	0

(d)

0	0	0	0	0
0	0	-3	3	-1
0	0	9	-9	3
0	0	-9	9	-3
0	0	3	-3	1

(e)

Fig. 5. $h_{5\times5}$ filters, from (a) to (e): $h_{5\times5spam}$, $h_{5\times5eu}$, $h_{5\times5eb}$, $h_{5\times5el}$, $h_{5\times5er}$

Furthermore, in [13] the features extracted from these four types of residual images are denoted as $Cooc_{1st}$, $Cooc_{2nd}$, $Cooc_{3rd}$ and $Cooc_{\{h_{n\times n}\}}$, where the type of $Cooc_{\{h_{n\times n}\}}$ feature-set consists of $Cooc_{\{f_{3\times3}\}}$ and $Cooc_{\{f_{5\times5}\}}$ two groups of features. In our work, we now use the HMCooc as our features. Specifically, our feature set includes $HMCooc_{1st}$, $HMCooc_{2nd}$, $HMCooc_{3rd}$ and $HMCooc_{\{h_{n\times n}\}}$. The $HMCooc_{\{h_{n\times n}\}}$ consist of four group of features, i.e., $HMCooc_{\{f_{3\times3}\}}$, $HMCooc_{\{f_{5\times5}\}}$, $HMCooc_{\{g_{5\times5}\}}$ and $HMCooc_{\{h_{5\times5}\}}$.

In [13], the features of $Cooc_{\{h_{n\times n}\}}$ consists of spam11, spam14, mm22h, mm22v, mm24 and mm41. There the 4th order co-occurrence features are derived from only horizontal and vertical directions and consist of two different kinds, i.e., spam and min/max (denote as mm) feature. There with certain identified symmetric properties, the dimension of co-occurrence features of spam has been reduced from 625 to 169. The dimension of min and max features have been merged (2×625) and reduced to 325.

In our method, The $HMCooc_{\{h_{n\times n}\}}$ feature-set consists of $HMCooc_{\{f_{3\times3}\}}$, $HMCooc_{\{f_{5\times5}\}}$, $HMCooc_{\{g_{5\times5}\}}$ and $HMCooc_{\{h_{5\times5}\}}$ four groups features. Here the $HMCooc_{\{g_{5\times5}\}}$ and $HMCooc_{\{h_{5\times5}\}}$ two groups of features have been added to our feature set. As said, this is because our mapping technology ends up with a reduced feature dimensionality from 625 to 120. This allows us to use some other features to enhance the performance while keeping similar feature dimensionality. Furthermore, we use features derived from all four directions: horizontal, vertical, diagonal, and minor diagonal.

3.2   More Details

Below we describe in more detail the features used in our method.

(1) $HMCooc_{\{h_{n\times n}\}}$ Type of Features

In our method, among the $HMCooc_{\{h_{n\times n}\}}$ type of features, we use the following four groups: $HMCooc_{\{f_{3\times3}\}}$, $HMCooc_{\{f_{5\times5}\}}$, $HMCooc_{\{g_{5\times5}\}}$ and

$HMCooc_{\{h_{5\times5}\}}$. The HMCooc also uses 4th order co-occurrence. Different from [13], we use not only those derived from horizontal and vertical, but also from major diagonal and minor diagonal. The way the residual image is generated is the same as that used in [13]. However, the quantization step, q, used in our work is $q = 2c$, and c is the value assumed by the central element of the filter mask. The threshold, T, used in our work is 2, which is the same as that used in [13].

Now we describe the $HMCooc_{\{f_{3\times3}\}}$ feature-set in detail as an example, and the $HMCooc_{\{h_{n\times n}\}}$ feature-set can be obtained as analogously. Firstly we define some notations: R_s, R_u, R_b, R_l and R_r. They are residual images calculate by using Eq. (1) with the filters $f_{3\times3}$ filters, from (a) to (e): $f_{3\times3spam}$, $f_{3\times3eu}$, $f_{3\times3eb}$, $f_{3\times3el}$ and $f_{3\times3er}$ respectively, and threshold $T = 2$, quantization step q $= 2c = 8$, as the same as done in [13]. We further define $Dmin1 = min(R_u, R_l)$, $Dmin2 = min(R_b, R_r)$, $Dmin3 = min(R_u, R_r)$, $Dmin4 = min(R_b, R_l)$ and $Dmin5 = min(Dmin1, Dmin2)$; in the same fashion we define Dmax1, Dmax2, Dmax2, Dmax3, Dmax4 and Dmax5 accordingly. We consider the HMCooc feature extraction as a function, and abbreviate it as HC. In this way, the HC(R,direction) means to calculate the HMCooc from the residual image, R, along the direction. As said, there are four directions, i.e., horizontal, vertical, diagonal and minor diagonal, which are abbreviated as hor, ver, diag, and mdiag, respectively.

In summary, our proposed features $HMCooc_{\{h_{n\times n}\}}$, consist of the following 10 categories as shown in Table 1.

Now we calculate the total number of features derived in this category. The number of features of spam14 is 360, the number of features for other types is 240 each, hence the total number of features derived from the $HMCooc_{\{h_{n\times n}\}}$ is 2,520. In feature extraction from $f_{3\times3}$, $f_{5\times5}$, $g_{5\times5}$, we can have 10 groups of features. For $h_{5\times5}$, we extract the following six groups of features: i.e., spam11, spam14, min22hv1, max22hv1, min24 and max24. Hence the total number of features derived from this type of is $3 \times (9 \times 240 + 360) + 5 \times 240 + 360 = 9,120$. That is, we extract 9,120 features from $HMCooc_{\{f_{3\times3}\}}$, $HMCooc_{\{f_{5\times5}\}}$, $HMCooc_{\{g_{5\times5}\}}$ and $HMCooc_{\{h_{5\times5}\}}$.

(2) Features Derived from the 1st-, 2nd-, and 3rd-order Differences
These features are derived from the 1st- order up to the 3rd-order difference along four directions. Note that these 1st-, 2nd-, and 3rd- order features are also generated and used in [13]. Specifically, the $Cooc_{1st}$ and $Cooc_{3rd}$ feature-sets consist of 11 feature sets, i.e., mm22h, mm34h, mm22v, mm24, mm34v, mm41, mm34, mm48h, mm48v, mm54, and spam14hv. The $Cooc_{2nd}$ feature-set consists of 6 feature sets, i.e., mm21, mm41, mm32, mm24h, mm24v and spam12hv. Again, only horizontal and vertical co-occurrence features are considered there. In this paper, the features extracted are the same as that in [13]. The only difference is that we do not merge the min and max features. Hence, in our framework, each kind of HMCooc feature has $120 \times 2 = 240$ features.

Since for this category, the way our features are extracted is the same as in [13], we do not list feature generation in detail. The readers are referred to [13] for the detail information. In summary, the numbers of features extracted

Table 1. Description of feature sets used in $HMCooc_{\{h_{n\times n}\}}$

Feature Name	Feature description
Spam11	$[HC(R_s, hor) + HC(R_s, ver)], HC(R_s, diag) + HC(R_s, mdiag)$
Spam14	$[HC([R_u, R_b], ver) + HC([R_l; R_r], hor),$ $[HC([R_u; R_b], hor) + HC([R_l, R_r], ver)],$ $[HC([R_u, R_b; R_l, R_r], diag) + HC([R_u, R_b; R_l, R_r], mdiag)]$
min22hv1	$[HC(min(R_u, R_b), ver) + HC(min(R_l, R_r), hor)],$ $[HC(min(R_u, R_b), hor) + HC(min(R_l, R_r), ver)]$
min22hv2	$[HC(min(R_u, R_b), diag) + HC(min(R_l, R_r), mdiag)],$ $[HC(min(R_u, R_b), mdiag) + HC(min(R_l, R_r), diag)]$
max22hv1	Same as min22hv1 except min is replaced by max
max22hv2	Same as min22hv1 except min is replaced by max
min24	$[HC(Dmin1; Dmin2; Dmin3; Dmin4], ver)+$ $HC(Dmin1; Dmin2; Dmin3; Dmin4], hor)],$ $[HC(Dmin1; Dmin2; Dmin3; Dmin4], diag)+$ $HC(Dmin1; Dmin2; Dmin3; Dmin4], mdiag)]$
max24	Same as min24 except min is replaced by max
min41	$[HC(Dmin5, ver) + HC(Dmin5, hor)],$ $[HC(Dmin5, diag) + HC(Dmin5, mdiag)]$
max41	Same as min41 except min is replaced by max

from the first three order filters are, respectively, the number of $HMCooc_{1st}$ and $HMCooc_{3rd}$ is 11×240, the number of $HMCooc_{2nd}$ is 6×240. The sub-total number of features is $6,720$.

Together with the above mentioned type of $9,120$ features, the total number of our features is $9,120 + 6,720 = 15,840$. In [13] the total number of features (i.e., TOP39 feature-set) used is $12,753$, which has achieved the accuracy of 86.45% in detecting stego images from cover images.

4   Experimentation

Two different experimental works and results are presented in this section. The first one is with a portion of features, while the second is with all of features. In both experiments, the steganalysis performance of the proposed features is compared with that reported in [13]. We evaluate the performance using the detection rate P_{corr} or detection error rate P_E, which is defined in [13] as well.

$$P_E = \min \frac{1}{2}(P_{FA} + P_{MD}(P_{FA})) \tag{11}$$

Or

$$P_{corr} = 1 - P_E \qquad (12)$$

where P_{FA} and P_{MD} are the probabilities of false alarm and missed detection.

4.1   Experiment Setup

We utilized the Bossbase ver. 0.92 [14] for all of our experiments. It consists of 9,074 cover images with size 512×512, The stego images also provide by the Boss oragizers with embeding rate at 0.4 bits per pixels. In each test, we calculate the average detection rate P_{corr} or detection error rate P_E on the 10 random splits.

4.2   Small Scale Experiment

In this experiment, a total of 1,807 features of six types (i.e., spam11, spam 14, mm22h, mm22v, mm24 and mm21) developed and reported in [13] as shown in Table 2 are utilized for steganalysis on Bossbase ver. 0.92 [14]. In each test, the randomly selected 8,074 pairs of stego and cover images are used for training and the remaining 1,000 pairs of image for testing. The FLD classifier is used. The tests are carried out by 10 times in each of which the training and testing images are randomly split. The accuracies of the tests are reported in Table 2. On the other hand the corresponding features implemented by using our proposed mapping technology are also tested. It is noted that in our methods, the min and max features have not been merged. So the $HMCooc$ consists of 10 feature sets with a total of 2,520 features, while Cooc consists of 6 feature sets with the total 1,807 features [13]. ·

From Table 2, it becomes clear that among six different cases (in each of which a type of features is generated by a different filter) there are five cases, the proposed mapping scheme achieves to a higher classification rate; the case of mm22v features is the only exception. This indicates that the mapping scheme does bring better performance in steganalysis. It is noted that the total number of features with HMCooc is a bit higher than that used in [13].

Table 3 reports the similar experiment, except now the four vertical consecutive elements in the residual image are considered for their co-occurrence. It can be observed that the performance achieved by the proposed $HMCooc_{\{f_{5\times5}\}}$ features owing to the proposed mapping technique constantly outperforms what the $Cooc_{\{f_{5\times5}\}}$ features [13] can achieve. Because of space constraint we do not list performance comparison on using the 1st-,2nd- and 3rd- order features. In experiments, on spam filter, the HMCooc features can achieve higher detection rates than that by the Cooc features reported in [13]. However, in the case of using min and max features, the HMCooc features perform a little bit worse than Cooc features as reported in [13]. The reason is that there are only 120 features for HMCooc while there are 325 or 328 features for Cooc [13].

Table 2. Detection rates achieved by $HMCooc_{\{f_{3\times3}\}}$ and that by $Cooc_{\{f_{3\times3}\}}$, 8074 pairs of images for training and 1000 pairs of images for testing FLD classifier used by 10 iterations on Bossbase ver. 0.92

$HMCooc_{\{f_{3\times3}\}}$				$Cooc_{\{f_{3\times3}\}}$				
feature	P_{corr} q=8	P_{corr} q=8	No. of features	feature	P_{corr} q=4	P_{corr} q=6	P_{corr} q=8	No. of features
spam11	0.7509	**0.7509**	240	spam11	0.7153	0.7125	0.7147	169
spam14	0.7490	**0.7490**	360	spam14	0.7100	0.7180	0.7045	338
min22hv1	0.7127	**0.7323**	240	mm22h	0.7045	0.7127	0.6971	325
min22hv2	0.6756		240					
max22hv1	0.7142	0.7240	240	mm22v	0.7426	**0.7550**	0.7361	325
max22hv2	0.6726		240					
min24	0.7366	**0.7621**	240	mm24	0.7177	0.7186	0.7060	325
max24	0.7268		240					
min41	0.7232	**0.7616**	240	mm41	0.7360	0.7431	0.7264	325
max41	0.7163		240					

Table 3. Detection rates achieved by $HMCooc_{\{f_{5\times5}\}}$ and that by $Cooc_{\{f_{5\times5}\}}$, 8074 pairs of images for training and 1000 pairs of images for testing FLD classifier used by 10 iterations on Bossbase ver. 0.92

$HMCooc_{\{f_{5\times5}\}}$				$Cooc_{\{f_{5\times5}\}}$				
feature	P_{corr} q=24	P_{corr} q=24	No. of features	feature	P_{corr} q=12	P_{corr} q=18	P_{corr} q=24	No. of features
spam11	0.7774	**0.7774**	240	spam11	0.7501	0.7566	0.7575	169
spam14	0.7761	**0.7761**	360	spam14	0.7483	0.7472	0.7442	338
min22hv1	0.7407	**0.7745**	240	mm22h	0.7029	0.7055	0.6945	325
min22hv2	0.7322		240					
max22hv1	0.7389	**0.7689**	240	mm22v	0.7544	0.7615	0.7595	325
max22hv2	0.7298		240					
min24	0.7698	**0.7871**	240	mm24	0.7364	0.7438	0.7414	325
max24	0.7662		240					
min41	0.7609	**0.7795**	240	mm41	0.7337	0.7376	0.7307	325
max41	0.7467		240					

Table 4. The detection error rate based on Our total 15,840 features on Bossbase ver. 0.92, 8,074 pairs of image for training, and 1,000 pairs of images for testing, using Ensemble Classifier.

Split	d_sub	L	P_E	P_{corr}
1	1800	82	0.1260	0.8740
2	2000	84	0.1170	0.8830
3	1600	82	0.1365	0.8635
4	2200	79	0.1305	0.8695
5	2000	77	0.1385	0.8615
6	2200	93	0.1290	0.8710
7	2000	74	0.1215	0.8785
8	1800	78	0.1330	0.8670
9	2000	83	0.1210	0.8790
10	2000	79	0.1300	0.8700
Average			**0.1283**	**0.8717**

4.3 Large-Scale Experiment

To evaluate the performance of our proposed HMCooc technique, we extract our features from the same dataset, i.e., BossBase ver. 0.92 [14,15], and use the same ensemble classifiers as used in [13]. The achieved experimental results are then compared with that reported in [13] which used the 4th order co-occurrence features.

The image dataset used is the BossBase ver. 0.92 [14] consisting of 9,074 pairs of cover and stego images. Stego images are generated by HUGO (Highly Undetectable Stegonagphy) [9] with the data embedding rate 0.4 bpp. In the experimental work, we conduct 10 tests, each time we randomly split the 9,074 pair of images into two parts: 8,074 pairs for training and the remaining 1,000 pairs of images for testing.

Table 4 presents the detection rate achieved by our proposed method. That is, the total 15,840 features generated by using our proposed mapping method are used. The average error rate is 12.83% over 10 random tests, equivalently the accuracy achieved is 87.17%. According to [13], the average error rate over 10 tests is 13.55% (i.e., the accuracy 86.45%) with 12,753 features (i.e., Top39 feature-set). In our experiments, it is found that the average accuracy of 86.99% in classification (i.e., 13.01% error rate) can be achieved by using all different quantization parameter, q, meaning that a total number of 34,671 features in [13] are used. It is known in the literature, e.g., in [13] and [12], in breaking HUGO, even 0.5% increase in detection accuracy is not easy as the detection is rather high like 86%, instead, it needs tremendous efforts.

Note that in Table 4, the d_sub and L are auto selected by ensemble classifier, with the default setting [20].

5   Discussion and Conclusions

In this work, the state-of-the-art in steganalysis on non-compressed images [13] has been studied. A novel mapping scheme has been proposed to reduce feature dimensionality drastically so as to achieve higher performance in steganalysis.

In utilizing four element co-occurrence matrixes for steganalysis [13], the dimensionality encountered is $5 \times 5 \times 5 \times 5$. Some symmetry properties have been utilized to reduce feature dimensionality. In this work, it has been found that the reduced feature dimension of $5 \times 4 \times 3 \times 2$ can outperform the state-of-the-art in breaking HUGO. It is noted that instead of $5 \times 4 \times 3 \times 2$ for dimensions of four consecutive elements horizontally, vertically, diagonally and minor-diagonally, any combination of four elements, say, $3 \times 4 \times 2 \times 5$ can achieve the same or very close detection rate. Other combination with more number of dimensions in total, such as $5 \times 4 \times 3 \times 5$, may achieve higher detection rate. In general, however, $5 \times 4 \times 3 \times 2$ achieves optimal performance because of a good balance between the feature diversity and the total number of features. That is, it is not always the case that the higher the feature dimension the better the performance. This has been shown in one of our experimental results. There with a total number of 15,840 features our new method can achieve 87.17% accuracy in BOSSbase ver. 0.92 [14], while the accuracy in the same dataset is 86.99% by using 34,671 features in [13].

Further study and research along this line is our future research in order to further boost steganalysis capability, which means higher steganalyzing capability and lower feature dimensionality.

Acknowledgement. This work has been partially supported by National Natural Science Foundation of China (61170271, 31100416) and Fujian Provincial Natural Science Fund of China (2010J01246).

References

1. Avcibas, M., Memon, N., Sankur, B.: Steganalysis Using Image Quality Metrics. In: SPIE, EI, Security and Watermarking of Multimedia Content, San Jose, CA (February 2001)
2. Farid, H., Siwei, L.: Detecting hidden messages using higher-order statistics and support vector machines. In: Petitcolas, F.A.P. (ed.) IH 2002. LNCS, vol. 2578, pp. 340–354. Springer, Heidelberg (2003)
3. Harmsen, J.J.: Steganalysis of Additive Noise Modelable Information Hiding. Master Thesis of Rensselaer Polytechnic Institute, Troy, New York, advised by Professor W. A. Pearlman (2003)
4. Xuan, G., Shi, Y.Q., Gao, J., Zou, D., Yang, C., Zhang, Z., Chai, P., Chen, C.-H., Chen, W.: Steganalysis based on multiple features formed by statistical moments of wavelet characteristic functions. In: Barni, M., Herrera-Joancomartí, J., Katzenbeisser, S., Pérez-González, F. (eds.) IH 2005. LNCS, vol. 3727, pp. 262–277. Springer, Heidelberg (2005)
5. Fridrich, J.: Feature-Based Steganalysis for JPEG Images and its Implications for Future Design of Steganographic Schemes. In: Fridrich, J. (ed.) IH 2004. LNCS, vol. 3200, pp. 67–81. Springer, Heidelberg (2004)

6. Sullivan, K., Madhow, U., Chandrasekaran, S., Manjunath, B.S.: Steganalysis of Spread Spectrum Data Hiding Exploiting Cover Memory. In: SPIE 2005, vol. 5681, pp. 38–46 (2005)

7. Zou, D., Shi, Y.Q., Su, W., Xuan, G.: Steganalysis Based on Markov Model of Thresholded Prediction-Error Image. In: IEEE International Conference on Multimedia and Expo., Toronto, Canada (2006)

8. Pevný, T., Bas, P., Fridrich, J.: Stegabalysis by subtractive pixel adjacency matrix. In: ACMM MSEC, Princeton, NJ, USA, September 7–8 (2009)

9. Pevný, T., Filler, T., Bas, P.: Using high-dimensional image models to perform highly undetectable steganography. In: Böhme, R., Fong, P.W.L., Safavi-Naini, R. (eds.) IH 2010. LNCS, vol. 6387, pp. 161–177. Springer, Heidelberg (2010)

10. Gul, G., Kurugollu, F.: A New Methodology in Steganalysis: Breaking Highly Undetectable Steganograpy (HUGO). In: Filler, T., Pevný, T., Craver, S., Ker, A. (eds.) IH 2011. LNCS, vol. 6958, pp. 71–84. Springer, Heidelberg (2011)

11. Fridrich, J., Kodovský, J., Holub, V., Goljan, M.: Steganalysis of Content-Adaptive Steganography in Spatial Domain. In: Filler, T., Pevný, T., Craver, S., Ker, A. (eds.) IH 2011. LNCS, vol. 6958, pp. 102–117. Springer, Heidelberg (2011)

12. Shi, Y.Q., Sutthiwan, P., Chen, L.: Textural features for steganalysis. In: Kirchner, M., Ghosal, D. (eds.) IH 2012. LNCS, vol. 7692, pp. 63–77. Springer, Heidelberg (2013)

13. Fridrich, J., Kodovský, J.: Kodovský: Rich Models for Steganalysis of Digital Images. IEEE Trans. on Info. Forensics and Security 7(3), 868–882 (2012)

14. Filler, T., Pevný, T., Bas, P.: BOSS (Break Our Steganography System) (July 2010), http://boss.gipsa-lab.grenoble-inp.fr

15. Bas, P., Filler, T., Pevný, T.: "Break our steganographic system": The ins and outs of organizing BOSS. In: Filler, T., Pevný, T., Craver, S., Ker, A. (eds.) IH 2011. LNCS, vol. 6958, pp. 59–70. Springer, Heidelberg (2011)

16. Haralick, R.M., Shanmugan, K., Dinstein, I.: Textural Features for Image Classification. IEEE Transactions on Systems, Man and Cybernetics SMC-3(6), 610–621 (1973)

17. Xuan, G., Shi, Y.Q., Huang, C., Fu, D., Zhu, X., Chai, P., Gao, J.: Steganalysis Using High-Dimensional Features Derived from Co-Occurrence Matrix and Classwise Non-Principal Components Analysis (CNPCA). In: Shi, Y.Q., Jeon, B. (eds.) IWDW 2006. LNCS, vol. 4283, pp. 49–60. Springer, Heidelberg (2006)

18. Shi, Y.Q., Chen, C.-H., Chen, W.: A markov process based approach to effective attacking JPEG steganography. In: Camenisch, J.L., Collberg, C.S., Johnson, N.F., Sallee, P. (eds.) IH 2006. LNCS, vol. 4437, pp. 249–264. Springer, Heidelberg (2007)

19. Shi, Y.Q., Sun, H.F.: Image and Video Compression for Multimedia Engineering: Fundamentals, Algortihms and Standards. CRC press LLC (2000)

20. Kodovský, J., Holub, V.: Ensemble classifier (2012), http://dde.binghamton.edu/download/ensemble/

Steganalysis of LSB Matching Based on the Sum Features of Average Co-occurrence Matrix Using Image Estimation

Yan-qing Guo[1,2], Xiang-wei Kong[1], Bo Wang[1], and Qian Xiao[1]

[1] Dalian University of Technology, Dalian, China, 116023
[2] State Information Center, Beijing, China, 100045

Abstract. A new LSB matching steganalysis scheme for gray images is proposed in this paper. This method excavates the relevance between pixels in the LSB matching stego image from the co-occurrence matrix. This method can acquire high accuracy near to 100% at high embedding rate. In order to increase the accuracy at low embedding rate, we strengthen the differences between the cover image and the stego image to improve the performance of our scheme. Two 8 dimensional feature vectors are extracted separately from the test image and the restoration image, and then the combining 16 dimensional feature vector is used for steganalysis with the FISHER linear classification. Experimental results show that the detection accuracy of this method is above 90% with the embedding rate of 25%; even when the embedding rate is 10%, the detection accuracy reaches 80%.Experiments show that this method is more reliable than other state-of-art methods.

Keywords: LSB matching, steganalysis, co-occurrence matrix, image restoration, feature classify.

1   Introduction

Digital steganography, an important branch of information hiding, is the art of invisible communication which can enhance the security of the information, and at the same time increase the difficulty for the network safety supervision. Steganalysis is the art of attacking steganography, which is useful for network safety supervision and for intercepting unsafe digital multimedia information. The cover objects for digital steganograpy are various, such as texts, audio clips, video clips, digital images etc. Because digital image has large redundancy allowance, small storage capacity etc, it is widely used in digital steganography. The embedding methods for images are various. According to the embedding domain, steganography can be classified into space domain and transform domain and so on. Among all the embedding methods, steganography in space domain is drawing the attention of researchers for its simple operation and large capacity, especially for the improvement algorithm of LSB——LSB matching, and our method is focusing on LSB matching.

Y.Q. Shi, H.J. Kim, and F. Pérez-González (Eds.): IWDW 2012, LNCS 7809, pp. 34–43, 2013.
© Springer-Verlag Berlin Heidelberg 2013

From the beginning of 2003, the researchers have been interested in LSB matching steganalysis. The most representative method was proposed by Harmsen and Pearlman etc [1] using the histogram characteristic function (HCF), depending on whether the function value of cover image is equal or greater than that of the stego image to distinguish the cover and stego images, but this approach is only effective for the BMP color image, and fail for the BMP gray image. Then Ker etc [2] did two improvements with Harmen's method: First, down sample the images; second, use the adjacency histogram instead of the normal histogram. The detection accuracy of LSB matching for gray images can reach 96%. In [3], a steganalysis method based on the correlation of pixel difference is proposed. The image histogram, smoothness of the difference histogram, gradient energy, the 1 and high dimension statistical distribution of pixel difference are used as the features for classification. Fridich [4] put forward a steganalysis method for LSB matching with good performance. This method called WAM extracts statistical moment of noise from wavelet domain to form the 27 dimensional feature vector. The detection accuracy of WAM reaches as high as 99% when the embedding rate is 1. However, the detection accuracy for low embedding rate is low; the method in this paper is to solve the problem of low detection accuracy at low embedding rate.

2   LSB Matching Model

LSB matching and LSB replacement are two widely used steganograpy method based on least significant bits of image pixels. Comparing with LSB replacement, LSB Matching is more secure. It can randomly add and subtract 1 to the image pixel's LSB, thus eliminate the effect of pair in LSB replacement, reduce the distortion of the cover image, and maintain the correlation between the adjacent pixels. It is also known as random ±1 LSB steganograpy, and the specific embedding method can be shown as follow:

$$I_s = \begin{cases} 1 & b \neq LSB(I_c) \, \& \, I_c = 0 \\ I_c \pm 1 & b \neq LSB(I_c) \, \& \, 0 < I_c < 2^L - 2 \\ I_c & b = LSB(I_c) \\ 2^L - 2 & b \neq LSB(I_c) \, \& \, I_c = 2^L - 1 \end{cases} \tag{1}$$

Where, I_C is the cover image, I_S is the stego image, b is one bit, L is the bits number of the image.

The LSB matching model can be expressed as $I_S = I_C + \eta$, where η is the secret message. The steganography method can be modeled as adding noise, and then the corresponding steganalysis method can be modeled as denoising.

LSB Matching method operates on the space domain of images, i.e. directly using the image pixels. From the human visual system, the images are nearly the same, people cannot find the differences before and after the secret message is embedded only with the human eyes; With respect to the image histogram, when a lot of information is embedded, image histogram becomes smoother. This can be seen as an image going through a low-pass filter, and the filter removes the high-frequency coefficients; With respect to the relevance of image pixels, the secret message weak the correlation and relationship between the pixels.

3   Sum Features of Average Co-occurrence Matrix Based Steganalysis

This section analyzes the correlation between the image pixels. After steganography, the changes of the pixel pairs' values in the edge area are less obvious than those in the smooth area, so we can use co-occurrence matrix to describe pixel difference in local area of the image, and construct sum features of average co-occurrence matrix for steganalysis. In order to strengthen the differences between cover images and stego images and improve the detection accuracy at low embedding rate, we combine with the technology of image estimation for steganalysis.

3.1   Analysis of Correlation between Image Pixels

Natural images are modeled as stationary source of local area by researchers. Objects have similar reflective characteristics of electromagnetic waves, which makes the pixels of local area have strong correlation. In the analysis of image, two hypotheses are admitted, one is the Markov assumption, that is a pixel value and the pixel values of its certain space neighborhood is correlated; the other is the translation invariance hypothesis ,that is the distribution of pixels in the neighborhood is independent on the absolute position of the neighborhood in the image [9].

In terms of the content of the image, the distribution of the pixels in a meaningful image is regular, and this regularity constitutes the content of the image. From the macroscopic view, image is sights that can be seen; from the microscopic view, it is a series of point sets or point pairs. These pixel sets or pairs have the same or close pixel value. There is a small critical region for the pixels in the smooth area of the image; but the distribution of the pixels in the edge area of the image fluctuates widely, the pixel differences in this part have large value.

Adjacent pixels are correlated in the image. LSB steganagraphy is modeled as adding noise. Due to the existence of noise, LSB steganagraphy will reduce the correlation between adjacent pixels. LSB Matching method changes pixel values in the range of [-1, 0, 1].The changes of the pixel pairs' values in the edge area are less obvious than those in the smooth area. Therefore, we mainly consider the changes in the smooth area during steganalysis. In the smooth area, the change of the correlation between pixels is more obvious, thus more suitable for steganalysis. For the relative smooth neighborhood, the distribution of the pixels in the neighborhood can be described using eq (2):

$$p - \varepsilon < (f(x, y) \mid x \in [x - \Delta x, x + \Delta x], y \in [y - \Delta y, y + \Delta y]) < p + \varepsilon \qquad (2)$$

Where, ε value is integer, $f(x, y) = p$ is the pixel value at location (x, y), (x, y) is the index of the image, Δx and Δy are the index increments.For more accurate depiction of the difference before and after steganography, in this paper ε takes 3.

3.2   Gray Level Co-occurrence Matrix

Gray level Co-occurrence Matrix (GLCM) was proposed in 1973 by Haralick. Firstly it was applied in the texture feature extraction, and had good superiority in texture analysis. Since then he put forward 14 gray statistical features for texture analysis, which were later widely used in image texture extraction, edge detection, and analysis of remote sensing image. Many researchers use co-occurrence matrix as a feature for steganalysis. Sullivan [5] used the co-occurrence matrix for the first time in spread spectrum steganalysis.129 features were selected from the co-occurrence matrix elements for classification. G. Xuan [6] also took the co-occurrence matrix in LSB and DCT domain for steganalysis, a total of 1029 elements in the main diagonal line and its top two diagonals were chosen as the features. In order to reduce dimensions, the CNPCA analysis method was adopt for classification. In [7] and [8], Fridrich et al employed co-occurrence matrix, histogram characteristics of DCT coefficients for detection of the secret message. In [10], a space domain steganalysis method was proposed.180 elements from the co-occurrence matrix of the difference matrix are used to detect the hidden message. As can be seen from the above examples, co-occurrence matrix has a lot of advantages in steganalysis. The brief introduction of the gray level co-occurrence matrix is as follow.

GLCM describes the correlation of the two pixels in the θ angle direction with the distance of d, denoted as $p(i,j,d,\theta)$, θ is $0°$, $45°$ $90°$ and $135°$ respectively. Fig.1 shows the gray level co-occurrence matrix. GLCM not only reflects the distribution characteristics of the luminance, but also reflects the distribution characteristics of the locations with the same or close luminance, including the comprehensive information about the direction, the adjacent interval, the amplitude of change. A digital image can be denoted as (x,y), the largest gray level is 255, gray level co-occurrence matrix meeting certain space requirements can be expressed by eq(3) :

$$p(i,j,d,\theta) = \begin{cases} \left[(x,y),(x+\Delta x, y+\Delta y)\right] \text{lf } f(x,y)=i, \\ f(x+\Delta x, y+\Delta y)=j; \\ x=0,1,2,...,N_x-1; y=0,1,2,...,N_y-1 \end{cases} \quad (3)$$

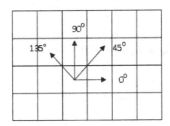

Fig. 1. Gray level co-occurrence matrix

Def 1:

Average co-occurrence matrix defines the average of four GLCMs that θ is $0°, 45°$ $90°$ and $135°$, the distance is d.

$$C_d = (C_{d0} + C_{d1} + C_{d2} + C_{d4})/4 \qquad (4)$$

Average co-occurrence matrix reflects the change of the pixels in four directions. Comparing with co-occurrence matrix in a single direction, Average co-occurrence matrix can reflect the distribution of pixels in the smooth area better, and show the correlation between the pixels better.

GLCM is composed by the elements in N diagonals, as shown in Fig.2. The i th diagonal is denoted as D_i, $i \in (-255, 255)$ and i is the Difference-value of the pixel pairs. Because the GLCM elements above and below main diagonal are symmetrical, therefore i can be considered only $i \in (0, 255)$.

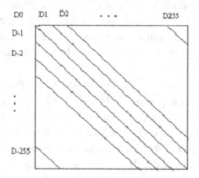

Fig. 2. Elements in the diagonal of the grayscale co-occurrence matrix

Def 2:

Sum feature of average co-occurrence matrix defines the sum of all the elements in all the GLCM's diagonals:

$$G_i = \sum D_i, \quad i = 0, 1, 2, ..., 255 \qquad (5)$$

In eq(5), i denotes the absolute difference between two pixels, when i is relatively small, the two pixel values are close, the two pixels locate in the smooth area of the image, the correlation between them is strong; As the value of i increases, the two pixels locates in the edge area of the image, the correlation is weak. The change due to data embedding in the edge area of the image is not significant. And if the image has complex textures, the edge information may cause interference to steganalysis. So combine eq (2), eq (5) is changed to eq (6):

$$G_i = \sum D_i, \quad i = 0, 1, 2, 3 \qquad (6)$$

If we use the Sum Features of the Average Co-occurrence Matrix to detect LSB matching, when the embedding rate is 100%, the detection accuracy is close to 100%. However, when the embedding rate is lower than 20%, the detection accuracy is only about 70%.

3.3   Image Estimation

Wavelet transform has low entropy, multi-resolution, decorrelation and multi-choice of wavelet basis and has significant superiority in the image denoising. Image noise energy generally concentrates in the high frequency part of the signal. The noisy signal is transformed to the frequency domain, and then the contradiction between the protection of local details and the suppression of noise become obvious. Wavelet transform has good time-frequency localization property, which may solve the contradiction above. In image processing, there exists a lot of denoising methods using wavelet transform, such as wavelet threshold denoising method, hard threshold denoising method, and the corresponding soft threshold denoising method, the wavelet energy filtering is the improvement of wavelet threshold denoising method, which uses the wavelet coefficients energy features to revise the wavelet coefficients, and filter out the noise, thus achieve the purpose of image restoration. The adaptive wavelet energy filter recovery method proposed here is different from the general method in which the wavelet coefficients shrinkage is done pixel by pixel, its wavelet coefficients shrinkage depends on the energy of all pixels in the neighborhood, and thus it has better adaptability.

Wavelet transform has different decomposition scales. There still exists some redundancy among the decomposition scales. A natural image usually has similar wavelet transform coefficients with the same resolution scales. The recovery method of adaptive wavelet energy filtering gives the wavelet energy shrinkage function and the recovery function.

Wavelet energy shrinkage function:

$$S_{m,n} = \frac{1}{N^2}\sum_{m=1}^{N}\sum_{n=1}^{N}d_{m,n}^2 \tag{7}$$

N is the filtering window size, $d_{m,n}$ are elements in the window function.

Recovery function:

$$\hat{d}_{ij} = \begin{cases} d_{ij}(1-\alpha\times\dfrac{\lambda^2}{S_{ij}}) & S_{ij} > \beta\times\lambda^2 \\[2mm] d_{ij} & other \end{cases} \tag{8}$$

$$\lambda^2 = 4\times\sigma^2\log\sqrt{N} \tag{9}$$

In eq (7), d_{ij} is the center element of the filtering window. Select odd number for the filtering window, and alpha, beta for undetermined coefficient. In eq (9), σ denotes noise variance. For a test image, σ is unknown and needs to be estimated from the image. In general, the energy of the noise after wavelet transform is mainly in HH frequency band. Here, use the wavelet coefficients of HH band after 1 level wavelet decomposition to estimate $\sigma = median(abs(d))/0.6745$.

The steps of image estimation:

Step 1: Calculate the first level wavelet decomposition of the test image, extract HH sub-band coefficients, and then calculate the local variance of HH sub-band coefficient, according to $\sigma = median(abs(d))/0.6745$;

Step 2: Calculate the second level wavelet decomposition of the test image, 6 high-frequency sub-bands are calculated ; use the energy shrinkage function and the recovery function to modify wavelet coefficients of three high-frequency sub-band in each level respectively, then another 6 high-frequency sub-bands are calculated;

Step 3: Merge the wavelet coefficients of the 12 sub-bands and reconstruct the image.

In order to validate the similarity between the estimation image after filtering and the original cover image, we use reconstruction bit error rate (BER), BER denotes the rate of the number of the pixels that the original cover image and corresponding estimation image have the same value and the total number of image pixels. Filtering the cover image and stego image respectively, the cover image BER is about 0.9 or so, the stego image BER is about 0.7 or so. Although estimation images of stego image and cover image are quite different, the difference highlights the difference between stego images and cover images. So extracting the sum features of the average GLCM from the estimation image can improve the steganalysis performance.

3.4   Feature Extraction

This section shows the detail of the feature extraction method and the flow diagram of our steganalysis approach, as shown in Fig.4.

Step 1: Use adaptive wavelet energy filter to get the estimation image from test image;

Step 2: Calculate the average GLCM C_1 , C_2 of the test image, according to eq (5); extract sum features $G_i, i = 0,1,2,3$ of C_1 , C_2 respectively, get 8 features;

Step 3: Calculate the average GLCM C_1^* , C_2^* of the estimate image, according to eq (5); extract sum features $G_i, i = 0,1,2,3$ of C_1^* , C_2^* respectively, get 8 features;

Step 4: Combine features from step3 and step4, get 16 average GLCM sum features.

Step 5: Use FISHER linear classifier for classification.

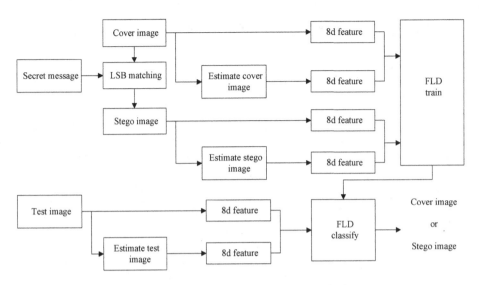

Fig. 3. Diagram of LSB matching steganalysis

4   Experimental Results

In order to verify the performance of the proposed method, we test out algorithm on the following database. The database consists of 485 uncompressed TIFF format images with the resolution of 1440 x960. All the images are converted into gray image. We generate stego images with the LSB Matching algorithm for different embedding rates of 100%, 75%, 50%, 25%, 15%, 10%. We randomly choose 200 images as the training set from the cover and the stego image database respectively, and the others for testing.

To compare the performance with other steganalysis methods, the 16 features using estimation image, the 8 features without using estimation image, WAM 27 features and improved HCF features are respectively classified by FISHER classifier. For different embedding rates and different false alarm rates, experimental results can be shown in ROC curve. Fig.4 shows detection accuracy of different methods when the embedding rate is 100% .Table 1 presents the details of the results for different embedding rates and different features (false alarm rate is 0.1).

Table 1. Average detection accuracy with the fisher classifier

Embedding rate %	16d features	8d features	WAM	Improved HCF
100	99.65%	99.30%	99.47%	96.90%
75	99.30%	98.42%	98.25%	96.84%
50	98.95%	97.72%	96.14%	81.05%
25	95.09%	91.40%	90.70%	62.46%
15	86.72%	76.49%	74.61%	60.42%
10	82.36%	73.51%	70.46%	58.42%

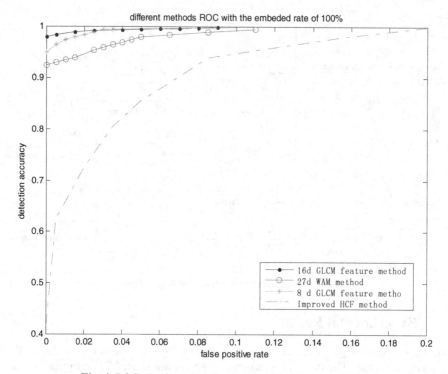

Fig. 4. ROC of different methods with embedding rate 100%

It is clear from Fig.4 and Table 1 that the detection accuracy of our method outperforms the other methods in detecting the LSB matching method for grayscale images with the same false alarm rate and the features using estimation image do better than the 8 features without using estimation image.

Experimental results show that when the embedding rate is lower than 25%, the detection accuracy is increased above 20% compared with the improved HCF feature, is increased about 10% compared with the feature without using estimation image, and is increased about 3% compared with WAM feature.

As shown, the detection accuracy of our proposed method is better than other methods.

5   Conclusion

This article starts from the correlation in the space domain of image, takes image as a local area stationary source, is based on characteristic of LSB matching, and proposes a steganalysis method based on the sum features of average co-occurrence matrix using estimation image. Experimental results show that the detection accuracy of this method is about 100% with the embedding rate of 100%; even in low embedding rate, the detection accuracy reaches 80%. Continuously improving the accuracy of image estimation is a new direction for steganalysis.

Acknowledgments. This work is supported by the National Natural Science Foundation of China (Grant No. 60971095) and China Postdoctoral Science Foundation (NO.20110490343).

References

1. Harmsen, J., Pearlman, W.: Steganalysis of additive noise modelable information hiding. In: Delp, E., Wong, P.W. (eds.) Proceedings SPIE, Electronic Imaging, Security, Steganography, and Watermarking of Multimedia Contents V, Santa Clara, California, USA, vol. 5020, pp. 131–142 (2003)
2. Ker, A.D.: Steganalysis of LSB matching in grayscale images. IEEE Signal Processing Letters 12(6), 441–444 (2005)
3. Zhang, T., Li, W.X., Zhang, Y., et al.: Steganalysis of LSB matching based on statistical modeling of pixel difference distributions. Information Sciences 180(23), 4685–4694 (2010)
4. Goljan, M., Fridrich, J., Holotyak, T.: New Blind Steganalysis and its Implications. In: Delp, E., Wong, P.W. (eds.) Proceedings SPIE, Electronic Imaging, Security, Steganography, and Watermarking of Multimedia Contents VIII, San Jose, California, USA, vol. 6072, pp. 1–13 (2006)
5. Sullivan, K., Madhow, U., Chandrasekaran, S.: Steganalysis of spread spectrum data hiding exploiting cover memory. In: Delp, E., Wong, P.W. (eds.) Proceedings SPIE, Electronic Imaging, Security, Steganography, and Watermarking of Multimedia Contents VII, San Jose, California, USA, vol. 5681, pp. 38–46 (2005)
6. Xuan, G., Shi, Y.Q., Huang, C., Fu, D., Zhu, X., Chai, P., Gao, J.: Steganalysis using high-dimensional features derived from co-occurrence matrix and class-wise non-principal components analysis (CNPCA). In: Shi, Y.Q., Jeon, B. (eds.) IWDW 2006. LNCS, vol. 4283, pp. 49–60. Springer, Heidelberg (2006)
7. Fridrich, J.: Feature-based steganalysis for JPEG images and its implications for future design of steganographic schemes. In: Fridrich, J. (ed.) IH 2004. LNCS, vol. 3200, pp. 67–81. Springer, Heidelberg (2004)
8. Pevný, T., Fridrich, J.: Towards multi-class blind steganalyzer for JPEG images. In: Barni, M., Cox, I., Kalker, T., Kim, H.-J. (eds.) IWDW 2005. LNCS, vol. 3710, pp. 39–53. Springer, Heidelberg (2005)
9. Wong, G.X., Ping, X.J., Xu, M.K., et al.: Steganalysis Based on Neighbor Image Pixels Correlation. Journal of Information Engineering University 8(1), 56–58 (2007)
10. Deng, Q.L., Lin, J.J.: Image steganalysis based on co-occurrence matrix. Microcomputer Information 12(1), 6–8 (2009)

Calibration Based Reliable Detector for Detecting LSB Matching Steganography

Fei Peng, Xiaolong Li, and Bin Yang

Institute of Computer Science and Technology, Peking University
Beijing 100871, China
{aniki,lixiaolong,yang_bin}@pku.edu.cn

Abstract. In this paper, a novel detector for detecting LSB matching steganography in gray-scale images is presented. We extend the previously introduced detectors, the one based on the center of mass of the histogram characteristic function (HCF-COM) and its calibrated version (C-HCF-COM), in two aspects. On one hand, to carry out detection, HCF-COM and C-HCF-COM computed from the first and second order difference images are combined together to build a feature set. On the other hand, the calibration used in C-HCF-COM, i.e., the downsample of original image, is changed to the Gaussian filtered image. With these extensions, our method significantly improves HCF-COM and C-HCF-COM. Its superiority over some state-of-the-art works is also demonstrated through extensive experiments.

Keywords: Steganography, steganalysis, LSB matching.

1 Introduction

Image steganography is designed to embed secret messages into digital images such that the existence of hidden data is undetectable. On the contrary, the detection of steganography is the goal of another topic of information hiding, steganalysis. Generally, steganalysis algorithms can be classified into two classes: blind and targeted. Regardless of the employed steganographic method, blind detector tries to decide whether the image contains hidden data or not. In contrast, targeted detector is intended to detect a specific steganography. We study the technique of targeted steganalysis in this work.

As an improvement of least-significant-bit (LSB) replacement, LSB matching (LSB-M) is an effective steganography which is hard to detect. The embedding procedure of LSB-M is simple: if the data bit to be embedded and the LSB of the corresponding cover pixel are different, the cover pixel value is randomly increased or decreased by 1. As a consequence, for decoder, it is easy to extract the embedded data by simply reading LSBs of stego image.

Many detectors against LSB-M have been proposed so far in the literature. In [1], Harmsen and Pearlman proved that the center of mass of the histogram characteristic function (HCF-COM) would decrease after LSB-M embedding, and they used HCF-COM as a discriminant to detect. To our best knowledge,

Y.Q. Shi, H.J. Kim, and F. Pérez-González (Eds.): IWDW 2012, LNCS 7809, pp. 44–53, 2013.

HCF-COM is the first effective detector of LSB-M. In [2], Ker pointed out that HCF-COM is highly related to image content, and he proposed the so-called calibrated HCF-COM (C-HCF-COM) to regularize the value of HCF-COM by taking the downsampled image as a calibration. After that, Li *et al.* [3] proposed to use difference image instead of the original one to compute C-HCF-COM. Recently, as an extension of [2], a new method is presented by Zheng *et al.* [4] by using the local variance histogram. Besides these HCF-COM based works, some other detectors are also proposed in recent years, e.g., the ones based on the statistics of amplitude of histogram local extrema [5,6,7], the compression-technique-based detectors [8,9,10,11], the statistical-moments-based detectors [12,13,14], the Markov-model-based detectors [15,16], etc.

Though many improvements have been achieved, HCF-COM and C-HCF-COM can be further investigated and improved. In this paper, we extend these detectors and propose a new one to detect LSB-M. Firstly, inspired by our previous work [17], the first and second order difference images are taken into consideration. We compute HCF-COM and C-HCF-COM from these residual images to build a 28-dimensional feature set to carry out detection using Fisher's linear discriminant (FLD). Secondly, we argue that in C-HCF-COM, the calibration is not necessarily the downsample of original image, and any denoised version of original image can be taken as a calibration. Actually, a better performance can be obtained if taking the Gaussian filtered image as calibration. In summary, with these extensions and by constructing a feature set of 28 features, the proposed detector obviously improves HCF-COM, C-HCF-COM, and some other state-of-the-art methods as well. It works well in detection of LSB-M.

The rest of this paper is organized as follows. In Section 2, the previous HCF-COM based steganalysis is briefly reviewed. In Section 3, the new detector is introduced in details. The evaluation of our detector is reported in Section 4, by comparing it with HCF-COM, C-HCF-COM, and some other state-of-the-art methods. Finally, we conclude our work in last section.

2   Related Works

As a result of LSB-M embedding, the stego image I_s is the sum of the cover image I_c and a noise N:

$$I_s(i,j) = I_c(i,j) + N(i,j) \tag{1}$$

where N is i.i.d. and independent of I_c. The distribution of N is symmetric about 0: $P(N = 0) = 1 - \alpha/2$ and $P(N = 1) = P(N = -1) = \alpha/4$, where α is the embedding rate. Denote h_c and h_s as the histogram of cover and stego image, respectively. Then,

$$h_s = f_\alpha * h_c \tag{2}$$

where f_α is a convolutional kernel: $f_\alpha(0) = 1 - \alpha/2$ and $f_\alpha(1) = f_\alpha(-1) = \alpha/4$. Let $\widehat{h}_c$ and $\widehat{h}_s$ be the discrete Fourier transform (DFT) of h_c and h_s, respectively. According to (2), we have:

$$\widehat{h}_s(k) = \left(1 - \alpha \sin^2 \frac{k\pi}{M}\right)\widehat{h}_c(k) \qquad (M = 256). \tag{3}$$

This property is the starting point of many steganalysis works of LSB-M.

In [1], for a gray-scale image I, Harmsen and Pearlman defined its HCF-COM as:

$$\mathcal{C}(I) = \frac{\sum_{k=0}^{M/2} k|\widehat{h}(k)|}{\sum_{k=0}^{M/2} |\widehat{h}(k)|} \qquad (M = 256) \tag{4}$$

where $\widehat{h}$ is DFT of the histogram of I. Using (3), Harmsen and Pearlman proved that

$$\mathcal{C}(I_s) \leq \mathcal{C}(I_c) \tag{5}$$

i.e., HCF-COM will decrease after LSB-M embedding. In this light, a threshold T is utilized to classify the image I as a cover if $\mathcal{C}(I) > T$ or a stego if otherwise.

HCF-COM is effective for detecting LSB-M. However, since the pixel-value histogram relies heavily on image content, the variation of HCF-COM is large. So, the distributions of $\mathcal{C}(I_c)$ and $\mathcal{C}(I_s)$ may seriously overlap, leading to the decrease of detection accuracy. To remedy this drawback, Ker [2] proposed the calibration technique in which the image I is downsampled to get the calibrated image $\widetilde{I}$:

$$\widetilde{I}(i,j) = \left\lfloor \frac{\sum_{u=0}^{1} \sum_{v=0}^{1} I(2i + u, 2j + v)}{4} \right\rfloor. \tag{6}$$

Then, Ker defined the C-HCF-COM of I as:

$$\mathcal{C}^*(I) = \frac{\mathcal{C}(I)}{\mathcal{C}(\widetilde{I})}. \tag{7}$$

Experimental results have shown that this normalized detector is much more reliable than HCF-COM.

For the downsampled images $\widetilde{I}_c$ and $\widetilde{I}_s$ (see Fig. 1), $\widetilde{I}_s$ can be viewed as the stego version of $\widetilde{I}_c$ by LSB-M with an embedding rate $\widetilde{\alpha}$ [18,19], where

$$\widetilde{\alpha} = \alpha - \frac{3}{4}\alpha^2 + \frac{3}{8}\alpha^3 - \frac{5}{64}\alpha^4 \tag{8}$$

which is small enough respecting to α. So, the mean-squared-error (MSE) between $\widetilde{I}_c$ and $\widetilde{I}_s$ is smaller than that of I_c and I_s. In this light, we may consider that $\widetilde{I}_c \approx \widetilde{I}_s$ and $\mathcal{C}(\widetilde{I}_c) \approx \mathcal{C}(\widetilde{I}_s)$. On the other hand, since $\widetilde{I}_c$ is the downsample of I_c, their histograms are similar, thus $\mathcal{C}(I_c) \approx \mathcal{C}(\widetilde{I}_c)$ and, accordingly, $\mathcal{C}^*(I_c) = \mathcal{C}(I_c)/\mathcal{C}(\widetilde{I}_c) \approx 1$. Take these assumptions into account and by (5), we have:

$$1 \approx \mathcal{C}^*(I_c) \approx \frac{\mathcal{C}(I_c)}{\mathcal{C}(\widetilde{I}_s)} \geq \frac{\mathcal{C}(I_s)}{\mathcal{C}(\widetilde{I}_s)} = \mathcal{C}^*(I_s). \tag{9}$$

By this equation, the reliability of C-HCF-COM is guaranteed and, importantly, the value of C-HCF-COM is close to the constant 1 and it is not widely distributed anymore.

Ker's work was improved in [3]. Instead of applying C-HCF-COM on original image, Li *et al.* [3] pointed out that the usage of difference image can yield a better result. Specifically, take the vertical difference image as example:

$$I^v(i,j) = I(i,j) - I(i+1,j) + 255 \tag{10}$$

Li *et al.* suggested calculating C-HCF-COM on I^v, i.e., taking

$$C^*(I^v) = \frac{C(I^v)}{C(\widetilde{I^v})} \tag{11}$$

to detect LSB-M, where $\widetilde{I^v}$ is the downsample of I^v. In this way, the performance of C-HCF-COM can be enhanced.

In a recent work [17], Cai *et al.* proposed to use histograms of the first and second order difference images to build a feature set to detect LSB-M. From the experimental results reported in [17], we see that Cai *et al.*'s method is better than many other works and the difference images are very useful in steganalysis of LSB-M.

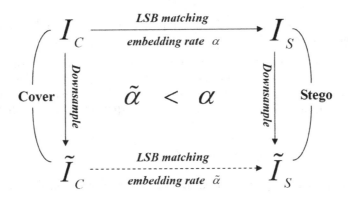

Fig. 1. Calibration (downsample) technique for the detection of LSB matching

3 Proposed Method

We first demonstrate the significance of difference images in the usage of HCF-COM and C-HCF-COM. Then, we show that in C-HCF-COM, any denoised version of original image can be taken as a calibration. Finally, we give the detailed feature extraction procedure.

3.1 Difference Images

The goal of steganalysis is to discriminate stego images from natural ones. An important approach to this issue is to explore usual image statistics. Since difference images can reflect image spatial correlations while data embedding may alter these correlations, they are obviously useful and have already shown their value in steganalysis [3,20,17]. Based on this consideration and inspired by our previous work [17], we argue that by exploiting difference images, the previous HCF-COM based detectors can be significantly improved. Specifically, we consider the first order (vertical, horizontal, diagonal, anti-diagonal) difference images $\{I^v, I^h, I^d, I^a\}$ and second order difference images $\{I^{x,y} : x, y \in \{v, h, d, a\}\}$. Here, for example, the vertical difference image I^v is defined in (10), and the second order difference image is defined by $I^{x,y} = (I^x)^y$. Notice that $I^{x,y} = I^{y,x}$ holds for each $x, y \in \{v, h, d, a\}$, thus we have only ten second order difference images.

Fig. 2 shows the receiver operating characteristic (ROC) curves for the following detectors, for 3000 images with an embedding rate of 1.0 bit per pixel (bpp):

- 1) HCF-COM [1],
- 2) C-HCF-COM [2],
- 3) C-HCF-COM computed on vertical difference image [3],
- 4) C-HCF-COM computed on the first and second order difference images (14 features),
- 5) HCF-COM and C-HCF-COM computed on the first and second order difference images (28 features).

This figure clearly illustrates the advantage of difference images. For example, comparing Ker's original C-HCF-COM with detector 4), it greatly increases the area under the ROC curve (AUC) from 0.73 to 0.91. Besides, we see that the best detection performance can be achieve when using HCF-COM and C-HCF-COM together.

3.2 Alterative Calibration

Our idea is motivated by (9). We argue that for a transformation of image I, $Cal(I)$, if the following conditions hold, $Cal(I)$ can be used as a calibration in C-HCF-COM (i.e., replace the downsampled image $\tilde{I}$ by $Cal(I)$ in computation of C-HCF-COM in (7)):

- For cover image I_c and its transformation $Cal(I_c)$, their histograms are similar.
- For cover image I_c and its stego version I_s, their transformations $Cal(I_c)$ and $Cal(I_s)$ have similar histograms.

In fact, with these conditions, we have $\mathcal{C}(I_c) \approx \mathcal{C}(Cal(I_c))$ and $\mathcal{C}(Cal(I_c)) \approx \mathcal{C}(Cal(I_s))$. Then, by (5), we see that

$$1 \approx \frac{\mathcal{C}(I_c)}{\mathcal{C}(Cal(I_c))} \approx \frac{\mathcal{C}(I_c)}{\mathcal{C}(Cal(I_s))} \geq \frac{\mathcal{C}(I_s)}{\mathcal{C}(Cal(I_s))}. \tag{12}$$

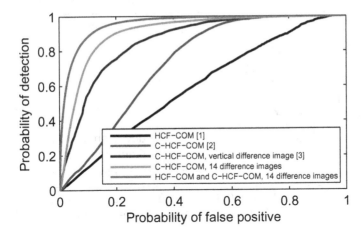

Fig. 2. ROC curves for the following detectors, for 3000 images with an embedding rate of 1.0 bpp: HCF-COM [1], C-HCF-COM [2], C-HCF-COM computed on vertical difference image [3], C-HCF-COM computed on 14 (the first and second order) difference images, HCF-COM and C-HCF-COM computed on 14 difference images. For the 4th and 5th detector, we first construct a multi-dimensional feature set and then use FLD to train and test.

So, if taking $\mathrm{Cal}(I)$ as calibration, the reliability of C-HCF-COM can also be guaranteed.

Based on the above discussion, instead of the downsampled image, the calibration in C-HCF-COM can be taken as any denoised version of I, since

- Cover images are usually natural ones with good perceptual quality. They contain only a low level of noise, and denoising algorithm may not significantly change their contents. So, a cover image and its denoised version have similar histograms.
- For a stego image, the embedding noise (see (1)) can be removed to some extent by denoising. So, for a cover image and its stego version, their denoised images are close enough to each other, and thus they have similar histograms.

We now give some experimental results to support our claim. Referring to Fig. 3, it shows ROC curves for the detector C-HCF-COM with different calibrations (we use here the original image but not the difference image), for 3000 images with an embedding rate of 1.0 bpp. From this figure, we see that by using either linear or nonlinear filter, the denoising-based calibration works well.

More experimental results will be provided in next section. We will see that by incorporating difference images, the Gaussian filtered image performs best among various choices of calibration.

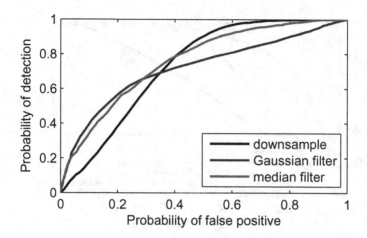

Fig. 3. ROC curves for the detector C-HCF-COM with different calibrations, for 3000 images with an embedding rate of 1.0 bpp. Here, the calibration is respectively the downsampled image (Ker's original C-HCF-COM [2]), denoised image by the Gaussian filter of size 3×3 with a standard deviation $\sigma = 0.5$, and denoised image by the median filter of size 3×3.

3.3   Feature Extraction Procedure

Consider a gray-scale image I. First, compute the first and second order difference images of I to get an image set denoted $\mathcal{S}_I$. This set contains 14 images. Then, for each image $J \in \mathcal{S}_I$:

- Get its calibration denoted Cal(J).
- Determine histograms of J and Cal(J): h and h_{Cal}. Take $h^* = h|_{[C-32,C+31]}$ and $h^*_{\text{Cal}} = h_{\text{Cal}}|_{[C-32,C+31]}$, where C is 255 for first order and 510 for second order difference images. We only take 64 bins since difference-histograms are concentrate distributions with two-sided exponential decay.
- Compute DFT of h^* and h^*_{Cal}, to get $\widehat{h}^*$ and $\widehat{h}^*_{\text{Cal}}$.
- Compute HCF-COM of J and Cal(J) by using $\widehat{h}^*$ and $\widehat{h}^*_{\text{Cal}}$, to get $\mathcal{C}(J)$ and $\mathcal{C}(\text{Cal}(J))$.

Finally, use the 28 features $\{\mathcal{C}(J), \mathcal{C}(J)/\mathcal{C}(\text{Cal}(J)) : J \in \mathcal{S}_I\}$ to train and test.

4   Experimental Results

The proposed detector is evaluated by comparing it with the following methods:

- HCF-COM [1] and C-HCF-COM [2].
- Targeted detectors of LSB-M: [6,3,7,4,17]. Particularly, for the method [17], two feature sets are considered. The first one contains 28 features by taking the histogram-bin-parameter $n = 1$ (see (10) of [17]), and the second one contains 70 features while the histogram-bin-parameter is $n = 4$.

Table 1. Comparison of AUC values between HCF-COM [1], C-HCF-COM [2], some state-of-the-art methods and our detector with five calibrations, for 3000 images with different embedding rates. In the last column, for each test image, the embedding rate is randomly selected from the range of $[0.1, 1.0]$.

Embedding rate (bpp)	1.0	0.5	0.4	0.3	0.2	0.1	0.1-1.0
Our method, downsample (28-D)	0.957	0.861	0.832	0.795	0.737	0.644	0.839
Our method, average filter (28-D)	0.953	0.839	0.805	0.771	0.714	0.628	0.818
Our method, Gaussian filter (28-D)	0.957	0.879	0.853	0.820	0.760	0.665	0.854
Our method, median filter (28-D)	0.952	0.861	0.830	0.796	0.737	0.644	0.834
Our method, Wiener filter (28-D)	0.952	0.839	0.805	0.770	0.713	0.628	0.818
Harmsen and Pearlman [1] (1-D)	0.592	0.544	0.535	0.527	0.517	0.508	0.550
Ker [2] (1-D)	0.732	0.580	0.554	0.540	0.523	0.508	0.602
Li et al. [3] (1-D)	0.848	0.746	0.700	0.657	0.599	0.548	0.743
Gao et al. [7] (50-D)	0.929	0.831	0.794	0.744	0.671	0.587	0.810
Zheng et al. [4] (6-D)	0.911	0.765	0.717	0.666	0.607	0.553	0.767
Cancelli et al. [6] (10-D)	0.848	0.710	0.668	0.629	0.582	0.539	0.715
Cai et al. [17] (28-D)	0.944	0.862	0.836	0.801	0.741	0.646	0.838
Cai et al. [17] (70-D)	0.982	0.909	0.878	0.845	0.782	0.686	0.884
Goljin et al. [13] (27-D)	0.821	0.705	0.684	0.656	0.614	0.563	0.687
Gul and Kurugollu [21] (50-D)	0.788	0.695	0.673	0.651	0.622	0.577	0.687

- Blind detectors: The wavelet-absolute-moments (WAM) based method of Goljin et al. [13], and a recently proposed method of Gul and Kurugollu [21] which is based on singular-value-decomposition (SVD).

Our experiments are conducted as follows.

- Test images: We download 3000 images from the USDA NRCS Photo Gallery[1]. After downloaded, these images are changed into gray-scale format. Then, in each image, a square area with maximum size is cropped. Finally, each cropped image is downsampled to 512×512 pixels.
- Classifier: For our detector and the methods using more than one feature, we take the parameter-independent classifier, FLD, to train and test. In each test, we randomly choose 25% of cover images and 25% of stego images for training, and the remaining 75% for testing. The procedure is repeated 100 times for cross-validation and ROC curves are vertically averaged to get the mean performance measured by AUC.
- Calibration: For our method, five calibrations are tested:
  - downsampled image,
  - denoised image by the average filter of size 3×3,
  - denoised image by the Gaussian filter of size 3×3 with a standard deviation $\sigma = 0.5$,
  - denoised image by the median filter of size 3×3,
  - denoised image by the Wiener filter of size 3×3.

---

[1] http://photogallery.nrcs.usda.gov

The comparison results are shown in Table 1. According to this table, we can conclude that:

- For our method, the Gaussian-filter-based calibration (the red one) is the best choice among the tested five cases, and, especially, the Gaussian-filter-based calibration is better than the downsample-based calibration.
- Our method significantly outperforms HCF-COM and C-HCF-COM. Moreover, our method is better than the previous HCF-COM based methods [3,7,4].
- Our method with Gaussian-filter-based calibration (the red one) performs rather well and it is better than the targeted detectors besides the one proposed by Cai *et al.* [17] which uses 70 features (the blue one). However, when Cai *et al.*'s method uses the same amount of features as ours (i.e., 28 features, the green one), our method is better.
- Our method is superior to the blind detectors including the WAM-based method [13] and the SVD-based method [21], since those detectors are not specifically designed for LSB-M and they may lose power in detection of LSB-M.

In summary, we suggest taking the Gaussian filtered image as calibration, and the detector obtained in this way works well in detection of LSB-M.

5   Conclusion

In this paper, we extended the previously introduced HCF-COM based detectors. We proposed to take HCF-COM and C-HCF-COM of difference images as features to carry out classification, and we showed that a better detection performance can be obtained if taking the Gaussian filtered image as calibration in C-HCF-COM. The effectiveness of our method is verified through extensive experiments. However, it should be mentioned that LSB-M is still hard to detect in the case of low embedding rate. The experimental results showed that our detector is not satisfactory enough when the embedding rate is 0.1 bpp. We will investigate more effective detector in the future.

References

1. Harmsen, J.J., Pearlman, W.A.: Steganalysis of additive noise modelable information hiding. In: Security and Watermarking of Multimedia Contents V. SPIE, vol. 5020, pp. 131–142 (2003)
2. Ker, A.D.: Steganalysis of LSB matching in grayscale images. IEEE Signal Process. Lett. 12(6), 441–444 (2005)
3. Li, X., Zeng, T., Yang, B.: Detecting LSB matching by applying calibration technique for difference image. In: Proc. of the 10th ACM Workshop on Multimedia & Security, pp. 133–138 (2008)
4. Zheng, E., Ping, X., Zhang, T., Xiong, G.: Steganalysis of LSB matching based on local variance histogram. In: Proc. IEEE ICIP, pp. 1005–1008 (2010)

5. Zhang, J., Cox, I.J., Doërr, G.: Steganalysis for LSB matching in images with high-frequency noise. In: Proc. IEEE MMSP, pp. 385–388 (2007)
6. Cancelli, G., Doërr, G., Cox, I.J., Barni, M.: Detection of +-1 LSB steganography based on the amplitude of histogram local extrema. In: Proc. IEEE ICIP, pp. 1288–1291 (2008)
7. Gao, Y., Li, X., Yang, B., Lu, Y.: Detecting LSB matching by characterizing the amplitude of histogram. In: Proc. IEEE ICASSP, pp. 1505–1508 (2009)
8. Boncelet, C., Marvel, L.: Steganalysis of +-1 embedding using lossless image compression. In: Proc. IEEE ICIP, vol. 2, pp. 149–152 (2007)
9. Boncelet, C., Marvel, L., Henz, B.: Rate insensitive steganalysis of +-1 embedding in images. In: Proc. IEEE ICIP, pp. 1272–1275 (2008)
10. Dong, J., Tan, T.: Blind image steganalysis based on run length histogram analysis. In: Proc. IEEE ICIP, pp. 2064–2067 (2008)
11. Yu, X., Babaguchi, N.: Run length based steganalysis for LSB matching steganography. In: Proc. IEEE ICME, pp. 353–356 (2008)
12. Xuan, G., Shi, Y.Q., Gao, J., Zou, D., Yang, C., Zhang, Z., Chai, P., Chen, C., Chen, W.: Steganalysis based on multiple features formed by statistical moments of wavelet characteristic functions. In: Barni, M., Herrera-Joancomartí, J., Katzenbeisser, S., Pérez-González, F. (eds.) IH 2005. LNCS, vol. 3727, pp. 262–277. Springer, Heidelberg (2005)
13. Goljan, M., Fridrich, J., Holotyak, T.: New blind steganalysis and its implications. In: Security, Steganography, and Watermarking of Multimedia Contents VIII. SPIE, vol. 6072, pp. 1–13 (2006)
14. Zhang, J., Zhang, D.: Detection of LSB matching steganography in decompressed images. IEEE Signal Process. Lett. 17(2), 141–144 (2010)
15. Zou, D., Shi, Y.Q., Su, W., Xuan, G.: Steganalysis based on Markov model of thresholded prediction-error image. In: Proc. IEEE ICME, pp. 1365–1368 (2006)
16. Pevny, T., Bas, P., Fridrich, J.: Steganalysis by subtractive pixel adjacency matrix. IEEE Trans. Inf. Forens. Security 5(2), 215–224 (2010)
17. Cai, K., Li, X., Zeng, T., Yang, B., Lu, X.: Reliable histogram features for detecting LSB matching. In: Proc. IEEE ICIP, pp. 1761–1764 (2010)
18. Ker, A.D.: Resampling and the detection of LSB matching in color bitmaps. In: Security, Steganography, and Watermarking of Multimedia Contents VII. SPIE, vol. 5681, pp. 1–15 (2005)
19. Li, X., Zeng, T., Yang, B.: A further study on steganalysis of LSB matching by calibration. In: Proc. IEEE ICIP, pp. 2072–2075 (2008)
20. Sun, Y., Liu, F., Liu, B., Wang, P.: Steganalysis based on difference image. In: Kim, H.-J., Katzenbeisser, S., Ho, A.T.S. (eds.) IWDW 2008. LNCS, vol. 5450, pp. 184–198. Springer, Heidelberg (2009)
21. Gul, G., Kurugollu, F.: SVD-based universal spatial domain image steganalysis. IEEE Trans. Inf. Forens. Security 5(2), 349–353 (2010)

LSB Replacement Steganography Software Detection Based on Model Checking

Zheng Zhao[1], Fenlin Liu[1], Xiangyang Luo[1,2], Xin Xie[1], and Lu Yu[3]

[1] Department of Network Engeering,
Zhengzhou Information Science and Technology Institute, Zhengzhou 450002, China
[2] State Key Laboratory of Information Security,
Institute of Information Engineering Chinese Academy of Science, Beijing 100093, China
[3] Department One, The Academy of National Defense Information,
430000 Wuhan, China
diyigemsn@hotmail.com, liufenlin@vip.sina.com,
{xiangyangluo,zhenggeda}@126.com, xiexin0011@gmail.com,

Abstract. Steganography software detection is one of effective approaches for steganography forensics using software analysis. In this paper a method of LSB replacement steganography software detection is proposed. Firstly three typical implementations of LSB replacement algorithms are analyzed and Finite Automatons description of them are presented. Secondly the control flow automatons are constructed for softwares to be detected. Finally, the model checking method for identifying LSB replacement steganography software is adopted. Experimental results show that the proposed method can reliably detect LSB replacement steganography softwares of different versions and those that are reimplemented relatively.

Keywords: steganography software, automaton, model checking, LSB replacement algorithm.

1   Introduction

Nowadays, some steganalysis focuses on stego-object. It is hard to accurately locate where the secret messages are embedded and extract them due to the lack of stganography algorithms, encoding schemes, random number generator, encrypted algorithms. However a larger number of steganography softwares for downloading and using spring up on the Internet[1] because of the increasing demand of covert communication. Aforementioned details can be obtained through detection and reverse analysis of steganography softwares on object computers used by steganographers, thus supporting steganalysis and forensics effectively.

Steganography software detection is one of the applications of software detection method. At present some related work has been done in malware detection and software piracy detection in the field of software detection. For example, sub-graph isomorphism[2],equivalent naturalization[3], heuristic scanning[4] and data mining[5] have been used in malware detection. In addition instruction set birthmark[6], API based birthmark[7], library function based birthmark[8], graph structure birthmark[9]

Y.Q. Shi, H.J. Kim, and F. Pérez-González (Eds.): IWDW 2012, LNCS 7809, pp. 54–68, 2013.

have been used in software piracy detection. There are three typical methods for detection of steganography sofwares.The hash value matching method[10]can rapidly detect steganography softwares. But the method is of no use if the hash value is changed by modification and deformation of steganography softwares. Learning from the idea of word-frequency statistics in text information processing, [11] proposes a method to detect steganography softwares based on code splitting in 2011. It shows a relatively high performance on variant identification of steganography softwares, while the rate of identification is low when the method is appliedon other steganography softwares having the same function. Based on the core instruction templates matching, [12] proposes an identification method for LSB replacement steganography softwares in 2012. The method constructs the templates of core codes of steganography softwares. Templates are used to detect steganography softwares. The proposed method has a high detection rate of the known steganography softwares. But it shows a low performance on detection of reimplemented steganography softwares.

According to the CEO of WeStone Technologies, Inc., as of December 1st, 2011 in their depository containing 836 data hiding products, 582 (70%) of which hide messages using LSB embedding[13]. In steganography algorithms, the LSB replacement steganography is widely applied into steganography softwares for the sake of simple implementation of the algorithm and high embedding capacity.So the detection of LSB replacement softwareshave important implications. For the low detection rate of steganography softwaresthat are reimplemented, a method based on model checking for detection LSB replacement steganography softwares is proposed in this paper learning from the method proposed in [14]. Experiment results show that the method can detect reimplemented and upgraded version steganography softwaresmore reliably.

2   A Detecting Architecture of Steganography Softwares Based on Model Checking

Model checking is an automated verification method that aims to verify theproperties of a model or system. Finite automaton(FA) is used to describe steganography behaviors. Control flow automaton(CFA) is used to stand for the state space of the software to be detected. And model checking method is adopted to verify whether a certain program contains steganography behavior. As is shown in figure 1, the detecting method for steganography softwares based on model checking consists of three steps.

Description of Steganography Behaviors. Analyze the implementations of steganography algorithm, construct a semantic-level FA for each implementation, reify semantic-level FAs as instruction-level FAs, and construct a database of steganography behavior FAs.

Construction of Model. Construct the control flow automaton(CFA) for the software to be detected as its state space. Through disassembling of the software we get the disassembled code, then build the CFA of the software to be detected.

Detection of Steganography Behaviors. With the description of steganography behaviors and CFA of the software to be detected, model checking method is used to verify whether a software contains steganography behaviors.

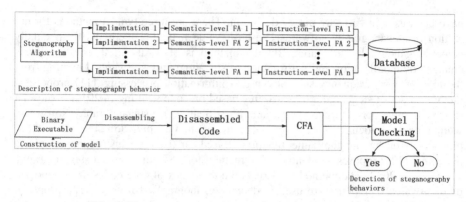

Fig. 1. The detecting procedure of steganography softwares

3   Description of LSB Replacement Steganography Behavior Based on Finite Automaton

In order to detect steganography softwares, we introduce a model checking approach. The behaviors of steganography are described as FAs. In the LSB replacement stega-nography softwares, thealgorithm of LSB replacement epitomizes the steganography behaviors. In this paper, we describe the process of LSB replacement algorithm, and build semantic-level FAs, then reify semantic-level FAs as instruction-level FAs which are called steganography behavior FAs in this paper. The steganography beha-vior FAs contain the necessary instructions and the dependence of instructions.

3.1   Implementations of LSB Replacement Algorithm

In LSB replacement steganography algorithm, the secret bit is used to replace the LSB of a pixel of an image so that messages can be hidden in spatial domain images. This algorithm has several implementations. Through analysis of LSB replacement steganography softwares, we obtain the following three typical implementations:

Implementation 1: reset the LSB of a pixel at first and judge the secret bit. If the secret bit is 1, add 1 to the pixel; otherwise, no operation.
Implementation 2: reset the LSB of a pixel at first and do or operation with the low-est bit of the pixel and the secret bit.
Implementation 3: get a pixel at first and set the lowest bit of the pixel 1or 0 depend-ing on the secret bit.

3.2   Construction of Steganography Behavior FAs

According to the implementation of LSB replacement algorithm, a semantic-level FA is given. This paper takes the implementation 1 in section 3.1 as an example to con-struct a semantic-level FA. Steps of this implementation are as follows:

Step1. reset the LSB of a pixel
Step2. determine whether the secret bit is 1
Step3. if the secret bit is 1, add 1 to pixel

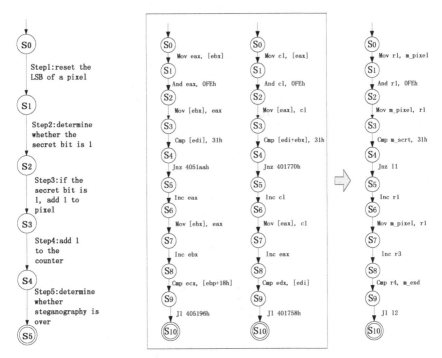

Fig. 2. Semantic-level FA M^{stc} **Fig. 3.** The different cases of operands are reduced using rule1

Step4. add 1 to the counter

Step5. determine whether steganography is over

As figure 2, a FA $M^{stc} = (S^{stc}, \Sigma^{stc}, \delta^{stc}, s_0^{stc}, F^{stc})$ is abstracted from the steps above, where

$S^{stc} = \{s_0, s_1, s_2, s_3, s_4, s_5\}$ is a finite set of states,

$\Sigma^{stc} = \{Step1, Step2, Step3, Step4, Step5\}$ is a finite alphabet. Each element in Σ^{stc} is a step of implementation 1,

$\delta^{stc} : S^{stc} \times \Sigma^{stc} \rightarrow 2^{S^{stc}}$ is the transfer function, $\delta^{stc}(s_0, Step1) = s_1$, $\delta^{stc}(s_1, Step2) = s_2$, $\delta^{stc}(s_2, Step3) = s_3$, $\delta^{stc}(s_3, Step4) = s_4$, $\delta^{stc}(s_4, Step5) = s_5$,

$s_0^{stc} = s_0$ is an initial state,

$F^{stc} = \{s_5\}$ is a non-empty set of final states.

M^{stc} completely describes the semantics of implementation 1. For detecting steganography softwares, we reify semantic-level FA M^{stc} as instruction-level FA M which describes steganography behaviors in instruction-level. Each element of Σ^{stc} can be express with several instructions. And the following 4 rules are adopted to construct an instruction-level FA to avoid means of equivalent deformation during the procedure of transforming the steps of algorithm into instruments, such as command operand replacement, equivalent instructions replacement, instruction transposition and irrelevant instruction insertion.

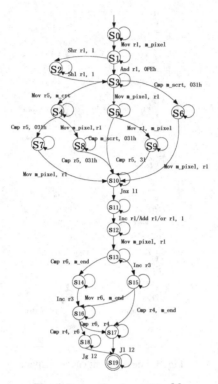

Fig. 4. Instruction-level FA *M*

Rule1. For operand replacement, the variables are utilized to replace register operands, memory reference operands, and instruction address operands in M. Thus different operand cases can be reduced. Let a specificinstruction I, its operand sequence is $< x_1,...,x_k >$, after operand replacement, we get operand sequence $< o_1,...,o_k >$. The rules of replacement are as follows: If x_i is a register, then x_i is replaced by a register variable r, $o_i = r$; If x_i is a memory reference operand, then x_i is replaced by a memory reference variable m, $o_i = m$; If x_i is an instruction address operand, then x_i is replaced by an instruction address variable l, $o_i = l$; If x_i is an immediate operand, then no replacement will be done, $o_i = x_i$, $1 \le i \le k$ .As shown in figure 3, the two different FAs which have different operands in their instructions can be reduced into a single FA with this rule.

Rule2. For equivalent instructions replacement, the equivalent instructions are reduced by expanding the set of states and transfer function of M. Suppose a subsequence Seq_1 of a sequence which is described by M and Seq_2 is an equivalent sequence to Seq_1. Expand the set of states and transfer function to describe Seq_2. Let $Seq_1 =< I_1^1,...,I_m^1 >$, $Seq_2 =< I_1^2,...,I_n^2 >$ and the transfer function $\delta(s_1, I_1^1) = s_2,...,$ $\delta(s_m, I_m^1) = s_{m+1}$ which can accept Seq_1 ,then add

$n-1$ states $s_1', ... s_{n-1}'$ to M and expand the transfer function with $\delta(s_1, I_1^2) = s_1', \delta(s_1', I_2^2) = s_2', ... \delta(s_{n-1}', I_n^2) = s_{m+1}$.

Rule3. For instruction transposition, the sequences of different order which have the same function can be treated as equivalent instructions. Instruction transposition can be reduced by expanding the set of states and transfer function of M.

Rule4. For irrelevant instruction insertion, the instructions which contain irrelevant instructions can be reduced by expanding the transfer function of M. For arbitrary state s and arbitrary I in M, expand the transfer function with $\delta(s, I) = s$.

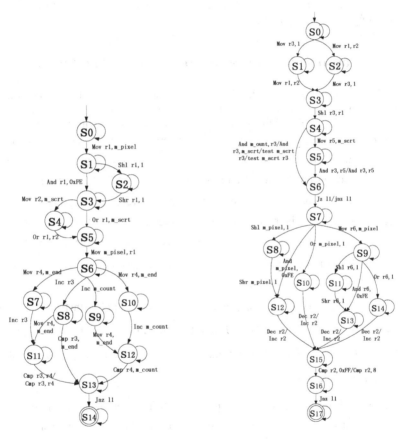

Fig. 5. The Instruction-level FA of imple-
mention 2

Fig. 6. The Instruction-levelFA of imple-
mention 3

By the rules above, M^{stc} is reified as steganography behavior FA $M = (V, S, \Sigma, \delta, s_0, F)$ as shown in figure 4, where

V is a set of variables including three types: register variables, memory reference variables and instruction address variables,

S is a set of finite states,

Σ is a finite alphabet in which each element $I = (op\_code, < o_1, ...o_k >)$, op_code is an arbitrary memonic and $< o_1, ...o_k >$ is a sequence of operands, where, if $o_i \in V$, o_i is a register variable or a memory reference variable or an instruction address variable; otherwise, o_i is a concrete operand. Particularly, if the length of the operand sequence is 0, then the instruction I has no operand,

$\delta : S \times \Sigma \rightarrow 2^S$ is a transition function,

$s_0 \in S$ is an initial state,

$F \subseteq S$ is a non-empty set of termination states.

We can get steganography behavior FAs of implementation 2 and 3 in the same way as is shown in figure 5 and figure 6.

4   The Construction of a Software' Control Flow Automaton

It is hard to construct a FA model for a whole software, so we treat every function respectively when constructing model for the software to be detected. By disassembling software P which is to be detected, we can get a sequence of instructions $Seq^P = < I_1, I_2, ..., I_n >$, and a set of execution order relations between instructions C^P. C^P is constructed as follows. If I_i is an unconditional jump instruction Jmp and I_j is the instruction on the target address, then $(I_i, I_j) \in C^P$. If I_i is a conditional jump instruction Jxx and I_j is the instruction on the target address, then $(I_i, I_j) \in C^P$ and $(I_i, I_{i+1}) \in C^P$. If I_i is the instruction Retn, then no such instruction I_j exists that $(I_i, I_j) \in C^P$. If I_i is other instruction and there exists an instruction I_{i+1}, then $(I_i, I_{i+1}) \in C^P$. With Seq^P and C^P, the CFA of the function can be constructed as $M^P = (S^P, \Sigma^P, \delta^P, s_0^P, F^P)$, where

S^P: for every instruction I_i in the sequence of disassembly instructions exists a state s_{I_i} in $S^P, 1 \le i \le n$. All the instructions in the instruction sequence correspond to a set of states $\{s_{I_1}, s_{I_2}, ..., s_{I_n}\}$ which has a one-to-one relationship with the instructions. And let s_f be the end state. $S^P = \{s_f\} \bigcup \{s_{I_1}, s_{I_2}, ..., s_{I_n}\}$.

Σ^P: a set of all instructions in the sequence of disassembly instructions Seq^P;

s_0^P: the initial state s_0^P is state s_{I_1} which corresponds to the entry instruction I_1, that is $s_0^P = s_{I_1}$;

F^P: every state in S^P is a termination state, that is $F^P = S^P$;

δ^P: we assume that $< I_1, I_2, ..., I_n >$ is an instruction sequence after being disassembled. For any $1 \le i, j \le n$, if there exists (I_i, I_j), s.t. $(I_i, I_j) \in C^P$, then there is a $\delta^P(s_{I_i}, I_i) = s_{I_j}$ in transition function of CFA; for the instruction I_i, if there does not exist any instruction I_j, s.t. $(I_i, I_j) \in C^P$, then there is a $\delta^P(s_{I_i}, I_i) = s_f$ in transition function of CFA.

As is shown in figure 7, the instruction sequence is the disassembly code of a function from which we can get the instruction sequence and the execution order relation of instructions, then we get CFA. When we construct the model of function in the software, we choose the functions defined by the software itself and some library functions.

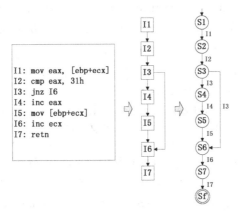

Fig. 7. Construction of CFA

5   The Method of LSB Replacement Steganography Software Detection

The steganography behavior FAs contain variables. If a steganography behavior FA M is used to detect a software P, every variable in M needs a value. The CFAs can be obtained based on P. Then test whether the intersection of M's language set and the CFAs' language is empty. At first the binding is described, then the algorithm of steganography behavior detection is proposed.

5.1   Binding

Let $B = \{(v, x) \mid v \in V, x \in X\}$, where V is a set of variables in the steganography behavior FA $M = (V, S, \Sigma, \delta, s_0, F)$, and X is a set of binding values in which there are three kinds of elements including registers, memory references and instruction addresses. If $\exists v_i, x_i$ s.t. $(v_i, x_i) \in B$, then we write $B(v_i) = x_i$, that is, we bind x_i to variable v_i

Let a steganography behavior FA $M = (V, S, \Sigma, \delta, s_0, F)$, while $V = \{v_1, v_2, ..., v_n\}$, if $\exists x_1, \exists x_2, ..., \exists x_n$, s.t. $B(v_1) = x_1$, $B(v_2) = x_2, ..., B(v_n) = x_n$, then a FA $B(M) = (S', \Sigma', \delta', s_0', F')$ can be obtained, while

$S' = S$;

$s'_0 = s_0$;

$F' = F$;

Σ' is an alphabet in which every element is got through binding with I. Let an element $I = (op\_code, < o_1, ..., o_k >)$ in Σ, then there is an element $I' = (op\_code',$ $< o'_1, ..., o'_k >)$ in Σ', where $op\_code' = op\_code$. For operand sequence $< o'_1, ..., o'_k >$, if $o_i \in V$, then $o'_i = B(o_i)$; otherwise $o'_i = o_i$. Bind a certain value to every variable in operands of the instruction I, then we get I' and we write $B(I)$.

δ': If there exists a $\delta(s_i, I) = s_j$ in transition function δ, then there correspondingly exists a $\delta'(s_i, B(I)) = s_j$ in transition function δ'.

Binding consistence $Consistent(B_1, B_2) \triangleq \forall v \in V, ((v, x_1) \in B_1 \wedge (v, x_2) \in B_2) \Rightarrow (x_1,$ $= x_2)$ where B_1 and B_2 are bindings[14]. For B_1 and B_2, if there does not exist a variable that binds different values, they are consistent; otherwise, they are not. Registers with different widths often have the same meaning, such as eax, ax and al, etc. If there are bindings {(r1, eax)} and {(r1, ax)}, they are considered as two consistent bindings.

Operation to reset the lowest bit of a pixel is described by M^{reset} in figure 8. And variables r1 and m_pixel are contained in M^{reset}. B_1 and B_2 are two different bindings of M^{reset}. After the binding, $B_1(M^{reset})$ and $B_2(M^{reset})$ can be treated as CFAs.

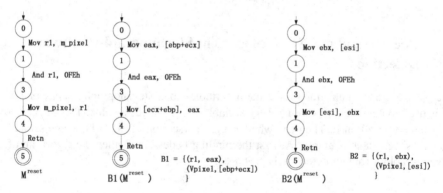

Fig. 8. Two bindings of FA M^{reset}

5.2   A Detection Algorithm

Model checking is used to detect steganography behaviors in softwares. $M^P = (S^P, \Sigma^P, \delta^P, s_0^P, F^P)$ and $M^{LSB} = (S^{LSB}, \Sigma^{LSB}, \delta^{LSB}, s_0^{LSB}, F^{LSB})$ are assumed to be a CFA of a certain software P that is to be detected and a steganography behavior FA respectively. At first, the alphabet Σ^{LSB} of M^{LSB} is expanded, $\Sigma^{LSB} \leftarrow \Sigma^{LSB} \bigcup \Sigma^P$. In this way, M^{LSB} can accept every instruction in M^P. The following language set is utilized to decide whether P is a LSB replacement steganography software.

$$\mathrm{Re}\,sult = (\bigcup_{M^P \in M^P_{All}} L(M^P)) \cap (\bigcup_{B \in B_{All}} L(B(M^{LSB}))) \tag{1}$$

$L(M^P)$ is the language accepted by the CFA of a function in P. M^P_{All} is a CFA set. Each element of the set is a CFA constructed by the functions which are defined by P itself and a part of library functions of P. B_{All} is a set of all the bindings of variables in the variable set V. We can detect whether or not there are some steganography behaviors in P just by judging whether the language set $\mathrm{Re}\,sult$ is empty or not. If the set is not empty, there are some steganography behaviors in P; otherwise, not. That is to say, if there is a binding B such that the intersection of the language $L(B(M^{LSB}))$ accepted by FA $B(M^{LSB})$ and the language $L(M^P)$ accepted by the CFA M^P is not empty, then there are code snippets in P which can achieve steganography.

Considering the algorithm reported in 2003[14], the LSB steganography software detection algorithm can be constructed. The input of the detection algorithm are the steganography behavior FA we construct and the CFA of the software to be detected. Whether the software has behaviors described by the FA can be outputted with our detection algorithm.

To detect steganography behaviors, an algorithm called SteganographyBehavior-Checking is constructedas follows.

Input: a steganography behavior FA $M^{LSB} = (S^{LSB}, \Sigma^{LSB}, \delta^{LSB}, s_0^{LSB}, F^{LSB})$,
a CFA $M^P = (S^P, \Sigma^P, \delta^P, s_0^P, F^P)$ of a software P detected.
Output: true if P is likely a steganography software,
false otherwise.
SteganographyBehaviorChecking(M^{LSB}, M^P)
foreach $s^P \in S^P$ **do** $L_{s^P} \leftarrow \Phi$

$L_{s_0^P} \leftarrow \{(s_0^{LSB}, \Phi)\}$
$WS \leftarrow \Phi$
do
    $WS \leftarrow \Phi$
    foreach $s^P \in S^P$
    if $L_{s^P} \neq \bigcup_{m \in \mathrm{Pr}\,evious(s^P)}^{\cdot} L_m$
      $L_{s^P} = \bigcup_{m \in \mathrm{Pr}\,evious(s^P)} L_m$
      $WS \leftarrow WS \bigcup \{s_i^P\}$
    foreach $s^P \in S^P$
      $NewL_{s^P} \leftarrow \Phi$
      foreach $(s^{LSB}, B) \in L_{s^P}$
        foreach $I^{LSB} \in \Sigma^{LSB}$
          if $(OperateCode(I_{s^P}^P) = OperateCode(I^{LSB}))$

$$NewBinding = BindingLike(I^{LSB}, I_{s^P}^P)$$

if $\delta(s^{LSB}, I^{LSB}) \neq \Phi \wedge NewBinding \neq \Phi$

$$\wedge BindingWith(I^{LSB}, Newbinding)) = I_{s^P}^P$$

foreach $s^{arv} \in \delta(s^{LSB}, I^{LSB})$

if $Consistent(NewBinding, B)$

add $(s^{arv}, NewBinding \cup L_{s^P})$ **to** $NewL_{s^P}$

if $NewL_{s^P} \neq L_{s^P}$

$$L_{s^P} \leftarrow NewL_{s^P}$$

$$WS \leftarrow WS \cup \{s^P\}$$

until $WS = \Phi$

return $\exists s^P \in S^P, \exists (s^{LSB}, B) \in L_{s^P}, s^{LSB} \in F^{LSB}$

In the algorithm SteganographyBehaviorChecking, the function $\Pr evious(s_i^P)$ returns a set of states which have been reached before the state s_i^P. And the function $OperateCode(I)$ returns the memonic of instruction I.

The function $BindingLike(I^{LSB}, I^P)$ returns a set. Suppose the operand sequence of instruction $I^{LSB} = (op\_code^{LSB}, < o_1^{LSB}, ..., o_k^{LSB} >)$ is $< o_1^{LSB}, ..., o_k^{LSB} >$, and the operand sequence of instruction $I^P = (op\_code^P, < o_1^P, ..., o_k^P >)$ is $< o_1^P, ..., o_k^P >$. For any $o_i^{LSB} \in V^{LSB}$, if o_i^{LSB} and o_i^P have the same type, then $(o_i^{LSB}, o_i^P) \in BindingLike(I^{LSB}, I^P)$, where $1 \leq i \leq k$; if there exists o_i^{LSB} s.t. $o_i^{LSB} \in V^{LSB}$ but types of o_i^{LSB} and o_i^P are different, then $BindingLike(I^{LSB}, I^P) = \Phi$, where $1 \leq i \leq k$.

Function $BindingWith(I^{LSB}, NewBinding)$ returns aninstruction I. Let $I^{LSB} = (op\_code^{LSB}, < o_1^{LSB}, ..., o_k^{LSB} >)$, then $I = (op\_code, < o_1, ..., o_k >)$, where $op\_code = op\_code^{LSB}$; If $o_i^{LSB} \notin V^{LSB}$, then $o_i = o_i^{LSB}$, if $o_i^{LSB} \in V^{LSB}$, then $o_i = binding(o_i^{LSB})$, $(o_i^{LSB}, binding(o_i^{LSB})) \in NewBangding$.

6   Experiments Result and Analysis

To illustrate the effectiveness and credibility of the presented method, 14 LSB steganography softwares, 9 other steganography softwares and15 non-steganography softwares are collected in the experiments. These 14 LSB replacement steganography softwares include some known steganography softwares and the reimplemented steganography softwares. The reimplemented softwares are developed by Microsoft Visual studio 2005; 9 other steganography softwares include multi-bit plane steganography softwares and format steganography softwares, etc; those 15 non-steganography softwares include image processing softwares, image format conversion softwares, image encryption softwares and some other softwares of different functions. The disassembly tool used in our experiment is IDA Pro v5.5.

In our experiment, the three steganography behavior FAs in 3.2 are used to be the description of LSB replacement behaviors. And three templates are construct based on [12] for comparing with proposed method. The results of experiments show that the proposed method can effectively detect softwares of different versions and reimplemented softwares, as is shown in table 1. In table 1, MC(Model Checking) is the detection result of proposed method and 1, 2 and 3 represent the implementation 1, 2 and 3; CIT(Core Insructions Tempate) is the detection result of paper[12] and Y means steganography behaviors has been detected and N not. The softwares A+file protection2.6 and WbStego4.3 are upgraded versions of A+fileprotection2.1 and WbStego4.1 respectively. MySteganography1, MySteganography2 and MySteganography3 are steganography softwares that are reimplemented by ourselves. And implementation 1, 2 and 3 are adopted respectively. The pseudocode of them are shown in the appendix. And the three softwares can be identified correctly by the proposed method. The method of [12] can only recognize some known steganography softwares, but the reimplementation steganography softwares can't be recognized.

As is shown in table 2, steganography behaviors can't be detected in other steganography softwares by proposed method. This is because steganography behavior FAs we construct only describe steganography behaviors of LSB replacement but not other steganography behaviors. The method of [12] can find a clip of instructions in the software steganos security suite which can match with a template, but the clip of

Table 1. Detection Results of LSB Replacement Steganography Software

NO	Name of software	Compiler	MC	CIT
1	A+file protection2.1	Microsoft Visual C++ 6.0	1	Y
2	A+file protection2.6	Microsoft Visual C++ 7.0	1	Y
3	Txt2bmp1.0.0.1	Microsoft Visual C++ 6.0	1	Y
4	Dstego1.0	Borland c++1999	2	Y
5	Wbstego3.5	Borland Delphi 4.0-5.0	3	N
6	Wbstego4.2	Borland Delphi 4.0-5.0	3	N
7	WbStego4.3	Borland Delphi 4.0-5.0	3	N
8	S-Tools1.0.0.1	Microsoft Visual C++ 4.X	3	Y
9	ST-BMP	-	3	Y
10	MySteganography1	Microsoft Visual C++ 9.0	1	N
11	MySteganography2	Microsoft Visual C++ 9.0	2	N
12	MySteganography3	Microsoft Visual C++ 9.0	3	N
13	eShow	Borland c++1999	-1	N
14	The third eye	Microsoft Visual C++ 6.0	-1	N

Table 2. Detection Results of Other Steganography Softwares

NO	Name of software	Compiler	Algorithm	MC	CIT
1	HideInBmp	Microsoft Visual C++ 6.0	Multi bit plane steganography	-1	N
2	Dialog	MASM32 / TASM32		-1	N
3	steganos security suite	Microsoft Visual C++ 7.0	Format steganography	-1	N
4	InPlainView1.0.0.1	Microsoft Visual C++ 6.0	PMK steganography	-1	Y
5	BMP_cryptogam	Borland C++ 1999		-1	N
6	steganopic	Microsoft Visual C++ 6.0	Gif image steganography	-1	N
7	Jphswin	Microsoft Visual C++ 5.0	Jpeg image steganography	-1	N
8	F5	Microsoft Visual C++ 9.0		-1	N
9	ST-wav	Microsoft Visual C++ 4.X	Audio file steganography	-1	N

Table 3. Detection Results of Non-steganography Softwares

NO	Name of software	Main function	Compiler	MC	CIT
1	VMProtect	Software protecter	Borland Delphi 4.0 -5.0	-1	N
2	Calc	calculator	Microsoft Visual C++7.0	-1	N
3	FrmtStegAnalysis	Format steganalysis	Microsoft Visual C++8.0	-1	N
4	Randomfile	Random file Generater	Microsoft Visual C++6.0	-1	N
5	insider	Decompression tool	Borland C++ 1999	-1	N
6	ViewPoint	Image browser	Borland C++1999	-1	N
7	watermark	Video watermarking tool	Microsoft Visual C++6.0	-1	N
8	daemon	Virtual CD-ROM	Microsoft Visual C++7.0	-1	N
9	PCKii	File protecter	Microsoft Visual C++6.0	-1	N
10	Advanced Batch Converter	Image format conversion tool	Borland Delphi 4.0 - 5.0	-1	N
11	Beyond_Compare	File comparison tool	Borland Delphi 6.0 - 7.0	-1	N
12	MD5Crack3	Encryption tools	Microsoft Visual C++7.0	-1	N
13	Watermarking	Image watermarking tool	Borland C++ 1999	-1	Y
14	Geotrans	Bitmap transformation tool	Microsoft Visual C++4.X	-1	Y
15	Picture Encryption	Image encryption tool	Microsoft Visual C++6.0	-1	Y

constructions doesn't appear in the core instruction clip in fact. With proposed method, no steganography behaviors are detected in non-steganography softwares as is shown in table 3. Some of the non-steganography softwares have something in common with steganography softwares, but they don't have steganography behaviors. The method of [12] misclassify the software Watermarking, Geotrans, Picture Encryption as steganography. Comparing with method of [12], the proposed method has a higher credibility.

No steganography behaviors are detected in eShow in our experiments. After the analysis we find other implementation is adopted when implementing LSB replacement steganography algorithm in eShow. When eShow gets a pixel, the xor operation is done with the high seven bit continuously, then xor with the secret bit and a bool value is got. At last the value is embed in the lowest bit of the pixel. The three steganography behavior FAs in this paper can't describe this implementation. In fact, there are a variety of implementations of LSB replacement steganography algorithm. However, only three common steganography behavior FAs are constructed in this paper. No steganography behaviors are detected in LSB replacement steganography software The third eye, though implementation 1 is adopted in it. This is because there are errors when reifying the semantic-level FA to the instruction-level FA. Not all implementations of LSB replacement algorithm are reduced in our steganography behavior FAs. Then undetected cases occur. The third eye gets bits from a secret message byte. The highest bit of secret message byte is got, then left shift the byte for next bit. But this case isn't reduced into implementation 1.

7   Conclusion

For the problem of low detection rate of reimplemented steganography, a LSB replacement steganography detection method based on model checking is proposed. Three implementations of LSB replacement algorithm is analyzed, the finite automaton description of steganography behaviors is constructed. The state space of the software to be detected is described by control flow automaton and model checking method is introduced for detecting steganography behaviors. The experimental results indicate that the method in this paper can reliably detect LSB replacement steganography softwares of different versions and those are reimplemented relatively. In addition the proposed method can effectively detect reimplimented steganography softwares and the steganography softwares of different versions.

The future work will be focused on the analysis of the implementation LSB replacement algorithm further, improvement of steganography behavior finite automaton as well as the exploration of other steganography algorithm.

Acknowledgments. This work is supported by the National Natural Science Foundation of China (Grant Nos. 60970141, 60902102, 61272489), Scientific and Technological Innovation Leading Talent of Zhenzhou(Grand No. 10LJRC182).

References

1. Steganography tools (2009), http://www.jjtc.com/Security/stegtools.htm
2. Moon, K.K.B.-R.: Malware Detection based on Dependency Graph using Hybrid Genetic Algorithm. In: Proceedings of GECCO 2010, Oregon, P-orland, pp. 1211–1218 (2010)
3. Walenstein, A., Mathur, R., Chouchane, M.R., Lakhotia, A.: Normalizing Metamorphic Malware Using Term Rewriting. In: Proceedings of the Sixth IEEE International Workshop on Source Code Analysis and Manipulation (SCAM 2006), Philadelphia, USA, pp. 75–84 (2006)
4. Schmall, M.: Classification and identification of malicious code based on heuristic techniques utilizing meta-languages. Ph.D. thesis, University of Hamburg (2003)
5. Schultz, M.G., Eskin, E., Zadok, E., Stolfo, S.J.: Data Mining Methods for Detection of New Malicious Executables. In: Proc. of the IEEE Symposium on Security and Privacy, pp. 38–49. IEEE Press, Oakland (2001)
6. Myles, G., Collberg, C.: K-gram Based Software Birthmarks. In: Proceeding of ACM Symposium on Applied Computing, pp. 314–318. ACM (2005)
7. Tamada, H., Okamoto, K.: Dynamic Software Birthmarks to Detect the Theft of Windows Applications. In: Proceedings of the International Symposium on Future Software Technology (2004)
8. Schuler, D., Dallmeier, V., Lindig, C.: A Dynamic Birthmark for Java. In: Proceedings of the 22nd IEEE/ACM International Conference on Automated Software Engineering, pp. 274–283 (2007)
9. Zhou, X., Sun, X., Sun, G., Yang, Y.: A Combined Static and Dynamic Software Birthmark Based on Component Dependence Graph. In: Proceedings of International Conference on Intelligent Information Hiding and Multimedia Signal Prcessing, pp. 1416–1421 (2008)
10. Muñoz, A.: StegSecret (2007), http://stegsecret.sourceforge.net
11. Zheng, D., Liu, F., Yang, C., Luo, X.: Identify Information Hiding Software Based on Software Birthmarking. In: International Conference on Infomation Security and Artificial Intelligence, vol. 3, pp. 530–534 (2010)
12. Zheng, Y., Liu, F., Yang, C., Luo, X.: Identification of stganography software Based on Core Insructions Tempate Matching. In: Proceedings of IEEE International Conference on Multimedia Information Networking and Security 2011, Special Session, vol. 1, pp. 494–498 (2011)

13. Fridrich, J., Kodovský, J.: Steganalysis of LSB Replacement Using Parity-Aware Features. In: Kirchner, M., Ghosal, D. (eds.) IH 2012. LNCS, vol. 7692, pp. 31–45. Springer, Heidelberg (2013)
14. Christodorescu, M., Jha, S.: Static Analysis of Executablesto Detect Malicious Patterns. In: Proc. 12th Usenix Security Symp., pp. 169–186 (2003)

Appendix: The Pseudo-codes of Reimplement LSB Replacement Steganography Softwares

MySteganography1, MySteganography2, MySteganography3 are three functions that implement LSB replacement steganography algorithm using different ways, which are parts of three reimplimented steganography softwares reported in this paper respectively. The pseudo-codes are as follows.

```
MySteganography1
{
foreach Bit ∈ SecretMessage //For every bit in the secret message
    Select aPixel ∈ Stego-picture //Select a pixel in the stego-picture
    aPixel := aPixel & 0xFE // Reset the least significant bit of thepixel
    if Bit = 1 //If the bit of secret message is 1, add 1 to the pixel
        aPixel := aPixel + 1
    Store aPixel to Stego-picture //Store the pixel
}
```

```
MySteganography2
{
foreach Bit ∈ SecretMessage //For every bit in the secret message
    Select aPixel ∈ Stego-picture //Select a pixel in the stego-picture
    aPixel := aPixel & 0xFE //Reset the least significant bit of the pixel
    aPixel := aPixel | Bit //Do or operation with the pixel and the bit of the secret
                    // message
    Store aPixel to Stego-picture //Store the pixel
}
```

```
MySteganography3
{
foreach Byte ∈ SecretMessage //For every byte in the secret message
    foreach Bit ∈ Byte
        Select aPixel ∈ Stego-picture //Select a pixel in the stego-picture
        if Bit = 1
            aPixel := aPixel & 1  //If the bit of secret message is 1, and 1 with the pixel
        else aPixel := aPixel & 0  //If the bit of secret message is 0, and 0 with the
                            //pixel
        Store aPixel to Stego-picture //Store the pixel
}
```

An Attempt to Generalize Distortion Measure for JPEG Steganography

Vasily Sachnev and Hyoung Joong Kim

Catholic University of Korea,
Center of Information Security Technologies,
Graduate School of Information Security and Management,
Korea University, Seoul 136-701, Korea
bassvasys@hotmail.com, khj-@korea.ac.kr

Abstract. In this paper, we present several methods to improve performance of the existing data hiding method for JPEG steganography. Recent JPEG steganographic methods usually exploit minimum distortion strategy, where each DCT coefficients has predefined distortion value. Such strategy uses the best solution for data hiding with minimum cumulative distortion. Steganographic methods based on hiding data using the best solution with minimum distortion have better chance to pass powerful steganalysis presented in literature. Thus, the key point for such methods is a way to compute distortion for each DCT coefficient. In this paper, we present three different ways to compute distortion and search for parameters, where proposed functions show the best results. BCH-based method has been used as a tool for data hiding. Experimental results show that the presented distortion functions with the best parameters show better results compared to traditional approaches.

Keywords: Minimal distortion, BCH coding, JPEG steganography, undetectable data hiding.

1 Introduction

The extreme growth of the communication technologies (i.e., internet, mobile communication) keeps attention on many aspects of information security. Important information has to be protected from threats and malicious actions. Hence, the steganography can be a very efficient tool for achieving high level of security. One of the most important purposes of information security is to hide existence of the secret communications. Here, the secret message has to be hidden to a cover signal (i.e., image, sound, or text). The modified image with hidden data has to be statistically undetectable from unmodified images.

The first steganographic methods exploit least-significant bit (LSB) substitution approach for hiding data to a set of quantized DCT coefficients. However, those methods failed against statistical analysis. Next generation of the steganographic methods were specifically designed to pass statistical analysis (i.e., steganalysis). For example, a method proposed by Provos [20] divides a set of the

Y.Q. Shi, H.J. Kim, and F. Pérez-González (Eds.): IWDM 2012, LNCS 7809, pp. 69–82, 2013.

DCT coefficients into two disjoint subsets. The fist subset of coefficients has been used for hiding data, the second subset of coefficients has been modified in order to preserve statistical features similar to features extracted from original images. Other methods in [3] and [17] use a similar approach. Another interesting idea has been presented by Solanki et al. [27]. They embed data into image in the spatial domain by using a technique robust against JPEG compression. As a result, their scheme provides less degradation onto the features of the DCT coefficients and finally passes old version of the steganalysis techniques.

Another promising direction in steganography area is based on reducing the number of modified coefficients. First steganographic techniques hides one bit of data to one coefficients. Thus, theoretical capacity for such method is quit high and equals to the number of available DCT coefficients. Traditionally only nonzero DCT coefficients have been used for data hiding. However, such strategy causes significant distortion and fails to pass steganalysis. Westfeld [28] first exploited methods from coding theory for hiding data into the set of nonzero DCT coefficients. Presented matrix encoding (ME) technique is based on the popular Hamming code. In general, his scheme hides many bits by flipping at most one coefficient in each block, if there is no shrinkage. ME was the first successful data hiding technique based on an error correcting code (ECC).

Fridrich et al. [6], [7], [8] [9], [11], [10], and [12] presented several brilliant ideas which contributed a lot to the steganography. Presented concept of the "minimal distortion" enhances security (i.e., decreasing efficiency of the steganalysis) by modifying the most suitable DCT coefficients. Presented approach estimates possible distortion for each DCT coefficients after flipping. Thus, method may always choose coefficients with "minimum distortion". Even now such strategy is still the most promising direction. The perturbed quantization (PQ) [9] steganography utilizes the wet paper coding. Note that, PQ may sufficiently hide data to already compressed image even without additional side information.

Later, Kim et al. [13] have improved the performance of the ME by using concept of "minimal distortion". Modified matrix encoding (MME) may change more number of coefficients (up to three) compared to ME. Experiments showed that the distortion impact after modifying one coefficient may be larger than that after modifying two or three coefficients. Presented method may always choose the best solution among flipping one, two or three coefficients with less distortion and, as a result, may pass steganalysis. Note that MME requires the original uncompressed image for computing necessary distortion impacts, but not for decoding.

Recently steganographers made several successful attempts to use more complex and powerful error correction codes for data hiding. Schönfeld and Winkler [25] have proposed a new way to hide data using more powerful structured BCH (Bose-Chaudhuri-Hochquenghem) code [2]. Zhang et al. [30] significantly decreased computational and storage complexity of the original BCH data hiding scheme proposed by Schönfeld and Winkler [25]. Presented method can easily find multiple solutions for hiding data and, by using the concept of the "minimal distortion", choose the best one with less distortion. As a result, their method may defeat steganalysis well compared to the existing methods. Later, Sachnev et al. [22] applied a heuristic optimization technique based on modifying the stream of the nonzero coefficients by inserting and removing coefficients 1 and -1. Their scheme used BCH implementation proposed by Zhang et al. [30] as a tool for data hiding. Presented method considerably outperforms the the steganography method proposed by Zhang et al. [30].

Recently, Filler and Fridrich [4] have proposed a remarkable framework which minimizes a distortion measure as a weighted norm of the difference between cover and stego feature vectors. In their approach, the distortion is not necessarily an additive function over the pixels because the features may contain higher-order statistics such as sample transition probability matrices of pixels or DCT coefficients modeled as Markov chains [1], [19], [26]. When the distortion measure is defined as a sum of local potentials, practical near-optimal embedding methods can be implemented with syndrome-trellis codes [5].

Most of the recent steganographic schemes presented in literature usually exploit different codes with a block structure. Data hiding based on this strategy divides set of the DCT coefficients into separate blocks and hides data to each block individually. In this paper we are using efficient BCH-based data hiding technique for steganography. Recent BCH-based steganographic methods show significant improvement over ME (matrix encoding) and MME (modified matrix encoding). Using better distortion function for such methods may improve results further.

In this paper we present three methods to define the most appropriate distortion function. Presented ideas may improve any steganographic scheme based on "minimum" distortion strategy. Chosen distortion function guarantees the best performance and has better chance to pass powerful steganalysis.

This paper is organized as follows. Section 2 explains the details of the BCH code for data hiding. Section 3 presents the proposed distortion function. In Section 4, we propose an iterative algorithm to compute distortion. Section 5, we present an analytical distortion function. Section 6 concludes the paper.

2   BCH-Based Steganography

The Bose-Chaudhuri-Hocquenghem (BCH) codes are the well-known and widely used family of the error correction codes. BCH code (n, k, t) can correct t bits by inserting $n - k$ additional bits to the original message k such that syndrome of n equal 0. In this paper, an efficient BCH-based data hiding technique presented by Zhang et al. [30] has been used for testing several distortion measures.

2.1   BCH Syndrome Coding

The generalized parity-check matrix H for BCH coding is presented as follows:

$$H = \begin{bmatrix} 1 & \alpha & \alpha^2 & \cdots & \alpha^{n-1} \\ 1 & (\alpha^3) & (\alpha^3)^2 & \cdots & (\alpha^3)^{n-1} \\ \vdots & & & & \vdots \\ 1 & (\alpha^{2t-1}) & (\alpha^{2t-1})^2 & \cdots & (\alpha^{2t-1})^{n-1} \end{bmatrix} \tag{1}$$

where α is the primitive element in $GF(2^m)$; and n is the size of a binary block V. Lets t be 2. Then, the parity-check matrix is expressed as follows:

$$H = \begin{bmatrix} 1 & \alpha & \alpha^2 & \alpha^3 & \cdots & \alpha^{n-1} \\ 1 & (\alpha^3) & (\alpha^3)^2 & (\alpha^3)^3 & \cdots & (\alpha^3)^{n-1} \end{bmatrix} \tag{2}$$

Assume that the original stream of binary data is $V = \{v_0, v_1, v_2, ..., v_{n-1}\}$, and the modified stream of binary data after data hiding is $R = \{r_0, r_1, r_2, ..., r_{n-1}\}$. The streams V and R over $GF(2^m)$ can be represented as $\mathbf{V}(x) = v_0 + v_1 \cdot x + v_2 \cdot x^2 + v_3 \cdot x^3 + ... + v_{n-1} \cdot x^{n-1}$, and $\mathbf{R}(x) = r_0 + r_1 \cdot x + r_2 \cdot x^2 + r_3 \cdot x^3 + ... + r_{n-1} \cdot x^{n-1}$, respectively.

The embedded message $\mathbf{m}$ can be computed as follows:

$$\mathbf{m} = \mathbf{R} \cdot H^T. \tag{3}$$

Thus, the hiding message $\mathbf{m}$ to $\mathbf{V}$ requires to find $\mathbf{R}$ such that $\mathbf{R} \cdot H^T = \mathbf{m}$.

The difference between $\mathbf{R}$ and $\mathbf{V}$ shows the number and location of the elements in V to be flipped.

$$\mathbf{R} = \mathbf{V} + \mathbf{E}. \tag{4}$$

or

$$\mathbf{E} = x^{u_1} + x^{u_2} + x^{u_3} + ... + x^{u_l}, \tag{5}$$

where $u = \{u_1, u_2, u_3, ..., u_l\}$ are positions of the elements in V to be flipped in order to get R.

Using Equations (3) and (4), the syndrome $\mathbf{S}$ is computed as follows:

$$\mathbf{S} = \mathbf{m} - \mathbf{V} \cdot H^T = \mathbf{E} \cdot H^T. \tag{6}$$

If t is 2, then

$$\mathbf{S} = [S_1 \ S_2]^T = \mathbf{E} \cdot H^T \tag{7}$$

or,

$$\begin{aligned} S_1 &= \alpha^{u_1} + \alpha^{u_2} + \alpha^{u_3} + ... + \alpha^{u_l}, \\ S_2 &= (\alpha^3)^{u_1} + (\alpha^3)^{u_2} + (\alpha^3)^{u_3} + ... + (\alpha^3)^{u_l} \end{aligned} \tag{8}$$

where $\alpha^{u_1}, \alpha^{u_2}, \alpha^{u_3}, ..., \alpha^{u_l}$ are unknown values.

Assume that $\beta_i = \alpha^{u_i}$, where $i = 1, 2, 3, ..., l$. Then,

$$\begin{aligned} S_1 &= \beta_1 + \beta_2 + \beta_3 + ... + \beta_l, \\ S_2 &= \beta_1^3 + \beta_2^3 + \beta_3^3 + ... + \beta_l^3. \end{aligned} \tag{9}$$

Define a new polynomial $\sigma(x)$:

$$\sigma(x) = (x - \beta_1) \cdot (x - \beta_2) \cdot (x - \beta_3) \cdots (x - \beta_l) \tag{10}$$

or

$$\sigma(x) = x^l + \sigma_1 \cdot x^{l-1} + \sigma_2 \cdot x^{l-2} + ... + \sigma_l. \tag{11}$$

The polynomial $\sigma(x)$ is the flip location polynomial. The roots β can be determined after getting coefficients of the polynomial $\sigma(x)$. The relationship between σ and β is derived as follows:

$$
\begin{aligned}
\sigma_1 &= \beta_1 + \beta_2 + \ldots + \beta_l, \\
\sigma_2 &= \beta_1 \cdot \beta_2 + \beta_2 \cdot \beta_3 + \ldots + \beta_{l-1} \cdot \beta_l, \\
\sigma_3 &= \beta_1 \cdot \beta_2 \cdot \beta_3 + \beta_3 \cdot \beta_4 \cdot \beta_5 + \ldots + \beta_{l-2} \cdot \beta_{l-1} \cdot \beta_l
\end{aligned}
\tag{12}
$$

The coefficients σ_1, σ_2, and σ_3 relay to syndrome components $\{S_1\ S_2\}$ by following the *Newton's identities*:

$$
\begin{aligned}
S_1 + \sigma_1 &= 0, \\
S_2 + \sigma_1 \cdot S_1^2 + \sigma_2 \cdot S_1 + \sigma_3 &= 0.
\end{aligned}
\tag{13}
$$

2.2   Lookup Tables

In order to get a flip location polynomial we utilized the method of Zhao et al. [29] based on the fast lookup tables for finding roots of quadratic and cubic polynomial of $\sigma(x)$. See detail in [29].

2.3   Solutions

Hiding message **m** to the binary stream V requires to find the positions of the coefficients to be flipped. The proposed scheme provides solutions of flipping one, two, or three coefficients. Thus, data hiding scheme presented in [30] has a choice between many different solutions. Their method will always choose solution with the lowest distortion.

2.4   Encoder and Decoder

The encoder and decoder is organized as follows:
    Encoders runs according to the following procedure. For the given bitmap image Im, message M, quality factor Q_f, and secret key K, process:

1) Divide image Im into non-overlapped 8 by 8 blocks of pixels and process DCT, quantization and rounding as presented in Equation (15). Remove DC coefficients and nonzero DCT coefficients. Compute round error e.
2) According to the size of the hidden message M and the number of nonzero coefficients, compute the parameter m and define BCH scheme by using following inequality:

$$
\left\lfloor \frac{N}{2^m - 1} \right\rfloor \cdot (2m) \geq |M|,
\tag{14}
$$

   where N is the number of available nonzero coefficients.
3) Divide message M and stream of nonzero coefficients into $\lfloor \frac{N}{2^m-1} \rfloor$ blocks.

4) Hide data to each block using guidelines from [30]. Obtain a modified stream of nonzero coefficients.
5) Recover the original sequence of the DCT coefficients from the modified stream using the secret key K and the pseudo-random generator. Add DC coefficients, and obtain the stego JPEG image Im'.

The **decoder** of the proposed steganographic method is organized as follows:
For the given modified JPEG image Im', quality factor Q_f, secret key K, and respected size of the payload $p = |P|$, process:

1) Read the DCT coefficients from the JPEG file. Permute them using the secret key K and the pseudo-random generator. Remove the DC coefficients. Obtain the stream of nonzero DCT coefficients C.
2) Divide C into the blocks according to the p and length of the C.
3) Decode data from each block using Equation (3).

3   Distortion Measure

For all methods based on the "minimal" distortion strategy, distortion for each coefficients have to be defined. Such methods always embed data (by modifying some DCT coefficients) according to the computed distortion. Thus, getting the best and the most optimal way to compute distortion for each coefficients is an open and hot issue for steganography. Slight modification in the distortion measure dramatically changes performance of the steganographic methods (see the subsection "Experimental results"). Such instability keeps interest among researchers to find a distortion measure with better performance.

The main objective of distortion measure is to penalize DCT coefficients correctly. Several distortion measures have been investigated in the previous works. For example, distortion impact of each DCT coefficient can be computed by using the modified round error e as follows:

DCT transformation and rounding operations according to JPEG compression standard is expressed as follows:

$$c = DCT(B), \quad C = \frac{c}{Q}, \quad C' = round(C), \tag{15}$$

where Q is the corresponding quantization coefficient, B is the 8×8 block from the bitmap image.

Round error:

$$E = 0.5 - |C - C'| \tag{16}$$

Distortion measure based on the modified round error may efficiently penalize DCT coefficients. If the magnitude of a DCT coefficient is very close to round barrier ($r(C) + 0.5$, where $r(x)$ is a round operation), DCT coefficients can be easily modified to $r(C) + 1$ with minimum distortion and vice versa.

As long as data hiding scheme uses only nonzero DCT coefficients, coefficient 1 and -1 can not be changed to 0, and, similarly, DCT coefficients 0 can not be changed to 1 or -1. Thus, Equation (16) has to be modified:

Round error suitable for steganography:

$$E = \begin{cases} 0.5 - |C - C'|, & \text{if } C \neq 1, -1 \\ 1.5 - |C|, & \text{overwise.} \end{cases} \tag{17}$$

Such modification prevents unacceptable changes.

As was mentioned before, modified round error E itself can be used as a distortion measure. For example, $D = f(E)$, such as $D = E$ or $D = E^x$, where x is some predefined constant. Unfortunately, such a design does not show good improvement. Better performances can be achieved by supporting the modified round error E by corresponding quantization coefficient from the quantization matrix Q. Then the distortion function may have the following shape:

$$D = f(E, Q), \quad D = E \cdot Q \tag{18}$$

Such a move is clear and logical. Quantization coefficients have been chosen in order to preserve high compression rate and low distortion. As long as each DCT coefficient has to be scaled by a corresponding quantization coefficient, the best candidates are DCT coefficients with smaller corresponding quantization coefficients.

Recent investigation showed that the steganography scheme may have much better result if $D = E^m \cdot Q^n$, where m and n are predefined constants. In our previous papers [21], [22] we already introduced distortion measure of this shape. Simple search over the integers numbers, such as $m = 1, 2, 3, ..$, $n = 1, 2, 3, ...$, and various combination of different m and n, gave the best solution for $D = E^2 \cdot Q^2$. In this paper, we extended this search and investigated float numbers for distortion function $D = E^m \cdot Q^n$.

3.1   Experimental Results

In this section, the best parameters m and n which cause minimum detection rate for the steganalysis have to be defined. BCH steganography presented by Zhang [30] has been used for testing different distortion measures. Experiments have been organized in the following order. A set of 4,000 bitmap images has been used for hiding data with different distortion function $D = E^m \cdot Q^n$ and for capacity 0.2 bits per nonzero coefficients (bpc). The output of each test is the testing accuracy of the SVM model built by using steganalysis presented by Kodovsky and Fridrich [14]. Their method utilizes 548 features extracted from the JPEG image and can deeply investigate an artificial changes. Experimental results are shown in Table 1.

Table 1. Experimental results for capacity 0.2 bpc

		1	1.25	1.4	1.5	1.6	1.7	1.75	2	3
	1	**68.21**							70.549	73.920
	1.25		**67.467**		68.337					
	1.4			**67.183**						
	1.5		67.948		**67.198**	67.221		68.021		
	1.6				67.568	**66.991**	67.239	68.300		
n	1.7					67.346	**66.201**	67.206		
	1.75				67.623	65.262	67.196	**66.54**	67.745	
	2	73.000			67.406			67.556	**66.83**	68.677
	3	85.990						68.393	68.504	**67.92**

Presented results clearly indicate that the proposed shape of the distortion function such as $D = E^m \cdot Q^n$ has better performance when $m = n$ (see Table 1). The best result has been obtained when $m = n = 1.7$, i.e., $D = (E \cdot Q)^{1.7}$. Any difference between m and n causes significant increasing of the testing efficiency of the steganalysis. It means that relationship between the modified round error E and the quantization coefficient Q is symmetric. For further investigation of the distortion function, we can state that $m = n$. The total improvement of the proposed method over the previous work is 0.602% in terms of the testing accuracy.

4 Iterative Approach for Computing Distortion Measure

In this section, we present an improved way to compute the distortion measure. Assume that distortion measure has a complicated shape and can not be simply presented as a function of the round error E. In the previous section we already showed that parameter m has to be equal to n. Thus, instead of computing distortion as $D = E^m \cdot Q^n$, let's introduce a distortion function F, such that $D = F(E) \cdot Q^{1.7}$. The exact shape of the distortion function F can be obtained iteratively in the predefined points E_i (see Figure 1) starting from $F(E_i) = E_i^2 \cdot Q_i^2$. During the first initial iteration, the distortion function F is the same with function $E^{1.7}$ in the predefined points. In general, distortion function F is a set of consecutive lines connected in the predefined points. The distortion value for some round errors E located between the predefined points can be obtained from the line equation $k \cdot E + b$, where $k = (E_i - E_{i-1})/(F(E_i) - F(E_{i-1}))$, $b = F(E_i) - k \cdot E_i$, and the index i has to satisfy the following condition $E_{i-1} < E < E_i$. Function's values y in the predefined points have to be defined iteratively.

In the initial stage, the predefined points $P_0 = \{p_1(E_1, y_1), p_2(E_2, y_2),...,$ $p_n(E_n, y_n)\}$ are located on the curve $y = E^{1.7}$ (similar to the illustration in the

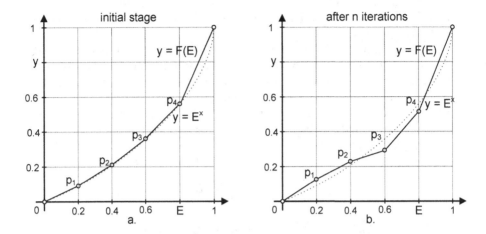

Fig. 1. Illustration of the distortion functions: a - in the initial stage; b - after n iterations

Figure 1.a), i.e., $(y_1 = E_1^{1.7}, y_2 = E_2^{1.7}, ..., y_n = E_n^{1.7})$. Note that vector Y_0 keeps all initial functions values, i.e., $Y_0 = \{E_1^{1.7}, E_2^{1.7}, ..., E_n^{1.7}\}$. The proposed iterative technique keeps modified round errors $(E_1, E_2, ..., E_n)$ unchanged and updates the output function's values $Y = \{y_1, y_2, ..., y_n\}$ as follows:

$$Y_i = Y_{i-1} + a, \qquad (19)$$

where a is an update vector.

1) *First iteration*

During the first iteration, the proposed algorithm has to collect enough initial data to start. In this experiment we randomly generate 10 different update vectors $a_I, a_{II}, ..., a_X$ as follows:

$$a = \frac{(2 \cdot rand(N) - 1) \cdot Y_0}{10}, \qquad (20)$$

where $rand()$ is a pseudo-random generator, $rand(N) \in [0; 1]$ generates N random values.

For each random update vector a, compute the modified distortion function $F(E)$ according to Equation (19).

Run a steganography-steganalysis test for each modified distortion function. Steganography-steganalysis test includes 1) hiding 0.2 bpc bits of message to a set of 4,000 bitmap images using the modified distortion function $F(E)$; 2) extracting 548 features according to the steganalysis method presented in [14]; 3) preparing image data sets for training and testing,

4) building the model according to the machine learning technique proposed by Kodovsky [15], 5) and testing set of images and getting testing accuracy and error probability.

Thus, steganography-steganalysis test for each distortion function finally results the testing accuracy, which can be better than for the distortion function $y = E^{1.7}$. Among 10 generated update vectors, choose the best vectors which produce result better than the distortion function $y = E^{1.7}$. Place the best update vectors to the matrix $B_{v \times l}$, where v is the number of chosen vectors, and l is the the number of predefined points.

2) *Second and other iterations*

Randomly generate 5 update vectors using the matrix B as follows:

$$a = \frac{rand(N) \cdot B'}{v}, \tag{21}$$

where $B' = \{\sum_{i=1}^{v} B(i,1), \sum_{i=1}^{v} B(i,2), ..., \sum_{i=1}^{v} B(i,n)\}$.

For each generated update vector, process as follows: 1) Compute a new distortion function; 2) Run steganography-steganalysis test using a new distortion function; 3) Obtain the testing accuracy and error probability.

Similar to the first iteration, matrix B has to be updated. All update vectors with the testing accuracy better than for the distortion function $y = E^{1.7}$ have to be placed to matrix B.

3) *Stop condition*

If after three iterations update vector with a better testing efficiency was not found, stop search.

Presented algorithm may update distortion function by using several update vectors with the best performances. Such approach performs suboptimal gradient search and may find better update vector after several iterations.

4.1   Experimental Result

In this section, we introduce the best results after running the proposed iterative algorithm several times. Presented distortion functions have been obtained after extensive computation process. The best distortion functions are displayed in Figure 2.

The first distortion function has the following parameters (see the left graph of Figure 2): 1) The number of predefined points is 9; 2) Number of iterations is 12; 3) The best update vector is $a = \{0, 0, 0.102, -0.108, -0.198, -0.342, -0.302, -0.2421, -0.151, 0.09, 0\}$; 4) Function's values in the predefined points are $Y_{best} = \{0, 0.01, 0.044, 0.081, 0.128, 0.1625, 0.252, 0.3675, 0.544, 0.9, 1\}$; 5) Testing accuracy is 65.81%; 6) Improvement over the distortion measure $D = E^2 \cdot Q^2$ is 1.02%.

The second distortion function has the following parameters (see the right graph of Figure 2): 1) The number of predefined points is 9; 2) Number of iterations is 9; 3) The best update vector is $a = \{0, 0, 0.98, 0, -0.1499, -0.31, -0.2506, -0.21, -0.09, 0, 0\}$; 4) Function's values in the predefined points are

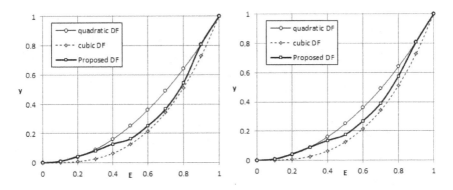

Fig. 2. Two distortion functions obtained by proposed iterative algorithm

$Y_{best} = \{0, 0.01, 0.044, 0.09, 0.136, 0.175, 0.27, 0.392, 0.576, 0.81, 1\}$; 5) Testing accuracy is 66.31%; 6) Improvement over the distortion measure $D = E^2 \cdot Q^2$ is 0.52%.

5 Search for Distortion Function

In this section we tried to find the distortion function among the analytical functions by using the results from the parameter optimization approach (section 3) and iterative approach (section4). Analytical functions have to have high correlation with the best distortion function obtained by using iterative approach. Eight different analytical functions have been tested (See Figure 3). The results are displayed in Table 2.

Table 2. Experimental results for different analytical distortion functions

	Analytical functions							
	1	2	3	4	5	6	7	8
Mathematical form	E^{1+E}	E^{1+2E}	$E^{1+1.5E}$	E^{1+3E}	E^{2+E}	$E^{1.5+2E}$	E^{2+2E}	$E^{1.5+1.5E}$
Testing accuracy	65.84	64.66	64.88	65.01	65.12	64.92	65.22	65.02
Improvement	1.1	2.08	1.86	1.73	1.62	1.82	1.52	1.72

Thus, the best distortion function has a shape E^{1+2E}. Total improvement for the proposed distortion function is 2.08%.

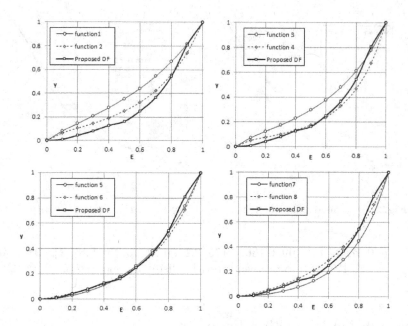

Fig. 3. Analytical functions and the best distortion functions obtained by proposed iterative algorithm

6   Conclusion

In this paper, we presented three connected approaches to get the best distortion function for JPEG steganography. The first approach is based on searching the best parameters for distortion measure $D = E^m \cdot Q^n$. The best result has been obtained for $m = n = 1.7$. Another important conclusion is that the modified round error E and corresponding quantization coefficients have symmetric properties. The results were always better if parameters m and n are equal. The second approach based on the iterative algorithm may search for the line-based distortion function which causes better result. The shape of the line-based distortion function with the best performance has been used for searching an analytical distortion function with similar to or even better testing accuracy. Finally we proposed the analytical function with the best results among all tested distortion measure. The total improvement over the previous works is 2.08% in terms of the testing accuracy.

Acknowledgment. This work was supported by the Catholic University of Korea, National Research Foundation of Korea, grand #2011 − 0013695, Information Technology Research Center, Culture Technology Research Center, Korea University, 3DLife, and IT R&D program (Development of anonymity-based u-knowledge security technology, 2007-S001-01).

References

1. Chen, C., Shi, Y.Q.: JPEG image steganalysis utilizing both intrablock and interblock correlations. In: Proceedings of the IEEE Internernational Symposium on Circuits and Systems, pp. 3029–3032 (2008)
2. Chien, R.T.: Cyclic decoding produce for the Bose-Chaudhuri-Hocquenghem codes. IEEE Transactions on Information Theory 11, 549–557 (1965)
3. Eggers, J., Bauml, R., Girod, B.: A communications approach to image steganography. In: Proceedings of SPIE: Security and Watermarking of Multimedia Contents IV, vol. 4675, pp. 26–37 (2002)
4. Filler, T., Fridrich, J.: Steganography using Gibbs random fields. In: Proceedings of ACM Multimedia and Security Workshop, pp. 199–212 (2010)
5. Filler, T., Judas, J., Fridrich, J.: Minimizing embedding impact in steganography using trellis-coded quantization. In: Proceedings of SPIE, vol. 7541, pp. 1–14 (2010)
6. Fridrich, J.: Minimizing the embedding impact in steganography. In: Proceedings of ACM Multimedia and Security Workshop, pp. 2–10 (2006)
7. Fridrich, J.: Feature-based steganalysis for JPEG images and its implications for future design of steganographic schemes. In: Fridrich, J. (ed.) IH 2004. LNCS, vol. 3200, pp. 67–81. Springer, Heidelberg (2004)
8. Fridrich, J., Filler, T.: Practical methods for minimizing embedding impact in steganography. In: Proceedings of SPIE, vol. 6505, pp. 2–3 (2007)
9. Fridrich, J., Goljan, M., Soukal, D.: Perturbed quantization steganography using wet paper codes. In: Proceedings of ACM Workshop on Multimedia and Security, pp. 4–15 (2004)
10. Fridrich, J., Goljan, M., Soukal, D.: Perturbed quantization steganography. ACM Multimedia and Security Journal 11(2), 98–107 (2005)
11. Fridrich, J., Pevny, T., Kodovsky, J.: Statistically undetectable JPEG steganography: Dead ends, challenges, and opportunities. In: Proceedings of ACM Workshop on Multimedia and Security, pp. 3–15 (2007)
12. Fridrich, J., Goljan, M., Soukal, D.: Wet paper coding with improved embedding efficiency. IEEE Transactions on Information Security and Forensics 1(1), 102–110 (2005)
13. Kim, Y.H., Duric, Z., Richards, D.: Modified matrix encoding technique for minimal distortion steganography. In: Camenisch, J.L., Collberg, C.S., Johnson, N.F., Sallee, P. (eds.) IH 2006. LNCS, vol. 4437, pp. 314–327. Springer, Heidelberg (2007)
14. Kodovsky, J., Fridrich, J.: Calibration revisited. In: Dittmann, J., Craver, S., Fridrich, J. (eds.) Proceedings of the 11th ACM Multimedia & Security Workshop, Princeton, NJ, September 7-8 (2009)
15. Kodovsk, J., Fridrich, J.: Steganalysis in high dimensions: fusing classifiers built on random subspaces. In: SPIE, Electronic Imaging, Media Watermarking, Security, and Forensics XIII, San Francisco, CA, January 23-26 (2011)
16. Lin, S., Costello, D.J.: Error Control Coding, 2nd edn. Prentice-Hall (2004)
17. Noda, H., Niimi, M., Kawaguchi, E.: Application of QIM with dead zone for histogram preserving JPEG steeganography. In: Proceedings of Initernational Conference on Image Processing, vol. II, pp. 1082–1085 (2005)
18. Pevny, T., Fridrich, J.: Multiclass blind steganalysis for JPEG images. In: Proceedings of SPIE, vol. 6072, pp. 257–269 (2006)
19. Pevny, T., Fridrich, J.: Merging Markov and DCT features for multi-class JPEG steganalysis. In: Proceedings of SPIE, San Jose, CA, vol. 6505, pp. 311–314 (2007)

20. Provos, N.: Defending against statistical steganalysis. In: Proceedings of 10th USENIX Security Symposium, Washington, DC, pp. 24–24 (2001)
21. Sachnev, V., Kim, H.J., Zhang, R., Choi, Y.S.: A novel approach for JPEG steganography. In: Kim, H.-J., Katzenbeisser, S., Ho, A.T.S. (eds.) IWDW 2008. LNCS, vol. 5450, pp. 209–217. Springer, Heidelberg (2009)
22. Sachnev, V., Kim, H.J., Zhang, R.: Less detectable JPEG steganography method based on heuristic optimization and BCH syndrome coding. In: Proceedings of ACM Workshop on Multimedia and Security, pp. 131–139 (2009)
23. Sallee, P.: Model-based steganography. In: Kalker, T., Cox, I., Ro, Y.M. (eds.) IWDW 2003. LNCS, vol. 2939, pp. 154–167. Springer, Heidelberg (2004)
24. Schöfeld, D., Winkler, A.: Embedding with syndrome coding based on BCH codes. In: Proceedings of ACM Workshop on Multimedia and Security, pp. 214–223 (2006)
25. Schönfeld, D., Winkler, A.: Reducing the complexity of syndrome coding for embedding. In: Furon, T., Cayre, F., Doërr, G., Bas, P. (eds.) IH 2007. LNCS, vol. 4567, pp. 145–158. Springer, Heidelberg (2008)
26. Shi, Y.Q., Chen, C.-H., Chen, W.: A markov process based approach to effective attacking JPEG steganography. In: Camenisch, J.L., Collberg, C.S., Johnson, N.F., Sallee, P. (eds.) IH 2006. LNCS, vol. 4437, pp. 249–264. Springer, Heidelberg (2007)
27. Solanki, K., Sarkar, A., Manjunath, B.S.: YASS: Yet another steganographic scheme that resists blind steganalysis. In: Furon, T., Cayre, F., Doërr, G., Bas, P. (eds.) IH 2007. LNCS, vol. 4567, pp. 16–31. Springer, Heidelberg (2008)
28. Westfeld, A.: F5–A steganographic algorithm: High capacity despite better steganalysis. In: Moskowitz, I.S. (ed.) IH 2001. LNCS, vol. 2137, pp. 289–302. Springer, Heidelberg (2001)
29. Zhao, Z., Wu, F., Yu, S., Zhou, J.: A lookup table based fast algorithm for finding roots of quadratic or cubic polynomials in the $GF(2^m)$. Journal of Huazhong University of Science and Technology (Nature Science Edition) 33(1), xx-xx (2005)
30. Zhang, R., Sachnev, V., Kim, H.J.: Fast BCH syndrome coding for steganography. In: Katzenbeisser, S., Sadeghi, A.-R. (eds.) IH 2009. LNCS, vol. 5806, pp. 48–58. Springer, Heidelberg (2009)

Optimal Data Embedding in 3D Models for Extraction from 2D Views Using Perspective Invariants

Yağız Yaşaroğlu and A. Aydın Alatan

Electrical and Electronics Engineering Dept., M.E.T.U.
Balgat 06531 Ankara, Turkey

Abstract. A 3D-2D watermarking method using a perspective projective invariant is proposed. Data is embedded in positions of six interest points on a 3D mesh, and extracted from any 2D view generated as long as the points remain visible. Determining interest point position change vectors, an important part of this method, is investigated. Different watermark embedding schemes including methods using heuristics and optimization of the watermark function are implemented. Simulations are done on random point sets and on six 3D mesh models with different watermark energies and view angles. Results show that the perspective invariant is suitable for 3D-2D watermarking using optimization based data embedding, confirming the new area of research that was introduced in previous work.

Keywords: 3D watermarking, steganography, projective invariants.

1 Introduction

Most 3D watermarking schemes deal with embedding and extracting information in 3D [4] while most 3D content is consumed in 2D. 2D watermarking can be used for embedding information in 3D content after 2D views are generated. However, there is another possibility: A content author may embed information in 3D content, for example a 3D mesh, generate 2D images and videos of it, and distribute them. The author may then extract the information that was embedded in 3D from a 2D image or video encountered at a later time. This is called 3D-2D watermarking, that is, information is embedded in 3D and extracted in 2D. A 3D-2D watermarking method enables the content author to embed information into the source model once, and distribute many 2D rendered views of the content, which is less costly than embedding information on every generated 2D view.

There has been little research in 3D-2D watermarking schemes. So far three directions were explored: In [7], watermark is embedded in apparent contours by modifying Fourier transform coefficients of the contour of 3D meshes. Contour is determined with respect to a specific camera position making this method dependent on camera position. Another method embeds data on texture images

Y.Q. Shi, H.J. Kim, and F. Pérez-González (Eds.): IWDW 2012, LNCS 7809, pp. 83–97, 2013.

of textured 3D objects [5]. To extract the watermark texture images need to be reconstructed, a process which depends on knowledge of camera and rendering parameters. Finally in [9], data is embedded in positions of five interest points on a mesh. Five point cross-ratio of interest points are used to extract embedded data. Since cross-ratio is a perspective invariant this method is camera position independent. Data embedded in the model can be retrieved as long as interest points remain visible in 2D views.

1.1   Perspective Invariants

A perspective invariant is a non-trivial constant function defined on a 3D model M, and its perspective projected 2D view m. That is, given that $m = T \cdot M$, the perspective invariant $f(M, m) = 0$ where T is any arbitrary perspective projection. The perspective invariant establishes a relationship between 3D models and their 2D perspective projected views independent of the projection.

Such a relationship provides a valuable tool for 3D-2D watermarking. Data is hidden in a model by modifying M and producing n different versions $\{M_i\}$. Given a 2D view generated from a model through any perspective transformation T, one can decide the source model by finding M_j that satisfies $f(M_j, m) = 0$.

Perspective invariant research has been mainly related to object identification, but there has been one study [9] that uses perspective invariants in 3D watermarking. Also, the idea of using perspective invariants in 3D-2D watermarking was investigated in [12], which laid the the groundwork of the work given in the present paper.

It is known that there is no general case perspective invariant on arbitrary 3D point sets [1]. However, by constraining the sets of points we can obtain usable perspective invariants. For example the cross ratio [3] requires four collinear points, and five point cross ratio [6] requires five coplanar points. Zhu et al. derived a perspective invariant for six points on two adjacent planes [13]. On the other hand, imposing constraints on point sets reduces the number of candidate points usable for embedding data. Therefore, more general perspective invariants are more suitable for use in 3D-2D watermarking. A more general perspective invariant given by YuanBin et al. in [11] is used in the proposed method, and is explained in detail in the next section.

2   General Perspective Invariant

In [11] the relationship between 6 3D points to their 2D perspective projections under the following constraints are specified:

Given 6 3D interest points $P_1, P_2, P_3, P_4, P_5, P_6$ and their perspective projected 2D counterparts $p_1, p_2, p_3, p_4, p_5, p_6$; 3D points P_1, P_2, P_3, P_4 should be non-coplanar, and 2D points p_1, p_2, p_3 should be non-collinear.

Under these constraints, the relative positions of six 3D interest points produce three coefficients $I = \{I_{12}, I_{13}, I_{14}\}$ [11]. The relative positions of 6 2D interest points produce five coefficients $K = \{K_{12}^{\lambda\tau}, K_{13}^{\lambda\tau}, K_{12}^{\rho\tau}, K_{13}^{\rho\tau}, K_{32}^{\lambda\rho}\}$ [11]. The perspective invariant is the function f given below.

$$f(I, K) = (K_{12}^{\lambda\tau} - 1)I_{13}I_{14} - \frac{K_{12}^{\lambda\tau} K_{13}^{\rho\tau} (K_{13}^{\lambda\tau} - 1)}{K_{13}^{\lambda\tau} K_{12}^{\rho\tau}} I_{12}I_{14}$$

$$+ (1 - \frac{K_{12}^{\lambda\tau} K_{13}^{\rho\tau}}{K_{13}^{\lambda\tau} K_{12}^{\rho\tau}})I_{12}I_{13} + (K_{13}^{\rho\tau} - \frac{K_{12}^{\lambda\tau} K_{13}^{\rho\tau}}{K_{13}^{\lambda\tau}})I_{14}$$

$$- (K_{12}^{\lambda\tau} \frac{K_{12}^{\lambda\tau} K_{13}^{\rho\tau}}{K_{13}^{\lambda\tau}})I_{13} + (\frac{K_{12}^{\lambda\tau} K_{13}^{\rho\tau}}{K_{12}^{\rho\tau}} - K_{13}^{\rho\tau})I_{12} = 0 \quad (1)$$

Fig. 1 is an image of $\log|f(I, K)|$ for fixed $P_1, P_2, P_3, P_4, P_5, P_6$ 3D vertex values and p_2, p_3, p_4, p_5, p_6 2D pixel values. p_1 value is varied across the image surface. At top left $p_1 = (0, 0)$ and at bottom right $p_1 = (800, 600)$. At red regions the function is undefined. Darker values are smaller. Blue dots are actual positions of p_1, p_2, p_3, p_4, p_5, and p_6. The thin dark line is composed of a series of local minima, about a pixel thick, as can be seen in the zoomed-in inset. This shows that a one pixel error in 2D interest point locations will result in large changes in $f(K, I)$ value.

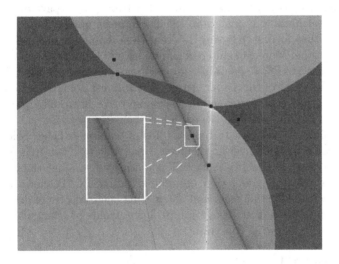

Fig. 1. Perspective invariant output. Small rectangle is zoomed-in.

This sensitivity to error is undesirable in 3D-2D watermarking. Due to this sensitivity $|f(I, K)|$ may not approach zero, causing a watermark to incorrectly be not detected. In this work it is investigated if the perspective invariant is suitable for watermarking despite this sensitivity, by implementing and evaluating different data embedding methods.

3   3D-2D Watermarking with Perspective Invariant

Watermarking process on a 3D model M using the general perspective invariant is given below:

1. Select six interest points in 3D $P = \{P_i\}, i \in [1, 6]$.
2. Embed data on 3D interest points by modifying their relative positions; creating different versions of the 3D model.
3. Calculate I coefficients for each version of the 3D model ($S_I = \{I_i\}, i \in [1, n]$).

If n versions of the model are created $\log_2(n)$ bits of information are embedded. After 2D views are generated from any viewpoint, data is extracted via:

1. Given a 2D view, detect interest points, $p = \{p_i\}, i \in [1, 6]$.
2. Calculate K coefficients using interest points.
3. Using the perspective invariant, find the I value that gives the minimum value of $|f(I_i, K)|$ for $I_i \in S_I$. This I value shows which version of the 3D model was used, and thus the embedded information is obtained.

3.1   Selection and Detection of Interest Points

Selection and detection of interest points is an important part of any practical 3D-2D watermarking application. Ideally, interest points should remain detectable when they are viewed using different camera angles, and under changing lighting conditions. Moreover, interest points should be detectable after data is embedded in the model. Repeatable interest point detection is a hard problem, and is not in the scope of this paper. To simplify interest point detection problem, and accurately judge performance of the perspective invariant, interest points are marked on 3D mesh models, as explained below.

Interest points are selected to be centroids of triangular faces. Selected faces are painted with distinct hues (red, green, blue, yellow, cyan, magenta), while unselected faces are left white. Since triangle centroids are invariant under perspective transformation, detection of interest points in 2D views is done by isolating regions of constant hue, and calculating their centers of gravity.

Interest points are selected randomly from centroids of triangular faces that conform with the following constraints:

- Selected face centroids should not be occluded,
- Angle between face normal and the vector connecting face centroid to camera center should be less than 60 degrees,
- Selected faces should not be adjacent (to prevent unwanted motion of adjacent faces during watermark embedding),
- First four selected faces' centroids should not be coplanar.

3.2   Embedding Data

Data is embedded in a model by changing positions of 3D interest points in a way that is not possible with a perspective transformation. This operation can be shown as $P_i' = P_i + v_i$ where v_i is the translation vector for i-th interest point. Watermark energy can be defined as the average of translation vector magnitudes, $s_w = \frac{\sum |v_i|}{6}$. Watermark energy will determine the amount of 3D mesh distortion and contribute to how robustly watermark is embedded.

It can be deduced from Fig. 1 that watermark energy alone will not determine the robustness of the embedded watermark. Direction of v_i is important, since the perspective invariant function's value is direction dependent around interest points. This fact can also be inferred from the observation that during data embedding, if 3D interest points are moved towards the camera, their 2D counterparts will not move, and embedded watermark will not be extracted.

To determine v_i, methods depending on heuristics and optimization are investigated in this work. In both cases the following ideas are used to aid in data embedding process: If interest points are moved parallel to image plane of the camera, largest interest point displacement will be generated on 2D views. If interest points are moved parallel to the face surface, 3D mesh distortion will be lower.

In the following discussion of data embedding methods, c_i is the vector connecting camera center and interest point P_i, and n_i is the normal vector of the face of the 3D mesh on which P_i resides. Both c_i and n_i are defined as unit vectors.

Data Embedding Using Heuristics. In data embedding methods using heuristics, each interest point is translated by a fixed amount along a direction. Displacement direction is heuristicaly selected based on view vector (c_i) and face normal (n_i). The following displacement directions are tested:

- Move towards or away from the camera: $v_i = s_w \cdot |c_i|$.
- Move perpendicular to c_i, parallel to image plane: $v_i = s_w \cdot |c_{i\perp}|$.
- Move perpendicular to face normal (parallel to face surface) and perpendicular to c_i (parallel to image plane): $v_i = s_w \cdot |n_i \times c_i|$.

Keeping translation parallel to image plane results in largest interest point displacement in generated 2D views, which is expected to create a large difference in the value of the watermark function. This expectation depends on the behavior of the perspective invariant. For the best performance, direction and magnitude of v should take into account the behavior of the perspective invariant. Embedding data optimally aims to address this problem.

Optimization Based Methods. When data is embedded in a 3D model to produce different model versions M_i, and a 2D image m_j obtained from one of the models, and its K coefficients K_j, it is expected that $|f(I_i, K_j)| = 0$ only for $i = j$. In other cases, $|f(I_i, K_j)|$ will be greater than zero. To maximize watermark detection performance, difference between these two values should be maximized.

On the other hand, a constraint on the amount of displacement of interest points should be imposed to limit the amount of 3D mesh distortion due to watermarking. Thus, the objective function O, that is to be maximized, is proposed below:

$$O = |\,|f(I_j, K_j)| - |f(I_i, K_j)|\,|$$
$$\text{where } i \neq j, |v_k| < \epsilon, \text{ and } P'_k = P_k + v_k, \ k \in [1,6]. \quad (2)$$

An optimization on this objective function should be carried out in 3D. In this case an 18-dimensional space (3 dimensions for 6 interest points) will be searched. The heuristics stated in the previous section might be used to reduce the dimensions; and hence, operation time of the search. Different data embedding approaches based on optimization and application of heuristics to reduce search space dimension is given below.

- **3D optimization:** Optimize in a 3D region centered around P_i.
- **2D optimization:** Optimize on the plane perpendicular to c_i, parallel to image plane, centered at P_i.
- **2D optimization:** Optimize on the plane perpendicular to n_i, parallel to face surface, centered at P_i.
- **1D optimization:** Optimize on face normal centered at P_i.
- **1D optimization:** Optimize on a line perpendicular to both face normal and view vector, centered at P_i.

Note that using camera location based heuristics is just an ad-hoc solution to reach an acceptable data embedding method. It is not mandatory to use camera location while embedding data. The proposed method of watermarking using perspective invariants is camera position independent. In fact, some of the data embedding methods, for example 3D optimization, do not utilize camera position. In general, the proposed method of watermarking using perspective invariants is camera position independent.

4   Simulations

Simulations are conducted in two phases. In the first phase randomly sampled 3D points independent of a model are used as interest points. Interest point detection is simulated by adding Gaussian noise onto 2D interest point coordinates. In the second phase, interest points are marked on 3D mesh models as explained in section 3.1. Interest point detection based on colored faces is applied.

In both phases, constrained Newton Conjugate-Gradient is used as the optimization method [10,8]. Optimization regions are defined as cubes, squares and line segments depending on the number of dimensions. Longest axis of the optimization region is set to be watermark strength upper bound value, that is, ϵ in equation 2.

4.1   Interest Point Detection on Synthetic Data

For each iteration of the experiment, six 3D interest points are randomly selected from a uniform distribution around the 3D origin. A perspective camera, located on the negative z-axis looking towards the origin is used to obtain 2D interest point coordinates. 2D coordinates are then scaled to correspond to pixel coordinates of a square image of 800 pixels on one side. Distribution of random 3D points and camera parameters are selected to be compatible with simulations with 3D mesh models. Gaussian noise is added to the pixel coordinates to simulate interest point detection. In this phase, since there are no models and no faces, only the following data embedding methods are simulated:

- 3D Optimization
- 2D Optimization on the plane perpendicular to view vector ($2D - c_\perp$)
- 1D Optimization along the view vector ($1D - c$)
- Heuristics: Along the view vector (c heuristics)
- Heuristics: Perpendicular to view vector ($c_\perp$ heuristics)

One bit of information is embedded by creating one additional version of the original model using selected data embedding method. Performance of the proposed system is investigated for a range of watermark energy upper bounds (0.05, 0.1, 0.15, 0.2), viewing angles ($0°$, $15°$, $30°$, $45°$) and 2D interest point Gaussian noise levels (0.0, 0.5, 1.0, 1.5). Watermark detection is defined to be successful if

$$|f(I_2, K_2)| < |f(I_1, K_2)| \tag{3}$$

where I_1 and K_1 are obtained from the original model and I_2 and K_2 are obtained from the modified model. For optimization based methods the following objective function is used:

$$O = |\,|f(I_2, K_2)| - |f(I_1, K_2)|\,| \text{ where } |v_k| < \epsilon, k \in [1, 6]. \tag{4}$$

If at any point in the iteration, selected interest points or their 2D counterparts fail to conform to perspective projection constraints given in Sect. 2, iteration is restarted using another set of random interest points.

In Fig. 2, performance of five data embedding methods is plotted against standard deviation of Gaussian noise added to 2D interest point coordinates, at $0°$ viewing angle, across all watermark energy levels. As can be seen, all methods exhibit perfect performance when there is no noise added, except c heuristics. This result is expected, since by moving 3D interest points towards the camera, no change is observed in 2D interest point locations. Detection performance degrades as noise strength is increased. Optimization based methods have better performance than heuristics based methods for any noise level, while 2D optimization shows the best performance, and other optimization methods closely following. At noise levels of 0.5 and 1.5 pixels standard deviation, detection performance drops to 95.3% and 88.6% for 2D optimization, and 92.8% and 82.7% for $c_\perp$ heuristics.

In Fig. 3, detection rate is plotted against viewing angle (from $0°$ to $45°$) for a noise level of 0.5 pixel standard deviation. Changing viewing angle in this range reduces performance of optimization and $c_\perp$ heuristics based methods by about

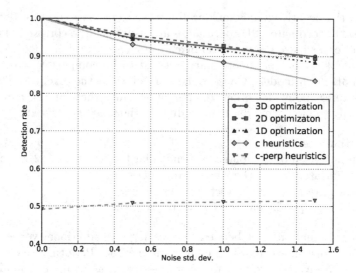

Fig. 2. Detection rate versus Gaussian noise standard deviation, plotted for different data embedding methods

3%. On the other hand, detection rate for c heuristics increases greatly with viewing angle, since when viewed from an angle, 2D interest points' translation towards the original camera position becomes more visible.

Finally, Fig. 4 displays detection rate against watermark energy at $0°$ viewing angle and 1.5 pixel noise standard deviation. This noise value is selected to distinctively evaluate different methods' performance. $c_\perp$ heuristics based method shows better performance by increasing watermark energy. Optimization based methods are ahead of heuristics based methods, although they do not exhibit a clear relationship in terms of detection rate. 3D, 2D and 1D optimization methods reach peak detection rates of 92.2%, 91.6% and 91.6%, respectively. $c_\perp$ heuristics follows with a peak detection rate of 85.8%.

Results obtained in this phase demonstrate that 3D-2D watermarking with perspective invariants is feasible, even when 2D interest point detection is noisy. 2D optimization among the optimization based methods, and $c_\perp$ among heuristics based methods have better performance when compared to others. Optimization based methods exhibit better performance, especially under higher noise levels and low watermark energies.

4.2   Interest Point Detection on 3D Models

In this phase, simulations are done on triangular faced mesh models with no textures. Mesh models are rendered in Blender 3D software. 2D views are rendered with a camera of 35 mm focal length. Camera is rotated around the model to the desired view angle. Given a 3D model, the following steps are performed in the watermark embedder:

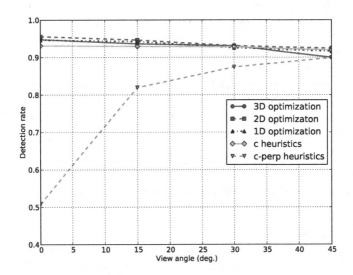

Fig. 3. Detection rate versus viewing angle, plotted for different data embedding methods

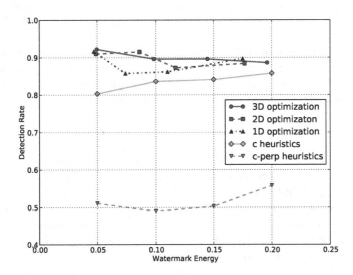

Fig. 4. Detection rate versus watermark energy (s_w), plotted for different data embedding methods

1. Interest points are randomly selected and marked.
2. Watermark is embedded by moving interest points according to the selected watermark energy and watermark embedding method.
3. 2D views are obtained for the original model (model-0) and the modified model (model-1), after rotating the camera by the specified view angle.
4. I coefficients for model-0 and model-1 are calculated.
5. Mesh distance values are calculated for each watermark embedded model using the Metro tool [2].
6. Signal to watermark ratios of 2D watermarked views to original model views are calculated.

If not exactly six interest points are detected, or detected interest points violate the perspective invariant constraint given in Sect. 2, the iteration is discarded. The iteration is considered a success if watermark for model-1 is successfully detected. Data is embedded using the following methods:

- 3D Optimization
- 2D Optimization on the plane perpendicular to view vector $(2D - c_\perp)$
- 2D Optimization on the plane perpendicular to face normal $(2D - n_\perp)$
- 1D Optimization along the face normal $(1D - n)$
- 1D Optimization on the line perpendicular to both $(1D - n \times c)$
- Heuristics: Along the line perpendicular to both $(n \times c)$

Performance of the proposed system is investigated for watermark strength values 0.025, 0.05, 0.075, 0.1, and view angles 0°, 7.5°, 15°. Higher strength values produce too pronounced distortion on models and thus were not simulated. Bigger view angles caused occlusion of interest points, causing too many discarded iterations.

Six models from Stanford 3D Scanning repository and Aim@Shape repository are used (Fig. 5). Mesh distortion is measured by Hausdorff distance. Hausdorff distance defined on two input meshes X and Y is given below, where $d(x, Y)$ is the Euclidean distance from a point x on X to the closest point on Y:

$$d_H(X, Y) = \max \left\{ \max_{x \in X} d(x, Y), \max_{y \in Y} d(y, X) \right\}$$

Detection rate of all data embedding methods for a viewing angle of 0° are given in Fig. 6. The x-axis denotes watermark energy (s_w). Overall, detection rates for optimization based methods are higher than $(n \times c)$ heuristics method, reaching 99.0% for 3D optimization at 0.021 watermark energy (cyan line) and 98.8% for 1D optimization on the line $n \times c$ at 0.019 watermark energy (red line). The $n \times c$ heuristics method exhibits at best 92.9% detection rate at 0.050 watermark energy. It can also be observed that optimization based methods show significantly better performance at lower watermark energies: When watermark energy is equal to 0.021, 3D optimization performs 10.1% better than heuristics based method.

For all methods, when watermark energy is increased beyond a level, detection rate is observed to decrease. The main reason for this unexpected situation is

Fig. 5. Mesh models used in simulations, with interest points marked

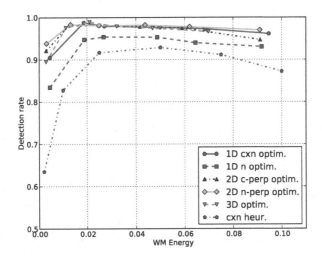

Fig. 6. Detection rate versus watermark energy bound or watermark energy (s_w or ϵ), plotted for different data embedding methods

the increased probability of self occlusion of faces after data embedding, and in consequence, increased localization errors in interest point detection at high watermark energy levels. In Table 1, performance of all data embedding methods is given at 0.1 watermark energy upper bound for two cases: All iterations included, and those iterations having interest point detection errors of more than 0.5 pixels discarded. The detection rate increase once again emphasizes importance of interest point detection and localization.

Table 1. Detection rate increase when interest point detection errors are removed at 0.1 watermark energy

Method	All	Errors discarded
3D Optimization	96.5%	98.2%
$2D - c_\perp$	94.7%	97.1%
$2D - n_\perp$	97.0%	98.2%
$1D - n$	93.1%	94.5%
$1D - n \times c$	96.1%	98.9%
$n \times c$ heuristics	87.2%	95.5%

As can be seen in Fig. 7, data embedding methods that displace interest points perpendicular to face normal (1D optimization along $n \times c$, 2D optimization on $n_\perp$, and $n \times c$ heuristics) produce lower mesh distortion, while optimization along the face normal results in the largest mesh distortion. In general, mesh distortion increases by increasing watermark energy almost linearly.

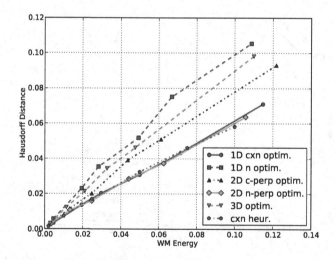

Fig. 7. Mesh distortion versus watermark energy bound or watermark energy (s_w or ϵ), plotted for different data embedding methods

Fig. 8 shows detection rate versus view angle characteristics for all data embedding methods. 3D optimization is observed to perform slightly better than other methods at 15° viewing angle, although detection performance degradation of only 1D optimization on n method is significant (2.5%). In (Fig. 9), signal to watermark ratio between 2D views of Model-0 and Model-1 is observed to be inversely related to watermark energy, as expected.

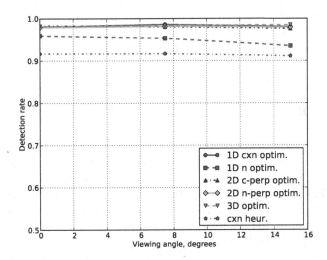

Fig. 8. Detection rate versus viewing angle, plotted for different data embedding methods

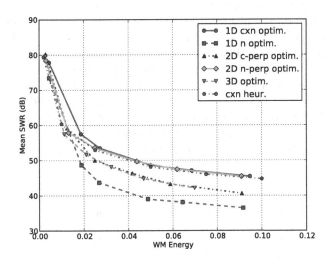

Fig. 9. Signal to watermark ratio versus watermark energy bound or watermark energy (s_w or ϵ), plotted for different data embedding methods

The results obtained in this phase indicate that optimization based methods continue to perform better than heuristics based methods, even when 3D models are used. On the other hand, reduced detection rate in higher watermark energy values demonstrate the difficulty and importance of interest point detection and localization after data is embedded in the mesh.

Data embedding methods that displace interest points perpendicular to face normal result in smaller mesh distortion in 3D, and higher signal to watermark ratio in 2D. On the other hand 3D optimization, despite being computationally costly, is both camera position independent and improves other methods by a small margin.

5   Conclusion

In this paper, a watermarking method that extracts data embedded in 3D models from arbitrary 2D views is presented. Proposed method utilizes a perspective invariant relating six minimally constrained 3D points and their 2D counterparts. Data is embedded by displacement of 3D interest points. Primary challenges of this watermarking method are identified to be noise sensitivity of the perspective invariant, and accurate 2D interest point detection.

An optimal data embedding method is developed to overcome the noise sensitivity of the perspective invariant. Also, a basic interest point detection scheme is devised to accurately judge perspective invariant performance.

Simulations conducted on point sets and mesh models highlight a number of observations. It is seen that optimally embedded data in 3D mesh models can be extracted from 2D views with 99.0% watermark detection performance when one bit of information is embedded into two models. Furthermore, optimization based methods have 10% higher watermark detection performance than heuristics based methods. In addition, peak detection rates are observed at lower watermark energies with optimization based methods, resulting in lower distortion in 3D meshes and 2D views. Detecting watermark on 2D views obtained with 15° camera angle does not produce significant performance degradation. However, even with the basic detection scheme, accurately detecting interest points remains a factor in watermark detection performance. Especially self occlusions caused by data embedding prevent watermark detection at high watermark energies.

These results show that it is possible to use perspective invariants in 3D-2D watermarking, especially when optimal data embedding methods are utilized. Further research will focus on interest point selection and detection. Using available features on textured models instead of marking interest points on models will be investigated.

References

1. Burns, J.B., Weiss, R.S., Riseman, E.M.: The non-existence of general-case view-invariants. In: Geometric invariance in computer vision, pp. 120–131. MIT Press, Cambridge (1992), http://portal.acm.org/citation.cfm?id=153634.153640
2. Cignoni, P., Rocchini, C., Scopigno, R.: Metro: Measuring error on simplified surfaces. Computer Graphics Forum 17(2) (1998); Journal of Pattern Recognition Research

3. Coelho, C., Heller, A., Mundy, J.L., Forsyth, D.A., Zisserman, A.: An experimental evaluation of projective invariants. In: Geometric Invariance in Computer Vision, pp. 87–104. MIT Press, Cambridge (1992), http://portal.acm.org/citation.cfm?id=153634.153638

4. Dugelay, J.L., Baskurt, A.: 3D Object Processing: Compression, Indexing and Watermarking, ch. 4. 3D Object Watermarking. Wiley & Sons Ltd., England (2008)

5. Garcia, E., Dugelay, J.: Texture-based watermarking of 3D video objects. IEEE Transactions on Circuits and Systems for Video Technology 13(8), 853–866 (2003)

6. Hartley, R.: Projective reconstruction and invariants from multiple images. IEEE Transactions on Pattern Analysis and Machine Intelligence 16(10), 1036–1041 (1994)

7. Bennour, J., Dugelay, J.-L.: Watermarking of 3D objects based on 2D apparent contours. In: Proc. of SPIE-IS&T Electronic Imaging, vol. 6072. SPIE (2006)

8. Jones, E., Oliphant, T., Peterson, P., et al.: SciPy: Open source scientific tools for Python (2001), http://www.scipy.org/

9. Koz, A.: Watermarking for 3D representations. Ph.D. thesis, Middle East Technical University (August 2007)

10. Nash, S.G.: Newton-Type Minimization via the Lanczos Method. SIAM Journal on Numerical Analysis 21, 770–788 (1984)

11. Wang, Y., Bin, Z., Ge, Y.: The invariant relations of 3D to 2D projection of point sets. Journal of Pattern Recognition Research 3(1), 14–23 (2008)

12. Yasaroglu, Y., Alatan, A.: Extracting embedded data in 3D models from 2D views using perspective invariants. In: 3DTV Conference: The True Vision - Capture, Transmission and Display of 3D Video (3DTV-CON), pp. 1–4 (May 2011)

13. Zhu, Y., Seneviratne, L.D., Earles, S.W.E.: New algorithm for calculating an invariant of 3D point sets from a single view. Image and Vision Computing 14(3), 179–188 (1996), http://www.sciencedirect.com/science/article/B6V09-3VVCMCX-2/2/16437141ad33485d7cc033de085ec66a

Consideration of the Watermark Inversion Attack and Its Invalidation Framework

Kazuo Ohzeki[1], YuanYu Wei[1], Yutaka Hirakawa[1], and Kiyosugu Sato[2]

[1] ISE, Shibaura Institute of Technology, 3-7-5 Toyosu, Koutouku,
Tokyo 135-8548 Japan
[2] IPE, College of Industrial Technology, 1-27-1 Nishikoya,
Amagasaki, Hyougo, 661-0047 Japan
{ohzeki,hirakawa}@sic.shibaura-it.ac.jp,
m710101@shibaura-it.ac.jp, kiyo@cit.sangitan.ac.jp

Abstract. This paper considers the problem of the inversion attack. We discuss a relation of a copyright owner and an attacker on an equal footing, the problem of the assumption of robustness, and the quantization error as a one-way function. Using an improved two-stage watermarking system, a framework that invalidates an inversion attack is proposed.

Keywords: watermark, inversion attack, quantization, one-way function.

1 Introduction

There are many attacks on digital watermarking, although not all are successful. One of these is the inversion attack, which belongs to the protocol group of attacks, and is not performed to specifically remove the watermark. Because inversion attacks can be applied unconditionally, we must consider a high degree of adverse effects. In this paper, we give an overview of research from around 1998, when such attacks were first announced, to the present. By examining the circumstances in detail, we can find ways to make inversion attacks difficult to apply unconditionally, and ultimately avoidable.

Conventionally, inversion attacks have been described mathematically. The simple model of embedding a digital watermark by the addition of a component, and its removal by subtraction, has been generally adopted. However, in practice, an embedded function (mapping) has many components, including the multiplication and division of real numbers, complex numbers, and irrational numbers. Therefore, we must take rounding errors into consideration. In addition, the introduction of a one-way function has been proposed as a means of avoiding simple addition. Deciphering such functions is not actually very difficult, and there has been much use of the surplus of integer modulo known as the hash function.

Moreover, in order that the counter measure of an attack might be the subject of a mathematical discussion, designers looked for the worst-case scenario, and proposed systems based on the maximum degree of pessimism. Other counter measures less than this maximum level were apt to be disposed. However, there is no necessity to

Y.Q. Shi, H.J. Kim, and F. Pérez-González (Eds.): IWDW 2012, LNCS 7809, pp. 98–110, 2013.

accept all of the unfair logic or an opinion of a particular attacker, such as in a Protocol Attack. The attacker should submit the things used as the basis of ownership of an image, e.g., the original picture and the embedding technique, embedding software, experimental data, etc. Naturally, the owner/embedder should submit the related information. Even if the framework is set up based on more detailed information, it does not necessarily serve to unfairly regulate an attacker.

We point out the defects of a conventional protocol relevant to an inversion attack. A framework that offers many keys to check the applicant's rights and the embedding of digital watermarking should be sufficiently complex, and should, to some extent, have the above robustness. We propose such a framework in this paper.

If an embedder is cooperating with information disclosure at the time of dispute, and a governmental verification organization sets up an agreement that carries out strict dispute processing, it is shown that an inversion attack can be made considerably more difficult, or even impossible.

2   Inversion Attack History

A timeline of inversion attacks is shown in Fig. 1, where appropriate discussions of each type are introduced with references.

It is claimed that [1] first raised the concept of an inversion attack, and this research has requested further development in the future. To forge a digital watermark, it was described that research on the strengthening of further robustness is possible. Moreover, it was described that research into a system that reinforces copyright with digital watermarking with the use of encryption is also important. The term "Inversion Attack" was described by Single Watermark Image Counterfeit Original (SWICO) system. The concept of SWICO is shown in Fig. 2. Thus, it was pointed out that an image whose watermark is forged can be constituted by the inverse operation. This is an explanation of the existence of the inversion attack. Even though it expressed the inverse of an embedded inverse operation using the most general function, the example of the image data of a concrete integer was separated from the general function.

In [2], the term "Inversion Attack" is used to refer to the contents [1]. This paper is related to the Spread Spectrum system and classifies many attacks into four categories, one of which ambiguity attacks includes the inversion attack. Other methods included in this category are the confusion attack, the fake-watermark attack, the fake-original attack, and the IBM attack. Although the SWICO attack is described in [1], it appears that terms such as "inversion attack" were subsequently used.

The term "inversion attack" is used once in [3], whereas the term "invertibility attack" is used nine times in its place. Although the author is a proposer of the concept of the inversion attack, the term SWICO attack and "invertibility attack" are used abundantly. In [3], a Zero-Knowledge Interactive Proof is included in the embedding of a digital watermark. This hides the embedding process, and operates the embedding and detection system.

The difference between an ambiguity attack and an inversion attack is also described in [4]. Ref. [5] concerns digital watermarks that use singular value decomposition (SVD), which is one-way and is said to be irreversible (i.e. it has non-invertibility). It is thought that digital watermarks incorporating this characteristic can robustly withstand an inversion attack. On the other hand, the disadvantage of this one-way method is that as a unique (singular) value changes with embedding, this deployment and embedding of SVD cannot extract the same data as the embedded watermark in detection.

Ref. [6] describes a system that opposes an inversion attack using a hash function for one-way operation. Although correct detection (legal positive) can be performed, many false positives exist. It is thus claimed to be one-way, but still produces many false positives.

This is because a hash was used. A hash divides image data by the value of the watermark key. The operation is to make an embedded image minutely changed such as for LSB. Influence of the change can be disregarded because it is minute change in watermark embedding. The disregarding is called the assumption of robustness, which was used in an inversion attacker's detection to identify two different embedded images as the same image.

Using SVD, the watermark can be embedded in a singular value decomposition space. This technique was used to realize one-wayness in [7]. By this system, because the embedding was not diagonal, it did not cause changes to the singular values. This SVD method has the feature that the embedded data is detected as it is. Thereby, reverse analyses, such as the inversion attack, are difficult.

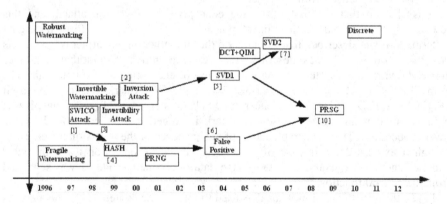

Fig. 1. Technical map of inversion attacks

In [8] and [9], the embedding system (which performs linear transformation, such as Chirp transformation and DCT, and quantization are studied. Calculating the number of cases when the coefficients of the linear transformation were changed minutely, the number of searches was shown to be sufficiently large, in terms of computational complexity, to be impossible on current computers. Ref [8] used pre-determined calculation tables, which were called ROM, for obfuscating embedding software. Therefore, the size of the transform block was restricted to smaller values.

In the above papers, the one-way function was an important measure against an inversion attack. Recently, in [10] quantization effects have been used in PRSG to invalidate the inversion attack. There has also been research focusing on systems that use a hash function. However, the attackers' techniques are many-sided and a pessimistic conclusion was reached. Although trials, such as SVD [11], also occurred, these were seldom taken up.

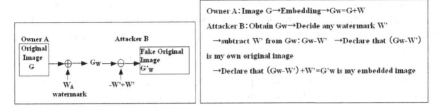

Fig. 2. Inversion Attack System. G is the original image of Owner A. W is a watermark of A. W_A is an embedded image. W' is a watermark of Attacker B.

3   Reconsideration of the Inversion Attack

We will consider some of the results from the proceeding chapter in detail. Table 1 is a score sheet for the detection by Owner A and by Attacker B for an image considered in [1]. In Test II, case 3 is normal. It is shown that after B receives the embedded image of A, B subtracts $W_B = X_B^0$ of B's watermark part from it, and A can detect A's watermark from the generated image as X_B^0. Furthermore, B cannot detect the watermark from A's original image. Cases 4 and 5 cannot occur without a fake. This table shows that there was apprehension about the possibility of Case 5 with an inversion attack.

Table 1. Determination of ownership from watermark presence (from Craver [1], p.577). Test I is for the detection of an embedded image by the owner. Cases 1 and 2 are only for Test I. Test II is for the detection of an original image by an opponent. X_A, X_B are watermarks in Ref. [1], which are represented W_A, W_B in this paper. "d" represents "don't care".

Scenario	Test I		Test II		Derived Ownership
	X_A	X_B	X_A^0	X_B^0	
Case 1	1	0	d	d	A
Case 2	0	1	d	d	B
Case 3	1	1	1	0	A
Case 4	1	1	0	1	B
Case 5	1	1	1	1	???

Here, there is an assumption of robustness in the possibility that Case 5 is valid. This means that when B subtracts the watermark W_B from an embedded image of A, the change caused by this subtraction can be ignored. However, such an assumption gives special facilities to B, which will generally be thought of as a bad step.

The assumption of robustness causes an object image to be changed minutely. Then, the assumption of robustness adds the inversion attack with other warping ability of geometrical category. The inversion attack belongs not only to a protocol attack, but also to a geometrical attack. In this paper, we consider only pure protocol attacks.

We consider how authentication of ownership is performed for a single image. We do not make another forged image by a different attack type. Inversion attacks are classified into protocol attacks (refer to Fig. 3), which carry out neither processing nor deletion of a watermark on an image. Mixtures of two or more attacks are considered separately.

The two-stage watermark system [12] is effective in dealing with the unfairness problem. The concept in [12] is improved here to have several factors that at the second stage both parties in a dispute must provide the original image, embedding information detection information and time-stamp data to a trusted third party (TTP) organization. The TTP judges the copyright by inspecting the provided data in a secret zone. The process builds a blind watermarking scheme because it uses the original images in detection. The blind watermarking system generally has greater robustness than the non-blind-type system.

Table 2, which shows an inversion attack in a pure protocol attack, improves Table 1. The first step does embed the digital watermark and publish the embedded image. A dispute then occurs, and verification by governmental or third party is the second step. Attacker B tries to detect G_A and G_B in the first step. However, we think that detection is performed inside B in a closed manner. In the second step, a governmental institution receives and saves the watermarks W_A and W_B that were first detected from A and B. Next, the institution receive the original images and detectors offered by A and B. Although the governmental institution performs detection processing, the probability that the watermark W_B of B will be detected from the original image G_A of A is nearly 0.

Table 2. Comparison of detection ability between Owner A and Attacker B. G_{WA} is a watermarked image of A, and G_{WB} is a watermarked image of B. G_A is the original image of A, and G_B is the original image of B. The inversion attack here is a pure protocol attack.

Stages	Images	Owner A	Attacker B of inversion attack	Blind Type
First	G_{wA}	Yes	Yes	keys are secret
	G_{wB}	Yes	Yes	
Second	G_A	No	No	detection of the
	G_B	Yes	No	original image

- Consideration of fairness

Conventionally, fair treatment in deciding truth or falsehood may not be made between embedding event of the owner of the media having embedded the watermark, and the detection event of the false watermark that an attacker describes. That is, watermark detection of the owner is strictly carried out, and it is said that attackers have only to present an indefinite possibility above the minimum level. This should be corrected so that both sides are in a fair position.

Even if the attacker generates an ambiguous state, the original owner's rights should not be lost. The inversion attack may not be validated even if an ambiguous state can be formed, and the original image that accompanies the watermarked one, the embedding technique, and the detection technique are verified in detail. The same idea of this unfairness was shown in [13], though expressed in a different way.

- Consideration of one-way function

A trial of one-way functions, which cancel an inversion attack, was considered and many hash functions, in particular, were tried. Systems that embed the bit sequence of the residual, when the image data is divided by the value of the secret key, were considered. Then, the one-way function with the hash function was invalidated by the above-mentioned assumption of robustness. If the assumption of robustness is not accepted, the hash functions still have one-way characteristics. However, embedding the residual bit sequence using a hash in an image has the problem that robustness becomes weak. Even when a 1 bit error in many bits occurs in bit sequences, authentication becomes impossible because of the different result in calculation. Concerning the one-way characteristics, although singular values in SVD are unique, decomposition matrices of SVD are not unique, which contributes one-way characteristic. Moreover, in a popular systems that use DCT and QIM, the operation of DCT uses the real numbers. Furthermore, there is a rounding operation when the inverse transform is carried out after embedding. Therefore, if a large number of rounded pixel patterns exist, the number of searches will increase. Thus, the linear

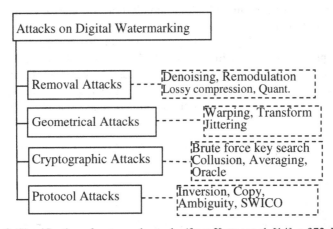

Fig. 3. Classification of watermark attacks (from Kutter et al. [14], p.372, Fig.1)

transform system has a finite 1:n asymmetrical function, which is a kind of one-wayness. If we add minute changes of coefficients to this linear transform system, the number of cases becomes so large that searching is impossible, as demonstrated in [9].

In this chapter, we considered three measures against inversion attacks;

- Reconsideration of the robustness assumption;
- The necessity for strict fairness;
- The one-way nature of the function.

4   Invalidation of an Inversion Attack

Based on the above consideration, we now attempt to formalize regulations for inversion attacks within the category of a pure protocol attack. First, based on the code of the above-mentioned fairness, protocols that favour an owner but are disadvantageous to an attacker should be adopted. Conversely, protocols that are detrimental to an owner and advantageous to an attacker should be impossible.

Cases with a large range of fairness, outside the framework of "Protocol by law" are not considered, and cases with a narrow range are shown in Fig. 4. If such regulation is applied, then an attacker has to perform embedding carefully at least at the level as the owner performs embedding even more carefully. It turns out that virtual claims, as if there was an original image from the inverse operation, which occurs in the former framework, can be eliminated.

Next, there are a variety of digital watermarks, from the very simple, such as LSB changes, to the complicated. Of course, a simple digital watermark is vulnerable, does not have robustness, and can be specified by a comparatively easy operation in many cases. Embedding can be seen as a function (or a mapping), and reverse engineering (RE) of the algorithm using embedding processing software is possible. When an embedding algorithm is found easily by this RE, its vulnerability is high. In order to suppress the vulnerability and increase robustness, some obfuscation of the embedding processing software is attempted [15].

In algorithm obfuscation, algorithm of a simple function can be easily estimated. For complicated function, from the input data and the output, the corresponding relation, which is the embedding algorithm, should be analyzed by attackers. Although an approximation function can be found by numerical analysis for this case, it is difficult to obtain a true function. For cases using DCT, quantization, inverse DCT, and rounding, the system becomes nonlinear. This requires numerical analysis that is of a similar complexity to finding the solution of a neural network [8].

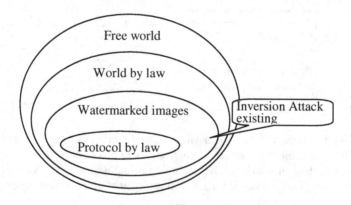

Fig. 4. Regulation of watermark detection

It is thought that the analysis becomes difficult to search for system and concrete coefficients as a digital watermark embedding uses a complicated algorithm. The authors considered conversion systems, for example using a nonlinear function and a gamma function before, evaluating how much complexity was required of an actual digital watermark. However, as transformation by discrete data resulted in the procession of discrete matrix coefficients of limited numbers after all, it turned out that a nonlinear continuous function could not be realized. On the other hand, QIM together with the Modified DCT group, which represents minute changes in the DCT coefficient, has nonlinear characteristics, requiring an almost unlimited number of search conditions [9].

We now describe a protocol that targeted inversion attacks by making a DCT+QIM embedding system into a reference model.

The embedding operation in [1] uses simple addition + and subtraction - with general operations defined by $\oplus$, and $\ominus$. This is shown in the application example of embedding using the hash function, which at the time was considered to be important. In contrast, the DCT+QIM method used now embeds with operations using real numbers and rounding after inverse DCT. Thus, it is assumed that Owner A performs a complicated embedding system using a degree of DCT and rounding. The embedding of a digital watermark should, therefore, not to provide a simple watermark W for Attacker B. We should make a system where a rounding error is inevitably added at random at the embedding, with the quantization error for B. Those who need authentication of ownership should use neither a system in which the embedding is simply destroyed, nor a system that is analysed easily. Indeed, there is no reason to use such vulnerable systems; everyone should use a more complex and unclear system.

The combination of embedding with a real number operation and rounding after the inverse DCT, as in the DCT+QIM method, causes complications in the embedding process of a digital watermark. In the inversion attack, the virtual watermark W_B is not fully used. As the watermark differs by only a minute quantity for every image, the inversion attack becomes difficult.

In Fig. 5, an example is shown that a coefficient is changed from the standard DCT, and the digital watermark embedding system using Modified-DCT (M-DCT) and quantization, which is also set to one of the embedded keys. After M-DCT, QIM at quantization part is carried out in embedding. Inverse M-DCT is performed after quantization. Rounding of integers is needed in order to convert the result into the image data, which can be displayed because most image format requires integer data.. This rounding of integers changes with the value of the original image.

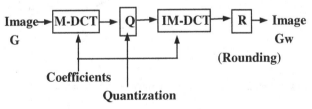

Fig. 5. Embedding system with M-DCT and Quantization

Therefore, such a system as an inversion attack that determines the fixed watermark data beforehand, does not produce the correct embedding. In the example of [9], which calculated the number of transform operations and the number of quantizations in the case of an orthogonal transform of small size, the computation times was found to exceed reasonable limits.

The above summary is shown in Fig. 6. A system whereby an owner's rights also become indefinite should be excluded, as such an ambiguous situation falls into the category of an Ambiguity Attack. The framework of fairness requires an owner and other parties to put forward embedding systems of similar difficulty, offering an original image, an embedding system, a detection system, processing software, etc. in the case of a dispute. This will suppress unjust and imperfect claims, and it is thought that the authentication degree of digital watermarks will increase sharply. In a conventional system, the inversion attacker shows nothing but insists a trick of protocol. The proposed system shown in Fig.6 additionally requests the inversion attacker to provide related information material that owners of original images must have. The original image, watermark W', embedding method/ software program and a detection method/program are examples of the related information materials. Governmental Organization verifies using these data with inspecting rounding effects in embedding calculation.

- **Fair judgement**
- **Do not use the robustness assumption**
- **Utilize Non-linear quantization characteristic as a one-way function**

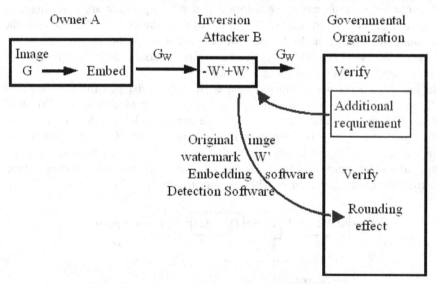

Fig. 6. Framework for invalidating an inversion attack

The assumption of robustness holds for two or more images obtained by attackers. Therefore, as this exceeds the category of a Protocol Attack, it is considered as an exception in this paper. Owing to this exception, the dispute gets to be limited to an event concerning one image set, namely an original image, a watermark-embedded image, an embedding machine, a corresponding detector, and corresponding watermark data. If another dispute event occurs when an attacker produces another image, which contains a minute change under the assumption of robustness, it is expected that the result will be the same as for the first examination considering it another independent dispute.

Generation of one-way function is theoretically difficult. A similar function can be generated using a system that applies a quantization error to the event, which consists of many pixels and in which the transform coefficients also produce variation.

- The number of full searches required for an attack

We will obtain the number of searches required in the usual attack method by estimating the transform coefficients, based on a full search of the system shown in Fig. 5. Basic considerations are given in [8] and [15]. The data used as evidence for the number of calculations is quoted from [16-18]. To obtain calculation times for matrix multiplications from experimental data, relations between larger sizes and smaller sizes are shown in Table 3. This Table 3 only shows partial calculation times such as multiplication. In a reference [8], a small-sized transform is used as a case in which obfuscation is incorporated. In this paper, in order to increase the robustness, new estimated values for 16×16 and 64×64 as in the case of the full search are also added in Table 4. Using the same technique as [8], there are 100 variable coefficient values for the 16th order, and 500 variable coefficient values for the 64th order.

Because the 16th transform matrix has 256 coefficients and the 64th transform matrix has 4096 coefficients, the total number of possible combinations is given by the 256th power of 100 and the 4096th power of 500, respectively. By this calculation method, we obtain the values of the rows for the 16th and 64th order cases shown in Table 4. When the event with the actual coefficient near 0 in a high frequency coefficient is contained, the number of kinds may decrease a little. In addition, as the 4th exponent calculation contained an error, it has been corrected.

In the case of attempting a full search attack to estimate the coefficients of the transform matrix, the computation time increases with the size of the matrix, and so the coefficient values with sufficient high orders cannot be found. Even performing parallel programming with improvements in CPU, Cuda, etc., the computation time is long enough to be unfeasible with current PC performance level.

5   Consideration

To make a complete watermark using a single embedding method to a media is difficult. However, a system with other devices can improve authentication ability. The performance can be evaluated by probability of safety, as for the case of RSA cryptography in which the security is computationally determined by using prime numbers that are as large as possible, increasing in size according to time and application seriousness. A two-stage watermarking system is effective by determining the specification in detail against the unfair behaviour of attackers. Even if the situation is ambiguous because an owner and an attacker are equal, the attacker always faces the risk that his intentional manipulation can be proved by TTP. Related to this two-stage watermarking system, methods using a computational one-way embedding function, and a rounding function are effective to improve authentication from the computational point of view.

Table 3(a). (from [15]) Time for Matrix Multiplication and Linear Equation by M-1800/2016 (sec) [16]

Order	Matrix Multiplication	Linear Equation
4th	1.01000E-05	8.13333E-06
8th	5.05000E-05	4.06667E-05
16th	0.000303000	0.000244000

Table 3(b). Time for Matrix Multiplication and Linear Equation by VP2600/10

Order	Matrix Multiplication	Linear Equation
4th	3.40000E-06	6.73333E-06
8th	1.70000E-05	3.36667E-05
16th	0.000102000	0.000202000

Table 3(c). Time for Matrix Inversion by Core2Duo,1.86GHz [17]

Order	Inverse Matrix	Order	Inverse Matrix
5th	3.46933E-07	320 th	0.040816327
10 th	2.42853E-06	640 th	0.285714286
20 th	1.69997E-05	1280 th	2
40 th	0.000118998	2560 th	15
80 th	0.000832986	5120 th	100

Table 3(d). Time for Matrix Multiplication and Linear Equation by Core2Duo, 2.66 GHz (E6700) [18] (Averaged and Clock adjusted)

Order	Matrix Multiplication	Linear Equation
4	3.2259E-07	4.86152E-07
8	1.61295E-06	2.43076E-06
16	9.6777E-06	1.45845E-05
32	6.77439E-05	0.000102092
65	0.000474207	0.000714643
125	0.00331945	0.005002499
250	0.023236152	0.035017493
500	0.162653061	0.245122449
1000	1.138571429	1.715857143
2000	7.97	12.011

Table 4. Estimated computation time in the case of full search of the system in Fig.5, including forward transform, quantization and inverse transform

Order	Computation time (sec)
4th	$(3.2E\text{-}7 \times 2 + 4.9E\text{-}7) \times 51^{\wedge}16$ $= 1.1E\text{-}6 \times 2.1E27 = 2.3\ E\ 21$
16th	$(9.7E\text{-}6 \times 2 + 1.5E\text{-}5) \times 100^{\wedge}256$ $= 3.4E\text{-}5 \times 1.0E512 = 3.4\ E\ 597$
64th	$(4.7E\text{-}4 \times 2 + 7.1E\text{-}4) \times 500^{\wedge}4096$ $= 1.7E\text{-}3 \times 9.6E1154 = 1.6E\ 1152$

6   Conclusion

The research progress into inversion attacks was investigated and some methods of invalidation were extracted. We separated the assumption of robustness from the inversion attack to consider the inversion attack as a pure protocol attack. As a protocol, we considered reconstruction, which rebalances fairness in favour of the owner rather than the attacker. We improved the two-stage watermarking system by adding specification items such as original images, embedding and detection information. With this two-stage system, improvements for an unfair problem and robustness can be observed qualitatively. The improvement of probability derived from the number of embedding cases can contribute security in the same way as other practical systems such as RSA, SSL and SSH.

It was shown that attacks by involving different original images induced by the assumption of robustness can be removed by excluding all the other images that should be treated in other cases. In terms of one-way functions, the number of searches for real coefficients expands sharply with the non-linearity of quantization and the number of transform coefficients. Thereby, the same effect as a one-way function can be realized. It is thought that by adopting these frameworks at the second stage of the two-stage watermarking system as standards for detection, inversion attacks can be made difficult. An embedding system using a variable transform and quantization was modelled, and we verified that the coefficient search of an attack became sufficiently large as to be unfeasible for analyzing.

For future study, a new standard for a watermarking embedding and detection system can be considered. Under this standard, we recommend using watermarking system, which restricts the effective working area, and which effectiveness of authentication is definitely better than in the conventional lawless system. We can further improve this standard in the future by gradually confining effective area of healthy watermarks.

Also, we focused only on a single attack in this paper, namely the inversion attack, to clarify the analysis of the problems. However, we hope to resolve all other attacks and to consider combined attacks.

References

1. Craver, S., Memon, N., Yeo, B.-L., Yeung, M.M.: Resolving Rightful Ownerships with Invisible Watermarking Techniques: Limitations, Attacks, and Implications. IEEE Journal on Selected Areas in Communications 16(4), 573–586 (1998)
2. Hartung, F., Su, J.K., Girod, B.: Spread spectrum watermarking: Malicious attacks and counter attacks. In: SPIE Proceedings, April 9, vol. 3657 (1999) ISBN: 9780819431288
3. Craver, S.: Zero Knowledge Watermark Detection. In: Pfitzmann, A. (ed.) IH 1999. LNCS, vol. 1768, pp. 101–116. Springer, Heidelberg (2000)
4. Adelsbach, A., Katzenbeisser, S., Veith, H.: Watermarking Schemes Provably Secure against Copy and Ambiguity Attacks. In: Proceedings of the 3rd ACM workshop on Digital rights management (DRM 2003), October 27-30, pp. 111–119. ACM, Washington, DC (2003)

5. Liu, R., Tan, T.: An SVD-based watermarking scheme for protecting rightful ownership. IEEE Transactions on Multimedia 4(1), 121–128 (2002)
6. Adelsbach, A., Katzenbeisser, S., Sadeghi, A.-R.: On the Insecurity of Non-invertible Watermarking Schemes for Dispute Resolving. In: Kalker, T., Cox, I., Ro, Y.M. (eds.) IWDW 2003. LNCS, vol. 2939, pp. 355–369. Springer, Heidelberg (2004)
7. Ohzeki, K., Sakurai, M.: SVD-Based Watermark with Quasi-One Way Operation by Reducing a Singular Value Matrix Rank. In: Proc. of the First International Conference on Forensic Applications and Techniques in Telecommunications, Information and Multimedia (e-forensics, Technical session B4. Watermarking, 1. January 21-23, Adelaide (2008)
8. Ohzeki, K., Wei, Y.: A New Watermarking System with Obfuscated Embedder and Quasi-Chirp Transform, IPSJ Tech. report Vol. 2011-CSEC-52 No.29 pp.1-10 (March 2011) (in Japanese)
9. Ohzeki, K., Wei, Y., Hirakawa, Y., Sato, K.: A New Watermarking Method with Obfuscated Quasi-Chirp Transform. In: Shi, Y.Q., Kim, H.-J., Perez-Gonzalez, F. (eds.) IWDW 2011. LNCS, vol. 7128, pp. 57–71. Springer, Heidelberg (2012)
10. Kang, X., Huang, J., Zeng, W., Shi, Y.Q.: Non-ambiguity of blind watermarking: a revisit with analytical resolution. Science in China Series F: Information Sciences 52(2), 276–285 (2009)
11. Ohzeki, K., Seo, Y., Gi, E.: Discontinuity of SVD Embedding Mapping Used for Watermarks. In: Meersman, R., Herrero, P., Dillon, T. (eds.) OTM 2009 Workshops. LNCS, vol. 5872, pp. 4–5. Springer, Heidelberg (2009)
12. Ohzeki, K., Seo, Y., Gi, E.: Numerical Analysis of Continuity of Quasi-One-way Mapping Developed for Watermarking, IPSJ SIG. Tech. Report Vol. 2009-CSEC-45 No.5 pp.1-8 (May 2009) (in Japanese)
13. Moulin, P.: Comments on "Why watermarking is nonsense". IEEE Signal Processing Magazine 20(6), 57–59 (2003)
14. Kutter, M., Voloshynovskiy, S.V., Herrigel, A.: The Watermark copy attack. In: Proc., of SPIE, Security and Watermarking of Multimedia Contents II, vol. 3971, pp. 371–930 (January 2000)
15. Ohzeki, K., Wei, Y.: An Obfuscation Method for a Detector of Watermarking, IPSJ SIG. Tech. Report vol. 2010-CSEC-48, No.26, pp.1–7 (March 2010) (in Japanese)
16. Watanabe, Y.: A Note on Numerical Computation and Speed. Advanced Computing Infrastructure Section, Research Institute for Information Technology 28(3), 207–231 (1995) (in Japanese), http://yebisu.cc.kyushu-u.ac.jp/~watanabe/RESERCH/MANUSCRIPT/KOHO/SPEED/speed.pdf
17. Yamamoto, Y.: Accelerating the Singular Value Decomposition of Rectangular Matrices using CUDA. Lecture Class and Workshop on GPGPU (June 24, 2009) (in Japanese), http://suchix.kek.jp/bridge/CUDA09/Docs/yamamoto_090624.ppt
18. Kusuhara, F.: Numerical Computation Library (old), Linear Algebra in kusuhara's wiki (in Japanese), http://www.rcs.arch.t.u-tokyo.ac.jp/kusuhara/fswiki/wiki.cgi?action=CATEGORY&category=Linear+Algebra

Geometrically Invariant Image Blind Watermarking Based on Speeded-Up Robust Features and DCT Transform

Huang Zhang and Xiao-qiang Li

School of Computer Engineering and Science, Shanghai University, Shanghai, China
xqli@staff.shu.edu.cn

Abstract. In this paper, we propose a novel robust image blind watermarking scheme based on Speeded-Up Robust Features (SURF) region and Discrete Cosine Transform (DCT). As SURF features are invariant to rotation and scaling, we employ SURF to extract feature points. Then circular patches are generated using the feature points. The watermark is embedding each circular patch based on DCT transform which can resist signal processing attacks. Multiple patches have been embedded watermark for resisting locally cropping attacks. Experimental results show that the proposed scheme is robust to both geometric attacks and signal processing attacks.

Keywords: geometrically invariant, watermarking, Speeded-Up Robust Features, DCT.

1 Introduction

With the development of computer technology, image can be easily modified, copied and distributed. As an effective method for solving this problem, digital watermarking is a promising way to protect the copyright of digital images[1]. Some information extracted from image used to be made watermark which can be embedded into the original image for copyright protection and ownership assertion. In this way, there has some challenging problem still not be resolved. For example, geometric attacks can desynchronize watermark information thus cause incorrect detection[2]. How to efficiently resist such attacks is still an open problem.

Geometric attacks include RST (rotation, scale, translation) and RBA (random bending) attack. Ruanaidh et al. first reported RST invariant watermarking in Fourier-Mellin domain[3], which is an invariant domain. The main drawback is that the watermarked images degrade much and they cannot resist cropping attacks, because the watermark is embedded in the global image. Bas et al. proposed a feature-based watermark synchronization method[4]. They used the Harris corner detector to extract interest points. Then the Delaunay tessellation was applied to the detected points, producing a set of triangles. The watermark was embedded into all triangles additively

Y.Q. Shi, H.J. Kim, and F. Pérez-González (Eds.): IWDW 2012, LNCS 7809, pp. 111–119, 2013.

in spatial domain. But Harris corner detector isn't scale invariant. Lee et al. developed a Scale-invariant feature transform (SIFT) based watermarking scheme[5]. SIFT was proposed by Lowe[6]. Compared with Harris corners, SIFT features are more stable and Scale invariant. They extracted feature points by SIFT and used them to generate a series of patches. The watermark was embedded into all patches. The scheme outperformed Bas' method.

SURF (Speeded-Up Robust Features) is a robust image detector & descriptor, first presented by Herbert Bay et al. in 2006[7]. It is partly inspired by the SIFT. SURF is several times faster than SIFT and also very robust against different image transformations like rotation, scaling and so on. Especially, about the JPEG compression, the stability of the SURF is much higher than the SIFT. Discrete Cosine Transform (DCT) is an image presentation in frequency domain[8], which transforms the spatial domain pixel values into the coefficients with low, medium and high frequency. Relative to the spatial domain, frequency domain can resist signal processing attacks better. In this paper, we propose a new image blind watermarking scheme using SURF feature points and DCT transform. First we employ SURF to extract feature points, and then circular patches are generated using the feature points. A rotation and scaling invariant watermark is generated on the patches. The watermark is embedded into multiple patches for resisting locally cropping attacks. The proposed scheme is robust to rotation, scaling, cropping, and signal processing attacks, especially the JPEG compression.

The rest of this paper is organized as follows. Section 2 reviews the related algorithm briefly. Our image watermarking scheme is illustrated in section 3. Section 4 is experimental results. The last section is conclusions.

2   Related Algorithm

2.1   SURF Points' Extraction

Speeded up robust feature (SURF) is a local invariant feature based on scale space theory, has almost the same performance as SIFT, yet it is about six times faster than SIFT because of the usage of integral image and box filter.

SURF detector is based on the estimation of Hessian matrix. Give a point $p = (x, y)$ in an image I, the Hessian matrix in x at scale σ is defined as

$$H(x, \sigma) = \begin{bmatrix} L_{xx}(x, \sigma) & L_{xy}(x, \sigma) \\ L_{xy}(x, \sigma) & L_{yy}(x, \sigma) \end{bmatrix} \tag{1}$$

where $L_{xx}(x,\sigma)$ is the convolution of the Gaussian second order derivative $\frac{\partial^2}{\partial x^2} g(\sigma)$ with the image I in point x, and similarly for $L_{xy}(x,\sigma)$ and $L_{yy}(x,\sigma)$. To reduce the computation time, SURF algorithm uses box filters to approximate the convolution of the Gaussian second order derivative. It can be evaluated at a very low computational cost using integral images. The integral image $I\sum(x)$ at a location x = (x, y) represents the sum of all pixels in the input image I within a rectangular region formed by the origin and x.

$$I\sum(x) = \sum_{i=0}^{i\leq x}\sum_{j=0}^{j\leq y} I(i,j) \tag{2}$$

The approximation of convolution is denoted by Dxx, Dxy and Dyy. Then we get The maxima of the determinant of the Hessian matrix can be computed with the function $\Delta(H)$ defined in equation (3) and then interpolated in scale and image space. Thus, stable and repeatable SURF points can be localized.

$$\Delta(H) = DxxDyy - 0.9\,Dxy^2 \tag{3}$$

2.2   DCT Transform

DCT transform is a typical scene for image processing and digital signal processing with advantages of high compression ratio, small bit error rate, good information integration ability and good synthetic effect of calculation complexity. Two dimensional DCT can be defined assimilative as:

$$f(x,y) = C(u)C(v)\sum_{u=0}^{N-1}\sum_{v=0}^{N-1} F(u,v)\cos\left[\frac{(2x+1)u\pi}{2N}\right]\cos\left[\frac{(2y+1)v\pi}{2N}\right] \tag{4}$$

The inverse of two dimensional DCT can be defined as:

$$F(u,v) = \frac{2}{N}C(u)C(v)\sum_{x=0}^{N-1}\sum_{y=0}^{N-1} f(x,y)\cos\left[\frac{(2x+1)x\pi}{2N}\right]\cos\left[\frac{(2y+1)y\pi}{2N}\right] \tag{5}$$

Where F(u, v) is cosine transform coefficient. For u and v are frequency variable; u, v=1, 2, 3..., N-1, if f(x, y) is N×N square of spatial domain. For x, y=0, 1, 2..., N-1. N is the number of horizontal and vertical pixels of pixel block.

3   Geometrically Invariant Watermarking Scheme

Because SURF is invariant to RST, we use SURF algorithm to get some feature points, generating circular patches around these feature points, then the watermark is embedded into all patches. These patches are invariant through geometrically transforming, so the watermark can be detected despite the image be attacked. The detailed diagram of watermark synchronization scheme is shown in figure 1.

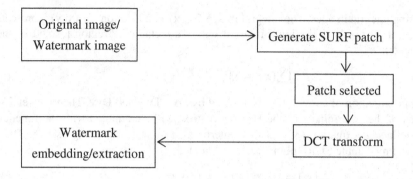

Fig. 1. Watermark synchronization scheme

3.1   Generation of the Regions for Watermarking

First run the SURF algorithm on the original image to get the feature points, and for each point, we make a circular patch by using only the coordinate (t1, t2) and scale s of extracted SURF features, as follows:

$$(x - t_1)^2 + (y - t_2)^2 = (ks)^2 \qquad (6)$$

The k is a factor to control the radius of the patch to get the embedding suitable size. The result is shown in figure 2(a). The figure shows that circles have different size, because feature point's scale would changes with the image's size, so these patches are invariant to image scaling as well as spatial modifications.

(a)   All SURF regions   (b) Remove overlapping region   (c) Remove small region

Fig. 2. SURF points and the circle regions

As shown in figure 2(a), these regions are too many and overlap each other, it's hard to embed watermark, thence remove these overlapping regions. Steps are as follows: first, choose a point which has the maximum response value (The best stability), then remove the regions which overlap with this point's region. Afterward the second maximum response value has been chosen, and so on. The result is shown in figure 2(b).

After removing overlapping regions, some regions are too small to embedding watermarking, thence remove these regions which radius less than 20, shown in figure 2(c). After these procedures the remaining regions are suitable for embedding watermarking, and stability for geometrically attacking and common attacking. Figure 3 shows circular patches from our proposed synchronization method in rotation, crop, JPEG compression, scaling of the image and spatial filters. Find that these patches are formulated robustly, even when the image is distorted.

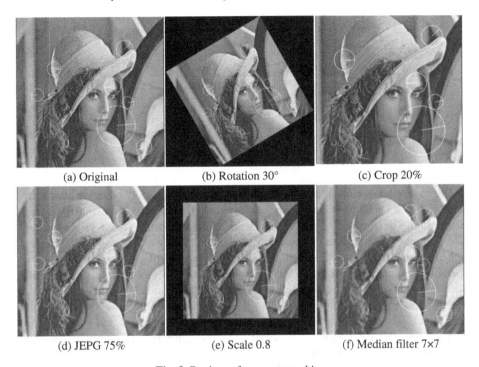

| (a) Original | (b) Rotation 30° | (c) Crop 20% |
| (d) JEPG 75% | (e) Scale 0.8 | (f) Median filter 7×7 |

Fig. 3. Regions after some attacking

3.2 Embedding Watermark

The proposed scheme embed watermark in DCT domain, DCT transform require the input must be a rectangle, hence generating a rectangle using the circular region similar to the figure 4.

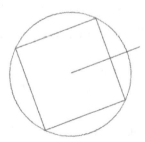

Fig. 4. Embed region generation

As shown in this figure, we employ the SURF point's orientations assignment as Y-axis, generating a square inside the circle. Orientations assignment is designed to resistance to rotation, so the square which generating by the previous method is rotation invariant.

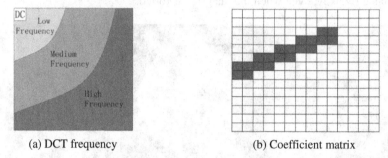

(a) DCT frequency   (b) Coefficient matrix

Fig. 5. Representation of DCT coefficients

The watermark is embedded into all regions for resisting locally cropping attacks by modifying the DCT coefficients. For each region, figure 5(a) shows the frequency distribution. The low frequency part represents a fairly important part in vision system, modifying the coefficient in this part may reduce the quality of image. The changes on high frequency part is not easy to affect the quality of image, but generally, some operations on images may remove these signals so as to affect robustness of watermark. Therefore, this scheme selects some locations in middle frequency coefficient to embed watermark like figure 5(b).

In figure 5(b) there has a 14×14 square embed 10 bit watermark, but generally, for each region, after filtering step, the square patch's minimum size is 28×28, and will embed more than 20 bit watermark.

Watermark can be expressed as: WM = { wm(k)| k=0, 1, 2, ..., M}, wm(k) equal 0 or 1. Assume square patch is N×N, the exact embed approach is as below:

$$
\begin{cases}
if(wm(k)=1) \begin{cases} DCT'\left(\left\lfloor\frac{N}{2}\right\rfloor-1-\left\lfloor\frac{k}{2}\right\rfloor,k\right) = \frac{DCT\left(\left\lfloor\frac{N}{2}\right\rfloor-1-\left\lfloor\frac{k}{2}\right\rfloor,k\right)+DCT\left(\left\lfloor\frac{N}{2}\right\rfloor-\left\lfloor\frac{k}{2}\right\rfloor,k\right)}{2}+S \\ DCT'\left(\left\lfloor\frac{N}{2}\right\rfloor-\left\lfloor\frac{k}{2}\right\rfloor,k\right) = \frac{DCT\left(\left\lfloor\frac{N}{2}\right\rfloor-1-\left\lfloor\frac{k}{2}\right\rfloor,k\right)+DCT\left(\left\lfloor\frac{N}{2}\right\rfloor-\left\lfloor\frac{k}{2}\right\rfloor,k\right)}{2}-S \end{cases} \\
if(wm(k)=0) \begin{cases} DCT'\left(\left\lfloor\frac{N}{2}\right\rfloor-1-\left\lfloor\frac{k}{2}\right\rfloor,k\right) = \frac{DCT\left(\left\lfloor\frac{N}{2}\right\rfloor-1-\left\lfloor\frac{k}{2}\right\rfloor,k\right)+DCT\left(\left\lfloor\frac{N}{2}\right\rfloor-\left\lfloor\frac{k}{2}\right\rfloor,k\right)}{2}-S \\ DCT'\left(\left\lfloor\frac{N}{2}\right\rfloor-\left\lfloor\frac{k}{2}\right\rfloor,k\right) = \frac{DCT\left(\left\lfloor\frac{N}{2}\right\rfloor-1-\left\lfloor\frac{k}{2}\right\rfloor,k\right)+DCT\left(\left\lfloor\frac{N}{2}\right\rfloor-\left\lfloor\frac{k}{2}\right\rfloor,k\right)}{2}+S \end{cases}
\end{cases}
\tag{7}
$$

After the above modification, we make each pair of two coefficient established a relations, when the watermark bit is 1, the above coefficient is greater than the below coefficient, and vice versa.

The S is the watermarking strength, the larger the value of S, the worse the invisibility. It also affects embedded intensity, but not an obvious rule. Based on the empirical study, we set the basis value of S to 1.6.

3.3   Extraction Watermark

The detecting procedure is similar as the embedding procedure. First run the SURF algorithm on the watermarking image, get feature regions, then filtering these regions, and generating square patches, convert to DCT domain. There are several patches in an image, and we try to detect the watermark from all patches. Then, utilize the following formula to get watermark.

$$\begin{cases} if(DCT\left(\left\lceil \frac{N}{2} \right\rceil - 1 - \left\lfloor \frac{k}{2} \right\rfloor, k\right) \geq DCT\left(\left\lceil \frac{N}{2} \right\rceil - \left\lfloor \frac{k}{2} \right\rfloor, k\right)) \ num_{k,1} + + \\ if(DCT\left(\left\lceil \frac{N}{2} \right\rceil - 1 - \left\lfloor \frac{k}{2} \right\rfloor, k\right) < DCT\left(\left\lceil \frac{N}{2} \right\rceil - \left\lfloor \frac{k}{2} \right\rfloor, k\right)) \ num_{k,0} + + \end{cases} \tag{8}$$

If $num_{k,1} > num_{k,0}$ wm(k)=1, else wm(k)=0.

4   Experimental Results

The proposed watermarking method was tested in a variety of images. We used many images having different information contents (Lena, Baboon, Sailboat, Airplane and so on) in JPG format of size 512x512 and grayscale resolution with 8bits per pixel. Figure 6 shows two test original images and watermarked versions respectively. As we embed the watermark into image local patch, the inserted watermark is invisible to the naked eyes. The peak signal to noise ratio (PSNR) values is higher than 40 dB.

(a) Original images   (b) Watermarked images

Fig. 6. Watermark invisibility

To evaluate our method, we considered a variety of attacks including signal processing attacks and geometric attacks. Employ watermark benchmarking software StirMark 4.0 to attack these test images. Experimental results are listed in Tables 1 and 2, respectively. It is an average value.

In Tables 1 detection ratio refers to the ratio of the number of extracted patches from attacked images to the number of correctly redetected patches from attacked images. The detection ratio increases when watermark synchronization is performed more strongly. In Tables 2 similarity is the average of similarity values between the original watermark and the extracted watermark from detected watermarked patches.

Table 1. Fraction of correctly detected watermark patches

Attack	Detection ratio	
	Our method	Literature[5]
JPEG 90%	97.2%	88.7%
JPEG 70%	91.5%	76.3%
JPEG 50%	75.3%	54.4%
JPEG 40%	61.2%	43.4%
Median Filter 4 × 4	75.1%	66.1%
Median Filter 7 × 7	78.3%	/
Gaussian 3 × 3	77.3%	74.8%
Rotation 5°	75.1%	68.0%
Rotation 15°	61.2%	55.9%
Rotation 30°	41.7%	48.6%
Scaling 0.8	57.8%	51.7%
Scaling 1.2	61.1%	66.1%
Crop 20%	73.4%	49.0%
Crop 50%	37.2%	16.2%

Table 2. Watermark similarity under attacks

Attack	Similarity	
	Our method	Literature[5]
JPEG 90%	0.934	0.698
JPEG 70%	0.813	0.623
JPEG 50%	0.775	0.532
JPEG 40%	0.614	0.477
Median Filter 4 × 4	0.732	0.609
Median Filter 7 × 7	0.719	/
Gaussian 3 × 3	0.763	0.671
Rotation 5°	0.771	0.641
Rotation 15°	0.564	0.538
Rotation 30°	0.618	0.514
Scaling 0.8	0.479	0.539
Scaling 1.2	0.513	0.614
Crop 20%	0.897	0.645
Crop 50%	0.582	0.446

In most of the attacks, our watermarking scheme could detect the inserted watermark from a considerable number of circular patches, and the similarity between the inserted and the detected watermark was high enough to prove ownership. Our scheme has an excellent performance in JPEG compressions, and also robust to other attacks, such as rotation, cropping, median Filter attacks. Our scheme is less robust to scaling down attacks, because when the watermarked image is scaled smaller or too bigger there is information loss. Despite this, our scheme has a better performance than the method of Lee et al. These results support the contention that our proposed watermarking scheme would be resilient to various image attacks.

5   Conclusions

By using the Speeded-Up Robust Features (SURF) and Discrete Cosine Transform (DCT), we have developed a geometrically invariant image blind watermarking. We use SURF to extract interest points and use them to generate patches. For each patch, an invariant watermark is produced using DCT transform. As we embed the watermark into local patches, the watermarked images are of high quality. The watermark is detected by comparing magnitudes of DCT coefficients.

The experimental results show that our proposed method can resist geometric attacks and signal processing attacks, such as scaling, rotation, JPEG compression and so on. Its robustness to a wide variety of attacks is suitable for many applications requiring high watermarking reliability and capacity, but the size of the watermark's bit is less that is a drawback. Future work will focus on the design of a watermark scheme which can embed more bits.

Acknowledgments. This work is supported by Shanghai Natural Science Foundation under Grant No. 10ZR1411700.

References

1. Cox, I.J., Miller, M.L.: The first 50 years of electronic watermarking. EURASIP Journal on Applied Signal Processing 2, 126–132 (2002)
2. Dong, P., Brankov, J.G., et al.: Digital watermarking robust to geometric distortions. IEEE Transaction on Image Processing 14(12), 2140–2150 (2005)
3. O'Ruanaidh, J.J.K., Pun, T.: Rotation, scale and translation invariant spread spectrum digital image watermarking. Signal Processing 66, 303 (1998)
4. Bas, P., Chassery, J.-M., Macq, B.: Geometrically invariant watermarking using feature points. IEEE Trans. Image Processing 11, 1014 (2002)
5. Lee, H.Y., Kim, H., Lee, H.K.: Robust image watermarking using local invariant features. Optical Engineering 45(3), 037002 (2006)
6. Lowe, D.G.: Distinctive image features from scale-invariant keypoints. In: Proc. IJCV 2004, vol. 2(60), pp. 91–110 (2004)
7. Bay, H., Tuytelaars, T., Van Gool, L.: SURF: Speeded Up Robust Features. In: Leonardis, A., Bischof, H., Pinz, A. (eds.) ECCV 2006, Part I. LNCS, vol. 3951, pp. 404–417. Springer, Heidelberg (2006)
8. Wu, W.-C., Ren, G.-R.: A DCT-Based Robust Image Watermarking Using Local Moment. In: 3rd ICMiA, pp. 122–126 (2011)

Self-embedding Fragile Watermarking Scheme Combined Average with VQ Encoding

Hongjie He, Fan Chen*, and Yaoran Huo

Sichuan Key Lab of Signal and Information Processing,
Southwest Jiaotong University, Chengdu 610031, China
{hjhe,fchen}@swjtu.edu.cn, hyr_2010@yahoo.cn

Abstract. Combined average encoding with vector quantization (VQ) encoding, a new self-embedding fragile watermarking scheme is proposed. To take into account watermark payload, localization accuracy and recovery quality, the 6-bit average-watermark of a 2×2 original block and the 8-bit VQ-watermark of a 4×4 block of image high-frequency component are generated and hidden in the corresponding mapping blocks of them based on secret key, respectively. To improve the tamper detection performance, the validity of a 2×2 block is determined by combining the average-watermark with the VQ-watermark. The average, VQ and inpainting recovery operations are executed in sequence to improve the recovery quality especially for a larger tampering ratio. Simulation results demonstrate that the proposed scheme not only provides a better invisibility and security against the known counterfeiting attacks, but also allows image recovery with an acceptable visual quality up to 70% tampering ratios.

Keywords: fragile watermarking, self-embedding, compression code, VQ encoding.

1 Introduction

The purpose of fragile watermarking is to achieve multimedia content authentication by imperceptibly embedding additional information into the host media [1,2]. Many fragile watermarking schemes have been developed for digital images to detect accurately the tampered areas [3] and further recover approximately the original content in the tampered areas [4], which is also called the self-correcting or self-embedding watermarking.

Self-embedding watermarking techniques for image authentication usually partition an image into blocks with the same size. All or part of watermark data of each block are a compression code (CC) of the block content and hidden in the other block of the image. The block CC is used to approximately reconstruct its original content if the block is tampered. The block CC directly affects the performance of self-embedding watermarking scheme, such as watermark payload, invisibility and recovery quality. The image compression technique is often

---

* Corresponding author.

Y.Q. Shi, H.J. Kim, and F. Pérez-González (Eds.): IWDW 2012, LNCS 7809, pp. 120–134, 2013.

adopted to balance the length of the block CC with recovery quality. Fridrich *et al* [4] firstly proposed that the block CC of a 8×8 block was generated by quantizing and encoding the important quantized DCT (discrete cosine transform) coefficients of itself. The length of the block CC based on DCT can adjust flexibly to the requirement of recovery quality [4]. The block CC based DCT was adopted and improved by many researchers [5-7]. Qian *et al* [6,7] proposed the multi-level encoding to generate the block CC with variable length for various types of blocks. The blocks were classified into different types according to their degrees of smoothness. The different types of blocks were encoded into different numbers of bits with rougher blocks having more bits and smoother blocks having fewer bits. The multi-level encoding can preserve adequate information of the image content with as few bits as possible. But, the type-code of each block has to be kept to reconstruct the block content successfully. This would increase the watermark payload and impair the quality of watermarked image. On the other hand, the VQ (Vector quantization) compression technique was also used to extract the index table from the host image as image content and generate the block CC. Yang [8] generated the 8-bit VQ-code watermark of each 4×4 block and maintained four copies of VQ-code watermark of the whole image. Since four times of embedding VQ-code watermark overcome the tampering coincidence problem [9] in the self-embedding watermarking, the quality of recovered image with a larger tampering ratio is enhanced. However, the watermark embedding payload is enlarged. Moreover, the embedded watermark data are not efficiently exploited especially for a smaller tampering ratio, leading to a limited quality of recovered content [9]. In addition, Lin *et al* [10] proposed that the recovery watermark was generated by encoding the average of block with size of 2×2 pixels. To improve the ability against the collage attack [11] and the constant average attack [12], a block-neighborhood based self-recovery fragile watermarking scheme [13] was proposed. In this method, the block-mapping sequence was randomly generated by the secret key and adopted the neighborhood characterization to design an automatic tamper detection method without adding the authentication watermark for each block. Compared with these self-embedding watermarking schemes [6-10] in which the additional authentication watermark was used to determine the validity of a block, this scheme [13] is invulnerable to the collage attack, but also improve the quality of tamper localization and recovery. However, two secure key-bits of each block did not contribute to the content recovery since they were used only for resisting the improved constant-average attack. That is to say, there is a watermark-data waste problem in method of [13] to some extent.

To address watermark-data waste problem, this work proposes a self-embedding fragile watermarking scheme that maintains good recovery quality and security. The average-watermark of the 2×2 block of the original image and the VQ- watermark of the 4×4 block of image high-frequency component are generated and embedded in the LSB of their corresponding mapping blocks based on secret key, respectively. The validity of a 2×2 block is determined by combining the average-watermark with the VQ-watermark. The proposed self-embedding watermarking combines the average-code with the VQ-code to produce the embedded watermark that contributes to the tamper detection and content recovery. As a result, the recovery quality and security are improved without increasing the watermark payload. Experimental results show that the proposed scheme provides a better invisibility and security against the known forgery attack such as the collage attack and the constant-average attack. Moreover, the proposed scheme allows image recovery with an acceptable visual quality up to 70% tampering ratio.

The remainder of this paper is organized as follows. In Section 2 the proposed self-embedding watermarking scheme is described. Experimental results are given in Section 3 and conclusions are given in Section 4.

2   Proposed Self-embedding Fragile Watermarking Method

This section describes in detail the proposed self-embedding fragile watermarking algorithm. To take into account watermark payload, localization accuracy and recovery quality, the 6-bit average-watermark of a 2×2 block and the 8-bit VQ-watermark of a 4×4 block are generated and hidden in the corresponding mapping 2×2 and 4×4 blocks, respectively. On the authentication side, the validity of a 2×2 block is determined by combining the average-watermark with the VQ-watermark. Three recovery operations, including average, VQ and inpainting, are adopted in sequence to improve the recovery quality. The proposed algorithm is described through three stages: watermark embedding, tamper detection, and tamper recovery.

2.1   Watermark Embedding

Similar to our previous methods, the original image data in the six MSB (most significant bit) planes are kept unchanged while the two LSB (least significant bit) planes are replaced with the watermark. But the mechanism for generating the watermark for content recovery is indeed different. In the proposed scheme, the watermark data are generated by encrypting the average-code of the original image and the VQ-code of image high frequency, respectively. The embedded watermark does not contain any additional redundancy and contributes to the tamper detection and content recovery. This way, the qualities of both the watermarked image and the recovered result are satisfactory. Fig.1 shows the proposed watermark embedding procedure. Suppose the size of a host image X be $4m \times 4n$ pixels, and N ($=2m \times 2n$) denote the number of 2×2 blocks in the original image. The embedding procedure consists of five steps.

Step.1 Binary random and two mapping sequences. According to the secret key, the binary random sequence $B = \{B_i | i = 1, \ldots, N\}$ is generated,

$$B_i = (b_{i1}, b_{i2}, \ldots, b_{i8}) \tag{1}$$

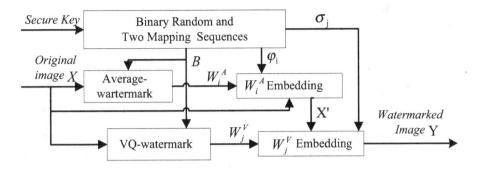

Fig. 1. Flow chart of watermark embedding procedure

At the same time, two mapping sequences Ψ of the integer interval $[1,N]$ and Λ of the integer interval $[1,N/4]$ are obtained,

$$\begin{cases} \Psi = (\varphi_1, \dots, \varphi_N) \\ \Lambda = (\sigma_1, \dots, \sigma_{N/4}) \end{cases} \tag{2}$$

The detailed procedure of generating mapping sequence refers to Ref. [10].

Step.2 Average-watermark. The original image X is partitioned into non-overlapping 2×2 block $X = \{X_i | i = 1, 2, \dots, N\}$. Each 2×2 block X_i can be expressed as,

$$X_i = \begin{bmatrix} x_{i1} & x_{i2} \\ x_{i3} & x_{i4} \end{bmatrix}, i = 1, 2, \dots, N \tag{3}$$

The average intensity of the block content is computed by truncating the two LSB planes of each pixel in block X_i,

$$a_i = round(1/4 \sum_{z=1}^{4} \lfloor x_{iz}/4 \rfloor) \tag{4}$$

where the round (.) returns the nearest integer of the argument, and $\lfloor . \rfloor$ is the largest integer less than or equal to the argument. Since the average value must fall into $[0,64]$, the average-code of block X_i, denote as $C_i^A = \{c_{i1}^A, \dots, c_{i6}^A\}$, are computed by,

$$c_{ik}^A = mod(\lfloor a_i/2^{k-1} \rfloor, 2), k = 1, \dots, 6 \tag{5}$$

where $mod(,)$ is the modulo operation. According to B_i from (1), the average-code C_i^A is encrypted to generate the average-watermark $W_i^A = \{w_{i1}^A, \dots, w_{i6}^A\}$,

$$w_{ik}^A = c_{ik}^A \oplus b_{ik}, k = 1, \dots, 6 \tag{6}$$

Step.3 VQ-watermark. The high-frequency component of block X_i is first generated by,

$$H_i = \begin{pmatrix} h_{i1} & h_{i2} \\ h_{i3} & h_{i4} \end{pmatrix} = \begin{pmatrix} x_{i1} - a_i & x_{i2} - a_i \\ x_{i3} - a_i & x_{i4} - a_i \end{pmatrix} \tag{7}$$

The high-frequency component of the original image, denote as H, can be obtained by assembling the high-frequency component of every blocks in the original image. Obviously, the size of high-frequency image H is the same as that of original image X. The high-frequency image is segmented into 4×4 image blocks $H = \{H_j | j = 1, \ldots, N/4\}$ and the code book $\{CB^l | l = 0, \ldots, 255\}$ is formed by VQ compression technique (The detailed procedure refers to Ref.[8]). Using Euclidean distance, we can find code word CB^l that is nearest to the block H_j. According to B_j generated by (1), the VQ-watermark $W_j^V = \{w_{j1}^V, \ldots, w_{j8}^V\}$ of block H_j are obtained by encrypting the index value l of code word CB^l,

$$w_{jk}^V = mod(\lfloor l/2^{k-1} \rfloor, 2) \oplus b_{jk}, k = 1, \ldots, 8 \tag{8}$$

Step.4 Average-watermark embedding. For each 2×2 block X_i, the average-watermark W_i^A are hidden in the first three pixels of the mapping block X_p, where $p = \varphi_i$ obtained by (2). The block $X_p' = (x_{p1}', \ldots, x_{p4}')$ is computed by,

$$x_{pz}' = \begin{cases} 4\lfloor x_{pz}/4 \rfloor + 2w_{i(z+3)}^A + w_{iz}^A, z = 1, 2, 3 \\ x_{pz}, z = 4 \end{cases} \tag{9}$$

Performing this step for all blocks in X, we can obtain the image $X' = (X_1', \ldots, X_N')$, in which the recovery-data has been embedded.

Step.5 VQ-watermark embedding. The image X' is partitioned into 4×4 blocks $X' = (X_1', \ldots, X_{N/4}')$. Each 4×4 block X_j' can be expressed as,

$$X_j' = \begin{bmatrix} x_{j1}' & \cdots & x_{j4}' \\ \vdots & \ddots & \vdots \\ x_{j13}' & \cdots & x_{j16}' \end{bmatrix} \tag{10}$$

Setting $q = \sigma_j$ generated by (2), the VQ-watermark W_j^V is embedded in the partial pixels of the mapping block X_q'. The watermarked block $Y_j = (y_{q1}, \ldots, y_{q16})$ is generated by,

$$y_{qz} = \begin{cases} 4\lfloor x_{qz}'/4 \rfloor + 2w_{j1}^V + w_{j2}^V, z = 6 \\ 4\lfloor x_{qz}'/4 \rfloor + 2w_{j3}^V + w_{j4}^V, z = 8 \\ 4\lfloor x_{qz}'/4 \rfloor + 2w_{j5}^V + w_{j6}^V, z = 14 \\ 4\lfloor x_{qz}'/4 \rfloor + 2w_{j7}^V + w_{j8}^V, z = 16 \\ x_{qz}', otherwise \end{cases} \tag{11}$$

2.2 Tamper Detection

Suppose Z represents the tested image, which can be a distorted watermarked image or unaltered one. A binary sequence $T = \{t_i | i = 1, 2, \ldots, N\}$ called the tamper detection mark (TDM) is used to represent the location of tampering [13], where N is the number of 2×2 blocks in the test image Z. As in the watermark insertion process, according to (1) and (2), the binary random sequence B, two mapping sequences Ψ and Λ are obtained by the same secret key. The tamper detection procedure includes the following steps.

Step.1 Average-watermark matching. According to the test image Z and the mapping sequence $\Psi = (\varphi_1, \ldots, \varphi_N)$, the average-watermark match-matrix $D^A = (d_1^A, \ldots, d_N^A)$ is calculated by,

$$d_i^A = \begin{cases} 0, if W_i^A = E_p^A \\ 1, otherwise \end{cases} \tag{12}$$

Where W_i^A is the computed average-watermark of the 2×2 block Z_i from (5), and E_p^A is the average-watermark extracted from the corresponding mapping block Z_p (where $p = \varphi_i$). The average-watermark TDM $T^A = \{t_i^A | i = 1, 2, \ldots, N\}$ is obtained by the block-neighborhood detection method proposed in [13]. That is,

$$t_i^A = \begin{cases} 1, if(d_i^A = 1)\&(\Gamma_i^A \geq \Gamma_p^A) \\ 0, otherwise \end{cases} \tag{13}$$

where $p = \varphi_i$, Γ_i^A and Γ_p^A denote the number of nonzero pixels that are adjacent to the ith and pth pixel in the D^A, respectively.

Step.2 VQ-watermark matching. Similar to Step.1, the VQ-watermark match-matrix $D^V = (d_1^V, \ldots, d_{N/4}^V)$ is calculated by,

$$d_j^V = \begin{cases} 0, if W_j^V = E_q^V \\ 1, otherwise \end{cases} \tag{14}$$

where $q = \sigma_i$, W_i^V and E_q^V are the computed and extracted average-watermark. To mark the validity of each 2×2 block, the VQ-watermark TDM $T^V = (T_j^V | j = 1, 2, \ldots, N/4)$ is obtained by,

$$T_j^V = \begin{cases} \begin{bmatrix} 1 & 1 \\ 1 & 1 \end{bmatrix}, if(d_j^V = 1)\&(\Gamma_j^V \geq \Gamma_q^V) \\ \begin{bmatrix} 0 & 0 \\ 0 & 0 \end{bmatrix}, otherwise \end{cases} \tag{15}$$

where Γ_j^V and Γ_q^V denote the number of nonzero pixels that are adjacent to the jth and qth pixel in the D^V, respectively. Note that T_j^V is a 2×2 block, so the size of T_j^V is the same as that of T^A.

Step.3 Tamper detection. Setting $\Omega = (\omega_1, \ldots, \omega_N)$, where $\omega_i = t_i^A + t_i^V$. Since value of t_i^V and t_i^A is 0 or 1, the value of ω_i must be an integer ranging from 0 to 2. Let ξ_i denotes the sum of eight pixels that are adjacent to the pixel ω_i in the Ω. The TDM $T = (ti | i = 1, 2, \ldots, N)$ is obtained by

$$t_i = \begin{cases} 1, if(\omega_i + \xi_i) > 4 \\ 0, otherwise \end{cases} \tag{16}$$

2.3   Tamper Recovery

After tamper detection, all blocks with size of 2×2 pixels in the test image are marked as either valid or invalid. The proposed recovery procedure is only for the tampered blocks and includes the three steps.

Step.1 Average recovery. According to the TDM T, the mapping sequence Ψ, and the binary random sequence B, the average-recovery image $R^A = \{R_i^A | i = 1, \ldots, N\}$ is obtained by,

$$R_i^A = \begin{cases} A_{ve}(E_{\varphi i}^A), if(t_i = 1)\&(t_{\varphi i} = 0) \\ Z_i, otherwise \end{cases} \tag{17}$$

where $A_{ve}(E_{\varphi i}^A)$ denotes the reconstructed average intensity by decrypting the average-watermark $E_{\varphi i}^A$ extracted from the associated block. At the same time, the destroyed template $\Delta = \{\Delta_i | i = 1, \ldots, N\}$, which size is the same as that of the test image, is generated by,

$$\Delta_i = \begin{cases} \begin{bmatrix} 1 & 1 \\ 1 & 1 \end{bmatrix}, if(t_i = 1)\&(t_{\varphi i} = 1) \\ \begin{bmatrix} 0 & 0 \\ 0 & 0 \end{bmatrix}, otherwise \end{cases} \tag{18}$$

Step.2 VQ recovery. According to B and Λ, the high-frequency image $H' = \{H_j' | j = 1, \ldots, N/4\}$ is first reconstructed by the extracted VQ-watermark. The average-recovery image R^A is divided into 4×4 blocks $R^A = \{R_j^A | j = 1, \ldots, N/4\}$. The VQ-recovery image $R^V = \{R_j^V | j = 1, \ldots, N/4\}$ is updated by,

$$R_j^V = \begin{cases} R_j^A + H_j', if(t_j = 1)\&(t_{\sigma i} = 0) \\ R_j^A, otherwise \end{cases} \tag{19}$$

Step.3 Inpainting recovery. According to the R_j^V and the destroyed template Δ, the inpainting operation proposed in [14] is adopted to further improve the quality of recovered image.

$$R = INP(R^V, \Delta) \tag{20}$$

where INP(.) is an inpainting operator, and R is the recovered image of the proposed method.

3   Experimental Results

We conduct numerous experiments to demonstrate the effectiveness of the proposed self-embedding fragile watermarking scheme and compare with the typical self-recovery watermarking schemes [8] and [13] in the performance. For quantitative evaluation, several measurements are introduced. (a) Watermark payload: the number of bits per pixel (bpp), (b) Invisibility: PSNR (peak signal-to-noise ratio) between the watermarked image and original one, (c) Restoration performance: PSNR between the recovered image and original one, (d) tamper detection performance: the PFA (Probability of false acceptance) and the PFR (Probability of false rejection) [13].

3.1   Watermark Payload and Invisibility

Generally, the watermark payload of the existing self-embedding schemes ranges from 1 to 3 bpp (bit per pixel). To ensure the invisibility of watermark, the watermarked image is commonly generated by substituting for the b (=1,2,3) LSB planes while keeping the MSB planes of the original image intact. Suppose that the original distribution of the data in the LSB planes is uniform, the PSNR of the watermarked image with respect to the original one is about [13],

$$PSNR \approx \begin{cases} 51.14dB, b = 1 \\ 44.15dB, b = 2 \\ 37.92dB, b = 3 \end{cases} \qquad (21)$$

The PSNR value of the watermarked image decreases with the increase of watermark payload. This indicates that the smaller the watermark payload is, the better the quality of watermarked image is.

In the proposed scheme, the embedded watermarks in a block of 4×4 pixels include the following parts: four average-watermark with length of 6 bits and one VQ-watermark with length of 8 bits. As a result, the watermark payload of the proposed scheme is (4×6+8)/16=2 bpp. That is, the watermark payload of the proposed scheme is the same as that of the schemes in [13] and [10]. From (21), PSNR of watermarked images generated by the proposed and He's schemes should be about 44 dB. On the contrary, PSNR of watermarked images generated by the schemes in [6,7,9] are about 38 dB from (21) due to the fact that their watermark payload are 3 bpp. The PSNR of watermarked images generated by Yang [8] is about 40 dB since a smoothing function was used in [8]. Therefore, the quality of the watermarked images generated by the proposed and He's [13] and Lin's [10] schemes is better than that by schemes in [6-9].

3.2   Restoration Performance under General Tampering

Self-recovery watermarking schemes enable the detection of tampering or replacement of a watermarked image. The distinction mainly lies in the tamper localization accuracy and the quality of recovered images. The quality of a recovered image depends highly on the localization accuracy and the complexity of image content. To demonstrate the tamper recovery ability of the proposed scheme under general tampering, two test images of size 512×512, a smooth Lena and a rough Baboon, are used to generate the watermarked images, which PSNR is about 44.12dB and 44.01 dB, as shown in Fig. 2(a) and 2(b). Figs. 2(c) and 2(d) are the tampered Baboon and Lena images, in which the tampered region is about 31% and 70% of the host image, respectively.

For the tampered images shown in Fig.2(c) and 2(d), Fig.3 shows the tamper detection and recovery results by the proposed scheme. The detection results are depicted in Figs. 3(a) and 3(b). It can be seen from Fig. 3(a) and 3(b) the proposed method effectively detect content modifications with high probability. The PFA and PFR of Fig. 3(a) are 0.06% and 0.78%, and those of Fig. 3(b) are 0.24% and 5.91%, respectively. The recovered images before inpainting operation are shown in Fig.3(c) and 3(d). There are many invalid pixels distributed randomly in the tampered region, as can be seen from Fig. 3(c) and 3(d). This impairs the quality of the recovered image. Since the invalid pixels are marked by the destroyed template and randomly distributed in tampered region, they could be reconstructed by the inpainting operation. The recovered images, shown in Fig.3(e) and 3(f), have the PSNR of 33.89 dB and 20.94 dB, respectively. The proposed scheme had a superior quality recovered images. This is mainly due to the fact that the proposed method would reconstruct the invalid pixels whose associated block is tampered using the inpainting operation. These results indicate that the tampered image can be recovered by the proposed scheme with an acceptable visual quality even the tamper ratio is up to 70% of the host image.

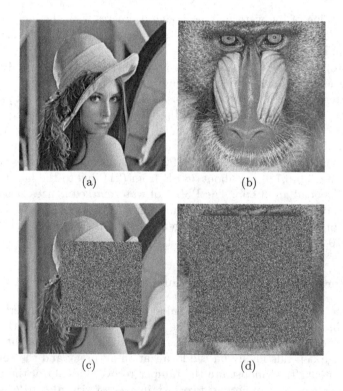

(a)   (b)

(c)   (d)

Fig. 2. Original and tampered images (a) Original Lena image, (b) Original Baboon image; (c) Tampered Lena with 31% tamper ratio, (d) Tampered Baboon with 70% tamper ratio

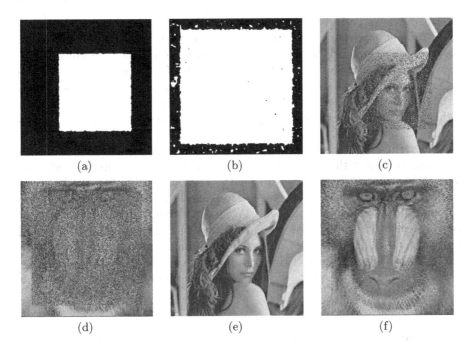

Fig. 3. Tamper detection and recovery results of Fig. 2(c) and 2(d). (a) and (b) are the detected results; (c) and (d) are the recovered images before inpainting operation; (e) and (f) are the recovered images

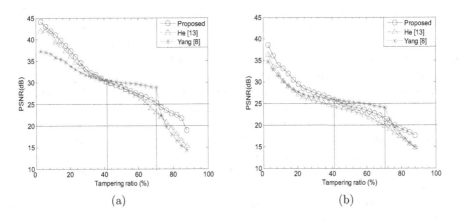

Fig. 4. Performance comparison of the restoration quality under general tampering with different tampering ratio (a) Lena, (b) Baboon

To further compare the quality of recovered images for the smoother Lena and rough Baboon images, the 2×2 image blocks were randomly modified with different tamper ratios, and the tampered blocks were detected and recovered, respectively. Fig.4 shows the performance comparison of experimental results under general tampering with different tampering ratios by the proposed, He's [13] and Yang's [8]schemes. Compared Fig. 4(a) with 4(b), the complexity of image content has much impact on the performance of tamper recovery. The recovery quality of Lena image is better than that of Baboon in the same tampering ratio for all self-embedding watermarking schemes. As seen from Fig.4, as the tampering ratio is no more than 40%, the PSNRs of the proposed scheme are highest. The PSNR value of the proposed scheme is larger than that of He's scheme [13] about 1 dB for Lena, but about 3 dB for Baboon. This indicates that the average-code is good for a smooth image. From Fig. 4(b), the schemes in [8] and [13] have the similar PSNR value in the same tampering ratio for rough Baboon image as the tampering ratio is small. This implies the VQ-code has more superiority than the average code since the average length of VQ-code is a one-third of that of average-code. When the tampering ratio is between 40 and 70 percent of the test image, the PSNRs of the scheme proposed by Yang [8] are highest. This is because Yang [8] maintained four copies of VQ-coding watermark of the whole image. However, Yang's scheme [8] is vulnerable to the collage attack. The security of self-embedding watermarking will be discussed in the following subsection.

3.3   Security

Self-embedding watermarking schemes enable the detection of general tampering of a watermarked image. However, not all fragile watermarking schemes have an ability against the collage attack. To demonstrate the ability against various malicious attacks, two tampered images obtained by the collage attack and multiple attacks are used to demonstrate the superiority of the proposed method.

The Water, Hill-water and Flinstones images with size of 512×512 pixels are chosen. The watermarked Water, Hill-water and Flinstones were generated by the proposed scheme with the same secret key, shown in Fig. 5(a)∼ 5(c), with PSNR of 44.14, 44.10 and 44.01 dB, respectively. To demonstrate the ability against the collage attack, the single-region collaged Water, Fig. 5(d), was constructed by copying the hill of Hill-water and pasting it onto the Water image while preserving their relative spatial location within image. The collaged region is about 26.7% of the tested image. To illustrate the performance under various malicious modifications, Fig. 5(e) is the multi-region tampered Water, in which there are five tampered regions tampered by the various counterfeiting attacks. For convenience of description, five tampered regions are marked as Ri ($i = 1, 2, \ldots, 5$), as shown in Fig. 5(e). These modifications can be classified into three attacks: (1) general tampering with a piece of white cloud marked R1; (2) VQ attack: R2 is replaced by a turtle of the watermarked Flinstones by a 2×2 block without preserving their relative spatial locations within the image, and R3 is replaced with the house in itself by pixel; and (3) collage attack: a turtle in the watermarked Flinstones was collaged onto R4 by the 2×2 block and a hill of the watermarked Hill-water was collaged onto R5 by the 8×8 block while preserving their relative spatial locations within the image.

Fig. 5. Watermarked images and tampered ones. Watermarked images (a) Water: 44.14 dB, (b) Hill-water: 44.10dB (c) Flinstones: 44.01 dB; Tampered images (d) Single-region collaged Water, and (e) multi-region tampered Water

Table 1. Performance comparison of tamper detection and recovery

Methods	Single-region collaged Water			Multi-region forged Water		
	PFA (%)	PFR(%)	PSNR (dB)	PFA (%)	PFR (%)	PSNR (dB)
Yang [8]	90.17	1.18	16.83	65.87	1.79	25.82
He [13]	5.47	0.52	27.43	0.85	0.19	36.18
Proposed	0.23	0.46	33.46	0.17	1.19	38.48

Performance comparison of various self-embedding watermarking methods on the single-region collaged Water and the multi-region tampered Water was investigated. Table 1 summarizes the quantitative results in terms of Rt (tamper ratio), PFA, PFR, and PSNR. Fig. 6 and Fig 7 show the tamper detection and recover results of the collaged Water, and the multi-region tampered Water by the proposed scheme, the methods in [8] and [13].

In the collage attack, since the authentication watermark of each block in Yang's scheme was the block-wise independent, Yang's scheme was not capable of withstanding the collage attack, indicated by the higher PFA of 90.17%. Accordingly, Yang's scheme could not recover the collaged image, indicated by PSNR of the recovered image is 16.83 dB. In contrast, the proposed and He's [13]

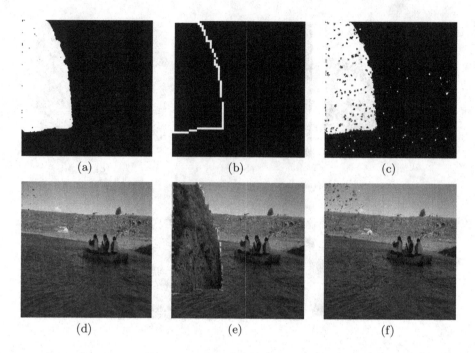

Fig. 6. Tamper detection and recovery results of Single-region collaged Water. Tamper detection results by (a) the proposed method, (b) Yang [8], and (e) He [13]; Recovered images by (f) the proposed method, (g) Yang [8], and (h) He [13].

methods would effectively resist the collage attack, evidenced by the lower PFA of 0.23% and 5.47%, respectively. Since the performance of tamper detection of the proposed scheme is better than that of He's scheme [13], the proposed method has the better recovery quality. PSNR of the recovered image by the proposed scheme is 35.27 dB, which is 6 dB higher than that of He's scheme. It indicates that the quality of the proposed scheme is the best in the collage attack, as evidenced by Figs. 6(d), 6(e) and 6(f).

For the multi-region tampered water image, the proposed and He [13] schemes exhibit much better tamper detection performance, indicated by the much lower PFA of 0.17% and 0.85%, respectively. The method reported in [8] cannot resist all the counterfeiting attacks, evidenced by the corresponding PFA of 65.87%. Moreover, quality of the recovered image by the proposed scheme tops other methods with the measure by the PSNR of 38.48 dB compared to the 36.18 dB by He's scheme, and 25.82 dB by Yang's scheme. The results are shown in Fig. 7. This demonstrates that the proposed method outperforms other self-recovery fragile watermarking algorithms in tamper detection and recovery under multi-region tampered image by the various counterfeiting attacks.

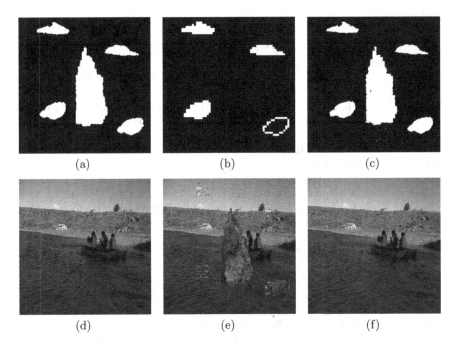

Fig. 7. Tamper detection and recovery results of multi-region tampered Water. Tamper detection results by (a) the proposed method, (b) Yang [8], and (e) He [13]; Recovered images by (f) the proposed method, (g) Yang [8], and (h) He [13]

4   Conclusion

In this paper, we proposed a novel self-embedding fragile watermarking method with high security and superior performance of tamper detection and recovery. The watermark data, including two parts, are generated by combining average encoding with VQ encoding. The validity of a 2×2 block is detected by the average-watermark and VQ-watermark, and the tampered blocks are recovered by executing the average, VQ and inpainting recovery operations in sequence. As a result, the embedded watermark data are used in both tamper detection and content recovery, leading to a better invisibility, detection performance and recovery quality. Also, the proposed scheme has a high security against the known counterfeiting attacks including the collage attack. Future research includes extending this approach capable of resisting signal processing operations, and analytic investigation on the tamper detection performance.

Acknowledgments. This work is supported in part by the National Natural Science Foundation of China (60970122, 61170226), the Research Fund for the Doctoral Program of Higher Education (20090184120021), the Science and Technique Foundation of Tibet Autonomous Region (2012) and the Fundamental Research Funds for the Central Universities (SWJTU09CX039, SWJTU10CX09).

References

1. Han, S.-H., Chu, C.-H.: Content-based image authentication: current status, issues, and challenges. Int. J. Inf. Secur. 9, 19–32 (2010)
2. Haouzia, A., Noumeir, R.: Methods for image authentication: a survey. Multimed Tools Appl. 39, 1–46 (2008)
3. Wong, P.W., Memon, N.: Secret and public key image watermarking schemes for image authentication and ownership verification. IEEE Trans. on Image Processing (10), 1593–1601 (2001)
4. Fridrich, J., Goljan, M.: Images with self-correcting capabilities. In: ICIP 1999, Kobe, Japan, October 25-28 (1999)
5. He, H., Zhang, J., Chen, F.: Adjacent-block based statistical detection method for self-embedding watermarking techniques. Signal Processing 89, 1557–1566 (2009)
6. Qian, Z., Feng, G., Feng, G.: Inpainting assisted self recovery with decreased embedding data. IEEE Signal Processing Letters 17(11), 929–932 (2010)
7. Qian, Z., Feng, G., Zhang, X., Wang, S.: Image self-embedding with high-quality restoration capability. Digital Signal Processing 21, 278–286 (2011)
8. Yang, C.W., Shen, J.J.: Recover the tampered image based on VQ indexing. Signal Processing 90, 331–343 (2010)
9. Zhang, X., Qian, Z., Ren, Y., Feng, G.: Watermarking with flexible self-recovery quality based on compressive sensing and compositive reconstruction. IEEE Trans. on Information Forensics and Security 6(4), 1223–1232 (2011)
10. Lin, P.L., Hsieh, C.K., Huang, P.W.: A hierarchical digital watermarking method for image tamper detection and recovery. Pattern Recognition 38(12), 2519–2529 (2005)
11. Fridrich, J., Goljan, M., Memon, N.: Cryptanalysis of the Yeung-Mintzer fragile watermarking technique. Electron. Imaging 11(4), 262–274 (2002)
12. Chang, C., Fan, Y., Tai, W.: Four-scanning attack on hierarchical digital watermarking method for image tamper detection and recovery. Pattern Recognit. 40, 654–661 (2008)
13. He, H., Chen, F., Tai, H.-M., Kalker, T., Zhang, J.: Performance analysis of a block-neighborhood-based self-recovery fragile watermarking scheme. IEEE Trans. on Information Forensics and Security 7(1), 185–196 (2012)
14. Elad, M., Starck, J.-L., Querre, P., Donoho, D.L.: Simultaneous cartoon and testure image inpainting using morphological component analysis (MCA). Appl. Comput. Harmon. Anal 10, 340–358 (2005)

An Efficient Fragile Web Pages Watermarking for Integrity Protection of XML Documents

Quan Wen[1] and Yufei Wang[2]

[1] Jilin University, Changchun, China
wenquan@jlu.edu.cn
[2] JiLin Normal University, Siping, China
yufei-522@hotmail.com

Abstract. This paper presents a novel web pages watermarking scheme for XML document named DSQC(Double Single Quotes Code). The watermark generated by PCA or hash function are embedded into XML original source code by making use of the XML attribute values feature which must be quoted either double or single. Experimental results demonstrate that the DSQC is a kind of semi-blind watermarking and sensitive for tamper, although the embedded watermark's amount is less than the ULC method. By comparing the time cost and sensitivity with experiment, the hash function is more effective than PCA.

Keywords: Digital Watermarking, Extensible Markup Language(XML), Principal Component Analysis(PCA), Tamper-proof.

1   Introduction

XML(Extensible Markup Language) is now as important for the Web as HTML. XML became the foundation of the Web due to its two important natures. One is using plain text to encode a hierarchical set of information. The other is using verbose tags to allow the document to be understood without any special reader or interpreter. Now XML is widely used in information exchanging, Web Service, Business-to-Consumer(B2C) and Business-to-Business(B2B) applications, etc[1]. Anyway, XML is everywhere!

Meanwhile, security of XML documents has become one of the most important issues about Web applications with XML[2-4]. Just like HTML, File Digest is a traditional, prevalent algorithm for the integrity protection of XML. A special version of digital signature for XML document in which a one-way hash function H is used is issued by the W3C[5]. MD2, MD5 and SHA-1, SHA-256 are well-known hash function and all of them are going to be tested with our watermarking scheme later.

For a better understanding of web page watermarking, this essay will start with a brief introduction of digital signature(ignore the encryption process for simplification). Suppose an XML document "M" needed to be signed before it's sent. The sender computes the digest of the XML document using a hash function(MD5, for example) which can be take as a 'digital fingerprint' of the original larger document. The 'digital fingerprint' H(M) then is attached to the end of the M, both the M and its

Y.Q. Shi, H.J. Kim, and F. Pérez-González (Eds.): IWDW 2012, LNCS 7809, pp. 135–144, 2013.

hash value have to be stored and transmitted. When the receiver gets the message M*, it generates the digest, H(M*). Then the H(M*) is compared with the attached digest value H(M). If they are identical, H(M)=H(M*), then the document is integral; otherwise, H(M)≠H(M*), it has been modified.

Since such signature has to be attached to the original XML document, additional storage and bandwidth are required to keep and transmit the whole signed XML document so that its integrity can be ensured. In order to conquer the drawback of the traditional digital signature, digital watermarking was proposed for protecting web page from tampering[6-8].

Digital watermarking is a feasible means for protecting digital intellectual property by embedding the watermarking into the original media. Watermarking has been proved a promising technology when it was proposed in 1990s[9]. From the point of academic view, Digital Watermarking can be divided into two types: Watermarking Algorithm and Watermarking Protocol. And the web page watermarking belongs to a kind of fragile text watermarking algorithm.

For the text fragile watermarking algorithm, Kazenbeisser et al.[10] proposed to embed watermarks by adding space and tag into the source code of HTML web pages(Space-Tab Coding, or STC for abbreviation). However, STC also has the problem of expanding file size. In order to resolve this problem, Zhao and Lu[6] used another watermark embedding method called Upper-Lower Coding(ULC) for HTML documents. It is based on the case-insensitivity of HTML tags. Then a modified ULC scheme was proposed by Wu and Chang[7]. But an apparent problem of ULC is that these watermarking algorithms belong to visible watermarking. Of course, the invisible watermarking is more secure than visible watermarking.

Among all the proposed web page watermarking, the scheme for XML document can seldom be found. Until now, only one XML watermarking method has been found[8]. But the presented algorithm in the 8th paper meets one problem which is the watermarked XML document cannot be directly used for web application only after validation. In order to resolve the above-mentioned problem in web page watermarking, this paper proposes a novel web page watermarking named DSQC for XML document in which the watermark is embedded by using the XML attribute value properties.

The rest of the paper is categorized as follows. In Section two we introduce the related work and the drawbacks of it; section three will focus on the watermarking method, separately with generating, embedding and validating; section four will show the simulation result; finally section five will make a conclusion.

2   Related Works

The first web page watermarking scheme was proposed for the HTML document[6]. Then, a modified scheme with hash function used to generate watermark was presented by Wu[8]. There is only one paper found out about XML document in which XOR method is used[7]. For the importance of XML today, more research should be pondered for XML document. The ULC embedding scheme was used in the all of proposed web page watermarking for HTML and XML. So let's introduce more detail for the ULC as follows.

2.1   Review of ULC Watermarking Scheme

Although different watermark generating algorithms(such as PCA or one-way hash function) will be used in ULC, the framework of watermarking scheme is similar to the following steps.

(1) Construct the digital number matrix H. The H is constructed from source codes of the original web page, in which English characters are mapped from "0" to "25", with both "a" and "A" mapped to "0", "b" and "B" mapped to "1" in the corresponding row vector of H, and so forth. For example, the text line "<Book><Author>" is mapped to(1, 14, 14, 10, 0, 20, 19, 7, 14, 17). And since the number of characters of each row in web page may be not the same, the "cyclic filling" is needed to expand the length of every row vector to the longest one. For instance, if the above row vectors is the longest one and another shorter one, such as(6, 9, 10, 10, 1)exists, then the shorter one will be expanded twice the origin to (6, 9, 10, 10, 1, 6, 9, 10, 10, 1). Finally, the alphabet document matrix H can be got. Suppose that $H \in F^{R \times C}$, where F represents either the real number domain or the complex number domain.

(2) Compute the matrix D from H. For amplify the changes in H, we get the matrix $D \in F^{R \times R}$ by $D = HH^t$, where t represents the transpose operation.

(3) Encrypt the matrix D to get the matrix I. In order to make the watermarking algorithm be non-invertibility[11], it used Shannon's Diffusion[12] to convolute the D matrix with a key K. And the K can be an image when input to MATLAB become an N x N matrix. The convolution equation is expressed with $I = D \otimes K$, where '$\otimes$'denotes the operation of convoluting and $I \in F^{(R+N-1)(R+N-1)}$.

(4) Generate watermark W from the matrix I. There two different ways for generating watermark information. One is PCA and another is one-way hash function. The PCA is more complicated than hash function, so it is illustrated as follows:

(a) Compute the covariance matrix V according to the equation:

$$V = \sum_{i=1}^{N} (I_i - \overline{I}_R)^t (I_i - \overline{I}_R) \tag{1}$$

where I_i is the ith row vector in I, t represents the transpose operation, and $\overline{I}_R \in F^{1 \times N}$ is the average vector of the row vectors in I, it is computed by following equation:

$$\overline{I}_R = \frac{1}{N} \sum_{i=1}^{N} I_i \tag{2}$$

(b) The eigen decomposition(ED) was applied to V by

$$V = ULU^{-1} \tag{3}$$

Where U^{-1} is the inverse matrix of U, L denotes a diagonal matrix with eigenvalue of V, whose diagonal elements are $\lambda_1, \lambda_2, ..., \lambda_N$ which are assumed be sorted in descending order($\lambda_1 \geq \lambda_2 \geq ... \geq \lambda_N$), and the columns of U, $u_1, u_2, ..., u_N$, are the eigenvectors of V.

(c) A subset of $u_1, u_2, ..., u_N$ are used as basis vectors of a feature space S:

$$S = span(u_1, u_2, ..., u_m), m \leq N \tag{4}$$

(d) Compute some feature vectors by projecting them into S by

$$Z_i = (I_i - \overline{I}_R) \cdot [u_1 u_2 \cdots u_m], i = 1, 2, .., N \tag{5}$$

Where $Z_i \in F^{1 \times m}$ can be taken as the coordinates of the original data in the feature space S. Z_i's can be called "the principle components".

(e) Chose the first R principle components as $Z_1, Z_2, ..., Z_R \in F^{1 \times R}$, and converted them into binary form, i.e. a sequence of '0' and '1'. Let z_{ij} denote the jth element of Z_i, $i = 1, 2, .., R$, $j = 1, 2, ... R$. Thus, each z_{ij} is converted to binary form β_{ij} , and all of them are connected to a binary sequence $W_i = \beta_{i1} \beta_{i2} ... \beta_{iR}$, which is taken as the watermark for the ith text line.

In the paper [7], authors propose one-way hash function instead of PCA to generate the watermark, and the hash function is more simple than PCA. The watermark W can be generated by

$$W = H(I) \tag{6}$$

where H represent the one-way hash function, such as MD5, SHA-1.

(5) Embed the watermark W. Through modifying the case of letters in HTML tags, as for ULC method, the watermark W is embedded in the original web page source code. The ULC modified the case of the letters in the HTML tags in the ith text line T_i: the jth letter was changed to lower case if the jth element of W_i is '0', otherwise upper case. If the number of letters is larger than the length of W_i, the letters index is modular by the length of W_i.

(6) Validate the watermarked web page. To validate whether a watermarked web page has been maliciously altered, the ULC scheme first generates a watermark W_G by the aforementioned embedding scheme such as PCA or hash function. Then, the watermark W_E is extracted from the detecting web page. The upper case letter is retrieved as '1', and the lower case letter as '0'. If $W_G = W_E$, then the integrity of the detecting web page is intact; otherwise, the page has been altered.

2.2   Problem and Solution

According to the above description, the main advantage of ULC method is that the watermarked web page will not increase file size. So it is more suitable for the web application. However, two problems exist in the ULC scheme.

(1) The ULC method is not blind watermarking. Although lower case to upper case is a little different, but most of web page source code is written with lower er case tag. Then the difference will be obvious when a lot of tag letters of original source code have been changed to upper case. So it is easy to find the web page has been watermarked. It is sure that ULC will become dangerous especially for a professional attacker.

(2) The ULC method is not appropriate for the XML document. For the XML XML Tags are Case Sensitive. The tag <Letter> is different from the tag <letter> in XML. And opening and closing tags must be written with the same case, for example as following:

```
<Message>This is incorrect</message>
<message>This is correct</message>
```

Although the ULC is modified by a good idea of XOR[8], the watermarked XML document can not be used before the validity because most of the tag pair in the watermarked XML source code have been modified incorrectly the same as showed above.

So, in order to resolve the above-mentioned two problems, we propose the following watermarking scheme named DSQC for XML document.

3   DSQC Watermarking Scheme

Because XML tags are case sensitive, we have to find another embedding method to replace of ULC. A feature can be noticed in XML: the attribute values must always be quoted with either single or double quotes. As most of XML document have many attributes, the watermark can be embedded by using those pair quote. In simple terms, the idea of watermarking is that: if a watermark bit is '0', the quote of attribute is double, otherwise it is single.

The watermarking method is named by **DSQC**(Double-Single Quotes Code). More details about DSQC are presented separately with watermark generating, watermark embedding and watermark validating as follows. Actually, DSQC has the same 6 steps as the ULC presented in section 2.1. The key point for the DSQC is in the step 5 and 6. The two steps are the embedding and extracting watermark process respectively.

3.1   Watermark Generating

The DSQC also uses the similar algorithm as ULC method to generate watermark W. As presented in Section 2.1, step 1 to 3 also executed to get the matrix I. But both of PCA and hash function are used for comparison.

3.2   Watermark Embedding

At the embedding step, XML tag letters won't be changed. Instead of changing the tag letters, it changes the attributes' quote pair to embed part of the watermark W. In general, the number of quote pair of attributes is little than the number bit of the watermark W. So we need select the important part of W suppose W_D to embed into the original XML document. The length of W_D should be equal to the pair quotes of the original XML. Briefly speaking, suppose the first row or column of matrix W can be chosen for embedding. Anyway, the more quote pair amount of the XML document is, the more appropriate it is for DSQC. In fact, most of XML document possess enough attribute quote to embedding watermark.

Suppose the double quote is used in XML attribute by default. So the embedding process is as easy as that: according to the watermark bit, if the bit is '0' the double quote won't be changed, otherwise the double quote is changed to '1'. For example, the following XML have 9 attributes, and the watermarking binary string W_D is [100110101] with length 9 can be embedded in it. The original and watermarked XML is showed Fig.1.

```
<xs:element name="note">
<xs:complexType>
  <xs:sequence>
    <xs:element name="to" type="xs:string"/>
    <xs:element name="from" type="xs:string"/>
    <xs:element name="heading" type="xs:string"/>
    <xs:element name="body" type="xs:string"/>
  </xs:sequence>
</xs:complexType>
</xs:element>
```

(a)

```
<xs:element name='note'>
<xs:complexType>
  <xs:sequence>
    <xs:element name="to" type="xs:string"/>
    <xs:element name='from' type='xs:string'/>
    <xs:element name="heading" type='xs:string'/>
    <xs:element name="body" type='xs:string'/>
  </xs:sequence>
</xs:complexType>
</xs:element>
```

(b)

Fig. 1. DSQC watermark embedding example with watermark binary:[100110101]. (a) Original XML message. (b) Watermarked XML message

3.3   Watermark Verification

To check whether a watermarked XML document has been tampered or not, we first generate a watermark with PCA or hash function as it is described in section 2.1. Afterward, the quote pair will be searched from the watermarked web page to retrieve the watermark. For everyone of searched quote pair, if it is double quote, the extracted watermark bit is '0', otherwise it is single quote, and the extracted watermark bit is '1'. Moreover, the DSQC can be non-invertible[11], because of the feature of PCA and hash function with the secret key K. More details about non-invertibility watermarking can be found in the papers[6-8].

4   Experimental Results

We use PCA and hash function to implement DSQC scheme in MATLAB. As for hash function, MD2, MD5, SHA-1 and SHA-256 are all used respectively. Firstly, the

```
<?xml version="1.0" encoding="UTF-8" ?>
<!DOCTYPE struts PUBLIC
    "-//Apache Software Foundation//DTD Struts Configuration
2.0//EN"
    " http://struts.apache.org/dtds/struts-2.0.dtd"><struts>
<package name="voteaction" extends="struts-default" names-
pace="/">
<action name="voteaction"
class="mvp.exportexcelaciton.VoteAction">
    <result name="success" >
        voteresult.jsp
    </result></action></package>
```

(a)

```
<?xml version="1.0" encoding='UTF-8' ?>
<!DOCTYPE struts PUBLIC
    "-//Apache Software Foundation//DTD Struts Configuration
2.0//EN"
    'http://struts.apache.org/dtds/struts-2.0.dtd'><struts>
<package name="voteaction" extends='struts-default' names-
pace='/'>
<action name="voteaction"
class='mvp.exportexcelaciton.VoteAction'>
    <result name="success" >
      voteresult.jsp
    </result></action></package>
```

(b)

Fig. 2. Effective test. (a) The original XML source code fragment. (b) The watermarked XML source code fragment.

effectiveness of the proposed watermarking scheme is tested. Fig.2 gives an example of experiment results. In Fig.2, the Fig.a is the original XML source code fragment, and the Fig.b is the watermarked XML source code fragment.

As shown in Fig.2, it is difficult to find the difference between (a) and (b) unless you are very careful or you know the DSQC method beforehand. The possibility of noticing the watermark will become even smaller when the XML size increases.

In addition, we list execution time of DSQC both with PCA and hash function in Table 1. It is that hash function is much faster than PCA especially when the file size increases.

As the amount of embedding watermark in DSQC is much less than ULC, we need test its sensitivity to the tampering of watermarked XML document. So, we just do a little change for the watermarked XML. Take the Fig.2(b) as a example, the line "voteresult.jsp" is modified with "voteresult.Jsp", just one letter changing from lower case to upper case. After that, the watermark W_T would be extracted from the tampered watermark XML and compared to the original watermark W_O. For all of 8 different size XML documents, the fragile test is carried out and the difference rate between W_T and W_O is drawn in Fig.3.

Of course, high difference rate between W_T and W_O will prove the DSQC is sensitive to tamper attack. As shown from Fig.3, both with PCA and hash function, the DSQC proves its sensitivity. At the same time, the hash function shows better fragile level than PCA method when the XML document size increased.

Table 1. The comparisons of DSQC method between one-way has function scheme and PCA scheme

File Size (KB)	Time(Seconds)									
	Embed					Validate				
	PCA	MD2	MD5	SHA-1	SHA-256	PCA	MD2	MD5	SHA-1	SHA-256
0.77	0.1262	0.0707	0.0703	0.0671	0.0882	0.1240	0.0665	0.0673	0.0656	0.0660
2.93	0.2520	0.0974	0.0788	0.0823	0.0798	0.2503	0.0924	0.0732	0.0727	0.0758
8.75	1.4477	0.2749	0.1115	0.1181	0.1279	1.3624	0.2654	0.0996	0.1088	0.1161
17.4	6.1423	0.8552	0.2001	0.2391	0.2626	6.2151	0.8348	0.1938	0.2116	0.2454
20.2	8.8153	1.1156	0.2383	0.2804	0.3061	8.8045	1.0848	0.2240	0.2583	0.2869
24.9	14.5933	1.5909	0.2704	0.3287	0.3883	14.4194	1.5637	0.2404	0.3004	0.3559
28.8	20.8547	2.1523	0.3779	0.4632	0.5259	20.8623	2.1279	0.3402	0.4225	0.4994
32.4	28.4948	2.6868	0.4607	0.5387	0.6375	28.4901	2.6584	0.4031	0.5116	0.5985

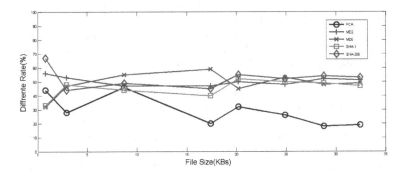

Fig. 3. The fragile test between PCA and one-way hash function

5   Conclusion

In this paper, we propose the DSQC a semi-invisible fragile watermark scheme for XML document. As the XML attribute values can be quoted either double or single, the watermark is embedded in original XML file using the XML feature. And extensive experimental results lead to the following conclusions. (1) The proposed DSQC is effective in protecting the integrity of XML documents. (2) The DSQC does not increase the file size of XML and it is semi-invisible at the same time. (3) The DSQC using hash function is faster and more sensitive than the PCA method. Therefore, we suggest that one-way hash function should be used for generating watermark in DSQC especially for large size XML document. Moreover, the DSQC is more practical, and it is easier to implement. In future, a complete invisible and with much bigger watermark method of watermarking web page will be a big challenge!

Acknowledgements. This work is granted by the Youth Science Foundation of JiLin Province(20100183).

References

1. Wu, J.: A Framework for Learning Comprehensible Theories in XML Document Classification. IEEE Transactions on Knowledge and Data Engineering 24(1), 1–14 (2012)
2. Jensen, M., Meyer, C., Somorovsky, J.: On the Effectiveness of XML Schema Validation for Countering XML Signature Wrapping Attacks. In: 2011 1st International Workshop on Securing Services on the Cloud (IWSSC), pp. 7–13 (2011)
3. Ammari, F.T., Lu, J.: Advanced XML Security: Framework for Building Secure XML Management (SXMS). In: 2010 Seventh International Conference on Information Technology: New Generations (ITNG), pp. 120–125 (2010)
4. Jager, T., Somorovsky, J.: How to Break XML Encryption. In: CCS 2011, Chicago, Illinois, USA, pp. 413–422 (2011)
5. Haron, G.R., Maniam, D., Ngiap, S.T.S.: Revisiting Secure Documents with XML Security: A Component-Based Approach. In: Developments in E-systems Engineering (DESE), pp. 257–262 (2010)

6. Zhao, Q., Lu, H.: PCA-based Web Page Watermarking. Pattern Recognition Society, Science Direct, 1334–1341 (2006)
7. Wu, C.-C., Chang, C.-C., Yang, S.-R.: An efficient fragile watermarking for web pages tamper-proof. In: Chang, K.C.-C., Wang, W., Chen, L., Ellis, C.A., Hsu, C.-H., Tsoi, A.C., Wang, H. (eds.) APWeb/WAIM 2007. LNCS, vol. 4537, pp. 654–663. Springer, Heidelberg (2007)
8. Yao, R., Zhao, Q., Lu, H.: A Novel Watermark Algorithm for Integrity Protection of XML Documents. International Journal of Computer Science and Network Security 6(2B), 202–207 (2006)
9. Petiteolas, F.A.R., Anderson, R.J., Kuhn, M.G.: Information hiding – A survey. Proc. of IEEE 1999, 1062–1078 (1999)
10. Katzenbeisser, S., Petitoclas, A.P.: Information Hiding Techniques for Steganography and Digital Watermarking. Artech House, Boston (2000)
11. Craver, S., Memon, N., Yeo, B.-L.: Resolving Rightful Ownerships with Invisible Watermarking Techniques: Limitations, Attacks, and Implications. IEEE Journal on Selected Areas in Communication 16(4), 573–586 (1998)
12. Stallings, W.: Cryptography and Network Security Principles and Practice. Prentice-Hall Inc., Englewood Cliffs (1999)

Image Information Hiding Based on Binary Holography of Iterative Conjugate-Symmetric Extension

Qiyin Zhao, Daqing Chen, Zhi Tao, and Jihua Gu[*]

School of Physical Science and Technology
Soochow University
Suzhou, China
jhgu@suda.edu.cn

Abstract. An image information hiding based on binary holography of iterative conjugate-symmetric extension hologram is proposed to significantly improve the method of binarizing traditional hologram. We binarize the conjugate symmetric extension hologram, and then iterate it between the spatial and transform domain. The binary hologram after iterative repetition loses much less information than the traditional binary interference hologram, so the reconstructed image is greatly improved. Binary hologram is embedded into the medium-frequency coefficient of discrete cosine transform (DCT) of the host image, and the watermark is extracted in the form of blind detection. The simulation results show that the algorithm has much better robustness to JPEG compression, cropping, filtering, noise contamination and other common image processing. Compared with traditional method of binary interference hologram, the robustness of the watermark has been significantly improved.

Keywords: information optics, digital hologram, digital watermark, hologram binarization, blind detection.

1 Introduction

Digital watermark is an efficient approach for copyright protection and data security maintenance of digital products by embedding invisible information into the media content. In the past years, watermark has gained significant attention with the rapid development of digital technology and communication network [1, 2].

Recently, the digital hologram and digital watermark technology based on optics theory are hot topics that have instigated much research works in the field of information security [3~7]. In 2002, Takai and Mifune [8] proposed the method of embedding digital hologram as the watermark information. In 2005, Chang et al. [9] improved this method that embedding digital holographic watermark in the discrete cosine transform

---

[*] Corresponding author.

Y.Q. Shi, H.J. Kim, and F. Pérez-González (Eds.): IWDW 2012, LNCS 7809, pp. 145–155, 2013.

(DCT) domain. The experiments show that the holographic watermark has good resistance to cropping attack. In 2006, ChiLiang Wei et al. [10] proposed the method to embed watermark in DCT domain based on JPEG model, it has excellent robustness to JPEG compression. In 2008, SuJuan Huang et al. [11] [12] proposed a new digital holographic method based on conjugate-symmetric extension without the interference procedure of imitating object light and reference light, and it has much high computational efficiency.

The holography used above are all grayscale images with a large amount of information. Under the same embedded conditions, the larger amount of the watermark information embedded in the host image, the worse transparency and robustness will be. Therefore, in order to reduce the watermarking information and further improve the practicality, GuoMing Li et al. [13] proposed hologram binary converting after obtaining the digital hologram, then taking the binary hologram as the watermark in 2011. But the direct binarization processing of the hologram will lose much holographic information and damage the reconstructed images.

In this letter, we propose a new method of image information hiding based on binary holography of iterative conjugate-symmetric extension to improve this deficiency. Firstly, binary the digital hologram of conjugate-symmetric extension; secondly, do inverse Fourier transform to the binary hologram and take the first half of phase of the result as the phase of the original watermark information; then, repeat the conjugate-symmetric extension holographic process. Finally, a satisfied result could be found through continued iterations of the process. We take many binary images and logo to do this experiment, simulation results show that this improved method converges in iterations. The iterated binary holograms lose less information, and the reconstructed image is greatly improved.

2   Digital Hologram Binarization

2.1   Binarization Algorithm of Traditional Interference Hologram

Let the gray values $m(x, y)$ of original watermark information be the amplitude of object light, and then modulated by a random-phase mask $\varphi(x, y)$ within the range $[-\pi, \pi]$ to improve the uniformity of Fourier transform field. The complex object light is expressed as

$$o(x, y) = m(x, y) \exp[i\varphi(x, y)] \tag{1}$$

The FT of Eq. (1) is expressed by

$$O(\xi, \eta) = \iint o(x, y) \exp[-2\pi i(\xi x + \eta y)] dx dy \tag{2}$$

and then interferes with a reference light **R**, which is denoted as

$$R(\xi, \eta) = R_0 \exp[2\pi i(a\xi + b\eta)] \tag{3}$$

where a and b are used to determine the location of the watermark image at the reconstruction plane. The detected intensity signal after interference can be expressed by

$$H(\xi,\eta) = |O(\xi,\eta) + R(\xi,\eta)|^2 = |O(\xi,\eta)|^2 + |R(\xi,\eta)|^2 \\ + O^*(\xi,\eta)R(\xi,\eta) + O(\xi,\eta)R^*(\xi,\eta) \tag{4}$$

The first and second terms in Eq. (4) have a significant impact to the reconstructed image, and must be discarded by calculating the power spectral density of the reference light and object light. That is,

$$H(\xi,\eta) = O^*(\xi,\eta)R(\xi,\eta) + O(\xi,\eta)R^*(\xi,\eta) \tag{5}$$

where **H** denotes the traditional digital hologram. Binarize the hologram **H** and obtain the binary hologram $H'(\xi,\eta) \in \{0,1\}$.

Intensity distribution of the reconstructed image is obtained by the inverse Fourier transform of the expression that multiplied by the binary hologram and illumination light. To simplify calculations, assume that the amplitude of illumination light is 1 and phase is 0. The intensity distribution at the reconstruction plane can be given by

$$o_R(x, y) = \iint H'(\xi,\eta) \exp[2\pi i(\xi x + \eta y)] d\xi d\eta \tag{6}$$

By substituting Eq. (3) and (5) into Eq. (6), we can obtain

$$o_R(x, y) = o(x - a, y - b) + o^*[-(x + a), -(y + b)] \tag{7}$$

Eq. (7) shows that two symmetrical images appear at the reconstruction plane. The locations are at the coordinates (a, b) and (-a, -b), respectively.

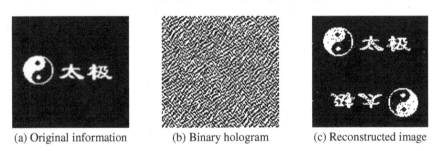

(a) Original information   (b) Binary hologram   (c) Reconstructed image

Fig. 1. Binary hologram of traditional interference algorithm and the reconstructed image

As shown in Fig. 1, Fig. 1(a) is the original watermark information with size of 128×128 pixels, Fig. 1(b) is the binary hologram of traditional interference algorithm and the reconstructed image is shown in Fig. 1(c). We can find out that the quality of reconstructed image by direct binarization hologram processing decreases significantly.

2.2   Binary Algorithm and Iterative Procedure Based on Conjugate Symmetric Extension Hologram

Digital Hologram by Conjugate-Symmetric Extension and Binarization

A novel holographic algorithm based on conjugate-symmetric extension is proposed by SuJuan Huang et al[11][12]. This method does not depend on simulation of inter-ference between object and reference lights to produce the hologram. The complex of the light wave to be recorded is extended to produce a conjugate symmetric function. The function is then Fourier transformed to generate a real valued distribution con-taining both amplitude and phase information of the object wave. The algorithm is highly efficient since it avoids simulation of wave interference.

Let the gray values $m(x, y)$ of original watermark information be the amplitude of object light, and then modulated by a random-phase mask $\varphi(x, y)$. The complex object light is expressed as

$$f_0(x, y) = m(x, y) \exp[i\varphi(x, y)] \tag{8}$$

A conjugate-symmetric extension $f(x, y)$ can be obtained as follows

$$f(x, y) = \begin{cases} f_0(x, y) & (x = 1, 2, ..., M/2-1; \ y = 1, 2, ..., N-1) \\ f_0^*(M - x, N - y) & (x = M/2+1, ..., M-1; \ y = 1, 2..., N-1) \\ 0 & (x = 0, \ or, \ y = 0, \ or, \ x = M/2) \end{cases} \tag{9}$$

Assuming that M and N are even, and the 2D discrete Fourier transform is

$$F(\xi, \eta) = \frac{1}{MN} \sum_{m=0}^{M-1} \sum_{n=0}^{N-1} f(x, y) \times \exp\left[-j2\pi(\frac{x\xi}{M} + \frac{y\eta}{N})\right] \tag{10}$$
$$(\xi = 0, 1, ..., M-1; \ \eta = 0, 1..., N-1)$$

By substituting Eq. (8) and (9) into Eq. (10), we can obtain

$$F(\xi, \eta) = \frac{2}{MN} \sum_{x=0}^{M/2-1} \sum_{y=0}^{N-1} \left\{ m(x, y) \times \cos\left[2\pi(\frac{x\xi}{M} + \frac{y\eta}{N})\right] - \varphi(x, y) \right\} \tag{11}$$

It is clear that the DFT is real valued distribution. The real-valued function $F(\xi, \eta)$ contains both the amplitude and phase of the complex object light.

Binarize the function $F(\xi, \eta)$ and obtain the binary hologram. As shown in Fig.2, Fig. 2(a) is the original watermark information with size of 63×127 pixels, Fig. 2(b) is the extended information, Fig. 2(c) is binary hologram by conjugate symmetric exten-sion and the reconstructed image is shown in Fig. 2(d). We can see that the quality of reconstructed image by binarization processing decreases significantly.

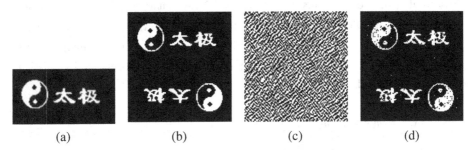

<table>
<tr><td>(a)</td><td>(b)</td><td>(c)</td><td>(d)</td></tr>
</table>

Fig. 2. Binary hologram by conjugate-symmetric extension and the reconstructed image. (a) Original information, (b) Extended information, (c) Binary hologram, (d) Reconstructed image

Iterative Procedure and Hologram Binarization

As shown in Fig. 3(a), with reference to the gray histogram of hologram before binarization, we can see that it has one peak and similar to the normal distribution. Analysis indicated that the direct binarization processing of the hologram will lose much holographic information and reduce quality of the reconstructed images.

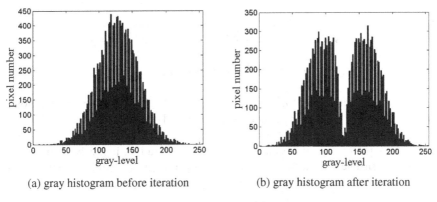

(a) gray histogram before iteration   (b) gray histogram after iteration

Fig. 3. Compare by gray histogram

In this letter, we propose an improved method against that drawback by iterating hologram in the spatial domain and transform domain based on conjugate-symmetric extension. The core of the iterative procedure is to find a particular spectral phase function that will yield a temporal intensity profile as close to the binary image as possible, when combined with the input intensity spectrum.

The Iteration Algorithm is shown in Fig. 4, where the input complex amplitude $f(x, y)$ is the conjugate symmetric extension of $f_0(x, y)$, $F(\xi, \eta)$ denotes the frequency spectrum corresponds to $f(x, y)$ and is a 2D real-valued function. First, the $f_0(x, y)$ is multiplied by initial phase $\exp[i\varphi_0(x, y)]$ and we get $f(x, y)$ by conjugate-symmetric extension of $f_0(x, y)$, then the real-valued spectrum $F(\xi, \eta)$ is obtained after the Fourier transform of $f(x, y)$. Next, binary $F(\xi, \eta)$ and we obtain $f'(x, y)$ by inverse Fourier transform, then the phase of $f_0(x, y)$ is replaced with the first half of phase of $f'(x, y)$ while the amplitude $m(x, y)$ is retained. Finally, we get a new $f(x, y)$ by conjugate symmetric extension. Repeat the process until a satisfied result could be found.

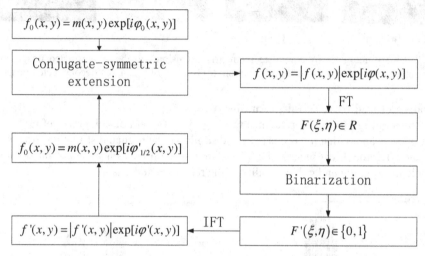

Fig. 4. Iterative schematic diagram

The gray histogram of hologram before binarization after 3000 times-iteration is shown in Fig. 3(b), it has two peaks on each side of the middle gray-level value. Binarize this hologram and obtain the binary hologram.

Fig. 5(a) is the binary hologram after 3000 times-iteration, Fig. 5(b) is the corresponding reconstructed image. Especially obviously, the quality of reconstructed image compared with Fig. 1(c) and Fig. 2(d), is greatly improved.

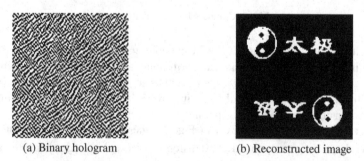

(a) Binary hologram   (b) Reconstructed image

Fig. 5. Binary hologram after iteration and the reconstructed image

3   Watermark Embedding and Extraction

The original information is converted into binary hologram which is embedded as watermark. In order to improve the watermark's transparency and resistance to JPEG compression, hologram is embedded into the middle-frequency DCT coefficient of the host image.

Embedding Algorithm

Here we assume that the host $\mathbf{X}$ is a gray image with the size of $N \times N$ where N can be divided by 8, thus the host can be divided into 8×8 sub-blocks, and watermark $\mathbf{H}$ is the binary hologram with the size of $M \times M$.

Watermark embedding scheme is described as follows:

- 1. Convert $\mathbf{H}$ into 1-Dimensional watermark sequence $\mathbf{W}$ by line-based scan, $\mathbf{W} = \{w(i), 0 \leq i < M^2\}$. Scramble $\mathbf{W}$ using the chaotic sequence produced by logistic equation. Meanwhile, chaos system can provide many secret keys by its sensitive dependence on initial values and parameters.
- 2. Partition the host image into blocks which contain of 8×8 pixels without any overlap. Use DCT to transform each block.
- 3. Generate two sets of random sequence $\mathbf{K_1}$, $\mathbf{K_2}$, followed Gaussian distribution with little correlation, $-1 < K_1(i) < 1, -1 < K_2(i) < 1; \ i = 1, 2, 3, 4$.
- 4. Embed the sequence into the medium-coefficients of the sub-blocks' DCT domain with Zigzag scan order. If $w(i) = 1$, $\mathbf{K_1}$ is embedded, otherwise, $\mathbf{K_2}$ is embedded.

Extraction Algorithm

Information extraction is the reverse process of information embedding. First of all, we use the discrete cosine transform algorithm to extract embedded information from the host image, and calculate the correlations with K1 and K2. Next, we obtain a one-dimensional binary sequence by paired comparison. Then, get binary hologram from the sequence, and the key will be in reverse order. Finally the hidden image can be reconstructed from the decrypted hologram by optical or digital Fourier transform.

4   Comparative Simulation Experiments

Watermark Embedding and Extraction Verification

Take the iterative binary hologram mentioned above as watermark to be embedded. As shown in Fig, 6, Fig. 6(a) is selected as the host image with size of 512×512 pixels. Fig. 6(c) is the binary hologram. Fig. 6(b) is the embedded image, and the hologram extracted is shown in Fig. 6(d). Fig. 6(e) shows two symmetrical images appear at the reconstruction plane.

Experiments Compared with the Traditional Method[13]

To verify robustness of the algorithm in this letter, we make experiments comparing with the binary algorithm of traditional interference hologram in the case of same embedding intensity. In order to eliminate observer's experience, environmental conditions and other factors, we evaluate the influence of embedding algorithm upon host image with the peak signal-to-noise ratio (PSNR). Normalized cross correlation (NC) is

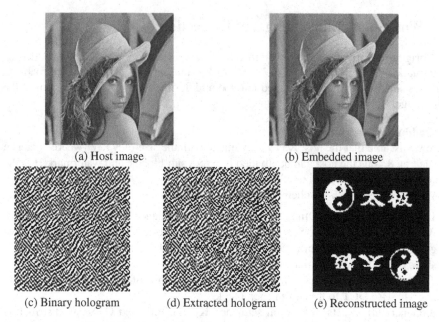

(a) Host image   (b) Embedded image

(c) Binary hologram   (d) Extracted hologram   (e) Reconstructed image

Fig. 6. Simulation of watermark embedding and extraction

Comparison Experiment by JPEG Compression

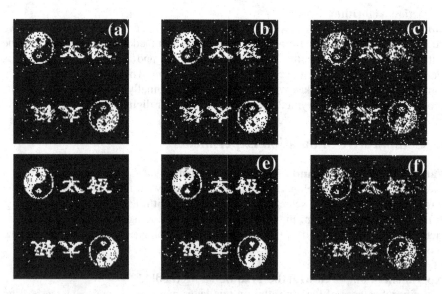

Fig. 7. Compare by JPEG compression with compression quality 80, 70 and 60. (a)~(c) Results by traditional method, (d)~(f) Results by proposed method.

used to make an objective assessment of the similarity between the extracted information and original information.

Fig. 7 shows results of JPEG compression experiment with compression quality 80, 70 and 60. The first row shows the results by the traditional interference binary holographic method and the next row shows the reconstructed images by proposed method. Tab. 1 summarizes the PSNR comparison of the host images and the NC coefficients of the extracted original information under the different JPEG compression quality, the NC coefficients of the extracted original information in the proposed method are all higher than that in traditional method. Both Fig. 7 and Tab. 1 show that the robustness of the proposed method compared with traditional method has been significantly improved.

Table 1. PSNR and NC comparison under different JPEG compression quality

	Traditional method		Proposed method	
Compress	PSNR/dB	NC/%	PSNR/dB	NC/%
80	38.16	91.33	38.17	96.19
70	36.54	86.31	36.52	93.00
60	35.36	68.98	35.40	83.09

Comparison Experiment by Cropping

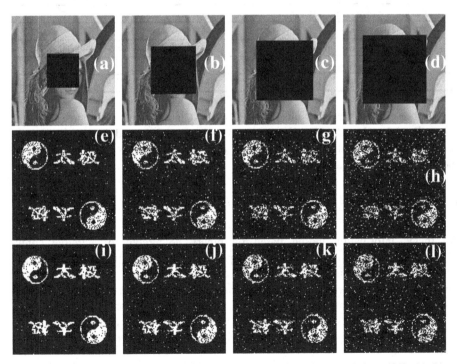

Fig. 8. Compare by cropping. (a) ~ (d) Embedded images cut out 10% to 40%, (e)-(h) Results by traditional method, (i) ~ (l) Results by proposed method.

As shown in the first row of Fig.8, the host images containing watermark are cut out 10% to 40%. The middle row shows the results of traditional method and the third row is the results by proposed algorithm. NC coefficients are shown in Tab. 2. Obviously, the robustness of the proposed method is much higher than the traditional algorithm.

Table 2. The robustness of cropping experiment

Crop / %	10	20	30	40
NC of the traditional method / %	93.05	82.87	76.87	65.09
NC of the proposed method / %	96.91	89.34	83.17	73.43

Comparison Experiment by other Attacks
The measurements of robustness to resist other attacks by traditional method and proposed method are shown in Tab. 3, respectively.

Table 3. The robustness to other attacks

Attack Type	NC of the traditional method / %	NC of the proposed method / %
Gaussian noise (sigma=0.02)	78.41	85.61
Salt and pepper noise (d=0.01)	64.25	74.61
Average filtering (3×3)	84.26	93.04
Median filtering (3×3)	80.45	90.06
Gaussian filtering (3×3, sigma=0.6)	96.07	98.89

All above experimental results show that the NC coefficients of proposed method are much higher than the traditional method in the case of embedding in same conditions. The proposed algorithm has greatly improved robustness than the traditional method of binary interference holograph.

5   Conclusion

An image information hiding based on binary holography of iterative conjugate-symmetric extension hologram is proposed in this paper. It achieves great improvement from the binary holograph of traditional interference method by iterating binary hologram between the spatial and transform domain. Binary hologram is embedded into the medium-frequency DCT coefficient of the host image. A large capacity of information can be embedded since the watermark is binary hologram. The technique has a good prospect in the digital image copyright protection and digital information hiding.

References

1. Petitcolas, F.A.P., Anderson, R.J., Kuhn, M.G.: Information hiding—a survey. Proceedings of IEEE 87(7), 1062–1078 (1999)
2. Cox, I.J., Miller, M.L.: The first 50 years of electronic watermarking. EURASIP J. of Applied Signal Processing 2, 126–132 (2002)
3. Javidi, B., Nomura, T.: Securing information by use of digital holography. Optics Letters 25(1), 28–30 (2000)
4. Kishk, S., Javidi, B.: Watermarking of three-dimensional objects by digital holography. Optics Letters 28(3), 167–169 (2003)
5. Seo, D.H., Kim, S.J.: Interferometric phase-only optical encryption system that uses a reference wave. Optics Letters 28(5), 304–306 (2003)
6. Okman, O.E., Akart, G.B.: Quantization index modulation-based image watermarking using digital holography. Opt. Soc. 24(1), 243–252 (2007)
7. Daqing, C., Jihua, G.: An image digital watermarking with phase retrieval algorithm and Fourier transformation hologram. Acta Optica Sinica 29(12), 3310–3316 (2009) (in Chinese)
8. Takai, N., Mifune, Y.: Digital watermarking by a holographic technique. Applied Optics 41(5), 865–873 (2002)
9. Chang, H., Tsian, T.: Image watermarking by use of digital holography embedded in the DCT domain. Applied Optics 44(29), 6211–6219 (2005)
10. Chiliang, Y., Jihua, G., et al.: An image digital watermark technique based on digital holography and discrete cosine transform. Acta Optica Sinica 26, 355–361 (2006) (in Chinese)
11. Huang, S., Wang, S., et al.: Digital watermark technology based on conjugate symmetric extension algorithm. Acta Physica Sinica 58(2), 952–958 (2009) (in Chinese)
12. Wang, S., Huang, S., et al.: Hologram-based watermarking capable of surviving print-scan process. Applied Optics 49(7), 1170–1178 (2010)
13. Guoming, L., Xianglin, L.: Holographic watermarking scheme based on DFT domain embedding. Computer Systems & Applications 20(5), 42–46 (2011) (in Chinese)

High Capacity Data Hiding for Halftone Image Authentication

Meng Guo and Hongbin Zhang

Computer Institute,
Beijing University of Technology, Beijing 100124, China
guome@126.com, zhb@public.bta.net.cn

Abstract. In an earlier paper [1], we propose a high capacity data hiding scheme for various types of binary images. The scheme ensures that in an M×N image block, the upper bound of the amount of bits that can be embedded is $\lfloor n\log_2((M{\times}N)/n + 1)\rfloor$ by changing at most n individual pixels. However, changing individual pixels in halftone images will introduce undesirable 'salt-and-pepper' noise, or local black or white clusters. In this paper, we propose a new scheme for halftone images which improves [1] in its capability to maintain better quality of the host image after data hiding by changing pixels in pairs rather than individually. The new scheme can still offer a high embedding efficiency. Experimental results show that the new scheme can maintain better image quality.

1 Introduction

Digital halftoning [2] is a technique to change multi-tone images into two-tone images, which look like the original multi-tone images when viewed from a distance. There are two main kinds of halftoning techniques, namely ordered dithering [2] and error diffusion [3]. Ordered dithering is computationally simple. It compares the pixel intensities with some pseudo-random threshold patterns or screens in order to determine its two-tone output. Error diffusion is more sophisticated with higher visual quality than ordered dithering.

Halftone images are very common in our daily lives and they are widely used in printing process, such as printing of books, magazines, newspapers and in computer printers. Since the halftoning is normally employed for image printing, it is desirable to hiding data into the halftone images for authentication and copyright control purposes. Most prior works on image data hiding focus on color and grayscale images in which the pixels take on a wide range of values, slightly changing the color of a small amount of pixels causes no perception by human eyes. But for halftone images, hiding data is more difficult. The halftone image pixels take on only two values, typically 0 and 1, resulting in lots of high-frequency noise and little intensity redundancy. Most existing watermarking schemes could not be applied to halftone images directly.

However, there are still a few existing techniques for data hiding in halftone images. Generally speaking, hiding data in halftone images can be divided into two classes. The first class of approaches is to hide data during the halftoning process [4][5][6]. Such methods can embed a fairly large amount of hidden information with

Y.Q. Shi, H.J. Kim, and F. Pérez-González (Eds.): IWDW 2012, LNCS 7809, pp. 156–168, 2013.

negligible visual distortion in halftone images. However, the original multi-tone images must be available before these methods can be applied. The second class of approaches is to hide data directly into the halftone image without involving the original multi-tone images [7][8]. Fu and Au proposed a series of methods that change the value of pseudo-randomly selected pixels in the halftone image with a combination of individual toggle or two complementary toggles [7][8]. The detector uses the same random number generator seed to create the sequence of pixels, which carry the message, and then it simply reads the values of those pixels. However, the embedding efficiency of these methods is rather low. In an earlier paper [1], we proposed a high embedding efficiency data hiding scheme for binary images by changing some individual pixels. Specifically, given an $M \times N$ image block, the scheme can embed as many as $\lfloor n\log_2((M \times N)/n + 1)\rfloor$ bits of data in block by changing at most n pixels. But for halftone images, changing individual pixels will introduce undesirable visual distortion, which appears as 'salt-and-pepper' noise, or local black or white clusters.

In this paper, we propose a new data hiding scheme without involving the original multi-tone image which improves [1] in terms of the visibility of the hiding effect by changing pixels in pairs rather than individually. The data hiding scheme proposed in this paper can be used for applications of fragile embedding such as authentication. The goal of image authentication is to verify that an image has not been altered since it left a trusted party. The major advantages of the proposed scheme lie in its larger capacity and better visual quality, which guarantee the authentication mark can be embedded in rather small halftone images.

The rest of this paper is organized as follows. Section 2 reviews out earlier scheme [1]. The revised new scheme is presented in Section 3. Experimental results are in Section 4, followed by a conclusion in Section 5.

2   A Review

Below, we review the data hiding scheme proposed in [1]. Through the review, we will point out the image quality problem for halftone images associated with it. This will motivate the work in this paper.

First, we introduce the definitions of some terms.

Definition 1. The set of all nonempty subsets of $\{1,2,\cdots,r\}$, is called the **complete set**, denoted by A_r, for example, if $r = 3$, $A_r = \{\{1\}, \{2\}, \{3\}, \{1,2\}, \{1,3\}, \{2,3\}, \{1,2,3\}\}$.

Definition 2. The **symmetric difference** of sets A and B, denoted by $A\Delta B$, is the set of elements which are in one of the sets, but not in both, for example, $\{1,2,3\} \Delta \{3,4\} = \{1,2,4\}$.

Definition 3. If any element of set A is a set, the **closure** of the set A, denoted by A^+, is a set that satisfies the following: $\forall a \in A^+$, $\exists b, c \in A \Rightarrow a \in A$ or $a = b\Delta c$. $(A^+)^n$ can be defined recursively as follows: $(A^+)^0 = A$; for all natural number n, $(A^+)^n = ((A^+)^{n-1})^+$.

Definition 4. If $(B^+)^n = A_r$, B is called the **n-th generating** set of complete set A_r, for example, for $r = 4$, $B = \{\{1\}, \{2\}, \{3\}, \{4\}, \{1,2,3,4\}\}$, it is not hard to verify that $(B^+)^1 = A_4$.

To facilitate discussion, we denote the n-th generating set of A_r as $G(n, r)$. Let $S(i, j)$ be set $\{i, i+1, i+2, \ldots, j-1, j\}$ and $A(i, j)$ denotes the set of all nonempty subsets of $S(i, j)$. The algorithm of generation of $G(n, r)$ is given as follows.

Algorithm 1.
Input: n, r
begin initialize $G(n, r) \leftarrow \{\}$, $index_1=0$, $index_2=0$, $r_1= r$
    for $i = 0$ **to** n **do**
    begin
            $index_1 = index_2+1$, $index_2 = index_2 + \lfloor r_1 / (n +1 - i) \rfloor$
            $G(n, r) = G(n, r) \cup A(index_1, index_2)$
            $r_1= r_1 - \lfloor r_1 / (n + 1 - i) \rfloor$
    end
    return $G(n, r)$
end

For example, $G(0,3) = \{\{1\}, \{2\}, \{3\}, \{1,2\}, \{1,3\}, \{2,3\}, \{1,2,3\}\}$; $G(1,4) = \{\{1\},\{2\},\{1,2\},\{3\},\{4\},\{3,4\}\}$

Definition 5. If B is the n-th generating set of A_r. A matrix I can serve as a **Grouping Index Matrix (GIM)**, if each element of B appears at least once in I.

The data embedding is described in Algorithm 2 in detail.

Algorithm 2.
The inputs to our scheme are as follows.
1) F is a host binary image block of size $M \times N$.
2) K is a random binary matrix of size $M \times N$. It is a secret key shared by the sender and the receiver.
3) I is a Grouping Index Matrix of size $M \times N$.
4) $s_1 s_2 \cdots s_r, s_i \in \{0,1\}$ is critical information consisting of r bits to be embedded in F.

The embedding process consists of five steps.
1) Compute $F \oplus K$, "$\oplus$" denotes the "Exclusive OR (XOR)" operation.
2) For each $i = 1,2 \cdots r$, compute the following set:

$$S_i = \left\{ (j,k) \middle| i \in I_{j,k} \right\} i = 1,2,\ldots,r.$$

3) For each $i = 1,2 \cdots r$, compute

$$Group_i = \left(\sum_{(j,k) \in S_i} [F \oplus K]_{j,k} \right) \bmod 2$$

4) For each $i = 1,2 \cdots r$, compute

$$Index_i = Group_i \oplus s_i, i = 1,2 \cdots r.$$

5) For each $i = 1,2 \cdots r$, compute $S = \{i | Index_i = 1\}$.

a) If $S = \Phi$, F does not need to be changed.

b) If $S \neq \Phi$, then there exist $a_1, a_2 \cdots, a_k$ in I, which satisfy $S = a_1 \Delta a_2 \Delta \cdots \Delta a_k$.
Find the positions of these elements, and flip the corresponding pixels in F.

Grouping Index Matrix I defined in Definition 5 can be used to construct a data hiding scheme capable of embedding r bits using at most $n + 1$ changes. If the generating set is generated by **Algorithm 1**, the upper bound of the capacity by changing at most n pixels in an $M \times N$ image block is $\lfloor n \log_2 ((M \times N)/n + 1) \rfloor$.

The above scheme can embed a large amount of data by small number of individual pixels changes. However, for halftone images, changing individual pixels will inevitably introduce undesirable visual distortion, which appears as 'salt-and-pepper' noise, or local black or white clusters as shown in Fig 1. This motivates the work in this paper.

Fig. 1. 'Salt-and-pepper' noise due to changing some individual pixels

3   Proposed Method

One problem of the earlier scheme is that it tends to have 'salt-and-pepper' noise by individual changes. To improve the visual quality, we propose a revised version for halftone images by changing pixels in pairs rather than individually.

Consider the example in Fig. 2. The center pixel called master pixel in Fig. 2(a) needs to be changed. Fig. 2(b) shows the effect after changing the center pixel individually. Fig. 2(b) gives poor visual quality due to creating the large 4-connected regions, which appears as 'salt-and-pepper' noise. This problem can be alleviated by flipping a neighbor pixel called slave pixel simultaneously as shown in Fig. 2(c).

To revise the earlier scheme by changing pixels in pairs, we should solve the following problems. (1) How to find the 'best' pairing pixels that minimizes the visual distortion. (2) How to ensure the extracted hidden information correctly by changing pairing pixels instead of individual pixels.

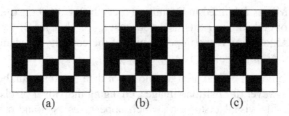

(a)   (b)   (c)

Fig. 2. Visual quality comparison between changing individual pixels and pairing pixels. (a) Original image block. (b) Image block with changing individual pixels. (c) Image block with changing pair pixels.

For binary pattern, the distance between two pixels plays a major role in their mutual interference perceived by human eyes. The nearer the two pixels are, the moresensitive it is to change one pixel when focusing on the other. Hence, diagonal neighbors have less effect on a center pixel in focus than horizontal or vertical neighbors. Based on these observations, we define the flippability of the pixels for halftone image. Let B is a 3×3 binary image block and the value of center pixel is B_c, $1 \le i, j \le 3$, the flippability of the center pixel is defined as

$$flip = \sum_{i, j} \left[\left| B(i, j) - B_c \right| \times W(i, j) \right] \tag{1}$$

where W is defined as follows:

$$W(i, j) = \begin{cases} 0 & \text{for } i=2 \text{ and } j=2 \\ \dfrac{1}{\sqrt{(i - 2)^2 + (j - 2)^2}}, & \text{otherwise.} \end{cases} \tag{2}$$

The flip is a measure of visual distortion caused by flipping a pixel in halftone images. The smaller flip is, the fewer 'salt-and-pepper' clusters effect caused by flipping the corresponding pixel is. In the earlier scheme [1], there exist some "redundancies" in Grouping Index Matrix. It means that there may have more than one choices of embedding changes for one piece of hidden information. Thus, we can choose the pixel with the minimum flip among the candidates as the master pixel to flip. After flipping the master pixel, it is necessary to change one of its neighbors to improve the visual quality. The candidates of the slave pixel are the neighbors with a different tone from the master pixel. The 'best' neighbor (the slave pixel) with minimum flip is chosen to change.

However, changing the slave pixels will corrupt the hidden information. Therefore, we redefine the Grouping Index Matrix (GIM) to overcome this by sacrificing some data hiding space.

Let a matrix $I_{halftone}$ of size $M×N$, $1 \le m \le M / 2$, $1 \le n \le N / 2$. The redefined GIM Ihalftone should satisfy the followings:

1. For all m and n, $I_{halftone}(2m-1, 2n) = \Phi$ and $I_{halftone}(2m, 2n-1) = \Phi$.
2. Each element of generating set appears at least once in the rest locations of $I_{halftone}$.

Actually, Grouping Index Matrix I_{halftone} can be designed to other forms. However, the above design can without sacrifice the embedding capacity a lot. Fig. 3 is an example of I_{halftone}. Φ means that the corresponding pixels do not belong to any group, that is to say, flipping the corresponding pixels will not affect the hidden information. In I_{halftone}, each corresponding master pixel in non-boundary regions has 4 candidate slave pixels. In this case, half of image pixels are used to embed data. However, the upper bound of the capacity does not decrease a lot. If the generating set is generated by Algorithm 1, the upper bound of the capacity by changing at most n master pixels in an $M \times N$ image block is $\lfloor n \log_2 ((M \times N) / 2n + 1) \rfloor$.

$$I_{halftone} = \begin{bmatrix} \{1\} & \Phi & \{2\} & \Phi & \{3\} & \Phi & \{1,2\} & \Phi \\ \Phi & \{1,3\} & \Phi & \{2,3\} & \Phi & \{1,2,3\} & \Phi & \{1\} \\ \{2\} & \Phi & \{3\} & \Phi & \{1,2\} & \Phi & \{1,3\} & \Phi \\ \Phi & \{2,3\} & \Phi & \{1,2,3\} & \Phi & \{1\} & \Phi & \{2\} \\ \{3\} & \Phi & \{1,2\} & \Phi & \{1,3\} & \Phi & \{2,3\} & \Phi \\ \Phi & \{1,2,3\} & \Phi & \{1\} & \Phi & \{2\} & \Phi & \{3\} \\ \{1,2\} & \Phi & \{1,3\} & \Phi & \{2,3\} & \Phi & \{1,2,3\} & \Phi \\ \Phi & \{1\} & \Phi & \{2\} & \Phi & \{3\} & \Phi & \{1,2\} \end{bmatrix}$$

Fig. 3. An example of GIM $I_{halftone}$, $I_{halftone}$ can be used to construct a data hiding scheme capable of embedding 3 bits using at most 1 master pixel change

4   Experimental Results

4.1   Objective Visual Quality Measures

Objective distortion measures such as Mean Squared Error (MSE), Peak Signal-to-Noise Ratio (PSNR), and Structural Similarity Index Measure (SSIM) not match well with the subjective assessment for halftone images. However, some objective distortion measures for halftone image have been defined in [8]. In this paper, we use the similar criteria to evaluate visual quality of our algorithms.

The distortion due to the proposed algorithm appears mainly in the form of "salt-and-pepper" artifacts due to local clusters of pixels. Large clusters are visually more disturbing than small ones. Thus a good way to measure visual quality is to measure the amount and the size of the "salt-and-pepper" clusters.   Let A be the locations of the master pixels which are modified by the algorithms. In [8], the authors defined the following five scores:

$$S_1 = \sum_{i=0}^{4} N_i, \quad S_2 = \sum_{i=0}^{4} (i+1)N_i, \quad S_3 = \frac{S_2}{S_1},$$

$$S_4 = \sum_{i=2}^{4} N_i, \quad S_5 = \sum_{i=0}^{4} iN_i = S_2 - S_1,$$

where N_i is the total number of elements in A having i neighbors with same pixel values in the 4-neighborhood after data hiding is performed. The N_0 corresponds to the number of visually pleasing isolated elements in A. The S_1 gives the total number of elements of A. The S_2 gives the total area covered by the clusters of A. The S_3 gives the average area per cluster. The S_4 is the number of elements of A associated with clusters of size 3 or more, which is useful because clusters of size 1 or 2 are not very visually disturbing. The S_5 is a perceptual measure with a linear penalty model. It gives a zero penalty score to isolated black or white pixels which look visually pleasing. It gives scores of 1, 2, 3 and 4 for clusters of size 2, 3, 4 and 5, respectively. In general, algorithms with smaller scores of S_1, S_2, S_3, S_4 and S_5 are better.

4.2   Results and Discussions

The proposed scheme is tested with several images. Due to limited space, this section only shows the results of three 256×256 test images: 'Lena', 'Peppers' and 'Trees'. These three images are halftoned by error diffusion using the Steinberg kernel and by ordered dithering using the '8×8 dispersed dot' screen. The new proposed scheme is compared with our earlier scheme [1] and DHSPT-CS4 [7]. To test the scheme under stress, 4096 bits of data are embedded in the original halftone images. The 4096 bits are a relatively large amount of data to be embedded. The scores (S_1 to S_5) of the algorithms are shown in Tables 1-6. Due to limited space, the corresponding selected images of 'Lena' and 'Peppers' are shown in Figs. 4-7. In Tables 7-10, we also compared the algorithms for different amount of embedded data.

According to Table 1, there are 890 (S_1) master pixels changes in our new proposed scheme. These clusters occupy a total area (S_2) of 1955 pixels. On the average, each cluster contains 2.197 pixels (S_3). Only 340 (S_4) out of the 890 'salt-and-pepper' clusters are of size 3 or larger which are visually disturbing. The S_5 is 1065. Although S_1 is larger than our earlier scheme, the S_2, S_3, S_4, S_5 are smaller than our earlier scheme and DHSPT-CS4. The corresponding images are shown in Fig. 4. In general, the new proposed scheme can improve the visual quality of the existing algorithms without reducing the embedding capacity, the visual quality refers to both subjective visual quality and objective scores S_1-S_5.

Table 1. Scores (S_1 to S_5) of various algorithms for error diffusion 'Lena'

	S_1	S_2	S_3	S_4	S_5
Proposed Scheme	890	**1955**	**2.197**	**340**	**1065**
Earlier Scheme	**639**	2163	3.385	477	1524
DHSPT-CS4	2063	4721	2.288	839	2658

Table 2. Scores (S_1 to S_5) of various algorithms for ordered dithering 'Lena'

	S_1	S_2	S_3	S_4	S_5
Proposed Scheme	886	**2239**	**2.527**	**481**	**1353**
Earlier Scheme	**632**	2421	3.831	509	1789
DHSPT-CS4	2084	5556	2.666	1211	3472

Table 3. Scores (S_1 to S_5) of various algorithms for error diffusion 'Peppers'

	S_1	S_2	S_3	S_4	S_5
Proposed Scheme	876	**1861**	**2.124**	**299**	**985**
Earlier Scheme	**641**	2082	3.248	452	1441
DHSPT-CS4	2003	4353	2.173	715	2350

Table 4. Scores (S_1 to S_5) of various algorithms for ordered dithering 'Peppers'

	S_1	S_2	S_3	S_4	S_5
Proposed Scheme	879	**2107**	2.397	**412**	**1228**
Earlier Scheme	**642**	2266	3.530	471	1624
DHSPT-CS4	2106	5039	**2.393**	992	2933

Table 5. Scores (S_1 to S_5) of various algorithms for error diffusion 'Trees'

	S_1	S_2	S_3	S_4	S_5
Proposed Scheme	878	**1483**	**1.689**	**158**	**605**
Earlier Scheme	**636**	1841	2.895	323	1205
DHSPT-CS4	2070	3656	1.766	452	1586

Table 6. Scores (S_1 to S_5) of various algorithms for ordered dithering 'Trees'

	S_1	S_2	S_3	S_4	S_5
Proposed Scheme	868	**1691**	**1.948**	**253**	**823**
Earlier Scheme	**634**	1944	3.066	382	1310
DHSPT-CS4	2042	4136	2.026	663	2094

Table 7. Scores of various algorithms for embedding 256 bits in error diffusion 'Lena'

	S_1	S_2	S_3	S_4	S_5
Proposed Scheme	40	**46**	**1.150**	**1**	**6**
Earlier Scheme	**32**	92	2.875	18	60
DHSPT-CS4	135	159	1.178	3	24

Table 8. Scores of various algorithms for embedding 512 bits in error diffusion 'Lena'

	S_1	S_2	S_3	S_4	S_5
Proposed Scheme	**79**	**107**	1.354	6	**28**
Earlier Scheme	81	220	2.716	37	139
DHSPT-CS4	265	384	1.449	29	119

Table 9. Scores of various algorithms for embedding 1024 bits in error diffusion 'Lena'

	S_1	S_2	S_3	S_4	S_5
Proposed Scheme	193	**281**	**1.456**	**17**	**88**
Earlier Scheme	**160**	459	2.869	86	299
DHSPT-CS4	489	1011	2.068	167	522

(a)

(b)

(c)

(d)

Fig. 4. (a) is the original Lena halftone image (error diffusion). (b) is the watermarked images with 4096 bits embedded by the proposed scheme. (c) is the watermarked images with 4096 bits embedded by our earlier scheme[1]. (d) is the watermarked images with 4096 bits embedded by DHSPT-CS4[7].

Table 10. Scores of various algorithms for embedding 2048 bits in error diffusion 'Lena'

	S_1	S_2	S_3	S_4	S_5
Proposed Scheme	384	**765**	**1.992**	**111**	**381**
Earlier Scheme	**316**	980	3.101	196	664
DHSPT-CS4	1049	2292	2.185	395	1243

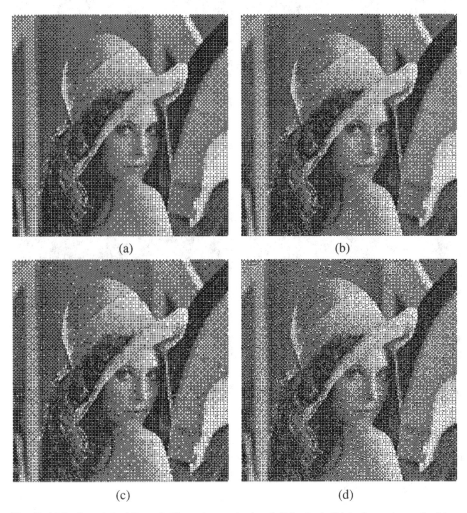

(a)

(b)

(c)

(d)

Fig. 5. (a) is the original Lena halftone image (ordered dithering). (b) is the watermarked images with 4096 bits embedded by the proposed scheme. (c) is the watermarked images with 4096 bits embedded by our earlier scheme[1]. (d) is the watermarked images with 4096 bits embedded by DHSPT-CS4[7].

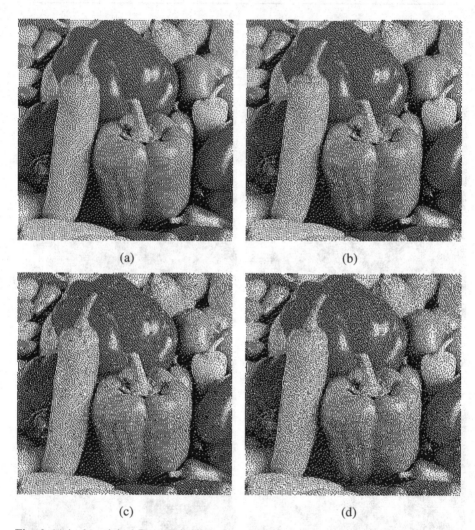

(a)   (b)

(c)   (d)

Fig. 6. (a) is the original Peppers halftone image (ordered dithering). (b) is the watermarked images with 4096 bits embedded by the proposed scheme. (c) is the watermarked images with 4096 bits embedded by our earlier scheme[1]. (d) is the watermarked images with 4096 bits embedded by DHSPT-CS4[7].

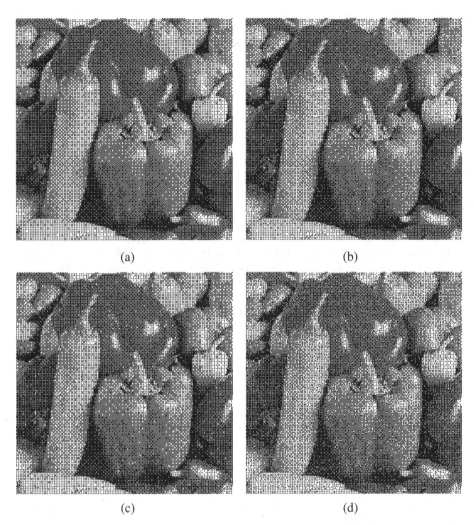

Fig. 7. (a) is the original Peppers halftone image (error diffusion). (b) is the watermarked images with 4096 bits embedded by the proposed scheme. (c) is the watermarked images with 4096 bits embedded by our earlier scheme[1]. (d) is the watermarked images with 4096 bits embedded by DHSPT-CS4[7].

5   Conclusion

In this paper, we proposed a new data hiding scheme for halftone images based on our earlier scheme [1]. The new proposed scheme can embed fairly large amount of data in halftone images without knowledge of the original multi-tone image and the half-toning method. Specifically, given an $M \times N$ image block, the scheme can embed as many as $\lfloor n \log_2((M \times N) / 2n + 1) \rfloor$ bits of data in the block by changing at most n master pixel(s) in that block. The major advantages of the proposed scheme lie in its larger capacity and better visual quality, which guarantee the authentication mark can be embedded in rather small halftone images.

Acknowledgment. This work was supported in part by the National Natural Science Foundation of China under grant 60775011.

References

1. Guo, M., Zhang, H.: High capacity data hiding for binary imageauthentication. In: Proc. Int. Conf. Pattern Recognition, pp. 441–1444 (2010)
2. Ulichney, R.: Digital Halftoning. MIT Press, Cambridge (1987)
3. Floyd, R.W., Steinberg, L.: An adaptive algorithm for spatial grayscale. In: Proc. SID 75 Dig.: Soc. Inf. Display, pp. 36–37 (1975)
4. Pei, S.C., Guo, J.M.: High-capacity data hiding in halftone imagesusing minimal-error bit searching and least-mean square filter. IEEETrans. Image Process. 15(6), 1665–1679 (2006)
5. Guo, J.M., Liu, Y.: Halftone-Image Security Improving Using Overall Minimal-Error Searching. IEEE Trans. Image Process. 20(10), 2800–2812 (2011)
6. Lien, B.K., Pei, W.D.: Reversible data hiding for ordered ditheredhalftone images. In: Proc. Int. Conf. Image Processing, pp. 4237–4240 (2009)
7. Fu, M.S., Au, O.C.: Data hiding watermarking for halftone images. IEEE Trans. Image Process. 11(4), 477–484 (2002)
8. Fu, M.S., Au, O.C.: Halftone image data hiding with intensity selection and connection selection. In: Sig. Proc.: Image Comm., pp. 909–930 (2001)

Coded Spread Spectrum Watermarking Scheme

Minoru Kuribayashi

Graduate School of Engineering, Kobe University
1-1 Rokkodai-cho, Nada-ku, Kobe, Hyogo, 657-8501 Japan
kminoru@kobe-u.ac.jp

Abstract. In conventional spread spectrum watermarking schemes, random sequences are used for the modulation of watermark information. However, because of the mutual interference among those sequences, it requires complicated removal operation to improve the performance. In this paper, we propose an efficient spread spectrum watermarking scheme by introducing the CDMA technique at the modulation of watermark information. In order to control the energy assigned to spread spectrum sequences, we propose a coded method that encodes watermark information into a constant weight codeword. If the weight and its code-length are properly selected, the performance of the method could outperform the conventional methods.

1 Introduction

Watermark embedding techniques can be roughly categorized into two classes: Quantization index modulation (QIM)-based approaches [1] which quantizes samples of host signal, and spread spectrum (SS)-based approaches where the watermark signal is added to many samples. The SS method, originally proposed by Cox et al. [3], is probably the most popular approach for data hiding, which spreads one watermark bit over the host signal.

1.1 Background

In the framework of SS method presented by Cox et al. [3] a SS sequence is embedded into frequency components of a digital image. Due to the high robustness against attacks and low embedding distortion, many researches have been investigated the SS method and its variants. At the detection, we calculate a correlation between the signal extracted from a copy and the original SS sequence. If the correlation score exceeds a certain threshold, we regard that the sequence is embedded in the copy. This kind of watermarking scheme is sometimes called "informed" watermarking.

The informed watermarking suffers from inherent host-interference under a blind extraction of the embedded signal. The detector can be formulated as a statistical decision problem [6], and its performance depends on the modeling of the host signals. For example, DCT coefficients are modeled as the generalized Gaussian [5][2], and DWT coefficients are modeled as the Laplacian [12].

Y.Q. Shi, H.J. Kim, and F. Pérez-González (Eds.): IWDW 2012, LNCS 7809, pp. 169–183, 2013.

Based on the statistical modeling of the host-interference, an optimal detector can be designed to maximize the performance. From the different point of view, Malvar and Florêncio [9] proposed an efficient method, called Improved Spread Spectrum (ISS) scheme, to minimize the host-interference by removing it at the embedding stage. Since the host-interference does not always degrade the watermark robustness as discovered in [7], the positive effect of the host-interference on the watermark detection is utilized to minimize the amount of degradation caused by the removal operation in [15].

In the conventional schemes, the SS sequences modulating watermark information are basically random sequences which are generated using a secret key. The main reason is to increase the secrecy of the watermark embedded into digital contents. Because of the randomness as reported in [11][10], however, it is difficult to effectively and efficiently remove the mutual interference among such random sequences, and its complexity increases with the number of those sequences, namely the amount of watermark information. Although an optimum detector can be obtained by considering the posterior probability under the condition of the Gaussian assumption for noise and attacks, it is NP-hard. Therefore, a sub-optimum detector has been proposed in [14] to compromise the performance.

1.2   Our Contribution

We introduce the idea of CDMA technique into the modulation of watermark information, and propose an efficient method to generate good SS sequences using orthogonal vectors and pseudo-random numbers. In order to reduce the computational complexity, we employ DCT basic vectors for the orthogonal vectors. The vectors are first modulated by the PN sequence such as M-sequence and Gold-sequence [4] specified by a secret key, and then, they are permuted randomly to increase the secrecy. Considering that SS sequences are embedded into those elements selected randomly from frequency components of a host data, it is noticed that the permutation of the sequence is performed by itself at this stage.

For the extension to the multibit embedding, it is generally required to consider the interference among SS sequences in the conventional scheme. However, the proposed SS sequences are basically orthogonal with each other, and hence, there is no interference in the correlation scores calculated from a watermarked data. At the detection, it is possible to calculate correlation scores at a time by performing DCT operation to the sequence extracted from the watermarked data. Furthermore, by performing a fast DCT algorithm, the computational costs are dropped in a logarithmic order.

We further propose an encoding method to the watermark information. Generally, each bit of the information is modulated by each SS sequence. In this case, the amount of energy assigned to each sequence is linearly decreased with the number of bits under a constant degradation level. In the proposed method, the watermark information is encoded into a constant weight binary codeword before embedding, and those sequences corresponding to the non-zero bits in the codeword are embedded as the watermark signal. The amount of energy assigned to each non-zero bit in the proposed method is inversely proportional to the number of the non-zero bits. Because the number of non-zero bits is much smaller than that of original bits, we can assign more energy to each sequence embedded as a watermark. Thus, the robustness against attacks of the proposed method could be higher than that of the conventional method. The relation between the energy assigned to each SS sequence is theoretically analyzed in this paper. Furthermore, some parameters required for the extension to the ISS method are investigated under the condition that the total distortion caused by the embedding operation is equal.

2   Spread Spectrum Watermarking

In this section, we review the basic operation of a conventional SS method and its improved version. Then, the extension to multibit embedding method is explained.

2.1   Basic Method

The SS watermarking method assumes that one bit of information is embedded in a vector with a length L. Let $\boldsymbol{x}$ be the vector of a host data, and $\boldsymbol{p}$ be a SS sequence. Then, the embedding operation is formulated as follows:

$$\boldsymbol{y} = \boldsymbol{x} + \alpha w \boldsymbol{p}, \tag{1}$$

where α is an embedding strength and $w \in \{\pm 1\}$ is the embedded bit. When a watermark is embedded in a frequency domain, the vector $\boldsymbol{x}$ could be selected from the coefficients of wavelet transform, DCT or DFT, etc. Assuming attacks to a watermarked data, the vector $\boldsymbol{y}$ is distorted by additive noise $\boldsymbol{e}$; namely $\boldsymbol{y}' = \boldsymbol{y} + \boldsymbol{e}$.

In a blind detection scenario, we first calculate the correlation score s:

$$s = \frac{\langle \boldsymbol{y}', \boldsymbol{p} \rangle}{\langle \boldsymbol{p}, \boldsymbol{p} \rangle}, \tag{2}$$

where $\langle \boldsymbol{a}, \boldsymbol{b} \rangle$ stands for the inner product of vectors $\boldsymbol{a}$ and $\boldsymbol{b}$. The embedded bit is then recovered by using the decision rule

$$w' = \text{sign}(s) = \begin{cases} 1 & \text{if } s > 0 \\ -1 & \text{otherwise} \end{cases}. \tag{3}$$

The main interference term involved in s is coming from $\boldsymbol{x}$ in this scenario, which is represented by h:

$$h = \frac{\langle \boldsymbol{x}, \boldsymbol{p} \rangle}{\langle \boldsymbol{p}, \boldsymbol{p} \rangle}. \tag{4}$$

Improved Spread Spectrum (ISS) [9] is one of the methods that reduce h at the embedding stage. It consists of precanceling the interference by the following operation:

$$y = x + (\alpha w - \lambda h)p \tag{5}$$

where λ controls the amount of interference reduced in this operation. If $\text{sign}(h) = \text{sign}(w)$, the host-interference plays a positive effect on the detection [15]. Therefore, it is better to set $\lambda = 0$ if $\text{sign}(h) = \text{sign}(w)$; otherwise, $\lambda > 0$.

2.2   Multibit Embedding

The basic method can be extended to convey more bits of information. Let w be the multibit message vector composed by k antipodal bits $w_t, 0 \le t \le k - 1$. Using k SS sequences p_t, the vector w is embedded as follows:

$$y = x + \alpha \sum_{t=0}^{k-1} w_t p_t. \tag{6}$$

From the code division multiplexing point of view, the sequences p_t should be orthogonal to each other. In the conventional schemes, however, the sequences are not strictly orthogonal. Because the number of orthogonal sequences is much smaller than that of random sequences, it has been supposed better to use the latter ones in order to prevent unauthorized modification by attackers. For example, a secret key is used by a pseudo random number generator to produce a SS sequence with zero mean.

Because of the non-orthogonality, it is required to reduce the interference among SS sequences as well as the host-interference in the multibit embedding scenario. As an expansion of ISS to the multibit embedding, these interference projected on each watermark sequence is canceled at the embedding stage by solving a group of linear equations (See [11][10]) by sacrificing the computational costs. In [14], step-by-step algorithms are presented as a sub-optimum solution that still requires a considerably high computational costs.

3   CDMA-Based Method

In a proposed method, we use orthogonal sequences produced from a secret key to modulate watermark information in a spread form. One simple way to produce orthogonal sequences from a secret key is to use pseudo random generator followed by the Gram-Schmidt algorithm. From the observation of the embedding process, it is noticed that a random permutation for basic orthogonal vectors is performed by itself because it is assumed that the host vector x is randomly sampled from a host data. Therefore, we focus on a method to produce good orthogonal sequences using a secret key.

The idea of proposed method comes from the method [8] which SS sequences are generated from the DCT basic vectors modulated by PN sequences. The main advantage is the low computational cost at the detector because the fast DCT algorithm can be applied for calculating the correlation scores. The procedures to generate such specific orthogonal sequences from watermark information and to calculate the correlation score are proposed in this section.

3.1 Spread Spectrum Sequence

There are several ways to embed a SS sequence into a digital content. From the studies of watermarking, it is advisable to utilize the frequency components for embedding because of the robustness against attacks. The frequency components are generally derived from an orthogonal transform such as DFT, DCT, DWT, and so on. Therefore, a vector x of a host data is assumed to be selected from the frequency components. Then, considering the secrecy, the selection rule should be governed by a secret key.

When a vector μ is embedded into a host vector x, the order of the elements in μ is automatically permuted at the inverse sampling operation that the watermarked vector y is placed in the randomly sampled frequency coefficients of a host data. By introducing a PN sequence such as M-sequence and Gold-sequence [4], the secrecy of the applied orthogonal sequences can be further enhanced. In addition, the host-interference as well as noise added to a watermarked data can be also spread over a detection sequence which is composed of correlation scores of k embedded bits.

The procedure to generate a SS sequence μ from watermark information $w = \{w_0, w_1, \ldots, w_{k-1}\}, w_t \in \{\pm 1\}$ is explained below. Let $d = \{d_0, d_1, \ldots, d_{L-1}\}$ be a sequence satisfying

$$d_t = \begin{cases} \beta w_t & \text{if } 0 \le t \le k-1 \\ 0 & \text{otherwise} \end{cases}, \tag{7}$$

where β is an embedding strength. A PN sequence $\rho = \{\rho_0, \rho_1, \ldots, \rho_{L-1}\}, \rho_t \in \{\pm 1\}$ is generated from a secret key. After performing inverse DCT to d, we obtain

$$\mu = \rho \otimes \text{IDCT}(d), \tag{8}$$

where $\otimes$ stands for an element-wise multiplication. Then, a watermarked data y is simply represented by $y = x + \mu$.

3.2 Correlation Score

At the detection, the correlation scores of k symbols w_t are calculated by a batch process in the proposed scheme. The inner products given in Eq.(2) can be substituted for the DCT operation.

$$d' = \text{DCT}(\rho \otimes y'), \tag{9}$$

where $d' = \{d'_0, d'_1, \ldots, d'_{L-1}\}$ is a detection vector. For $0 \le t \le k-1$, the embedded bit is recovered by using the decision rule $w'_t = \text{sign}(d'_t)$.

The validity of Eq.(9) is discussed from the theoretical point of view. In the proposed scheme, each bit w_t is modulated by the t-th DCT basic vector amplified by β. Even though a PN sequence is multiplied at the embedding, it is canceled at the detection as given in Eq.(9). The effect of the PN sequence is the spread of noise because of the following reason. Without the knowledge of the selection of frequency components and the applied PN sequence, an injected signal into a watermarked data is spread over the sequence d'. Let ϕ_t be a t-th DCT vector. Then, it is obvious that the inner product of a DCT vector is $\langle \phi_t, \phi_t \rangle = 1$. The DCT operation is represented by

$$(d')^T = \begin{bmatrix} \phi_0 \\ \phi_1 \\ \vdots \\ \phi_{L-1} \end{bmatrix} (\rho \otimes y')^T, \tag{10}$$

where T stands for the transposition. Therefore, the t-th element can be interpreted as the inner product:

$$d'_t = \frac{\langle \phi_t, \rho \otimes y' \rangle}{\langle \phi_t, \phi_t \rangle}. \tag{11}$$

Since $y' = x + \mu + e$, Eq.(11) can be rewritten by

$$d' = \langle \phi_t, \rho \otimes x \rangle + \langle \phi_t, \rho \otimes \rho \otimes \mathtt{IDCT}(d) \rangle + \langle \phi_t, \rho \otimes e \rangle \tag{12}$$
$$= h_t + \langle \phi_t, \mathtt{IDCT}(d) \rangle + e_t \tag{13}$$

where $h_t = \langle \phi_t, \rho \otimes x \rangle$ is the host-interference and $e_t = \langle \phi_t, \rho \otimes e \rangle$ is a noise term. Due to the multiplication of a PN sequence, the host-interference h_t is approximately modeled as additive white Gaussian noise. The second term implies the calculation of the t-th DCT coefficient, namely,

$$\langle \phi_t, \mathtt{IDCT}(d) \rangle = d_t. \tag{14}$$

As a consequence, the detection vector d' derived from Eq.(9) is just equal to the list of correlation scores of k embedded bits and the other unallocated elements. With the assistance of fast DCT algorithm, the computational cost to calculate the vector d' is reduced to a logarithmic scale.

3.3   Host-Interference Removal Operation

In order to extend the above scheme to ISS, we first calculate the host-interference vector $h = \{h_0, h_1, \ldots, h_{L-1}\}$,

$$h = \mathtt{DCT}(\rho \otimes x), \tag{15}$$

and then, produce a watermarked data as follows:

$$y = x + \mu - \rho \otimes \mathtt{IDCT}(\lambda \otimes h), \tag{16}$$

where $\boldsymbol{\lambda} = \{\lambda_0, \lambda_1, \ldots, \lambda_{L-1}\}$ is a control vector. As mentioned in Sect.2.1, these parameters should be $\lambda_t \geq 0$ for $0 \leq t \leq k - 1$ depending on the embedded bit w_t and the host-interference h_t. Note that we should set $\lambda_t = 0$ for $k \leq t \leq L-1$ because they never interfere the detection of k embedded bits.

The above ISS operation is to remove the host-interference term involved in a detection vector $\boldsymbol{d'}$ at the embedding stage. Therefore, it is possible to perform the ISS operation in the detection domain, namely, we calculate $\boldsymbol{d} - \boldsymbol{\lambda} \otimes \boldsymbol{h}$ before producing a SS sequence. Thus, Eq.(16) can be rewritten to

$$y = x + \rho \otimes \mathtt{IDCT}(d - \lambda \otimes h). \tag{17}$$

4   Coded Spread Spectrum Watermarking

In order to embed k-bit watermark information into a host data, it is required for the conventional methods including the CDMA-based method explained above to embed k independent sequences. In the CDMA-based method, the total energy of watermark signals is $k\beta^2$, where β^2 is the energy given for each sequence. Because of the transparency required for a watermarked data, the total energy must be limited to a certain threshold. Thus, with the increase of k, β^2 is linearly decreased. By encoding the watermark, we improve the distortion-energy behavior in this section. For convenience, the method proposed in this section is called "coded method".

4.1   Embedding

The idea of coded method is to encode k-bit watermark information into a codeword which has a constant weight $\tilde{k}$ and length $\tilde{L} \leq L$. At the embedding, we select $\tilde{k}$ out of $\tilde{L}$ SS sequences specified by the watermark information. The parameters $\tilde{k}$ and $\tilde{L}$ must satisfy the following condition:

$$2^k \leq \binom{\tilde{L}}{\tilde{k}} = \frac{\tilde{L}!}{\tilde{k}!(\tilde{L} - \tilde{k})!} < 2^{k+1}. \tag{18}$$

The mapping operation from k-bit information into a codeword $\boldsymbol{c}$ with weight $\tilde{k}$ and length $\tilde{L}$ has been proposed by Schalkwijk[13]. Based on the algorithm, we propose an encoding algorithm from watermark information $\boldsymbol{w}$ into its corresponding codeword.

Let $C(\tilde{k}, \tilde{L})$ be a set of vectors with a constant weight $\tilde{k}$ and length $\tilde{L}$. The procedure to encode watermark information $\boldsymbol{w}$ into a vector $\boldsymbol{c} \in C(\tilde{k}, \tilde{L})$ is described in Algorithm 1.

Different from the CDMA-based method, a vector $\tilde{\boldsymbol{d}}$ with length L is produced by

$$\tilde{\boldsymbol{d}} = \tilde{\beta}\boldsymbol{c}||\mathbf{0}^{L-\tilde{L}} = \{\tilde{\beta}c_0, \tilde{\beta}c_1, \ldots, \tilde{\beta}c_{\tilde{L}-1}, 0, \ldots, 0\}, \tag{19}$$

where "$||$" stands for a concatenation and $\mathbf{0}^{L-\tilde{L}}$ is a zero vector with length $L - \tilde{L}$. It is worth-mentioning that the length L of a vector must be a power of 2 in a fast DCT algorithm, and hence, the zero vector is padded to the codeword.

Algorithm 1. Encode $\boldsymbol{w}$ into $\boldsymbol{c}$

Require: $\tilde{k} \ll k$, $\tilde{L} \le L$, $\boldsymbol{w} = \{w_0, w_1, \ldots, w_{k-1}\}$, $w_t \in \{\pm 1\}$
Ensure: $\boldsymbol{c} = \{c_0, c_1, \ldots, c_{\tilde{L}-1}\}$, $c_t \in \{0, 1\}$

$\quad W \leftarrow \sum_{t=0}^{k-1} \dfrac{w_t + 1}{2} 2^t$;

$\quad \ell \leftarrow \tilde{k}$;

$\quad$ **for** $t = 0$ **to** $\tilde{L} - 1$ **do**

$\qquad$ **if** $W \ge \dbinom{\tilde{L} - t - 1}{\ell}$ **then**

$\qquad\quad W = W - \dbinom{\tilde{L} - t - 1}{\ell}$;

$\qquad\quad \ell = \ell - 1$;

$\qquad\quad c_{\tilde{L}-t-1} = 1$;

$\qquad$ **else**

$\qquad\quad c_{\tilde{L}-t-1} = 0$;

$\qquad$ **end if**

$\quad$ **end for**

Since the weight of $\boldsymbol{c}$ is $\tilde{k}$, only $\tilde{k}$ out of L elements are nonzero in the vector $\tilde{\boldsymbol{d}}$. Using the vector $\tilde{\boldsymbol{d}}$, the same operation in CDMA-based method is performed to embed the watermark information $\boldsymbol{w}$, Thus, the watermarked data $\boldsymbol{y}$ is represented by

$$\tilde{\boldsymbol{y}} = \boldsymbol{x} + \tilde{\boldsymbol{\mu}}, \tag{20}$$

where

$$\tilde{\boldsymbol{\mu}} = \boldsymbol{\rho} \otimes \text{IDCT}(\tilde{\boldsymbol{d}}). \tag{21}$$

In order to extend the coded method to ISS, we introduce a control vector $\tilde{\boldsymbol{\lambda}}$ similar to the CDMA-based method, and calculate the watermarked vector $\tilde{\boldsymbol{y}}$ as follows.

$$\tilde{\boldsymbol{y}} = \boldsymbol{x} + \boldsymbol{\rho} \otimes \text{IDCT}(\tilde{\boldsymbol{d}} - \tilde{\boldsymbol{\lambda}} \otimes h) \tag{22}$$

4.2 Detection

At the detection, we first extract the vector $\boldsymbol{y}' = \tilde{\boldsymbol{y}} + \boldsymbol{e}$ from a watermarked data, and then, calculate $\tilde{\boldsymbol{d}}'$ similar to Eq.(9). Different from the the decision rule in the CDMA-based method, we recover the codeword $\boldsymbol{c}'$ from $\tilde{\boldsymbol{d}}'$ as follows. Since the weight of codewords is constant in the coded method, it is sufficient to select largest $\tilde{k}$ elements from the first $\tilde{L}$ elements of $\tilde{\boldsymbol{d}}'$. Therefore, we first find the $\tilde{k}$-th largest element $D_{\tilde{k}}$ in $\tilde{\boldsymbol{d}}'$, and then, determine the $\tilde{k}$ elements in the codeword $\boldsymbol{c}'$ as follows:

$$c_t' = \begin{cases} 1 & \text{if } \tilde{d}_t' \ge D_{\tilde{k}} \\ 0 & \text{otherwise} \end{cases}, \quad 0 \le t \le \tilde{L} - 1 \tag{23}$$

By decoding the codeword $\boldsymbol{c}'$ using Algorithm 2, the watermark information $\boldsymbol{w}'$ is recovered in the coded method.

Algorithm 2. Decode $\boldsymbol{c'}$ into $\boldsymbol{w'}$

Require: $\tilde{k} \ll k$, $\tilde{L}$, $\boldsymbol{c'} = \{c'_0, c'_1, \ldots, c'_{\tilde{L}-1}\}$, $c'_t \in \{0, 1\}$
Ensure: $\boldsymbol{w'} = \{w'_0, w'_1, \ldots, w'_{k-1}\}$, $w'_t \in \{\pm 1\}$
  $W' = 0$;
  $\ell = 0$;
  for $t = 0$ **to** $\tilde{L} - 1$ **do**
    if $c'_t = 1$ **then**
      $\ell = \ell + 1$;
$$W' = W' + \binom{t}{\ell};$$
    end if
  end for
  for $t = 0$ **to** $k - 1$ **do**
    if $W' \bmod 2 = 1$ **then**
      $w'_t = 1$;
    else
      $w'_t = -1$;
    end if
    $W' = \lfloor W'/2 \rfloor$;
  end for

---

5 Consideration

Both in the conventional multibit SS method and the proposed CDMA-based method, watermark information $\boldsymbol{w}$ is represented by antipodal signal. It means that watermark information is modulated by Binary Phase Shift Keying (BPSK) before embedding. On the other hand, the watermark information is encoded into a constant weight codeword $\boldsymbol{c}$ in the coded method. From the communication technique point of view, we can say that Pulse Position Modulation (PPM) is performed to the watermark information. After such modulations, the SS communication technique is performed to transmit these modulated signals over a host data regarding as a communication channel. In the proposed two methods, the SS sequences are based on DCT basic vectors. Even though a PN sequence is multiplied, the operation of the SS technique in the proposed methods is merely the orthogonal transformation of these modulated signals, and hence, the energy preservation law is satisfied. Therefore, we study the characteristics of the proposed methods from the energy point of view.

5.1 Embedding Strength

When $\tilde{\beta}^2$ energy is given for each sequence in the coded method, the total energy is $\tilde{k}\tilde{\beta}^2$. Under the condition that the total energy embedded in a host data is equal to that of the CDMA-based method, namely $k\beta^2 = \tilde{k}\tilde{\beta}^2$, $\tilde{\beta}^2$ is much larger than β^2 because $\tilde{k} \ll k$. Thus, there is a relation between β and $\tilde{\beta}$.

Table 1. Some examples of parameters $\tilde{k}$ and $\tilde{L}$

k	$\tilde{k}$	$\tilde{L}$	γ
64	6	4873	3.266
	7	1918	3.024
	8	972	2.828
80	7	9324	3.651
	8	3863	3.162
	9	1975	2.981
	10	1170	2.828
96	9	6751	3.266
	10	3525	3.098
	11	2092	2.954
	12	1366	2.828
112	11	5714	3.191
	12	3424	3.055
	13	2236	2.935
	14	1562	2.828
128	12	8610	3.266
	13	5230	3.138
	14	3432	3.024
	15	2395	2.921
	16	1757	2.828

$$\tilde{\beta} = \gamma\beta, \tag{24}$$

where

$$\gamma = \sqrt{\frac{k}{\tilde{k}}}. \tag{25}$$

In the CDMA-based method, k antipodal signals $d_t \in \{\pm\beta\}, 0 \le t \le k - 1$ are embedded into a host data in a spread form, and those signals are detected by checking $\mathrm{sign}(d_t')$. It is noticed that the difference between those two antipodal signals is 2β. On the other hand, the signals d_t are $\tilde{\beta}$ or 0 in the coded method, hence the difference between signals is $\tilde{\beta}$. Therefore, if $\gamma > 2$, then the coded method is superior to the CDMA-based method. Table 1 shows some numerical examples of parameters k, $\tilde{k}$, $\tilde{L}$, and γ that satisfy Eq.(18).

5.2   Comparison

It is clear that the performance of the CDMA-based scheme expected to be equal to the conventional SS schemes if the ISS operation completely removes the host-interference at the embedding in the conventional schemes. The advantage of the CDMA-based method from the conventional SS schemes is the computational complexity both at the embedding and detection. At the embedding in

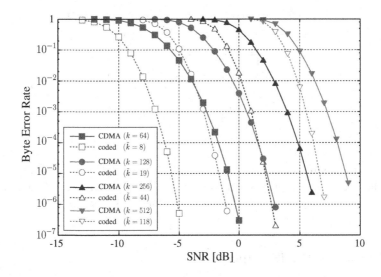

Fig. 1. Comparison of the byte error rate when $L = 1024$

the CDMA-based scheme, the amount of host-interference is easily performed by calculating the DCT coefficients as given in Eq.(15), and the interference is removed by Eq.(16). Due to the fast algorithm, the amount of computational cost can be reduced by a logarithmic order compared with the conventional schemes. In addition, the conventional schemes must solve a group of linear equations to remove the interference among SS sequences, which complexity increased with the number of watermark bits.

For the comparison of the CDMA-based method and coded method, we measure the detection error rate under the following condition. The SS sequences μ and $\tilde{\mu}$ with a same length L are generated from randomly selected k-bit watermark information w, and they are transmitted over AWGN channel. We define the byte error rate as the number of incorrectly received watermarks divided by the total number of transmitted watermarks. In our experiments, by randomly selecting 10^9 watermarks w, we count the number of incorrect ones at the detection by changing the SNR defined as

$$SNR = \frac{\text{the total energy of watermark}}{\text{the total energy of noise}}. \tag{26}$$

The noise is added to the modulated signal y and y' which are generated from k-bit watermark information. the byte error rate is expected to be increased with k in both schemes. We compare the improvement rate of the coded method by changing k. Figure 1 shows the result when the length of the SS sequence is $L = 1024$. The detailed parameters of constant weight codewords are enumerated in Table 2. From this figure, it is observed that the coded method is better than the CDMA-based method and the byte error rate of the coded method is

Table 2. Parameters of constant weight codewords

k	$\tilde{k}$	$\tilde{L}$	γ
64	8	972	2.828
128	19	865	2.596
256	44	1018	2.412
512	118	1022	2.083

approaching to that of the CDMA-based method with the increase of k. From the results, we can say that it is recommended to encode watermark information into a constant weight codeword before calculating the SS sequence under the above condition.

5.3   Analysis of the ISS Operation

The above analysis is valid only if the host-interference is completely removed. In order to consider the realistic case, we analyze the amount of energy removed by ISS operation assuming that the vector $\boldsymbol{h}$ follows Gaussian distribution with zero mean and variance σ_h^2, namely $\mathcal{N}(0, \sigma_h^2)$. The removal of the host-interference is controlled by the vectors $\boldsymbol{\lambda}$ and $\tilde{\boldsymbol{\lambda}}$ for the CDMA-based method and the coded method, respectively, because $\boldsymbol{\lambda} \otimes \boldsymbol{h}$ and $\tilde{\boldsymbol{\lambda}} \otimes \boldsymbol{h}$ are removed in Eq.(17) and Eq.(22). For simplicity, we introduce thresholds $T \geq 0$ and $\tilde{T} \geq 0$ to control the amount of removed energy instead of those vectors.

If $(\tilde{d}_t = 0) \cap (h_t < 0)$ and $(\tilde{d}_t \neq 0) \cap (h_t > 0)$, the removal of the host-interference should be avoided in the coded method because the host interference plays a positive effect on a detection vector in these cases. In order to control the amount of energy removed by the ISS operation, we should perform the removal operation except for these cases.

Suppose that we reduce the amount of remained host-interference term to less than $\tilde{T}$ if $\tilde{d}_t = 0$. Then, the detection sequence becomes $d'_t < \tilde{T}$ under a noiseless case. In order to satisfy this condition, it is sufficient to set $\tilde{\lambda}_t h_t = h_t - \tilde{T}$ only when $h_t > \tilde{T}$. On the other hand, if $\tilde{d}_t \neq 0$, we control the detection sequence to be $d'_t > \beta - \tilde{T}$ by setting $\tilde{\lambda}_t h_t = h_t + \tilde{T}$ only when $h_t < -\tilde{T}$. It is noticed that the host-interference h_t is controlled to be $\pm\tilde{T}$ if $(\tilde{d}_t = 0) \cap (h_t > \tilde{T})$ and $(\tilde{d}_t \neq 0) \cap (h_t < -\tilde{T})$. Therefore, the energy $\tilde{\epsilon}_t$ removed by the ISS operation is represented by

$$\tilde{\epsilon}_t = \begin{cases} h_t^2 - \tilde{T}^2 & \text{if } \left((\tilde{d}_t = 0) \cap (h_t > \tilde{T})\right) \cup \left((\tilde{d}_t \neq 0) \cap (h_t < -\tilde{T})\right) \\ 0 & \text{otherwise.} \end{cases} \tag{27}$$

By a statistical analysis, the expectation of $\tilde{\epsilon}_t$ under the conditions $(\tilde{d}_t = 0) \cap (h_t > \tilde{T})$ and $(\tilde{d}_t \neq 0) \cap (h_t < -\tilde{T})$ can be derived as follows:

$$\mathbb{E}[\tilde{\epsilon}_t] = \mathbb{E}[h_t^2 - \tilde{T}^2] = \mathbb{E}[h_t^2] - \tilde{T}^2 = \sigma_h^2 - \tilde{T}^2. \tag{28}$$

Remember that the Probability Density Function (PDF) of h_t is assumed to be $\mathcal{N}(0, \sigma_h^2)$. Because of the symmetry of the PDF centering on zero, the above condition can be simplified into $h_t > \tilde{T}$. Here, we obtain

$$\Pr[h_t > \tilde{T}] = \frac{1}{2}\text{erfc}\left(\frac{\tilde{T}}{2\sigma_h^2}\right), \tag{29}$$

where

$$\text{erfc}(x) = \frac{2}{\sqrt{\pi}} \int_x^\infty e^{-t^2} dt. \tag{30}$$

Therefore, for a given threshold $\tilde{T}$, $\mathbb{E}[\tilde{\epsilon}_t]$ is represented by

$$\mathbb{E}[\tilde{\epsilon}_t] = \frac{\sigma_h^2 - \tilde{T}^2}{2}\text{erfc}\left(\frac{\tilde{T}}{2\sigma_h^2}\right). \tag{31}$$

Since all host-interference $h_t, 0 \le t \le \tilde{L} - 1$ should be removed in the coded method, the total energy $\tilde{\varepsilon}$ of the removed signal is given by

$$\tilde{\varepsilon} = \tilde{L}\mathbb{E}[\tilde{\epsilon}_t] = \frac{\tilde{L}(\sigma_h^2 - \tilde{T}^2)}{2}\text{erfc}\left(\frac{\tilde{T}}{2\sigma_h^2}\right). \tag{32}$$

Similarly, the energy ϵ_t of the CDMA-based method can be represented as follows.

$$\epsilon_t = \begin{cases} h_t^2 - T^2 & \text{if } ((w_t = 1) \cap (h_t > T)) \cup ((w_t = -1) \cap (h_t < -T)) \\ 0 & \text{otherwise} \end{cases} \tag{33}$$

By a statistical analysis, the expectation of ϵ_t is represented by

$$\mathbb{E}[\epsilon_t] = \mathbb{E}[h_t^2 - T^2] = \mathbb{E}[h_t^2] - T^2 = \sigma_h^2 - T^2. \tag{34}$$

In the CDMA-based method, only k host-interference elements $h_t, 0 \le t \le k-1$ is removed by ISS operation, and hence, the total energy ε is given by

$$\varepsilon = k\mathbb{E}[\epsilon_t] = \frac{k(\sigma_h^2 - T^2)}{2}\text{erfc}\left(\frac{T}{2\sigma_h^2}\right). \tag{35}$$

Under the constraint that the amount of distortion caused by both the watermark embedding and the ISS operations, we obtain the following relationship between the CDMA-based and coded methods.

$$k\beta^2 + \varepsilon = \tilde{k}\tilde{\beta}^2 + \tilde{\varepsilon} \tag{36}$$

Considering the above relationship, we have to determine optimal parameters $\tilde{k}$, $\tilde{\beta}$, and $\tilde{T}$ for the coded method. It is noticed that the host vector $\boldsymbol{x}$ affects the determination of those parameters because its corresponding variance σ_h^2 is one of the important factor in the above relationship. It implies that we should pay attention on the selection of the vector $\boldsymbol{x}$ from a host data (e.g. sampling from the frequency components of an image).

6   Concluding Remarks

We proposed an efficient method to generate SS sequences from a secret key based on the CDMA technique. The proposed SS sequences are the DCT basic vectors modulated by the PN sequence specified by the secret key. The systematic generation of the sequences enables us to calculate the correlation scores of multibit watermark information simultaneously, and its computational costs can be reduced by employing the fast DCT algorithm. Because watermark information is embedded into the elements sampled from the frequency components of a host data using a secret key, the SS sequences are permuted by itself at the embedding stage, which enhances the secrecy of the watermark. Thanks to the PN sequence used in the embedding operation, a noise added to a watermarked data is spread over the whole samples which suppresses unexpected peaks appeared in a detection sequence.

We also proposed an encoding method to control the energy assigned to the SS sequences. By encoding watermark information into a constant weight codeword, the number of the sequences is drastically reduced in the proposed method, and hence, we can get higher peaks at the detection sequence. From our theoretical analysis, it is revealed that the amount of distortion caused by the watermark embedding and the host-interference removal operation must be controlled by carefully selecting parameters $\tilde{k}$, $\tilde{\beta}$, and $\tilde{T}$ in the coded method.

Acknowledgment. This research was partially supported by the Ministry of Education, Culture, Sports Science and Technology, Grant-in-Aid for Young Scientists (B) (24760299).

References

1. Chen, B., Wornel, G.W.: Quantization index modulation: a class of provably good methods for digital watermarking and information embedding. IEEE Trans. Inform. Theory 47(4), 1423–1443 (2001)
2. Cheng, Q., Huang, T.S.: An additive approach to transform-domain information hiding and optimum detection structure. IEEE Trans. Multimedia 3(3), 273–284 (2001)
3. Cox, I.J., Kilian, J., Leighton, F.T., Shamson, T.: Secure spread spectrum watermarking for multimedia. IEEE Trans. Image Processing 6(12), 1673–1687 (1997)
4. Gold, R.: Maximal recursive sequences with 3-valued recursive cross-correlation functions. IEEE Trans. Information Theory 14(1), 154–156 (1968)
5. Hernández, J.R., Amado, M., Pérez-González, F.: Dct-domain watermarking techniques for still images: detector performance analysis and a new structure. IEEE Trans. Image Processing 9(1), 55–68 (2000)
6. Hernández, J.R., Pérez-González, F.: Statistical analysis of watermarking schemes for copyright protection of images. Proceedings of the IEEE, 1142–1166 (1999)
7. Kumar, S.K., Sreenivas, T.: Increased watermark-to-host correlation at uniform random phase watermarks in audio signals. Signal Processing 87(1), 61–67 (2007)
8. Kuribayashi, M.: Hierarchical spread spectrum fingerprinting scheme based on the cdma technique. EURASIP J. Information Security (502782), 16 pages (2011)

9. Malvar, H.S., Florêncio, D.A.F.: Improved spread spectrum: a new modulation technique for robust watermarking. IEEE Trans. Signal Processing 51(4), 898–905 (2003)
10. Mayer, J., Bermudez, J.C.M.: Multi-bit informed embedding watermarking with constant robustness. In: Proc. ICIP 2005, vol. 1, pp. 669–672 (2005)
11. Mayer, J., Silva, R.A.: Efficient informed embedding of multi-bit watermark. In: Proc. ICASSP 2004, vol. 3, pp. 389–392 (2004)
12. Ng, T.M., Garg, H.K.: Maximum-likelihood detection in DWT domain image watermarking using Laplacian modeling. IEEE Signal Processing Letters 12(4), 285–288 (2005)
13. Schalkwijk, J.P.M.: An algorithm for source coding. IEEE Trans. Information Theory IT-18(3), 395–399 (1972)
14. Senda, K., Kawamura, M.: Statistical-mechanical approach for multiple watermarks using spectrum spreading. In: Kurosawa, K. (ed.) ICITS 2009. LNCS, vol. 5973, pp. 231–247. Springer, Heidelberg (2010)
15. Zhang, P., Xu, S., Yang, H.: Selective host-interference cancellation: a new informed embedding strategy for spread spectrum watermarking. IEICE Trans. Fundamentals E95-A(6), 1065–1073 (2012)

Enhancement of Method for Preventing Unauthorized Copying of Displayed Information Using Object Surface Reflection

Takayuki Yamada[1], Seiichi Gohshi[2], and Isao Echizen[1,3]

[1] Graduate University for Advanced Studies, Japan
[2] Kogakuin University, Japan
[3] National Institute of Informatics, Japan
{nii20081705,iechizen}@nii.ac.jp, gohshi@cc.kogakuin.ac.jp

Abstract. A enhancement is described for a previously proposed method for preventing unauthorized copying of information shown on a display [1]. Our previously proposed method utilizes the difference in spectral sensitivity between humans and imaging devices. A near-infrared light source is used to create noise added to the entire display area in only the photographic image without affecting the viewer's perception. Unauthorized copying of displayed information can thus be prevented without adding a new function to digital cameras. However, it is not effective against cameras equipped with a short wavelength pass filter (SWPF) to eliminate the noise. We propose a countermeasure that makes it effective against such filters. A countermeasure was established in which the near-IR rays reflected off the filter are detected by using the IR object surface reflection of the filter with four IR camcorders placed at end of the display. The proposed enhancement was implemented on a prototype illegal recording prevention unit installed on a 17-inch liquid crystal display. Testing showed that, with this enhancement, the unit can effectively detect a digital camera with an attached SWPF.

Keywords: Illegal recording, Information leakage, Short wavelength pass filter, Specular reflection, Infrared ray, Filter detection.

1 Introduction

Technologies to prevent unauthorized copying through encryption are widely used to prevent the disclosure of personal and/or confidential information and to protect the copyright of pictures and images, but digital information that has been converted to an analog form and shown on a display can be captured with a digital camera, thereby making the encryption useless (the analog hole problem). There have been several such cases of disclosure of confidential and personal information. In one case, a Japanese air traffic controller posted secret American flight information, including detailed flight plans for Air Force One, on his blog [2].

The use of digital watermarking has been widely used to control the distribution of pictures and images shown on cinema screens and displays [3–7]. Such methods use

Y.Q. Shi, H.J. Kim, and F. Pérez-González (Eds.): IWDW 2012, LNCS 7809, pp. 184–197, 2013.
© Springer-Verlag Berlin Heidelberg 2013

watermarks to embed unique information in pictures and images, the purpose being to identify the location where the illegal recording occurred by detecting the watermark in unauthorized copies. While using digital watermarking may psychologically deter normally honest people from illegally recording pictures and images, it is unable to prevent the actual act of illegal recording using a digital camera or other photographic equipment. Also, even if it were possible to detect the time and place of the illegal recording from the distributed content, it would be difficult to identify the offender without equipment in the movie theater or other location (surveillance cameras etc.). In addition, there are concerns about the increasingly high quality of unauthorized images due to continuing improvements in the functions of display devices and photographic equipment. The prevention of unauthorized copying of information presented on displays is essential to preventing information disclosure and protecting copyrights.

For these reasons, we have previously proposed a method that prevents the use of digital cameras to make unauthorized copies of information shown on a display [1]. It is based on the difference in spectral sensitivity between humans and imaging devices. By installing a near-infrared light source, which superimposes noise on the recorded images without adding any new functions to digital cameras. It supports copyright protection for picture and image content and prevents disclosure of confidential and personal information through the unauthorized copying of displayed information, an increasingly serious problem. This method is broadly applicable to the unauthorized photographing of works of art, factory equipment and other objects subject to photographic restrictions.

However, it is ineffective if the digital camera or camcorder used for the recording is equipped with a short wavelength pass filter (SWPF). Therefore, we implemented a countermeasure to make our method effective even against SWPF-equipped cameras and camcorders. IR rays reflected off the filter are detected by exploiting the IR specular reflection properties of the SWPF. This countermeasure uses light-emitting diodes (LEDs) to create noise and to serve as a light source for detection. Four IR camcorders with an attached visible range cut filter capture images of the audience area, and a PC is used to detect specular reflection from an SWPF. The proposed enhancement was implemented on a prototype illegal recording prevention unit installed on a 17-inch liquid crystal display. Experimental evaluation with the prototype showed that the enhanced unit can effectively detect a camera equipped with an SWPF in real time.

2   Elimination of IR Noise Using SWPF

According to the International Commission on Illumination (CIE), the wavelengths of visible light range from 380 to 780 nm [8]. However, the image sensor devices, such as the CCDs and CMOSs, used in digital cameras and camcorders can generally detect light between 200 and 1100 nm, which gives them the high level of luminous sensitivity needed for recording in the dark. Our previously proposed recording prevention method uses IR light of 870 nm to add noise to images displayed on a screen without it being detected by the human eye [1]. It is, however, ineffective when an

SWPF is used to filter out the IR light. Such a filter allows short wavelength light to pass and blocks long wavelength light, i.e., IR light. SWPFs can be classified into IR cut filters and IR absorption filters.

An IR cut filter is a planar object with a dielectric multilayer. It reflects the IR light received from several directions back in a single outgoing direction (specular reflection). An IR absorption filter is also a planar object that reflects the incoming IR light back in only one direction. However, since the wavelength penetration depends on the quantity of the absorber mixed into the glass, the IR reflection is lower than that of an IR cut filter and has almost the same reflectance as the reflection from a glass surface. In contrast, non-specular reflectors, such as scatter plates, have various shapes and surface treatments, so they reflect the incident IR light back in various directions (diffuse reflection). The filter detection algorithm can thus detect the use of an SWPF by analyzing the reflection images picked up by an IR camcorder.

3   Filter Detection

3.1   Principle

As illustrated in Fig. 1, IR emission units (IR LEDs) are used to corrupt the recorded content by adding noise signals that are invisible to the naked eye but are picked up by a camera's CCD or CMOS device [9]. They are also used to detect SWPFs. An SWPF is a glossy planate filter, so it reflects incoming IR light in only one direction (specular reflection). An SWPF attached to a camcorder used for illegal recording is naturally aligned parallel to the display. The IR light emitted by the IR emission units is specularly reflected by the SWPF and captured as video images by four camcorders with high IR sensitivity placed at end of the display. A filter-detection algorithm running on a PC detects the SWPF by analyzing these images.

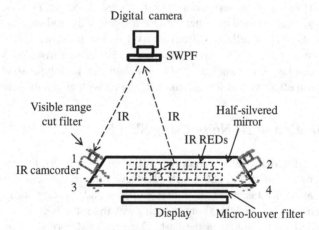

Fig. 1. Method for SWPF detection

3.2   Illegal Recording and Detection Areas

To limit the area in which illegal recording is possible, a micro-louver filter is attached to the front of the display. The "illegal recording area (G,C,A,B,D,H)" is indicated by the dashed diagonal lines in Fig. 2.   The IR rays emitted by the IR emission units pass through the entire area of the half-silvered mirror surface in front of the display. Since a pirate points a digital camera towards the display and records the images, all we have to do is place IR camcorders for detection in the unit. The four solid lines in Fig. 2 indicate the view angles of the two IR camcorders (1 and 2) set at each end of the display for detecting reflection from an SWPF. The gray-shaded triangular area (A,B,O) in front of the unit is outside the view angles of the two IR camcorders. To cover this blind area, we added two more IR camcorders (3 and 4) inside the half-silvered mirror, with one at each end. They are placed inwards aslant and thus cover most of the blind area, as indicated by the lightly dotted lines. As a result, the system can detect an SWPF attached to a digital camera anywhere in the detection area (E,C,A,O,B,D,F) regardless of whether it is aligned parallel to the screen.

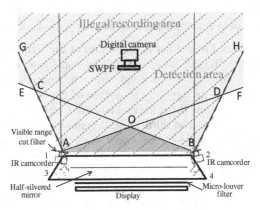

Fig. 2. Illegal recording and detection areas

3.3   Object Surface Reflection

The reflections from all object surfaces in the detection area must be measured in order to distinguish the reflection of a SWPF from those of other objects. In our method, as described in section 3.1, the radiant intensity of the light source is equal to the radiant intensity of the IR light source plus the radiant intensity of the display:

$$I_e(\lambda) = I_i(\lambda)K_m(\lambda) + I_d(\lambda)K_p(\lambda)(1 - K_m(\lambda)), \tag{1}$$

where
$I_i(\lambda)$: radiant intensity of IR light source,
$I_d(\lambda)$: radiant intensity of display,
$I_e(\lambda)$: radiant intensity of light source,
$K_p(\lambda)$: reflectance of   micro-louver filter,
$K_m(\lambda)$: reflectance of   half-silvered mirror,
$(0 \leq K_m(\lambda), K_p(\lambda) \leq 1)$.

According to the Phong shading model [10] of object reflection, when there is a light source, an object, and a camcorder, the spectral radiance $L_Q(\lambda)$ for one pixel can be expressed as

$$L_Q(\lambda) = I_e(\lambda)K_d(\lambda)\cos\theta/\,r^2 + I_e(\lambda)K_s(\lambda)(\cos\varphi)^n + I_a(\lambda)K_a(\lambda), \qquad (2)$$

Where
r: distance of object from light source,
θ: angle between light source and normal vector of object surface,
φ: angle between camcorder and regular reflection,
$I_e(\lambda)$: radiant intensity of light source,
$I_a(\lambda)$: radiant intensity of ambient light source,
$K_d(\lambda)$: diffuse reflectance of light source,
$K_s(\lambda)$: specular reflectance of light source,
$K_a(\lambda)$: reflectance of ambient light,
$(0 \leq K_d(\lambda),\ K_s(\lambda),\ K_a(\lambda) \leq 1)$.

Because a micro-louver filter is used to restrict the illegal recording area, the spectral radiance falls into one of two cases depending on the positions of the IR camcorders.

Case (1): IR Camcorders 1 and 2 Set at Each End of the Display

The first term of Eq. (2), the diffuse reflection element, shows that the light reflects randomly and diffuses equally. The second term, the specular reflection element, shows that the light reflects strongly on the surface of the object. When the decrease N in reflection intensity is large, the reflection is more specular, and, when it is small, the reflection is more diffuse. The third term, the ambient light element, shows the brightness imparted to the surface of the object when the light is not directly from a light source. We consider the light source as the IR light source, the camcorders as IR camcorders, and the object as an SWPF and use the Phong shading model.

Since the display can be regarded as a source of visible range light, a half mirror with very high reflectance is used. Since the specular reflection from an SWPF reflects the entering IR light in one direction, a visible range cut filter (long wavelength pass filter; LWPF) is used for the IR camcorders to eliminate the effect of the visible range light. Since the specular reflection from an SWPF at any location in the detection area can be observed the IR light sources, which are reflected over the entire display by the half-silvered mirror, the effect of visible light is excluded.

As a result, the radiant intensity of the light source $I_e(\lambda)$, the reflectance of the half-silvered mirror $K_m(\lambda)$, and coefficients K_d, K_a, and φ of the reflection model are given by

$$I_e(\lambda) \cong I_i(\lambda)K_m(\lambda). \qquad (3)$$

$$K_m(\lambda) \cong 1,\ K_d(\lambda) \cong\ 0,\ K_a(\lambda) \cong 0,\ \varphi \cong\ 0, \qquad (4)$$

and Equation (1) becomes

$$L_Q(\lambda) \cong I_i(\lambda)K_s(\lambda). \qquad (5)$$

Here,

$$0 \leq K_s(\lambda) \leq 1. \qquad (6)$$

If the IR-cut filter specular reflectance is K_s, and if the IR-absorption filter specular reflectance is K_s',

$$0 \leq K_s' \leq K_s(\lambda) \cong 1. \tag{7}$$

This relationship can be used to express both cases.

Case (a): IR-cut filter

$$L_Q(\lambda) \cong I_i(\lambda). \tag{8}$$

Case (b): IR-absorption filter

$$L_Q(\lambda) \leq I_i(\lambda) \tag{9}$$

If the object surface is curved or is not a specular one, the specular reflection is lower, and the diffuse reflection is higher. Since the increment in the diffuse reflection element is inversely proportional to the square of the distance from the light source, the diffuse reflection element is smaller than spectral radiance $L_Q(\lambda)$ if the object is an SWPF. This can be found by measuring the IR reflection, making it possible to distinguish between an SWPF and other objects.

A key point here is that the reflective objects remain fixed in relation to the display for a certain amount of time. Even if some of them happen to be facing the display, when they are moved, they are automatically eliminated as a candidate SWPF by a motion estimation algorithm. Moreover, even if an object is fixed and facing the display for a certain amount of time, whether or not it is an SWPF can be determined by target detection on the basis of its shape and area.

Case (2): IR Camcorders 3 or 4 Set Inside the Half-Silvered Mirror
The spectral radiance for one pixel is given by

$$L_Q'(\lambda) = L_Q(\lambda)(1-K_m(\lambda))+ I_i(\lambda)K_p(\lambda)(1- K_m(\lambda)). \tag{10}$$

Using the average radiant intensity of the IR light source $\bar{I}_i(\lambda)$ and the average spectral radiance $\bar{L}_Q(\lambda)$, we can express this relation as

$$\bar{L}_Q(\lambda) = \bar{I}_i(\lambda)K_p(\lambda)(1- K_m(\lambda)). \tag{11}$$

The effect of the second term in Eq. (10) is excluded by using

$$\delta = L_Q'(\lambda) - \bar{L}_Q(\lambda) \cong (1-K_m(\lambda))L_Q(\lambda) \cong CL_Q(\lambda), \tag{12}$$

where C is a constant. That is, δ can be regarded as a constant multiple of $L_Q(\lambda)$. As a result, as in case (1), we can distinguish the reflection from an SWPF from those of other objects. Any object in the room from the beginning is eliminated by background subtraction.

3.4   Stabilization of IR Noise Effect

When the radiation angle of the IR LEDs is narrower than the visible range of a camera used for illegal recording so that the radiant intensity of the IR light source is insufficient for IR-absorption filter detection, the larger the display, the lower the IR noise effects at the edges when a person approaches the screen and views the image from the front. The narrow radiant angle of the IR LED increases the IR noise effect. To stabilize this effect, we use six panels to integrate the IR LEDs so that their radiation angle is larger near the display edge. As shown in Fig. 3, the panels have a length of 2a and are symmetrically arranged with the center line running from the SWPF to the center of the screen.

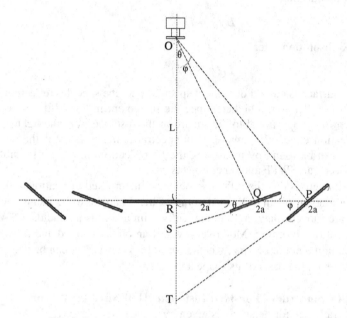

Fig. 3. Relationship between SWPF and six IR panels

As a result, the radiant intensity of the IR LEDs decreases quickly in inverse proportion to the square of the distance between the SWPF and the unit. Rather than arrange the panels in parallel, they are arranged as shown in the figure so that the IR LED radiant intensity in front of the screen at distance L is higher. As shown in Fig. 3, by defining a sign for each panel, we can derive the optimal angle for each one by using the similar triangles of algebra geometry.

$$\theta = \arctan(3a/L) \tag{13}$$

$$\varphi = \arctan(5a/L) \tag{14}$$

Thus, we can effectively prevent recording from the good front of illegal recording conditions by placing six IR panels with a length of $2a$ at the derived angles.

3.5   Filter Detection Algorithm

The algorithm used for detecting specular reflection from an SWPF is shown in Fig. 4. The inputs are two sets of IR camcorder video images. They are used to eliminate reflective objects already in the environment.

Set (a) images: shot in room without audience
Set (b) images: shot in room with audience

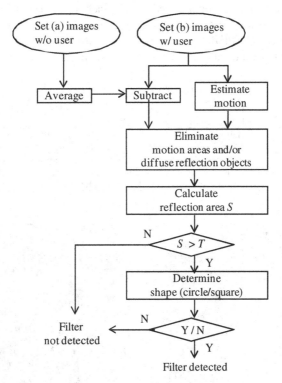

Fig. 4. Filter detection algorithm

The process flow of the algorithm comprises nine steps.

Step 1 Input set (a) video images.

Step 2 Average processed image frames and generate one averaged image frame.

Step 3 Do steps 4 through 7 for each series of the image frames in set (b) video images.

Step 4 Subtract pixel values of averaged image frame of set (a) generated in step 2 from those of each image frame of set (b).

Step 5 Estimate the motion areas in set (b) from the image frames processed in step 4.

Step 6 Eliminate the motion areas in set (b) by using the results of the motion estimation (step 5), and eliminate the diffuse reflection objects in set (b).

Step 7 Calculate average pixel value for each reflection area S in set (b) images and compare with threshold T. If value exceeds threshold, go to step 8.

Step 8 Determine shape of reflection area. Detect attack if shape is circle or square.

4   Prototype

Photographs of the prototype unit installed on a 17-inch liquid crystal display (LCD) are shown in Fig. 5. It has three main components (Table 1): an IR emission part, an IR reflective part, and an SWPF detection part. Even though the unit sits in the front of the display, it does not affect the user's viewing of or listening to the display device.

Table 1. Main components of prototype unit

IR emission part	IR LEDs (peak wavelength: 870 nm; no.: 1728; angle of radiation: ±11°), LWPF (cut-on wavelength: 850 nm)
IR reflective part	Half-silvered mirror (transmittance: 8%; reflectance: 92%), Micro-louver filter (viewing angle: 60°; transmittance: 80%)
SWPF detection part	IR camcorder (1/3-in. CCD; no. of effective pixels: a quarter of a million; angle of view: 92.6°), Visible range cut filter (cut-on wavelength: 780 nm), PC (OS: Windows 7; CPU: Core i7; RAM: 8 GB)

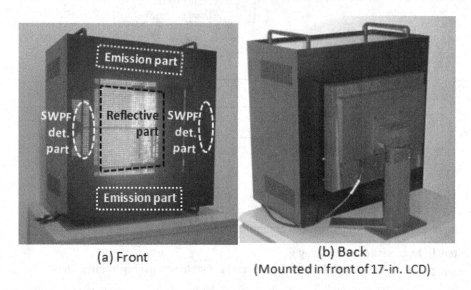

(a) Front   (b) Back
                  (Mounted in front of 17-in. LCD)

Fig. 5. Unit overview

IR Emission Part

The IR emission part consists of six IR LED panels, each with an LWPF, at the top of the unit and another six at the bottom. Each panel has 144 reflective IR LEDs with a peak wavelength of 870 nm, so there are 1728 (144×6×2) IR LEDs in total.

The designed viewing distance for HDTV is about 3 times the height of the display (3H), i.e., at the point where the pixel structure becomes invisible to someone with 20/20 (1.0) eyesight [11]. Since we used a 17-inch LCD, we positioned the IR panels at a distance of 777 mm (about 1 m) from the display. Given an IR panel length of $2a$ (60 cm) and distance L of ~1 m, we obtain the following angles by using the algorithm described in section 3.5.

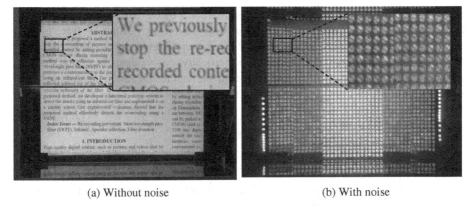

(a) Without noise   (b) With noise

Fig. 6. Digital camera images of displayed text without and with noise

$$\theta = \arctan(90/1000) \cong 5.14°$$
$$\varphi = \arctan(150/1000) \cong 8.53° \ . \tag{15}$$

IR Reflective Part

The IR reflective part consists of a half-silvered mirror and a micro-louver filter. The mirror lets light from the display pass through and reflects the IR rays without interfering with normal viewing of the display. Its use enables IR noise to be added to the entire display area. Since the transmittance and reflectance of a half-silvered mirror affect display viewability, a preliminary experiment was conducted to evaluate the legibility of the displayed information and the degree of the disturbance in images recorded with a digital camera. On the basis of the results, we used a half-silvered mirror with 8% transmittance and 92% reflectance. The micro-louver filter limits the area in which illegal recording is possible, as described in section 3.3. We set the filter so that the viewing angle was 60° on the basis of the radiation angle of the IR LEDs in the IR emission part.

SWPF Detection Part

This part does not need an IR light source for detection because it uses the IR light emitted from all the LCDs for detection. It consists of four IR camcorders, each with an attached visible range cut filter, and a PC for analysis. As described in section 3.3 and shown in Fig. 2, an IR camcorder was set at each end of the display, and the two other IR camcorders were set inside the half-silvered mirror, with one at each end. The images recorded by these camcorders were analyzed to detect specular reflections by using the filter detection algorithm running on the PC.

5   Evaluation

5.1   Method

We evaluated the ability of the prototype unit to detect an SWPF (an IR-cut filter and an IR-absorption filter) by placing objects that would normally be in a room at distances of 1 m from it (Fig. 7). We classified the objects into four categories, as shown in Table 2. The camcorders used for illegal recording (Group D) were placed one at a time at the position shown in Fig. 2. They were oriented so that they recorded the whole display at maximum size. More specifically, an evaluator faced the display and used a hand-held digital camera to record the whole display at maximum size. Since the values of the pixels in the image was saturated by IR noise reflected from the half-silvered mirror, using a ND filter, spectral radiance enters into the IR camcorders was made in 1/800.

Threshold T was set as follows.

Case (A): Evaluator   outside of blind area

> T was set to 500 so that the IR-absorption filter can detect by the corner of the last in the room.

Case (B): Evaluator inside blind area

> T was set to 50 so that the IR-absorption filter can detect in the blind area which is most far distance from the unit.

In each case (A) and (B), the distance between the evaluation objects and the prototype unit was 1 m and 0.2 m.

Table 2. Evaluation objects

Group	Category	Objects
A	**Room facilities**	(1) Desk (2) Chair
B	**User belongings (moving)**	(3) Eyeglasses (4) Watch (5) Tie clip (6) ID card (7) Pen
C	**Things user carry into room (static)**	(8) Drinking glass (9) Plastic bottle (10) Nylon bag
D	**Things pirates carry into room**	(11) Digital camera with attached SWPF

 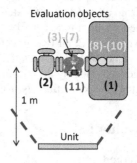

Fig. 7. Evaluation objects

Because IR noise is added to the entire display area, the legibility of a digital photographic image of the displayed information is degraded. Example images of displayed text without and with added noise captured using respectively a digital camera and a cellular phone with a camera are shown in Fig. 6. Using a scientific paper as an evaluation sample, we judged legibility by using a six-grade subjective evaluation (in ascending order, 1: Illegible, 2: Barely legible, 3: Fairly legible, 4: Legible without difficult, 5: Legible, 6: Very legible) and found that, when there was IR noise, the evaluation grade was 1 (Illegible) [1].

6 Results

We obtained results for SWPF detection for an IR-cut filter and an IR-absorption filter inside and outside the blind area. The reflections from the objects already in the room (1 and 2) were eliminated by the background subtraction step in the filter detection algorithm, and the reflections from the user's belongs (3–7) were eliminated by the motion estimation step, so only the SWPF remained to be detected. When an SWPF was detected, a red circle appeared in the recorded image and a beep sounded. These red circle areas correctly corresponded to a camera with an attached SWPF. The SWPF was detected within one second, virtually in real time.

Case (A): Evaluator Outside of Blind Area (IR camcorders 1–4)
(1) IR-Cut Filter Attached to Camera
The detection results for the IR-cut filter are shown in Fig. 8. Since an IR-cut filter has high IR reflectance, the average pixel value for reflection area S was high, making it is easy to distinguish the filter from other reflection objects. The average pixel values for the areas detected as an IR-cut filter were 219, 234, 209, and 205 for IR camcorders 1–4, respectively.

(2) IR-Absorption Filter Attached to Camera
The detection results for the IR-absorption filter are shown in Fig. 9. The average pixel values were less than those for the IR-cut filter and were the same as those for glass. The average pixel values for the areas detected as an IR-absorption filter were 201, 194, 67, and 84 for IR camcorders 1–4, respectively.

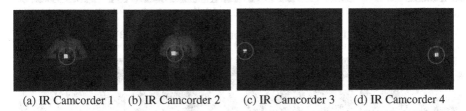

(a) IR Camcorder 1   (b) IR Camcorder 2   (c) IR Camcorder 3   (d) IR Camcorder 4

Fig. 8. Evaluation results for IR-cut filter in Case (A)

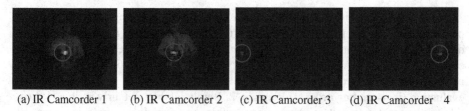

(a) IR Camcorder 1   (b) IR Camcorder 2   (c) IR Camcorder 3   (d) IR Camcorder 4

Fig. 9. Evaluation results for IR-absorption filter in Case (A)

Case (B): Evaluator Inside Blind Area (IR Camcorders 3 and 4; IR Camcorders 1 and 2 Outside of Angle of View)
(1) IR-Cut Filter Attached to Camera
The detection results for the IR-cut filter are shown in Fig. 10. Since an IR-cut filter has high IR reflectance, the average pixel value for reflection area S was high, making it is easy to distinguish the filter from other reflection objects by subtracting the background image. The average pixel values for the areas detected as an IR-cut filter were respectively 246 and 245 for IR camcorders 3 and 4.

(2) IR-Absorption Filter Attached to Camera
The detection results for the IR-absorption filter are shown in Fig. 11. Detection of the IR-absorption filter was more difficult because the values of the pixels in the image after background subtraction were low. The average values for the areas detected as an IR-absorption filter were respectively 66 and 113 for IR camcorders 3 and 4. The more difficult detection is attributed to specular reflection from the IR-absorption filter penetrating the half-silvered mirror and reaching the IR camcorders. However, in case (B), since the detection area is an area that compensates for the blind area of the two IR camcorders set outside the half-silvered mirror, the IR camcorders for detection and the reflective objects are closer. Therefore, when an IR-absorption filter is in the blind area, the reflection intensity is sufficient for IR-absorption filter detection.

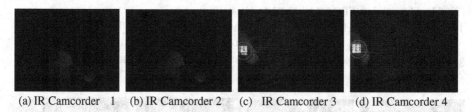

(a) IR Camcorder 1   (b) IR Camcorder 2   (c) IR Camcorder 3   (d) IR Camcorder 4

Fig. 10. Evaluation results for IR-cut filter in Case (B)

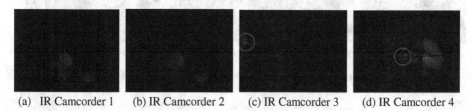

(a) IR Camcorder 1   (b) IR Camcorder 2   (c) IR Camcorder 3   (d) IR Camcorder 4

Fig. 11. Evaluation results for IR-absorption filter in Case (B)

7   Conclusion

As consumer cameras become smaller and more powerful, illegal recording of displayed content will become an even more serious problem. Even though existing technical countermeasures using digital watermarking might create a mental deterrence, they are unable to prevent it. The previous method could prevent illegal recording of displayed content that actually prevents recording, but it was ineffective against camcorders equipped with an SWPF. We have enhanced the previous method so that it can detect the IR specular reflection from an SWPF. Testing using our prototype system showed that this enhancement enables the previous method to detect a camera with an attached SWPF. We plan to enhance the method so that the position of an SWPF can be calculated from the separate images recorded using the four IR cameras.

References

1. Yamada, T., Gohshi, S., Echizen, I.: iCabinet: Stand-alone implementation of a method for preventing illegal recording of displayed content by adding invisible noise signals. In: Proc. of the ACM Multimedia 2011 (ACM MM 2011), pp. 771–772 (2011)
2. Fackler, M.: Japan Investigates Online Posting of Obama Flight Plans. The New York Times (September 10, 2011), http://www.nytimes.com/2011/09/11/world/asia/11japan.html
3. Haitsma, J., Kaler, T.: A Watermarking Scheme for Digital Cinema. In: Proc. of the 8th International Conference on Image Processing (ICIP 2001), vol. 2, pp. 487–489 (2001)
4. Gohshi, S., Nakamura, H., Ito, H., Fujii, R., Suzuki, M., Takai, S., Tani, Y.: A New Watermark Surviving After Re-shooting the Images Displayed on a Screen. In: Khosla, R., Howlett, R.J., Jain, L.C. (eds.) KES 2005. LNCS (LNAI), vol. 3682, pp. 1099–1107. Springer, Heidelberg (2005)
5. Nakamura, H., Gohshi, S., Fujii, R., Ito, H., Suzuki, M., Takai, S., Tani, Y.: A Digital Watermark that Survives after Re-shooting the Images Displayed on a CRT Screen. Journal of the Institute of Image Information and Television Engineers 60(11), 1778–1788 (2006)
6. Nakashima, Y., Tachibana, R., Babaguchi, N.: Watermarked Movie Soundtrack Finds the Position of the Camcorder in Theater. IEEE Trans. on Multimedia 11(3), 443–454 (2009)
7. Lee, M., Kim, K., Lee, H.: Digital Cinema Watermarking for Estimating the Position of the Pirate. IEEE Transactions on Multimedia 12(7), 605–621 (2010)
8. Schanda, J. (ed.): Colorimetry: Understanding the CIE system. Wiley-Interscience (2007)
9. Holst, G., Lomheim, T.: CMOS/CCD Sensors and Camera Systems. Society of Photo Optical (2007)
10. Zhang, H., Daniel Liang, Y.: Computer graphics using Java 2D and 3D. Prentice Hall (2006)
11. Ardito, M., Gunetti, M.: The impact of display parameters on the quality perceived by the viewers. In: Proceedings of International Conference on Consumer Electronics, pp. 112–113 (1995)

Image Splicing Verification Based on Pixel-Based Alignment Method

Rimba Whidiana Ciptasari[1,2], Kyung-Hyune Rhee[3], and Kouichi Sakurai[1]

[1] Graduate School of Information Science and Electrical Engineering
Department of Informatics, Kyushu University, Fukuoka, Japan
[2] Faculty of Informatics, Telkom Institute of Technology, Bandung, Indonesia
[3] Department of IT Convergence and Application Engineering, Pukyong National
University, 599-1, Daeyeon 3-Dong, Nam-Gu, Busan 608-737, Korea

Abstract. Due to the easy manipulation and alteration of digital images using widely available software tools, forgery detection is emerged as a primary goal in image forensics. A common form of manipulation is to combine parts of the image fragment into another different image to remove objects from the image. Inspired by the image registration concept, we exploit the correlation-based alignment method to automatically identify the spliced region in any fragment of the reference images. We show the efficacy of the proposed scheme on revealing the source of spliced regions. We anticipate this scheme to be the first concrete technique towards appropriate tools which are necessary for exposing digital forgeries.

Keywords: Image splicing, image alignment, edge detection, membership function, interpolation.

1 Introduction

1.1 Background

In today's digital age, the creation and manipulation of digital images referred to as photomontage are made simply by the advent of low-cost and high-resolution digital cameras and sophisticated editing software. Consequently, a photograph, which has been accepted as a proof of the recorded event, no longer possesses a unique quality. Digital image forgeries, often leaving no obvious traces of having been subjected to any of manipulation operations, are somewhat indistinguishable from authentic photographs.

An image can be tampered in many ways and at varying degrees, like compositing, duplicating, enhancing, with various intents. Image enhancement comprises change of the color of object, blurring out the object, or change of the weather condition. Another common manipulation is known as region duplication in which a continuous portion of pixels are copied and pasted to a different location in the same image. Image composite involves combining two or more image regions to create a new image. These kind of manipulations are often

Y.Q. Shi, H.J. Kim, and F. Pérez-González (Eds.): IWDW 2012, LNCS 7809, pp. 198–212, 2013.

referred to as image splicing in which we focus on. In addition, image splicing is conducted without further post-processing such as smoothing of boundaries among different regions. Since the artifacts introduced by image splicing are almost imperceptible, image splicing detection still remains a challenging task.

1.2 Related Work

A number of passive detections focused on image splicing have been developed over the past several years. *Ng et al.* [1] improved the performance of bicoherence features of [8] to detect image splicing. Both the original bicoherence and their estimated features were computed to obtain stronger discrimination power between authentic and spliced images. Then, support vector machine (SVM) was applied to train these features and classify given images. By detecting the inconsistency in lighting with respect to different parts in an image, Johnson and Farid have developed a technique of image splicing detection [2]. To identify the suspicious splicing areas, Hsu and Chang [3] computed the geometry invariants from the pixels and estimated the camera response function. *Dong et al.* [6] analyzed the spliced artifact on image run-length representation and edge statistics.

As an alternative to the image splicing detection, we used interpolation technique and reference images to identify the suspicious regions. In the previous work [7], we exploited normalized cross-correlation function to locate the peak value throughout reference images which can be used as evidence of tampering.

1.3 Challenge Issue

Generally speaking, we classify all proposed outstanding works into two categories: pixel-based approach and machine learning-based framework. Several general techniques have been proposed in the former category. Popescu and Farid [10] exploited expectation/maximization (EM) algorithm to detect re-sampling's lattice of the original image. Prasad and Ramakrishnan [11] have a propensity to investigate the properties of a re-sampled discrete sequence and proposed deterministic techniques to detect re-sampling. *Ye et al.* [5] investigated blocking artifacts introduced during JPEG compression. For the latter category, Farid and Lyu [13] built a classification scheme to differentiate between natural image and tampered image. *Avcibas et al.* [14] constructed a classifier by employing image quality metrics as the essential features. *Chen et al.* [4] extracted the image features by exploiting the magnitude and phase of a given test image. *Dong et al.* [6] and *Sutthiwan et al.* [16] employed SVM to train image features as well.

However, all aforementioned detection methods typically do not provide direct evidence from which the spliced/tampered regions are derived. They are only able to determine whether the given image is tampered. Despite our previous work can identify the source of tampered regions, the use of peak correlation coefficient can suffer from a lack of accuracy and precision.

Motivated by pixel-based alignment concept [19], we formulate a tampered image problem as locating the best correlation between the suspicious region and its reference. Thus, the challenge issue lies on how to incorporate and describe the form of these correlations to assess the authenticity of an image.

1.4   Contribution

We propose a novel scheme for spliced image detection which involves only the images that are similar, in terms of color, texture, or shape, to the targeted image as depicted in Fig 1. To retrieve these similar images, we directly employ a content-based image retrieval (CBIR) technique. CBIR is a popular scheme in image retrieval, we do not need discuss in detail in this article since it is beyond the scope of our research. In order to have a meaningful scheme, we assume that these similar images are definitely authentic ones. Further, based on its results, we select only the representative images as references. On the other side, given a targeted image, an edge detector is employed to detect edge pixels suspicious of containing any spliced artifacts. Assume that spliced regions introduce discontinuity in their intensities. To find accurately the spliced artifacts, we exploit an interpolation technique to reconstruct the gray-value at the both-side locations nearby the detected edge pixels. By utilizing membership functions, the error rate of the intensities' reconstruction is used to determine whether the artifacts fall into spliced candidates. Once the spliced artifact is found, we have two spliced-region candidates. To precisely select the appropriate one, we align two images, i.e. each region candidate and the reference. If the region candidate can be correctly overlaid on the reference image, the targeted image is considered as the spliced one.

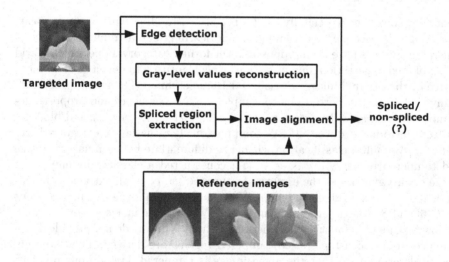

Fig. 1. General scheme of spliced image detection

We fundamentally adopt the concept of pixel-based alignment, which is one part of image registration. Image registration is the process of overlaying two or more images of the same scene taken at different times, from different viewpoints, and/or by different sensors. In other words, given a template image $t(\mathbf{x})$ sampled at discrete pixel locations $\{\mathbf{x}_i = (x_i, y_i)\}$, we wish to find where it is located in a reference image $f(\mathbf{x})$.

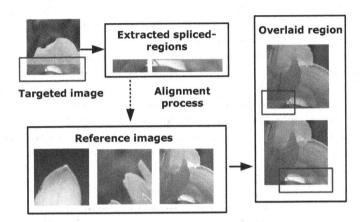

Fig. 2. Exposing image splicing using pixel-based alignment method

Figure 2 illustrates our basic idea to evaluate the authenticity of an image using alignment method. Suppose there exists a targeted image, which is the spliced one, and N reference images that are similar to the targeted one. The spliced region is highlighted in the red box. In this case, the spliced artifact is introduced in the vertical direction, thus causing the region to be divided into two areas. Once the spliced region candidates are extracted, we overlay each region on each reference image to locate the best match entities. The results confirm that both extracted regions are properly overlaid on the third reference, emphasizing the occurrence of splicing condition.

2   Methods

For exposition purpose, we first enlighten the concept of correlation-based alignment and its completion on splicing detection. The complete depiction based on statistics approach is then presented.

2.1   Correlation-Based Alignment

We employ one of the pixel-based alignments referred to as correlation-based approach. In this approach, *normalized cross-correlation* (NCC) is commonly used,

$$\varsigma(u,v) = \frac{\sum_{x,y}\left[f(x,y) - \overline{f}_{u,v}\right]\left[t(x-u,y-v) - \overline{t}\right]}{\sqrt{\sum_{x,y}\left[f(x,y) - \overline{f}_{u,v}\right]^2 \sum_{x,y}\left[t(x-u,y-v) - \overline{t}\right]^2}} \tag{1}$$

where f is the reference image , $\overline{t}$ is the mean of the spliced region, and $\overline{f}$ is the mean of $f(x,y)$ in the region under the spliced region. The correlation coefficient ς is in the range [0,1], with larger value indicating higher level of similarity. ς close to -1 means the matching entities are inverse of each other, ς close to 1 refers to matching entities are exactly the same, and $\varsigma=0$ is an indication of no relationship between the matching entities.

Figure 3 depicts the mechanism of alignment process. Suppose we have a spliced region t of size $m \times n$, which is shown as the red box, we wish to find where it is located in a reference image f of size $p \times q$. The complete correlation coefficient $\varsigma(u,v)$ is obtained by moving the center of the region so that the center of t visits every pixel in f. At the end, we locate the peak value in $\varsigma(u,v)$ to find where the best match occurred. It is possible to have multiple locations in $\varsigma(u,v)$ with the same peak value, indicating several matches between t and f [20].

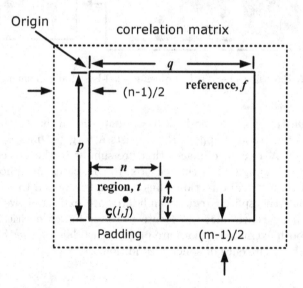

Fig. 3. The mechanism of correlation-based alignment

Let us assume the peak value is located in (i,j) shown as a black dot. What we have now is a correlation matrix ς of size $(p+m-1) \times (q+n-1)$ due to the padding. We exploit the formulas below to approximately locate the expected position of region t within reference f.

$$col_{offset} = j - n, \tag{2}$$

$$row_{offset} = i - m, \tag{3}$$

where col_{offset} refers to a column onset of a region t in the reference f, and row_{offset} denotes the row onset of a region t in the reference f. If both col_{offset} and row_{offset} are equal to zero, it reflects that the onset position of region t is exactly on the origin. Thus the difference between its peak position and the row/column's size is considered as the beginning location of region t. Note that either the col_{offset} or row_{offset} could be negative or exceed matrix dimension of reference f. If this condition occurs, the region t cannot be aligned on reference f.

To evaluate whether the region t is the spliced area, we extract the suspected region from the reference image starting from row_{offset} and col_{offset}. If the suspected region is exactly the same as region t, it is considered as the spliced area. In practical, however, it is infrequent to obtain such condition. To make convincing forgeries, the tampered images have undergone some manipulations with the aid of sophisticated photo editing software. In this case, the region t is no longer exactly the same as its original but it still introduces a high value in correlation coefficient. Therefore, a specific threshold τ is necessary to be determined to evaluate the splicing condition.

2.2   Spliced Artifacts Identification

We define a spliced image as an image derived by combining image portions from different images without further post-processing such as smoothing of boundaries among different portions. To authenticate the given image, we devise the following definition.

Definition 1 (suspected spliced-image). Suppose there are n extracted regions $A=\{a_1, a_2, \cdots, a_n\}$ derived from a given image I, and m reference images $B=\{b_1, b_2, \cdots, b_m\}$. Assume that there exists at least one a_i such that $a_i \subseteq b_j$ for $i=1,\cdots,n$ and $j=1,\cdots,m$. Then, image I is said to be a suspected spliced-image.

As we suppose that spliced artifacts are introduced as edge features, edge detection is the first exploited approach. Given a targeted image, $I_t(x,y)$ for $x = 0$, $1, \ldots, M$ - 1 and $y = 0, 1,\ldots, N$ - 1. *Roberts cross operator*, which implements basic first order edge detection and uses two convolution masks, is conducted to detect edges on $I_t(x,y)$. Let us denote $I_e(x,y)$, where the component of $I_e(x,y)$ is in $\{0,1\}$, is the resulting of edge-detected image. We then construct two edge matrices E_h and E_v to be a $m \times n$, $n=3$, $m \in [0, L\text{-}1]$, where L is the number of detected edges. E_h and E_v respectively contains detected edges in both horizontal and vertical directions whose $(i,1)^{th}$, $(i,2)^{th}$, and $(i,3)^{th}$ entries represents the row/column index, onset of an edge, and the number of edge pixels, correspondingly.

Assume an edge segment has been identified. The spliced region may be viewed as an area in which the intensity on the either side of the detected edge changes abruptly. It is expected that the spliced portions demonstrate their prediction errors in large difference, thus makes the splicing detection more efficient.

In doing so, we accomplish bilinear interpolation to the detected edges which can be expressed as

$$v(x, y) = ax + by + cxy + d \tag{4}$$

where the four coefficients are determined from the four equations in four unknown variables that can be written using the four nearest neighbors of point (x,y).

As previously described, we focus on the edge detected in horizontal and vertical directions. We reconstruct the gray-level value on two locations, e.g. the edge pixels, and the pixels adjacent to the edge pixel. For the latter case, the adjacent pixels may be located on top and bottom area of detected edge (horizontal direction), or on left and right side of the detected edge (vertical direction). The interpolation is then accomplished to these adjacent pixels along the detected edge. Next, we compute the error prediction residual. As a result, there are two residual matrices, MSE_p and MSE_{ratio} which refer to prediction error and prediction error ratio, respectively.

In practice, of course, the spliced artifacts are often introduced hardly noticeable. Thus it is fairly hard to identify the spliced region and likely fall into an uncertainty problem. Inspired by Ye et al in [21], we consider that exploiting membership function is most adequate in representing uncertainty in measurement. In order to identify the spliced artifacts, we investigate on several parameters: prediction error, prediction error ratio, and a number of occurrences of detected edge pixels. In order to provide a comprehensible understanding, we define the following definition for the first two parameters.

Definition 2 (Prediction-error). Suppose $I'=\{i_1,i_2,\ldots,i_n\}$ represents predicted pixel intensities and $I=\{i_1,i_2,\ldots,i_n\}$ indicates corresponding original intensity values on a detected edge of n edge pixels with I' and $I\epsilon \{0,\ldots,255\}$. Then, **prediction-error** refers to MSE of I' from I.

Definition 3 (Prediction-error-ratio). Let us assume the detected edge segment is in horizontal direction. Suppose $I'_T=\{i_1,i_2,\ldots,i_n\}$ and $I'_B=\{i_1,i_2,\ldots,i_n\}$ represents predicted pixel intensities of top and bottom region, respectively, with elements I'_T and $I'_B \epsilon \{0,\ldots,255\}$ of number of edge pixels n. If there exists MSE_T and MSE_B which stand for mean squared prediction error of top and bottom region, respectively, then **prediction-error-ratio** is defined as ratio of MSE_T to MSE_B.

Either the prediction-error-ratio or prediction-error of spliced region often occurs in an extreme value, whereas the authentic one is in average rate. In terms of edge pixel occurrences, the spliced region may have an extreme occurrence, while the authentic one emerges on average rate. Based on these observations, the following rules are devised:

1. The candidate spliced region has an extreme prediction error and large deviation, whereas the prediction error of a non-spliced region is on average value.
2. The candidate spliced region has a prediction error ratio in an extreme value and has large deviation, whereas the ratio of a non-spliced region is in small value.
3. The candidate spliced region has an extreme occurrence and large deviation, whereas the non-spliced region occurs on average amount.

We use sigmoid and Gaussian membership functions to calculate the degree of membership for each rule above denoted as

$$\mu_i^E = \begin{cases} 1 & \text{if } X \geq \gamma_i, \\ \dfrac{1}{1 + exp\left(-\dfrac{(X - \gamma_i)^2}{(X - \alpha_i)\sigma_i^2}\right)} & \text{otherwise .} \end{cases} \quad (5)$$

$$\mu_i^{av} = exp\left(-\frac{\left(X - \overline{\beta}\right)^2}{X . \sigma_i^2}\right). \quad (6)$$

Symbol i refers to the rule. For each rule, X refers to prediction error, prediction error ratio, and number of occurrence of edge pixels. Akin to X, σ^2 for each rule refers to standard deviation of prediction error, prediction error ratio, and number of occurrence of edge pixels. Parameter β of each rule refers to the average of acceptable prediction error, prediction error ratio, and occurrence. Lastly, γ and α respectively represents maximum and minimum acceptable value of prediction error, prediction error ratio, and occurrence of edge pixels.

The authenticity is determined by comparing two variables, namely D_S which refers to the degree of spliced region, and D_A represents degree of non-tampered region, and are denoted as

$$\begin{cases} D_S = max\left\{\mu_1^E, \mu_2^E, \mu_3^E\right\} \\ D_A = max\left\{min\left(1 - \mu_1^E, 1 - \mu_2^E, 1 - \mu_3^E\right), min\left(\mu_1^{av}, \mu_2^{av}, \mu_3^{av}\right)\right\} \end{cases} \quad (7)$$

If $D_S > D_A$, then the region is identified as a spliced region; otherwise it is considered as a non-spliced region. Parameters μ_1^E, μ_2^E, and μ_3^E refer to degree of tampered region, while μ_1^{av}, μ_2^{av}, and μ_3^{av} denote degree of non-tampered region.

Once the spliced artifacts identified, we obtain two candidate spliced regions. To verify the authenticity of a given image, correlation-based alignment method is then conducted. If any region candidate precisely aligned on either reference images, the given image is said to be spliced image, and vice versa. See Algorithm 1 for a detailed description.

Algorithm 1. Spliced_Verification(I_t, I_r)

Input:

I_t : a given image.

I_r : reference images, $I_r = \{s_1, s_2, \cdots, s_n\}, n$ is the number of reference images.

1: $\langle E_h, E_v \rangle \leftarrow$ edge_detection(I_t)

2: $\langle MSE_p, MSE_{ratio} \rangle \leftarrow$ interpolation(E_h, E_v)

3: $R \leftarrow$ region_extraction(MSE_p, MSE_{ratio})

   $R = \{r_1, r_2, \cdots, r_m\}$, m is the number of extracted regions.

4: **for all** $r \in R$ **do**

5:     $e_i \leftarrow$ alignment(r_i, s_j)

6:     **if** $r_i = e_i$ **then**

7:         **print** "It is a forgery"

8:     **else**

9:         **compute** NCC(r_i, e_i) $\Leftrightarrow e_i$ is visually similar to r_i

10:         **if** $\varsigma(r_i, e_i) \geq \tau$ **then**

11:             **print** "It is a forgery"

12:         **else**

13:             **print** "It is a non-tampered"

14:         **end if**

15:     **end if**

16: **end for**

---

3 Experimental Results

In this section, we evaluate the quantitative performance of the proposed spliced detection method on a set of generated spliced images.

3.1 Synthesized Spliced Images

We exploit an available public image dataset provided by Columbia DVMM Research Lab [22]. It consists of 933 authentic and 912 spliced image blocks of size 128 × 128. Each class is divided into five categories, i.e. smooth, texture, smooth-smooth, smooth-texture, and texture-texture. However, all spliced region on provided images are roughly derived from the image itself. To evaluate our proposed approach, we have to construct different spliced image dataset. We collect 217 authentic from provided images and construct 219 spliced images based on authentic ones. We construct the spliced images in the following way:

  a. For each authentic image, we first collect several arbitrary images with different scene.
  b. We randomly choose region(s) from references, copy the region(s), and paste onto the authentic one.
  c. The size of a spliced region is arbitrary in order to yield an unnoticeable artifact.

Fifteen examples of smooth, texture, and smooth-texture images used in our experiment are depicted in Figure 4.

Fig. 4. Examples of synthesized spliced images used in our experiments. The first, second, and third rows depict consecutively samples of smooth, texture, and smooth-texture images.

3.2 Sensitivity

From the digital forensics point of view, it is important to quantify the sensitivity of our detection method. Consider the following four categories: True positives (TP) are examples correctly identified as spliced images. False positive (FP) refers to examples incorrectly identified as spliced images. True negative (TN) corresponds to examples correctly rejected as spliced images. Finally, False negative (FN) refers to examples incorrectly rejected as spliced images. We define the True Positive Rate (TPR) as the fraction of spliced images that are correctly identified, i.e. TPR= TP/(TP+FN), and False Positive Rate (FPR) as the fraction of non-spliced images that are misclassified as spliced images, i.e. FPR=FP/(FP+TN).

We evaluate the images, either spliced or authentic images, into three categories: smooth, texture, and smooth-texture. The total number of samples used in experiment is 435 images. The parameters are configured as follows. The threshold τ is set to 0.9. The parameter γ_1 and α_1 set to 6581.31 and 3023, respectively. In terms of ratio, the parameter γ_2 and α_2 is correspondingly set to be 120 and 44. And, we let respectively γ_3 and α_3 be 25 and 15. These membership function parameters are investigated by exploiting the following outlier formula.

$$outlier = \begin{cases} ub & \text{if } 1.5\,(IQR) > Q_3 \\ lb & \text{if } 1.5\,(IQR) < Q_1 \end{cases} \tag{8}$$

where $Q_1(.)$, $Q_2(.)$, and $Q_3(.)$ represent quartile function, and IQR (*interquartile range*) is computed as $Q_3 - Q_1$. We observe that spliced features tend to exhibit an outlier value over others. Thus, to determine γ_i and α_i values, we experimentally observe outliers which are greater than ub (upper bound).

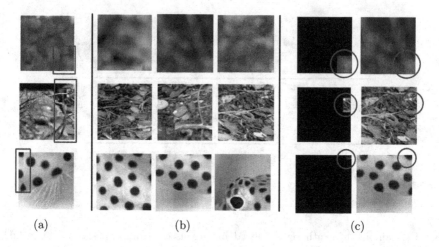

(a)   (b)   (c)

Fig. 5. Alignment results on given spliced images. (a) shows the given spliced images. The red box exhibits the spliced region and red circles represent its actual position. (b) depicts reference images that correspond to the first column. The spliced regions' positions located in corresponding reference images and the results of alignment processes are shown in (c).

Figure 5 depicts several examples of aligning the extracted region throughout reference images. It illustrates that correlation-based alignment is able to distinguish a typical pattern, e.g. smooth, repetitive, and geometrical pattern. By exploiting correlation-based alignment, it can precisely reveal the source of spliced region. The right most columns show the location of spliced region found on its corresponding reference. Thus it reflects that the given image falls into the tampered one. On the other side, our scheme principally relies on how accurate the detector algorithm identifies the spliced artifacts. We observe that Robert's detector utilizes 2-D mask with a diagonal preference which means that diagonal edge direction is of interest. Images that occur with various directions in intensity are likely undetectable. Thus the average of true positive is approximately 85.68%.

For non-spliced image, a true negative occurs when our method is able to disarrange the extracted regions on reference images or the correlation is below a specific threshold τ. Figure 6 is the sample results of our proposed scheme against a repetitive pattern. The extracted regions of such a pattern are supposed to introduce their correlation coefficient in high value. The given images, however, can be correctly identified as negative examples.

In terms of diagnostic parameters, for the smooth type, our scheme achieves true positive greater than 88% with an average of 0.03 false positive. Image with texture pattern attains approximately 95% with an average of 0.01 false positive, while true positive texture-smooth pattern can roughly be reached to 92% with an average of 0.02 false positive. This is consistent with the result reflected by receiver operating characteristics (ROC) graphs depicted in Fig. 7.

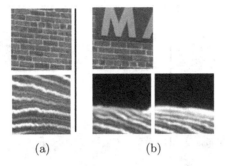

(a)   (b)

Fig. 6. (a) shows authentic images, and their corresponding reference images are given in (b). We deliberately select typical samples, such as repetitive or geometrical pattern, to exhibit the reliability of our scheme.

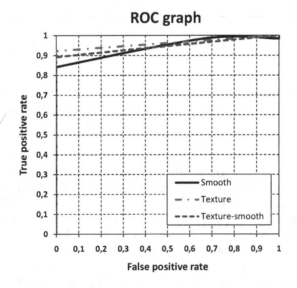

Fig. 7. ROC graph of the three image types showing that texture pattern achieves the best accuracy compare to other two types

3.3   Realistic Detection

It is desirable to evaluate any detection system in practical situation. Investigation on alleged forgery images that has raised public's attention is one reasonable way. In this section, we evaluate our scheme against several convinced spliced images provided by Fourandsix Technologies, Inc.[1]

Figure 8 depicts that our method is able to reveal the regions that are suspicious of the tampered parts of the image. The regions below the images,

---

[1] Image source: `http://www.fourandsix.com/photo-tampering-history/`

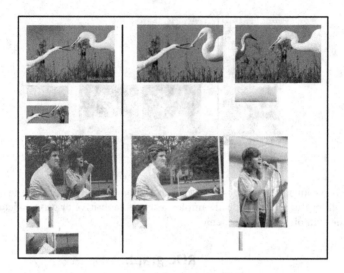

Fig. 8. Detection results of our method on a set of realistic forgery images

both forgery and reference images, demonstrate the extracted suspicious regions. These images have undergone some convinced effects by using state-of-the-art image retouching algorithms and tools, thus these tampered regions cannot be overlaid on their references. Their correlation coefficients, however, achieve a considerable value greater than 0.9. For example, the splicing bird photo, the first extracted region has its corresponding region on the first reference. Although the tampered region is not fully extracted, its correlation coefficient equals to 0.9725. It states that our scheme precisely detects the tampering. While another extracted region, which is subjected to the tampered one, has no corresponding region in any references. Of course, since it is a spliced portion, such scene cannot be found in any references. Similarly, the first two suspicious regions of KerryFonda's photo have their corresponding regions on the references. Their correlation coefficients achieve 0.909591 and 0.945296, respectively. While another suspicious region containing spliced portion has no corresponding region on any reference. Among ten collected images from outside the dataset, our accuracy is still left behind that of evaluation over dataset.

4   Concluding Remark

Image source identification is the main design of our approach, particularly in revealing the tampering evidence of a given image. We have described one of the pixel alignment techniques, that is correlation-based, to automatically identify such a spliced area in any region of the reference images. High value of peak of correlation coefficient does not guarantee it belongs to a spliced region. Low value of peak of correlation might belong to a spliced region. This technique is able to overcome such situations as well as distinguish images with typical pattern, such as geometrical patterns.

Despite having attained well performance in exposing digital forgeries, our approach relies on edge artifact detection. The forgeries which do not introduce any edges are hard to be detected, or might cause fault extraction. The bird image shown in Fig. 8 indicates such a case. Our expectation is that those two birds can be separately extracted. As a future work, we are currently exploring other approaches to improve the detection performance for such cases. We believe, however, that this technique still provide usefulness in digital forensics environment, for example in case of providing proofs of tampering in the court of law.

Acknowledgments. The first author is partially supported by Telecommunication Advancement Foundation Japan, and fully supported by the Directorate General of Higher Education, Ministry of National Education, Indonesia. The second author acknowledges support provided by Grant NRF-2011-013-D00121 from the National Research Foundation of Korea.

References

1. Ng, T.T., Chang, S.F., Sun, Q.: Blind Detection of Photomontage using Higher Order Statistics. In: IEEE International Symposium on Circuits and Systems, vol. 5, pp. 688–691 (2004)
2. Johnson, M.K., Farid, H.: Exposing digital forgeries by detecting inconsistencies in lighting. In: ACM Multimedia and Security Workshop (2005)
3. Hsu, Y.-F., Chang, S.-F.: Detecting image splicing using geometry invariants and camera characteristics consistency. In: IEEE International Conference on Multimedia and Expo. (ICME) (2006)
4. Chen, W., Shi, Y.Q., Su, W.: Image Splicing Detection using 2-D Phase Congruency and Statistical Moments of Characteristic Function. In: Society of Photo-Optical Instrumentation Engineers (SPIE) Conference Series, vol. 6505, art. No. 65050R. SPIE, Washington (2007)
5. Ye, S., Sun, Q., Chang, E.C.: Detecting Digital Image Forgeries by Measuring Inconsistencies of Blocking Artifact. In: IEEE International Conference on Multimedia and Expo. (ICME) (2007)
6. Dong, J., Wang, W., Tan, T., Shi, Y.Q.: Run-Length and Edge Statistics Based Approach for Image Splicing Detection. In: Kim, H.-J., Katzenbeisser, S., Ho, A.T.S. (eds.) IWDW 2008. LNCS, vol. 5450, pp. 76–87. Springer, Heidelberg (2009)
7. Ciptasari, R.W., Rhee, K.-H., Sakurai, K.: An Image Splicing Detection Based on Interpolation Analysis. In: Lin, W., Xu, D., Ho, A., Wu, J., He, Y., Cai, J., Kankanhalli, M., Sun, M.-T. (eds.) PCM 2012. LNCS, vol. 7674, pp. 390–401. Springer, Heidelberg (2012)
8. Farid, H.: Detecting Digital Forgeries Using Bispectral Analysis. Technical Report AIM-1657, AI Lab, Massachusetts Institute of Technology (1999)
9. Ng, T.T., Chang, S.F., Lin, C.Y., Sun, Q.: Passive-blind Image Forensics. In: Zeng, W., Yu, H., Lin, C.Y. (eds.) Multimedia Security Technologies for Digital Rights, ch. 15, pp. 383–412. cademic Press, Missouri (2006)

10. Popescu, A.C., Farid, H.: Exposing Digital Forgeries by Detecting Traces of Resampling. IEEE Transaction on Signal Processing 53(2), 758–767 (2005)
11. Prasad, S., Ramakrishnan, K.R.: On Resampling Detection And Its Application To Detect Image Tampering. In: IEEE International Conference on Multimedia and Expo. (ICME) (2006)
12. Pan, X., Lyu, S.: Region Duplication Detection using Image Feature Matching. IEEE Transaction on Information Forensics and Security 5(4), 857–867 (2010)
13. Farid, H., Lyu, S.: Higher-order Wavelet Statistics and their Application to Digital Forensics. In: IEEE Workshop on Statistical Analysis in Computer Vision (in Conjunction with CVPR) (2003)
14. Avcibas, I., Bayram, S., Memon, N., Sankur, B., Ramkumar, M.: A Classifier Design for Detecting Image Manipulations. In: IEEE International Conference on Image Processing, ICIP (2004)
15. Bayram, S., Avcibas, I., Sankur, B., Memon, N.: Image Manipulation Detection. Journal of Electronic Imaging 15(4), 041102 (2006)
16. Sutthiwan, P., Shi, Y.Q., Zhao, H., Ng, T.-T., Su, W.: Markovian Rake Transform for Digital Image Tampering Detection. In: Shi, Y.Q., Emmanuel, S., Kankanhalli, M.S., Chang, S.-F., Radhakrishnan, R., Ma, F., Zhao, L. (eds.) Transaction on DHMS VI. LNCS, vol. 6730, pp. 1–17. Springer, Heidelberg (2011)
17. Wang, W., Farid, H.: Exposing digital forgeries in video by detecting duplication. In: Proceeding ACM Workshop on MMSec, Dallas, TX (2007)
18. Ng, T.T.: Statistical and Geometric Methods for Passive-blind Image Forensics. Ph.D. Dissertation, Columbia University (2007)
19. Szeliski, R.: Image Alignment and Stitching: A Tutorial. Computer Graphics and Vision 2(1), 1–104 (2006), doi:10.1561/0600000009
20. Gonzalez, R.C., Woods, R.E.: Digital Image Processing, 3rd edn. Pearson Prentice Hall (2008)
21. Ye, S.M., Sun, Q.B., Chang, E.C.: Error resilient content-based image authentication over wireless channel. In: IEEE Int. Symp. Circuits and Systems (ISCAS), Kobe, Japan, pp. 2707–2710 (2005)
22. Ng, T.T., Chang, S., Sun, Q.: A data set of authentic and spliced image blocks. In: ADVENT Technical Report 203-2004-3. Columbia University (June 2004), http://www.ee.columbia.edu/trustfoto

Multimedia Operator Chain Topology and Ordering Estimation Based on Detection and Information Theoretic Tools

Pedro Comesaña[1] and Fernando Pérez-González[1,2,⋆]

[1] Signal Theory and Communications Department, University Vigo
E. E. Telecomunicación, Campus-Lagoas Marcosende, Vigo 36310, Spain
[2] Gradiant (Galician Research and Development Center in
Advanced Telecommunications), Vigo 36310, Spain
{pcomesan,fperez}@gts.tsc.uvigo.es
http://www.gts.tsc.uvigo.es/gpsc/

Abstract. The extensive use of multimedia editing tools suitable for non-skilled users has significantly reduced the trust on audiovisual contents. Simultaneously, a new branch of multimedia security, named multimedia forensics, has been developed to cope with this problem. Nevertheless, most of the schemes proposed so far are heuristic and ad-hoc solutions that try to deal with a particular signal processing operator (or a simple combination of them). In a previous work by the authors, fundamental limits to forensics applications are provided, based on the use of two well-known measures, originated at the detection and information theory fields. In the current work the suitability of those measures for establishing the topology and ordering of the operator chain a multimedia content has gone through is illustrated. The provided results show that in general different operator chains can be distinguished, although in some particular cases (e.g., comparison between double and triple quantization) the considered operator chains can be completely indistinguishable.

Keywords: Multimedia forensics, ordering detection, topology detection, operator parameter estimation.

1 Introduction

In the last decades the number of multimedia contents and their impact in our lives has dramatically increased. The cost reduction of capture devices, especially digital cameras, and the growth of digital networks where those contents can be

⋆ Research supported by the European Union under project REWIND (Grant Agreement Number 268478), the European Regional Development Fund (ERDF) and the Spanish Government under projects DYNACS (TEC2010-21245-C02-02/TCM) and COMONSENS (CONSOLIDER-INGENIO 2010 CSD2008-00010), and the Galician Regional Government under projects "Consolidation of Research Units" 2009/62, 2010/85 and SCALLOPS (10PXIB322231PR).

Y.Q. Shi, H.J. Kim, and F. Pérez-González (Eds.): IWDW 2012, LNCS 7809, pp. 213–227, 2013.

published have converted multimedia contents not only in valuable proofs of our personal evolution and social life, but also in a weapon that can be used to harm the public image of individuals. Therefore, multimedia contents have evolved to be considered precious assets with both implicit and explicit value that one would like to preserve. However, together with this growth, a huge number of editing tools available in applications for non-skilled users have proliferated during this time, thus compromising the reliability of those contents, and strongly constraining their use in some applications, for example as court evidence. As a consequence, trust on multimedia contents has steadily decreased.

In this context, multimedia forensics, an area of multimedia security, has appeared as a possible solution to the decrease of confidence on multimedia contents. The target of multimedia forensics can be summarized as assessing the processing, coding and editing steps a content has gone through. Although much effort has been paid to this topic in the last years, most of the proposed solutions are somewhat heuristic ad-hoc methods that do not answer to the question of what is the optimal way of detecting the operators the contents have undergone, or how easily different operator chains can be distinguished. Answers to those fundamental questions are provided in a previous work by the authors [4], proposing the use of detection and information theoretic measures. The target of this work is to provide distinguishability results on a number of new scenarios not analyzed so far, as well as illustrating the suitability of those measures for identifying the operator chain ordering.

The remaining of this paper is organized as follows: previous approaches to multimedia forensics problems, paying special attention to JPEG and double JPEG quantization, are summarized in Sect. 2; the proposed measures are presented in Sect. 3. Sect. 4 presents some experimental results on three relevant practical scenarios, while Sect. 5 reports results on the use of those measures for distinguishing the ordering of operators in processing chains. Finally, Sect. 6 summarizes the main conclusions of this work and discusses future lines.

2   Previous Works on Quantization and Double Quantization Detection and Estimation

In this section we give a brief overview of some state-of-the-art forensics methods dealing with quantization; our interest in that operator is related to the scenarios analyzed in Sect. 4, which in turn are just an example of the applicability of the measures we propose to use in forensics. By no means we try to be exhaustive, but simply provide a rough picture of some of the solutions that have been proposed in the last years, emphasizing their ad-hoc and/or heuristic nature.

One of the first works in the literature dealing with the single quantization detection and estimation is due to Fan and Queiroz [6], where the detection statistic depends on the difference between the histogram of the pixel differences across blocks and within blocks. Once the quantization is detected, a Maximum Likelihood (ML) estimator, based on assuming that the AC DCT coefficients follow a Laplacian distribution, is used for estimating the quantization step. A completely different approach was proposed by Lin *et al.* in [8], where in order to check the suitability of a candidate transform, the authors try to estimate the pdf of the original (unquantized) coefficients by interpolating the histogram of the observed coefficients, and then compute the normalized correlation between this pdf approximation and the observed histogram; if the obtained value is high, then the considered transform will likely be the one used in coding. In another relevant work [11], the variability of the integral of the AC DCT coefficients in different intervals is exploited in order to detect the quantization artifacts; the same idea is then used to determine the transform encoder.

Concerning double quantization, in [9] Lukas and Fridrich propose a method for estimating the first quantization matrix; they study some characteristic features that appear in DCT coefficient histograms when those coefficients are quantized; although several strategies are proposed, the most successful one is based on neural networks. An alternative approach is proposed by Fu *et al.* in [7], where a generalized version of Benford's law is exploited for JPEG detection and estimation, and double JPEG detection. In [12], Milani *et al.* also exploit the distribution of the most significant digits of DCT coefficients, modeled according to Benford's law, to estimate the number of compression stages the image has gone through. In another proposal, Luo *et al.* [10] study the blocking artifacts introduced by misaligned double JPEG coding; with the help of a SVM that information is used to determine if an image is a JPEG original or it was cropped from other JPEG image and re-saved as JPEG. The non-aligned double JPEG artifacts on the pdf of the DCT coefficients are exploited in [1] for locating image forgeries.

3   Distinguishability Measures

This section summarizes the reasons for using the distinguishability measures exploited in Sects. 4 and 5. Since an extensive motivation of their use was already provided in [4], the current work will just recall their advantages and definitions (the interested reader is referred to [4]).[1] First of all, the desirable characterisitcs of our distinguishability measures are enumerated:

- they should be capable of reliably determining if a multimedia content has gone through an arbitrary chain of operators which are arranged in a particular ordering and topology.
- they should allow to quantify how easily two different chains of operators (characterized by their ordering and topology, and where in some circumstances additional knowledge on the operator parameters is assumed) can be distinguished.

---

[1] During the celebration of IWDW 2012, Dr. Rainer Böhme pointed to the authors the links between the approach proposed in [4] and [2]. Despite the evident similarities, we would like to mention that in [2] the Kullback-Leibler Divergence is proposed to be used only when analyzing counter-forensic attacks; furthermore, the theoretical framework proposed in [4] enables the formalization of a series of scenarios, for example, the case where the attacker assumes some *a priori* information on the input signal distribution, or on the operator chain parameters.

- some optimality criterion should be followed; for example, minimizing the false positive probability (i.e., determining that the considered content has gone through a given operator chain, when it has not) for a given false negative probability (i.e., saying that the content has not undergone a given operator chain, when indeed it has).
- it is also desirable the detection scheme to be blind, meaning that deterministic knowledge of the original multimedia content should not be required, although some kind of *a priori* information about the original statistical distribution will typically be assumed to be known.

Based on these requirements, the use of two different measures is proposed for distinguishing operator chains.

3.1 Detection-Theoretic Measure

From a detection theory point of view the problem of determining which distribution out of two possible candidates produced a given observation, is modeled as a binary hypothesis test; it is well known that the most powerful test (i.e., that one minimizing the probability of false positive for a given false negative probability) in that scenario is given by the Neyman-Pearson Lemma, which uses the likelihood-ratio between the so-called null hypothesis (denoted by θ_0) and the alternative hypothesis (denoted by θ_1), i.e., $\Lambda(\mathbf{x}) = \frac{p(\theta_0|\mathbf{X})}{p(\theta_1|\mathbf{X})}$, where $\mathbf{x}$ denotes the n-dimensional signal under test. Assuming that no *a priori* information about the different hypotheses is available, the former ratio is equivalent to

$$\mathrm{LLR}(\mathbf{x}) = \log\left(\frac{p(\mathbf{x}|\theta_0)}{p(\mathbf{x}|\theta_1)}\right),$$

for the discrete case (the continuous counterpart has an analogous form). For the sake of notational simplicity we will use $p(\mathbf{x}|\theta_i) = p_i(\mathbf{x})$.

Be aware that θ_0 and θ_1 define the considered operator chain topology (i.e., how the operators are linked, in parallel or series) and ordering, as well as the specific parameters characterizing each operator. Therefore, the generality objective is achieved by this measure, as it can be useful, among others, for detecting:

- the ordering and topology of the operator chain whenever a fixed set of operators, each of them using fixed parameters, is considered;
- the presence of different operators in chains sharing the same topology;
- the use of different operator parameters in processing chains using the same operators with common ordering and topology;
- combinations of the previous scenarios.

3.2 Information-Theoretic Measure

Concerning information-theoretic measures devoted to quantify the differences between two pdfs/pmfs, probably the most used choice is the Kullback-Leibler divergence (a.k.a. Kullback-Leibler distance and relative entropy). This measure was used, for example, for quantifying the statistic detectability of the watermark embedding in steganography [3]. For the discrete case it is defined as

$$D(p_0||p_1) = \sum_{\mathbf{x} \in \mathcal{X}} p_0(\mathbf{x}) \log \left(\frac{p_0(\mathbf{x})}{p_1(\mathbf{x})} \right),$$

where $\mathcal{X}$ is the discret alphabet where $\mathbf{x}$ takes values. The KLD is non-negative, being null if and only if the two considered distributions are the same almost everywhere; indeed, in order to provide an intuitive insight, one can say that the closer two distributions are, the smaller their KLD is.

Concerning the relationship between both measures, it is a well-known result that the relative entropy version of the Asymptotic Equipartition Property establishes that if $\mathbf{X}$ is a sequence of random variables drawn i.i.d. according to $p_0(\mathbf{x})$, then $\frac{1}{n} \log \left(\frac{p_0(\mathbf{X})}{p_1(\mathbf{X})} \right) \to D(p_0||p_1)$, where convergence takes place in probability [5]. In plain words, this result shows that when the contents produced under the null hypothesis are i.i.d. and the dimensionality of the considered problem goes to infinity, then the two measures whose use is proposed for forensic applications are asymptotically equivalent. This confirms that both measures are good candidates for quantifying the distinguishability between different operator chain topologies, and/or operator chains with different operator parameters, providing a coherent framework.

Finally, the Chernoff-Stein Lemma [5] states that the false positive probability error exponent achievable for a given non-null false negative probability asymptotically converges to $D(p_0||p_1)$ (as long as that measure takes a finite value) when the dimensionality of the problem goes to infinity.

4   Studied Scenarios

In this section the mentioned distinguishability measures are used for quantifying the closeness between the distributions corresponding to different operator parameters of three operator chains, i.e., for quantifying how easily the use of different processing parameters in those operator chains could be identified. The operator parameters used for generating the considered samples (i.e., those corresponding to the null hypothesis) will be denoted by the subindex 0, while 1 will refer to the tested values (corresponding to the alternative hypothesis). In case that a subindex were already used for denoting the corresponding parameter (e.g., Δ_i), a second subindex will be added for denoting the null or alternative hypothesis (i.e., $\Delta_{i,j}$, where $j = 0, 1$).

The used distinguishability measures will be those introduced in Sect. 3, i.e., the LLR of the observed signal for the null and alternative hypotheses, and the KLD; in the latter case two choices are considered for the null hypothesis distribution: the theoretical distribution, and its empirical counterpart, i.e., the histogram of the considered content.

4.1   Scenario 1: Quantization; Gamma Correction; Quantization

- **Operator chain description:** the input content (e.g., an image) is quantized (with quantization stepsize Δ_1), for example due to Analog to Digital Conversion. Then, the obtained digital content goes through gamma correction with parameter γ in order to improve the contrast; as the levels of the output signal do not belong to a lattice (i.e., they are not equidistant), a second quantization (with quantization stepsize Δ_2) is performed in order to produce a content with equidistant coding levels. The last quantization stepsize is assumed to be known.
- **Application scenario:** an image is captured using a lossless format (such as TIFF), and then it is gamma-corrected to improve its contrast; as the output of the corrector is in general a real number, a second quantization must be performed in order to produce an output TIFF image. In this example of use, compression algorithms (e.g., JPEG) are not considered, as the quantization and the gamma correction should be performed in the same domain; given that the gamma correction is usually applied in the pixel domain, that should be also the case for the quantization, while those compression algorithms most of times work in a transform domain (as the DCT). Since the considered processing operates pointwise, the dependence among neighboring pixels of natural images can be neglected for our analysis. Although an accurate pdf model would probably require a more complicated characterization, since these scenarios just try to illustrate the usefulness of the proposed measures, we will model the pixels by an i.i.d. Gaussian with mean $\mu_X = 128$ and variance $\sigma_X^2 = 240$, truncated to lie in the interval $[0, 255]$.
- **PMF theoretical model:** in this case it will be useful to introduce the pmf of the signal at the output of the first quantizer, which is given by

$$p^{\text{quant}_1}(k\Delta_1|\Delta_1) = \begin{cases} \mathcal{Q}\left(\frac{k\Delta_1 - \Delta_1/2 - \mu_X}{\sigma_X}\right) - \mathcal{Q}\left(\frac{k\Delta_1 + \Delta_1/2 - \mu_X}{\sigma_X}\right), & \text{if } k \in \mathbb{N}, k > 0, \text{ and } k < \left(\frac{255}{\Delta_1} - \frac{1}{2}\right) \\ 1 - \mathcal{Q}\left(\frac{\Delta_1/2 - \mu_X}{\sigma_X}\right), & \text{if } k = 0 \\ \mathcal{Q}\left(\frac{k_1\Delta_1 - \Delta_1/2 - \mu_X}{\sigma_X}\right), & \text{if } k = k_1 \\ 0, & \text{otherwise} \end{cases}$$

where $k_1 = \lceil \frac{255}{\Delta_1} - \frac{1}{2} \rceil$, and $\mathcal{Q}(x) = \int_x^\infty \frac{e^{\frac{-\tau^2}{2}}}{\sqrt{2\pi}} d\tau$. Based on this distribution, the pmf of the operator chain output in this scenario is given by

$$p^1(k\Delta_2|\Delta_1, \gamma, \Delta_2) = \sum_{m \in \mathcal{M}_k} p^{\text{quant}_1}(m\Delta_1|\Delta_1),$$

where $\mathcal{M}_k = \left\{ m : Q_{\Delta_2}\left(255\left[\frac{m\Delta_1}{255}\right]^\gamma\right) = k\Delta_2 \right\}$, $Q_\Delta(\cdot)$ is the uniform scalar quantizer with stepsize Δ.

- **Known/unknown parameters:** the first quantization stepsize will be denoted by Δ_1, and the gamma correction parameter by γ; both are assumed to be unknown to the forensics analyst. On the other hand, the second quantization stepsize Δ_2, as well as the mean and variance of the input signal will be assumed to be known.

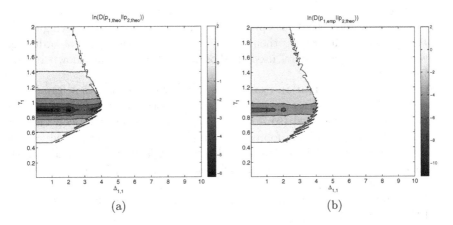

Fig. 1. Theoretical (a) and empirical (b) KLD for Scenario 1. $\Delta_{1,0} = 1$, $\gamma_0 = 0.9$, $\Delta_{2,0} = \Delta_{2,1} = 4$, $n = 10^6$.

- **Results:** Figs. 1, and 2 show the theoretical and empirical KLDs, as well as the LLR for $\Delta_{1,0} = 1$ (first quantization stepsize for the null hypothesis), $\gamma_0 = 0.9$ (gamma correction factor for the null hypothesis), $\Delta_{2,0} = \Delta_{2,1} = 4$ (the second quantization stepsize used for producing the input content is assumed to be known, as it can be easily estimated by the forensics analyst), and $n = 10^6$. As one would expect, the minimum of the considered functions are located at $\Delta_{1,1} = 1$ and $\gamma_1 = 0.9$, showing that for this case, the two hypotheses would be least distinguishable.

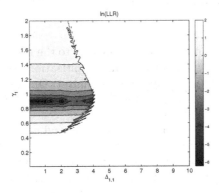

Fig. 2. LLR for Scenario 1. $\Delta_{1,0} = 1$, $\gamma_0 = 0.9$, $\Delta_{2,0} = \Delta_{2,1} = 4$, $n = 10^6$.

4.2   Scenario 2: Gamma Correction; Quantization; Quantization

- **Operator chain description:** this scenario is very similar to the previous one, but in this case the first quantization and the gamma correction are swapped. The relevance of considering these two related scenarios is that later we will show that the proposed measures are able to distinguished between them, illustrating their ability for determining operator ordering, even when the parameters used in those operators are not known by the forensics analyst.

– **Application scenario:** an example of use of this scenario is a framework where we have a camera with an analog gamma corrector; then, the corrected analog signal is digitized (so a first fine quantization must be considered). Finally, trying to fool the forensics analyst, or just in order to reduce the size of the produced image, a second quantizer is used (e.g., the original signal could use 12 bits for coding each color component of a pixel, while the output of the second quantizer could use just 8).

– **PMF theoretical model:** in this case the pmf of the signal at the output of the first quantizer is

$$
p^{\text{quant}_2}(k\Delta_1|\Delta_1) =
\begin{cases}
Q\left(\dfrac{255\left(\frac{k\Delta_1-\Delta_1/2}{255}\right)^{1/\gamma}-\mu_X}{\sigma_X}\right) - Q\left(\dfrac{255\left(\frac{k\Delta_1+\Delta_1/2}{255}\right)^{1/\gamma}-\mu_X}{\sigma_X}\right), & \begin{array}{l}\text{if } k \in \mathbb{N}, k > 0, \\ \text{and } k < \left(\frac{255}{\Delta_1}-\frac{1}{2}\right)\end{array} \\[2em]
1 - Q\left(\dfrac{255\left(\frac{\Delta_1/2}{255}\right)^{1/\gamma}-\mu_X}{\sigma_X}\right), & \text{if } k = 0 \\[2em]
Q\left(\dfrac{255\left(\frac{k_2\Delta_1-\Delta_1/2}{255}\right)^{1/\gamma}-\mu_X}{\sigma_X}\right), & \text{if } k = k_2 \\[1em]
0, & \text{otherwise}
\end{cases}
$$

where $k_2 = \lceil\frac{255}{\Delta_1} - \frac{1}{2}\rceil$. Based on this distribution, the pmf on this scenario is given by

$$
p^2(k\Delta_2|\gamma, \Delta_1, \Delta_2) = \sum_{m\in\mathcal{L}_k} p^{\text{quant}_2}(m\Delta_1|\Delta_1),
$$

where $\mathcal{L}_k : \{m : Q_{\Delta_2}(m\Delta_1) = k\Delta_2\}$.

– **Known/unknown parameters:** similarly to the previous case, the gamma correction parameter γ, and the first quantization stepsize Δ_1 will be assumed to be unknown to the forensics analyst. On the other hand, the second quantization stepsize Δ_2, as well as the mean and variance of the input signal will be assumed to be known.

– **Results:** Figs. 3, and 4 show the theoretical and empirical KLDs, as well as the LLR for $\gamma_0 = 0.9$ (gamma correction factor under the null hypothesis), $\Delta_{1,0} = 1$ (first quantizer stepsize for the null hypothesis), $\Delta_{2,0} = \Delta_{2,1} = 4$ (second quantizer stepsizes for the null and alternative hypothesis, respectively), and $n = 10^6$. Again, as one would expect the minima of the considered functions are located at $\gamma_1 = 0.9$ and $\Delta_{1,1} = 1$. It is interesting to note that values of γ_1 even slightly smaller than γ_0 produce very large values of the considered target functions. Finally, one can observe that the cases where $\Delta_{1,1} > \Delta_{2,0}$ are easily discarded; this is due to the presence of centroids with non-null probability that will not be feasible under the alternative hypothesis.

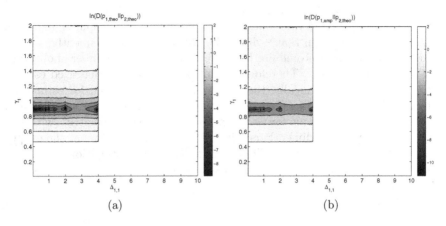

Fig. 3. Theoretical (a) and empirical (b) KLDs for Scenario 2. $\gamma_0 = 0.9$, $\Delta_{1,0} = 1$, $\Delta_{2,0} = \Delta_{2,1} = 4$, $n = 10^6$.

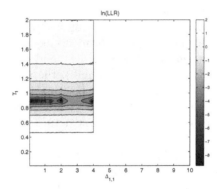

Fig. 4. LLR for Scenario 2. $\gamma_0 = 0.9$, $\Delta_{1,0} = 1$, $\Delta_{2,0} = \Delta_{2,1} = 4$, $n = 10^6$.

4.3 Scenario 3: Filtered White Gaussian Signal with Channel h = (1, h(1), h(2))

- **Operator chain description:** this scenario considers the effect of filtering white Gaussian signal (with mean $\mu_X = 0$) with an FIR filter of order 2. This example must be regarded as a very simple case of filtering detection and estimation, where those tasks are assisted by the knowledge of the input distribution to the filter. Additionally to its inherent interest, we think that the study of this framework is also worthy due to the addition of memory.
- **Application scenario:** this scenario must be regarded as a filtering toy example, showing the power of the proposed measures for dealing with systems with memory. Indeed, due to the memory constraint and the subsequent correlation between vector components, if one wants to obtain the empirical results in this scenario by using the histogram, as we did in the

previous sections, then an n-dimensional histogram should be considered; nevertheless, for large values of n one would expect the output signal to be sparsely distributed in that n-dimensional space, and consequently the histogram computation would not be feasible for a realistic number of observed n-dimensional vectors. Therefore, in this scenario a parameterized estimation is followed; specifically, the observed samples are used for estimating by ML the corresponding Gaussian pdfs, parameterized by the sample mean (assumed to be the same for each sample) and covariance matrix (with size $n \times n$). A set of L n-dimensional filtered vectors (i.e., vectors at the output of the filter under analysis) will be considered in this estimation.

– **PDF theoretical model:** in this case it is well known that

$$f^3(\mathbf{x}|\mu_Y, \Sigma) = \frac{e^{-\frac{1}{2}(\mathbf{X}-\mu_Y)^T \Sigma^{-1}(\mathbf{X}-\mu_Y)}}{(2\pi)^{n/2} |\Sigma|^{1/2}}, \tag{1}$$

where μ_Y is the mean of the filtered content (so if we are computing the theoretical pdf, based on $\mu_X = 0$, it is evident that $\mu_Y = 0$) and Σ is the covariance matrix, which for the theoretical pdf, assuming that $\mathbf{h} = (1, h(1), h(2))$ is used, will be the result of substracting to the symmetric Toeplitz matrix with main diagonal elements equal to $1 + h(1)^2 + h(2)^2$, first diagonal elements equal to $[1 + h(2)]h(1)$, and second diagonal elements $h(2)$ (all the remaining elements being null), the matrix whose element at position $(1,1)$ is $h(1)^2 + h(2)^2$, that at position $(2,2)$ is $h(2)^2$, and those at $(2,1)$ and $(1,2)$ are $h(2)h(1)$ (i.e., the steady regime covariance matrix, minus the disturbances from the Toeplitz structure due to the filter boundary effect).

On the other hand, in this scenario the use of the histogram for dealing with the empirical pdf would be impractical. Instead, the ML estimation of the mean and covariance matrix will be performed; the estimates will be replaced in (1).

– **Known/unknown parameters:** for the sake of simplicity we will assume that $h(0) = 1$. The other two coefficients of the filter will be assumed to be unknown by the forensics analyst.

– **Results:** Figs. 5, and 6 show the theoretical and empirical KLDs, and the LLR for the considered scenario. The filter used under the null hypothesis is $\mathbf{h}_0 = (1, 0.4, -0.2)$, and $\sigma_X^2 = 2$. It is worth highlighting the almost triangular shape of the level curves for all the 3 proposed measures; this fact can be shown to be related to the stability triangle of $\mathbf{h}_0$.

5   Distinguishing Operator Chain Topologies

In the scenarios studied in the previous section we have checked the distinguishability capabilities of the proposed measures when the same operators in the same ordering and topology are compared, i.e., we were just analyzing how easily the impact of the same operator chain could be distinguished for different

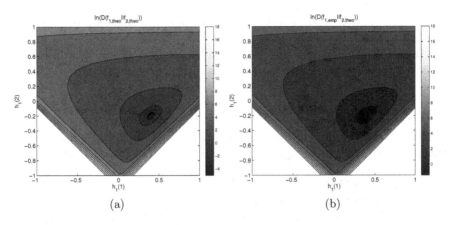

Fig. 5. Theoretical (a) and empirical (b) KLD for Scenario 3. $\mathbf{h}_0 = (1, 0.4, -0.2)$, $n = 10^4$, $L = 10^2$, $\sigma_X^2 = 2$.

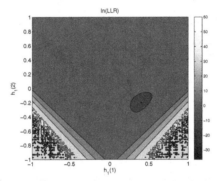

Fig. 6. LLR for Scenario 3. $\mathbf{h}_0 = (1, 0.4, -0.2)$, $n = 10^4$, $L = 10^2$, $\sigma_X^2 = 2$.

operator parameters. Indeed, in all the scenarios considered so far the null hypothesis belongs to the alternative hypothesis search space, so there was at least a point, where the parameters corresponding to the alternative hypothesis are equal to those corresponding to the null hypothesis, that yields a null value of the KLD between the theoretical pmf corresponding to the null hypothesis and its alternative hypothesis counterpart, as well as a null value of the LLR.

In the last two scenarios this framework will be changed. First, we will compare two pairs of the operator chains using the same elementary operator but a different number of times; namely, double vs. triple quantization. Then, we will focus on the study of ordering, analyzing two different operator chains composed by the same elementary operators.

The comparison measures used here will be based on those described in Sect. 3; specifically, since we are interested in determining which is the closest alternative distribution to the null distribution, the proposed comparison measures are

$$\min_{\psi_1 \in \Psi_1} D(f(\mathbf{x}|\psi_0)\|f(\mathbf{x}|\psi_1)), \quad \text{and} \quad \min_{\psi_1 \in \Psi_1} \log\left(\frac{f(\mathbf{x}|\psi_0)}{f(\mathbf{x}|\psi_1)}\right),$$

Ψ_1 is the set of values where the alternative hypothesis operator parameters are searched for. A detailed motivation of these measures can be found in [4].

5.1   Scenario 4: Double Quantization vs. Triple Quantization

In this section the pdfs and samples produced by using 2 and 3 serially concatenated quantizers are compared. The detailed analysis of each those operator chains can be found in [4]; similarly to there, we will model original signal coefficients in the DCT domain by a Laplacian distribution. Denoting by $p^{\text{theo},k\text{-q}}$ the theoretical pmf when k quantizers are considered, and by $p^{\text{emp},k\text{-q}}$ the corresponding histogram, the obtained results for $n = 10^6$ are the following

$$\min_{(\Delta_{1,1},\Delta_{2,1})\in\mathbb{R}^+\times\mathbb{R}^+} D(p^{\text{theo},2\text{-q}}(\mathbf{x}|\Delta_{1,0}=5,\Delta_{2,0}=9)\|p^{\text{theo},3\text{-q}}(\mathbf{x}|\Delta_{1,1},\Delta_{2,1},\Delta_{3,1}=9)) = 0,$$

$$\min_{(\Delta_{1,1},\Delta_{2,1})\in\mathbb{R}^+\times\mathbb{R}^+} D(p^{\text{emp},2\text{-q}}(\mathbf{x}|\Delta_{1,0}=5,\Delta_{2,0}=9)\|p^{\text{theo},3\text{-q}}(\mathbf{x}|\Delta_{1,1},\Delta_{2,1},\Delta_{3,1}=9)) = 1.5\cdot10^{-5},$$

$$\min_{(\Delta_{1,1},\Delta_{2,1})\in\mathbb{R}^+\times\mathbb{R}^+} \log\left(\frac{p^{\text{theo},2\text{-q}}(\mathbf{x}|\Delta_{1,0}=5,\Delta_{2,0}=9)}{p^{\text{theo},3\text{-q}}(\mathbf{x}|\Delta_{1,1},\Delta_{2,1},\Delta_{3,1}=9)}\right) = 0,$$

$$\min_{\Delta_{1,1}\in\mathbb{R}^+} D(p^{\text{theo},3\text{-q}}(\mathbf{x}|\Delta_{1,0}=4,\Delta_{2,0}=7,\Delta_{3,0}=9)\|p^{\text{theo},2\text{-q}}(\mathbf{x}|\Delta_{1,1},\Delta_{2,1}=9)) = 0.0438,$$

$$\min_{\Delta_{1,1}\in\mathbb{R}^+} D(p^{\text{emp},3\text{-q}}(\mathbf{x}|\Delta_{1,0}=4,\Delta_{2,0}=7,\Delta_{3,0}=9)\|p^{\text{theo},2\text{-q}}(\mathbf{x}|\Delta_{1,1},\Delta_{2,1}=9)) = 0.0435,$$

$$\min_{\Delta_{1,1}\in\mathbb{R}^+} \log\left(\frac{p^{\text{theo},3\text{-q}}(\mathbf{x}|\Delta_{1,0}=4,\Delta_{2,0}=7,\Delta_{3,0}=9)}{p^{\text{theo},2\text{-q}}(\mathbf{x}|\Delta_{1,1},\Delta_{2,1}=9)}\right) = 0.0435,$$

while when the same operator chain topology and ordering is considered

$$\min_{\Delta_{1,1}\in\mathbb{R}^+} D(p^{\text{theo},2\text{-q}}(\mathbf{x}|\Delta_{1,0}=5,\Delta_{2,0}=9)\|p^{\text{theo},2\text{-q}}(\mathbf{x}|\Delta_{1,1},\Delta_{2,1}=9)) = 0,$$

$$\min_{\Delta_{1,1}\in\mathbb{R}^+} D(p^{\text{emp},2\text{-q}}(\mathbf{x}|\Delta_{1,0}=5,\Delta_{2,0}=9)\|p^{\text{theo},2\text{-q}}(\mathbf{x}|\Delta_{1,1},\Delta_{2,1}=9)) = 2.1\cdot10^{-5},$$

$$\min_{\Delta_{1,1}\in\mathbb{R}^+} \log\left(\frac{p^{\text{theo},2\text{-q}}(\mathbf{x}|\Delta_{1,0}=5,\Delta_{2,0}=9)}{p^{\text{theo},2\text{-q}}(\mathbf{x}|\Delta_{1,1},\Delta_{2,1}=9)}\right) = 0,$$

$$\min_{(\Delta_{1,1},\Delta_{2,1})\in(\mathbb{R}^+)^2} D(p^{\text{theo},3\text{-q}}(\mathbf{x}|\Delta_{1,0}=4,\Delta_{2,0}=7,\Delta_{3,0}=9)\|p^{\text{theo},3\text{-q}}(\mathbf{x}|\Delta_{1,1},\Delta_{2,1},\Delta_{3,1}=9)) = 0,$$

$$\min_{(\Delta_{1,1},\Delta_{2,1})\in(\mathbb{R}^+)^2} D(p^{\text{emp},3\text{-q}}(\mathbf{x}|\Delta_{1,0}=4,\Delta_{2,0}=7,\Delta_{3,0}=9)\|p^{\text{theo},3\text{-q}}(\mathbf{x}|\Delta_{1,1},\Delta_{2,1},\Delta_{3,1}=9)) = 1.5\cdot10^{-5},$$

$$\min_{(\Delta_{1,1},\Delta_{2,1})\in\mathbb{R}^+\times\mathbb{R}^+} \log\left(\frac{p^{\text{theo},3\text{-q}}(\mathbf{x}|\Delta_{1,0}=4,\Delta_{2,0}=7,\Delta_{3,0}=9)}{p^{\text{theo},3\text{-q}}(\mathbf{x}|\Delta_{1,1},\Delta_{2,1},\Delta_{3,1}=9)}\right) = 0.$$

It is interesting to note that whenever the 2 quantizers scenario is considered as null hypothesis and the 3 quantizers scenario is the alternative hypothesis, the obtained results indicate that both scenarios cannot be distinguished. This result, although probably a bit surprising at first sight, can be easily explained; it means that whenever 3 quantizers are considered for the alternative hypothesis, one can find quantization stepsizes for the first and second quantizers such that the output of the total system is equivalent to that produced by just those two quantizers (the null hypothesis). In other words, there is at least one subcase within the alternative hypothesis search space that yields the same results that the null scenario. Indeed, in the considered framework several of those cases exist; just for the sake of illustration, we will enumerate some of them:

- $(\Delta_{1,1}, \Delta_{2,1}) = (5, 5)$: due to the idempotence of the two first quantizers, the cascade of the three quantizers in the alternative hypothesis is equivalent to the cascade considered by the null hypothesis.
- $(\Delta_{1,1}, \Delta_{2,1}) = (5, 9)$: one can follow a reasoning similar to the previous point, but considering in this case the last two quantizers.
- $(\Delta_{1,1}, \Delta_{2,1}) = (5/(2k+1), 5)$, where k is any non-negative integer value: the output of the second quantizer is the same that if one had $(\Delta_{1,1}, \Delta_{2,1}) = (5, 5)$, as the quantization region boundaries corresponding to $\Delta = 5$ are a subset of those corresponding to $\Delta = \frac{5}{2k+1}$.
- $(\Delta_{1,1}, \Delta_{2,1}) = (5, 9/(2k+1))$, with k any non-negative integer number: following a reasoning similar to the previous case, but considering the relationship between the quantization regions corresponding to the second and third quantizers.
- $(\Delta_{1,1}, \Delta_{2,1}) = (5, 5/k)$, where k is any positive integer number: if that relationship between the quantization stepsizes holds, then the second quantizer does not modify the quantized values, and consequently the same values will be obtained at the output of the third quantizer.
- $(\Delta_{1,1}, \Delta_{2,1}) = (5, \xi)$, where $0 < \xi < 1$: since the minimum distance between the points in $5\mathbb{Z}$ and $9\mathbb{Z}+4.5$ (the quantizaton boundaries of the third lattice) is 0.5, if the quantization distortion is smaller than 0.5, then a change in the chosen centroid of the third lattice is not possible. The mentioned constraint on the quantization distortion is verified if $\Delta_{2,1} < 1$.
- $(\Delta_{1,1}, \Delta_{2,1}) = (5, \Delta_2^*)$, where Δ_2^* is any positive real number verifying

$$\left\{ \forall k \in \mathbb{Z}, \exists (k_2, k_3) : k_2 = \text{round}\left(\frac{k_1 \Delta_1}{\Delta_2}\right), k_3 = \text{round}\left(\frac{k_2 \Delta_2}{\Delta_3}\right), k_3 = \text{round}\left(\frac{k_1 \Delta_1}{\Delta_3}\right) \right\}.$$

Be aware that no every $\Delta_2^* > 0$ is a feasible solution to the previous problem, as the two values assigned to k_3 should coincide. Intuitively, the last formula means that we can consider any value of $\Delta_{2,1}$, as long as the result of quantizing the output of the first quantizer ($k_1 \Delta_1$, for any integer k_1) with the third quantizer, is equivalent to quantizing it first with the second quantizer, and then with the third one. Note that this last bullet is not implied by the previous ones; for example, $\Delta_2^* = 1.2$ verifies this constraint, while it does not satisfy any of the previous conditions.

On the other hand, whenever the triple quantization scenario is considered as the null hypothesis (i.e., the content under test is produced by going through three quantizers), it is easily distinguished from the double quantization case.

Finally, we would like to emphasize that the values of $D(p^{\mathrm{emp},k\text{-}\mathsf{q}}||p^{\mathrm{theo},k'\text{-}\mathsf{q}})$ correspond to consider a particular sample ($n = 10^6$), changing for each realization; in any case, the obtained results were always in the same order of magnitude that the reported data.

5.2   Scenario 5: Gamma;Quantization;Quantization vs. Quantization;Gamma;Quantization

When dealing with the comparison between the operator chains described in Scenarios 1 and 2 one has to consider the swapping of the location of the first quantizer and the gamma corrector. Denoting by $p^{\mathrm{theo},i}$ the theoretical pmf for the ith scenario, and by $p^{\mathrm{emp},i}$ the corresponding histogram, the obtained results are the following,

$$\min_{(\gamma_1,\Delta_{1,1})\in\mathbb{R}^+\times\mathbb{R}^+} D(p^{\mathrm{theo},1}(\mathbf{x}|\Delta_{1,0}=1,\gamma_0=0.9,\Delta_{2,0}=4)||p^{\mathrm{theo},2}(\mathbf{x}|\gamma_1,\Delta_{1,1},\Delta_{2,1}=4)) = 2.8\cdot10^{-3},$$

$$\min_{(\gamma_1,\Delta_{1,1})\in\mathbb{R}^+\times\mathbb{R}^+} D(p^{\mathrm{emp},1}(\mathbf{x}|\Delta_{1,0}=1,\gamma_0=0.9,\Delta_{2,0}=4)||p^{\mathrm{theo},2}(\mathbf{x}|\gamma_1,\Delta_{1,1},\Delta_{2,1}=4)) = 2.9\cdot10^{-3},$$

$$\min_{(\gamma_1,\Delta_{1,1})\in\mathbb{R}^+\times\mathbb{R}^+} \log\left(\frac{p^{\mathrm{theo},1}(\mathbf{x}|\Delta_{1,0}=1,\gamma_0=0.9,\Delta_{2,0}=4)}{p^{\mathrm{theo},2}(\mathbf{x}|\gamma_1,\Delta_{1,1},\Delta_{2,1}=4)}\right) = 2.8\cdot10^{-3},$$

$$\min_{(\gamma_1,\Delta_{1,1})\in\mathbb{R}^+\times\mathbb{R}^+} D(p^{\mathrm{theo},2}(\mathbf{x}|\gamma_0=0.9,\Delta_{1,0}=1,\Delta_{2,0}=4)||p^{\mathrm{theo},1}(\mathbf{x}|\Delta_{1,1},\gamma_1,\Delta_{2,1}=4)) = 5.1\cdot10^{-4},$$

$$\min_{(\gamma_1,\Delta_{1,1})\in\mathbb{R}^+\times\mathbb{R}^+} D(p^{\mathrm{emp},2}(\mathbf{x}|\gamma_0=0.9,\Delta_{1,0}=1,\Delta_{2,0}=4)||p^{\mathrm{theo},1}(\mathbf{x}|\Delta_{1,1},\gamma_1,\Delta_{2,1}=4)) = 5.2\cdot10^{-4},$$

$$\min_{(\gamma_1,\Delta_{1,1})\in\mathbb{R}^+\times\mathbb{R}^+} \log\left(\frac{p^{\mathrm{theo},2}(\mathbf{x}|\gamma_0=0.9,\Delta_{1,0}=1,\Delta_{2,0}=4)}{p^{\mathrm{theo},1}(\mathbf{x}|\Delta_{1,1},\gamma_1,\Delta_{2,1}=4)}\right) = 4.9\cdot10^{-4},$$

while when the null hypothesis belongs to the search space of the alternative hypothesis (i.e., the same operator chain topology and ordering is considered)

$$\min_{(\gamma_1,\Delta_{1,1})\in\mathbb{R}^+\times\mathbb{R}^+} D(p^{\mathrm{theo},1}(\mathbf{x}|\Delta_{1,0}=1,\gamma_0=0.9,\Delta_{2,0}=4)||p^{\mathrm{theo},1}(\mathbf{x}|\Delta_{1,1},\gamma_1,\Delta_{2,1}=4)) = 0,$$

$$\min_{(\gamma_1,\Delta_{1,1})\in\mathbb{R}^+\times\mathbb{R}^+} D(p^{\mathrm{emp},1}(\mathbf{x}|\Delta_{1,0}=1,\gamma_0=0.9,\Delta_{2,0}=4)||p^{\mathrm{theo},1}(\mathbf{x}|\Delta_{1,1},\gamma_1,\Delta_{2,1}=4)) = 1.44\cdot10^{-5},$$

$$\min_{(\gamma_1,\Delta_{1,1})\in\mathbb{R}^+\times\mathbb{R}^+} \log\left(\frac{p^{\mathrm{theo},1}(\mathbf{x}|\Delta_{1,0}=1,\gamma_0=0.9,\Delta_{2,0}=4)}{p^{\mathrm{theo},1}(\mathbf{x}|\Delta_{1,1},\gamma_1,\Delta_{2,1}=4)}\right) = 0,$$

$$\min_{(\gamma_1,\Delta_{1,1})\in\mathbb{R}^+\times\mathbb{R}^+} D(p^{\mathrm{theo},2}(\mathbf{x}|\gamma_0=0.9,\Delta_{1,0}=1,\Delta_{2,0}=4)||p^{\mathrm{theo},2}(\mathbf{x}|\gamma_1,\Delta_{1,1},\Delta_{2,1}=4)) = 0,$$

$$\min_{(\gamma_1,\Delta_{1,1})\in\mathbb{R}^+\times\mathbb{R}^+} D(p^{\mathrm{emp},2}(\mathbf{x}|\gamma_0=0.9,\Delta_{1,0}=1,\Delta_{2,0}=4)||p^{\mathrm{theo},2}(\mathbf{x}|\gamma_1,\Delta_{1,1},\Delta_{2,1}=4)) = 1.38\cdot10^{-5},$$

$$\min_{(\gamma_1,\Delta_{1,1})\in\mathbb{R}^+\times\mathbb{R}^+} \log\left(\frac{p^{\mathrm{theo},2}(\mathbf{x}|\gamma_0=0.9,\Delta_{1,0}=1,\Delta_{2,0}=4)}{p^{\mathrm{theo},2}(\mathbf{x}|\gamma_1,\Delta_{1,1},\Delta_{2,1}=4)}\right) = 0.$$

Similarly to the previous scenario, the results for $D(p^{\mathrm{emp}}||p^{\mathrm{theo}})$ depend on the particular sample ($n = 10^6$), but for different samples the obtained results are in the same order of magnitude. These results show that the proposed measures are able to distinguish between very similar operator chains; specifically, the proposed measures prove to be useful tools for determining the ordering of operators in complex chains.

6   Conclusions and Future Work

This work uses two measures, coming from detection and information theory, for analyzing the distinguishability of different operator parameters working on fixed operator chains, as well as for detecting the ordering and topology of similar chains. The reported results are promising, since the methods based on the proposed measures rightly estimated the applied parameters and operator chains. In the future work, special attention will be paid to experiments with real images, as well as to the comparison with existing ad-hoc schemes in the literature.

References

1. Bianchi, T., Piva, A.: Analysis of non-aligned double JPEG artifacts for the localization of image forgeries. In: Proc. of the IEEE WIFS. Iguaçu Falls, Brazil, pp.1–6 (December 2011)
2. Böhme, R., Kirchner, M.: Counter-Forensics: Attacking Image Forensics. In: Digital Image Forensics. Springer (2012)
3. Cachin, C.: An information-theoretic model for steganography. In: Aucsmith, D. (ed.) IH 1998. LNCS, vol. 1525, pp. 306–318. Springer, Heidelberg (1998)
4. Comesaña, P.: Detection and information theoretic measures for quantifying the distingsuishability between multimedia operator chains. In: IEEE WIFS 2012, Tenerife, Spain, pp. 211–216 (December 2012)
5. Cover, T.M., Thomas, J.A.: Elements of Information Theory. Wiley (2006)
6. Fan, Z., de Queiroz, R.L.: Identification of bitmap compression history: JPEG detection and quantizer estimation. IEEE Transactions on Image Processing 12(2), 230–235 (2003)
7. Fu, D., Shi, Y.Q., Su, W.: A generalized Benford's law for JPEG coefficients and its applications in image forensics. In: Proc. SPIE 6505, San Jose, CA, vol. 6505, p. 65051L (January 2007)
8. Lin, W.S., Tjoa, S.K., Zhao, H.V., Liu, K.J.R.: Digital image source coder forensics via intrinsic fingerprints. IEEE Transactions on Informations Forensics and Security 4(3), 460–475 (2009)
9. Lukas, J., Fridrich, J.: Estimation of primary quantization matrix in double compressed JPEG images. In: Proc. of DFRWS (2003)
10. Luo, W., Qu, Z., Huang, J., Qiu, G.: A novel method for detecting cropped and recompressed image block. In: Proc. of the IEEE ICASSP, Honolulu, HI, pp. 217–220 (April 2007)
11. Luo, W., Wang, Y., Huang, J.: Detection of quantization artifacts and its applications to transform encoder identification. IEEE Transactions on Information Forensics and Security 5(4), 810–815 (2010)
12. Milani, S., Tagliasacchi, M., Tubaro, S.: Discriminating multiple JPEG compression using first digit features. In: Proc. of the IEEE ICASSP, Kyoto, Japan, pp. 2235-2256 (March 2012)

Distinguishing Computer Graphics
from Photographic Images Using Local Binary Patterns

Zhaohong Li[1,2,3], Jingyu Ye[1], and Yun Qing Shi[1]

[1] Department of Electrical and Computer Engineering,
New Jersey Institute of Technology, Newark, NJ 07102, USA
`{zhl,jy58,shi}@njit.edu`
[2] School of Electronic and Information Engineering
Beijing Jiaotong University, Beijing, 100044, China
`zhhli2@bjtu.edu.cn`
[3] Shanghai Key Laboratory of Integrate Administration Technologies for Information Security,
Shanghai, 200240, China

Abstract. With the ongoing development of rendering technology, computer graphics (CG) are sometimes so photorealistic that to distinguish them from photographic images (PG) by human eyes has become difficult. To this end, many methods have been developed for automatic CG and PG classification. In this paper, we explore the statistical difference of uniform gray-scale invariant local binary patterns (LBP) to distinguish CG from PG with the help of support vector machines (SVM). We select YCbCr as the color model. The original JPEG coefficients of Y and Cr components, and their prediction errors are used for LBP calculation. From each 2-D array, we obtain 59 LBP features. In total, four groups of 59 features are obtained from each image. The proposed features have been tested with thousands of CG and PG. Classification accuracy reaches 98.3% with SVM and outperforms the state-of-the-art works.

Keywords: Image forensics, computer graphics, local binary patterns, image authentication.

1 Introduction

In recent years, computer graphics (CG) provide people entertainments with incredibly photorealistic visual scene produced by advanced rendering software such as 3D Studio Max, Accurender, Photoshop, SketchUp and so on. However, also because of the photorealistic rendering, CG can be used as a forgery of photo image in journalism, scientific research, justice and other areas for malicious social, economy or political purpose. We can foresee that the rendering software will become even more advanced and powerful, and be able to produce highly realistic images to deceive human eyes. Therefore, distinguishing CG from PG (photographic images) automatically has turned out to be an important topic in digital image forensics.

Since photographic images are generated by digital cameras, it is expected that the distinct physical generation pipelines of camera must introduce unique intrinsic

Y.Q. Shi, H.J. Kim, and F. Pérez-González (Eds.): IWDW 2012, LNCS 7809, pp. 228–241, 2013.

characteristics into PG, which are absent in CG. Based on this assumption, some distinguishing methods have been reported [1-4]. Dehnie et al. [1] used pattern noise caused by imperfections of camera sensors to distinguish CG from PG. Ng et al. [2] proposed a geometry-based image model to reveal certain image processing differences, such as gamma correction in PG. Dirik et al. [3] developed four features that capture traces of Color Filter Array (CFA) and demosaicking in camera image processing pipeline, and another feature to capture chromatic aberration for the discrimination of CG and PG. In their later work [4], Dirik et al. introduced two features. The first one was a revisit to the third demosaicking feature proposed in [3]. The second one measured the sensor noise power changes all across the image. Both of the features can achieve high classification accuracies with high quality PG images.

Apart from the aforementioned methods which focus on one or two stages of camera image processing pipeline, works reported in [5-13] are based on difference of image statistical features caused by difference of whole image formation procedures of CG and PG. Ng et al. [5] studied three types of natural image statistics derived from the power spectrum, wavelet transform and local patch of images to distinguish CG from PG. Wu et al. [6] employed several visual features derived from color, edge, saturation and texture features extracted with the Gabor filter as discriminative features. Chen et al. [7] formed the distinguishing features by using statistical moments of characteristic function of wavelet subbands and their prediction-errors. Sutthiwan et al. [8] employed second-order statistics to capture the significant statistical difference between computer graphics and photographic images. Chen et al. [9] built an alpha-stable distribution model to characterize the wavelet decomposition coefficients of natural images, and extracted the fractional lower order moments in the wavelet domain. Li et al. [10] extracted the variance and kurtosis of second-order difference signals and the first four order statistics of predicting error signals as distinguishing features in the HSV color space. Pan et al. [11] extracted a set of features derived from hidden Markov tree model to classify natural images and computer graphics. Zhang et al. [12] presented an approach combining imaging features and visual features from different image components. Wu et al. [13] took several highest histogram bins of the difference images as features to carry out classification, and these simple histogram features worked well.

Image statistical features [5-13] have been proved to be useful in CG and PG classification. And it is mentioned in [14] that "Texture is an innate property of virtually all surfaces". This inspires us that features developed for texture classification could potentially play a role in CG and PG classification. In this paper, we take a close look at the uniform gray-scale invariant LBP [15], which has been developed as an efficient local texture descriptor. In this popular technology (as of February 2012 [15] has been cited almost 1900 times according to Google), the features describe a texture by calculating the local binary patterns in the entire image, which is measured by histograms. The number of bins is suppressed from 256 (8 neighbors) to 59 by separating 'uniform' and 'non-uniform' patterns and merging 'non-uniform' patterns to one bin. Hence, for each image, 59 local binary patterns are extracted, respectively, from Y and Cr components, and their prediction-error 2D arrays. Support vector machines are built for classification of thousands of CG and PG. Compared with the results in literatures, the classification accuracy reported in this paper is higher.

The rest of the paper is organized as follows. The LBP features and the features extraction are introduced in Section 2. Experimental results and discussions are presented in Section 3 and Section 4 concludes the paper.

2   Proposed Method

LBP is a simple yet efficient method for texture classification, which has been proved to be powerful for texture classification in various texture analysis tasks [16]. However, LBP has not been applied for classifying between CG and PG. This motivates us to employ LBP to find the differences between CG and PG based on image structure information relating to texture.

2.1   Review of LBP

LBP is an efficient texture descriptor, which is defined as follows [15],

$$LBP_{P,R} = \sum_{p=0}^{P-1} s(g_p - g_c) 2^p \tag{1}$$

Where

$$s(x) = \begin{cases} 1, & x \geq 0 \\ 0, & x < 0 \end{cases} \tag{2}$$

and g_c is the gray value of the central pixel, $g_p (p = 0, ..., P - 1)$ correspond to the gray values of its P neighbors that form a circle with radius of $R(R > 0)$. According to Equations (1) and (2), the differences between central pixel and its neighbors are binarized. If the gray value of a neighbor pixel is smaller than that of the central pixel, a binary 0 is recorded for this pixel; otherwise, a binary 1 is recorded. Then the binary string is referred to as local binary pattern, which can also be converted to one of the 255 decimal numbers ranging from 0 to 255. Fig.1 shows an example of LBP calculation.

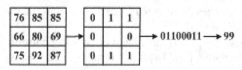

Fig. 1. An example of LBP calculation

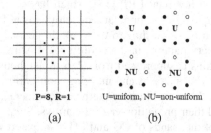

Fig. 2. (a) Constellation of neighborhood; (b) Examples of 'uniform' and 'non-uniform' local binary patterns [15]

If we set R = 1 and P = 8, the circularly neighbor set is shown in Fig. 2(a).There gray values of neighbors which do not fall exactly in the center of pixels are estimated by interpolation. After the LBP pattern of each pixel is identified, the corresponding histogram with a total of $2^8 = 256$ bins is built to represent the whole image texture. Furthermore, the concept of 'uniform' local binary patterns is introduced in [15]. The U value of a LBP pattern is defined as,

$$U(LBP_{P,R}) = |s(g_{P-1} - g_c) - s(g_0 - g_c)|$$
$$+ \sum_{p=1}^{P-1} |s(g_p - g_c) - s(g_{p-1} - g_c)| \tag{3}$$

The uniform LBP refers to the pattern in which the number of spatial transitions (bit-wise 0/1 changes) is equal to or less than two($U \leq 2$). Some examples of uniform and non-uniform LBP patterns are given in Fig.2 (b), where black and white circles correspond to bit values of 0 and 1, U means uniform, and NU means non-uniform.

As the uniform patterns provide the vast majority, sometimes over 90 percent, of all 3×3 patterns present in the observed textures [15], those 'non-uniform' local binary patterns are merged into one bin in the histogram, thereby suppressing the number of bins from 256 to 59 if $R=1$ and $P =8$. The combined 59 bins are then used as distinguishing features in our proposed method.

2.2   Feature Extraction

The next problem we consider is the color model used for extracting LBP. There are various color models used in color image processing, such as RGB model, HSV model and YCbCr model. It has been reported in [17] that features derived from YCbCr give the best performance among several different color systems. Y is luminance, meaning that light intensity, and Cb and Cr are the blue-difference and red-difference chroma components, which makes YCbCr color model is suitable to capture the differences between CG and PG both in brightness and color. Further, the YCbCr color model has been adopted by the most popularly used JPEG images. Therefore, we extract LBP features in the YCbCr color model rather than other color models.

2.2.1   Feature Extraction Framework
In addition, the prediction-error image, which is in essence a spatial domain highpass filtered image, tells a better story about image statistics with less influence from image content [8]. Following that, we use JPEG tool box to get the JPEG coefficients arrays of Y, Cb, and Cr components, and then extract the features from the three JPEG coefficients arrays and their prediction-error arrays, respectively.

The prediction-error image is the difference between the original image and its predicted version [18]. Considering a 2×2 image pixel block, prediction of a pixel value is achieved by Equation (4),

$$\hat{x} = \begin{cases} \max(a,b), & c \leq \min(a,b) \\ \min(a,b), & c \geq \max(a,b) \\ a + b - c & otherwise \end{cases} \tag{4}$$

where a, b are, respectively, the immediately horizontal and vertical neighbors of the pixel x, c is the diagonal neighbor of x as shown in Fig.3, and $\hat{x}$ is the prediction value of x.

Fig. 3. Pixel x and its neighbors for prediction

To conclude, from each color component, we extract the LBP features from the original JPEG coefficients array, and its prediction-error 2D array, resulting in a total of $59 \times 2 = 118$ features. The feature extraction framework of one color component is shown in Fig. 4.

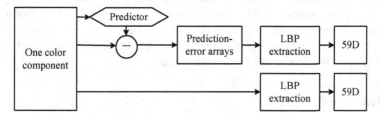

Fig. 4. Feature extraction framework for one color component

2.2.2   Correlation Analysis among Color Components

An interesting fact, that features derived from Cr and Cb components are much more strongly correlated than any other combinations of two components, YCr and YCb, has been reported in [8]. To examine if this is true for the LBP as well. we investigate the correlation among LBP features extracted from different color components and their prediction-error arrays.

Here we measure the correlation level by the correlation coefficient $\rho_{X,Y}$ between two random vectors X and Y,

$$\rho_{X,Y} = \frac{E\left((X - \mu_X)(Y - \mu_Y)\right)}{\delta_X \delta_Y} \tag{5}$$

where μ_X and μ_Y are the expected values of vectors X and Y, σ_X and σ_Y are the standard deviations of vectors X and Y, respectively.

The average correlation coefficients of feature vectors from any two color components in the YCbCr color model for the given image and their prediction-error arrays are calculated from 1964 CG and 1964 PG which are training samples in the experiments reported late in Section 3. F_Y, F_{Cb} and F_{Cr} mean the LBP features extracted from Y, Cb and Cr components, and F_{EY}, F_{ECb} and F_{ECr} mean the features extracted from their prediction-error arrays, respectively.

Table 1. Average correlation coefficient values of scaled feature vectors from any two color components in YCbCr color model

	of 1964CG	of 1964PG
$\rho_{F_Y F_{Cb}}$	0.6771	0.6567
$\rho_{F_Y F_{Cr}}$	0.6494	0.5798
$\rho_{F_{Cb} F_{Cr}}$	0.9360	0.9090
$\rho_{F_{EY} F_{ECb}}$	0.6704	0.7024
$\rho_{F_{EY} F_{ECr}}$	0.6486	0.6677
$\rho_{F_{ECb} F_{ECr}}$	0.9546	0.9422

As shown in Table 1, correlations between the features derived from Cr and Cb components of the test images and their prediction-error arrays are very high, while the features from any other combinations of YCb and YCr are less correlated. Further, the correlation of F_Y and F_{Cb} is a little bit stronger than that of F_Y and F_{Cr}. This fact also exists in the features derived from their prediction-error arrays. It indicates that using all of features constructed from three color components will not improve the feature effectiveness significantly but rather increases computational complexity drastically. Therefore, in our image feature extraction process, we only select Y and Cr components.

3   Experiments and Discussions

In experiments, all the CG and PG in our database are color images in JPEG format with moderate to good visual quality. The CG database contains 2455 images collected from [19] and [20]. More than 50 rendering softwares, e.g., 3D Studio Max, After Effects, and AutoCad, were used to generate those photorealistic CG images, whose resolutions range from 500×500 to 800×800. The PG database contains also 2455 digital camera images of resolution 500×500 to 800×800. Part of the images in the PG database is from [19], the rest are collected by our group. The images contents in both CG and PG database spans a variety of outdoor and indoor scenes, including flowers, trees, animals, characters and architectures, etc.

3.1   Experimental Setting

In our experiments, we use Support Vector Machine (SVM) of polynomial kernel [21] as the classifier.

To train the SVM classifier, 4/5 of the images are randomly selected as the training set (1964 CG and 1964 PG). The rest 1/5 form testing set. The experiments are repeated for 20 times to secure reliable classification results.

The performance of our LBP features are compared with methods proposed in [4,8,13]. Method [4] is implemented by ourselves. The codes of the methods [8,13] are obtained from the authors. For fair comparison, we train and test the methods [8,13] using the same SVM kernel function with the same parameters used in our proposed method on our image database.

3.2   Experimental Results

The comparison between our method and the previous works [4,8,13] are presented in Table 2, where True Positive (TP) represents the correct detection rate of CG, True Negative (TN) represents the detection rate of PG images, and the accuracy is the arithmetic average of TP and TN.

From Table 2, it is observed that the proposed method outperforms these state-of-the-art works with higher accuracy. The accuracy of our method with 236-D features is about 1% higher than that of [8] which employed higher dimensional feature vectors, and it is about 2.5% higher than that reported in [13].

It has been reported in [4] that both of the proposed two features are effective in classifying between CG and PG. However, in our experiments, both features proposed in [4] failed in classifying CG from PG in our database. Our further investigation in this regard is reported in Section 3.4.

Table 2. Classifier test accuracy

Method	Feature size	TP	TN	Accuracy
Feature 1 of [4]	1	0.0473	0.9719	0.5096
Feature 2 of [4]	1	0.9287	0.4701	0.6994
Markov features of [8]	324	0.9727	0.9764	0.9745
Histogram Bins of [13]	112	0.9559	0.9596	0.9577
LBP	236	0.9846	0.9820	0.9833

Furthermore, the averaged Receiver Operating Characteristics (ROC) curves are shown in Fig.5 (a), and the top left region of Fig.5 (a) is enlarged as shown in Fig. 5(b), where "LBP" is the ROC curve of the proposed method while "Markov" and "Histogram Bins" are ROC curves of methods in [8] and [13], respectively. From these figures, we see that the proposed method is slightly better than [8], while our improvement over [13] is obvious.

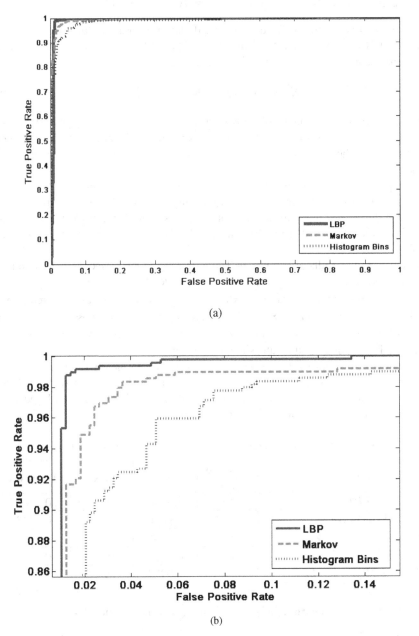

(a)

(b)

Fig. 5. (a) ROC among different methods; (b) the enlarged top left region of part (a)

3.3   Variance and Multi-resolution in Classifying CG and PG

LBP is an effective technique for texture classification. In order to further enhance its capability, the variance and multi-resolution in [15] have been further introduced . The rotation invariant measure of local variance is defined as:

$$VAR_{P,R} = \frac{1}{P}\sum_{p=0}^{P-1}(g_P - \mu)^2, \text{ where } \mu = \frac{1}{P}\sum_{p=0}^{P-1} g_P. \tag{6}$$

As $VAR_{P,R}$ is a complementary of $LBP_{P,R}$ in describing the local image texture, we then investigate whether it can improve the classification accuracy in classification of CG from PG. In the multi-resolution analysis the LBP features with different (P, R) parameters are utilized.

The experimental works have been conducted to examine if these two techniques can further enhance the performance of classifying CG from PG. In the experiments, we just use those 'non-uniform' local binary patterns as R=1 and P =8, together with the LBP features extracted from R=2 and P =8. The combined features are used to classify CG from PG.

The experiment results are shown in Table 3. There $LBP_{1,8}$ means the combined LBP features of F_Y, F_{Cr} F_{EY}, and F_{ECr} when $R=1$ and P =8, $VAR_{Y(1,8)}$ and $VAR_{EY(1,8)}$ denote the local variance extracted from Y component and its prediction-error arrays when $R=1$ and P =8, $LBP_{Y(2,8)}$ and $LBP_{EY(2,8)}$ mean the LBP features extracted from Y component and its prediction-error arrays when $R=2$ and P =8, respectively. The experimental results show that using either the local variance or multi-resolution does not improve the performance further while increase the feature size. This indicates that these two techniques developed in [15] are effective for texture classification. But, they are not effective for classification of CG from PG. Hence, we do not include these two groups of features in our work.

Table 3. Classifying accuracy using local variance and multi-resolution

Method	Feature size	TP	TN	Accuracy
$LBP_{1,8}$	236	0.9846	0.9820	0.9833
$LBP_{1,8} + VAR_{EY(1,8)}$	236+16	0.9846	0.9830	0.9838
$LBP_{1,8} + VAR_{EY(1,8)} + VAR_{Y(1,8)}$	236+32	0.9836	0.9815	0.9825
$LBP_{1,8} + LBP_{EY(2,8)}$	236+59	0.9826	0.9796	0.9811
$LBP_{1,8} + LBP_{EY(2,8)} + LBP_{Y(2,8)}$	236+118	0.9824	0.9803	0.9814

3.4   Discussions on Features of [4] for Distinguishing CG and PG

In [4], Dirik and Memon proposed two features, one is based on CFA pattern number estimation and the other is based on CFA based noise analysis. Feature 1 considers that PG has been initially interpolated with one kind of Bayer demosaicking patterns, and then if it is reinterpolated with all kinds of CFA, the right CFA pattern should yield significantly smaller mean squared error than others patterns. Feature 2 relies on the fact that sensor noise power in CFA interpolated pixels should be significantly lower than non-interpolated pixels. It was reported that the detection accuracies of both features can reach as high as 99% for distinguishing CG from PG. But the PG dataset used in [4] is restricted to high quality images. This restriction also exists for the method [13]. However, in our database, both GG and PG may have undergone some manipulations, e.g., JPEG compression as shown below, which may destroy the traces of demosaicing in PG. This is why the features in [4] cannot differentiate CG and PG on our database.

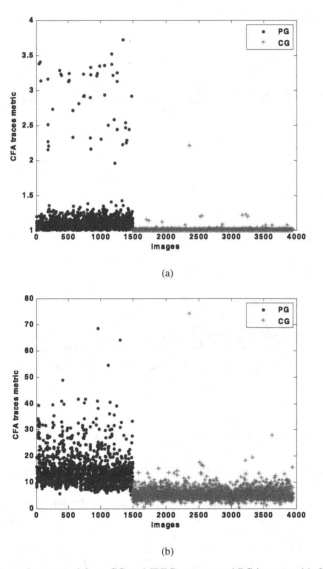

(a)

(b)

Fig. 6. (a) Feature 1 computed from CG and JPEG compressed PG images with QF of 100; (b) Feature 2 computed from CG and JPEG compressed PG images with QF of 100

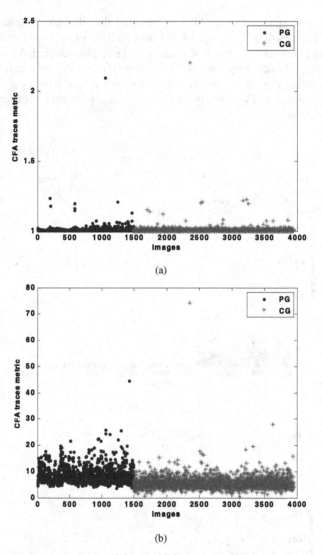

(a)

(b)

Fig. 7. (a) Feature 1 computed from CG and JPEG compressed PG images with QF of 80; (b) Feature 2 computed from CG and JPEG compressed PG images with QF of 80

Inspired by this, we further investigate both features of [4] in PG databases with different JPEG compression quality factors. Here, we use the same CG database as the one used in the above experiments. However, the PG databases are built based on the Dresden Image Database[22]. First, we download 1488 raw PG images captured by the following cameras: Nikon_D70, Nikon_D70s, and Nikon_D200, and use the software Dcraw with default set to read them. Then we compress these images with JPEG quality factors (QF) of 100, 90, and 80, respectively. Finally, we get four different PG databases, and then we test using both of the features [4] in each of the PG databases.

The values of Feature 1 and Feature 2 are computed from the 2455 CG images and two JPEG compressed PG databases with QF of 100 and 80, respectively. The resulting feature plots are shown in Fig. 6 and Fig. 7. From Fig.6, we can see that there are clear boundaries between the features generated from CG and those from PG. While in Fig. 7, Feature 1 and Feature 2 derived from PG are obviously weakened, which makes the features of CG and PG are hardly to differentiate.

Fig.8 shows the classification accuracies achieved by applying Feature 1 and Feature 2 in 4 different PG databases, respectively. The classification accuracies are above 90% when testing the features derived from raw PG images and JPEG compressed PG images with QF of 100, but they decrease dramatically once the QF decreases to 90 or 80. It can be concluded that the features in [4] is effective when PG are raw images or JPEG images with very high quality factor. However, the features are very sensitive to JPEG compression. As seen, the traces of demosaicing in PG will be substantially weakened when the images are compressed with quality factor equals to 90 or 80, which results in the failure of distinguishing CG from PG.

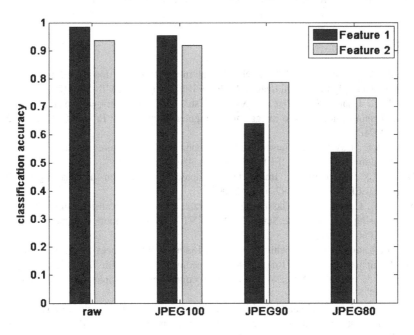

Fig. 8. Classification accuracies of Feature 1 and Feature 2 in raw PG images, JPEG compressed PG images with QF of 100, 90, and 80, respectively

4   Conclusion

In this paper, a novel method for computer graphics identification from photographic images has been presented. We extract Local Binary Patterns (LBP) as distinguishing features from YCbCr color model, and combine features from Y, Cr components and their prediction-error 2D arrays. Compared to the state-of-the-art works, the proposed method has achieved higher classification accuracy.

The multi-resolution and variance developed for the LBP technology [15] have been investigated through our experiments. The experimental results seem that using either the multi-resolution or variance does not improve the performance further.

Besides, it has been found that the features proposed in [4] have good performance in distinguishing computer graphics from photographic images only when photographic image is compressed with very high JPEG compression quality factor (QF), e.g., QF=100. The performance drops dramatically as the QF drops, and ends up with total failure with further drop of the QF factor.

Acknowledgments. We would like to thank Dr. Xiaolong Li, Dr. Bin Yang; and Dr. Patchara Sutthiwan for their kindness by providing us with their codes. We also appreciate Guanshuo Xu for his kindly suggestions. The first author was supported by the Basic Research Foundation of Beijing Jiaotong University (No. 2011JBM004) and Supported by the Opening Project of Shanghai Key Laboratory of Integrate Administration Technologies for Information Security (No. AGK2012003).

References

1. Dehnie, S., Sencar, T., Memon, N.: Digital image forensics for identifying computer generated and digital camera images. In: Proc. IEEE ICIP, pp. 2313–2316 (2006)
2. Ng, T.-T., Chang, S.-F., Hsu, J., Xie, L., Tsui, M.-P.: Physics- motivated features for distinguishing photographic images and computer graphics. In: Proc. ACM Multimedia, pp. 239–248 (2005)
3. Dirik, A.E., Bayram, S., Sencar, H.T., Memon, N.: New features to identify computer generated images. In: Proc. IEEE ICIP. IV, pp. 433–436 (2007)
4. Dirik, A.E., Memon, N.: Image tamper detection based on demosaicing artifacts. In: Proc. IEEE ICIP, pp. 1497–1500 (2009)
5. Ng, T.-T., Chang, S.-F.: Classifying Photographic and Photorealistic Computer Graphic Images using Natural Image Statistics. ADVENT Technical Report, Columbia University, #220-2006-6 (2004)
6. Wu, J., Kamath, M.V., Poehlman, W.F.S.: Detecting Differences between Photographs and Computer Generated Images. In: Proceedings of the 24th IASTED International Conference on Signal Processing, Pattern Recognition, and Applications, SPPRA 2006, pp. 268–273 (2006)
7. Chen, W., Shi, Y.Q., Xuan, G.R.: Identifying Computer Graphics Using HSV Color Model and Statistical Moments of Characteristic Functions. In: Proc. ICME, pp. 1123–1126 (2007)
8. Sutthiwan, P., Cai, X., Shi, Y.Q., Zhang, H.: Computer graphics classification based on Markov process model and boosting feature selection technique. In: Proc. IEEE ICIP, pp. 2913–2916 (2009)
9. Chen, D.M., Li, J.H., Wang, S.L., Li, S.H.: Identifying Computer Generated and Digital Camera Images Using Fractional Lower Order Moments. In: IEEE Conference on Industrial Electronics and Applications (ICIEA), pp. 230–235 (2009)
10. Li, W.X., Zhang, T., Zheng, E.G., Ping, X.J.: Identifying Photorealistic Computer Graphics Using Second-order Difference Statistics. In: Seventh International Conference on Fuzzy Systems and Knowledge Discovery (FSKD), pp. 2316–2319 (2010)

11. Pan, F., Huang, J.: Discriminating computer graphics images and natural images using hidden markov tree model. In: Kim, H.-J., Shi, Y.Q., Barni, M. (eds.) IWDW 2010. LNCS, vol. 6526, pp. 23–28. Springer, Heidelberg (2011)

12. Zhang, R., Wang, R.D.: Distinguishing Photorealistic Computer Graphics from Natural Images by Imaging Features and Visual Features. In: International Conference on Electronics, Communications and Control (ICECC), pp. 226–229 (2011)

13. Wu, R.Y., Li, X.L., Yang, B.: Identifying computer generated graphics VIA histogram features. In: Proc. ICIP, pp. 1933–1936 (2011)

14. Haralick, R.M., Dinstein, Shanmugan, K.: Textural features for image classification. IEEE Transaction on Systems, Man and Cybernetics 3(6), 610–621 (1973)

15. Ojala, T., Pietikainen, M., Maenpaa, T.: Multiresolution gray-scale and rotation invariant texture classification with local binary patterns. IEEE Transactions on Pattern Analysis and Machine Intelligence 24, 971–987 (2002)

16. Mäenpää, T., Pietikäinen, M.: Texture analysis with local binary patterns. In: Handbook of Pattern Recognition and Computer Vision, 3rd edn., pp. 197–216 (2005)

17. Chen, W.: Detection of Digital Image and Video Forgeries, Ph.D. Dissertation, Dept. of ECE, NJIT (2008)

18. Weinberger, M.J., Seroussi, G., Sapiro, G.: LOCO-I: a low complexity, context-based, lossless image compression algorithm. In: Proceedings of Data Compression Conference, DCC 1996, pp. 140–149 (1996)

19. http://www.creative-3d.net, http://www.3dlinks.com

20. Friedman, J., Hastie, T.: Additive logistic regression: a statistical view of boosting. The Annals of Statistics 28(2), 337–407 (2000)

21. Chang, C.-C., Lin, C.-J.: LIBSVM: a library for support vector machines. ACM Transactions on Intelligent Systems and Technology 2, 27:1–27:27 (2011), Software available at http://www.csie.ntu.edu.tw/~cjlin/libsvm

22. Gloe, T., Böhme, R.: The 'Dresden Image Database' for benchmarking digital image forensics. Presented at the Proceedings of the 2010 ACM Symposium on Applied Computing, Sierre, Switzerland (2010)

Detecting Removed Object
from Video with Stationary Background

Leida Li[1,2], Xuewei Wang[1], Wei Zhang[1], Gaobo Yang[3], and Guozhang Hu[4]

[1] School of Information and Electrical Engineering,
China University of Mining and Technology, Xuzhou 221116, China
[2] Shanghai Key Laboratory of Integrate Administration Technologies
for Information Security, Shanghai 200240, China
[3] School of Information Science and Engineering, Hunan University,
Changsha 410082, China
[4] Department of Neurosurgery, China-Japan Union Hospital, Jilin University,
Changchun 130033, China

Abstract. This paper presents a method for detecting the removed object in video captured by stationary camera. The method is based on an observation that the removed object, while not distinguishable by human eyes, leaves artifacts that can be detected by computers. In this paper, the block based motion estimation method is employed to extract motion information from adjacent video frames. Then the magnitude and orientation of the motion vectors are used to differentiate the authentic region and the forged region. By exploring the discrepancies in motion vectors, the position of the removed object can be revealed. The efficiency of the proposed method is demonstrated by experiments.

1 Introduction

Blind multimedia forensic has become an attractive research field during the past few years. With this technique, the authenticity of an image/video can be determined by analyzing the characteristics of the suspicious data directly. While most of the prior work has been focused on image forensics [1], video contents are also frequently used in our daily life, such as TV broadcasting and surveillance applications. Particularly, video contents have been widely used in judicial forensics, where they are commonly used as evidence in the courtroom. For these applications, the authenticity of the video is critically important.

Recently, several video forensic methods have been proposed. Wang et al. proposed several methods to expose video forgeries [2,3,4,5]. In [2], they addressed two techniques to detect the duplicated frames and duplicated regions across frames. They also reported a forensics method for interlaced and Deinterlaced videos [3]. For the deinterlaced video, the correlations introduced by the camera or deinterlacing algorithms were quantified. Disturbances of these correlations can signify possible tampering. For the interlaced videos, the motion between fields of a single frame and across fields of neighboring frames is investigated to detect tampering. More recently, they presented a method to detect

Y.Q. Shi, H.J. Kim, and F. Pérez-González (Eds.): IWDW 2012, LNCS 7809, pp. 242–252, 2013.

the re-projected video [4]. The camera parameters estimated from the videos are employed to expose the forgery. In [5], specific static and temporal statistical perturbations were investigated during double MPEG compression of the video, whose presence would expose the presence of possible tampering. In the work of Chen and Shi, the probability distribution of the first digits of the non-zero MPEG quantized AC coefficients is explored [6]. Disturbance of the probability distribution can be used as an evidence of double compression. While the method can expose double MPEG compression, double compression of the video many not necessarily indicate video forgery. Kobayashi et al. employed the noise characteristics for detecting video tampering in static scene [7,8]. Su et al. proposed to detect frame deletion in video based on motion-compensated edge artifact [9]. In [10], the ghost shadow artifact is extracted and used to disclose the removed object. Su et al. also addressed a method to detect the logo-removal forgery in video by estimating the inconsistency of blur [11]. In [12,13], the authors employed the multimodal fusion of residue features to detect video tampering.

Most of the existing video forensic methods aim to deal with a specific kind of video forgery, such as frame deletion, frame duplication, logo removal. In this paper, we propose a method to detect the object removal forgeries for surveillance videos with stationary backgrounds. The discrepancies in motion vector fields are employed as a sign of tampering. Specifically, the magnitude and orientation of the motion vectors between adjacent video frames are extracted, and the abnormal characteristics of them can be used to determine and locate the forged regions. We show the efficiency of the proposed scheme by conducting several experiments.

2   Proposed Method

The proposed method aims at exposing the traces of object removal forgery in static scene videos, especially surveillance videos. Our idea is to detect the removed object by finding the area with abnormal motion characteristics. For surveillance applications, the background of the video is usually static with moving object. As a result, the motion features between the background and the foreground are different. Furthermore, the motion vectors in the foreground shall have obvious coherence. If the object is removed from the video, the motion vectors will be distributed non-uniformly. Fig.1 shows an example of object removal forgery in two adjacent video frames and the corresponding motion vector (MV) fields. In this example, the moving car is removed from the video.

It is observed from Fig.1 that: (1) The motion vectors in the background area are very small compared to the foreground area. Most of them are approaching zero. (2) The distribution of the motion vectors in the foreground area between the authentic video and the forged video are quite different. For the authentic video, the MVs distribute almost uniformly, regardless of the magnitude or the orientation. By contrast, the distribution of the MVs for the tampered video is disordered. The non-uniform distribution of the MVs is caused by the traces of forgery when removing the moving object. As a result, if we can correctly

244 L. Li et al.

Fig. 1. Motion vector fields extracted from authentic video and tampered video. Left: original frames and the MV field; Right: tampered frames and the MV field.

identify the regions where the MVs show abnormality, the region can be detected, indicating possible forgery. The proposed method is based on this finding, and it operates as follows. For a possibly tampered video, the motion vectors between the adjacent frames are first computed. Then the moving objects are detected by comparing the magnitudes of the MVs. The next step is to estimate the uniformity of the MVs, and the presence of non-uniform MVs in a foreground area is employed as the evidence of video tampering.

2.1 Detection of Moving Object

As we are processing video with stationary background, the motion vectors between the background and foreground are quite different. In this paper, the moving objects are detected by comparing the magnitudes and orientations of the MVs. Let the motion vectors be denoted by $\{V_{i,j}, i = 1, 2, \cdots, \mathcal{S}, j = 1, 2, \cdots, \mathcal{T}\}$, where $\mathcal{S}$ and $\mathcal{T}$ are the maximum row index and column index of the MVs. Each MV consists of a magnitude part and an angular part. In this paper, the magnitude and orientation of the MV is denoted by $\{M_{i,j}, i = 1, 2, \cdots, \mathcal{S}, j =$

$1, 2, \cdots, \mathcal{T}\}$ and $\{A_{i,j}, i = 1, 2, \cdots, \mathcal{S}, j = 1, 2, \cdots, \mathcal{T}\}$. The average magnitude and orientation of the MVs are first computed.

$$M_{mean} = \frac{\sum_{i=1}^{\mathcal{S}} \sum_{j=1}^{\mathcal{T}} |M_{ij}|}{\mathcal{S} \times \mathcal{T}} \tag{1}$$

$$A_{mean} = \frac{\sum_{i=1}^{\mathcal{S}} \sum_{j=1}^{\mathcal{T}} |A_{ij}|}{\mathcal{S} \times \mathcal{T}} \tag{2}$$

It should be noted that the angle is represented in radian so that the MVs with orientations horizontally to the right can be represented by either 0 or 2π.

The background and the moving object can be detected by comparing the magnitude and orientation of each motion vector to the average values. Let the background and the object be denoted by S_{bkg} and S_{obj}, they can be obtained as follows.

$$B_{ij} \in \begin{cases} \mathcal{S}_{bkg}^M, & if \;\; M_{ij} < M_{mean} \\ \mathcal{S}_{obj}^M, & if \;\; M_{ij} \geq M_{mean} \end{cases} \tag{3}$$

$$B_{ij} \in \begin{cases} \mathcal{S}_{bkg}^A, & if \;\; A_{ij} < A_{mean} \\ \mathcal{S}_{obj}^A, & if \;\; A_{ij} \geq A_{mean} \end{cases} \tag{4}$$

where B_{ij} is the block corresponding to the motion vector V_{ij}. $\mathcal{S}_{bkg}^M$ and $\mathcal{S}_{obj}^M$ denote the background and object determined by the magnitudes of the MVs, while $\mathcal{S}_{bkg}^A$ and $\mathcal{S}_{obj}^A$ are the background and object determined by the angular parts. Based on Eqs.(3) and (4), we can obtain two results of the detected moving objects. In this paper, we propose to obtain the final result by applying the $\mathcal{OR}$ operation.

$$S_{obj} = \mathcal{S}_{obj}^M \bigcup \mathcal{S}_{obj}^A \tag{5}$$

In determining the area with moving object, the logical $\mathcal{OR}$ operation can guarantee a complete contour of the region.

2.2   Determining Forgery by Inconsistency of MV Orientation

If a moving object is removed from the original video, it is very likely that the tampered area has some computer detectable artifacts. Therefore, the tampered area can be readily detected. However, it should also be noted that normal moments can also be detected at the same time. Fig.2 shows an example of the detection result on a video with two moving cars, where only one is removed.

It is known from Fig.2 that the two moving objects can both be detected. In order to determine the tampered region, further processing is required. It has been shown in Fig.1 that the major differences between the normal moving

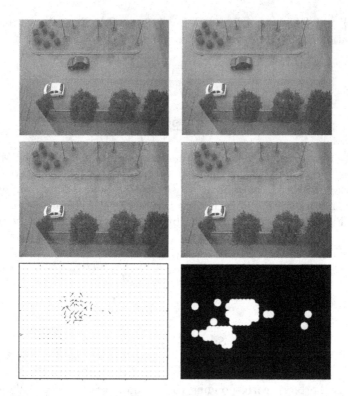

Fig. 2. Forgery detection in a video with two moving targets. First row: original video; Second row: tampered video; Third row: MV field and initial detection result.

area and tampered area is that the distribution of MVs are quit uniform for the normal movement. Based on this finding, our next step is to differentiate the normal moving area from the tampered moving area. In this paper, we propose to locate the tampered area according to the non-uniformity of the MVs. Specifically, the standard deviation of the MVs within the initial detected areas are computed. In order to achieve this goal, the foreground areas are first determined using regional growth. Then each detected area is denoted by a set $\Omega_i, i = 1, 2, \cdots, N$, where N is the total number of moving areas.

In order to compute the variance of the angle of the MVs, each MV is assigned a unique angle within the range $[0\ 2\pi)$. Then the variance of each region is computed and denoted by $\sigma_i, i = 1, 2, \cdots, N$. In order to differentiate the normal moving region and the tampered region, a threshold is employed, which is denoted by T_h in this paper. As the MVs distribute quite irregularly, the variances of the tampered regions are bigger than those in the normal moving regions.

$$\Omega_i \in \begin{cases} \text{Tampered region,} & if \quad \sigma_i \geq T_h \\ \text{Normal region,} & if \quad \sigma_i < T_h \end{cases} \qquad (6)$$

2.3   Post-processing

For the initial detection result, several small isolated regions can be detected. Typically, these are falsely detected areas, and they should be removed to obtain the final result. In this paper, these regions are removed by mathematical morphological operation. Furthermore, in order to identify the tampered region and the normal moving area, two different colors are used to mark the contours of the detected regions.

3   Experimental Results

In this section, we conduct some simulations to demonstrate the efficiency of the proposed method. Our method is mainly designed to detect the object removal forgery in video with stationary backgrounds, especially surveillance videos. As a result, the videos used in our experiments are all captured by stationary camera.

Fig. 3. Forgery detection in a video with one moving target. First row: original video; Second row: tampered video; Third row: detection map and detection result.

Fig.3 shows an example of the detection result on a surveillance video captured in the campus. A car is passing through the camera in the original video. In the tampered video, the car is removed. This may occur when an object is removed purposely, mainly with the aim to hide the existence of such object. It is seen from the figure that the tampered video frames look very natural, and the traces of tampering are not visible to the naked eyes. It is known from the figure that the detection result clearly indicates the existence of an object in the places marked by the red contour.

Fig.4 shows another video downloaded from the internet [14]. During forgery, the moving care is removed. The detection result shows the forged region clearly.

Fig. 4. Forgery detection on a video with one moving target. First row: original video; Second row: tampered video; Third row: detection map and detection result.

In the next experiment, videos with two or more moving targets are employed to evaluate the performance of the proposed scheme. In Fig.5, the original video contains two moving cars. In order to create a forgery, the blue car is removed. In Fig.6, three people are passing by the camera in the original video. The middle person is removed to create the forged video. In both cases, it is hard to notice the trace of tampering by the naked eyes.

It is known from Figs.5 and 6 that the removed regions can be readily detected. Apart from the tampered region, the regions with normal movement can also be located as well. In order to differentiate them, the forged regions are marked with red color while the normal movement regions are marked with green color. In other words, the proposed method can not only expose the object removal forgery, but also can indicate the normal movement. This is important when we need to locate the tampered regions in an automatic manner.

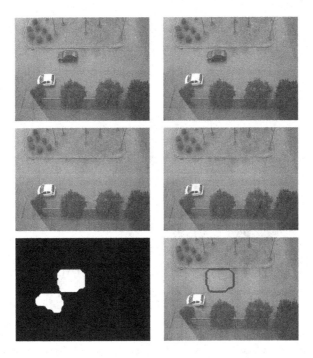

Fig. 5. Forgery detection on a video with two moving target. First row: original video; Second row: tampered video; Third row: detection map and detection result.

The proposed method can be improved to process videos with moving backgrounds. Unlike the situation of stationary camera, the moving camera will produce motion vectors. Furthermore, the magnitudes of the MVs in the backgrounds may have significant values, even bigger than those in the moving objects. Therefore, the moving object and the background cannot be determined using Eqs.(3) and (4) directly. However, by incorporating a threshold into Eqs.(3) and (4), the moving object and the moving background can be detected by the following two formulas.

$$B_{ij} \in \begin{cases} \mathcal{S}_{bkg}^{M}, & if \;\; |M_{ij} - M_{mean}| \leq T_M \\ \mathcal{S}_{obj}^{M}, & if \;\; |M_{ij} - M_{mean}| > T_M \end{cases} \qquad (7)$$

$$B_{ij} \in \begin{cases} \mathcal{S}_{bkg}^{A}, & if \;\; |A_{ij} - A_{mean}| \leq T_A \\ \mathcal{S}_{obj}^{A}, & if \;\; |A_{ij} - A_{mean}| > T_A \end{cases} \qquad (8)$$

While Eqs.(7) and (8) can differentiate the moving object and background, it is based on an assumption that the motion of the camera is different to the motion of the object, either in speed or direction. In reality, this assumption is commonly satisfied.

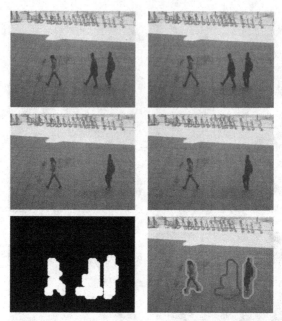

Fig. 6. Forgery detection on a video with three moving target. First row: original video; Second row: tampered video; Third row: detection map and detection result.

Fig. 7. Forgery detection on a video with moving targets and moving camera. First row: original video; Second row: tampered video; Third row: detection map and detection result.

Fig.7 shows the simulation results on a video captured by moving camera with multiple moving objects. In the original video, there are three moving cars. After tampering, the red car is removed. From the simulation results, we know that the tampered region can be detected, which is denoted by the red contour. Except for the tampered region, the normal moving objects are also marked correctly.

4   Conclusion

Video contents have been widely used in our daily life as well as many scenarios, where the authenticity of the data is critically important. The main contribution of this paper is that we present a method to detect the object removal forgery in videos. Specifically, we establish our method based on video with stationary backgrounds, especially surveillance videos. The motion vector features between the adjacent video frames are investigated to achieve this goal. The proposed method can locate the tampered regions. Furthermore, it can also identify the normal movement automatically. We have done some experiments to demonstrate the efficiency of the proposed scheme.

While some promising results have been obtained in this work, we have also found that if the object is removed by a person with sophisticated skills, our method may fail because of the difficulty to estimate the indiscrepancies of the motion vectors. Furthermore, the following issues should be considered in the future. 1. Currently, the discrepancy of the motion vectors is measured by variance of the MVs, which is very simple. The next step is to find other motion vector characteristics to depict the distribution of the MVs and improve the performance of the scheme in face of moving backgrounds. 2. The proposed method operates on the video frames directly. It should be improved to handle compressed videos. 3. The current work focus on the detection of rigid object removal. Non-rigid object forgery detection is more common in reality, so this should be considered. 4. Video inpainting is a technique to repair the removed regions in video while maintaining its visual quality. In order to create satisfactory forgeries, one may adopt the video inpainting technique to generate the forged video. This will pose a new challenging for video forensics. As a result, to develop video forensics methods that can deal with video inpainting processing is needed.

Acknowledgements. This work is supported by the Opening Project of Shanghai Key Laboratory of Integrate Administration Technologies for Information Security (AGK2012002), the Fundamental Research Funds for the Central Universities (2012QNA59), National Natural Science Foundation of China (60802077, 60702065), Pre-phase Project of the National Basic Research Program of China (2010CB334706), New Century Excellent Talents in University (NCET-11-0134), Key Project of Hunan Provincial Natural Science Foundation (11JJ2053) and China Postdoctoral Science Foundation (201104586, 20100471415).

References

1. Farid, H.: A survey of image forgery detection. IEEE Signal Processing Magnazine 26(2), 16–25 (2009)
2. Wang, W.H., Farid, H.: Exposing digital forgeries in video by detecting duplication. In: Proc. MMSec 2007, ACM Multimedia and Security Workshop, pp. 35–42 (2007)
3. Wang, W.H., Farid, H.: Exposing digital forgeries in interlaced and de-interlaced video. IEEE Transactions on Information Forensics and Security 2(3), 438–449 (2007)
4. Wang, W., Farid, H.: Detecting re-projected video. In: Solanki, K., Sullivan, K., Madhow, U. (eds.) IH 2008. LNCS, vol. 5284, pp. 72–86. Springer, Heidelberg (2008)
5. Wang, W.H., Farid, H.: Exposing digital forgeries in video by detecting double MPEG compression. In: Proc. MMSec 2006, ACM Multimedia and Security Workshop, pp. 37–47 (2006)
6. Chen, W., Shi, Y.Q.: Detection of double MPEG compression based on first digit statistics. In: Kim, H.-J., Katzenbeisser, S., Ho, A.T.S. (eds.) IWDW 2008. LNCS, vol. 5450, pp. 16–30. Springer, Heidelberg (2009)
7. Kobayashi, M., Okabe, T., Sato, Y.: Detecting video forgeries based on noise characteristics. In: Wada, T., Huang, F., Lin, S. (eds.) PSIVT 2009. LNCS, vol. 5414, pp. 306–317. Springer, Heidelberg (2009)
8. Kobayashi, M., Okabe, T., Sato, Y.: Detecting forgery from static-scene video based on inconsistency in noise level functions. IEEE Transactions on Information Forensics and Security 5(4), 883–892 (2010)
9. Su, Y.T., Zhang, J., Liu, J.: Exposing digital video forgery by detecting motion-compensated edge artifact. In: Proc. CiSE 2009, International Conference on Computational Intelligence and Software Engineering, pp. 1–4 (2009)
10. Zhang, J., Su, Y.T., Zhang, M.Y.: Exposing digital video forgery by ghost shadow artifact. In: Proc. MiFor 2009, ACM Workshop on Multimedia in Forensics, pp. 49–53 (2009)
11. Su, Y.T., Zhang, J., Han, Y., Chen, J.: Exposing digital video logo-removal forgery by inconsistency of blur. International Journal of Pattern Recognition and Artificial Intelligence 24(7), 1027–1046 (2010)
12. Chetty, G.: Blind and passive digital video tamper detection based on multimodal fusion. In: Proc. of the 14th WSEAS International Conference on Communications, pp. 109–117 (2010)
13. Chetty, G., Biswas, M., Singh, R.: Digital video tamper detection based on multimodal fusion of residue features. In: Proc. International Conference on Network and System Security, pp. 606–613 (2010)
14. http://v.youku.com/v_show/id_XMTcwMzU4ODQ0.html

Audio Forgery Detection Based on Max Offsets for Cross Correlation between ENF and Reference Signal

Yongjian Hu[1,2], Chang-Tsun Li[1], Zhisheng Lv[2], and Bei-bei Liu[2]

[1] Department of Computer Science, University of Warwick, Coventry CV4 7AL, UK
[2] School of Electronic and Information Engineering,
South China University of Technology, Guangzhou 510640, P.R. China
{Yongjian.Hu,ctli}@dcs.warwick.ac.uk, eeyjhu@scut.edu.cn

Abstract. The electric network frequency (ENF) is likely to be embedded in audio signals when the electronic recording devices are connected to electric power lines. If an audio signal is edited, the embedded ENF will be altered inevitably. In order to assess audio authenticity, this paper proposes a new method based on the max offset for cross correlation between the extracted ENF and the reference signal. By comparing the max offsets on a block-by-block basis, we can determine whether the audio signal in question was digitally edited as well as the location at which the editing manipulation occurs. The validity and effectiveness of our method have been verified by experiments on both synthetic composite signals and real-world audio signals.

Keywords: Electric network frequency, audio forgery detection, max offset for cross correlation, single-frequency reference signal.

1 Introduction

With wide applications of various multimedia devices, digital audio recording becomes more common in human life. Meanwhile, audio editing also becomes a simple task and even non-professionals can easily tamper with audio without leaving any traces [1]. Therefore, as a branch of digital forensics, audio forgery detection has become more and more important [2].

When recording with digital equipment connected to an electrical outlet, the electric network frequency (ENF), designed to be 50 Hz (e.g., in most of European countries and China) or 60 Hz (e.g., in US), will most likely be embedded in the recorded audio signals. By examining consistency of the ENF we can assess whether the audio was altered. It is worth mentioning that in real electric network the ENF is not always fixed precisely at 50 Hz or 60 Hz but varies over time because of the differences between the produced power and the consumed power. However, the fluctuation range of the ENF is small and is often less than 0.6 Hz [3]. In [3-6], the ENF extracted from speech signals was compared with the recorded real-time ENF to determine the continuity and consistency of the audio signals. But these methods need to record a large number of ENF signals to constitute the reference signal database, and the detection of whether the audio signal was altered would rely on human

Y.Q. Shi, H.J. Kim, and F. Pérez-González (Eds.): IWDW 2012, LNCS 7809, pp. 253–266, 2013.

observations. In [7], Nicolalde *et al.* discussed an audio authenticity method based on the spectrum distances and the ENF phases change. In [8], the same authors used a high-precision Fourier analysis method for improving estimation of the ENF phases. However, their phase estimation methods are sensitive to the resolution of frequency estimation. To acquire a precise estimation of the phase, the resolution must be high; otherwise, the estimation error would be large. High resolution often means high computational complexity. On the other hand, the narrow-band pass filter used to extract the ENF also has bandwidth limitation, which would affect the accuracy of phase estimation.

In this paper, we propose a simple and efficient method for detection of audio forgery. We first introduce the concept of max offset, and then elaborate on how to use the max offsets to detect audio forgery. Our method can determine whether the audio signal in question was edited. If the audio signal was edited, our method can further tell where the editing operations occur.

The remainder of the paper is organized as follows. In Section 2, we briefly review the method of phase estimation using discrete Fourier transform (DFT) in [7]. In Section 3, we propose the basic idea of our method and elaborate on the max offset for cross correlation between the ENF and the reference signal. In Section 4, we describe how to implement the proposed method in detail. In Section 5, we test our method on synthetic composite signal as well as real-world audio signals to evaluate its performance. In Section 6, we briefly discuss the computational complexity of the proposed method. We summarize our method in Section 7.

2   Using DFT for Estimation of Phase of Single-Frequency Signals

The frequency and phase of a single-frequency signal was estimated using the DFT in [7] and [8]. This section briefly reviews the DFT method for phase estimation. Let $s(n) = \sin(2\pi n f_0 / f_s + \theta_0)$ denote a M-sample signal with the sampling frequency f_s. After processed by a smoothing window $w(n)$ (e.g., Hann), the signal becomes $x(n) = s(n)w(n)$. The N_{DFT}-point ($N_{DFT} \geq M$) DFT transform of $x(n)$ can be expressed as $X(k)$ as follows:

$$X(k) = \sum_{n=0}^{N_{DFT}-1} x(n)e^{-j\frac{2\pi}{N_{DFT}}kn} \tag{1}$$

If $|X(k)|$ gets the maximum value at k_{max}, the tone frequency of the signal can be estimated by

$$\hat{f}_0 = k_{max}\frac{f_s}{N_{DFT}} \tag{2}$$

The resolution of $\hat{f}_0$ is f_s / N_{DFT}. The greater the value of N_{DFT} is, the better the accuracy of $\hat{f}_0$, at the expense of increasing computational burden [8]. The initial phase of the signal can be simply estimated by the angle of $X(k_{max})$

$$\hat{\theta}_0 = \arg[X(k_{max})] \tag{3}$$

For a given test audio signal, the method in [7] applies a sliding window to it. Each window/block covers N samples. The phase of the ENF in each window can thus be estimated. If one moves the window across the whole signal in a way of partial overlapping and estimates the phase of ENF in every window, one can easily detect audio authenticity by comparing the phase differences.

   The DFT method in [7] has several drawbacks. Firstly, it relies on the accuracy of estimation of the ENF phase. Although the ENF is ideally supposed to be a single frequency signal, the ENF extracted by the band-pass filter from a practical audio signal often contains other frequency components from the voice and background noise. These components interfere with the accuracy of estimation of the ENF phase. Secondly, the frequency fluctuation of the practical ENF caused by real electric networks also interferes with the accuracy of estimation of the ENF phase. Thirdly, in order to estimate the ENF phase more accurately, a larger sliding window with more samples is preferred. However, the use of a larger sliding window would increase computational complexity. On the other hand, it lowers the precision for the location of audio editing.

3   The Max Offset for Cross Correlation between the Extracted ENF and the Reference Signal

We propose a method to detect audio authenticity based on the offset for maximizing the cross correlation between the extracted ENF and a reference signal. This offset is called the *max offset* in this work for simplicity. Assume that the extracted ENF $x(n)$ is a composite signal with center frequency f_0. It contains L frequency components (i.e., harmonics).

$$x(n) = A_0 \sin(2\pi n f_0 / f_s + \theta_0) + \sum_{i=1}^{L} a_i \sin(2\pi n f_i / f_s + \theta_i) \tag{4}$$

where a_i, f_i, θ_i refer to amplitude, frequency and initial phase for the i-th component, respectively. Here $|f_i - f_0| < 1$. We then introduce a reference signal with the same frequency as the ENF:

$$r(n) = \sin(2\pi n f_0 / f_s) \tag{5}$$

The cross correlation between the extracted ENF $x(n)$ and the reference signal $r(n)$ can be calculated as follows:

$$R_{x,r}(\tau) = \frac{1}{N}\sum_{n=0}^{N-1}[A_0\sin(2\pi n\frac{f_0}{f_s}+\theta_0)+\sum_{i=1}^{L}a_i\sin(2\pi n\frac{f_i}{f_s}+\theta_i)]\sin(2\pi(n+\tau)\frac{f_0}{f_s})$$

$$=\frac{1}{N}\sum_{n=0}^{N-1}\left\{\frac{A_0}{2}[\cos(-2\pi\tau\frac{f_0}{f_s}+\theta_0)-\cos(2\pi n\frac{2f_0}{f_s}+2\pi\tau\frac{f_0}{f_s}+\theta_0)]\right\}+$$

$$\frac{1}{N}\sum_{n=0}^{N-1}\left\{\sum_{i=1}^{L}\frac{a_i}{2}[\cos(2\pi n\frac{f_i-f_0}{f_s}-2\pi\tau\frac{f_0}{f_s}+\theta_i)-\cos(2\pi n\frac{f_i+f_0}{f_s}+2\pi\tau\frac{f_0}{f_s}+\theta_i)]\right\} \quad (6)$$

$$=\frac{A_0}{2N}\left\{\sum_{n=0}^{N-1}[\cos(-2\pi\frac{\tau}{N_0}+\theta_0)]-\sum_{n=0}^{N-1}[\cos(2\pi\frac{2n}{N_0}+2\pi\frac{\tau}{N_0}+\theta_0)]\right\}+$$

$$\sum_{i=1}^{L}\frac{a_i}{2N}\left\{\sum_{n=0}^{N-1}[\cos(2\pi n\frac{\Delta f_i}{f_s}-2\pi\frac{\tau}{N_0}+\theta_i)]-\sum_{n=0}^{N-1}[\cos(2\pi n\frac{2f_0+\Delta f_i}{f_s}+2\pi\frac{\tau}{N_0}+\theta_i)]\right\}$$

where $\Delta f_i = f_i-f_0, N_0 = \frac{f_s}{f_0}, n=1,2,\cdots,N, \tau=0,1,\cdots N_0-1$. Here τ refers to the

offset. For a given signal, if N is an integral multiple of N_0 and $\theta_0 = 2\pi\frac{\tau}{N_0}$, we

obtain

$$\frac{1}{N}\sum_{n=0}^{N-1}[\cos(-2\pi\frac{\tau}{N_0}+\theta_0)]=1 \quad (7)$$

$$\frac{1}{N}\sum_{n=0}^{N-1}[\cos(2\pi\frac{2n}{N_0}+2\pi\frac{\tau}{N_0}+\theta_0)]=\frac{1}{N}\sum_{n=0}^{N-1}[\cos(2\pi\frac{2n}{N_0}+2\theta_0)] \quad (8)$$

We can find that the cycle of $\cos(2\pi\frac{2n}{N_0}+2\theta_0)$ is $\frac{N_0}{2}$, so

$$\frac{1}{N}\sum_{n=0}^{N-1}\cos(2\pi\frac{2n}{N_0}+2\theta_0)=0.$$

$$\frac{1}{N}\sum_{n=0}^{N-1}[\cos(2\pi n\frac{\Delta f_i}{f_s}-2\pi\frac{\tau}{N_0}+\theta_i)]=\frac{1}{N}\sum_{n=0}^{N-1}\cos(2\pi n\frac{\Delta f_i}{f_s}-\theta_0+\theta_i) \quad (9)$$

For $\Delta f_i = f_i-f_0, 0<|\Delta f_i|<1$ (i.e., $\Delta f_i \ll f_s$), $N<f_s$ and the randomness of $\theta_i-\theta_0$, the value of (9) is a random variable between -1 and 1, so

$$\frac{1}{N}\sum_{n=0}^{N-1}\cos(2\pi n\frac{\Delta f_i}{f_s}-\theta_0+\theta_i)=\xi_i, |\xi_i|<1.$$

$$\frac{1}{N}\sum_{n=0}^{N-1}\cos(2\pi n\frac{2f_0+\Delta f_i}{f_s}+2\pi\frac{\tau}{N_0}+\theta_i)\approx\frac{1}{N}\sum_{n=0}^{N-1}\cos(2\pi\frac{2n}{N_0}+\theta_0+\theta_i)=0 \quad (10)$$

From (7) to (10), equation (6) can be rewritten as:

$$R_{x,r}(\tau) \approx \frac{A_0}{2} - \sum_{i=1}^{L} \frac{a_i}{2} \xi_i, \qquad \qquad |\xi_i| < 1 \qquad \qquad (11)$$

With respect to an audio signal with high SNR, we have $A_0 \gg a_i, i = 1, ..., L$, meaning that the harmonics often have little impact on $R_{x,r}(\tau)$. For audio forgery, we are only interested in the offset at which $R_{x,r}(\tau)$ gets the max value. This offset value is denoted as the max offset τ_{max}. Note that we do not need to really calculate the value of $R_{x,r}(\tau)$ for finding out τ_{max}. What we need to do is to increase τ by a small increment each time and calculate the correlation value. The largest cross correlation value corresponds to the max offset. Theoretically, τ_{max} is the nearest integer of $\frac{\theta_0}{2\pi} N_0$ and is irrelevant to N. As a spatial domain method, the proposed method is insensitive to resolution f_s / N_{DFT}.

In summary, for an audio signal in question, we first divide the signal into overlapped blocks using a sliding window of size N, and then calculate τ_{max} in each block. We can determine audio forgery by investigating the differences between the max offsets from neighboring blocks. If τ_{max} values of all the blocks are the same or almost constant, the differences are 0 or near 0. In this case, the audio signal is detected as being original; otherwise the audio signal is likely to have been edited.

4   Implementation of the Proposed Method

We propose to use the difference between the max offsets from different blocks for the detection of audio forgery. The algorithm diagram is shown in Fig.1.

Below we describe how to visually and automatically judge the differences between the max offsets from blocks, respectively.

4.1   Visual Method

Our visual method includes the following seven steps.

1. Down-sample the audio signal in question to frequency f_d to reduce computational cost. To ensure that the number of ENF samples per cycle is the same, f_d may be 1000 Hz or 1200 Hz, depending on the ENF being 50 Hz or 60 Hz.
2. Extract the ENF from the down-sampled audio signal through a linear-phase bandpass filter (BPF). The center frequency of the filter should be the same as the ENF, and the pass band width could be between 0.6 Hz and 1.4 Hz [8].

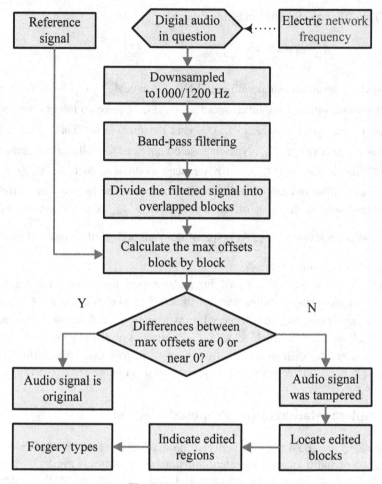

Fig. 1. Algorithm diagram

3. Divide the ENF signal into blocks. Each block contains N_C cycles of ENF, and thus $N = N_C \times N_0$. Here $N_0 = f_d / f_0$. Adjacent blocks have an overlap of $(N_C - 1)$ cycles.

4. Generate a single-frequency reference signal $r(n)$ whose frequency is the same as the ENF. Sample it using f_d. According to formula (6), calculate the cross correlation between the extracted ENF and the reference signal, and determine the max offset τ_{max} for every block.

5. Observe τ_{max} values of all blocks. If τ_{max} values are the same or approximately same, the ENF is detected as being original. If τ_{max} leaps at some points, the ENF is likely to be edited.

6. If the ENF is detected as being edited, locate the boundaries at which τ_{max} values leap.

7. Determine the type of forgery according to the content of the located edited region. Specifically, the voice part is for insertion editing while the silent part is for deletion editing.

4.2   Automatic Method

The difference between τ_{max} values from two adjacent blocks can be expressed as

$$\Delta\tau_{max}(i) = \tau_{max}(i+1) - \tau_{max}(i), \qquad i = 1,2,3,\cdots N_{Block} - 1 \tag{12}$$

where N_{Block} is the number of blocks. We first label the blocks where $\Delta\tau_{max}(i) \neq 0$. Assume that there are P such blocks, labeled as $i_1, i_2, i_3, \cdots i_p$. We then calculate the following variables

$$D_t(k) = i_{k+1} - i_k \tag{13}$$

$$D_{os}(k) = \left| \Delta\tau_{max}(i_{k+1}) + \Delta\tau_{max}(i_k) \right| \tag{14}$$

where $k = 1, 2, \cdots P-1$. $D_t(k)$ refers to the time interval between adjacent blocks i_k and i_{k+1}. $D_{os}(k)$ refers to the absolute of sum of the two differences for these two blocks.

In order to reduce false alarms, we define the threshold of time interval T_t and the threshold T_{os} for the absolute sum of differences of the max offsets below:

$$T_t = \min(N_{T0}, N_{Td}) \tag{15}$$

where $N_{T0} = \dfrac{N_{BLOCK}}{P+1}$. N_{T0} is introduced for decreasing false alarms caused by the ENF fluctuation. N_{Td} is related to the pass-band of the filter and can be selected experimentally. $N_{Td} = 60$ for our experiments. We set $T_{os} = 2$ to reduce false alarm errors caused by the fluctuations of τ_{max}. We will use examples to further explain T_{os} and T_t in Section 5.

To realize the automatic detection, we define F as

$$F = \sum_k \frac{D_{os}(k)}{D_t(k) \times T_d} \tag{16}$$

where $T_d = 1/f_d$ is the down-sampling period. F reflects the change of the max offsets in the short time interval. If an audio signal is original, F is very small; otherwise, F is large. If we calculate $\lg F$, we can readily discriminate between the original signal and the edited signal with the threshold 0.

5   Experiment and Discussion

5.1   Synthetic Composite Signal

We first evaluate the validity and effectiveness of the proposed method on a simulated ENF signal. As discussed in Section 3, an extracted ENF can be simulated as a composite signal by (4). We randomly assume $A_0 = 0.1$, $M = 6$, $a_1 = 0.0015$, $a_2 = 0.001$, $a_3 = 0.0005$, $a_4 = 0.0005$, $a_5 = 0.001$, $a_6 = 0.0015$, $f_0 = 50$ Hz, $f_1 = 49.4$ Hz, $f_2 = 49.6$ Hz, $f_3 = 49.8$ Hz, $f_4 = 50.2$ Hz, $f_5 = 50.4$ Hz, $f_6 = 50.6$ Hz, $f_s = 8000$ Hz, and $\theta_0 = \pi/4$, $\theta_1 = \pi$, $\theta_2 = \pi/2$, $\theta_3 = \pi/3$, $\theta_4 = \pi/4$, $\theta_5 = \pi/5$, $\theta_6 = \pi/6$. On the other hand, according to (5), the reference signal can be assumed to be $r(n) = 2\sin(2\pi n f_0 / f_s)$.

To simulate an edited audio signal, we interchange two segments of the synthetic signal. The resulting signal has four boundaries, as shown in Fig. 2(a). We down-sample this edited signal to 1000 Hz and then use a band-pass filter with 1.2 Hz pass band to process it. The extracted ENF of the edited signal is shown in Fig. 2(b).

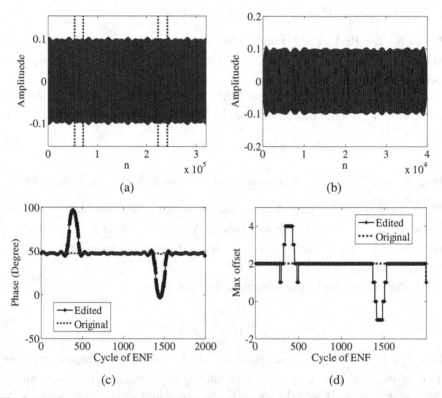

Fig. 2. (a) Edited signal; (b) Extracted ENF from the edited signal; (c) Estimated phases using the DFT method in [7]; (d) Max offsets using our method; (e) Edited regions determined using (d).

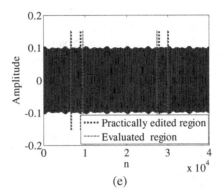

(e)

Fig. 2. (*Continued.*)

Fig. 2(c) gives the results using the DFT method in [7]. The estimated phases of all blocks in the signal are used to judge audio forgery. The phases from blocks of the original signal remain almost the same, but the phases from blocks of the edited signal change apparently at the edited regions. However, the starting and ending points of editing cannot be accurately located due to the slope of the phase estimation curve. Fig. 2(d) gives the results from the proposed method. The max offsets for all blocks of the original signal are almost constant while the max offsets of the edited signal for the blocks at the boundaries change abruptly. Since the boundaries are almost vertical, we can easily determine the starting and ending points of the alterations except three false alarms, with two occurring immediately before and after the first really edited region and another at the end cycle of the ENF. Note that the max offsets at the boundaries increase and drop in a manner of ladder. The ladder-like jump is caused by the non-sharp cut-off characteristic of the band-pass filter. We now explain how to remove the false alarms. Assume that the far left false alarm occurs at two consecutive blocks i_k and i_{k+1}. So $\Delta\tau_{\max}(i_k) = -1$ and $\Delta\tau_{\max}(i_{k+1}) = 1$. Obviously, $D_{os} = |\Delta\tau_{\max}(i_{k+1}) + \Delta\tau_{\max}(i_k)| = 0$. If we set T_{os} greater than 0, we can avoid this false alarm. Generally, we set $T_{os} = 2$ to balance false alarm and missed detection. Similarly, we can remove the other two false alarms. Note that we introduce D_t as an extra constraint for performing D_s. In other words, we perform D_s only when the time interval is small enough. The threshold T_t can be calculated by (16). Fig. 2(e) indicates the edited regions corresponding to the boundaries in Fig. 2(d). We can observe that the deviations between the estimated editing boundaries and the actual boundaries are small.

5.2   Real Voice Signal

We then test the proposed method on real voice signals. The real voice recordings are derived from two public databases, AHUMADA and GAUDI [8]. The recordings are in Spanish and digitized with 16-bit quantization. The sampling rates are 8 kHz in the case of telephone and 16 kHz in the case of microphone signals, respectively [9]. The signals taken for the experiments are neither digitally saturated nor having a low signal-to-noise ratio (SNR). Since they come from Spain, the nominal ENF of all the audio signals is 50 Hz. Overall there are 100 pieces of audio: 50 by female and 50 by male speakers [8].

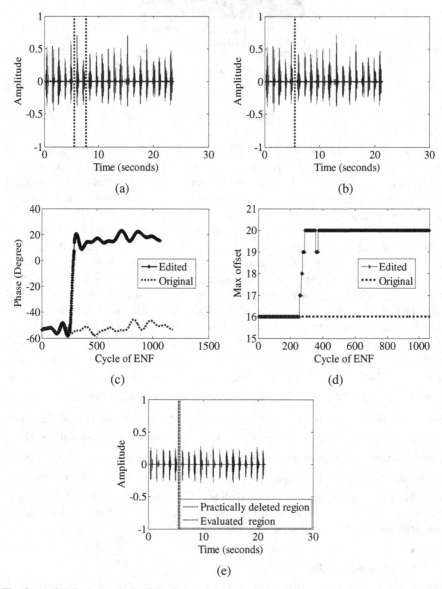

Fig. 3. (a) Original signal; (b) Edited signal (deletion); (c) Estimated phases using the DFT in [7]; (d) Max offsets using our method; (e) Evaluated edited region based on (d)

Detect Deletion and Insertion Forgery by Visual Method
Two audio signals from the test audio corpus are edited by deletion and insertion, respectively. Fig. 3(a) shows the original audio signal. The region between two dash lines is intentionally deleted to obtain the audio signal in Fig. 3(b). Fig. 3(c) gives the estimated ENF phases using the DFT method in [7] while Fig.3 (d) gives the max offsets using the proposed method. We can see that, although both the estimated phases and the

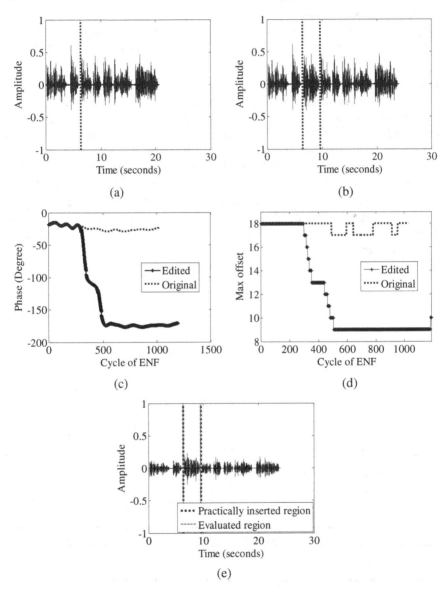

Fig. 4. (a) Original signal; (b) Edited signal (insertion); (c) Estimated phases using the DFT method in [7]; (d) Max offsets using our method; (e) Edited region based on (d)

max offsets show apparent change at the editing boundaries, it is difficult for the former to precisely locate the starting and ending points of editing. In contrast, the use of max offsets can easily locate the starting and ending points. Fig. 3(e) shows that the practical edited position and the estimated position in the down-sampled audio signal are very close. Taking into account the fact that the voice activity is absent in the estimated edited area, we can judge that it is a deletion forgery.

Fig. 4 gives an example of inserting an audio segment into a speech signal. From Fig. 4(c) and (d), we can observe that the proposed method can locate the starting and ending points of editing region clearly. Furthermore, from the estimated boundaries (see Fig. 4 (e)), this region can be judged as being an insertion forgery operation.

Automatic Detection

We test our automatic detection method on the database that contains the whole 100 original audio files and 130 intentionally edited audio files. Among the 130 edited audio recordings, half of them have an audio portion deleted while the other half have a portion of audio inserted. To increase the difficulty of detection, the inserted fragments come from the same file to avoid strong short-time spectral changes. Fig. 5 shows the values of $\lg F$ for different audio files. We can find that the original audio files and the forgery audio files can be easily discriminated by F values. Table 1 gives the detection rates of the automatic method. The average precision is above 95%. Note that a few wrong decisions can be seen in Fig. 5, which is mainly caused by the setting of T_{os} and T_t.

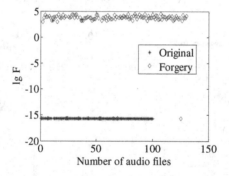

Fig. 5. lg F values for original audio files and forgery audio files

Table 1. Precision of our automatic method

	Correct detection rate (%)	Erroneous detection rate (%)
Edited signal	94.62	5.38
Original signal	96	4

6   Computational Complexity Comparison

We use an example to briefly compare the computational complexity of our visual method and the DFT method in [7]. Table 2 gives the time taken by these two methods for the detection of the signal in Fig. 4 (b). It can be seen that the DFT method requires over twice the time of our method. Moreover, with the increase of N_{DFT} and the length of audio signal, the time needed by the DFT method increases more rapidly than that of our method. For the detection of other signals, we can obtain similar results.

Table 2. Comparison between our method and the method in [7] in terms of running time

Parameter	the method in [7]	our method
$N_{DFT} = 500, N = 60$	0.547s	0.219s
$N_{DFT} = 1000, N = 120$	0.640s	0.234s
$N_{DFT} = 2000, N = 240$	1.047s	0.250s

7   Conclusion

In this paper, we have proposed a novel method for audio forgery detection. Our major contribution is the introduction of the max offset. After calculating the max offsets for cross correlation between the blocks of the ENF and the reference signal, we can determine audio forgery by comparing the change of max offsets from different blocks. The change of max offsets can also help indicate the boundaries of edited region. Since our method is a spatial domain method and does not need to carry out DFT, the computational load is much lighter than the typical method in literature. We have proposed both visual detection and automatic detection. The former can be used for both forgery detection and the location of edited region while the latter can be used for fast forgery detection of a large amount of audio files. Our future work will focus on decreasing erroneous detection rates and increasing the accuracy of locating the boundaries of edited region.

Acknowledgement. This work was partially supported by the EU FP7 Digital Image and Video Forensics project (Grant Agreement No. 251677, Acronym: DIVeFor) and the Fundamental Research Funds for the Central Universities, SCUT (Project No. 2012ZM0027). The authors would like to thank Dr. D. P. Nicolalde Rodriguez for offering the source code and audio database for [7].

References

1. Sanders, R.W.: Digital authenticity using the electric network frequency. In: Proc. AES 33rd Int. Conf. Audio Forensic, Theory and Practice, Denver, CO (2008)
2. Maher, R.: Audio forensic examination: Authenticity, enhancement, and interpretation. IEEE Signal Processing Magazine 26(2), 84–94 (2009)
3. Grigoras, C.: Digital audio recording analysis: The electric network frequency (ENF) criterion. Speech Language Law 12(1), 63–76 (2005)
4. Kajstura, M., Trawinska, A., Hebenstreit, J.: Application of the Electrical Network Frequency (ENF) Criterion: A case of a digital recording. Forensic Science International 155(2), 165–171 (2005)
5. Grigoras, C.: Applications of ENF criterion in forensic audio, video, computer and telecommunication analysis. Forensic Science International 167(3), 136–145 (2007)
6. Huijbregtse, M., Geradts, Z.: Using the ENF criterion for determining the time of recording of short digital audio recordings. Computational Forensics, 116–124 (2009)
7. Nicolalde, D.P., Apolinario, J.A.: Evaluating digital audio authenticity with spectral distances and ENF phase change. In: 2009 IEEE International Conference on Acoustics, Speech and Signal Processing, Taipei, Taiwan, pp. 1417–1420 (2009)
8. Nicolalde Rodriǧuez, D.P., Apolinario, J.A., Biscainho, L.W.P.: Audio Authenticity: Detecting ENF Discontinuity with High Precision Phase Analysis. IEEE Transactions on Information Forensics and Security 5(3), 534–543 (2010)
9. Ortega-García, J., González-Rodríguez, J., Marrero-Aguiar, V.: AHUMADA, a large speech corpus in Spanish for speaker characterization and identification. Elsevier Speech Communication 31, 255–264 (2000)

A Novel Video Inter-frame Forgery Model Detection Scheme Based on Optical Flow Consistency

Juan Chao[1], Xinghao Jiang[1,2], and Tanfeng Sun[1,2,3,*]

[1] School of Information Security Engineering Shanghai Jiao Tong University,
Shanghai 200240, China
{xhjiang,tfsun}@sjtu.edu.cn
[2] National Engineering Lab on Information Content Analysis Techniques,
GT036001, Shanghai 200240, China
[3] Department of Electrical and Computer Engineering, New Jersey Institute of Technology,
Newark 07102, USA

Abstract. In this paper, a novel video inter-frame forgery detection scheme based on optical flow consistency is proposed. It is based on the finding that inter-frame forgery will disturb the optical flow consistency. This paper noticed the subtle difference between frame insertion and deletion, and proposed different detection schemes for them. A window based rough detection method and binary searching scheme are proposed to detect frame insertion forgery. Frame-to-frame optical flows and double adaptive thresholds are applied to detect frame deletion forgery. This paper not only detects video forgery, but also identifies the forgery model. Experiments show that our scheme achieves a good performance in identifying frame insertion and deletion model.

Keywords: optical flow consistency, frame deletion, frame insertion, forgery model identification.

1   Introduction

The development of digital equipment has made surveillance videos important evidences in court. How to detect the integrity and authenticity of videos has become an importance field in information security [1].

Video forgery detection includes active detection and passive detection. Active video forgery detection based on watermark and digital signature has been researched for years and has got much progress [2]. Active detection depends on watermark or signature. However, most cameras don't have such functions, making it impossible.

Passive video forgery detection extracts internal features of videos and has caught much attention nowadays. Prof. A. De proposed a method to uncover video forgery based on readout noise introduced by the Readout from camera CCD [3]. M. Kobayashi tried to detect suspicious surveillance videos with noise characteristics [4]. D.D. Liao proposed a method to detect double H.264/AVC compression detection

---

* Corresponding author.

Y.Q. Shi, H.J. Kim, and F. Pérez-González (Eds.): IWDW 2012, LNCS 7809, pp. 267–281, 2013.
© Springer-Verlag Berlin Heidelberg 2013

using quantized nonzero AC coefficients [5]. W.H. Wang and H. Farid proposed a video tampering tracing technique in de-interlaced and interlaced video [6].

Digital video forgery includes inter-frame forgery and intra-frame forgery. Intra-frame forgery is similar to image forgery. Intra-frame forgery detection is much easier comparing with inter-frame forgery detection, since image forgery detection research has got many achievements. M. K. Johnson proposed an image forgery detection method based on the lighting inconsistencies [7]. A. Swaminathan detected image forgery via intrinsic fingerprints of both inside and outside processing operations [8].

From above discussion, this paper focuses on detecting forgery and identifying forgery model, which has not been considered by other researchers. They mainly focus on if a video has been tampered but don't analyze the forgery model. In section 2, the optical flow generation and how inter-frame forgery affects it are introduced. Section 3 gives the framework and detailed procedures of our scheme, experiments are shown in section 4 and a brief conclusion will be conducted in the last section.

2   Optical Flow Analysis for Inter-frame Forgery Video Frames

The Lucas Kanade optical flow is proposed by B.D. Lucas and T. Kanade, it has been widely used in layered motion, mosaic construction and face coding, but has never been used in video forgery detection. In this paper, we found that the optical flow is sensitive to inter-frame forgery and analysis will be given to prove it. Based on this finding, we innovatively use it in our inter-frame forgery detection.

2.1   Optical Flow Generation in the Video

The main steps to extract the Lucas Kanade optical flow are as follows:

1. Given two images, a spatial sampling is conducted to reduce the computational complexity. For each image, take its odd rows to form an odd image and their even rows to form an even image as is shown in figure 1.

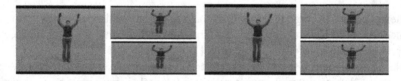

Fig. 1. Spatial sampling of image1 and image2

2. A pyramid is built for each image. In the figure below, the picture in the bottom is the original image, and the fours above it are the pyramid built on it.

Fig. 2. 5-layer pyramid of odd image1 and odd image 2

3. Estimate motion vectors in both X and Y directions of each layer in figure 2 from top to bottom. The first frame in figure 3 is the motion vector between the top layers. Accordingly, the last one is the motion vector between the bottom layers.

Fig. 3. Motion vectors of the five pyramid layers

4. Expand the motion vector in the top layer twice in both X and Y directions and add it to its lower layer, then smooth the sum of this two layers. Repeat these steps until the bottom layer. In the top row below, the first figure is the first motion vector in figure 3; the second is the sum of the first expanded motion vector and second motion vector in figure 3; accordingly, the last figure is the sum of all motion vectors in figure 3. The five pictures in the bottom row are the smoothing results of relative figures in the top row; the last is the final optical flow between the odd image 1 and odd image 2 in figure 1.

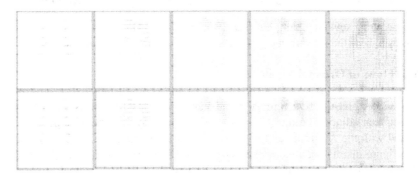

Fig. 4. Sum of motion vectors of the five pyramid layers before and after smoothing

5. Below is the optical flow figures extracted with image1 and image2, odd image1 and odd image 2, even image 1 and even image 2. The odd optical flow and the even one are almost the same, while the original one is the sum of the two, reducing the computing complexity while keep the optical flow feature.

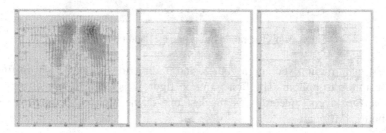

Fig. 5. Optical flow of original images, odd images and even images

6. For two frames *M* and *N*, two optical flow figures $OFX_{(m,n)}$ and $OFY_{(m,n)}$ which are the optical flow vectors in the 2D space are computed by adding the absolute values of the optical flow in each pixel *(i, j)*with equation (1).

$$S_{(m,n)}(x) = \sum_{i=1}^{width} \sum_{j=1}^{height} OFX_{(m,n)}(i,j) \tag{1}$$

Where $S_{(m,n)}(x)$ is the sum of optical flow values between frame M and frame N in the X direction, and X can be replace with y to calculate $S_{(m,n)}(y)$, which is the sum of optical flow values between frame M and frame N in the Y direction, width and height are the number of pixels in each row and each column of the optical flow figure.

2.2   Analyzing Video Features of Inter-frame Forgery by Optical Flow

In this section, several examples based on the KTH video database are given to demonstrate how the inter-frame forgery affects the optical flow consistency.

Optical Flows of Original Video
In above figure, these six adjacent frames in the top row are extracted from an original video, and the five figures in the second row are the Lucas Kanade optical flows between adjacent frames in the top flow, that's to say, the Kth optical flow is computed with the Kth frame and the $(K+1)^{th}$ frame. In above figure, the optical flow in each figure mainly focuses on the upper half. The two histograms in the third row are the total optical flow values in X and Y directions of the five optical flow figures. From the histograms, the five bars in both X and Y directions are almost the same, which means their optical flows are consistent.

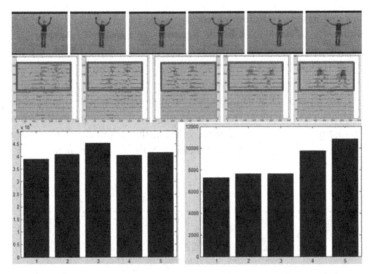

Fig. 6. Original video frames and their optical flows

Optical Flows of Frame Insertion Video

In above figure, these first three frames and last three frames in the top are extracted from two different videos. Among these five Lucas Kanade optical flow figures in the middle row, the third one is computed by the third and fourth frames and it is quite different from the others. From the optical value histogram in the bottom row, the third optical flow bar is in X direction and Y direction are much higher than others, which means that the optical flow are no longer consistent due to the insertion.

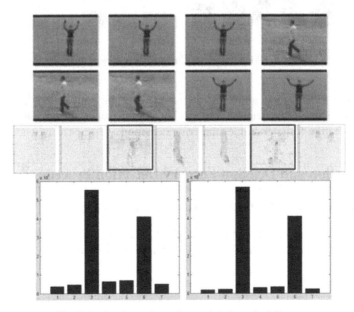

Fig. 7. Video frame insertion and their optical flows

Optical Flows of Frame Deletion Video

In above figure, these six frames in the top row are extracted from the same video, but they are not adjacent in the original video, the first three frames are the 6th, 7th, 8th frames and the last frames are the 151th, 152th, 153th frames. Though 142 frames are deleted, there is not much visible difference. However, in the optical flow figures, the third optical flow figure spreads almost the whole figure, compared to the other four where the optical flows focus mainly in the upper half. From the two optical flow histograms, the optical flow value at the deletion point is about 3 times than other points in the X direction and about 5 times larger than others in the Y direction.

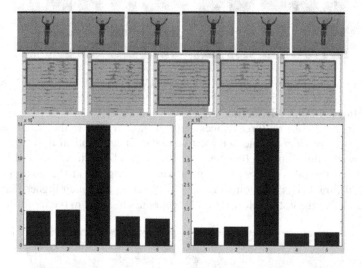

Fig. 8. Video frame deletion and their optical flows

From these three figures above, it can be seen that the optical flow is sensitive to frame insertion and frame deletion forgery. Thus in this paper, the optical flow is used as the main feature for inter-frame tampering detection.

3   Insertion and Deletion Forgery Detection Procedure

3.1   Framework of Inter-frame Forgery Detection Scheme

In this paper, an optical flow consistency based inter-frame forgery detection scheme is proposed. The main framework of our algorithm is as follows:

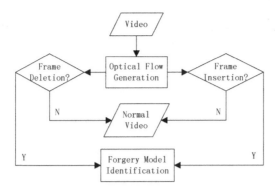

Fig. 9. Framework of inter-frame forgery detection scheme

The detailed scheme of our algorithm is:

1. For a given video, first generate the optical flow as is given in Section 2.
2. The optical flow is used to detection frame insertion and frame deletion forgery separately according to the procedures in Section 3.2 and 3.3.
3. If forgery is detected, identity their tampering model according to the difference between frame insertion and frame deletion.
4. If no frame insertion or deletion is detected, than mark a video as normal.

With this scheme, our algorithm can not only detect inter-frame forgery, but also identify forgery model, i.e. identify if it's frame insertion or frame deletion.

3.2   Frame Insertion Forgery Detection Procedure

For frame insertion forgery, a window based rough detection is proposed. By dividing a video into windows and computing the optical flow between the first frame and the last frame in each window, the detection time has been largely reduced. From figure 7 it's clear that the optical flow at an insertion point is hundreds of times larger than others, and the optical flow between two non-adjacent frames in figure 8 is only several times larger than that of adjacent frames. Even though the window mechanism will compute the optical flow of two non-adjacent frames and increase the optical flow value by several times, compared to the hundreds of times for insertion forgery, the window mechanism won't influence the optical flow much, but greatly fasten the detection speed. So the window mechanism is proposed for fast rough insertion detection.

In this paper, window mechanism is not used in frame deletion since inconsistency of deletion forgery is smaller comparing with insertion forgery. If window mechanism is applied, it will narrow this inconsistency further and result in more missed detections.

Below is the detailed process of the video frame insertion detection method.

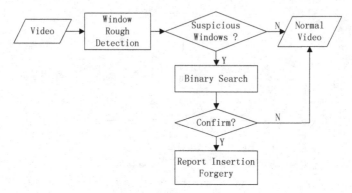

Fig. 10. Frame insertion forgery detection procedure

1. Each video is divided into equal-size windows. Here the window size is 16, because the optimal size for binary search is 2^n, and 16 is less than the frame rate (25Fps), ensuring that there won't be an integrate insertion in a window.

2. Then compute the Lucas Kanade optical flows $S_k(x)$ in X and $S_k(y)$ in Y direction between the first and the last frame in each window with equation 1 where X can be replaced with Y, but m and n are replaced with the first frame and last frame in a window.

3. Compute the average optical flow in X and Y directions with below equation (where X can be replaced with Y). *NOW* is the number of   windows in a video; *AOF(x)* is the average optical flows in the X direction :

$$AOF(x) = \frac{1}{NOW} \sum_{k=1}^{NOW} S_k(x) \qquad (2)$$

4. When the optical flow in a window K meets equation (3) either in X direction or Y direction where $T=2$, it means that the optical flow in this window is larger than the threshold and this window should be further detected.

$$S_k(x) \geq T * AOF(x) \qquad (3)$$

5. Suspicious windows are binary researched to locate shift point. Each window is divided into two equal sub windows, optical flows between the first frame and the last frame in each sub window are computed in both X and Y direction.   If the optical flows in left sub window and right sub window meet equation (4) where X can be replaced with Y, then a shift point may exist in the left sub window; go on with binary search in the left sub window until window size is 1. Here L means the left sub window, and R is the right sub window.

$$S_L(x) \geq T * S_R(x) \qquad (4)$$

Else if the optical flow in X direction or Y direction meets equation (5) where X can be replaced with Y for the Y direction, then a shift point may exist in the right sub window, go on binary searching it until the sub window size is 1.

$$S_R(x) \geq T * S_L(x) \tag{5}$$

If a shift point is detected, then frames before and after this point are quite different in their optical flows. If optical flow between frame K and $(K+1)$ and that between frame $(K+1)$ and $(K+2)$ meet (4), then $(K+1)$ is a shift point. Else if two optical flows meet (5); then $(K+2)$ is a shift point.

If the optical flows meet none of the two equations (4) and (5), then it means that there is no shift point in this suspicious window.

6. After the binary research in all suspicious windows, further detection is conducted to identify insertion part. For each point I and J, three optical flows will be computed: optical flow between $(I-2)$ and $(I-1)$, optical flow between $(I-1)$ and $(J+1)$, optical flow between $(J+1)$ and $(J+2)$. If they are similar, it means that the video frames before the shift point I and after the shift point J come from the same video, so frames between these two shift points are inserted.

3.3 Frame Deletion Forgery Detection Procedure

For frame deletion forgery, the differences of optical flows are much smaller than frame insertion forgery. So in our method, optical flows between all adjacent frames are computed. Below is the detailed procedure of the frame deletion forgery detection.

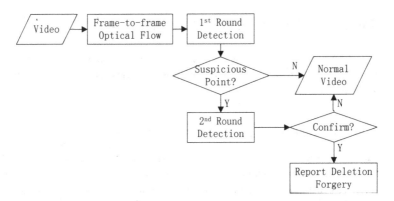

Fig. 11. Frame deletion forgery detection procedure

1. Each video is firstly divided into individual frames.
2. Then compute the Lucas Kanade optical flow between the Ith frame and the $(I+1)^{th}$ frame.

3. Compare each optical flow with its adjacent frames. If it meets equation (6) in X direction or Y direction where X can be replaced with Y, then it's a suspicious deletion position. Where T_1 is 2 in this paper.

$$S_{(k,k+1)}(x) \geq \frac{T_1}{4} \sum_{i=-2, i \neq 0}^{2} S_{(k-i,k-i+1)}(x) \tag{6}$$

4. Compute the average optical flow in both X and Y directions with below equation, where $S_{(k,k+1)}(x)$ is computed with equation (1); NOF is the number of optical flow figures in a video; $AOF(x)$ is the average optical flow in the X. Replace the X in this equation with Y to get the average optical flow:

$$AOF(x) = \frac{1}{NOF-1} \sum_{k=1}^{NOF-1} S_{(k,k+1)}(x) \tag{7}$$

5. When the optical flow of the suspicious point in X direction or Y direction meets equation (8), it means that the optical flow between these two frames is much larger than average optical flow and some frames have been deleted between them. Where T_2 is 3.5 in this paper.

$$S_{(k,k+1)}(x) \geq T_2 * AOF(x) \tag{8}$$

6. Compare all $S_{(k,k+1)}(x)$ in the video, if none of the optical flow meets the equation (8) in neither X direction nor Y direction, then this video hasn't been tampered with frame deletion.

4   Simulation Experiments and Results

Video forgery model detection research just began in recent years and there are no other optical flow based video forgery detection methods, so here in this paper we didn't do comparison with other researchers' work.

4.1   Evaluation Standards

To evaluate the detection efficiency, the recall rate (R_r) and precision rate (R_p) are used, which are common standard in video and image related detection and classification research. The recall rate is the percentage of correctly detected videos among all tampered videos; a high recall rate can well prove the detection accuracy. The precision rate is the percentage of correctly detected videos among all the detected ones; a high precision rate can well demonstrate a low false alarm rate.

$$R_r = \frac{N_c}{N_c + N_m} \times 100\% \tag{9}$$

$$R_p = \frac{N_c}{N_c + N_f} \times 100\% . \tag{10}$$

Where N_c is the number of correctly detected video forgeries; N_m is the number of missed video forgeries; N_f is the number of falsely detected video forgeries.

4.2   Test Video Databases

Original Video Database
In this section, a large number of simulation experiments based on KTH database are conducted to evaluate our algorithm. The frame rate of videos in our test is 25Fps.

Frame Insertion Video Database Built with CBCD Scripts
The first test video database is generated with TRECVID Content Based Copy Detection (CBCD) scripts. To use the script, we first generate two folders: Reference and Non-reference, and then this script can automatically generate frame insertion videos by insertion a randomly chosen Reference video segment to a randomly chosen Non-reference video with random length.

Frame Insertion Video Database with OpenCV Library
To demonstrate that our frame insertion forgery detection method is robust to different kinds of frame insertion tools, we tried to generate another test video database with the OpenCV function library in C and C# coding language on visual studio 2010.   Below is the frame insertion forgery database generation procedure with OpenCV.

For each video I, we insert N frames from video $(I+1)$ to it. These N frames are selected randomly from video $(I+1)$ and they are inserted to video I. In our test, we test different values of N $(N=100, N=25)$ to evaluate the robustness to different insertion length. $N=100$ (4s) is chosen as a representation of long insertion, and $N=25$ is chosen to represent a short insertion based on the assumption that only video segments with meaningful activities are inserted and a meaningful activity will last for at least 1s.

Frame Deletion Video Database with OpenCV Library
Since the CBCD scripts can only generate frame insertion videos, we generated frame deletion forgery database with the OpenCV function on visual studio 2010.

For each video I, we delete N frames in it from K to $(K+N-1)$. In our test, we test different values of N $(N=100, N=25)$ so as to evaluate the robustness of the proposed frame deletion forgery detection algorithm.

4.3   Experiment on Frame Insertion Forgery Model's Detection

Test Results of Frame Insertion Database Built with CBCD Scripts
From the experiment in table 1, 3000 frame insertion videos are tested. The frame insertion detection recall rate reaches 95.43% and the precision rate reaches 95.34%.

Table 1. Test Results with Frame Insertion Database 1

N_c	N_m	N_f	$R_r(\%)$	$R_p(\%)$
2863	137	140	95.43	95.34

Test Results of Frame Insertion Database Built with OpenCV Library

In the table above, different frame insertion numbers are tested. The detection recall rate is 94.33% with 100 frames insertion, while with 25 frames insertion, it drops to 92.67%. The detection precision rate with 100 frames insertion is 97.92%, but for 25 frames insertion, it reaches 98.58%. From the results, it can be found that when inserting fewer frames, the detection recall rate will drop, which is consistent to the theory that our visual system can find large changes easily but will skip the small changes. Accordingly, the low recall rate means that in the first round of window detection, less suspicious are detected, and in binary search round, more suspicious windows are rejected. Accordingly, less false detections occur in the first round and more false detections are rejected in the binary search, so precision rate increases with fewer frames inserted.

Table 2. Test results Frame Insertion Database 2

	N_c	N_m	N_f	$R_r(\%)$	$R_p(\%)$
$N=100$	566	34	12	94.33	97.92
$N=25$	556	44	8	92.67	98.58

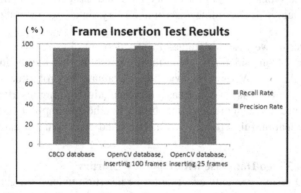

Fig. 12. Frame insertion detection results comparison with different test database

From figure 12, frame insertion detection results of three databases are similar. So we can conclude that our video frame insertion detection method achieves a well robustness with different tampered videos and different frame insertion lengths.

From the three groups of recall rates and precision rates, we can conclude that for frame insertion detection, the higher the recall rate, the lower the precious rate. This is because a fixed threshold is used among all databases, and when the recall rate is high for a database, it means the threshold is low for this insertion type, which will cause more false detections in this database, so the precision rate will increase.

4.4   Experiment on Frame Deletion Forgery Model's Detection

Test Results of Frame Deletion Database Built with OpenCV Library

From the experiment result above, the frame deletion is a little worse than frame insertion. For frame insertion, the lowest recall rate is above 92% and the lowest precision rate is above 95%, but for frame deletion, the recall rate and precision rate are both lower than 90%. It is because in frame insertion, frames are inserted from other videos, while different videos are usually recorded with different camera or different parameters, so frames from different videos have bigger optical flow inconsistency.

Table 3. Test Results with Frame Deletion Database 3

	N_c	N_m	N_f	$R_r(\%)$	$R_p(\%)$
$N=100$	514	86	61	85.67	89.39
$N=25$	507	93	90	84.50	84.92

From the results, we can find that the recall rate and precision rate of deleting 25 frames are lower than those of deleting 100 frames, which is consistent to the fact that if fewer frames are deleted, it will be harder to be detect, so the recall rate is lower when deleting fewer frames. As with the precision rate, it's different with frame insertion. For frame insertion, a fixed threshold T is used in the first round detection, and with a fixed threshold, the false detection will be reduced with fewer frames inserted, so the precision rate will increase. But for frame deletion, adaptive thresholds are used, and when fewer frames are deleted, frames around the shift point are much similar. So the adaptive threshold mechanism will drop down the threshold to guarantee the recall, but lower threshold will induce more false detection caused by fast movements such as jogging, so the precision will also increase with fewer frames deleted.

From above analysis, we can conclude that our detection scheme can achieve a relatively stable performance to different frame deletion forgery.

From experiments in 4.3 to 4.4, we can conclude that out method achieves a good performance in identifying both frame insertion forgery model and frame deletion forgery model. In addition, the proposed method is robust to different tampering tools and different inserted and deleted frame numbers.

4.5   Analyzing Detection Effect on Threshold Parameter Selection

It our experiment, we used adaptive threshold for the $T1$ and $T2$ in equation (6) and (8), below figures give the test results with different $T1$ and $T2$.

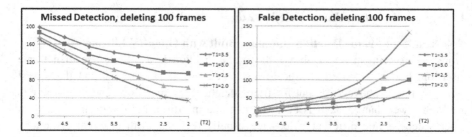

Fig. 13. Testing results of deleting 100 frames with different threshold *T1* and *T2*

From the two figures above, for a fixed *T1*, when *T2* increases, the missed detection number increases, but the false detection number decreases. This is because the threshold *T2* will filter false deletion after detecting suspicious deleting shift points. The bigger the threshold *T2* is, more false detections will be filtered, thus the false detection rate will decrease, but at the same time, bigger *T2* will increase the danger to filter true detections, causing the missed detection rate to increase.

With a fixed *T2*, the missed detection number will increase as *T1* increases, while the false detection number drops. This is because the smaller *T1* is, more frames will be detected as suspicious deletion shift points, thus it will decrease missed detection rate. Accordingly, it will increase the danger of regarding normal frames as frame deletion shift points, thus increasing the false detection number.

As is analyzed above, the missed detection number is inversely proportional to the false detection number; however, we can still achieve a balance recall rate and precision rate of frame deleting detection. We can conclude that our adaptive threshold mechanism can obtain an optimal value for *T1* and *T2* to balance the recall rate and precision rate.

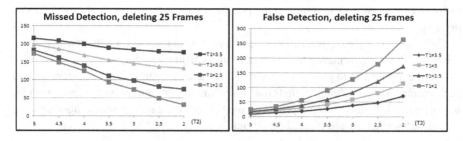

Fig. 14. Testing results of deleting 25 frames with different threshold *T1* and *T2*

From the comparison of figure 13 and 14, the influence of *T1* and *T2* while deleting 25 frames is similar with deletion 100 frames, but still there is some difference. With the same *T1* and *T2*, the missed detection number and false detection number of deleting 25 frames are both a little larger than deleting 100 frames, so the detection recall rate and precision rate of deleting 25 frames are lower than 100 frames. This result is consistent to the analysis and conclusion in 4.4.

5   Conclusion

In this paper, a novel video inter-frame forgery detection scheme based on Lucas Kanade optical flow consistency is proposed. It is based on the assumption that for adjacent frames in original videos, their optical flows are consistent, and inter-frame forgery will disturb this optical flow consistency. In this paper, a window based rough detection and binary search based precise detection is proposed for frame insertion forgery detection. And for frame deletion forgery detection, frame-to-frame mechanism and double adaptive thresholds are proposed to detect the tiny difference in optical flow, so as to detect deletion forgery. By detecting different forgery models separately according to their difference, our algorithm can not only well detect video inter-frame forgery, but also identify the forgery model. Experiments show that the recall rate reaches 95% and the precision rate reaches 98% of frame insertion forgery detection. For frame deletion forgery detection, the detection rates are a little lower than insertion forgery, but still the recall rate reaches 85% and precision rate reaches 89%. Future work will focus on detecting frame duplication and improve the recall rate and precision rate of detecting frame deletion.

Acknowledgement. We would like to thank Prof. Y. Q. Shi at NJIT in U.S.A. for the fruitful technical discussions and selfless help. The work of this paper is sponsored by the National Natural Science Foundation of China (No. 61071153, No. 61272249), the National New Century Excellent Talents Support Plan of Ministry of Education, China (No. NECT-10-0569). It is also under the Project of International Cooperation and Exchanges supported by Shanghai Committee of Science and Technology (No. 12510708500).

References

1. Rocha, A., Scheirer, W., Boult, T., et al.: Vision of the Unseen: Current Trends and Challenges in Digital Image and Video Forensics. ACM Computing Surveys 43(5), article number:26 (2011)
2. Zhou, Z.Y., Tang, X.H.: Integrity Authentication Scheme of Color Video Based on the Fragile Watermarking. In: International Conference on Electronics, Communications and Control (ICRCC), Ningbo, China, pp. 4354–4358 (2011)
3. De, A., Chadha, H., Gupta, S.: Detection of forgery in digital video. In: The 10th World Multi Conference on Systemics Cybernetics and Informatics, vol. V, pp. 229–233 (2006)
4. Kobayashi, M., Okabe, T., Sato, Y.: Detecting Video Forgeries Based on Noise Characteristics. In: Wada, T., Huang, F., Lin, S. (eds.) PSIVT 2009. LNCS, vol. 5414, pp. 306–317. Springer, Heidelberg (2009)
5. Liao, D.D., Yang, R., Liu, H.M., et al.: Double H.264/AVC compression detection using quantized nonzero AC coefficients. In: Conference on Media watermarking, Security, and Forensics, San Francisco, CA, vol. 7880, article number: 78800Q (2011)
6. Wang, W.H., Farid, H.: Exposing Digital Forgeries in Interlaced and De-Interlaced Video. IEEE Transactions on Information Forensics and Security 2(3), 438–449 (2007)
7. Johnson, M.K., Farid, H.: Exposing Digital Forgeries in Complex LightingEnvironments. IEEE Transaction on Information Forensics and Security 2(3), 450–461 (2007)
8. Swaminathan, A., Wu, M., Ray Liu, K.J.: Digital Image Forensics via IntrinsicFingerprint. IEEE Transaction on Information Forensics and Security 3(1), 101–117 (2008)

Countering Universal Image Tampering Detection with Histogram Restoration[*]

Luyi Chen[1], Shilin Wang[2], Shenghong Li[1], and Jianhua Li[1]

[1] Dept. of Electrical Engineering, Shanghai Jiaotong University, Shanghai, China
lychen1109@gmail.com, {shli,lijh888}@sjtu.edu.cn
[2] School of Information Security, Shanghai Jiaotong University, Shanghai, China
wsl@sjtu.edu.cn

Abstract. In this paper, we point out state-of-the-art algorithm in natural image splicing detection, namely the transition probability matrix feature proposed by Shi, et al., can be attacked by modifying block discrete cosine transform (BDCT) coefficients without significantly degrading quality of the spliced image. BDCT coefficients of the spliced image are modified so that its distance to a close authentic image in feature space is minimized. The minimization is accomplished with a greedy algorithm. The modification makes the spliced image statistically similar to the authentic image so as to reduce the effectiveness of detection algorithm. The performance of the algorithm is evaluated on Columbia Image Splicing Detection Evaluation Dataset. With the proposed anti-forensics post processing, detection accuracy and true positive rate reduces to 69.4% and 62.5% respectively, while the processed images still maintain average peak signal-to-noise ratio (PSNR) at 42.22db.

Keywords: Anti-forensics, Splicing Detection, Information Security, Gaussian Mixture Model, Multivariate Statistics.

1   Introduction

In the last few years, accompanying wide-spreading of powerful digital image manipulating software, more and more fake images has brought troubles for governments, companies and individuals. As a result, a young research area, called image forensics, emerges. Different from traditional media authentication approach like watermarking, it does not rely on previously embedded metadata, but merely using intrinsic property of the media itself to evaluate its processing history and origin. A number of algorithms have been developed to detect double compression history of JPEG images [1], copy and move [2-3], resampling [4] and splicing [5]. Intrinsic properties that have been exploited in digital image forensics include direction of light source [6], statistics of pixel values in spatial and frequency domain, quantization table used in compression, CFA patterns used in sensor and model of the camera.

[*] This work is supported by National Science Foundation of China (61271316, 61071152), 973 Program of China (2013CB329605) and Chinese National "Twelfth Five-Year" Plan for Science & Technology Support (2012BAH38B04).

Y.Q. Shi, H.J. Kim, and F. Pérez-González (Eds.): IWDW 2012, LNCS 7809, pp. 282–289, 2013.

But the problem is far from being solved. Nearly every forensic tool mentioned above has assumed that the image forger has not taken any countering measure to remove its trace. In reality, like every information security field, vulnerabilities in existing forensic tools will be exploited, and modified images will not only fool our eyes, but also pass safely though detection programs. Thus there is urgent need to re-evaluate all existing forensic tools to take countering measure into account.

Currently there are not many publications in this anti-forensics area. We have just seen a few published works in hiding resampling trace [7], recreating CFA [8], removing contrast enhancement trace [9] and hiding JPEG compression history [10].

In this paper, we deal with another problem in anti-forensics, countering universal tampering detection. A typical image tampering usually involves splicing, resizing, rotation, blurring and compression, etc. There are two basic approaches to detect tampered images. One approach is to detect specific processing. The other approach is blind detection without knowing specific processing history of the image. Thus the latter is also called universal tampering detection. This approach usually extracts low dimensional features from the image and uses machine learning to generate prediction model.

Most of the universal tampering detection algorithms are borrowed from steganalysis research [11]. We propose in the paper that anti-forensics research can also learn from steganography research. Lots of steganography algorithm follows the idea of histogram restoration. Part of the embeddable components is reserved to compensate for the changes caused by message embedding. Algorithms such as F5, OutGuess, and MB1 follow this approach.

There are two differences between steganography and anti-forensics. Goal of steganography is to embed a message while keeping the changes undetectable. Anti-forensics does not have the requirement to transmit a message, so the modification is more flexible. While steganography algorithm manages to restore the histogram to its original shape, there is no clear objective in anti-forensics restoration. We propose to use a close authentic image in feature space as approximation of its authentic counterpart.

A good restoration needs a good image model. Traditional algorithms such as F5, OutGuess and MB1 only restore its first order histogram, which has been approved not secure enough. A detector only needs to use a second order feature. While currently there are some algorithms proposed to restore second order histogram, the detector can always use a richer model. To the best of our knowledge, there is currently no good high dimensional natural image model can serve the needs of statistically restoration in steganography or anti-forensics.

The lack of a good image model has been dealt with by the lately proposed HUGO algorithm [12]. HUGO uses a weighted L1 distance to reach minimum embedding impact in feature space. The feature used is discriminative features used in steganalysis, namely SPAM feature with a very large threshold. It uses a large threshold, T=90, to prevent over-fitting to the feature.

Idea proposed in this paper is similar to HUGO. The set of feature we use is Markov transition probability matrix feature, which is a universal tampering detection algorithm proposed by Shi, et al [5]. It is currently state-of-the-art in terms of detection accuracy and computing complexity. Since this feature models joint probability in DCT domain, we target our algorithm at JPEG images.

The paper is organized in the following way. In section 2, universal blind tampering detection algorithm is reviewed. Our proposed algorithm is introduced in section 3. In section 4, we provide experimental result on Columbia Splicing Detection Evaluation Dataset. Section 5 concludes the whole paper.

2   Universal Image Tampering Detection

Machine learning is one of the basic approaches used in universal image tampering detection. Ideally, we can train a natural image model and a tampered image model. Then a suspicious image's probability under two models is calculated. The image is predicted to be in class where it has a higher probability. Such generative model is hard to train, so a popular approach is to extract a set of low dimensional features and then use discriminative learning to train the prediction model.

Quite a lot of publications belong to low dimensional feature category. Features are usually selected through experiment or borrowed from other research problems, such as steganalysis. These include bicoherence features, high order moment features, transition probability matrix features, run-length features and 2D phase congruency features, etc. Among them, transition probability matrix features is by far the most effective feature in terms of detection accuracy and feature extraction complexity. The feature extraction steps can be briefly described as follows:

1. If the image is not already in JPEG format, it is transformed with 8x8 BDCT.
2. The absolute value of the coefficients is calculated and rounded to the nearest integer, which forms a BDCT coefficient array.
3. Difference of adjacent elements on BDCT coefficients array along different directions is calculated and processed with a threshold T.
4. Markov chain is used to capture transition probability on the difference arrays.
5. Every element on the transition probability matrix is used as feature by a classifier to check the authenticity of images.

The feature has two forms. One is conditional probability form. Elements in the matrix is defined as

$$M(x, y) = P(d_{i,j+1} = y \mid d_{ij} = x), \tag{1}$$

where d_{ij} and $d_{i,j+1}$ are adjacent elements on the difference array of BDCT coefficients, and M is the probability matrix. After the processing with threshold T, x and y are integers between $-T$ and T. The other form is joint probability form or co-occurrence matrix, which is defined as

$$M(x, y) = P(d_{i,j+1} = y, d_{ij} = x), \tag{2}$$

with the same definition of parameters in the equation. There two forms have been proved to have similar performance in splicing detection. Difference between (1) and

(2) is that (2) keeps marginal distribution of the elements. In this paper, we use the joint probability form for two reasons: one is to make sure that post-processing takes marginal distribution into consideration; the other is co-occurrence matrix is easy to be modified, which has been pointed out by others [12].

2.1   From Steganography to Anti-forensics

Since most universal image tampering detection algorithms are borrowed from steganalysis, modern steganography research can contribute to anti-forensics as well. HUGO is a recently introduced steganography algorithm. Different from other algorithms that try to compensate for the message embedding, HUGO uses high dimensional features to locate pixels that introduce the least distortion. This motivates us to use similar approach to locate those pixels that can change feature distribution most efficiently so that the processed image looks similar to an authentic image but the distortion is minimized. The distortion we considered is the one between the original tampered image and the one after anti-forensics processing.

3   Histogram Restoration in Feature Space

The basic idea of the proposed approach is to slightly change BDCT coefficients of the image so that they are statistically indistinguishable to authentic images without introducing too much distortion. There are two approaches to restore the image in feature space. One is to use a generative model to restore the image to a common model. The other is to restore the image to its authentic counterpart.

In the first approach, we have tried to model the joint probability matrix with Gaussian Mixture Model (GMM), but the result is not good. There are two possible reasons: one is that GMM is too simple to capture the high dimensional joint probability; the other one is that there are not enough images in the dataset to learn an accurate model.

In the second approach, we define the authentic counterpart as an authentic image close to the tampered image in feature space. The authentic counterpart is statistically similar to the tampered image so that the latter can be efficiently modified with low distortion. The concept of counterpart is similar to the original image in steganography.

As we introduced in section 2, Markov transition probability feature is good enough to be used as a feature space for histogram restoration. There are a couple of parameters need to be decided, which will be discussed in the next subsection.

3.1   Algorithm Parameters

HUGO uses a very large threshold, T=90, so that the dimension of the feature space is 6×10^{7}. Images in our experimental dataset are relatively small, which is all 128x128, so that we choose T=10, and already get acceptable result. Generally larger T is better.

We have a couple of options for the measure of distance between samples in feature space. We have tried L1 distance, L2 distance, Mahalanobis distance and even a weighted L1 distance like the one used in HUGO. L2 distance gives the best result. Our analysis is that L2 distance is consistent with the distance measure used in Gaussian RBF kernel,

$$K(x, y) = e^{-\gamma * |x-y|^2}, \tag{3}$$

which is used in our classifier. Although other classifiers do not use this information directly, we have also observed significant decreasing of detection accuracy with a GMM-based Bayes classifier.

We modify the image in BDCT domain. We only modify non-zero AC components, which is a common setting in steganography.

In order to prevent from introducing too much noise in the post-processing, the maximum distortion which can be introduced into every BDCT coefficient needs to be bounded. We name this bound as K.

To find a global optimized solution to this problem is still difficult, we introduce a sub-optimal greedy algorithm, which can get satisfied result in acceptable time.

3.2   Component Visiting Strategy

To a 128x128 image block, there are 16384 BDCT coefficients. When every coefficient can change ±K from its original value, there are $(2K+1)^{16384}$ possible modifications. Searching for the global optimization solution is an NP-hard problem. Change of one coefficient will affect multiple bins in the histogram, so there's no closed-form expression of the gradient of the objective function.

Because of this, we propose to use greedy algorithm to find a suboptimal solution. There are two steps in the greedy algorithm. First every non-zero component is visited from upper-left to lower-right. The maximum change of distance every component can bring to the image is recorded as its potential. In the second step, non-zero components are visited again in descending order of their potential. The modification takes place in the second step. The visiting strategy insures the most efficient non-zero components are visited first.

4   Simulation Result and Discussion

The performance of the algorithm is evaluated on Columbia Splicing Detection Evaluation Dataset [13]. There are totally 1831 images in the dataset, 921 of which are authentic images and 910 are spliced images.

Markov transition probability features can be extracted in different directions, such as horizontal, vertical, diagonal and minor diagonal. For simplicity, we only use horizontal direction in both our anti-forensics processing and detection. The threshold used in anti-forensics processing is 10, while the threshold used in detection is 3.

For every spliced image, we choose a unique authentic image as its authentic counterpart. The authentic counterpart is selected in the following way. The spliced images are visited in random order. For every spliced image, we choose the authentic image which is closest to it in feature space as its authentic counterpart. Every authentic image can only be chosen once. When all spliced images are visited, we calculate sum of L2 distance of all pairs of images. The process is repeated 100 times, the solution which has the lowest sum distance is used. This is certainly not the optimal solution, but it is simple and fast. Visual effect of the proposed algorithm is shown in Figure 1.

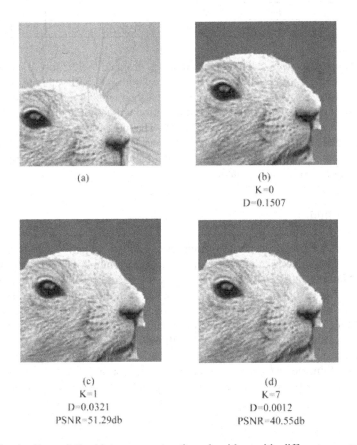

(a)

(b)
K=0
D=0.1507

(c)
K=1
D=0.0321
PSNR=51.29db

(d)
K=7
D=0.0012
PSNR=40.55db

Fig. 1. Visual effect of the histogram restoration algorithm with different parameters. (a) Authentic image, (b) Spliced image without histogram restoration, (c) Restored image with K=1, (d) Restored image with K=7. D is L2 distance to (a) in feature space.

We use LibSVM with Gaussian kernel [14] to evaluate the detection accuracy. 2/3 of the samples are used as training set, 1/3 is used as test set. The result is in Table 1.

Table 1. Test accuracy of restored images. K=0 means without restoration. AC is accuracy, TP is true positive and TN is true negative.

K	AC	TP	TN	PSNR (db)
0	0.863	0.878	0.849	N/A
1	0.824	0.793	0.856	52.72±2.09
2	0.779	0.746	0.811	49.17±2.47
3	0.739	0.695	0.783	46.94±2.67
4	0.716	0.658	0.774	45.34±2.81
5	0.705	0.616	0.792	44.11±2.93
6	0.700	0.629	0.770	43.10±3.01
7	0.694	0.625	0.761	42.22±3.05

When K increases to 7, the average PSNR has dropped to 42.22db. We assume this is the limit to the current setting. Further increasing of K will generate perceptually visible distortion to the image. In reality, the forger will be able to select a better authentic counterpart than us, thus the modification will be more efficient.

There is one limitation in our algorithm. The post-processed image should be stored in JPEG format. Transform the image back to spatial domain will introduce rounding errors which will affect transition probability matrix in frequency domain, thus making the result unpredictable.

5   Conclusion

In this paper, we proposed an anti-forensics algorithm which is able to reduce the effectiveness of universal tampering detection algorithm. We modify the tampered image in Markov transition probability matrix feature space. We also propose to use L2 distance as measure of distance between samples in the feature space and a greedy algorithm to calculate the suboptimal solution. The effectiveness of the method is evaluated on Columbia Splicing Detection Evaluation Dataset. We are able to reduce the detection accuracy significantly while still maintain high PSNR.

Our future research direction is to extend the algorithm to spatial domain so that the processed image can be saved in difference format. We will also do more experimental study to evaluate the over-fitting problem in this algorithm, and work on possible improvements.

References

1. Pevny, T., Fridrich, J.: Detection of Double-Compression in JPEG Images for Applications in Steganography. IEEE Transactions on Information Forensics and Security 3(2) (2008)
2. Fridrich, J., Soukal, D., Lukáš, J.: Detection of copy-move forgery in digital images. In: Digital Forensic Research Workshop (2003)
3. Ryu, S.-J., Lee, M.-J., Lee, H.-K.: Detection of copy-rotate-move forgery using zernike moments. In: Böhme, R., Fong, P.W.L., Safavi-Naini, R. (eds.) IH 2010. LNCS, vol. 6387, pp. 51–65. Springer, Heidelberg (2010)

4. Popescu, A.C., Farid, H.: Exposing digital forgeries by detecting traces of resampling. IEEE Transactions on Signal Processing 53(2), 758–767 (2005)
5. Shi, Y.Q., Chen, C., Chen, W.: A Natural Image Model Approach to Splicing Detection. In: The 9th workshop on Multimedia & Security, pp. 51–62. ACM, New York (2007)
6. Johnson, M.K., Farid, H.: Exposing digital forgeries by detecting inconsistencies in lighting. In: The 7th workshop on Multimedia and Security. ACM (2005)
7. Kirchner, M., Böhme, R.: Hiding Traces of Resampling in Digital Images. IEEE Transactions on Information Forensics and Security 3(4) (2008)
8. Kirchner, M., Bohme, R.: Synthesis of color filter array pattern in digital images. In: Proc. of SPIE. SPIE, San Jose (2009)
9. Cao, G., et al.: Anti-Forensics of Contrast Enhancement in Digital Images. In: MM&Sec 2010. ACM, Rome (2010)
10. Stamm, M.C., et al.: Anti-Forensics of Jpeg Compression. In: ICASSP. IEEE (2010)
11. Shi, Y.Q., Chen, C.-H., Xuan, G., Su, W.: Steganalysis versus splicing detection. In: Shi, Y.Q., Kim, H.-J., Katzenbeisser, S. (eds.) IWDW 2007. LNCS, vol. 5041, pp. 158–172. Springer, Heidelberg (2008)
12. Pevný, T., Filler, T., Bas, P.: Using high-dimensional image models to perform highly undetectable steganography. In: Böhme, R., Fong, P.W.L., Safavi-Naini, R. (eds.) IH 2010. LNCS, vol. 6387, pp. 161–177. Springer, Heidelberg (2010)
13. Ng, T.-T., Chang, S.-F.: A Dataset of Authentic and Spliced Image Blocks, ADVENT Technical Report, #203-2004-3, Columbia University (2004)
14. Chang, C.-C., Lin, C.-J.: LIBSVM: a library for support vector machines. ACM Transactions on Intelligent Systems and Technology 2(3) (2011)

Face Verification Using Color Sparse Representation

Wook Jin Shin, Seung Ho Lee, Hyun-seok Min, Hosik Sohn, and Yong Man Ro

Image and Video Systems Lab.,
Korea Advance Institute of Science and Technology (KAIST),
Yuseong-gu, Daejeon, Republic of Korea
{wookja,leesh09,hsmin,sohnhosik}@kaist.ac.kr,
ymro@ee.kaist.ac.kr

Abstract. This paper proposes an effective method for face verification using color sparse representation. In the proposed method, sparse representations are separately applied to multiple color bands of face images. The complementary residuals obtained from the multiple color face images are merged by means of score-level fusion, yielding improved discrimination capability for face verification. Experimental results using two public face databases (CMU Multi-PIE and Color FERET) showed that the proposed face verification method is highly robust under challenging conditions, compared to the conventional methods using grayscale sparse representation.

Keywords: Face verification, color sparse representation, information fusion.

1 Introduction

In recent years, biometric identity verification has gained much attention as an alternative solution to traditional cryptographic key-based verification mechanisms [1]. The fundamental problem of the key-based verification lies in a difficulty of key management. The cryptographic key can be easily forged, lost, and stolen. On the other hand, biometric data is extremely difficult to copy and share as it reflects the physiological and/or behavioral traits of a human. Hence, the uniqueness of biometric data makes biometric identity verification a prominent solution to enhance security.

Among a variety of biometric modalities, face verification has played a great role in many applications, such as biometric access control system, video surveillance systems, etc. [2]. In face verification, given a pair of face images, the goal is to determine whether they are coming from a single class or not. For successful face verification, the matching of faces should be robust to the challenging conditions such as variations of pose, illumination, and expression present in face images.

To fulfill the above requirement, designing an effective classifier is one of the crucial tasks in face verification. For this, a variety of classifiers have been introduced for face verification purposes [3-6]. In particular, sparse representation classifier has proven to be a highly powerful tool for face recognition due to its robustness to a variety of image distortion. In [6], Wright et al. suggested recognition framework for robust face recognition using sparse representation. The experimental results of [6]

Y.Q. Shi, H.J. Kim, and F. Pérez-González (Eds.): IWDW 2012, LNCS 7809, pp. 290–299, 2013.

showed that the sparse representation based classification outperforms other classifiers such as nearest neighbor (NN) and nearest subspace (NS) for face identification/verification.

The above-mentioned work demonstrated that sparse representation is a prominent classifier that offers robust face recognition accuracy. However, this work is limited to use only grayscale information of face images. It is important to note that, for face recognition, the use of facial color information is known to significantly improve discrimination capability [7-8]. In particular, the effectiveness of color information can be significant when face images are taken under variations in illumination and facial pose [8]. However, in scientific literature, no efforts have been thus far made to investigate color sparse representation for face recognition.

In this paper, we propose a new face identity verification method based on color sparse representation. In the proposed method, color face images in training set are converted to different color band images via color space conversion. After that, dictionaries associated to each color band are constructed using the corresponding color band images. In the testing phase, we convert probe color face image in the same way. Then, we compute the sparse solution vectors and the corresponding residual errors by separately applying sparse representation to each of the color bands. As illustrated in Fig. 2, distinct sparse solution vectors (derived from multiple color band images) can provide complementary cues to each other, which allow for reliable discrimination of face images. To facilitate the complementary effect for face images, the resultant residual scores (each of which is computed from a single color band) are combined at score-level. The combined residual score is then used for verification of the probe image. For details on verification criteria, please refer to Section 2. To the best of our knowledge, this is the first attempt to make effective use of color information in the area of face verification based on sparse representation.

To verify the usefulness of the proposed method, comparative and extensive experiments have been conducted using two publicly available face databases (DBs): CMU Multi-PIE [9] and Color FERET [10]. The two DBs are used to evaluate the verification capability under variations in illumination and facial pose, respectively. Experimental results show that the proposed color sparse representation based face verification can significantly improve that using conventional sparse representation that rely only on grayscale information. In addition, the proposed face verification clearly outperforms some state-of-the-art methods.

The rest of this paper is organized as follows: Section 2 details the proposed color face verification method. Section 3 presents experimental results and conclusion is drawn in Section 4.

2   Color Sparse Representation for Face Verification

In this section, we describe the proposed color sparse representation for face verification. Fig. 1 shows the framework of the proposed method which is composed of multiple sparse coding systems. Each of the sparse coding systems is associated with a particular color band. Given a *RGB* face image, multiple color band images are

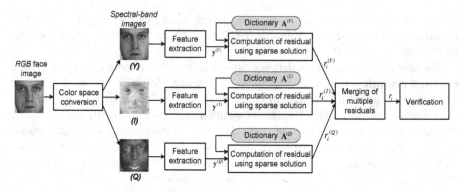

Fig. 1. Framework of the proposed face verification using color sparse representation. Note that *YIQ* color space is used as an example.

obtained through using color space conversion. In general, K color band images are assumed to be obtained. These color band images obtained from training set are used as training samples. On each of the training samples, feature extraction is performed for the purpose of dimensionality reduction (in this paper, downsampling and randomfaces are used). After that, K dictionaries are generated for the corresponding K color bands. Using the feature vectors of training samples, we construct a dictionary for the k-th color band as follows:

$$\mathbf{A}^{(k)} = [\mathbf{A}_1^{(k)}, \mathbf{A}_2^{(k)}, ..., \mathbf{A}_C^{(k)}] \in \mathfrak{R}^{d \times N} \tag{1}$$

where $\mathbf{A}_i^{(k)}$ is the dictionary consisting of d-dimensional feature vectors associated with the i-th class. N denotes the number of entire training face images. Note that feature vector is normalized to have unit length before generating the dictionary $\mathbf{A}^{(k)}$.

Since the construction of dictionary is separately performed on each color band, the vertical lengths of the resulting dictionaries remain unchanged (i.e., they are always d rather than increased). This allows us to keep underdetermined dictionaries as in [6] even when large number of color bands is used (three color bands in the case of Fig. 1).

Using the dictionary $\mathbf{A}^{(k)}$, the feature vector $\mathbf{y}^{(k)}$ of a given probe face image can be approximated as follows:

$$\mathbf{y}^{(k)} = \mathbf{A}^{(k)} \mathbf{x}^{(k)} \in \mathfrak{R}^d, \tag{2}$$

where $\mathbf{x}^{(k)}$ corresponds to the sparse solution vector for the k-th color band. In order to choose the sparsest solution among the all possible solutions, we employ ℓ^1-minimization constraint. By ℓ^1-minimization, the sparsest solution can be obtained by solving the following criteria:

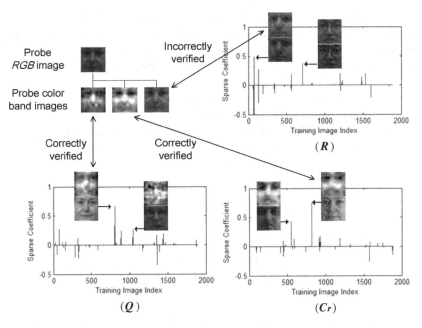

Fig. 2. Examples of sparse coefficients that are separately derived from three different color bands (e.g., R, Q, and C_r) of a probe face image. Training face images corresponding to the first and second largest sparse coefficient values are indicated for illustration purpose.

$$\hat{\mathbf{x}}_1^{(k)} = \arg\min\left\|\mathbf{x}^{(k)}\right\|_1 \quad \text{subject to} \quad \mathbf{A}^{(k)}\mathbf{x}^{(k)} = \mathbf{y}^{(k)} \tag{3}$$

where $\left\|\cdot\right\|_1$ denotes ℓ^1-norm. Once the sparsest solution $\hat{\mathbf{x}}_1^{(k)}$ is obtained, we compute the residuals $r_i^{(k)}(\mathbf{y}^{(k)})$ for each class, which can be computed as follows:

$$r_i^{(k)}(\mathbf{y}^{(k)}) = \left\|\mathbf{y}^{(k)} - \mathbf{A}^{(k)}\delta_i(\hat{\mathbf{x}}_1^{(k)})\right\|_2^2, \quad i = 1,2,...,C, \tag{4}$$

where $\delta_i(\cdot)$ indicates the characteristic function that selects the coefficients associated with the i-th class. From using equations from (1) to (4), the residuals for all of K color bands can be readily computed.

Fig. 2 shows the distributions of sparse coefficients separately computed from three distinct color bands (e.g., R, Q, and C_r) of a color face image. As shown in Fig. 2, the distributions of the sparse coefficients are different along the training image index, which means they contain distinct discriminative information for face verification. The sparse coefficients for R color band (related to luminance information [7]) in Fig. 2 are undesirable since the identity of the training face image having the largest coefficient value does not correspond to that of the probe image. This could be mainly due to varying lighting conditions across face images. On the other hand, for Q and C_r color bands (which are related to chromaticity of color), we can see that the training face images with the largest coefficient values and the probe face image have the same identity (although the two face images have quite different luminance). From the above observation, the sparse solutions from multiple color bands could be complementary to each other, improving discrimination capability for reliable face verification.

Here, we combine multiple residuals (each of which is obtained from a single color band) by using score-level fusion technique [11] so that we consolidate complementary effect of multiple color bands in sparse representation at once. To produce a fused residual, sum rule [11] is employed. The combination of the residuals can be defined as follows:

$$r_i = \sum_{k=1}^{K} \lambda_k r_i^{(k)}(\mathbf{y}^{(k)}), \quad i = 1,2,...,C, \tag{5}$$

where λ_k $(k=1,...,K)$ denotes weight value. In this paper, we choose equal weights for all color bands (i.e., $\lambda_k = 1/K$). Prior to the fusion, z-score normalization [11] is applied to all $r_i^{(k)}$ to have zero mean and unit variance within color band.

Finally, using each combined residual associated to i-th class, we make the final decision by the following criteria:

$$verification(\mathbf{y},i) = \begin{cases} 1 & if \ r_i \leq \tau \\ 0 & if \ r_i > \tau \end{cases}, \quad i = 1,2,...,C, \tag{6}$$

where τ is a global threshold used for verification. As a result of (6), the value 1 indicates that the feature vector $\mathbf{y}$ of a given probe face image is verified to belong to the class (or identity) i, vice versa.

3   Experimental Results

To evaluate the verification performance of the proposed method, two public face DBs: CMU Multi-PIE [9] and Color FERET [10] were used. The face images used in the experiment were cropped from the original images according to the locations of two eyes, and rescaled the cropped images to the size of 44×44 pixels (see Fig. 3). In order to investigate the stability of the proposed method in terms of verification accuracy under different color configurations, three color representations: 'RIQ' (R from RGB, I and Q from YIQ) [7]', 'RQC_r (C_r from YC_bC_r) [7]', and 'YC_bC_r (Y from YIQ) [8]' were used, since these color representations were known to provide richer discrimination capability for face representation than simple RGB color representation as reported in [7-8]. For the purpose of reducing vertical length of dictionary (i.e., to keep the dictionary in the condition of underdetermined), downsampling and Randomfaces [6] were used.

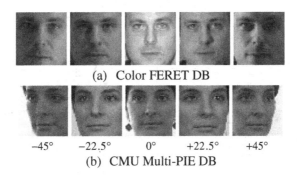

(a) Color FERET DB

−45°   −22.5°   0°   +22.5°   +45°

(b) CMU Multi-PIE DB

Fig. 3. Example images used in the experiments (a) CMU Multi-PIE DB (b) Color FERET DB

To make a decision in verification, the global threshold was set to have 200 evenly sampled values varying in the range from the minimum residual value to the maximum residual value among values computed using all the testing samples. In our experiments, Equal Error Rate (EER) [12] was used as the measurement for face verification performance. Using a False Rejection Rate (FRR) versus False Acceptance Rate (FAR) curve, EER is obtained at the point where FRR is equal to FAR [12]. To obtain reliable experimental results, 20 independent runs of experiments were executed. Thus, all the results reported below were the data averaged over 20 runs.

Firstly, we evaluated the robustness of the proposed method against extensive variations in illumination using CMU Multi-PIE DB. From CMU Multi-PIE DB, 3,733 facial images of 129 classes (i.e., clients) were collected. In this dataset, at least 13 face images per class were included. As shown in Fig. 3(a), the face images from CMU Multi-PIE DB are subject to severe illumination changes, which makes the face verification challenging. By using a random partition, the facial images were divided into training and testing set. The training set consisted of 1,896 images while the rest of images were used as the testing set. To measure the verification performance, each testing image was examined whether it belongs to its corresponding class (true attempt) and whether it belongs to the remaining classes (false attempts). We measured EER with 6 different dimensionalities of feature vectors: 16, 36, 64, 100, 144, and 196, which correspond to the square numbers of 4, 6, 8, 10, 12, and 14, respectively. Fig. 4 shows comparison results between the proposed face verification with color sparse representation and the one using grayscale sparse representation. As shown in Fig. 4, the proposed color sparse representation method significantly reduces EER in comparison with the grayscale based sparse representation, regardless of the color configuration used.

We further assessed the usefulness of the proposed method under variations in pose using Color FERET DB. For this, a total of 987 facial images of 70 classes (i.e., clients) were collected. In this dataset, at least 10 face images per class were included. The face images from FERET DB include five different pose angles ranging from −45° to +45° as shown in Fig. 3(b). Also note that all the images have neutral facial expression and illumination. The face data set was randomly partitioned into the training and testing set. To construct dictionary, 812 training images were used

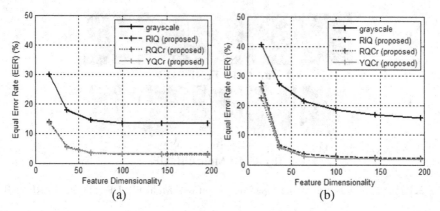

Fig. 4. EER on CMU Multi-PIE DB (a) Result using downsampling (b) Result using Randomfaces

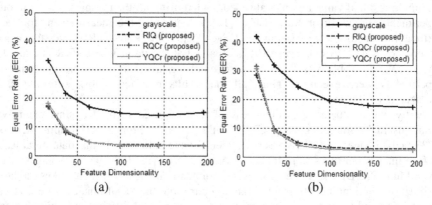

Fig. 5. EER on Color FERET DB(a) Result using downsampling (b) Result using Randomfaces

whereas the remaining 175 images were used for testing. The comparison results are given in Fig. 5. It is shown that the proposed color methods constantly outperform the grayscale based sparse representation. The improvement of EER is more than 10% for any feature dimension examined in this experiment. It demonstrates the effectiveness of our color face verification method under pose variations.

We performed additional experiment to make a comparison with other state-of-the-art methods; face verifications using LBP [13], Gabor wavelet [14], Local Directional Pattern (LDP) [15], and color LBP [16] features. For this comparison, the same face dataset collected from CMU Multi-PIE DB and Color FERET DB were used. For the methods using LBP, color LBP, and LDP descriptors, each cropped face image was rescaled to the size of 112×112 pixels. For LBP and color LBP, we selected $LBP_{8,2}$ operator (i.e., $P = 8$ and $R = 2$) [13], [16]. For obtaining Gabor representation, five scales and eight orientations were used to construct a set of Gabor filter banks [14].

Table 1. Performance comparison of the proposed FR with other state-of-the-art FR methods on CMU Multi-PIE DB. Note the image size is 112×112 pixels except the proposed color face verification.

Method	EER
LBP [13]	23.00%
Gabor [14]	12.46%
LDP [15]	21.78%
Color LBP [16]	25.49%
Color Sparse Representation (proposed method)	**1.89%**

Table 2. Performance comparison of the proposed FR with other state-of-the-art FR methods on Color FERET DB. Note the image size is 112×112 pixels except the proposed color face verification.

Method	EER
LBP [13]	23.30%
Gabor [14]	14.32%
LDP [15]	21.29%
Color LBP [16]	21.07%
Color Sparse Representation (proposed method)	**2.79%**

For the five above-mentioned face verification methods, we used Regularized Linear Discriminant Analysis (RLDA) for low-dimensional feature extraction, which was reported to achieve the best performance among four different low-dimensional feature extraction methods present in [16]. Also, for the methods using color information (i.e., color LBP and the proposed method based on color sparse representation), RQC_r color configuration was used. As seen in Table 1 and Table 2, the proposed method using color sparse representation performs clearly better than other four state-of-the-art methods. Specifically, for CMU Multi-PIE DB, the proposed face verification method is able to attain 20.51%, 11.53%, 18.50%, and 18.28% improvement in terms of EER, compared to the methods using LBP, Gabor, LDP, and color LBP features, respectively. Similarly, the improvement of 21.11%, 10.57%, 19.89%, and 23.6% in terms of EER were attained compared to each of four methods, respectively. This result sufficiently demonstrates the effectiveness of the proposed face verification method using color sparse representation.

4   Conclusion

In this paper, we proposed a simple yet effective color sparse representation based face verification. In the proposed method, sparse representation is applied to each of multiple color bands of a face image, and the corresponding residuals are obtained. The resultant residuals are combined via score-level fusion, consolidating the evidence from the multiple color band images. Experimental results demonstrated that the proposed face verification method is highly effective under challenging conditions.

The experiments conducted in this paper have been limited to a small number of color configurations consisting of three color bands, such as RQC_r. Hence, in-depth investigation about the effectiveness of various subsets of color bands in sparse representation will be studied in our future work. Also, although we used uniform (equal) weights in this paper to combine multiple residuals, the way of determining weights for each color band will be considerably explored. To this end, we plan to combine multiple results obtained from different color bands based on a boosting algorithm [17]. By finding the optimal subset of color bands, a higher face verification performance will be attained.

Acknowledgment. This research was partially supported by a grant (No. 10040218) from the R&D Program (Industrial Strategic Technology Development) funded by the Ministry of Knowledge Economy (MKE), Republic of Korea.

References

1. Jain, A.K., Ross, A., Prabhakar, S.: An Introduction to Biometric Recognition. IEEE Trans. on. Circuits and Systems for Video Technology 14(1), 4–20 (2004)
2. Zhao, W., Chellappa, R., Phillips, P.J., Rosenfeld, A.: Face recognition: A literature survey. Journal of ACM Computing Surveys 35(4), 399–458 (2003)
3. Duda, R., Hart, P., Stork, D.: Pattern Classification, second edition, 2nd edn. John Wiley & Sons (2001)
4. Ho, J., Yang, M., Lim, J., Lee, K., Kriegman, D.: Clustering Appearances of Object under Varying Illumination Conditions. In: IEEE Int'l Conf. on Computer Vision and Pattern Recognition (2003)
5. Vapnik, V.: The Nature of Statistical Learning Theory. Springer (2000)
6. Wright, J., Yang, A., Ganesh, A., Sastry, S., Ma, Y.: Robust Face Recognition via Sparse Representation. IEEE Trans. on Pattern Analysis and Machine Intelligence 31(2), 210–227 (2009)
7. Choi, J.Y., Ro, Y.M., Plataniotis, K.N.: Color Face Recognition for Degraded Face Images. IEEE Trans. on Systems, Man, and Cybernetics 39(5), 1217–1230 (2009)
8. Shih, P., Liu, C.: Improving the Face Recognition Grand Challenge Baseline Performance Using Color Configurations Across Color Spaces. In: Proc. IEEE Int'l Conf. on Image Processing (2006)
9. Gross, R., Matthews, I., Cohm, J., Kanade, T., Baker, S.: Multi-PIE. In: Proc. IEEE Int'l Conf. on Automatic Face and Gesture Recognition (2008)
10. Phillips, P.J., Moon, H., Rizvi, S.A., Rauss, P.J.: The FERET Evaluation Methodology for Face Recognition Algorithms. IEEE Trans. on Pattern Analysis and Machine Intelligence 22(10), 1090–1104 (2000)
11. Ross, A., Jain, A.K.: Information Fusion in Biometrics. Pattern Recognition Letters 24(13), 2115–2125 (2003)
12. Sanderson, C., Paliwal, K.K.: Fast feature for face authentication under illumination direction changes. Pattern Recognition Letters 24(14), 2409–2419 (2003)
13. Ahonen, T., Hadid, A., Pietikäinen, M.: Face Description with Local Binary Pattern: Application to Face Recognition. IEEE Trans. on Pattern Analysis and Machine Intelligence 28(12), 2037–2041 (2006)

14. Liu, C., Wechsler, H.: Gabor Feature Based Classification using the Enhanced Fisher Linear Discriminant Model for Face Recognition. IEEE Trans. on Image Processing 11(4), 467–476 (2002)
15. Jabid, T., Kabir, M.H., Chae, O.: Local Directional Pattern (LDP) for Face Recognition. In: IEEE Int'l Conf. on Consumer Electronics (2010)
16. Choi, J.Y., Ro, Y.M., Plataniotis, K.N.: Using Colour Local Binary Pattern Features for Face Recognition. In: IEEE Int'l Conf. on Image Processing (2010)
17. Choi, J.Y., Ro, Y.M., Plataniotis, K.N.: Boosting color feature selection for color face recognition. IEEE Trans. on Image Processing 20(5), 1–10 (2011)

Rapid Image Splicing Detection
Based on Relevance Vector Machine

Bo Su[1], Quanqiao Yuan[1], Yujin Zhang[2], Mengying Zhai[2], and Shilin Wang[1]

[1] School of Information Security Engineering, Shanghai Jiao Tong University
{subo,Danial00,wsl}@sjtu.edu.cn
[2] Department of Electronic Engineering, Shanghai Jiao Tong University
Shanghai, P.R. China 200240
{yjzhang82,janezmy}@sjtu.edu.cn

Abstract. Image splicing detection has become one of the most important topics in the field of information security and much work has been done for that. We focus on its practical application, which considers not only detection rate but also the time consumption. This paper combines Run-length Histogram Features (RLHF) in spatial domain and Markov based features in frequency domain for capturing splicing artifact. Principal Component Analysis (PCA) is adopted to reduce the dimensions of the features in order to reduce the computational complexity in classification. Furthermore, this paper introduces Relevance Vector Machine (RVM) as a classifier and introduces its advantage over Support Vector Machine (SVM) in theory. Simulation shows that the performance of combined features is better than each feature alone. RVM consumes much less test time than SVM at the price of a negligible decline of detection rate. Therefore, the proposed method meets the requirements of a fast and efficient image splicing detection.

Keywords: RLHF, Markov, PCA, RVM, Image Chroma.

1 Introduction

As digital image equipment and processing software spring up, tamper of digital images becomes rather easy and convenient. When photo record of what have happened is not reliable, it is a great threat to our society security especially in aspects like news media, military, and legal argument. Image forensic has become one of the most important topics in the field of information security.

Digital image forensic detection can be categorized into two major types: active detection [1] and passive detection [2]. The former method detects image forensic by verify digital signature or check watermark embedded before the reception of images. This method has a great constraint because it requires built-in standardized watermarking functionality in image equipment, which makes these devices more expensive and less universal. This kind of detection is only available for the equipment with such function itself and not convenient for others. Passive approaches for image

Y.Q. Shi, H.J. Kim, and F. Pérez-González (Eds.): IWDW 2012, LNCS 7809, pp. 300–310, 2013.

forensic detection have no demand for any watermark or prior knowledge and only exploit the knowledge of images themselves. Their blind nature makes passive detection exceling active detection in many applications.

The purpose of image forensic is to change the original content and create feint, so cropping and pasting regions from the same or different images to form another image should be a common operation. This is defined as image splicing and often regarded as a symbol for forensics.

Many passive image splicing detection methods have come out in recent years. Shi et al. [3] has proposed a nature model consists of statistical features including moments of characteristic functions of wavelet sub-bands and Markov transition probabilities to capture the difference between authentic and forensic images. Johnson and Farid [4] analyzed the lighting inconsistency in an image to detect splicing images. The disadvantage of this approach is that it can't detect splicing images taken under the same or rather similar light conditions. Another scheme was proposed by Farid [5] to detect splicing images based on different JPEG compression quality. It can handle cases that the tampered region has been compressed with lower quality than its host image but is not effective for other cases. Fridrich and Lukas in [6] showed that the high-medium frequency component of the sensor pattern noise was an equivalent of "bullet scratches" for digital images and could be used for reliable forensic identification. Pan and lyu [7] caught SIFT features from different image regions and compared them, then used their correlations to output a map indicating region to be duplicated from another region with high possibility.

Most of the prior researches only focused on splicing detection rate, while we want to pay attention to the time consumption for practical application at the same time. This paper adopts PCA to reduce the multi-features and replace SVM by RVM as the classifier in order to facilitate testing and calculation. Early works that employed statistical features of splicing image bias toward either spatial domain or frequency domain alone, and we give an approach which combines both of them together and correspondingly get a better classification rate according to our experiments.

The rest of the paper is organized as follows. The model for capturing splicing features based on Run-length Histogram and Markov is given in section 2. In section 3, Relevance Vector Machine (RVM) is briefly described and its advantages over SVM are presented. Then, we give our experiment results and analysis in Section 4. Conclusion and discussion are provided in Section 5.

2   A Statistical Model for Capturing Splicing Artifacts

For a nature image, it has its own smoothness, consistency, continuity and periodicity. So values of pixels in image matrix should obey some particular statistical disciplines. When splicing operation is conducted, these disciplines will be disturbed and that is why statistical features in proposed method have detection capability. With two most common domains-spatial and frequency to describe signal, we develop a model to represent images splicing features by Run-length Histogram Features (RLHF) in the former and Markov based features in the later. As research in [8] presents, features extracted in chroma space have a better discrimination result over luminance space.

2.1   Run-Length Histogram Features

Galloway in [9] proposed the use of a run-length matrix for texture feature extraction and Jing Dong developed run-length histogram features for blind image steganalysis in [10]. In this paper, we take advantage of run-length histogram features (RLHF) to capture the difference that separates spliced images from nature images.

2.1.1   Run-Length Matrix
In run-length matrix, a run is defined as a string of consecutive pixels which have the same gray level intensity along a specific orientation (typically horizontal in 0, diagonal in 45, vertical in 90, minor diagonal in 135). For a given image gray matrix, the elements $P_\theta(m,n)$ in run-length matrix is defined as the number of runs with gray level m and run length n along θ direction.

2.1.2   Run-Length Histogram
For a run-length matrix $P_\theta(m,n)$, calculate the sum of elements in each column and we can get a n length vector $P_\theta(n) = [p_\theta(1), p_\theta(2), ..., p_\theta(n)]$, which is defined as run-length histogram, with its element defined as

$$p(j) = \sum_{i=1}^{M} p(i,j), \qquad j = 1, ..., N. \tag{1}$$

Image splicing operation will change the correlation between neighbor pixels, exactly the local texture information, and the change will be captured by the RLHF. As Galloway analyzes in [9], short runs occupies most of runs, that is, short runs hold most of the RLHF information. In this paper, the threshold value in formula (1) is designed as M=30. For most texture of image, RLHF in orientation 0 and orientation 90 is already enough to catch the splicing operation. A general block diagram is given in Fig. 1 and we get 30*2=60 dimension of RLHF.

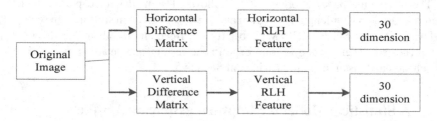

Fig. 1. General block diagram of RLHF extraction procedure

2.2   Markov Based Features

RLHF is a kind of feature reflecting the statistical changes in spatial domain caused by image splicing and we want to get such features in frequency domain. Markov based features proposed by Shi et al. in [3] carry out that intention perfectly. A brief introduction is given out here.

2.2.1   Block Discrete Cosine Transform (BDCT)

For the block discrete cosine transform (BDCT)'s capability in decorrelation and energy compaction, it is widely used in image or video processing like compression and denoise. The BDCT in this paper is set to have a block size as 8*8, and then the transform is given by

$$F(s,t) = \frac{2}{n} \sum_{x=0}^{n-1} \sum_{y=0}^{n-1} \Delta(x)\Delta(y)\cos\frac{\pi s(2x+1)}{2n} \cos\frac{\pi t(2y+1)}{2n} f(x,y) \qquad (2)$$

Where $\Delta(x) = \begin{cases} \frac{1}{\sqrt{2}}, x = 0 \\ 1, otherwise \end{cases}$, and $s, t \in \{0, 1, \dots, n-1\}$.

2.2.2   Difference 2-D Array

As many researches indicate, one of the main obstacles for splicing detection is the interference from the image content. A difference 2-D array is introduced to eliminate this interference. Difference 2-D arrays are defined as $F_\theta(u, v)$, given by following equations.

$$F_h(u, v) = [F(i, j)] - [F(i+1, j)]. \qquad (3)$$

$$F_v(u, v) = [F(i, j) - F(i, j+1)]. \qquad (4)$$

$$F_d(u, v) = [F(i, j) - F(i+1, j+1)]. \qquad (5)$$

$$F_m(u, v) = [F(i+1, j) - F(i, j+1)]. \qquad (6)$$

Where (u, v) represents the difference array coordinate, (i, j) stands for original array coordinate, θ represents different directions (horizontal(h), vertical(v), diagonal(d), and minor-diagonal(m)), and [*] means round operation. This paper exploits difference array in horizontal and vertical direction to represent splicing features.

2.2.3   Markov Transition Probability Matrix

Under the assumption that pasted parts are additive to the host image and the additive noise is independent to the host image, the distribution of the spliced image is the convolution of the distribution of the host image and that of the additive noise [3]. When additive splicing noise obeys Gaussian distribution, the splicing operation will cause the disturbance of concentration along the main diagonal of Markov transition probability matrix of the difference array. And this statistical artifact can be employed to detect splicing.

Because the coefficients of difference 2-D array have a vast range, it's needed to turn to a threshold technique. If the value of an element in a difference array is larger than T or smaller than –T, it will be represented by T or –T. This procedure results in a transition probability matrix $P_{(2T+1)*(2T+1)}$. In horizontal and vertical direction, the element in the matrix is given by

$$p\{F_h(u + 1, v) = n | F_h(u, v) = m\}$$
$$= \frac{\sum_{v=0}^{N-2} \sum_{u=0}^{N-2} \delta(F_h(u, v) = m, F_h(u + 1, v) = n)}{\sum_{v=0}^{N-2} \sum_{u=0}^{N-2} \delta(F_h(u, v) = m)}. \tag{7}$$

$$p\{F_v(u, v + 1) = n | F_v(u, v) = m\}$$
$$= \frac{\sum_{v=0}^{N-2} \sum_{u=0}^{N-2} \delta(F_v(u, v) = m, F_v(u, v + 1) = n)}{\sum_{v=0}^{N-2} \sum_{u=0}^{N-2} \delta(F_v(u, v) = m)}. \tag{8}$$

The general block diagram of Markov feature extraction procedure is presented in Fig.2. We preform 8*8 BDCT on images and then form horizontal and vertical difference 2-D arrays from them. These difference 2-D arrays are modeled by Markov process and the transition probability matrix is calculated for each difference array. A threshold technique is developed before Markov process. With threshold T=3, we get (2T+1)* (2T+1)=49 parameters for each direction and totally get 98 dimension of Markov based features.

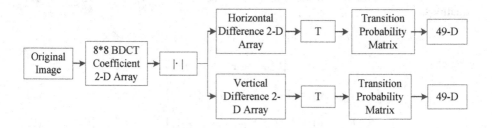

Fig. 2. General block diagram of Markov feature extraction procedure

2.3   Chroma Spaces

Chroma spaces refer to color difference spaces, where luminance component is removed and most content details of the image, regarded as interferences for the splicing detection, are slipped too. Wang et al. [11] has conducted experiments that justified the effectiveness of chroma spaces over RGB space. In YCbCr color space, Y is the luminance component and Cb (Cr) is the blue-difference (red-difference) chroma component. Cb (or Cr) component has less image content and then is more effective for splicing detection. The conversion from RGB space to YCbCr is given as

$$\begin{bmatrix} Y \\ Cr \\ Cb \end{bmatrix} = \begin{bmatrix} 0.299 & 0.578 & 0.114 \\ 0.500 & -0.4187 & -0.0813 \\ -0.1687 & -0.3313 & 0.500 \end{bmatrix} \begin{bmatrix} R \\ G \\ B \end{bmatrix} + \begin{bmatrix} 0 \\ 128 \\ 128 \end{bmatrix}. \tag{9}$$

3   Relevance Vector Machine

Considering the disadvantages of SVM [12-13], Tipping [12] originally proposed the relevance vector machine (RVM). RVM adopts a fully probabilistic framework and introduces a prior over the model weights controlled by a set of parameters, one associated with each weight, whose most probable values are iteratively estimated from the data. In practice, we find that the posterior distributions of many of the weights are sharply peaked around zero. Then we term those training vectors associated with the remaining non-zero weights relevance vectors according to the principle of automatic relevance determination which motivates the presented approach [15-16], and sparsity is well obtained. The most charming feature of RVM lies in that it employs dramatically fewer kernel functions in parallel with performance comparable to an equivalent SVM.

In this paper, we give a brief review of RVM for classification, and more details can be found in [12]. For two-class classification, the purpose is to predict the posterior probability of membership of one of the classes given the input $\mathbf{X}$. Following statistical convention, we generalize the linear model by applying the sigmoid link function $\sigma(y) = 1/(1 + e^{-y})$ to $y(x)$ and, adopting the Bernoulli distribution for $P(t|\mathbf{X})$, the likelihood is given,

$$P(\mathbf{t}|\mathbf{w}) = \prod_{n=1}^{N} \sigma\{y(x_n; w)\}^{t_n} [1 - \sigma\{y(x_n; w)\}]^{1-t_n}, \ t_n \in \{0,1\}. \tag{11}$$

If we calculate $\mathbf{w}$ through Maximum Likelihood directly, most of elements in $\mathbf{w}$ will not be zero. Let's recall that one disadvantage of SVM is that too much support vectors lead to overfitting. We want to avert this problem, so we assume the prior distribution of w_i as independent normal distribution with zero-mean. Then we can get,

$$p(w_i|\alpha_i) = N(w_i|0, \alpha_i^{-1}). \tag{12}$$

$$p(\mathbf{w}|\boldsymbol{\alpha}) = \prod_{i=0}^{N} \frac{\alpha_i}{\sqrt{2\pi}} \exp\left(-\frac{\alpha_i w_i^2}{2}\right). \tag{13}$$

Where $\boldsymbol{\alpha} = [\alpha_0, \alpha_1, \alpha_2, \dots, \alpha_{0N}]^T$ is defined as the hyperparameters introduced to control the strength of the prior over its associated weight.

From Bayes' rule, we have the formula as

$$p(\mathbf{w}|\mathbf{t}, \boldsymbol{\alpha}) = \frac{p(t|w)p(w|\alpha)}{p(t|\alpha)}. \tag{14}$$

Where $p(t|w)$ is the likelihood, $p(w|\alpha)$ is the prior, and $p(w|\alpha)$ is regarded as evidence. We exploit the approximation procedure proposed in [15] based on Laplace's method to calculate unanalyzable weights:

4   Experiments and Results

4.1   Image Dataset

The image splicing database we test our algorithm on is the Columbia Uncompressed Image Splicing Detection Evaluation Database [17]. It contains a total of 363 images in our database, with 183 of them authentic images and 180 spliced ones. The real images are taken with four kinds of cameras: Canon G3, Nikon D70, Canon EOS 350D Rebel XT, and Kodak DCS330. They are all in uncompressed RAW or BMP forms with size range from 757*568 to 1152*768. The splicing images are created from the authentic images set with Adobe Photoshop. The tamper operation is only copy and paste without post processing in order to focus on the effects of splicing. Each spliced image contains contents from exactly two cameras. Most of them are indoor scenes like lab, desk, books and so on, with only 27 images (about 15%) is taken outdoors on a cloudy day. Examples are shown as Fig 3.

Fig. 3. Image examples of Authentic and Spliced images in the database

4.2   Feature Extraction

With theory support in the early sections, we design our algorithm for splicing image detection on the database specially. Firstly, we read in the images and get the Cb or Cr component in YCbCr color space. Secondly, we perform Markov and RLHM algorithm to exact totally 158 dimension of feature for the whole 363 images, then combine them and normalize. Finally, we play PCA [14] to reduce the dimension of the features to 20. According to experiment results, the relationship of detection rate with dimension of features is shown in Fig 4, and we choose 20 as the final dimension of features.

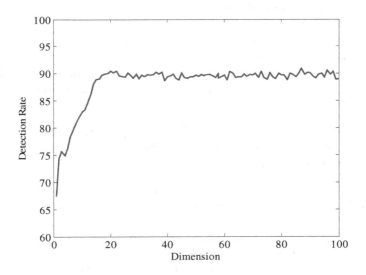

Fig. 4. Relation between detection rate and dimension

4.3   Classifier

The relevant vector machine (RVM) is a kind of supervised machine learning method like SVM. It exploits the advantages of probability and preforms better than SVM for over-fitting. The theory part has been presented in the early part. In this paper, we use basic part of Sparse Bayes V1.1 [13] code and update it for our experiment. The whole flow diagram of algorithm is given as Fig.5.

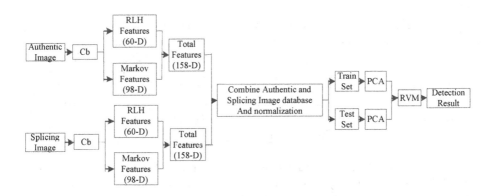

Fig. 5. Flow Diagram of the Algorithm

4.4   Experiment Results and Analysis

4.4.1   Comparison of Detection Rate

To better verify the effectiveness of our algorithm, we further extract RLH features, Markov based features independently from the database and perform both SVM and RVM in classification. Experiment results are shown in Table 1 and we can draw some conclusion as follows:

- Our proposed RLH features alone can achieve a detection rate of 82.3% by SVM, which is not as good as Markov based features. But we will get a better performance with these two methods together.

- The detection rate with RVM is a little worse than SVM as a whole, but difference is rather slight, especially for our 20 dimension of features with only 0.5%.

Table 1. Comparison between RVM and SVM of detection rate

	Dimension	RVM	SVM
RLH Feature	60	80.2	82.3
Markov Feature	98	87.3	86.3
RLH + Markov	158	89.8	91.3
After PCA	20	90.4	90.9

4.4.2   Comparison of Time Consumption

To better prove our algorithm is excellent for real time applications, we compare the time consumption of each method of feature extraction and classifier. Experiment results are shown in Table 2and some conclusion can be drawn:

Table 2. Comparison between RVM and SVM of time consumption

	D	Train	Test	Time Consumption	
				RVM	SVM
RLH Feature	60	181	181	0.0025	0.02
Markov Feature	98	181	181	0.0015	0.015
RLH + Markov	158	181	181	0.002	0.02
After PCA	20	181	181	0.0008	0.006

- PCA can reduce the time consumption with a rather mild decrease or even increase in detection rate generally as it always performs. When playing PCA, considerable time is needed for getting transform matrix. But for a special test image, the time consumption is about 0.000006s, negligible compared with SVM or RVM.
- RVM is able to reduce time consumption at a large degree and about 7 times faster for 20 dimensions of features classification compared with SVM.

Together with the conclusion prior, our experiment results witness that RVM can save a lot time with negligent decrease in detection rate. To better explain this result, we give our explanation as follows.

From the theory part in section 3.2, RVM is a kind of Bayes model. To avoid over-fitting in SVM caused by too many support vectors, it predefine the probability distribution of weights as $w_i \sim N(0, \alpha_i^{-1})$, where α_i is a super parameter and assumed to obey Gamma distribution. Most α_i will get bigger after numbers of iteration with w_i tending to zero correspondingly. Then vectors relevant to these w_i will turn 'irrelevant' and only fewer vectors are left, which are named as 'relevant vector' and form the sparse model. Table 3 show that the number of relevant vectors (RVs) are smaller than that of support vectors (SVs), which verify that RVM is more sparse than SVM.

Table 3. Comparison of the number of RVs and SVs

	Dimension	(RVs)	(SVs)
RLH Feature	60	24	120
Markov Feature	98	9	85
RLH + Markov	158	14	110
After PCA	20	12	65

5   Conclusion

This paper has designed a splicing image detection method which combines RLHF in spatial domain and Markov based features in frequency domain and achieves a rather good result. Furthermore, with PCA and RVM, we reduce the time consumption in vast scale without imperceptible decrease of detection rate. This makes our method more effective when dealing with real time detection. To make the method well-founded and more persuasive, we give a brief theory derivation and experiment analysis for RVM's advantage over SVM.

Most research concentrate their attention on the detection rate of the proposed method, which is of cause one of the most important thing. But the time consumption for real application is also needed to take into consideration. Our method has achieved both these two purposes successfully and should be more practical.

The detection rate of 90.4% is good but not enough, research for more effective features and their better combinations is still needed. More researches focused on detection time consumption should be conducted. And also, the Columbia Image Splicing Detection Evaluation Dataset [17] contains so few color images and image content is too single. More complex and integrate splicing image database is needed to test the proposed method effectively.

Acknowledgements. This work is funded by National Natural Science Foundation of China (61071152, 61271316), 973 Program (2010CB731403, 2010CB731406) of China and National "Twelfth Five-Year" Plan for Science & Technology Support (2012BAH38 B04).

References

1. Zhang, Z., Qiu, G., Sun, Q., Lin, X., Ni, Z., Shi, Y.Q.: A Unified Authentication Framework for JPEG 2000. In: IEEE International Conference on Multimedia and Expo., vol. 2, pp. 915–918. IEEE Press, New York (2004)
2. Ng, T.T., Chang, S.F., Lin, C.Y., Sun, Q.: Passive-blind Image Forensics. In: Zeng, W., Yu, H., Lin, C.Y. (eds.) Multimedia Security Technologies for Digital Rights, ch. 15, pp. 383–412. Academic Press, Missouri (2006)
3. Shi, Y.Q., Chen, C., Chen, W.: A Natural Image Model Approach to Splicing Detection. In: 9th Workshop on Multimedia and Security, pp. 51–62. ACM, New York (2007)
4. Johnson, M.K., Farid, H.: Exposing Digital Forgeries by Detecting Inconsistencies in Lighting. In: 7th Workshop on Multimedia and Security, pp. 1–10. ACM, New York (2005)
5. Farid, H.: Exposing Digital Forgeries from JPEG Ghost. IEEE Transactions on Information Forensics and Security 4(1), 154–160 (2009)
6. Fridrich, J., Lukas, J.: Digital Bullet Scratches for Images. In: Proceeding of IEEE International Conference on Image Processing, Genova, Italy (2005)
7. Pan, X., Lyu, S.: Detecting image region duplication using SIFT features. In: 2010 Acoustics Speech and Signal Processing, ICASSP 2010 (2010)
8. Wang, W., Dong, J., Tan, T.: Effective image splicing detection based on image chroma. In: 2009 International Conference on Image Processing, ICIP 2009 (2009)
9. Galloway, M.M.: Texture analysis using gray level run lengths. Cornput. Graphics Image. Proc. 4, 172–179 (1975)
10. Dong, J., Tan, T.N.: Blind image steganalysis based on run-length histogram analysis. In: 15th International Conference of Image Processing (ICIP 2008), pp. 2064–2067 (2008)
11. Wang, W., Dong, J., Tan, T.: Effective Image Splicing Detection Based on Image Chroma. In: 16th IEEE International Conference on Image Processing, pp. 1257–1260. IEEE Press, New York (2009)
12. Tipping, M.E.: The Relevance Vector Machine. In: Solla, S.A., Leen, T.K., Müller, K.-R. (eds.) Advances in Neural Information Processing Systems 12, pp. 652–658. MIT Press (2000)
13. Tipping, M.E.: Sparse Bayesian learning and the relevance vector machine. Journal of Machine Learning Research, 211–244 (2001)
14. Abdi, H., Williams, L.J.: Principal Component Analysis. Wiley Interdisciplinary Reviews: Computational Statistics 2, 433–459 (2010)
15. MacKay, D.J.C.: The evidence framework applied to classificationnetworks. Neural Comput. 4(5), 720–736 (1992)
16. MacKay, D.J.C.: Bayesian non-linearmodeling for the prediction competition. ASHRAE Transactions, ASHRAE 100(2), 1053–1056 (1994)
17. Columbia DVMM Research Lab. Columbia Image Splicing Detection Evaluation Dataset (2004),
   http://www.ee.columbia.edu/ln/dvmm/downloads/authsplcuncmp/

An Efficient Speech Content Authentication Algorithm Based on Coefficients Self-correlation Degree

Zhenghui Liu and Hongxia Wang

School of Information Science and Technology,
Southwest Jiaotong University, Chengdu 610031, China
zhenghui.liu@163.com, hxwang@swjtu.edu.cn

Abstract. In this paper, the definition of coefficients self-correlation degree is given. Based on coefficients self-correlation degree, an efficient speech content authentication algorithm is proposed, which is aimed at some shortcomings in the existing content-based speech content authentication schemes. At the same time, the frequency domain watermark embedding method of pseudo-Zernike moments based on discrete cosine transform is given. Watermark bit is generated by coefficients self-correlation degree and embedded by quantizing the pseudo-Zernike moments of discrete cosine transform domain low-frequency coefficients. Compared with the existing audio watermark algorithms based on pseudo-Zernike moments, the algorithm increases the embedding capacity and improves the efficiency greatly. Experimental evaluation results show that the proposed scheme is effective.

Keywords: speech content authentication, speech characteristic, tamper localization, coefficients self-correlation degree.

1 Introduction

There are abundant audio content authentication algorithms [1~5]. However, the speech content authentication schemes are rarely. Comparing with audio signals, speech signals are more likely to cause attacker's interest and be attacked. If the attacked signals are not detected, the authentication client will consider the attacked speech signal is veracity, which will cause serious consequences. So, the research of speech content authentication is more realistic meaning and practical value.

There are some shortcomings for some existing watermark schemes: (1) Some watermark is embedded in public and fixed frequency points, which results that attackers can tamper watermark in frequency domain easily. The detailed discussion of this is described in [6]. (2) For the scheme proposed in [7], the watermark bits are embedded in the lest significant bits (LSBs), which is very fragile to common signal processing operations. In practical applications, for the convenience of storage, the format of special requirements and many other reasons, speech signal will inevitably be subject to a certain degree of common signal processing operations. In this situation, the scheme is unsuitable. (3) For the content-based audio content authentication

Y.Q. Shi, H.J. Kim, and F. Pérez-González (Eds.): IWDW 2012, LNCS 7809, pp. 311–326, 2013.

algorithm [5], on the one hand, the features used to generate watermark are public, and attackers can get the features easily. On the other hand, the watermark embedded and extracted method is known to attackers, it is possible for attackers to extract the watermark embedded. Then, for one watermarked audio frame, attackers search to find another audio content having the same features and watermark extracted and to substitute the frame, which will not be detected at the authentication client. We call this attack as feature-analysed substitution attack.

Consideration of the above problems and the practical value of speech content authentication, an efficient speech content authentication algorithm based on coefficients self-correlation degree (CSCD) is proposed. Firstly, the definition and calculation of CSCD are given. Secondly, the robustness of CSCD of speech signal and the pseudo-Zernike moments (p-ZMs) of discrete cosine transform (DCT) domain low-frequency coefficients are analyzed experimentally. Watermark bits are generated by CSCD and embedded by quantizing the p-ZMs of DCT domain low-frequency coefficients. In this paper, for the features used to generate and extract watermark are secrets, the algorithm is robust against the feature-analysed substitution attack. Compared with the existing audio watermark algorithms based on p-ZMs, the method increases the embedding capacity and improves the efficiency greatly. Theoretical analysis and simulation results show that the proposed algorithm is inaudible, and can distinguish the common signal processing operations and the malicious attacks, meanwhile has excellent ability of tamper detection.

The organization of this paper is as follows. Section 2 introduces the theoretical foundation of the proposed scheme. Section 3 and 4 describe the watermark embedding and extracting algorithm, respectively. Section 5 analyzes the performance of the algorithm theoretically. In section 6, simulation results and comparison with other reported algorithms are presented, which illustrate the effectiveness of the proposed scheme. Finally, we summarize the conclusion in section 7.

2   Theoretical Foundation

2.1   The Coefficients Self-correlation Degree

Denote A as the speech signal. The transformation of frequency domain is performed on A, and the l-th frequency domain coefficients is denoted by F_l. The coefficients self-correlation degree (CSCD) in frequency domain is defined as

$$D = \sqrt{\sum_{l=1}^{L} |F_l| \times |F_{l+h}|} \tag{1}$$

where D represents the CSCD of A, and F_{l+h} is the h-th coefficient behind F_l, $h \geq 0$. $|F_l|$ represents the amplitudes of F_l. In Eq. (1), when $l+h > L$, $F_{l+h} = F_{l+h-L}$. And the D value reflects the degree of the closeness of $|F_l|$ and $|F_{l+h}|$. The greater D is, the closer $|F_l|$ and $|F_{l+h}|$ is. On the contrary, the smaller D is, the larger the difference between $|F_l|$ and $|F_{l+h}|$ is.

2.2   The Robustness of Pseudo-zernike Moments of DCT Domain Low-Frequency Coefficients

Suppose $A = \{a(l), 1 \leq l \leq La\}$ is the test speech signal.

(1) DCT is performed on A, and the DCT domain coefficients are denoted by DA. The front of t ($t < n, t = t' \times t'$) DCT domain low-frequency coefficients are denoted by $LDA(l'), 1 \leq l' \leq t$.

(2) $LDA(l'), 1 \leq l' \leq t$ is mapped into 2D form by using the following projection

$$\begin{cases} t = N \times N + M, \ 0 \leq M < 2N + 1 \\ LDA(i, j) = LDA((i-1) \cdot N + j), \ 1 \leq i, j \leq N \end{cases} \tag{2}$$

where $LDA(i, j)$ is the corresponding 2D form after projection, M is the rest of samples, N is the width or height in $LDA(i, j)$, the value of which is as large as possible under the constrain of Eq. (2).

(3) The p-ZMs of $LDA(i, j), 1 \leq i, j \leq t'$ are calculated by the following mathematical expression [8,9].

$$E_{an} = \sum_m |A_{nm}|, \quad E_{bn} = \sum_m |\hat{A}_{nm}| \tag{3}$$

where $|A_{nm}|$ is the amplitude of p-ZMs of order n with repetition m, and $|\hat{A}_{nm}|$ is the corresponding version of $|A_{nm}|$ after undergoing some signal processing, $0 \leq n \leq n_{max}$. E_{an} and E_{bn} represent the total amplitude of all moments with the given order n before and after undergoing some signal processing operations, respectively. The process is shown in Fig. 1.

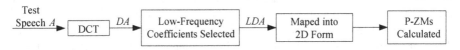

Fig. 1. The calculation of p-ZMs of DCT domain low-frequency coefficients

We select 12 speech segments randomly, containing adult male voice, adult female voice and children voice, which are 16-bit quantified mono WAVE format signal sampled at 22.05 kHz. And La=10240, t=100.

Fig. 2(a) and (b) show the variation of p-ZMs of DCT domain low-frequency coefficients after undergoing re-sampling operation with different sampling rate and low-pass filtering under different cutoff frequency, respectively. The test results are the statistical average value of the 12 speech segments, from which we can see that the low order p-ZMs of DCT domain low-frequency coefficients are very robust to common signal processing operations. Based on the analysis, the frequency domain watermark embedding method of p-ZMs is proposed in section 3.

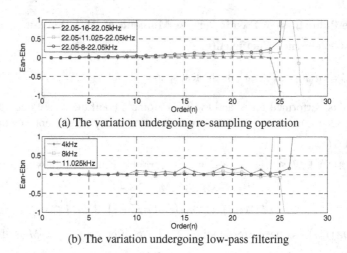

(a) The variation undergoing re-sampling operation

(b) The variation undergoing low-pass filtering

Fig. 2. The variation of p-ZMs of DCT domain low-frequency coefficients undergoing re-sampling operation and low-pass filtering

2.3 The Robustness of Coefficients Self-correlation Degree

In this section, the robustness of CSCD is analyzed experimentally. The test speech signals and the statistical method of the test results are same as that in section 2.2. It's worth noting that La=102400 in this section.

A is cut into 100 frames, and the i-th frame is denoted by $A(i)$, which has 1024 samples. Then DCT is performed on $A(i)$, and the front of 169 DCT domain low-frequency coefficients are selected. The number of DCT domain low-frequency coefficients selected is obtained by experiment.

The CSCD of the DCT domain low-frequency coefficients is calculated using the Eq. (1), in which h=20. $Ca(i)$ and $Cb(i)$ represent the value of CSCD of the i-th frame before and after undergoing common signal procession operations, respectively.

Fig. 3(a) and (b) show the variation of CSCD undergoing low-pass filtering under different cutoff frequency and undergoing MP3 compression under different bit rates, respectively. From the test results, we can conclude that the CSCD of speech signal is very robustness to common signal procession operations.

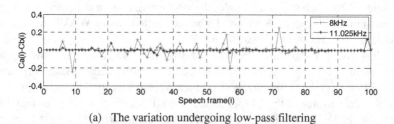

(a)   The variation undergoing low-pass filtering

Fig. 3. The variation of CSCD undergoing low-pass filtering and MP3 compression

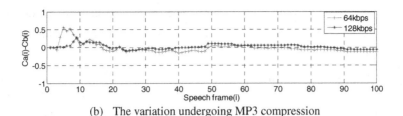

(b)   The variation undergoing MP3 compression

Fig. 3. (*Continued.*)

3   Watermark Generating and Embedding Scheme

The original speech signal is denoted by $A = \{a(l), 1 \le l \le LA\}$, and the watermark generation and embedding process is shown in Fig. 4.

Step 1: Preprocessing

(1) The pseudo-random sequence $X = \{x_r | r = 1, 2, ...\}$ is generated based on Logistic map (4), and adopt k (k is the secret key of the watermarking system) as the initial value of the Logistic map

$$x_{r+1} = \mu x_r (1 - x_r), x_0 = k, 3.5699 \le \mu \le 4 \tag{4}$$

where $x_r \in (0,1), r = 1, 2, \cdots$. Let denote $B = \{b_r | b_r \in \{0,1\}, r = 1, 2, \cdots\}$, b_r can be generated by

$$b_r = \begin{cases} 0, & x_r < 0.5 \\ 1, & x_r \ge 0.5 \end{cases} \tag{5}$$

(2) B is cut into some segments, and each segment has m samples. Each segment is cut into T non-overlapping sub-segments, and each sub-segment has m_1 samples. The t-th sub-segment of the i-th segment is denoted by $B_{i,t}$.

$$B_{i,t} = \left\{ b_{i,t}(r) | b_{i,t}(r) = b_r, (i-1) \times m + (t-1) \times m_1 + 1 \le r \le (i-1) \times m + t \times m_1 \right\} \tag{6}$$

where $1 \le t \le T$, and $T = m / m_1$.

(3) Denote $T_{i,t} = c + Z_{i,t} \bmod Z$, where c and Z are positive integers, and $Z_{i,t}$ is the decimal integer of $B_{i,t}$.

(4) A is cut into P non-overlapping frames, and each frame has I samples, where $I = LA / P$. The i-th frame is denoted by A_i, $1 \le i \le P$.

(5) A_i is cut into two segments. The first and the second segment are denoted by FA_i and SA_i, respectively. FA_i has M samples and SA_i has N samples, where $M + N = I$.

Step 2: Watermark generation

(1) DCT is performed on FA_i, and the front of $T_{i,1} \times T_{i,1}$ DCT domain low-frequency coefficients are denoted by $LA_i(g), 1 \leq g \leq T_{i,1} \times T_{i,1}$. Then CSCD of $LA_i(g)$ is calculated by the Eq. (1), and the result is denoted by $C_i, 1 \leq i \leq P$.

(2) The highest bit value of $\lfloor C_i \rfloor$ is denoted by H_i. H_i is converted into binary bits, which is denoted by $W_i = \{w_{i,t} | w_{i,t} \in (0,1), 1 \leq t \leq T\}$ (If the bit number of W_i is less than T, then the method of left cycle shift will be taken to meet the condition). W_i is the watermark generated of the i-th frame.

Step 3: Watermark embedding

(1) SA_i is divided into T segments. The t-th segment is denoted by $SA_{i,t}$, $1 \leq t \leq T$, and each segment has N/T samples.

(2) DCT is performed on $SA_{i,t}$, and the corresponding coefficients are denoted by $DSA_{i,t}$, $1 \leq t \leq T$. Denote $DSA_{i,t}(g), 1 \leq g \leq T_{i,t} \times T_{i,t}$ as the front $T_{i,t} \times T_{i,t}$ DCT domain low-frequency coefficients of the t-th segment.

(3) $DSA_{i,t}(g), 1 \leq g \leq T_{i,t} \times T_{i,t}$ is mapped into 2D form by using the Eq. (2). Then the p-ZMs of the 2D signals are calculated using the Eq. (3), and the results are denoted by $S_{i,t}, i = 1, 2, \cdots P, 1 \leq t \leq T$.

(4) The highest bit value of $\lfloor S_{i,t} \rfloor$ is denoted by $H_{i,t}$, and the second highest bit value of $\lfloor S_{i,t} \rfloor$ is denoted by $L_{i,t}$. Then the watermark is embedded as follows

$$L'_{i,t} = \begin{cases} 2, & w_{i,t} = 0 \\ 7, & w_{i,t} = 1 \end{cases} \tag{7}$$

The value of $L_{i,t}$ is replaced by $L'_{i,t}$, and the corresponding result is denoted by $S'_{i,t}$, $i = 1, 2, \cdots P, 1 \leq t \leq T$. For example, if $S_{i,t} = 34.58$, then $H_{i,t} = 3$, and $L_{i,t} = 4$.

(5) Scaling the value of $DSA_{i,t}(g), 1 \leq g \leq T_{i,t} \times T_{i,t}$ using the factor $\alpha_{i,t}$, and the corresponding DCT domain low-frequency coefficients of SA_i is denoted by $DSA'_{i,t}$. $\alpha_{i,t}$ can be calculated by

$$\alpha_{i,t} = \frac{S'_{i,t}}{S_{i,t}} \tag{8}$$

(6) Inverse DCT is performed on $DSA'_{i,t}, i = 1, 2, \cdots P, 1 \le t \le T$, and the signal obtained is the watermarked speech signal.

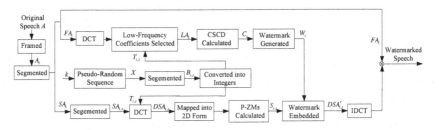

Fig. 4. The process of watermark generation and embedding

4   Content Authentication

Suppose $A^* = \{a^*(l), 1 \le l \le LA\}$ is the watermarked speech signal, and the process of content authentication is shown in Fig. 5.

Step 1: Preprocessing

(1) According to the step 1 in section 3, we can obtain the pseudo-random sequence $X = \{x_r | r = 1, 2, \ldots\}$ and the binary sequences B. Then B is cut into some segments, and each segment is cut into T non-overlapping sub-segments. The t-th sub-segment of the i-th segment is denoted by $B_{i,t}$ (see the Eq. (6)), $1 \le t \le T$, $T = m/m_1$.

(2) Denote $T_{i,t} = c + Z_{i,t} \bmod Z$, and the meaning of c, Z and $Z_{i,t}$ are similar to that in section 3.

(3) A^* is cut into P non-overlapping frames. Each frame has I samples, and the i-th frame is denoted by A_i^*, $I = LA/P$, $1 \le i \le P$. A_i^* is cut into two segments. The first and the second segment are denoted by FA_i^* and SA_i^*, respectively. FA_i^* has M samples and SA_i^* has N samples, where $M + N = I$.

Step 2: Watermark generating

(1) DCT is performed on FA_i^*, and the front of $T_{i,1} \times T_{i,1}$ DCT domain low-frequency coefficients are denoted by $LA_i^*(g), 1 \le g \le T_{i,1} \times T_{i,1}$. Then CSCD of $LA_i^*(g)$, $1 \le g \le T_{i,1} \times T_{i,1}$ is calculated by Eq. (1), and the result is denoted by $C_i^*, 1 \le i \le P$.

(2) The highest bit value of $\lfloor C_i^* \rfloor$ is denoted by H_i^*. H_i^* is converted into binary sequences $W_i^* = \{w_{i,t}^* | w_{i,t}^* \in (0,1), 1 \le t \le T\}$. If the bit number of W_i^* is less than T, then the method of left cycle shift will be taken to meet the condition. W_i^* is the watermark generated of the i-th frame.

Step 3: Watermark extraction and content authentication

(1) SA_i^* is cut into T segments. The t-th segment is denoted by $SA_{i,t}^*, 1 \le t \le T$.

(2) DCT is performed on $SA_{i,t}^*$, and the corresponding coefficient is denoted by $DSA_{i,t}^*$. Denote $DSA_{i,t}^*(g), 1 \le g \le T_{i,t} \times T_{i,t}$ as the front $T_{i,t} \times T_{i,t}$ DCT domain low-frequency coefficients of the t-th segment.

(3) $DSA_{i,t}^*(g), 1 \le g \le T_{i,t} \times T_{i,t}$ is mapped into 2D form by using the Eq. (2). Then the p-ZMs of the 2D signals are calculated by using the Eq. (3), and the results are denoted by $S_{i,t}^*, i = 1, 2, \cdots P, 1 \le t \le T$.

(4) The second highest bit value of $S_{i,t}^*$ is denoted by $L_{i,t}^*$, and the watermark extracted of the i-th frame is denoted by $\hat{W}_i^* = \{ \hat{w}_{i,t}^*, | \hat{w}_{i,t}^* \in (0,1), 1 \le t \le T \}$, $\hat{w}_{i,t}^*$ is generated by the following rule.

$$\hat{w}_{i,t}^* = \begin{cases} 0, & \lfloor L_{i,t}^*/5 \rfloor = 0 \\ 1, & \lfloor L_{i,t}^*/5 \rfloor = 1 \end{cases} \tag{9}$$

(5) Content authentication

If $\sum_{t=1}^{T} w_{i,t}^* \oplus \hat{w}_{i,t}^* = 0$, it indicates that the i-th speech frame is original.

If $\sum_{t=1}^{T} w_{i,t}^* \oplus \hat{w}_{i,t}^* \ne 0$, it indicates that the i-th speech frame has been tampered.

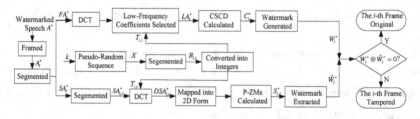

Fig. 5. The process of content authentication

5   Performance Analysis

5.1   Embedding Capacity

The definition of embedding capacity is the number of watermark bits embedded in per second. Let denote V_w as the embedding capacity of the proposed scheme and f_s(Hz) as the sampling rate of the original speech signal. The number of frames in per second is f_s/I, where I represents the length of each frame. According to section 3, the number of watermark bits embedded in each frame is T. So, the embedding capacity is computed by

$$V_w = \frac{T \cdot f_s}{I}(bit/s) \tag{10}$$

For the proposed scheme, one watermark bit is embedded in 1 segment. While in [8,9], one watermark bit is embedded in 9 segments. So, the embedding capacity V'_w of the proposed scheme in [8,9] is computed by

$$V'_w = \frac{T \cdot f_s}{9I}(bit/s) \tag{11}$$

From the Eq. (10) and (11), we can obtain that the embedding capacity of the proposed scheme is 9 times as that in [8,9] theoretically.

5.2   Inaudibility Analysis

The inaudibility means that the watermark embedded is to be inaudible, which reflects the change degree of original speech after watermarking. In this paper, signal to noise ratio (SNR) is used to test the inaudibility objectively. The definition of SNR is as follow [5]

$$SNR = 10 lg \left(\frac{\sum_{n=1}^{LA} a(l)^2}{\sum_{l=1}^{LA} \left(a(l) - a'(l) \right)^2} \right) \tag{12}$$

where $a(l)$ is the original speech signal, and $a'(l)$ is the watermarked speech signal.

5.3   Time Efficiency Analysis

In the following, the time efficiency of the proposed scheme is compared with that in [8,9]. Denote A as the original signal, which is cut into some segments, and $A_i = \{a(j), 1 \le j \le n\}$ is denoted as one segment of A. Supposed 1 watermark bit will be embedded in speech signal A. In [8,9], 9 continuous segments are needed, and the pseudo-Zernike transform are performed on all the speech samples($9 \times n$). In this paper, the pseudo-Zernike transform are performed on m ($m < n$) DCT domain low-frequency coefficients of A_i only. So, the efficiency of the proposed scheme is $9 \times n/m$ times as that in [8,9] theoretically.

5.4   The Ability against Feature-Analysed Substitution Attack

For some existing content-based speech (audio) content authentication algorithms, the watermark embedding and content authentication process can be described as shown in Fig. 6(a) and (b), respectively. For these schemes, the features used to generate watermark are public to attackers, which are vulnerable to feature-analysed substitution attack. The steps can be described as follows.

Supposed that A^* is the watermarked speech signal.

(1) Attackers calculated the features used to generate watermark, and the result is denoted by C. Let W' be the watermark ciphertext generated by C and the secret key K, and W' is calculated by the following expression.

$$W' = f(C, K) \qquad (13)$$

where $f(\cdot)$ is the function of watermark generation.

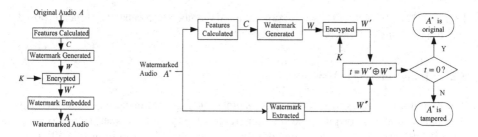

(a) Watermark embedding   (b) Content authentication

Fig. 6. The process of watermark embedding and content authentication

(2) For some existing watermark schemes, the watermark extraction process doesn't need the secret key [5]. It is possible for attackers to extract the watermark ciphertext W' from A^*. Then attackers find other speech (A_1^*) having the same features and watermark extracted as A^* to substitute A^*.

For the authentication client, the features of A_1^* is C, and the watermark generated by C and the secret key K is W'. Meanwhile the watermark extracted from A_1^* is W' too. The content substituted can get through the verification at the authentication client. So, the authentication client can't detect the feature-analysed substitution attack.

Based on the analysis above, we conclude that the content-based content authentication algorithms need to satisfy the principle that the features used to generate watermark and the watermark extracted need to be secrets for attackers(as shown in Fig. 7). For one scheme, if the condition is satisfied, it is difficult for attackers to obtain the features used to generate watermark and the watermark extracted. So the scheme is robust against feature-analysed substitution attack.

For the scheme proposed in this paper, the watermark extraction and content authentication method (shown in Fig. 5) meet the condition. The DCT domain low-frequency coefficients used to generate and extract watermark are unknown to attackers. So, the proposed scheme is against the feature-analysed substitution attack. In the following, the ability against the feature-analysed substitution attack is analysed theoretically.

According the watermark generation and embedding method, the watermark embed is T binary bits. If one frame is subject to feature-analysed substitution attack, the probability that the watermark generated and extracted are equal is $1/2^T$, which is the probability that the frame substituted is not detected. That is, for one frame, the ability against feature-analysed substitution attack A_s is

$$A_s = 1 - \frac{1}{2^T} \qquad (14)$$

where T represents the length of watermark embedded in each frame.

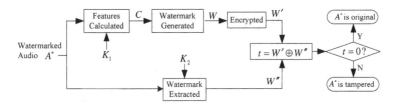

Fig. 7. The process of content authentication method robust against feature-analysed substitution attack

6   Simulation Results

In the following, the inaudibility, the robustness to common signal processing operations and the tamper location ability against malicious tampers are tested. We choose 16-bit quantified mono speech signal sampled at 22.05 kHz as the test speech, which is WAVE format. The order of p-ZMs is 17, and other important parameters are set as follows: k=0.6, $\mu = 3.7$, c=4, Z=10, LA=512000, P=100, M=1024, N=4096, m=16, m_1=4, T=4.

6.1   Inaudibility Test

Different type voice, containing adult male voice, adult female voice and children voice, were chosen to evaluate the inaudibility. Table 1 lists the SNR values, from which we can concluded that the inaudibility of the proposed scheme is good.

Table 1. The SNR values of different type voice

Voice type	SNR(dB)
Adult male voice	37.5237
Adult female voice	36.2543
Children voice	36.1301

6.2   The Robustness to Common Signal Processing Operations

It is known that some existing speech content authentication schemes are fragile to common signal processing operations [4,7], which is unsuitable under some circumstances. Considering the practical applications, the scheme proposed is robust to common signal processing and fragile to hostile attacks. In the following, the bit error rate (BER) is used to measure the reliability, and the values are compared with the robust watermark scheme [11]. The definition of BER is shown as [10]

$$\text{BER} = \frac{1}{P \times T} \sum_{i=1}^{P} \sum_{t=1}^{T} w_{i,t}^* \otimes \hat{w}_{i,t}^* \tag{15}$$

where $\otimes$ is the exclusive or (XOR) operator, and $P \times T$ is the total number of watermark bits in this paper.

Table 2. The BER values under various common signal processing

Ref.[11]		Our	
Common signal processing	BER	Common signal processing	BER
MP3 Compression (48kbps)	0.4578	MP3 Compression (48kbps)	0.3572
MP3 Compression (96kbps)	0	MP3 Compression (96kbps)	0.0361
MP3 Compression (128kbps)	0	MP3 Compression (128kbps)	0
Denoiser (-80dB)	0.0078	Denoiser (-80dB)	0
Denoiser (-60dB)	0.0361	Denoiser (-60dB)	0.0067
Re-sampling (44.1→8→44.1kHz)	0.0009	Re-sampling (22.05→8→22.05kHz)	0
Low pass filtering (11.025kHz)	—	Low pass filtering (11.025kHz)	0

The BER values of male voice under various common signal processing operations are listed and compared with [11] in Table2. It's worth noting that, the audio sampling rate is 44.1kHz in [11], while the speech sampling rate is 22.05kHz in this paper. The comparison is just used to indicate that the proposed scheme in this paper is robustness to common signal processing operations.

6.3   Tamper Location Test

The tamper location results of the watermarked speech signal subject to common signal processing operations and malicious tampers are shown in the following section, in which $TA(i)=0$ means the corresponding speech frame is not maliciously attacked, while $TA(i)=1$ means the corresponding speech frame is maliciously attacked.

(1) The tamper location result of non-attack

Fig. 8 shows the watermarked speech signal with non-attack and the corresponding tamper location result. Fig. 8(b) shows that the number of speech frames attacked is 0 when the watermarked audio is non-attacked.

(2) The tamper location result of silent attack

The watermarked speech samples 20481~35840 were kept silent. Fig. 9 shows the watermarked speech signal attacked and the corresponding location result.

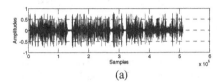
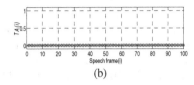

(a)   (b)

Fig. 8. The watermarked speech with non-attack and the corresponding tamper location result

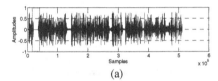
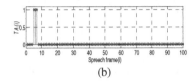

(a)   (b)

Fig. 9. The watermarked speech silent attacked and the corresponding tamper location result

(3) The tamper location result of insertion attack

Insert 5120 samples at the 317440-th sample of the watermarked speech. Fig. 10 shows the maliciously tampered watermarked speech signal and the corresponding location result.

(4) The tamper location result of deletion attack

The watermarked speech samples from the 463159-th to the 473399-th were deleted. Fig. 11 shows the maliciously tampered watermarked speech signal and the corresponding location result.

(5) The tamper location result of feature-analysed substitution attack

Supposed that attackers select one frame (the 44-th) randomly, denoted by F, to perform the feature-analysed substitution attack, as follows

① F is cut into 5 segments, and the i-th segment is denoted by F_i, $1 \leq i \leq 5$.

② DCT is performed on F_1, and the DCT domain low frequency coefficients are selected(supposed 36 coefficients) which is used to obtain CSCD and generate watermark. The CSCD is $C=5.0432$. According the watermark generating method, watermark generated is $W = \{1101\}$.

③ Attackers search to find other 4 speech segments, denoted by F_i', $2 \leq i \leq 5$, from which the watermark extracted is W. For F_i', $2 \leq i \leq 5$, the DCT domain low frequency coefficients used to extract watermark are 36, 64, 36, and 49, respectively. Then substitute the content of F_i by using F_i', $2 \leq i \leq 5$, to perform the feature-analysed substitution attack.

The DCT domain low frequency coefficients used to generate and extract watermark are related to the secret k (k=0.6), see section 4. That is the DCT domain low frequency coefficients attackers selected randomly are different to that of authentication client selecting with high probability. So, the watermark generated by F_i is distinct to that extracted from F_i' at the authentication client, $2 \leq i \leq 5$. Fig. 12 shows the watermarked speech signal attacked and the corresponding location results.

(6) In the following, on the basis of the test above, we verify the robustness of the proposed scheme to common signal processing operations, which is necessary for content authentication algorithms in some situations. And the false alarm probability, which is the probability of declaring speech frame without tampers as tampered speech farme by authentication client [5] is analyzed too.

The watermarked speech signal (Fig. 12(a)) is re-sampled (22.05→16→22.05kHz). Fig. 13 shows the processed signal and the corresponding location result.

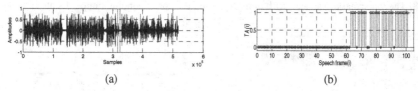

(a)   (b)

Fig. 10. The watermarked speech subject to insertion attack and the corresponding tamper location result

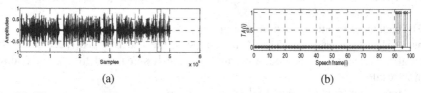

(a)   (b)

Fig. 11. The watermarked speech subject to deletion attack and the corresponding tamper location result

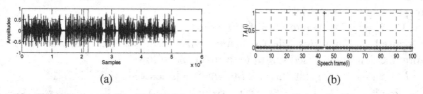

(a)   (b)

Fig. 12. The watermarked speech subject to feature-analysed substitution attack and the corresponding tamper location result

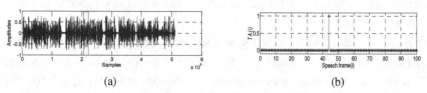

(a)   (b)

Fig. 13. The watermarked speech subject to feature-analysed substitution attack and re-sampling operation and the corresponding tamper location result

According to the simulation results above, we can conclude that the tamper location ability against malicious tampers of the proposed scheme is excellent; and the maliciously tampered speech can also be detected after being subjected to common signal processing operations, which reflect that the proposed scheme can distinguish the common signal processing operations and the malicious attacks, and the false alarm probability is 0.

7   Conclusion

An efficient speech content authentication algorithm based on coefficients self-correlation degree is proposed in this paper. The definition and properties of coefficients self-correlation degree in frequency domain are given, and the robustness of pseudo-Zernike moments of discrete cosine transform domain low-frequency coefficients is analyzed. Watermark bits are generated by coefficients self-correlation degree and embedded by quantizing the pseudo-Zernike moments of discrete cosine transform domain low-frequency coefficients. The watermark embedding method increases the embedding capacity and improves the efficiency. Experimental results show that the proposed speech content authentication algorithm is efficient.

Acknowledgments. This paper is supported by the National Natural Science Foundation of China (grant Nos. 61170226, 60970122), the Fundamental Research Funds for the Central Universities (grant Nos. SWJTU11CX047, SWJTU12ZT02), and the Young Innovative Research Team of Sichuan Province (grant No. 2011JTD0007). We also thank the anonymous reviewers for their constructive suggestions.

References

1. Ma, Z., Zhang, X., Yang, J.: A Novel Dual Watermarking Scheme for Audio Copyright Protection and Content Authentication. In: Tan, Y., Shi, Y., Tan, K.C. (eds.) ICSI 2010, Part II. LNCS, vol. 6146, pp. 149–156. Springer, Heidelberg (2010)
2. Chen, N., Zhu, J.: A Multipurpose Audio Watermarking Scheme for Copyright Protection and Content Authentication. In: IEEE International Conference on Multimedia and Expo., pp. 221–224 (2008)
3. Li, J., Wang, R.D.: Audio Aggregation Zero-Watermarking Algorithm Based on(k,n/k=n). In: IEEE International Conference on Signal Processing Systems, pp. 644–648 (2010)
4. Jiang, W.Z.: Fragile Audio Watermarking Algorithm Based on SVD and DWT. In: IEEE International Conference on Intelligent Computing and Integrated Systems, pp. 83–86 (2010)
5. Wang, H.X., Fan, M.Q.: Centroid-based Semi-Fragile Audio Watermarking in Hybrid Domain. Science in China Series F-Information Sciences 53, 619–633 (2010)
6. Xie, L., Zhang, J.S., He, H.J.: A Novel Robust Audio Watermarking Scheme Based on Nonuniform Discrete Fourier Transform. Chinese Journal of Computers 29(9), 1711–1721 (2006)

7. Chen, O.T.C., Liu, C.H.: Content-dependent watermarking scheme in compressed speech with identifying manner and location of attacks. IEEE Transactions on Audio, Speech, and Language Processing 15(5), 1605–1616 (2007)
8. Wang, X.Y., Ma, T.X., Niu, P.P.: A Pseudo-Zernike Moments Based Audio Watermarking Scheme Robust Against Desynchronization Attacks. Computers and Electrical Engineering 37(4), 425–443 (2011)
9. Xiang, S.J., Huang, J.W., Yang, R., Wang, C.T., Liu, H.M.: Robust audio watermarking based on low-order zernike moments. In: Shi, Y.Q., Jeon, B. (eds.) IWDW 2006. LNCS, vol. 4283, pp. 226–240. Springer, Heidelberg (2006)
10. Lei, B.Y., Song, I.Y., Li, Z.: Blind and Robust Audio Watermarking Scheme Based on SVD–DCT. Signal Processing 91(8), 1973–1984 (2011)
11. Wang, X.Y., Niu, P.P., Yang, H.Y.: A Robust, Digital-Audio Watermarking Method. IEEE Multimedia 16(3), 60–69 (2009)

Saliency-Based Region Log Covariance Feature for Image Copy Detection

Xin He, Huiyun Jing, Qi Han, and Xiamu Niu

Department of Computer Science and Technology, Harbin Institute of Technology, No.92, West Da-Zhi Street, Harbin, China

Abstract. This paper introduces a novel global feature-based image copy detection approach. Firstly, Space-based and Object-based saliency detection methods are combined to generate salient region represented by an ellipse. Then the covariance matrix of various image features extracted from the elliptically salient region is formed and log covariance matrix is applied on the covariance matrix for low computational complexity. 28 independent numbers from log covariance matrix are regarded as the region feature vector, the similarity of which can be measured by L_2 norm. The experimental results show that our proposed approach achieves similar or better performance than GIST and log covariance matrix based SCOV for image copy detection.

Keywords: Saliency detection, Global feature, Log covariance matrix, Image copy detection.

1 Introduction

With the rapid development of network technology and widespread application of multimedia, more and more multimedia data are distributed through networks. However, their rapid distribution on the networks has created new problems to multimedia publishers, owners and carriers, such as copyright infringements and waste of storage space and network bandwidth. Therefore, copyright protection and management has become a pressing and important issue.

Digital watermarking and content-based copy detection (CBCD) are two general techniques for fighting piracy and protecting intellectual property, which are different from digital tampering detection [1]. Watermarking approach embeds identifying information of a producer, owner, distributor and user into the media prior to distribution. The watermark can be extracted to prove ownership even when the watermarked media is corrupted by intentional or unintentional operations such as translation, rotation, cropping and scaling. Watermarking approach has two obvious disadvantages as follows. First, watermarking approach changes the media content, which will lead to degrade the media content quality. Second, watermarking approach must be performed before distributing the media. Once the media is distributed without watermarking, watermarking approach will fail to protect the media content. In contrast to watermarking, CBCD does not

Y.Q. Shi, H.J. Kim, and F. Pérez-González (Eds.): IWDW 2012, LNCS 7809, pp. 327–335, 2013.

introduce any distortion to the media or involve any form of embedding operation. CBCD uses the media itself to extract a distinctive feature as an identifier. Therefore, CBCD approaches have emerged in recent years for monitoring illegal copies and copyright protection.

A variety of approaches have been proposed for content-based image copy detection. The key issue of CBCD is to extract transformation-invariant features from potential copies and the original images. Therefore, most current approaches can be generally divided into two categories: global feature-based approach [2–4] and local feature-based approach [5–8]. Global feature-based approaches are generally easy to extract and compact to storage, yet they usually fail to detect the copies with local transformations. Although local feature-based approaches have been proven to be relatively more robust compared to global feature-based approaches, they are too computationally expensive and require a huge amount of storage space.

Inspired by Zheng [4], a novel global feature-based approach for image copy detection is proposed in this paper. The framework of our approach is shown in Fig. 1. Different from Zheng [4], our saliency map combines space and salient-object saliency. Moreover, the log coyariance matrix computed from a covariance matrix is applied as a feature vector, which lies in Euclidean space and has low computational complexity and high discrimination.

The rest of this paper is organized as follows. The details of our previous saliency detection methods are described and a simple region extraction method combining two kinds of saliency detection is introduced in Section 2. Section 3 details log covariance matrix based feature vector extraction method, where only 7 features are used. Experimental results and comparisons are presented and discussed in Section 4, and conclusions are given in Section 5.

2 Saliency Detection and Region Extraction

Visual attention is the ability of the Human Visual System (HVS) to select regions of interest that contain salient information and thus reduces the computational complexity. There are many models to functionally account for visual attention. The saliency based visual attention model is widely used due to fast, stimulus-driven and independent of the knowledge in the scene. Visual saliency makes important or interesting regions/parts pop out from their neighbors, and immediately grabs our perceptual attention. Extracted salient regions/parts facilitate further processing to perform high-level tasks such as video compression [9], objects discovery [10] and product search [11].

Generally saliency detection can be classified into space-based saliency detection and salient object-based saliency detection. Space-based saliency detection is associated with the prediction of human eye fixation data [12–16]. Space-based saliency detection has worked well in finding a few fixation locations in natural images, but has not been able to accurately detect where the salient object should be [17]. So the focus of salient object-based saliency detection is to detect the salient objects/regions [17–20]. With a more comprehensive consideration of

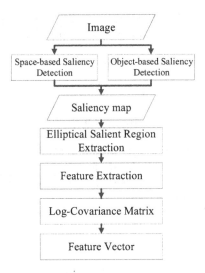

Fig. 1. The framework of our approach

image saliency, we combine space-based saliency detection and salient object-based saliency detection to extract a salient region represented by an ellipse. Our previous works [21, 22] have designed the two kinds of saliency detection algorithms, which are simple and efficient.

2.1   Space-Based Saliency Detection

Our space-based saliency detection [21] is achieved by extracting DCT magnitude of local region and using local and global kernel density estimation. DCT magnitude represents the energy information of local region in the image.

In the first stage, 2D-DCT operates on 3×3 block around pixel **i**. The absolute values of DCT coefficients are considered as the feature of each pixel. For the sake of robustness, we use $F_i = [f_i^1 f_i^2, \ldots, f_i^6]$ to represent the feature of pixel **i**.

In the second stage, we perform a kernel density estimation to compute $K_{global}(F_i)$ as follows.

$$K_{global}(F_i) = \frac{\sum_{j=1}^{M} \kappa(F_i - F_j)}{\sum_{i=1}^{M} \sum_{j=1}^{M} \kappa(F_i - F_j)} \tag{1}$$

where M is the total number of pixels in the image.

In the third stage, we choose 7×7 window around pixel **i** as the center-surround region of pixel **i**. Each window has 49 features which is represented as $F_1, F_2, \ldots, F_{49}$. Then we use the following equation to calculate $K_{local}(F_i)$

$$K_{local}(F_i) = \frac{1}{\sum_{j=1}^{49} \exp(\frac{-1+\rho(F_i, F_j)}{\sigma^2})} \tag{2}$$

where $\rho(F_i, F_j)$ is equal to $trace(\frac{F_i^T F_j}{\|F_i\|\|F_j\|})$ and σ is set to 0.007 as default value. The final stage calculates the space-based saliency of each pixel as follows.

$$S_{ss}(i) = \frac{K_{local}(F_i)}{K_{global}(F_i)} \tag{3}$$

2.2   Salient Object-Based Saliency Detection

Our salient object-based saliency detection [22] utilizes the generic knowledge of salient regions, including spatial information and contrast information.

Given an image, we firstly use region based contrast method[20] (RC) to compute saliency of region contrast.

$$S_{rc}(r_k) = \sum_{r_k \neq r_i} \exp(-D_s(r_k, r_i)/\delta_s^2)\omega(r_i)D_c(r_k, r_i) \tag{4}$$

where r_k and r_i denote the regions segmented by graph-based image segmentation method, $\omega(r_i)$ is the weight of region r_i, $D_c(\cdot, \cdot)$ is the color distance metric between the two regions, $D_s(\cdot, \cdot)$ is the spatial distance metric between the two regions, and δ_s is the strength of spatial weighting.

Secondly, saliency of spatial distribution is measured as follow.

$$S_{sd}(r_k) = \frac{M}{\sum_{i=1}^{M}((x_{r_k}^i - \overline{x_{r_k}})^2 + (y_{r_k}^i - \overline{y_{r_k}})^2)} \tag{5}$$

where M is the number of pixels belonging to the region r_k, and $\overline{x_{r_k}}$ and $\overline{y_{r_k}}$ respectively represent the mean of x coordinates and y coordinates of the pixels belonging to the region r_k.

The two saliency maps are normalized and linearly combined into the final object-based saliency map as follows.

$$S_{os}(r_k) = \frac{1}{2}(\mathcal{N}(S_{sd}(r_k)) + \mathcal{N}(S_{rc}(r_k))) \tag{6}$$

where $\mathcal{N}(\cdot)$ normalizes the value to be in [0,1].

2.3   Elliptically Salient Region Extraction

For simple and fast extraction of salient region, we firstly binarize the saliency map using a threshold as follows.

$$S_{bw} = \begin{cases} 1, & S_{ss} \geq T_{ss} \text{ or } S_{os} \geq T_{os}, \\ 0, & \text{otherwise.} \end{cases} \tag{7}$$

In order to achieve invariance, an ellipse is fitted to the salient region irregular shape. Then the elliptically salient region is used to extract features.

3   Saliency-Based Log Covariance Matrix

Once the elliptically salient region has been generated, these following features $\mathcal{F} = \{\mathbf{f_n}\}$ are chosen to form covariance descriptors according to: spatial information, color information, and gradient information.

$$\mathcal{F}(x,y) = [Dist\ R\ G\ B\ \frac{\partial I}{\partial x}\ \frac{\partial I}{\partial y}\ \sqrt{(\frac{\partial I}{\partial x})^2 + (\frac{\partial I}{\partial y})^2}]^T \tag{8}$$

where $Dist(\cdot,\cdot)$ represents the distance of each pixel (x,y) from the center, $R(\cdot,\cdot)$, $G(\cdot,\cdot)$ and $B(\cdot,\cdot)$ are RGB values of each pixel, $\frac{\partial I}{\partial x}(\cdot,\cdot)$ and $\frac{\partial I}{\partial y}(\cdot,\cdot)$ are the intensity gradients along x and y, respectively.

Then the covariance matrix is defined on $\mathcal{F}$ as follows.

$$\mathcal{C} = \frac{1}{N-1}\sum_{n=1}^{N}(\mathbf{f_n} - \mu)(\mathbf{f_n} - \mu)^T \tag{9}$$

where μ is the mean feature vector in $\mathcal{F}$. The covariance matrix provides a natural way to fuse multiple feature vectors. $\mathbf{f_n}$ is 7 dimensional and $\mathcal{C}$ is a 7×7 matrix.

Riemannian metric is applied to measure the similarity of two covariance matrices [23].

$$\rho(\mathcal{C}_1,\mathcal{C}_2) = \sqrt{\sum_{i=1}^{7}\ln^2 \lambda_i(\mathcal{C}_1,\mathcal{C}_2)} \tag{10}$$

where $\lambda_i(\mathcal{C}_1,\mathcal{C}_2)$ are the generalized eigenvalues of $\mathcal{C}_1$ and $\mathcal{C}_2$, computed from

$$\lambda_i\mathcal{C}_1\mathbf{x_i} - \mathcal{C}_2\mathbf{x_i} = 0 \tag{11}$$

where $\mathbf{x_i} \neq 0$ are the generalized eigenvectors.

However covariance matrix does not lie on a Euclidean space and Riemannian metric has high computational complexity. In order to solve this problem, a novel log covariance matrix has been proposed on the covariance matrix [24]. The log covariance matrix is computed as follows.

Given a $d \times d$ covariance matrix $\mathcal{C}$, the singular value decomposition (SVD) of $\mathcal{C}$ is denoted as $\mathcal{C} = UDU^T$, where $D = diag(\lambda_1, \lambda_2, \ldots, \lambda_d)$ is the diagonal matrix of eigenvalues, and U is an orthonormal matrix. Then the log covariance matrix $\mathcal{L}$ is defined as follows.

$$\mathcal{L} = \log(\mathcal{C}) = U \cdot diag(\log(\lambda_1), \log(\lambda_2), \ldots, \log(\lambda_d)) \cdot U^T \tag{12}$$

Then, the distance between two covariance matrices $\mathcal{C}_1$ and $\mathcal{C}_2$ can be simply and easily measured by Euclidean norm, specifically,

$$\rho(\mathcal{C}_1,\mathcal{C}_2) = \| \log(\mathcal{C}_1) - \log(\mathcal{C}_2)\| = \|\mathcal{L}_1 - \mathcal{L}_2\| \tag{13}$$

Because $\mathcal{C}$ is a 7×7 symmetric matrix, $\mathcal{L}$ is also a 7×7 symmetric matrix. Due to its symmetry, $\mathcal{L}$ has only 28 independent numbers. Then 28 numbers are extracted from $\mathcal{L}$ and regarded as the region feature vector $\mathbf{V} = [v_1 \ v_2 \ \dots \ v_{28}]$. The L_2 norm is used to compute the similarity of two region feature vectors. It is apparent that region feature vector has the advantages of low computational complexity compared to covariance matrix.

4   Experimental Results

Our proposed approach has been applied for image copy detection. We performed experiments on a publicly available Copydays dataset provided by Douze et al. [25], which is composed of their holidays photos. The Copydays dataset contains 157 original images and the following three kinds of artificial attacks are chosen for evaluation.

1. Cropping (ranging from 10 to 80: 10, 15, 20, 30, 40, 50, 60, 70, 80);
2. Scale (1/16 pixels) and JPEG compression (JPEG quality factors: 15, 20, 30, 50 and 70);
3. Rotation (90,180) and Flipping (vertical, horizontal).

Each original image in turn is used as query image to retrieve the attacked copies of the image. The precision is defined as follows.

$$\text{Precision} = \frac{\text{number of relevant images retrieved}}{\text{number of images retrieved}} \quad (14)$$

Three global feature-based image copy detection approaches are evaluated in our experiments. GIST [25, 26]: L_2 norm is used for similarity measure; Log covariance matrix based Salient Covariance (SCOV) [4]: log covariance matrix is used to form a feature vector and L_2 norm is used for similarity measure; Our approach: L_2 norm is used for similarity measure. The experimental results are shown in Table 1, Table 2 and Table 3.

Table 1. Precision performance for cropped copy detection

Feature	% of cropping							
	10	20	30	40	50	60	70	80
GIST	1	1	1	0.96	0.72	0.42	0.21	0.11
SCOV(LoG)	1	0.99	0.97	0.91	0.82	0.72	0.55	0.43
Our approach	1	0.99	0.98	0.95	0.88	0.72	0.58	0.43

Table 1 and Table 2 show our approach achieves better performance than SCOV(LoG) under 30% to 50% of cropping, and achieves similar results with SCOV(LoG) under others. Table 3 shows that our approach is robust against rotation attack and invariant against flipping attack compared to GIST and SCOV(LoG).

Table 4 shows the dimensions of SCOV and our approach. Compared with 45 dimension of SCOV, our feature vector is only 28 dimensional, which is more compact than SCOV.

Table 2. Precision performances for JPEG compressed copy detection

Feature	jpeg quality factor				
	15	20	30	50	75
GIST	1	1	1	1	1
SCOV(LoG)	0.98	0.99	1	1	1
Our approach	0.98	0.99	1	1	1

Table 3. Precision performances for rotation and flipping copy detection

Feature	rotation		flipping	
	90	180	vertical	horizontal
GIST	0.013	0.09	0.19	0.39
SCOV(LoG)	0.81	0.96	0.96	1
Our approach	0.94	0.96	0.96	1

Table 4. The dimension of feature vector

	SCOV	Our approach
Dimension	45	28

5   Conclusions and Future Work

We have proposed a novel saliency-based region log covariance feature for image
copy detection. Based on space and salient object saliency detection, elliptically
salient region is firstly extracted. And in the elliptical region, seven features of
each pixel are used to form region covariance matrix. For low computational
complexity of similarity measure, log covariance matrix is applied on the covariance matrix. Finally, due to symmetry of the log covariance matrix, a region
feature vector is formed by 28 independent numbers in the log covariance matrix,
the similarity of which can be measured by L_2 norm. Compared to GIST and
log covariance matrix based SCOV, experiments on a public dataset indicate our
approach has the similar or better performance.

Acknowledgments. This work is supported by the National Natural Science
Foundation of China (60832010, 61100187), the Fundamental Research Funds
for the Central Universities (Grant No. HIT. NSRIF. 2010046) and the China
Postdoctoral Science Foundation (2011M500666).

References

1. Popescu, A.C., Farid, H.: Exposing digital forgeries by detecting traces of resampling. IEEE Transactions on Signal Processing 53(2), 758–767 (2005)
2. Kim, C.: Content-based image copy detection. Signal Processing: Image Communication 18(3), 169–184 (2003)
3. Hsiao, J.H., Chen, C.S., Chien, L.F., Chen, M.S.: A new approach to image copy detection based on extended feature sets. IEEE Transactions on Image Processing 16(8), 2069–2079 (2007)
4. Zheng, L., Qiu, G., Huang, J., Fu, H.: Salient covariance for near-duplicate image and video detection. In: 2011 18th IEEE International Conference on Image Processing (ICIP), pp. 2537–2540 (2011)
5. Berrani, S.A., Amsaleg, L., Gros, P.: Robust content-based image searches for copyright protection. In: Proceedings of the 1st ACM international workshop on Multimedia Databases, MMDB 2003, pp. 70–77. ACM, New York (2003)
6. Ke, Y., Sukthankar, R., Huston, L.: Efficient near-duplicate detection and sub-image retrieval. In: Proceedings of the 12th Annual ACM International Conference on Multimedia, MULTIMEDIA 2004, pp. 869–876. ACM, New York (2004)
7. Jégou, H., Douze, M., Schmid, C., Pérez, P.: Aggregating local descriptors into a compact image representation. In: 2010 IEEE Conference on Computer Vision and Pattern Recognition (CVPR), pp. 3304–3311 (June 2010)
8. Ling, H., Cheng, H., Ma, Q., Zou, F., Yan, W.: Efficient image copy detection using multiscale fingerprints. IEEE Multimedia 19(1), 60–69 (2012)
9. Itti, L.: Automatic foveation for video compression using a neurobiological model of visual attention. IEEE Transactions on Image Processing 13(10), 1304–1318 (2004)
10. Luo, Y., Yuan, J., Xue, P., Tian, Q.: Saliency density maximization for efficient visual objects discovery. IEEE Trans. Circuits Syst. Video Techn. 21(12), 1822–1834 (2011)
11. He, J., Feng, J., Liu, X., Cheng, T., Lin, T.H., Chung, H., Chang, S.F.: Mobile product search with bag of hash bits and boundary reranking. In: 2012 IEEE Conference on Computer Vision and Pattern Recognition (CVPR). IEEE (2012)
12. Itti, L., Koch, C., Niebur, E.: A model of saliency-based visual attention for rapid scene analysis. IEEE Transaction on Pattern Analysis and Machine Intelligence 20(11), 1254–1259 (1998)
13. Bruce, N.D.B., Tsotsos, J.K.: Saliency based on information maximization. Advances in Neural Information Processing Systems 18, 155–162 (2006)
14. Zhang, L., Tong, M.H., Marks, T.K., Shan, H., Cottrell, G.W.: Sun: a bayesian framework for saliency using natural statistics. Journal of Vision 8(7), 32–51 (2008)
15. Gao, D., Mahadevan, V., Vasconcelos, N.: On the plausibility of the discriminant center-surround hypothesis for visual saliency. Journal of Vision 8(7), 13–31 (2008)
16. Seo, H.J., Milanfar, P.: Static and space-time visual saliency detection by self-resemblance. Journal of Vision 9(12), 1–27 (2009)
17. Liu, T., Sun, J., Zheng, N., Tang, X., Shum, H.: Learning to detect a salient object. In: Proc. IEEE Cont. on Computer Vision and Pattern Recognition (CVPR), Minneapolis, USA (June 2007)
18. Hou, X., Zhang, L.: Saliency detection: a spectral residual approach. In: Proc. IEEE Cont. on Computer Vision and Pattern Recognition (CVPR), Minneapolis, USA (June 2007)
19. Achanta, R., Hemami, S., Estrada, F., Susstrunk, S.: Frequency-tuned salient region detection. In: Proc. IEEE Cont. on Computer Vision and Pattern Recognition (CVPR), Miami, USA, pp. 1597–1604 (June 2009)

20. Cheng, M., Zhang, G., Mitra, N., Huang, X., Hu, S.: Global contrast based salient region detection. In: Proc. IEEE Cont. on Computer Vision and Pattern Recognition (CVPR), Colorado Springs, USA, pp. 409–416 (June 2011)
21. He, X., Jing, H., Han, Q., Niu, X.: A novel bayes' theorem-based saliency detection model. IEICE Transactions on Information and Systems E94-D(12), 2545–2548 (2011)
22. He, X., Jing, H., Han, Q., Niu, X.: Salient region detection combining spatial distribution and global contrast. Optical Engineering 51(4), 047007-1–047007-4 (2012)
23. Tuzel, O., Porikli, F., Meer, P.: Region covariance: A fast descriptor for detection and classification. In: Leonardis, A., Bischof, H., Pinz, A. (eds.) ECCV 2006. LNCS, vol. 3952, pp. 589–600. Springer, Heidelberg (2006)
24. Arsigny, V., Fillard, P., Pennec, X., Ayache, N.: Log-euclidean metrics for fast and simple calculus on diffusion tensors. Magnetic Resonance in Medicine 56(2), 411–421 (2006)
25. Douze, M., Jégou, H., Sandhawalia, H., Amsaleg, L., Schmid, C.: Evaluation of gist descriptors for web-scale image search. In: Proceedings of the ACM International Conference on Image and Video Retrieval, CIVR 2009, pp. 19:1–19:8 (2009)
26. Oliva, A., Torralba, A.: Modeling the shape of the scene: A holistic representation of the spatial envelope. International Journal of Computer Vision 42, 145–175 (2001)

Blind Detection of Electronic Voice Transformation with Natural Disguise

Yong Wang, Yanhong Deng, Haojun Wu, and Jiwu Huang

School of Information Science and Technology, Sun Yat-sen University,
Higher Education Mega Center, PanYu, Guangzhou 510006, China
isswy@mail.sysu.edu.cn

Abstract. Electronic voice transformation with natural disguise ability is a common operation to change a person's voice and conceal his or her identity, which can easily cheat human ears and automatic speaker recognition(ASR) systems and thus presents threaten to security. Till now, few efforts have been reported on detection of electronic transformation, which aims to distinguish disguised voices from original voices. Therefore in this paper we investigate the principle of electronic voice transformation, and propose a blind detection approach using MFCC(Mel Frequency Cepstrum Coefficients) as the acoustic features and VQ-SVM (Vector Quantization-Support Vector Machine) as the classification method. By extensive experiments, it is demonstrated to have classification accuracy higher than 98% in most cases, indicating that the proposed approach has good performance and can be used in forensic applications.

Keywords: Electronic voice transformation, disguise, detection, forensic.

1 Introduction

Voice disguise can be classified into two categories: voice conversion and voice transformation[1][2]. Voice conversion is to transform one's voice to imitate a target person provided with the target's acoustic information, while voice transformation is to change the sound without any target. Both conceal speaker's identity and present threaten to security. However, since no target information is needed, voice transformation is much easier to implement and be adopted in criminal cases than voice conversion. Therefore, in this paper we will focus on detection of voice transformation disguise.

Voice transformation can be implemented by non-electronic and electronic means. Non-electronic means includes the alteration of voice by using a mechanic system like a mask over the mouth, a pen in the mouth or pinching the nostril. Electronic means is achieved by softwares or electronic devices. Generally, by sophisticated algorithm the electronic output sounds more natural than the non-electronic one and presents greater confusion, since people may be easier to be cheated by transformed voices that sound natural. Moreover, electronic

Y.Q. Shi, H.J. Kim, and F. Pérez-González (Eds.): IWDW 2012, LNCS 7809, pp. 336–343, 2013.

Speech Record

Fig. 1. MFCC extraction process

voice transformation has been incorporated into many softwares and electronic devices in recent years, and has been adopted in more criminal cases than before. However, research efforts on forensic of electronic voice transformation is still very insufficient. Hence in this paper we will examine detection of electronic voice transformation, which can be used in many forensic applications, especially in those related to speaker recognition. For example in forensic speaker recognition(FSR), the detection results can be used a a reference to aid the recognition decision making.

There are several voice transformation methods. Since our aim is to investigate the one with natural disguise ability that presents threaten both to human ears and to automatic speaker recognition(ASR) systems, we will focus on phase vocoder based transformation [3] because it presents the most natural disguise ability among the existing voice transformation methods, and it is prevailing.

Time and frequency characteristics of a signal, being related by Fourier transform, are not independent but of a duality relationship. Since 1950s, large collection of voice transformation solutions have been proposed which break this tradition tie between pitch and rate of playback. Among them, the most frequently used techniques are based on 'signal models' [4] and implemented by short-time Fourier transform(STFT), also referred to as phase-vocoder, that change the prosody by pitch modification[3]. The phase-vocoder based method has been incorporated in many professional and popular softwares for speech and music processing. One of such leading benchmarks is Adobe Audition[5]. In this paper we will examine the blind detection of phase vocoder prototype transformation[6] and further verify our proposed approach by its implementation in Adobe Audition.

Most of the adjacent existing researches focus on investing effects of transformation on ASR systems [1][7][8][9][10][11][12]. However, there have been no reported research efforts on blind detection of voice transformation till now. Therefore in this paper, based on the study of voice transformation principle, we will propose a blind and robust detection approach to distinguish disguised voices from original voices using MFCCs(Mel Frequency Cepstrum Coefficients)[9] as the acoustic features and VQ-SVM(Vector Quantization - Support Vector Machine)[13][14] as the classification method.

The structure of this paper is as follows. In Section 2 we introduce the model of electronic voice transformation and MFCC extraction process. In Section 3 we present our proposed blind detection approach using MFCC and VQ-SVM. Experimental results are given in Section 4. Finally we summarize conclusions and future works in Section 5.

2 Model of Electronic Voice Transformation and MFCC Extraction

In applications of audio processing, the most widely used analysis/synthesis method is short-time Fourier transform(STFT) which begins by windowing a signal to short segments. Fast Fourier transform(FFT) is then applied to each segment and the resulting spectral components can be manipulated in a variety of ways. However, due to the resolution limitation, the FFT bin frequencies generally do not represent the true frequencies(also called instantaneous frequencies). For example using a window of size 2048 and a sampling rate of 44.1kHz, the resolution in frequency domain is only 21.5Hz, which is far too coarse in lower frequency band.

By insight of the relationship between phase and frequency, phase vocoder employs phase information that the STFT ignores to improve frequency estimation. The core of phase vocoder is to compute the deviation from the FFT bin frequency to the instantaneous frequency by using phase information. Instantaneous frequency can then be computed by adding the deviation and the FFT bin frequency. Finally three numbers obtained from the FFT analysis for each sinusoid, namely bin magnitude, bin frequency and bin phase are reduced to just magnitude and transient frequency. The entire procedure can be referred to [3]. We now present it in a simple form in Equ.(1)-(3).

Firstly speech signal $x(n)$ is windowed by hamming or hanning window by Equ.(1).

$$F(k) = \sum_{n=0}^{N-1} x(n) \cdot w(n) e^{-j\frac{2\pi kn}{N}} \quad 0 \leqslant n < N \tag{1}$$

Then instantaneous magnitude $|F(k)|$ and instantaneous frequency $w(k)$ are calculated by Equ.(2) and Equ.(3) respectively,

$$|F(k)| = |\sum_{n=0}^{N-1} x(n) \cdot w(n) e^{-j\frac{2\pi kn}{N}}| \quad 0 \leqslant n < N \tag{2}$$

$$w(k) = (k + \Delta) * Fs/N \tag{3}$$

where Fs is the sampling frequency and Δ is the deviation from the kth bin frequency.

For voice transformation, transient frequency $w(k)$ is modified by Equ.(4), where α is the scale factor.

$$w'(\lfloor k * \alpha \rfloor) = w(k) * \alpha \quad 0 \leqslant k, k * \alpha < N/2 \tag{4}$$

In order to maintain the signal energy, transient magnitude is modified by Equ.(5)

$$|F'(\lfloor k * \alpha \rfloor)| = \sum_{\lfloor k*\alpha \rfloor \leqslant k*\alpha < \lfloor k*\alpha \rfloor + 1} |F(k)| \tag{5}$$

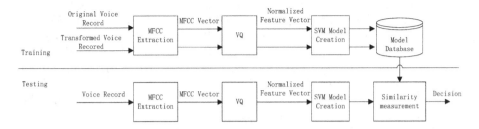

Fig. 2. Generic system using MFCCs as the feature and VQ-SVM as the classification method

The instantaneous phase $\phi'(k)$ is then calculated via the instantaneous frequency $\omega'(k)$ and the transformed FFT coefficients is obtained by Equ.(6).

$$F'(k) = |F'(k)|e^{j\phi'(k)} \tag{6}$$

Inverse FFT is performed on $F'(k)$ and the transformed signal can be obtained.

From the above transformation procedure, we know that the distribution of spectra magnitude $|F(k)|$ is changed after the transformation. Since the voice spectrum carries the natural acoustic features of vocal tract, we think that voice transformation would alter such natural features, and thus the magnitude $|F(k)|$ can be used to distinguish transformed voices from original voices. However, if $|F(k)|$ is used, the computation load will be so heavy that the whole classification process will be extremely slow. Hence we turn to MFCCs which converts the spectrum magnitudes into mel-frequency cepstrum with much less feature data, and which maintains the vocal tract acoustic features.

MFCC extraction process is shown in Fig.1. We can learn that MFCC is computed from spectrum magnitudes $|F(k)|$. The filter bank is to combine the spectrum magnitudes in each mel subband to form one contribution that reflects the vocal tract acoustic features. Furthermore the MFCC extraction algorithm compresses the data amount to shorten the classification process. In this paper a 12-order MFCC vector is extracted from each frame and the whole feature is the combination of MFCC vectors from all the frames.

3   Classification Algorithm

Durations of different speech signals are usually different. Since MFCCs are extracted along the time axis, the lengths of MFCC vectors, i.e., the numbers of MFCC vectors from different speech signals are usually different too. However, SVM requires the input features to have the same length. Hence we use VQ(vector quantization) to normalize their lengths.

Suppose $X = \{x_1, x_2, \cdots, x_T\}$ is the MFCCs consisting of T number of vectors extracted from T frames, each of which has dimension N. VQ aims to convert X into K separate clusters($K \ll T$). Each cluster is represented by a code vector, c_i, which is the centroid of the cluster. The whole set of code vectors $C = \{c_1, c_2, ..., c_K\}$ is used as the normalized feature vectors input into SVM.

SVM has become the state-of-the-art classification method in many pattern recognition applications in recent years. In most applications SVM is a binary classifier which models the decision boundary in hyper-plane with the maximum margin of separation between two classes. Reported efforts have shown that the best results for SVMs in speech applications have been obtained using the generalized linear discriminant sequence (GLDS) kernel[15][16], which creates a single characteristic vector using the sequence of features extracted from a speech signal. Hence in our SVM configuration GLDS is used as the kernel.

Generic classification system is shown in Fig.2. In training phase, MFCCs of original and transformed speech records are extracted and input into VQ box to normalize the lengths, then the normalized feature vectors are input into SVM to create the models of original and transformed speech records. In testing phase, the same process is carried on the test speech record to create its model and to calculate the similarity between the test speech record and the two models obtained in training phase. Finally a decision is made.

4   Experiments

4.1   Experiment Setup

1. Corpus

   TIMIT[17] is used as the corpus for the experiments. TIMIT is a popular corpus which has been designed for the development of automatic speech recognition systems and can be used in many other speech applications. It contains 630 speakers, 192 females and 438 males, from 8 major dialect regions of America. Each speaker reads 10 sentences to obtain a total number of 6300 records in it. All the sentences are recorded as as wav format of 16kHz sampling rate, 16-bit quantization and mono channel. The duration of each record lasts around 3 seconds.

2. Transformation methods

   Prototype of phase vocoder transformation[6] and its implementation in Adobe Audition are performed on TIMIT records to obtained transformed records. The transformation scaling factors are [0.55 : 0.05 : 1.45] which cover the range that is commonly used in real applications. Scaling factor 1.0 is excluded since it does not modify the records.

3. Training and testing configuration

   In order to simulate the real forensic scenario, we permute the 6300 records, and divide them in half into a training subset and a testing subset each of which contains 3150 records. Each record in the training subset is transformed with scaling factors [0.55 : 0.05 : 1.45] to obtained 18 transformed records. Original and transformed records in the training subset are then input into VQ-SVM to train the two models. The resulting models are used in testing phase where records in testing subset are also transformed, and

Table 1. Classification results of scenario 1 in case of phase vocoder prototype

scaling factor	0.55	0.60	0.65	0.70	0.75	0.80	0.85	0.90	0.95
TP	100%	100%	100%	100%	100%	100%	100%	98.79%	93.81%
TN	100%	100%	100%	100%	100%	100%	99.94%	99.37%	96.03%
accuracy	100%	100%	100%	100%	100%	100%	99.97%	99.08%	94.92%
scaling factor	1.05	1.10	1.15	1.20	1.25	1.30	1.35	1.40	1.45
TP	95.62%	96.63%	97.94%	98.48%	98.79%	99.27%	99.49%	99.49%	99.65%
TN	97.37%	98.29%	98.92%	99.40%	99.62%	99.78%	99.81%	99.90%	99.90%
accuracy	96.50%	97.46%	98.43%	98.99%	99.21%	99.53%	99.65%	99.70%	99.78%

Table 2. Classification results of scenario 1 in case of Adobe Audition

scaling factor	0.55	0.60	0.65	0.70	0.75	0.80	0.85	0.90	0.95
TP	99.65%	99.46%	99.37%	98.89%	98.48%	97.30%	66.70%	88.13%	72.16%
TN	99.81%	99.81%	99.37%	98.95%	97.81%	97.08%	73.21%	86.60%	73.08%
accuracy	99.73%	99.64%	99.37%	98.92%	98.15%	97.19%	69.96%	87.37%	72.62%
scaling factor	1.05	1.10	1.15	1.20	1.25	1.30	1.35	1.40	1.45
TP	58.63%	84.98%	79.97%	100%	100%	100%	99.97%	100%	100%
TN	65.08%	89.33%	99.05%	99.97%	100%	100%	100%	100%	100%
accuracy	61.86%	87.16%	89.51%	99.99%	100%	100%	99.99%	100%	100%

are input into VQ-SVM along with the original records. SVM outputs *accuracy*, the true classification rate, *TP*, the true classification rate for identifying transformed records, and *TN*, the true classification rate for identifying original records.

4.2   Classification Performance

For a thorough investigation we take into consideration the following two scenarios.

1) Scenario 1: Classification between the original records and the transformed records with one scaling factor, which reveals the different effects brought by different transformation degrees.

2) Scenario 2: Classification between the original records and all of the transformed records, which yields the overall performance.

Detection results of scenario 1 in case of phase vocoder prototype transformation is given in Table 1, from which we can have the following observations.

1) The farther the scaling factor is from 1.0, the higher accuracy, TP and TN are achieved, which coincides the fact that the more the records are modified the more difference will be introduced between original and transformed records.

2) TP, TN, and accuracy with scaling factors [0.95,1.05] are apparently much lower than those with other scaling factors, which is considered to be acceptable in this paper, since in real applications scaling factors in range of [0.95 1.05] are of small modification, and they generally does not change the speaker's identity.

3) With scaling factors outside [0.95 1.05] most of the accuracy, TP and TN are over 97% to 100%, indicating the proposed detection approach can distinguish the transformed and original records at a high classification rate.

Detection results in scenario 2 in case of phase vocoder prototype transformation are TP = 95.81%, TN = 98.41%, and accuracy = 97.11%. Since there has been no reported research efforts on such detection, comparison and evaluation are quite difficult to make. However, since the detection results are to be used as reference for the FSR decision making and a FSR system generally yields a much lower accuracy[18], we think that the performance of our proposed approach is acceptable.

Detection results of scenario 1 in case of Adobe Audition is given in Table 2, from which we can see that with scaling factors between [0.85 1.15], TP, TN and accuracy are much lower than the counterparts in case of phase vocoder prototype. They further lower the classification rates in scenario 2: TP = 75.37%, TN = 94.83%, and accuracy = 85.10%. Although detailed algorithms used in Adobe Audition are not open sources, by perception of the acoustic quality, we find that with scaling factors between [0.85 1.15], the signal transformed by Adobe Audition sounds smoother than the one transformed by the prototype. By observation of the frequency domain, we also notice that there are fewer abrupt spectral components in the former than in the latter. This smoothing post-processing by Adobe Audition removes those abrupt characteristics that are not produced by human vocal tract, and makes a transformed record sound more closer to the one that are uttered by vocal tract. With a larger transformation degree, such smoothness declines and the detection rates become similar to the counterparts in case of prototype.

5   Conclusions

In summary, in this paper the principle of voice electronic transformation is thoroughly investigated, and a blind detection using MFCCs as the acoustic features and VQ-SVM as the classification approach is proposed to distinguish disguised voices form original voices. Extensive experiments are conducted. The results show that in most cases high TP, TN and accuracy are achieved indicating that the detection results can be used as reference for forensic works. There are still many open issues worthy of investigation in future works. We will continue to improve the performance of our proposed approach, and trace other disguise methods with natural ability if they emerge.

Acknowledgements. This work is supported by the National Natural Science Foundation of China (NSFC) under Grants 61100168, the Research Fund for the Doctoral Program of Higher Education of China under Grant 20110171120052, the Fundamental Research Funds for the Central Universities under Grants 12lgpy38, and the National Natural Science Foundation of China (NSFC) under Grants F020703.

References

1. Perrot, P., Aversano, G., Chollet, G.: Voice disguise and automatic detection: Review and perspectives. In: Stylianou, Y., Faundez-Zanuy, M., Esposito, A. (eds.) WNSP 2005. LNCS, vol. 4391, pp. 101–117. Springer, Heidelberg (2007)
2. Masthoff, H.: A report on voice disguise experiment. Forensice Linguistics 3(1), 160–167 (1996)
3. Laroche, J.: Time and Pitch Scale Modification of Audio Signals. In: Applications of Digital Signal Processing to Audio and Acoustics in the International Series in Engineering and Computer Science, vol. 437, ch. 7, pp. 279–309. Springer, US (2006)
4. McAulay, R., Quatieri, T.: Speech analysis/Synthesis based on a sinusoidal representation. IEEE Trans. on Acoustics, Speech and Signal Processing 34(4), 744–754 (1986)
5. http://www.adobe.com/products/audition.html
6. Phase vocoder based voice transformation source code, http://www.dspdimension.com/smbPitchShift.cpp
7. Perrot, P., Chollet, G.: The question of disguised voice. The Journal of the Acoustical Society of America 123(5), 3878 (2008)
8. Künzel, H., Gonzalez-Rodriguez, J., Ortega-Garcia, J.: Effect of voice disguise on the performance of a forensic automatic speaker recoginition system. In: Proc. of Odyssey, pp. 153–156 (2004)
9. Reynolds, D., Rose, R.: Robust text-independent speaker identification using Gaussian mixture speaker models. IEEE Trans. Speech Audio Processing 3(1), 72–83 (1995)
10. Bonastre, J.-F., Matrouf, D., Fredouille, C.: Artificial impostor voice transformation effects on false acceptance rates. In: Proc. of Interspeech, pp. 2053–2056 (2007)
11. Matrouf, D., Bonastre, J.-F., Costa, J.P.: Effect of impostor speech transformation on automatic speaker recognition. In: Proc. of COST275 Workshop "Biometric on the internet", Hatfied, UK (2005)
12. Matrouf, D., Bonastre, J.-F., Fredouille, C.: Effect of voice transformation on impostor acceptance. In: Proc. of Int. Conf. on Acoustics, Speech, and Signal Processing, Toulouse, France (2006)
13. Linde, Y., Buzo, A., Gray, R.: An algorithm for vector quantizer design. IEEE Trans. Commun. 28, 84–94 (1980)
14. Libsvm Tool, http://www.csie.ntu.edu.tw/cjlin/libsvm
15. Campbell, W.M., Campbell, J., Reynolds, D.A., Torres-Carrasquillo, P.: Support vector machines for speaker and language recognition. Computer Speech and Language 20(2), 210–229 (2006)
16. Campbell, W.M., Singer, E., Torres-Carrasquillo, P.A., Reynolds, D.A.: Language recognition with support vector machines. In: Proc. Odyssey: The Speaker and Language Recognition Workshop, pp. 41–44 (2004)
17. TIMIT Acoustic-Phonetic Continuous Speech Corpus, http://www.ldc.upenn.edu/Catalog/CatalogEntry.jsp?catalogId=LDC93S1
18. Campbell, J.P., Shen, W., Campbell, W.M., Schwartz, R., Bonastre, J.-F., Matrouf, D.: Forensic speaker recognition. IEEE Signal Processing Magazine 26(2), 95–103 (2009)

Robust Median Filtering Detection
Based on Filtered Residual

Anjie Peng[1,2] and Xiangui Kang[1,2]

[1] School of Information Science and Technology, Sun Yat-Sen University,
Guangzhou, 510275, China
`isskxg@mail.sysu.edu.cn`
[2] State Key Laboratory of Information Security (Institute of Information Engineering,
Chinese Academy of Sciences, Beijing 100093)

Abstract. In multimedia forensics, exposing an image's processing history
draws much attention. Median filtering is a popular noise removal tool, which
has been used as a popular anti-forensics tool recently. An image is usually
saved in a compressed format such as the JPEG format. While the detection of
median filtering from a JPEG compressed image is difficult because typical filter characteristics are suppressed by JPEG quantization and block artifacts. In
this paper, we introduce a novel forensic trace – median filter residual. Median
filtering is first applied on a test image, and the difference between the initial
image and the filtered output image is called the median filter residual. The filtered residual is used as the forensic fingerprint. Thus, the interference from the
image edge and texture which is regarded as a major limitation of the existing
forensic methods can be reduced. Experimental results on a large image database show that the proposed method is very robust to JPEG post- compression,
and achieves much better performance than the existing state-of-the-art works.

Keywords: Digital image Forensics, Median filter residual, Transition
probability.

1   Introduction

Blind forensics technology can verify the authenticity of multimedia without access to
its original source, which is very important when contents can be shaved easily. Some
content preserving manipulations, such as: filtering [1-3], re-sampling [4], compression [5], and contrast enhancement [6] do not damage the authentic value of an image
in general, but their blind detection is forensically important [1-3].

The median filtering is a popular noise removal tool and image enhancement tool.
It can affect forensic methods and steganalysis methods in various ways. First, a median filter is capable of removing statistical traces of the blocking artifacts by JPEG
compression and defeat JPEG forensic algorithms [7]. It is also an effective counter-
forensics tool for hiding traces of re-sampling [9]. Additionally, the actual state of an
image prior to manipulation may influence the set of tools available to analyze the
image, or how to interpret the evidence derived from these tools. For example, in
steganalysis, the choice of a suitable spatial-domain detector might depend upon the
actual state of a cover image and its properties [10].

Y.Q. Shi, H.J. Kim, and F. Pérez-González (Eds.): IWDW 2012, LNCS 7809, pp. 344–357, 2013.

An image is usually saved in a compressed format such as the JPEG format. Recently, in multimedia forensics and steganalysis, exposing the processing history has drawn much attention [1-3]. A forensic method is generally required to be robust against lossy compression, due to the task of exposing the processing history of a possibly severely compressed multimedia. However, this is a challenging work because JPEG post compression may destroy the trace that could be utilized to detect median filtering.

In this paper, we propose to perform median filtering on a test image first and output the filtered image. We then obtain the difference between the test image and the median filtered image, which is called the median filter residual (MFR). The median filter residual is used as the forensic fingerprint. Thus, the interference from the image edge and texture, which is regarded as a limitation of the existing forensic methods, can be reduced. Then model the MFR as second-order Markov chains, calculate the transition probability as the feature, and input such feature to a support vector machine (SVM) to train a classifier. The trained classifier is applied to discriminate a median filtered image from a non-filtered image. Because the edge and texture of a test image is reduced in the MFR fingerprint, our approach can detect median filtering from JPEG compressed images with quality factor as low as 50 reliably, and outperforms the existing state-of-the-art works [1-2] quite a lot. The proposed method also distinguishes median filtering from other manipulations such as Gaussian filtering, average filtering, downscaling, and up-scaling etc.

The rest of this paper is organized as follows. In Section 2, we will briefly review existing works on detection of median filtering. In Section 3, the extraction of MFR fingerprint and the feature for median filtering are introduced. In Section 4, the proposed algorithm is compared with the sate-of-the-art methods [1-2], and our experimental results are reported. Finally, we draw the conclusion in Section 5.

2   Prior Related Works

The median filter replaces a pixel with the median of pixels in a small window of size $w \times w$. 3×3 and 5×5 median filtering are the most widely used forms of median filtering, especially the former. Median filtering is performed window by window, with the windows overlapping each other. For example, input a $M \times N$ image $x(i, j)$, and output a filtered image $y(i,j)$ as follows:

$$y(i, j) = median \ \ (x(i + h, j + v)), (h, v) \in (-\frac{w - 1}{2},..., 0,..., \frac{w - 1}{2}),$$
$$(i, j) \in (1,..., M) \times (1,..., N) \tag{1}$$

A theoretical analysis of the general relationship between the input and output distributions of median filter is very cumbersome, because it is a non-linear smoother. Hence, the analysis of median filtering has been largely confined to some specific features of interest [1].

The median filter can remove noise and preserve edges in an image, which can produce constant or nearly constant regions called streak (linear patches) or amorphous blotches [11]. Bovik analyzed this phenomenon quantitatively, and obtained the probability that the median values stemming from overlapping windows are equal.

The median value is close to the mean value (DC) in a $w \times w$ window. Assume the central pixel of a local 3×3 window is $x(i, j)$, we define the deviation energy as:

$$E(i, j) = \sum_{h=-1}^{h=1} \sum_{v=-1}^{v=1} (x(i+h, j+v) - x(i, j))^2 \tag{2}$$

After the central pixel is replaced by the median value, the deviation energy within this local $w \times w$ window is minimized. The deviation energy is reduced window by window. In general, the average deviation energy of a median filtered image is lower than that of a non-median filtered image. This characteristic is helpful to discriminate a filtered image from a non-filtered image, which is used to enhance the detection of median filtering in the following experiments.

There are some existing forensic methods of median filtering. Swaminathan et al. [12] developed a reliable technique based on the intrinsic fingerprints in digital images, to differentiate a median filtered image from an unmodified digital camera image; the true positive rate of median filtering is 70-80% at a false positive rate of 10%. Chuang et al. [13] introduced a tampering detection approach based on the empirical frequency response. Their proposed approach could distinguish median filtering from other kinds of content preserving manipulation, e.g., JPEG compression, up-sampling, down-sampling, average filtering, and histogram equalization, with an accuracy of about 90%. While these early techniques can successfully detect median filtering, they require either an accurate estimate or direct knowledge of the camera model used to capture an image. As a result, their performance is sensitive to the training data used.

Kirchner and Fridrich [1] and Cao et al. [3] take the first order difference of an input image as the forensics fingerprint. Assuming an input image is $x(i, j)$, the first order difference is defined as follows:

$$e_{i,j}^{(k,l)} = x(i, j) - x(i + k, j + l), (i, j) \in (1,..., M) \times (1,..., N) \tag{3}$$

where $(k, l) \in \{(0,1), (0,-1), (1,0), (1,1), (1,-1), (-1,0), (-1,1), (-1,-1)\}$. Assume $H^{(k,l)} = \{..., h_{-2}^{(k,l)}, h_{-1}^{(k,l)}, h_0^{(k,l)}, h_1^{(k,l)}, h_2^{(k,l)}, ...\}$ is the corresponding histogram of $e_{i,j}^{(k,l)}$. Streaking resulting from median filtering tends to increase the ratio $\rho^{(k,l)} = h_0^{(k,l)} / h_1^{(k,l)}$. Kirchner and Fridrich [1] proposed using the ratio $\rho^{(k,l)}$ as a detection statistic for median filtering. For a median filtered image, it means $\rho^{(k,l)} \gg 1$. They also developed a weighted median of this ratio to lessen the influence of saturation in an image. In order to improve the robustness against JPEG compression which defeats the method of using a weighted median of $\rho^{(k,l)}$, Kirchner and Fridrich [1] used a subtractive pixel adjacency matrix (SPAM) feature [16] to describe the first order difference $e_{i,j}^{(k,l)}$, as show in Equation 3. The detector obtained reliable results for an uncompressed image and JPEG post-compressed image with quality factor 90 and 80 on a 512 × 512 grayscale image. However, the SPAM method shares the following weakness: the robustness of the detector against compression rapidly decreases when the size of the test image and the compression quality factor become small. For example, the performance of a 3 × 3 median filtering detector severely degrades when a 512 × 384 test image is JPEG compressed with quality factor less than 90.

Cao *et al.* [3] proposed that the probability of zeros $h_0^{(k,l)}$ in the first-order difference $e_{i,j}^{(k,l)}$ of a test image in textured regions is the statistical fingerprint of median filtering. Their experimental results show that median filtering is detectable with high accuracy in the case of a median filtered image versus an original non-compressed image. However, their methods are not robust to JPEG post-compression.

Fig. 1. Example showing (a) Original image, (b) first-order difference, (c) MFR fingerprints

Median values originating from overlapping filter windows are dependent upon each other. The degree of dependence is related to the size of the window and the distance of the pixels. Yuan [2] proposed that local dependence among the pixels within a 3 × 3 window is a specific characteristic of median filtering, and constructed a 44-D feature, which is called the median filtering feature (MFF in short), to detect median filtering. The MFF method achieves better performance of detecting 3× 3 median filtering than that of the SPAM method [1], and comparable robustness to JPEG compression with the SPAM method on detection of 5 × 5 median filtering. The MFF method can also discriminate median filter from other smoothers such as a Gaussian filter and, moving average filter *etc.*

Overall, the robustness against JPEG post-compression remains a challenging problem. For example, the performance of a 3 × 3 median filtering detectors severely degrades when a 512 × 384 8-bit grayscale image is JPEG compressed with a quality factor less than 90. [1] and [3] take the first order difference $e_{i,j}^{(k,l)}$ as the forensic trace. However, the first order difference $e_{i,j}^{(k,l)}$ contains largely the edge and texture information of an image. Fig. 1a shows an original image, Fig. 1b shows its first order difference $e_{i,j}^{(1,0)}$. The edge and texture are very obvious in the first order difference (Fig. 1b). The edge and texture interfere with the median filtering detector, and thus deteriorate the performance. Chen *et al* [19] also used the first and second order differences as forensic fingerprints. Yuan [2] used the local dependence among the pixels within a 3 × 3 window. However, the local content of an image, such as edge and texture also has large impact on the detector.

3   Median Filter Residual

In order to remove the interference from the image content, such as edge and texture, we propose to extract the MFR fingerprint as follows. Apply 3 × 3 median filtering on a test image $x(i, j)$ and obtain the output image $y(i, j)$. The median filter residual $d(i, j)$ is obtained using Equation 4. Fig. 1c shows that the median filter residual contains less image content, i.e., edge and texture, compared with the image (first order) difference.

$$d(i, j) = y(i, j) - x(i, j),$$
$$(i, j) \in (1, \cdots, M) \times (1, \cdots, N)$$

(4)

It can be observed that MFR extracted from an already filtered image is different from that extracted from a non-altered image. Assume $H = \{\ldots, h_{-2}, h_{-1}, h_0, h_1, h_2, \ldots\}$ is the corresponding histogram of $d(i, j)$. Fig. 2 shows the histogram of $d(i, j)$ for 1338 images in UCID image database. The figure only displays the histogram of $d(i, j)$ ranging from -100 to 100. Fig. 2 (left) shows the histogram of the two kinds of MFR

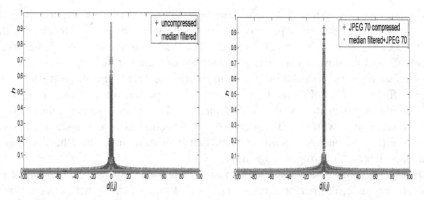

Fig. 2. Histogram of MFR for 1338 uncompressed images (left) and JPEG 70 compressed images (right) in UCID database

extracted from the filtered uncompressed images (green) and the non-filtered uncompressed images (red). It can be observed that h_0 is much larger for a pre-filtered image than that for a non- altered image. Therefore, the quantity of h_0 or the ratio $\rho = h_0 / h_1$ can be adopted to differentiate a median filtered image from a non-filtered image in the case of no post-compression. However, for a JPEG post-compressed image, h_0 or $\rho = h_0 / h_1$ is no longer suitable for the detection of median filtering any more. Fig. 2 (right) shows the histograms of the two kinds of MFR extracted from JPEG 70 compressed images. The red color is the histogram of MFR from JPEG 70 compressed images and the green color is that of MFR from median filtered and JPEG 70 post-compressed images. It shows that there is a significant overlapping region for h_0 bins in the histograms of the two kinds of MFR fingerprint in Fig. 2 (right). "Median filtered+JPEG70" denotes the composite operation of median filtering and JPEG compression with quality factor 70. The histogram of the MFR from pre-filtered images has larger kurtosis, and the variance of the MFR is smaller.

The second-order Markov chains [1] are employed to model $d(i, j)$. First, dividing fingerprint $d(i, j)$ into overlapping windows of size 3 × 3. Then, calculating the horizontal and vertical transition probabilities as follows [16 - 18]:

$$P^{h,v}_{z_2,z_1,z_0} = P(d_{i+h,j+v} = z_2 | d_{i,j} = z_1, d_{i-h,j-v} = z_0)$$
$$s.t. \quad (h,v) \in \{(0,1),(1,0),(0,-1),(-1,0)\}$$
(5)

where $z_n \in Z$ ($n = 0, 1, 2$), h and v are horizontal and vertical displacement from the center (i, j) of a 3 × 3 window respectively. As median filter is a symmetric operator, the overall transition probability along four directions (horizontal left, horizontal right, vertical up and vertical down) are averaged as follows:

$$P(z_2,z_1,z_0) = (P^{1,0}_{z_2,z_1,z_0} + P^{-1,0}_{z_2,z_1,z_0} + P^{0,1}_{z_2,z_1,z_0} + P^{0,-1}_{z_2,z_1,z_0})/4$$
(6)

The $d(i, j)$ mainly consists of small (absolute) integer value (Fig. 2). It is feasible to limit the dimension of $P(z_2,z_1,z_0)$ by truncating z_n ($n = 0, 1, 2, z_n \in Z$) as shown in Equation 7 when its absolute value is larger than a threshold t ($t>0$). After truncation, the dimension of the feature is $L = (2t+1)^3$.

$$z_n = \begin{cases} t, & z_n \geq t \\ z_n, & -t < z_n < t \\ -t, & z_n \leq -t \end{cases}$$
(7)

In order to reduce the influence of smooth windows and saturated windows, whose deviation energy in a window defined in Equation 2 is small, we ignore all these windows when computing transition probabilities $P^{h,v}_{z_2,z_1,z_0}$. In implementation, if the deviation energy $E(i, j)$ of one 3 × 3 window is less than a threshold T, the window will be ignored in the calculation of the transition probabilities $P^{h,v}_{z_2,z_1,z_0}$ for all directions. As mentioned in Section 2, the average deviation energy of a median filtered image is generally lower than that of a non-median filtered image, so setting up a threshold T is helpful in discrimination between a filter image and a non-filtered image. In our experiments, the parameter T is chosen to be 300 empirically.

When handling a JPEG compressed image, we also ignore the 3×3 window which contains a pixel in the boundary of 8×8 JPEG block with the aim of eliminating the impact of JPEG block artifact.

We propose to use the transition probabilities $P(z_2, z_1, z_0)$ of MFR $d(i, j)$ as forensic feature, which is called MFRTP in short form in the sequel.

4   Experimental Results

To evaluate the performance of the proposed approach, we employ the UCID image database which consists of 1338 uncompressed RGB images of size 512×384 [14]. Many of the images in the UCID database have significant regions of either saturated pixels or largely smooth patches. Some images are out of focus or contain blur from camera shake. This database is widely used in forensic works [2-3], [6]. All of the images are converted to gray-scale images before any further processing. The size of the training set is approximate 60% (850) of the database size. The rest of the images constitute the testing image set.

We employ C-SVM with Gaussian kernel $k(x,y)=\exp(-\gamma\|x-y\|^2)$ ($\gamma>0$) as classifier[15]. The experimental procedure of MFRTP is as follows:

1). For all images with size of $M \times N$, extract the MFR by performing 3×3 median filtering, then compute the transition probability of the MFR using Equation 5. The truncating threshold t (Equation 7) controls the dimension of the extracted feature. The dimension of the extracted feature affects the detection results. The larger is t, the better result can be obtained at the cost of computation time. In order to reduce the computing time of the C-SVM, $t = 3$ is suitable for both the detection results and efficiency, thus the dimensionality of the extracted feature is $L = (2t+1)^3 = 343$.
2). Search for the best parameter of c and γ in the multiplicative grid $(c, \gamma) \in \{(2^i, 2^j)|4i \in Z,\ 4j \in Z \}$ using five-fold cross-validation, and the step size of i, j are 0.25.
3). Use those parameters to get the classifier model on the training set.
4). Use the classifier model to perform a classification on the testing image set.

The performance of the proposed algorithm is evaluated using the area under the ROC curves (AUC in short form) and the minimal average decision error P_e under the assumption of equal priors and equal costs:

$$P_e = \min(\frac{P_{fp} + 1 - P_{tp}}{2})$$ (8)

where P_{fp} and P_{tp} denote the false positive (FP) and true positive rates (TP), respectively.

Table 1. Pe and AUC (%) for median filtering detectors against JPEG compression

		MF3			MF5		
		MFRTP (343-D)	MFF (44-D)	SPAM (343-D)	MFRTP (343-D)	MFF (44-D)	SPAM (343-D)
JPEG 90	P_e (%)	0.31	1.84	2.05	0.31	1.54	0.82
	AUC(%)	99.96	99.64	99.64	99.98	99.75	99.93
JPEG 70	P_e (%)	1.33	3.89	11.6	1.23	2.36	2.36
	AUC(%)	99.89	98.56	94.12	99.93	99.23	99.61
JPEG 50	P_e (%)	2.25	7.38	17.0	1.33	3.38	4.30
	AUC(%)	99.53	96.65	89.41	99.87	98.96	98.82

We compare the proposed method with the state-of-the-art works – both the SPAM method [1] and Yuan's median filter feature (MFF) method [2]. For the sake of fair comparison, only the horizontal and vertical features are adopted for both MFRTP and SPAM methods, and both methods have the same dimension (i.e. 343-D) of features. MFF method has 44 dimensions of feature [2]. SVM training for the three methods is similar. The ROC curves of detecting 3 × 3 median filtering (MF3 in short form) and 5 × 5 median filtering (MF5 in short form) are shown in Figs 3-7. The detailed classification results are shown in Table 1. "Original VS MF3" denotes that the original unmodified image is the negative sample, and the 3 × 3 median filtered image is the positive sample. "MF3+JPEG70" denotes the composite operation of median filtering and JPEG post-compression with quality factor 70.

The result of detecting 3 × 3 median filtering is shown in Fig. 3. For the uncompressed gray-scale image set, MF3 can be detected perfectly at both false positive rate and P_e equal 0 (Table 1) for all three methods. For JPEG post-compressed image, it can be observed that the proposed MFRTP classifier achieves much better ROC performance than both the SPAM classifier and the MFF classifier. The ROC curve of the proposed MFRTP method is always above the ROC curves of other two methods. It demonstrates that the proposed MFRTP method is much more robust against JPEG compression than the other methods. In particular, the advantage of the MFRTP method over the other two comparison methods grows when the JPEG compression quality becomes small (Fig. 3). The minimal average decision error P_e of MFRTP classifier is P_e = 0.31%, 1.33%, 2.25% for JPEG 90, JPEG 70, JPEG 50 respectively. While P_e of the SPAM classifier is P_e = 2.05%, 11.6%, 17.0% respectively, P_e of the MFF classifier is P_e = 1.84%, 3.89%, 7.38% respectively (Table 1).

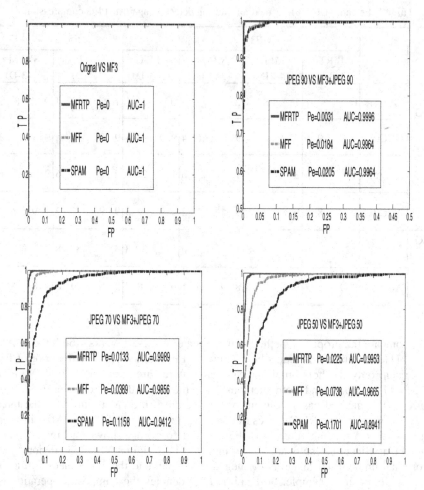

Fig. 3. ROC curves showing 3 × 3 median filtering detection performance on uncompressed images (top left), JPEG 90 compressed images (top right), JPEG 70 compressed images (bottom left), JPEG 50 compressed images (bottom right)

A similar improvement in performance is observed for the detection of 5 × 5 median filtering. The detection results of MF5 are shown in Fig. 4 and Table 1. Better performance than both comparison methods, is achieved in the detection of 5 × 5 median filtering on different JPEG post-compressed images, such as JPEG 90, JPEG 70 and JPEG 50. The minimal average decision error P_e of MFRTP classifier is P_e = 0.31%, 1.23%, 1.33% for JPEG 90, JPEG 70, JPEG 50 respectively. While P_e of the SPAM classifier is P_e = 0.82%, 2.36%, 4.30% respectively, P_e of the MFF classifier is P_e = 1.54%, 2.36%, 3.38% respectively (Table 1).

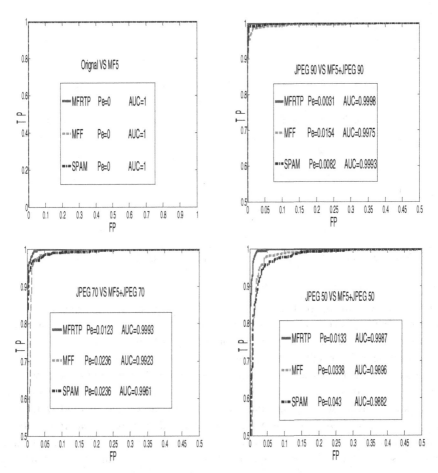

Fig. 4. ROC curves showing 5 × 5 median filtering detection performance on uncompressed images (top left), JPEG 90 compressed images (top right), JPEG 70 compressed images (bottom left), JPEG 50 compressed images (bottom right)

The detection results of both MF3 and MF5 show that the performance of the MFRTP classifier is excellent when the JPEG compression quality changes from 90 to 50. The performance of SPAM classifier deteriorates severely when the JPEG compression quality is low. The MFRTP classifier achieves much better robustness against JPEG post-compression than both comparison methods.

The dimension of the extracted feature affect the detection results, we do the experiments to verify the influence of this factor. Threshold t controls the dimension of the extracted feature. To see how this parameter affects the result, we choose $t \in \{1, 2, 3\}$

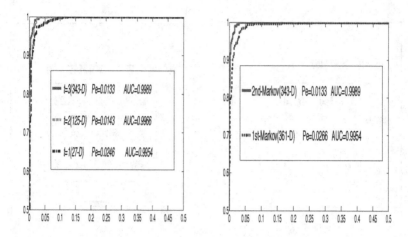

Fig. 5. ROC curves of MF3 detector with different dimensionality on JPEG 70 compressed images

and perform experiments on the images with JPEG post-compression quality 70. Fig. 5a shows that the best result achieves at $t = 3$, while the results for $t = 2$ and $t = 1$ drops slightly. In order to reduce the computing time of the C-SVM, $t = 3$ is suitable for both the detection results and efficiency.

We also test the results when adopting second-order Markov chains and first-order Markov chains to model the MFR fingerprint respectively. On the JPEG 70 post-compressed images, we compare the second-order Markov model (343-D feature) with first-order Markov model, which adopts similar dimension of feature *i.e.* 361-D feature, in the detection of 3 × 3 median filtering. Fig. 5b shows that the detection results of second-order Markov chain model are better than that of first-order Markov chain model. In Fig. 5b, "2nd-Markov" denotes "second-order Markov chain model", and "1st -Markov" denotes "first-order Markov chain model".

Finally, we test whether the proposed MFRTP method and the comparison methods can differentiate median filtering from other popular tools including average filtering (AVE), Gaussian filtering (GAU), up-scaling operations (UpRes) and down-scaling operations (DownRes). The interpolation adopted in a rescaling operation is bilinear. The up-scaling factor is set to 1.1, while the downscaling factor is 0.9. For an image without post-processing by JPEG compression, three methods can distinguish median filtering (MF3 or MF5) from other operations perfectly well, the minimal average decision error P_e of the three classifiers achieves zero. For the case of an image post-processed by JPEG 70, experiment result shows that MFRTP can

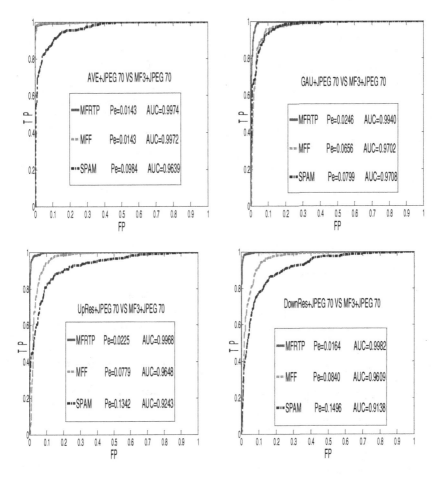

Fig. 6. ROC curves showing each technique's ability to discriminate 3×3 median filtering from average filtering (top left), Gaussian filtering (top right), upscaling (bottom left), and downscaling(bottom right) in JPEG compressed images using a quality factor of 70

discriminate MF3 from other four operations with high accuracy (the worst value of P_e is only 2.46%)(Fig. 6). For MF5 detection, we obtain similar results. The proposed classifier can distinguish MF5 from other manipulations with high accuracy (Fig. 7) and the proposed method outperforms both comparison methods, achieving the best performance.

In this paper, we do not discuss the case of median filtering pre-compression, *i.e.*, median filtering of already JPEG compressed images because a low pre-compression quality can even increase the detector's performance.

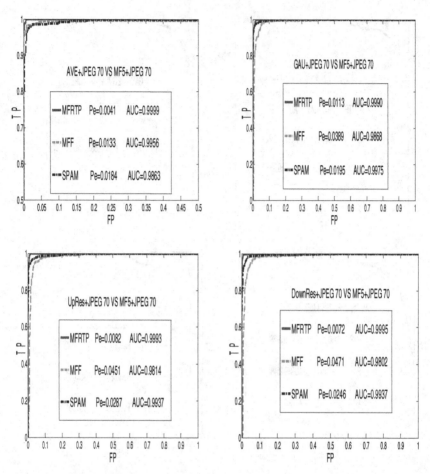

Fig. 7. ROC curves showing each technique's ability to discriminate 3×3 median filtering from average filtering (top left), Gaussian filtering (top right), upscaling (bottom left), and downscaling(bottom right) in JPEG compressed images using a quality factor of 70

5   Conclusion

In this paper, we propose to use the median filter residual to detect median filtering, which eliminate the interference from the image edge and texture. Experimental results show the proposed method is very robust to JPEG post-compression even with quality factor as low as 50 and achieves much better performance than the existing state-of-the-art works. Our method can also distinguish median filtering from other linear smoothers/manipulation in the case of JPEG post compression. The developed method is suitable in forensics of image processing history and can enhance security in resisting the anti-forensic attack. The developed technique can be applied to detect compressive sensing compression and other signal manipulation and this would be a part of our future work.

Acknowledgement. This work was supported by NSFC (61070167), 973 program (2011CB302204), PFMEC (20110171110042) and NSFC (U1135001). The authors thank Dr. H. Yuan for providing the code of MFF scheme in [2].

References

1. Kirchner, M., Fridrich, J.: On detection of median filtering in digital images. In: Proc. SPIE, Electronic Imaging, Media Forensics and Security II, vol. 7541, pp. 1–12 (2010)
2. Yuan, H.: Blind Forensics of Median Filtering in Digital Images. IEEE Trans. Inf. Forensics Security 6(4), 1335–1345 (2011)
3. Cao, G., Zhao, Y., Ni, R., Yu, L., Tian, H.: Forensic detection of median filtering in digital images. In: Proc. 2010 IEEE Int. Conf. Multimedia and Expo. 2010, pp. 89–94 (2010)
4. Popescu, A.C., Farid, H.: Exposing digital forgeries by detecting traces of re-sampling. IEEE Transactions on Signal Processing 53(2), 758–767 (2005)
5. Luo, W.Q., Huang, J.W., Qiu, G.P.: JPEG error analysis and its applications to digital image forensics. IEEE Trans. Inf. Forensics Security 5(3), 480–491 (2010)
6. Stamm, M., Liu, K.J.R.: Forensic estimation and reconstruction of a contrast enhancement mapping. In: International Conf. on Acoustics, Speech and Signal Processing, Dallas, Texas, USA (2010)
7. Stamm, M.C., Ray Liu, K.J.: Anti-Forensics of Digital Image Compression. IEEE Trans. Inf. Forensics Security 6(3), 1050–1065 (2011)
8. Dirik, A.E., Memon, N.: Image tamper detection based on demosaicing artifacts. In: International Conference Proceedings on Image Processing, Cairo, pp. 1497–1500 (2009)
9. Kirchner, M., Bohme, R.: Hiding traces of resampling in digital images. IEEE Trans. Inf. Forensics Security 3(4), 582–592 (2008)
10. Ker, A.D., Bohme, R.: Revisiting weighted stego-image stegoanalysis. In: Proceedings of SPIE, Electronic Imaging: Security, Forensics, Steganography and Watermarking of Multimedia Contents X, vol. 6819, p. 5 (2008)
11. Bovik, A.C.: Streaking in median filtered images. IEEE Transactions on Acoustics, Speech and Signal Processing 35(4), 493–503 (1987)
12. Swaminathan, A., Wu, M., Liu, K.J.: Digital image forensics via intrinsic fingerprints. IEEE Trans. Inf. Forensics Security 3(1), 101–117 (2008)
13. Chuang, W.H., Swaminathan, A., Wu, M.: Tampering identification using empirical frequency response. In: Proc. IEEE Int. Conf. Acoust., Speech and Signal Processing, pp. 1517–1520 (2009)
14. Schaefer, G., Stich, M.: UCID-An uncompressed color image database. In: Proceedings of SPIE, Storage and Retrieval Methods and Applications for Multimedia, pp. 472–480 (2004)
15. Chang, C.-C., Lin, C.-J.: LIBSVM: a library for support vector machines. ACM Transactions on Intelligent Systems and Technology 2, 27:1–27:27 (2011)
16. Pevý, T., Bas, P., Fridrich, J.: Steganalysis by subtractive pixel adjacency matrix. IEEE Trans. Inf. Forensics Security 5(2), 215–224 (2010)
17. Shi, Y.Q., Chen, C.-H., Chen, W.: A Markov Process Based Approach to Effective Attacking JPEG Steganography. In: Camenisch, J.L., Collberg, C.S., Johnson, N.F., Sallee, P. (eds.) IH 2006. LNCS, vol. 4437, pp. 249–264. Springer, Heidelberg (2007)
18. Zo, D., Shi, Y.Q., Su, W., Xuan, G.: Steganalysis based on Markov model of thresholded prediction-error image. In: Proc. IEEE Int. Conf. Multimedia and Expo., Toronto, Canada, July 9-12, pp. 365–1368 (2006)
19. Chen, C., Ni, J., Huang, R., Huang, J.: Blind median filtering detection using statistics in difference domain. In: Kirchner, M., Ghosal, D. (eds.) IH 2012. LNCS, vol. 7692, pp. 1–15. Springer, Heidelberg (2013)

Reversible Data Hiding in Encrypted Images Using Pseudorandom Sequence Modulation[*]

Xinpeng Zhang[1], Chuan Qin[2], and Guangling Sun[1]

[1] School of Communication and Information Engineering
Shanghai University
Shanghai 200072, P.R. China
[2] School of Optical-Electrical and Computer Engineering
University of Shanghai for Science and Technology
Shanghai 200093, P.R. China
xzhang@shu.edu.cn

Abstract. This work proposes a novel reversible data hiding scheme for encrypted images based on a pseudorandom sequence modulation mechanism. In the first phase, a content owner encrypts the original image for content protection. Then, a data-hider replaces a small proportion of data in LSB planes of encrypted image with the additional data and modifies the rest data in LSB planes according to the pseudorandom sequences modulated by the replaced and embedded data. With the encrypted image containing additional data, an additional-data user knowing the data-hiding key can extract the embedded additional data. And a content user with the encryption key may decrypt the encrypted image containing additional data to obtain the principal original content. If someone receives the decrypted image and has the data-hiding key, he can also successfully extract the additional data and perfectly recover the original image by exploiting the spatial correlation in natural image.

Keywords: reversible data hiding, image encryption, image recovery.

1 Introduction

While the encryption techniques convert plaintexts into unintelligible data for privacy protection, the data-hiding techniques embed additional information into digital multimedia for copyright protection, content annotation or covert communication. In recent years, the combination of the encryption and data-hiding techniques has attracted considerable research interests. In some works on joint encryption and data-hiding [1, 2], a part of data in digital multimedia products are used to carry watermark information and the rest data are encrypted, so that the copyright and privacy are simultaneously protected. With the aid of encryption techniques, different versions of multimedia products containing the information of various users can be produced for

[*] This work was supported by the Natural Science Foundation of China (61073190, 61103181 and 60832010), the Research Fund for the Doctoral Program of Higher Education of China (20113108110010), and the Alexander von Humboldt Foundation.

Y.Q. Shi, H.J. Kim, and F. Pérez-González (Eds.): IWDW 2012, LNCS 7809, pp. 358–367, 2013.

tracing pirates. For example, by employing a watermarking protocol in [3], the seller encrypts the original multimedia product, and then permutes and embeds an encrypted fingerprint provided by the buyer in the encrypted domain. This protocol ensures that the seller cannot know the buyer's watermarked version while the buyer cannot know the original product. Another anonymous fingerprinting scheme based on Okamoto–Uchiyama encryption is presented in [4]. In [5], the content owner encrypts the signs of original DCT coefficients and the content-users decrypt only a subset of the coefficients according to different keys, so that a series of versions containing different fingerprints are generated for the users.

The reversible data hiding for encrypted images is studied in [6-9]. Although there have been a number of works on reversible data hiding [10-14], most of them are only suitable for unencrypted images. Using the schemes in [6-9], when a content owner encrypts original images, an inferior assistant or a content administrator may append additional data within the encrypted images though he does not know the encryption key. After receiving an encrypted image containing additional data, someone knowing both the cryptographic and data-hiding keys can extract the additional data and recover the original image without any error. However, with the scheme in [6], when a receiver decrypts the encrypted image containing additional data, the quality of decrypted image will be significantly degraded due to the disturbance of additional data. In [7] and [8], the data-hiding operation modifies only the cover data in least-significant-bit (LSB) planes, so that the quality of decrypted image is good. But a receiver without the knowledge of the cryptographic key cannot extract the additional data in encrypted domain even though he knows the data-hiding key. With the separate method presented in [9], although the embedded data can be extracted in encrypted domain by using the data-hiding key, it is impossible to perform the data extraction and image recovery from a decrypted image without the knowledge of cryptographic key.

This work proposes a novel reversible data hiding scheme for encrypted images, in which the additional data are embedded into encrypted images using a pseudorandom sequence modulation mechanism, and the embedded data can be completely separated from the original image content after decryption at receiver side. Furthermore, a decryption on the encrypted image containing additional data results in an image very similar to the original version, and the data extraction can be performed in both the plain and encrypted domains. In other words, the drawbacks of previous schemes in [6-9] are avoided.

2   Proposed Scheme

Figures 1-3 sketch the phases of the proposed scheme. A content owner encrypts the original image using an encryption key to produce an encrypted image for content protection. Then, a data-hider replaces a small proportion of data in LSB planes of encrypted image with the additional data and modifies the rest data in LSB planes according to the pseudorandom sequences modulated by the replaced and embedded data. This way, an encrypted image containing additional data is generated. With the encrypted image containing additional data, an additional-data user knowing the data-hiding key can extract the embedded additional data. And a content user with the encryption key may decrypt the encrypted image containing additional data to obtain an image similar to the original one. Since the data embedding operation affects only the LSB, the quality of the decrypted image is satisfactory. If someone receives the decrypted image and has the data-hiding key, he can successfully extract the additional data and perfectly recover the original image. The detailed phases of the proposed scheme are as follows.

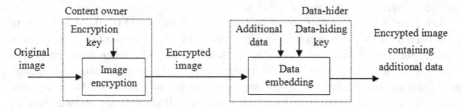

Fig. 1. Sketch of image encryption and data embedding

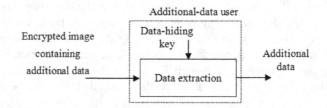

Fig. 2. Sketch of data extraction in encrypted domain

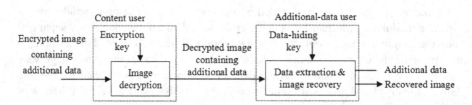

Fig. 3. Sketch of data extraction and image recovery in plain domain

2.1   Image Encryption

In this phase, the content owner encrypts the original image using a standard stream cipher. Denote the pixels in an original uncompressed image with a size of $N_1 \times N_2$ as $p_{i,j}$ ($1 \leq i \leq N_1$ and $1 \leq j \leq N_2$), and assume each pixel is represented by 8 bits $b_{i,j,0}$, $b_{i,j,1}$, ..., $b_{i,j,7}$. Then,

$$P_{i,j} = \sum_{u=0}^{7} b_{i,j,u} \cdot 2^u \tag{1}$$

and

$$b_{i,j,u} = \left\lfloor P_{i,j} / 2^u \right\rfloor \bmod 2, \quad u = 0,1,\ldots,7 \tag{2}$$

An exclusive-or operation is used to produce an encrypted image,

$$B_{i,j,u} = b_{i,j,u} \oplus r_{i,j,u} \tag{3}$$

where the pseudorandom bits $r_{i,j,u}$ are derived from an encryption key. In short, the encryption operation conceals the original values of all bits in the image, but does not change their positions. Actually, the encryption operation is same as that in [7].

2.2   Data Embedding

When having an encrypted image, the data-hider can embed some additional data into it by using a pseudorandom sequence modulation mechanism. After dividing the encrypted image into K non-overlapping blocks sized by $s \times s$ ($K \cdot s^2 = N_1 \cdot N_2$), the data-hider will embed M additional bits into each block. The values of s and M will be discussed later. For each block, collect and pseudo-randomly permute the encrypted bits in the 3 LSB planes to reorganize them as a vector $\mathbf{V}_k = [V_k(1), V_k(2), \ldots, V_k(3 \cdot s^2)]$, where the permutation way is determined by a data-hiding key and k is the block index ($1 \le k \le K$). Denote the M bits to be embedded into the k-th block as $\mathbf{w}_k = [w_k(1), w_k(2), \ldots, w_k(M)]$. The data-hider replaces the first M bits of $\mathbf{V}_k$ with $\mathbf{w}_k$,

$$V'_k(m) = w_k(m), \qquad m = 1,2,\ldots,M; \quad k = 1,2,\ldots,K \tag{4}$$

Furthermore, the rest bits in $\mathbf{V}_k$ should be modified by the following way. According to the data-hiding key, generate 2^{2M} pseudorandom binary sequences with a same length ($3 \cdot s^2 - M$) for each block. The elements in the pseudorandom sequences are i.i.d. with uniform distribution on the set $\{0, 1\}$. Denote the sequences as $\mathbf{s}_{k,l} = [s_{k,l}(1), s_{k,l}(2), \ldots, s_{k,l}(3 \cdot s^2 - M)]$, where $1 \le k \le K$ and $0 \le l \le 2^{2M} - 1$. Concatenate the first M bits of $\mathbf{V}_k$ and the M embedded bits, and calculate the decimal value of the concatenated string d_k,

$$d_k = \sum_{m=1}^{M} \left[V_k(m) \cdot 2^{m-1} \right] + \sum_{m=1}^{M} \left[V'_k(m) \cdot 2^{M+m-1} \right], \qquad k = 1,2,\ldots,K \tag{5}$$

Then, modify the last ($3 \cdot s^2 - M$) bits in $\mathbf{V}_k$ using the d_k-th pseudorandom sequence,

$$V'_k(m+M) = V_k(m+M) \oplus s_{k,d_k}(m), \qquad m = 1,2,\ldots,3s^2 - M; \quad k = 1,2,\ldots,K \tag{6}$$

After obtaining the new vectors $\mathbf{V'}_k$, put the bits in them into the original positions by an inverse permutation to generate an encrypted image containing additional data. We denote the u-th bits at position (i, j) in the generated image as $B'_{i,j,u}$ ($0 \le u \le 7$, $1 \le i \le N_1$ and $1 \le j \le N_2$). Clearly, $B'_{i,j,u}$ in the 5 most-significant-bit (MSB) planes are same as the corresponding $B_{i,j,u}$, while a half of $B'_{i,j,u}$ in the 3 LSB planes are inverse to the corresponding $B_{i,j,u}$ on average. The embedding rate, a ratio between the amount of embedded bits and the total number of cover pixels, is

$$R = M/s^2 \tag{7}$$

2.3   Data Extraction and Image Recovery

Then, we will discuss the data extraction from the encrypted image containing additional data, the decryption of the encrypted image containing additional data, and the data extraction and content recovery from a decrypted image.

Firstly, consider an additional-data user having the data-hiding key but not the encryption key. Although he does not know the image content due to the absence of encryption key, he can easily extract the additional data from the encrypted image containing them. After dividing the image into K non-overlapping blocks and reorganizing the 3 LSB in each block as a vector according to the data-hiding key, the additional-data user may collect the first M bits of each vector to retrieve the additional data. This way, the data extraction is implemented in encrypted domain.

Secondly, consider a content user with the encryption key. The content user may decrypt the encrypted image containing additional data to obtain the principal original content. The decryption operation is same as the encryption,

$$b'_{i,j,u} = B'_{i,j,u} \oplus r_{i,j,u} \tag{8}$$

where $r_{i,j,u}$ are derived from the encryption key. The gray values of decrypted pixels are

$$p'_{i,j} = \sum_{u=0}^{7} b'_{i,j,u} \cdot 2^u \tag{9}$$

Since the data-embedding operation does not alter any MSB of encrypted image, the decrypted MSB must be same as the original MSB. On the other hand, since the LSB have been changed by the pseudorandom binary sequences, the distribution of the data in the 3 LSB-planes of decrypted image is uniform. Assuming the distribution of the 3 LSB of original image is also uniform, the average energy of difference between the original and encrypted images is

$$E_D = \frac{1}{64} \cdot \sum_{\alpha=0}^{7} \sum_{\beta=0}^{7} (\alpha - \beta)^2 \tag{10}$$

So, the approximate PSNR is

$$\text{PSNR} \approx 10 \cdot \log_{10}\left(255^2/E_D\right) = 37.9 \text{ dB} \tag{11}$$

That implies that the affection of additional data in decrypted image is not serious. Note that the additional data still exist in the decrypted image.

At last, consider that an additional-data user has the data-hiding key and receives the decrypted image from the content user. In this case, the additional-data user can extract the additional data and recover the original content from the decrypted image by exploiting the spatial correlation in natural image. The detailed procedure of data extraction and image recovery is as follows. Divide the decrypted image into K blocks, and reorganize the 3 LSB in k-th block as a vector $\mathbf{v}_k = [v_k(1), v_k(2), \dots, v_k(3 \cdot s^2)]$. For each integer l falling into $[0, 2^{2M}-1]$, calculate its binary representation

$$t_l(m) = \lfloor l/2^{m-1} \rfloor \bmod 2, \quad m = 1, 2, \dots, 2M \tag{12}$$

and modify the vector $\mathbf{v}_k$ to get a new vector $\mathbf{v}_{k,l}$,

$$v_{k,l}(m) = v_k(m) \oplus t_l(m) \oplus t_l(m+M), \qquad m = 1, 2, \dots, M \tag{13}$$

$$v_{k,l}(m+M) = v_k(m+M) \oplus s_{k,l}(m), \qquad m = 1, 2, \dots, 3s^2 - M \tag{14}$$

Because there are 2^{2M} possible l, we can get 2^{2M} modified versions of vector $\mathbf{v}_k$. For each modified vector $\mathbf{v}_{k,l}$, put the $3s^2$ bits in it into their original positions to generate a candidate block $\mathbf{C}_{k,l}$. If the integer l is same as d_k, the corresponding candidate block is just the original block since the operations of (13) and (14) in plain domain counteract the operations of (5) and (6) in encrypted domain. Otherwise, a half of bits in 3 LSB planes of the corresponding candidate block should be different from those in original block on average since the different pseudorandom sequences are independent mutually. Then, the additional-data user measures the fluctuation in the candidate blocks,

$$f_{k,l} = \sum_{u=2}^{s-1}\sum_{v=2}^{s-1}\left|c_{k,l}(u,v) - \frac{c_{k,l}(u-1,v)+c_{k,l}(u,v-1)+c_{k,l}(u+1,v)+c_{k,l}(u,v+1)}{4}\right| \tag{15}$$

where $c_{k,l}(u,v)$ are the pixel values in candidate block $\mathbf{C}_{k,l}$, and find the minimum of $f_{k,l}$ for each given k,

$$\hat{d}_k = \arg\min_l f_{k,l} \tag{16}$$

Due to the spatial correlation in natural image, the fluctuation measurement of original block is usually lower than those of disturbed versions. So, the additional-data user may regard the candidate block with minimal $f_{k,l}$ as the recovered content of the k-th block, and retrieve the M embedded bits

$$\hat{w}_k(m) = \lfloor \hat{d}_k/2^{m+M-1} \rfloor \bmod 2, \quad m = 1, 2, \dots, M \tag{17}$$

Thus, the original image can be recovered and the additional data can be extracted in a block-by-block manner. That implies the data extraction can also realized in the plain domain.

3   Experimental Results

The gray image Man sized 512×512 shown in Figure 4(a) was used as the original image in the experiment, and its encrypted version is shown in Figure 4(b). Then, we let $M = 4$ and $s = 32$ to embed 1024 additional bits into Figure 4(b) to produce an encrypted image containing additional data as shown in Figure 4(c). Using the data-hiding key, the embedded additional data can be extracted from Figure 4(c). When we decrypted the image in Figure 4(c), PSNR in the decrypted image when regarding the original image as a reference was 37.9 dB, which verifies the theoretical value in (11) and is same as the PSNR value in [7] and significantly better than the PSNR value in [6], 13.3 dB. The decrypted image is given as Figure 4(d). Furthermore, with the data-hiding key, the embedded data could be successfully extracted and the original image could be perfectly recovered from Figure 4(d).

Clearly, a smaller s or a larger M corresponds to a higher embedding rate. On the other hand, a smaller s implies fewer pixels in each block and a larger M implies more candidate versions for each block, leading to higher risk of incorrect data-extraction and content-recovery. Tables 1 and 2 list the embedding rates and extracted-bits error rates with respect to different values of s and M when Man was used as the original image. If s is too small and M is too large, the data extraction as well as the content recovery may be unsuccessful. Figure 5 compares the performance between the proposed scheme and the method in [7], and it can be seen the proposed scheme outperforms the method in [7]. In addition, while the data-extraction is allowed only in plain domain using the method in [7], it can be implemented in both the plain and the encrypted domains using the proposed scheme.

Table 1. Embedding rates with respect to different s and M when using the cover Man

		M				
		1	2	3	4	5
	16	0.0039	0.0078	0.0117	0.0156	0.0195
	20	0.0025	0.0050	0.0075	0.0100	0.0125
s	24	0.0017	0.0035	0.0052	0.0069	0.0087
	32	0.0010	0.0020	0.0029	0.0039	0.0049
	40	0.0006	0.0013	0.0019	0.0025	0.0031

Table 2. Extracted-bit error rates with respect to different s and M when using the cover Man

		M				
		1	2	3	4	5
	16	0.0068	0.0111	0.0142	0.0278	0.0389
	20	0.0032	0.0043	0.0041	0.0082	0.0127
s	24	0	0	0	0.0021	0.0021
	32	0	0	0	0	0.0018
	40	0	0	0	0	0

(a)

(b)

(c)

(d)

Fig. 4. (a) Original Man, (b) its encrypted version, (c) an encrypted image containing embedded data, and (d) a decrypted image containing embedded data with PSNR 37.9 dB

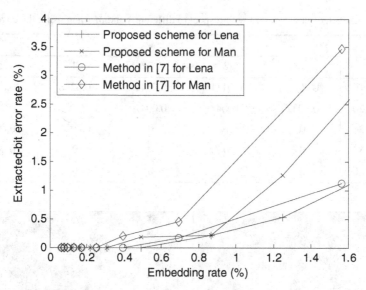

Fig. 5. Performance comparison between the proposed scheme and the method in [7]

4   Conclusion

This work proposes a novel reversible data hiding scheme for encrypted images based on pseudorandom sequence modulation, in which a part of data in LSB planes of encrypted image is replaced with the additional data and the rest data in LSB planes are modified by the pseudorandom sequences modulated by the replaced bits and embedded data. Then, the additional-data user with the data-hiding key can easily extract the additional data in encrypted domain. Since the data embedding operation affects only the LSB, a direct decryption may result in an image with principal original content. By finding the modulated sequences corresponding to the minimal fluctuation, the embedded data can be extracted from the decrypted image and the original content can also be recovered without any error when the embedding rate is not too high.

References

1. Lian, S., Liu, Z., Ren, Z., Wang, H.: Commutative Encryption and Watermarking in Video Compression. IEEE Trans. on Circuits and Systems for Video Technology 17(6), 774–778 (2007)
2. Cancellaro, M., Battisti, F., Carli, M., Boato, G., Natale, F.G.B., Neri, A.: A Commutative Digital Image Watermarking and Encryption Method in the Tree Structured Haar Transform Domain. Signal Processing: Image Communication 26(1), 1–12 (2011)
3. Memon, N., Wong, P.W.: A Buyer–Seller Watermarking Protocol. IEEE Trans. on Image Processing 10(4), 643–649 (2001)

4. Kuribayashi, M., Tanaka, H.: Fingerprinting Protocol for Images Based on Additive Homomorphic Property. IEEE Trans. Image Processing 14(12), 2129–2139 (2005)
5. Kundur, D., Karthik, K.: Video Fingerprinting and Encryption Principles for Digital Rights Management. Proceedings of the IEEE 92(6), 918–932 (2004)
6. Puech, W., Chaumont, M., Strauss, O.: A Reversible Data Hiding Method for Encrypted Images. In: Proc. SPIE, Security, Forensics, Steganography, and Watermarking of Multimedia Contents X, vol. 6819 (2008)
7. Zhang, X.: Reversible Data Hiding in Encrypted Image. IEEE Signal Processing Letters 18(4), 255–258 (2011)
8. Hong, W., Chen, T.-S., Wu, H.-Y.: An Improved Reversible Data Hiding in Encrypted Images Using Side Match. IEEE Signal Processing Letters 19(4), 199–202 (2012)
9. Zhang, X.: Separable Reversible Data Hiding in Encrypted Image. IEEE Trans. Information Forensics & Security 7(2), 526–532 (2012)
10. Tian, J.: Reversible Data Embedding Using a Difference Expansion. IEEE Trans. on Circuits and Systems for Video Technology 13(8), 890–896 (2003)
11. Ni, Z., Shi, Y.-Q., Ansari, N., Su, W.: Reversible Data Hiding. IEEE Trans. on Circuits and Systems for Video Technology 16(3), 354–362 (2006)
12. Celik, M.U., Sharma, G., Tekalp, A.M., Saber, E.: Lossless Generalized-LSB Data Embedding. IEEE Trans. on Image Processing 14(2), 253–266 (2005)
13. Hong, W., Chen, T.-S., Chang, Y.-P., Shiu, C.-W.: A High Capacity Reversible Data Hiding Scheme Using Orthogonal Projection and Prediction Error Modification. Signal Processing 90, 2911–2922 (2010)
14. Chang, C.-C., Lin, C.-C., Chen, Y.-H.: Reversible Data-Embedding Scheme Using Differences between Original and Predicted Pixel Values. IET Information Security 2(2), 35–46 (2008)

Optimal Histogram-Pair and Prediction-Error Based Image Reversible Data Hiding[*]

Guorong Xuan[1], Xuefeng Tong[1], Jianzhong Teng[1], Xiaojie Zhang[1], and Yun Qing. Shi[2]

[1] Computer Science, Tongji University, Shanghai, China
[2] ECE, New Jersey Institute of Technology, Newark, New Jersey, USA
grxuan@tongji.edu.cn, shi@njit.edu

Abstract. This proposed scheme reversibly embeds data into image prediction-errors by using histogram-pair method with the following four thresholds for optimal performance: embedding threshold, fluctuation threshold, left- and right-histogram shrinking thresholds. The embedding threshold is used to select only those prediction-errors, whose magnitude does not exceed this threshold, for possible reversible data hiding. The fluctuation threshold is used to select only those prediction-errors, whose associated neighbor fluctuation does not exceed this threshold, for possible reversible data hiding. The left- and right-histogram shrinking thresholds are used to possibly shrink histogram from the left and right, respectively, by a certain amount for reversible data hiding. Only when all of four thresholds are satisfied the reversible data hiding is carried out. Different from our previous work, the image gray level histogram shrinking towards the center is not only for avoiding underflow and/or overflow but also for optimum performance. The required bookkeeping data are embedded together with pure payload for original image recovery. The experimental results on four popularly utilized test images (Lena, Barbara, Baboon, Airplane) and one of the JPEG2000 test image (Woman, whose histogram does not have zero points in the whole range of gray levels, and has peaks at its both ends) have demonstrated that the proposed scheme outperforms recently published reversible image data hiding schemes in terms of the highest PSNR of marked image verses original image at given pure payloads.

Keywords: Reversible image data hiding, prediction error, neighborhood fluctuation, histogram pair scheme, gray level histogram modification.

1   Introduction

Reversibility requires that not only the hidden data can be extracted correctly but also the marked image can be inverted back to the original cover image exactly after the hidden data extraction. Research on reversible, also called lossless, image data hiding has attracted great interests recently, which can be manifested by the dramatically and

[*] This research is largely supported by Shanghai City Board of education scientific research innovation projects (12ZZ033) and National Natural Science Foundation of China (NSFC) on project (90304017).

Y.Q. Shi, H.J. Kim, and F. Pérez-González (Eds.): IWDW 2012, LNCS 7809, pp. 368–383, 2013.

continuously increasing number of publications on this subject, e.g., [1-14] (just a rather incomplete list). This is because reversible data hiding has found wide applications in image content authentication, e-banking and e-government, to name a few.

In the beginning stage, module 256 addition was used to achieve reversibility [1]. However, it has been realized that module 256 addition may damage image quality severely, and hence has been less used nowadays [15,16]. Lower bit-plane compression has shown to be able to fulfill reversible data hiding [2,3] with improved visual quality. The data embedding rate is however not high though. Note that when the data embedding is conducted in integer wavelet transform (IWT) domain [3], one or two sides of histogram of the image in which data is embedded may need to be shrunk towards the center (referred to as histogram modification) in order to keep reversibility. Difference expansion method [4] has largely boosted the amount of data that can be reversibly embedded. Histogram manipulation method [5] has demonstrated high quality of image with data losslessly embedded. Along this line, via quite some progressive improvements [e.g., 6,7], histogram-pair method [8] works on high frequency wavelet subbands further significantly improves lossless data embedding efficiency. Reversibly embedding data into prediction-error [9] is another effective scheme to largely boost embedding effectiveness in terms of the PSNR of the image with data hidden with respect to the original image versus data embedding rate. While many advanced reversible data hiding works [e.g., 10,11,12,13] have continued to appear in the literature, indicating this is a promising research subject for digital world; the work using sorting and prediction [13] may have provided generally the best performance in the literature at this stage.

In this paper, to achieve optimum performance (the highest PSNR at given capacity without overflow and/or underflow) we propose a scheme to reversibly embed data into image prediction-errors by using histogram-pair method with the following four thresholds: embedding threshold, fluctuation threshold, left- and right-histogram shrinking thresholds. The embedding threshold is used to select only those prediction-errors, whose magnitude does not exceed this threshold, for possible reversible data hiding. The fluctuation threshold is used to select only those prediction-errors, whose associated neighbor fluctuation does not exceed this threshold, for possible reversible data hiding. The left- and right-histogram shrinking thresholds are used to possibly shrink histogram from the left and/or right towards the center by a certain amount for reversible data hiding. An initial and short version of this framework was reported in [14], where only two thresholds were presented and without demonstration of how to achieve the optimality. Furthermore, in [14], the possible left- and/or right-histogram end shrinking is designed and conducted to only achieve reversibility, i.e., they have never been considered and manipulated to achieve the optimality in reversible data embedding. There are also some other minor differences between two schemes.

In order to facilitate the readers who may not know the principle of histogram-pair reversible data hiding [8] to follow this paper, a very simple example is presented here. In Fig. 1, the original image (9 pixels only) has 4 different pixel values: {6,7,8,9}. The to be embedded data are four bits: [1,0,0,1]. In Fig. 1 (a), the original image is shown, its histogram is [h(6),h(7),h(8),h(9)]=[4,3,1,1]. In Fig. 1 (b) histogram modification is made, i.e., a pixel with gray value 9 is changed to 8 in order to avoid overflow after data embedding. The information of this change needs to be embedding into image as well so as to recover the original image exactly after the hidden data has been extracted. The histogram is hence changed to [h(6),h(7),h(8),h(9)]=[4,3,2,0]. In Fig. 2(c), a histogram-pair [h(6),h(7)]=[4,0] is created by change three pixels' gray values from 7 to 8, and two gray values from 8 to 9. The histogram is thus changed to [h(6),h(7),h(8),h(9)]=[4,0,3,2]. The [4,0] is referred to as a histogram pair, which can be used for data embedding. In Fig. 2(d), four bits, [1,0,0,1] are embedded into this histogram-pair, that is, the histogram-pair [h(6),h(7)]=[4,0] changes to [h(6),h(7)]=[2,2]. That is, after four bits embedding, the histogram changes to [h(6),h(7),h(8),h(9)]=[2,2,3,2]. As said, during the embedding process the bookkeeping data need to be embedded into the image for the image recovery late and this detail is not shown here.

6	7	6
6	8	7
7	6	9

(a)

6	7	6
6	8	7
7	6	8

(b)

6	8	6
6	9	8
8	6	9

(c)

6	8	7
7	9	8
8	6	9

(d)

Fig. 1. Simple example of data hiding by histogram-pair (a) original image, (b) histogram modification, (c) creation of histogram-pair, (d) after data embedded

As shown above, because histogram shifting is used in data embedding which may lead to underflow and/or overflow, it is sometimes necessary for us to shrink one or two ends of image histogram towards the center. Note that some frequently used images, e.g., Lena, Barbara, and Airplane have two ends of their histogram being zero. However, Baboon image has its left-side of histogram non-zero, and Woman image, a JPEG2000 test image, has both sides of its histogram non-zero. Hence under these two circumstances it is necessary to shrink one-side or both sides of image histogram towards the center to reversibly embed data. Fig. 2 illustrates this procedure. Different from our previous work, where the image gray level histogram shrinking towards the center is conducted only for avoiding underflow and/or overflow, in this work how much to shrink the histogram also becomes two of four thresholds to seek optimal reversible data hiding.

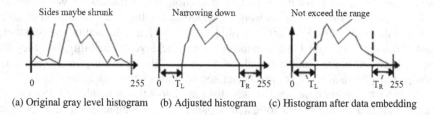

(a) Original gray level histogram   (b) Adjusted histogram   (c) Histogram after data embedding

Fig. 2. Histogram modification in reversible data hiding

The rest of the paper is organized as follows. The principle of four thresholds is presented in Section 2. The block diagram of the proposed scheme and a short example to illustrate the algorithm are shown in Section 3. In Section 4, experimental works on four popularly used test images and one of JPEG2000 test image are presented. In doing so, how to achieve optimality by using the proposed algorithm is demonstrated. The conclusion and discussion are made in Section 5.

2   Four Thresholds

In our work, a pixel, x, and its eight-neighbor, x_1, x_2, x_3, x_4, x_5, x_6, x_7, x_8, depicted in Eq. 1, are considered. The proposed method can also work with other types of neighbor, say, the four-neighbor. However, it can be shown that the eight-neighbor works more efficient than, say, the four-neighbor.

$$\begin{bmatrix} x_1 & x_4 & x_6 \\ x_2 & x & x_7 \\ x_3 & x_5 & x_8 \end{bmatrix} \tag{1}$$

The prediction error, P_E, is defined as follows, where the prediction of the central pixel, $\bar{x}$, is derived from its eight-neighbors.

$$P_E = x - \bar{x} \qquad where \qquad \bar{x} = \left[(1/12)\left(\sum_{i=1,3,6,8} x_i + \sum_{i=2,4,5,7} 2x_i \right) \right] \tag{2}$$

The fluctuation value, F, associated with the above-mentioned eight-neighbor, is defined as follows. That is, the related average value, $\bar{x}$, is equal to the above-mentioned prediction of the central pixel. The fluctuation value depends on eight neighbor pixels values.

$$F = (1/3)\left(\sum_{i=1,3,6,8}(x_i - \bar{x})^2 + \sum_{i=2,4,5,7} 2(x_i - \bar{x})^2 \right) \tag{3}$$

(1) Fluctuation threshold, T_F

In this reversible data hiding algorithm, for each candidate pixel, we calculate the fluctuation using Eq. 3 from its surrounding 8-eighbors, and compare it with the fluctuation threshold T_F. If the calculated fluctuation, F, is larger than or equal to the fluctuation threshold, T_F, i.e., $F \geq T_F$, the pixel is untouched. Only when the calculated fluctuation, F, is smaller than T_F, a bit can possibly be embedded.

(2) Embedding threshold, T

For a pixel under consideration, which has satisfied the fluctuation threshold, T_F, it may be selected to embed a bit, or it may be expanded without data embedding, or remaining non-touched at all, depending on the embedding threshold T.

Specifically, P_E has the following three possible different situations. Let us consider $P_E \geq 0$ and $T \geq 0$. First, $P_E = T$, a bit of data will be embedded: $P_E = P_E + b$, b

is a bit that we want to be added at this time. Second, $P_E > T$, we do not embed data, instead the P_E is extended, i.e., $P_E = P_E + 1$. Third, $P_E < T$, do nothing. If $P_E < 0$ and $T < 0$, similarly we have three different situations. All details are shown in Fig. 3.

(3) Right-histogram threshold, T_R

Right-histogram threshold is such a threshold that the gray level at right histogram will be shrank by T_R to make largest gray level become smaller than 255, prior to data embedding [8,14]. Different from [8,14], however, in this paper this threshold is adjusted not only to prevent   underflow and/or overflow but also to achieve the optimal performance in reversible data hiding.

(4) Left-histogram   threshold, T_L

Similarly, left-histogram threshold is such a threshold that the gray level at left histogram will be shrank by T_L to make the smallest gray level larger than 0 prior to data hiding. Here the T_L is designed not only to prevent underflow but also to achieve the optimal performance in reversible data hiding.

3   Proposed Algorithm

In this section, we first present the principle of the proposed optimal algorithm, then the block diagrams of data embedding and retrieval, finally a simple example to illustrate the data hiding and extraction. To save the space, all of the formulae which have appeared in the block diagrams are not shown in the text again.

3.1   Proposed Optimal Algorithm

With the embedding threshold T, fluctuation threshold T_F, left- and right-histogram adjustment thresholds T_L and T_R, under the constraints of no underflow and/or overflow, and the give embedding requirement, our proposed reversible data hiding scheme can be expressed as follows.

$$[T, T_F, T_L, T_R] = \underset{\substack{neither\ underflow\ nor\ overflow \\ meeting\ embedding\ capacity}}{\arg\max} [\ PSNR(Payload)\ ] \qquad (4)$$

As an example, take a look at the case in which a payload of 0.3 bpp is required to be embedded into the Baboon image. In Table 1(a), it is shown in this case, as T=-5, T_F=2200, T_L=T_R=0, the PSNR of the stego image that can be achieved is 37.42 dB, which is higher than other PSNR values reported in Table 1(a). However, this is not the optimal PSNR with the payload of 0.3 bpp. After a thorough search among all of the four thresholds, it is shown that the PSNR can reach 37.97 dB for the following combination of the four thresholds: T=-7, T_F=800, T_L=5, T_R=0; and it is the highest possibly achieved, hence the optimal PSNR value achieved at the embedding rate of 0.3 bpp. This is one of distinct differences with and an improvement over the prior work [14]. In Table 1, "UNF" means underflow.

Table 1. PSNR improvement by T_L and T_R for Baboon image

(a) Baboon at $T_L=0$

PSNR=37.42 ,paylaod=0.3, T=-5, T_F=2200 at T_L=0,T_R=0				
T\T_F	2000	2100	2200	2300	2400
-6	UNF	UNF	37.17	37.11	37.07
5	37.41	37.37	37.29	37.26	37.21
-5	37.34	37.42	37.42	37.38	37.36
4	36.72	36.74	36.68	36.67	36.65
-4	UNF	UNF	UNF	UNF	UNF

(b) Baboon at $T_L=5$

PSNR=37.97 ,paylaod=0.3, T=-7, TF=800 at T_L=5,T_R=0				
T\T_F	600	700	800	900	1000
-8	37.74	37.91	37.81	37.72	37.66
7	37.52	37.93	37.89	37.86	37.81
-7	37.34	37.82	37.97	37.86	37.77
6	37.07	37.48	37.70	37.89	37.82
-6	36.78	37.19	37.49	37.62	37.72

3.2   Block Diagram

The block diagrams of data embedding and retrieval for the proposed algorithm are shown in Fig. 3 and Fig. 4, respectively.

Note that there is another difference between the proposed algorithms with that reported in [8,14]. That is, instead of from one-side of a histogram, say, T=4, to reversibly embed data, if the to-be embedded data have not been all embedded, the algorithm embeds data in T=-4, and so on, in this proposed algorithm, differently, we scan the image and embed data into both t_P=4 as well as t_N=-4 as the first step. If the data have not been completely embedded, we are to embed data to the next pair of

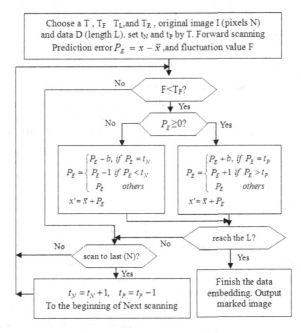

Fig. 3. Flowchart of data embedding

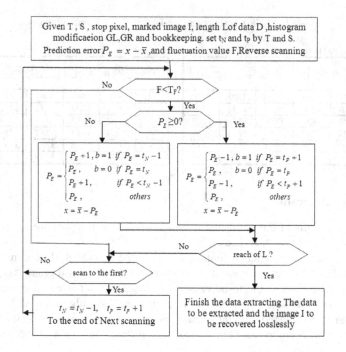

Fig. 4. Flowchart of data extracting of proposed scheme

t_P=3 and t_N=-3. That is, the data embedding in an order of $\{4,-4\},\{3,-3\},\{2,-2\}$, $\{1,-1\},\{0\}$. Note that it can also be: $\{-4,3\},\{-3,2\},\{-2,1\},\{-1,0\}$. Furthermore, depends on the situation, it is not necessary that the data embedding process has to end up at $\{0\}$, it can end at any value in the sequence prior to 0, e.g., it can end, respectively, at -4 and 3 in the two sequences listed above. As long as the required amount of data has been embedded, the algorithm stops. Our experimental results have demonstrated that this strategy can lead to a higher PSNR of a stego image versus the original image for the case where the pure payload (amount of data that needs to be embedded) is not large.

3.3   An Illustrative Example

For simplification, the fluctuation value F of a pixel under consideration in this example only depends on the four neighbors sounding this pixel.

Below, a simplified example is used to illustrate: 1) how data can be embedded into an original image to generate a stego image (the image with the data hidden inside); 2) how the hidden data can be extracted out without any error, and the stego image can turn back to the original image without any difference. In doing so, to simplify the procedure, we do not use 8-neighbor in prediction; instead, 4-neighbor is used in the demonstration. That is, Eq. (3) is now simplified as:

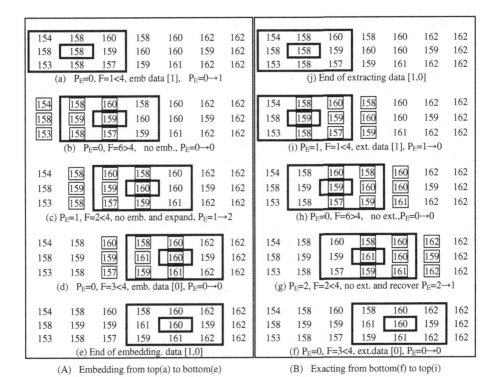

(A) Embedding from top(a) to bottom(e)   (B) Exacting from bottom(f) to top(i)

Fig. 5. Embedding and exacting data [1,0] with T= 0 , $T_F = 4$, $T_L = 0$, $T_R = 0$

$$F = (x2-\bar{x})^2 + (x4-\bar{x})^2 + (x5-\bar{x})^2 + (x7-\bar{x})^2, \text{ and } \bar{x} = floor\{(x2+x4+x5+x7)/4\},$$
i.e., the prediction of the central pixel x is derived from 4-neighbor pixels of the central pixel instead of 8-neighbor pixels. Further we assume that T_L and T_R have been satisfied in this illustration example. In Fig. 5, it is shown step-by-step in the left-hand side from the top to the bottom how two bits [1,0] are embedded into this piece of the image, and in the right side from the bottom to the top step by step how the embedded data [0,1] can be retrieved.

(A) Embedding:

a) In the top of the left side of Fig. 5, a 3x3 window is opened centered at the pixel of gray value 158. The predicted value for the window center is 158, hence the prediction error is 0, and the fluctuation is 1, which is smaller than the threshold T_F of 4. Hence, the 1st bit, 1, can be embedded into the prediction error, i.e., $P_E=0\rightarrow1$. That is, the central pixel after this step changes from 158 to 159.

b) The 3x3 window center is now moved towards the right hand side by one pixel. Using 4-neighbor, the estimated central pixel value is 159. Hence the prediction error is 0. The fluctuation value F=6. Hence, there is no data embedding. At the same time, the central pixel value remains to be 159.

c) Now the window center moves to the next pixel, whose gray value is 160 as shown in the sub-figure (c). Hence, the $P_E=1$, $F=2<4$, no data embedding here, instead the P_E is extended to 2, i.e., $P_E =1 \rightarrow 2$, thus making the central pixel gray value 160 $\rightarrow$ 161.

d) The window center moves to the following point 160 as in sub-figure (d). The prediction error $P_E=0$, $F=3<4$, hence the 2nd bit, 0, is embedded, the central pixel remains to be 160. $P_E=0 \rightarrow 0$.

At this point two bits [1,0] have been embedded and the algorithm stop, as shown in sub-figure (e). The point becomes the end point.

(B) Extracting:

The decoding starts from the ending point of data embedding, as shown in (f), backwards to the starting point of data embedding in (j). Due to the space constraint, the detail in step-by-step has been omitted here.

One important observation is made here. That is, take a look at Fig. 5 (e) and Fig. 5 (f). All of 8 neighbor pixels in (d) are identical to all of 8 neighbor pixels in (f). Hence, the fluctuation value F in both cases are the same, and $F=3$. It can be observed that the eight neighbors in any specific 3x3 structure, hence the associated fluctuation F, during the data embedding is identical to the eight neighbors of a corresponding 3x3 structure in data extraction but in a reverse order. This is a key element to guarantee the reversibility.

Note that the procedure of embedding is fulfilled by a sequence of scanning the image gray level. Each scanning is scanned from the top-left to the bottom-right of an image.

4   Experimental Results

The results of applying the proposed algorithm to the following four frequently-utilized test images: Lena, Barbara, Airplane and Baboon [17] and one of the JPEG2000 test image Woman [18] have been reported in this section. It is observed that the first four test images have been widely utilized in reversible data hiding research community. It is observed that almost all of these four popularly used images have the two sides of their histograms empty (except the left side of Baboon image's histogram), while their histograms are different from each other. On the other hand, it is noticed that the both ends of the histogram of Woman image have peaks. Therefore, it is recommended that the reversible data hiding community should pay attention to Woman image and test the proposed reversible data hiding algorithm on Woman image. In this section, we first present our test results on Woman image in detail. Afterwards, we present the summarized test results on the rest four test images:

4.1   Test Results on Woman Image

The size of Woman has been reduced from 1920 ×1536 to 960×768 by using Photoshop, and shown in Fig. 6 (a). The histogram of Woman image is shown in Fig. 7. It is observed that its histogram has non-zero peaks at the two sides of its histogram. By applying our proposed algorithm, the marked image with a pure payload of 0.7 bpp is shown in Fig. 6 (b), and detailed results are shown in Table 2.

(a) Original image   (b) Marked with 0.7 bpp embedded

Fig. 6. Woman image (960×768)

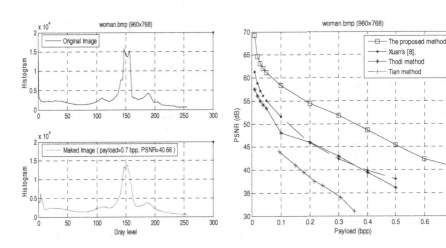

Fig. 7. Histogram of woman Image   **Fig. 8.** Data embedding for woman

Table 2. Data embedding into Woman image using the proposed method

Payload (bpp)	PSNR (dB)	T	T_F	T_L	T_R	Payload (bits) (bpp×N)	Book-keeping (bit)	Cycle	Scan	Real payload (bit)	t_N	t_P	S	Time (sec)
0.01	69.22	-2	8	0	0	7372	0	1	1	7372	-2	1	-2	0
0.02	64.67	1	17	0	1	14745	1176	1	1	15921	-1	1	-1	1
0.03	63.15	0	6	0	1	22118	1176	1	1	23294	-	0	0	4
0.04	62.05	0	7	0	1	29491	1176	1	1	30667	-	0	0	8
0.05	61.18	0	7	0	1	36864	1176	1	1	38040	-	0	0	12
0.1	58.38	0	11	0	1	73728	1176	1	1	74904	-	0	0	19
0.2	54.35	1	50	1	1	147456	6327	1	1	153783	-1	1	-1	26
0.3	51.84	-1	130	1	1	221184	6327	1	1	227468	-1	0	-	35
								2	1	43	-1	0	-1	35
0.4	48.70	-2	80	2	2	294912	12212	1	1	100042	-2	1	-	45
									2	207082	-1	0	0	54
0.5	45.38	-2	60	3	3	368640	17826	1	1	97183	-2	1	-	63
									2	206323	-1	0	-	73
								2	1	82960	-2	1	1	81
0.6	42.34	-2	600	3	3	442368	17826	1	1	119036	-2	1	-	90
									2	231988	-1	0	-	100
								2	1	109170	-2	1	1	110
0.7	40.66	-2	300	4	4	516095	26849	1	1	113211	-2	1	-	120
									2	228200	-1	0	-	131
								2	1	107204	-2	1	-	141
									2	94329	-1	0	-1	149

In Table 2, the t_N, t_P, which have been introduced in Section 3.2 and included in Fig.3 and Fig.4, indicate specific threshold value the threshold T assumes at the left side and right side of the histogram of prediction-errors during the algorithm execution. The S stands for the stop point in data embedding, which is either the last t_N or the last t_P used in the algorithm. With the S and threshold T, the algorithm can retrieve data correctly. The "Time" listed in the right-most column of Table 2 is the time consumed in each case. Note that there are "Cycle" and "Scan" in Table 2. Take a look at the case of 0.5 bpp embedding. There are two cycles. In Cycle 1, there are two scans. In Scan 1, the first pair of $\{t_N, t_P\}$ is equal to $\{-2, 1\}$ and the second pair is $\{t_N, t_P\}=\{-1, 0\}$. Since the required amount of data has not been completely embedded in Cycle 1 while the t_P has reached 0, Cycle 2 embedding is conducted with $\{t_N, t_P\}=\{-2,1\}$. Since 0.5 bpp has been embedded for the image, there is no need to another scan, and the algorithm stops. The real payload is the sum of payload and bookkeeping. The bookkeeping data are used to store the histogram modification information for data extracting and the original image recovery. For example, at 0.5 bpp case, the real payload is the payload, 368,640 bits, plus bookkeeping, 17,826 bits, equal to 386,466 bits. The real payload 386,466 can also be calculated through the circle and scan as 97183 (Circle 1, Scan 1) plus 206323 (Circle 1, Scan 2) and plus 82960 (Circle 2, Scan 1).

The performance comparison on the Waman iamge in terms of PSNR versus pure payload among our proposed method, and three prior-arts: Difference expansion method [4], Prediction-error expansion method [9], and Optimal histogram-pair based method [8] are shown in Fig. 8.

Table 3. Results of optimal thresholds T vs. T_F (left), T_L vs. T_R (right) with different payload for Woman Image

PSNR=64.67,bpp=0.02,T_L=0,T_R=1				
$T \backslash T_F$	11	14	17	20	23
2	UNF	UNF	Fail	Fail	Fail
-2	UNF	UNF	Fail	Fail	Fail
1	UNF	UNF	64.67	64.65	64.62
-1	63.93	63.89	63.87	63.83	63.83
0	64.62	64.57	64.56	64.54	64.52

PSNR=64.67,bpp=0.02,T=1,T_F=17				
$T_L \backslash T_R$	4	0	1	2	3
4	50.06	OVF	50.34	50.3	50.22
3	51.72	OVF	52.15	52.09	51.95
0	Fail	OVF	64.67	Fail	Fail
1	57.92	OVF	60.07	59.69	58.98
2	54.6	OVF	55.48	55.34	55.06

PSNR=62.05,bpp=0.04,T_L=0,T_R=1				
$T \backslash T_F$	1	4	7	10	13
1	Fail	UNF	Fail	Fail	Fail
-1	Fail	UNF	Fail	Fail	Fail
0	Fail	62.01	62.05	61.97	61.88
-2	Fail	UNF	Fail	Fail	Fail
2	Fail	UOF	Fail	Fail	Fail

PSNR=62.05,bpp=0.04,T=0,T_F=7				
$T_L \backslash T_R$	4	0	1	2	3
4	49.77	OVF	50.03	49.99	49.91
3	51.4	OVF	51.78	51.72	51.61
0	59.1	OVF	62.05	61.49	60.47
1	57.09	OVF	58.69	58.42	57.9
2	54.1	OVF	54.83	54.72	54.49

PSNR=58.38,bpp=0.1,T_L=0,T_R=1				
$T \backslash T_F$	3	7	11	15	19
1	Fail	UNF	Fail	Fail	Fail
-1	Fail	UNF	Fail	Fail	Fail
0	Fail	OVF	58.38	58.26	58.15
-2	Fail	UOF	Fail	Fail	Fail
2	Fail	UOF	UOF	Fail	Fail

PSNR=58.38,bpp=0.1,T=0,T_F=11				
$T_L \backslash T_R$	4	0	1	2	3
4	48.56	OVF	OVF	48.78	48.69
3	50.16	OVF	OVF	50.54	50.38
0	56.89	OVF	58.38	58.12	57.64
1	54.96	OVF	56.58	56.25	55.64
2	52.46	OVF	OVF	53.1	52.85

PSNR=51.84,bpp=0.3,T_L=1,T_R=1				
$T \backslash T_F$	110	120	130	140	150
-2	UOF	UOF	UOF	UOF	UOF
1	OVF	OVF	OVF	OVF	OVF
-1	51.76	51.82	51.84	51.8	51.76
0	Fail	Fail	Fail	Fail	Fail
2	UOF	UOF	UOF	UOF	UOF

PSNR=51.84,bpp=0.3,T=-1,T_F=130				
$T_L \backslash T_R$	4	0	1	2	3
4	47.7	OVF	OVF	47.88	47.81
0	Fail	UOF	Fail	Fail	Fail
1	51.19	OVF	51.84	51.69	51.48
2	50.1	OVF	OVF	50.44	50.31
3	48.76	OVF	OVF	49	48.9

PSNR=45.38,bpp=0.5,T_L=3,T_R=3				
$T \backslash T_F$	20	40	60	80	100
-3	Fail	UOF	UOF	UOF	UOF
2	Fail	UOF	OVF	OVF	OVF
-2	Fail	UOF	45.38	45.32	45.24
1	Fail	Fail	OVF	OVF	OVF
-1	Fail	Fail	Fail	Fail	Fail

PSNR=45.38,bpp=0.5,T=-2,T_F=60				
$T_L \backslash T_R$	1	2	3	4	5
1	UOF	UOF	Fail	Fail	Fail
2	UOF	UOF	Fail	Fail	Fail
3	OVF	OVF	45.38	45.31	45.23
4	OVF	OVF	44.9	44.83	44.76
5	OVF	OVF	44.16	44.11	44.04

PSNR=40.66,bpp=0.7,T_L=4,T_R=4				
$T \backslash T_F$	100	200	300	400	500
-3	UOF	UOF	UOF	UOF	UOF
2	OVF	OVF	OVF	OVF	OVF
-2	Fail	Fail	40.66	40.42	40.21
1	Fail	Fail	Fail	Fail	Fail
-1	Fail	Fail	Fail	Fail	Fail

PSNR=40.66,bpp=0.7,T=-2,T_F=300				
$T_L \backslash T_R$	2	3	4	5	6
2	UOF	UOF	Fail	Fail	Fail
3	UOF	UOF	Fail	Fail	Fail
4	OVF	OVF	40.66	40.64	40.59
5	OVF	OVF	40.41	40.38	40.33
6	OVF	OVF	40.09	40.04	40.01

In Table 3, the performance (PSNR at given data embedding rate) of optimal thresholds T vs. T_F with some values of T_L and T_R (left), T_L vs. T_R with some values of T and T_F (right) at different payload for Woman Image are listed. The sub-table of thresholds T vs. T_F under fixed T_L and T_R are provided on the left. The sub-table of thresholds T_L vs. T_R under fixed T and T_F are provided on the right. The highest PSNR of the stego image with respect to the original image in each sub-table has been indicated with a small box, from which one can observe the optimal "T and T_F" or "T_L and T_R". That is, the optimal embedding results for various embedding rate with all of four thresholds have been listed in Table 3 for the Woman image. There "UOF" means both underflow and overflow, "UF" means underflow, "OF" means overflow, and "Fail" means embedding failure (i.e., the required amount of data cannot be embedded with the corresponding set of thresholds).

4.2   Test Results on Four Commonly Utilized Test Images

The curves of PSNR vs. payload for Lena, Barbara, Baboon and Airplane images are shown in Fig. 9 to Fig. 12, respectively.

4.3   Performance Summary on All of Five Test Image

The optimal thresholds utilized and the resultant PSNR achieved on the above-mentioned five test images by applying the proposed method with various data embedding rates ranging from 0.01 to 0.7 bpp are listed in Table 4, where, as said in Section 4.1, S is the stop value of the embedding threshold T. It is observed that as embedding rate is between 0.01 bpp and 0.7 bpp, T_L and T_R are all zero for Lena, Barbara and Airplane, meaning the optimality can be achieved as both T_L and T_R being zero for these payloads. It is sure if more data are embedded then the thresholds T_L and T_R will not be zero any more. For Woman and Baboon, however, the optimality often achieved with non-zero T_L and T_R even with the payload below 0.7 bpp because of their different histogram distribution, i.e., non-zero at both or one ends.

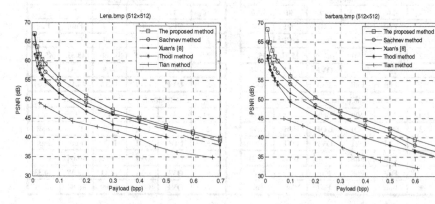

Fig. 9. Embedding for Lena   **Fig. 10.** Embedding for Barbara

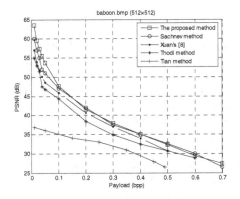

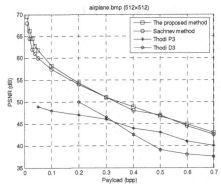

Fig. 11. Embedding for Baboon

Fig. 12. Embedding for Airplane

Table 4. PSNR and optimal thresholds on five test images with different payloads

Woman												
bpp	0.01	0.02	0.03	0.04	0.05	0.1	0.2	0.3	0.4	0.5	0.6	0.7
PSNR	69.22	64.67	63.15	62.05	61.18	58.38	54.35	51.84	48.70	45.38	42.34	40.66
T	-2	1	0	0	0	0	1	-1	-2	-2	-2	-2
T_F	8	17	6	7	7	11	50	130	80	60	600	300
T_L	0	0	0	0	0	0	1	1	2	3	3	4
T_R	0	1	1	1	1	1	1	1	2	3	3	4
S	-2	-1	0	0	0	0	-1	-1	0	1	1	-1
Lena												
bpp	0.01	0.02	0.03	0.04	0.05	0.1	0.2	0.3	0.4	0.5	0.6	0.7
PSNR	67.08	63.78	61.79	60.38	59.22	55.44	50.87	47.29	45.16	43.18	41.47	39.89
T	-4	4	3	-4	3	2	-1	2	-2	-3	-4	-5
T_F	14	26	21	36	32	48	100	100	250	200	250	550
T_L	0	0	0	0	0	0	0	0	0	0	0	0
T_R	0	0	0	0	0	0	0	0	0	0	0	0
S	-4	4	-3	-3	-2	-2	0	1	0	-1	3	-1
Barbara												
bpp	0.01	0.02	0.03	0.04	0.05	0.1	0.2	0.3	0.4	0.5	0.6	0.7
PSNR	68.28	64.89	62.76	61.19	60.04	55.97	50.50	47.07	44.67	42.32	39.57	37.40
T	-4	-4	-4	-3	-3	2	-3	-3	-4	-6	-6	-6
T_F	18	30	38	23	31	65	85	100	120	250	320	250
T_L	0	0	0	0	0	0	0	0	0	0	0	0
T_R	0	0	0	0	0	0	0	0	4	2	3	0
S	3	3	-4	-3	2	-2	1	-1	-1	-1	-5	2
Baboon												
bpp	0.01	0.02	0.03	0.04	0.05	0.1	0.2	0.3	0.4	0.5	0.6	0.7
PSNR	63.51	59.57	57.29	55.46	53.75	47.65	41.60	37.99	35.01	32.29	29.46	27.44
T	-5	3	3	3	-3	-3	-4	-7	-11	-12	-13	-13
T_F	85	110	180	310	510	540	660	800	1100	2400	2200	2400
T_L	0	0	0	0	0	0	0	4	7	9	17	22
T_R	0	0	0	0	0	0	0	0	0	0	15	0
S	-5	3	3	3	2	1	-1	-1	0	0	8	4
Airplane												
bpp	0.01	0.02	0.03	0.04	0.05	0.1	0.2	0.3	0.4	0.5	0.6	0.7
PSNR	69.58	66.31	64.57	62.83	61.91	58.25	54.28	50.99	48.86	46.76	44.90	42.95
T	1	1	1	1	1	1	-1	1	-2	-3	-4	-5
T_F	3	4	4	6	6	10	17	26	37	52	94	220
T_L	0	0	0	0	0	0	0	0	0	3	0	4
T_R	0	0	0	0	0	0	0	0	0	0	0	1
S	-1	-1	1	1	-1	1	-1	0	-1	-3	-1	4

5   Discussion and Conclusion

The research on reversible data hiding has made rapid progress in the past decade. An optimal histogram-pair and prediction-error based method has been reported in the paper. Instead of based on two thresholds [8,14], i.e., embedding threshold T and fluctuation threshold T_F, the four thresholds have been utilized in this new algorithm. That is, the left- and right-histogram shrinking parameters used in [6,7,8,14] have now become two additional thresholds, i.e., the left- and right-shrinking thresholds, respectively, in this proposed algorithm. They are adjusted not only to avoid overflow and/or underflow but also for optimal performance in reversible data embedding. The performance of this proposed algorithm has been further enhanced, in particular for Woman image, which is a JPEG2000 test image, whose histogram has peaks on both of its right and left ends. On this Woman image, the proposed scheme achieves 2.22dB, 3.35dB and 3.62dB higher PSNR at the embedding rates of 0.01 bpp, 0.1 bpp and 0.5 bpp, respectively, compared with what reported in [14]. Since the proposed algorithm works on prediction-error image, its performance is much higher than what reported in [8]. Another advancement made in this paper over [8,14] is that the optimization has been concretely conducted and demonstrated in this paper for the first time. That is, the optimality has been mentioned in [8,14], but there have been no concrete procedures.

One observation is made here. That is, in addition to Lena image, whose histogram has its two ends widely empty, we suggest that Woman image with both sides of its histogram having peaks should be added as a test image for the reversible data hiding community in reporting and comparing the performance of various reversible data hiding algorithms.

Compared with the state-of-the-art reversible data hiding scheme [4][9][13] whose embedding strategy can be represented by $2P_E+b$, where P_E stands for error or prediction-error and b stands for the bit to be embedded, our histogram-pair based scheme is in spirit of P_E+b. The performance comparison reported in this paper indicates that the strategy of P_E+b is more efficient then $2P_E+b$ in terms of the PSNR verses data embedding rate. Specifically, compared with Sachnev et al.'s method [13], perhaps the most advanced scheme reported in the literature, on 12 different payloads ranging from 0.01 bpp to 0.7 bpp, our proposed scheme has achieved on average 1.94 dB improvement for Lena image, 2.33 dB for Barbara image, 1.28 dB for Baboon image, and 1.01 dB for Airplane image.

Note that Ni et al.'s method [5] is the first method that uses the P_E+b approach and image histogram shifting. There is no, however, consideration and procedure for achieving the optimality in terms of the PSNR of stego image versus data embedding rate. In terms of performance, the proposed method has been far more advanced than what reported by the method [5].

References

1. Honsinger, C.W., Jones, P., Rabbani, M., Stoffel, J.C.: Lossless recovery of an original image containing embedded data. US Patent: 6,278,791 (2001)
2. Fridrich, J., Goljan, M., Du, R.: Invertible authentication. In: Proc. SPIE Photonics West, Security and Watermarking of Multimedia Contents III, San Jose, California, vol. 397, pp. 197–208 (January 2001)

3. Xuan, G., Zhu, J., Chen, J., Shi, Y.Q., Ni, Z., Su, W.: Distortionless data hiding based on integer wavelet transform. IEE Electronics Letters 38(25), 1646–1648 (2002)
4. Tian, J.: Reversible data embedding using a difference expansion. IEEE Transaction on Circuits and Systems for Video Technology 13(8), 890–896 (2003)
5. Ni, Z., Shi, Y.Q., Ansari, N., Su, W.: Reversible data hiding. In: Proceedings of IEEE International Symposium on Circuits and Systems (ISCAS), Bangkok, Thailand, vol. 2, pp. 912–915 (May 2003); Also appear in Ni, Z., Shi, Y. Q., Ansari, N., Su, W.: Reversible data hiding. IEEE Transactions on Circuits and Systems for Video Technology 16(3), 354-362 (2006)
6. Xuan, G., Shi, Y.Q., Yang, C., Zheng, Y., Zou, D., Chai, P.: Lossless data hiding using integer wavelet transform and threshold embedding technique. In: IEEE International Conference on Multimedia and Expo (ICME 2005), Amsterdam, Netherlands (July 2005)
7. Xuan, G., Yao, Q., Yang, C., Gao, J., Chai, P., Shi, Y.Q., Ni, Z.: Lossless data hiding using histogram shifting method based on integer wavelets. In: Shi, Y.Q., Jeon, B. (eds.) IWDW 2006. LNCS, vol. 4283, pp. 323–332. Springer, Heidelberg (2006)
8. Xuan, G., Shi, Y.Q., Chai, P., Cui, X., Ni, Z., Tong, X.: Optimum histogram pair based image lossless data embedding. In: Shi, Y.Q., Kim, H.-J., Katzenbeisser, S. (eds.) IWDW 2007. LNCS, vol. 5041, pp. 264–278. Springer, Heidelberg (2008)
9. Thodi, D.M., Rodríguez, J.J.: Reversible watermarking by prediction-error expansion. In: Proceedings of 6th IEEE Southwest Symposium on Image Analysis and Interpretation, Lake Tahoe, CA,USA, March 28-30, pp. 21–25 (2004); Also appear as Thodi, D.M., Rodriguez, J.J.: Expansion embedding techniques for reversible watermarking. IEEE Trans. Image Process 16(3), 721–730 (2007)
10. Kamstra, L., Heijmans, H.J.A.M.: Reversible data embedding into images using wavelet techniques and sorting. IEEE Transactions on Image Processing 14(12), 2082–2090 (2005)
11. Coltuc, D., Chassery, J.M.: Very fast watermarking by reversible contrast mapping. IEEE Signal Processing Letters 14(4), 255–258 (2007)
12. Lee, S., Yoo, C.D., Kalker, T.: Reversible image watermarking based on integer-to-integer wavelet transform. IEEE Transactions on Information Forensics and Security 2(3), pt. 1, 321–330 (2007)
13. Sachnev, V., Kim, H.J., Nam, J., Suresh, S., Shi, Y.Q.: Reversible watermarking algorithm using sorting and prediction. IEEE Transactions on Circuits and Systems for Video Technology 19(7), 989–999 (2009)
14. Xuan, G., Shi, Y.Q., Teng, J., Tong, X., Chai, P.: Double-threshold reversible data hiding. In: IEEE International Symposium on Circuits and Systems (ISCAS 2010), Paris, France (May 2010); Also appear in Xuan, G., Shi, Y.Q., Chai, P., Teng, J., Ni, Z., Tong, X.: Optimum histogram pair based image lossless data embedding. In: Shi, Y.Q. (ed.) Transactions on DHMS IV. LNCS, vol. 5510, pp. 84–102. Springer, Heidelberg (2009)
15. Shi, Y.Q.: Reversible data hiding. In: Cox, I., Kalker, T., Lee, H.-K. (eds.) IWDW 2004. LNCS, vol. 3304, pp. 1–12. Springer, Heidelberg (2005)
16. Ni, Z., Ni, Z., Shi, Y.Q., Ansari, N., Su, W., Sun, Q., Lin, X.: Robust lossless image data hiding designed for semi-fragile image authentication. IEEE Transactions on Circuits and Systems for Video Technology 18(4), 497–509 (2008)
17. http://sipi.usc.edu/database
18. Source JPEG2000 (JPSEC), ISO/IEC 15444-8 (April 2007)

An Improved Algorithm for Reversible Data Hiding in Encrypted Image

Jie Yu[1], Guopu Zhu[1,*], Xiaolong Li[2], and Jianquan Yang[1]

[1] Shenzhen Institutes of Advanced Technology, Chinese Academy of Sciences,
Shenzhen, GD 518055, China
{jie.yu,jq.yang}@siat.ac.cn, guopu.zhu@gmail.com
[2] Institute of Computer Science and Technology, Peking University,
Beijing 100871, China
lixiaolong@pku.edu.cn

Abstract. Recently, Zhang [1] proposed a reversible data hiding algorithm for encrypted image, which can reversibly embed data into encrypted image without knowing the original image content. However, in data extraction of this algorithm, the error-rate is large especially for high capacity case. In this paper, to remedy the above problem, an improved method is presented. By our improvement, the error-rate is significantly decreased and the visual quality of the decrypted marked image is enhanced as well.

Keywords: Image encryption, reversible data hiding, signal processing in the encrypted domain (SPED).

1 Introduction

In recent years, more and more attention has been paid to signal processing in the encrypted domain (SPED) for the sake of data security and privacy. Generally, SPED can be applied in following scenario: some important digital signals need to be sent by their owners to other parties for processing, but the other parties may be not trustworthy, so the signals should be encrypted before they are sent out. In this case, the signals to be processed by other parties are in cyphertext format. SPED is more difficult to be implemented compared with normal signal processing. However, its feasibility has been demonstrated by many existing works such as data hiding in encrypted image [2–5], signal transformation in encrypted domain [6–8], content retrieval over encrypted multimedia database [9], encrypted image and video compression [10, 11], feature extraction from encrypted image [12], etc.

This paper focuses on the reversible data hiding technique for encrypted image, in which secret data is embedded into encrypted image in a reversible way, i.e., one can recover both the hidden data and original image from the marked encrypted image. By now, only a few works have been done on this topic [1, 13–15].

---

* Corresponding author.

Y.Q. Shi, H.J. Kim, and F. Pérez-González (Eds.): IWDW 2012, LNCS 7809, pp. 384–394, 2013.
© Springer-Verlag Berlin Heidelberg 2013

In [13], the original image is first encrypted by the content owner, then secret data is embedded into the encrypted image by the data-hider using a reversible algorithm. Once the receiver gets the marked encrypted image, it can extract the embedded data and meanwhile recover the original image as well. However, in this algorithm, the content owner has to send the encryption key along with the encrypted image to data-hider, thus the privacy of the original image is easily leaked to data-hider. In this light, the algorithm is not secure if the data-hider is not trustworthy. In [1], Zhang proposed a new algorithm in which data-hider can embed data into the encrypted image without using the encryption key. Thus the data-hider cannot obtain the original image and the leakage of image privacy is avoided. In another work [14], Zhang also proposed a separable reversible data hiding algorithm for encrypted image, which mainly studied the separability of the encryption key and the data-hiding key. Recently, Hong et al. [15] improved Zhang's algorithm [1] in the extraction and image recovery phase by using a better fluctuation function and the side match technique.

This paper focuses on the analysis and improvement of the algorithm of Ref. [1]. In Zhang's algorithm [1], a fluctuation function was devised to extract the embedded data. However, the error-rate of data extraction is large, and thus the original image cannot be well recovered. In this paper, to remedy this problem, an improved algorithm of [1] is proposed. The novel algorithm is based on a detailed theoretical analysis about the fluctuation function. By our improvement, the extraction error is significantly decreased. In addition, the proposed algorithm is also advantageous in increasing the PSNR of decrypted marked image versus original image.

The rest of this paper is organized as follows. First in Section 2, Zhang's algorithm is introduced and analyzed in detail. Then, an improved algorithm is presented in Section 3. The experimental results are reported in Section 4. Finally, we draw our conclusions in Section 5.

2   Zhang's Algorithm

In [1], Zhang proposed a reversible data hiding algorithm for encrypted image, in which the data-hider can reversibly embed data into the encrypted image without using the encryption key used by the content owner. In other word, by this method, the data-hider can implement reversible data embedding directly in the encrypted image, without knowing the original image content. Zhang's algorithm includes three key procedures:

1. *Image encryption:* The content owner generates a pseudo random bit stream as encryption key and uses the key to encrypt the original image by a bitwise exclusive-or operation. Then the encrypted image is sent to the data-hider.
2. *Data embedding:* First, the data-hider divides the encrypted image into non-overlapping blocks sized by $s \times s$, and one data bit will be embedded into each block. Then, according to a data-hiding key, for each image block, the data-hider randomly divides its pixels into two equal-sized sets S_0 and S_1.

For data embedding, flip the l least significant bits (LSB) of each pixel in S_0 if the data bit to be embedded is 0; otherwise, flip the l LSB of each pixel in S_1. In [1], l is fixed as 3. Finally, the marked encrypted image is sent to receiver. Notice that, for an image of $M \times N$ pixels, the embedding capacity of Zhang's algorithm is $\lfloor \frac{M}{s} \rfloor \times \lfloor \frac{N}{s} \rfloor$, where $\lfloor \cdot \rfloor$ denotes the floor function.

3. *Data extraction and image recovery:* After decrypting, the receiver divides the received image into blocks and separates each block into S_0 and S_1 in the same way as in data embedding. Then, for a decrypted block, let H_0 and H_1 be the new block obtained by flipping the l LSB of each pixel in S_0 and S_1, respectively. As proved in [1], H_0 or H_1 is the original image block, and the other one is the modified block where the l LSB of each pixel are flipped. So, to determine which one is the original one, Zhang proposed the following fluctuation function

$$f = \sum_{u=2}^{s-1} \sum_{v=2}^{s-1} \left| p_{u,v} - \frac{p_{u-1,v} + p_{u,v-1} + p_{u+1,v} + p_{u,v+1}}{4} \right| \qquad (1)$$

where $p_{u,v}$ is the value of pixel (u, v) of the block. Denote, respectively, f_0 and f_1 as the fluctuation function of H_0 and H_1. Finally, the receiver can extract the embedded data and recover the original image block as follows: if $f_0 < f_1$, H_0 is the original block and the embedded data is 0; otherwise, H_1 is the original block and the embedded data is 1. Here, the basic idea is that, the original image block is assumed to be less fluctuate than its modified version.

Although Zhang's algorithm can reversibly embed data into encrypted image without knowing the original image content, it has a certain error in data extraction, and thus the original image cannot be completely recovered especially for the case of high capacity (i.e., the block size $s \times s$ is small). Since the fluctuation effect is the key point of data extraction, we then flip more LSB to increase the fluctuation and a better performance is expected. But, according to our experimental results in Fig. 1, we observe that the extraction error does not decrease monotonically when increasing the flipped LSB number, l. The lowest extraction error is generally archived when l is 3 or 4.

We now explain why Zhang's algorithm does not work as expected. Without loss of generality, assume that H_0 is the original image block and H_1 is the modified one. Denote $p_{u,v}^L$ and $p_{u,v}^M$ as the l LSB and the $(8 - l)$ most significant bits (MSB) of $p_{u,v}$, respectively. Then, we know that

$$p_{u,v} = p_{u,v}^M + p_{u,v}^L. \qquad (2)$$

When flipping the l LSB of $p_{u,v}$, $p_{u,v}^L$ will changed to

$$\overline{p}_{u,v}^L = 2^l - 1 - p_{u,v}^L \qquad (3)$$

while $p_{u,v}^M$ remains unchanged, then $p_{u,v}$ will changed to

$$p_{u,v}^M + 2^l - 1 - p_{u,v}^L. \qquad (4)$$

Table 1. The probability of $d_{u,v}^M = 0$ with respect to the flipped LSB number l

l	1	2	3	4	5	6	7	8
The probability of $d_{u,v}^M = 0$	0.122	0.196	0.298	0.420	0.557	0.704	0.849	1.000

Let

$$d_{u,v}^L = p_{u,v}^L - \frac{p_{u-1,v}^L + p_{u,v-1}^L + p_{u+1,v}^L + p_{u,v+1}^L}{4} \tag{5}$$

and

$$d_{u,v}^M = p_{u,v}^M - \frac{p_{u-1,v}^M + p_{u,v-1}^M + p_{u+1,v}^M + p_{u,v+1}^M}{4}. \tag{6}$$

Then, according to (1) and (2), the fluctuation functions of H_0 and H_1, f_0 and f_1, can be written as

$$f_0 = \sum_{u=2}^{s-1} \sum_{v=2}^{s-1} |d_{u,v}^M + d_{u,v}^L| \tag{7}$$

and

$$f_1 = \sum_{u=2}^{s-1} \sum_{v=2}^{s-1} |d_{u,v}^M - d_{u,v}^L|. \tag{8}$$

Due to the strong correlation of MSB, the probability of $d_{u,v}^M = 0$ is high and it increases rapidly when increasing l (see Table 1[1]). Particularly, when $l = 8$, $d_{u,v}^M = 0$ for all (u, v), then $f_0 = f_1$. In this case, whatever the embedded bit is, the extracted bit is always 1. It means that a kind of error in data extraction is derived from the MSB correlation, and the larger the number of filliped LSB is, the more the kind of error happens to Zhang's algorithm.

3   Improved Algorithm

In order to reduce the extraction error derived from the MSB correlation, here we propose an improved algorithm. The new algorithm also includes three procedures:

1. *Image encryption:* This procedure is exactly the same as that of Zhang's.
2. *Data embedding:* First, divide the encrypted image into blocks of $s \times s$ pixels and separate the pixels in each block into two sets S_0 and S_1 as did in Zhang's algorithm. Then, depending on a data-hiding key, each bit of all l LSB of the encrypted image is selected as an active bit with probability p, where $p \in (0, 1]$ is a given number. Finally, for each block, flip all active bits in S_0 if the data bit to be embedded is 0; otherwise, flip all active bits in S_1.

---

[1] The values in Table 1 and 2 are calculated using the test set of 1200 images, which is described in Section 4.

Table 2. The probabilities of $|d_{u,v}^L| < |\widetilde{d}_{u,v}^L|$ and $f_0 < f_1$, when $d_{u,v}^M = 0$ for all (u,v) in image block, for different block size s, flipped LSB number l and parameter p. Here, f_0 denotes the fluctuation function of the original image block, while f_1 denotes that of the modified image block.

	$s = 4$				$s = 8$			
	$l = 3$		$l = 5$		$l = 3$		$l = 5$	
	$p = 0.5$	$p = 0.7$	$p = 0.5$	$p = 0.7$	$p = 0.5$	$p = 0.7$	$p = 0.5$	$p = 0.7$
$|d_{u,v}^L| < |\widetilde{d}_{u,v}^L|$	0.823	0.795	0.906	0.889	0.856	0.828	0.933	0.919
$f_0 < f_1$	0.962	0.949	0.985	0.980	0.999	0.999	1.000	1.000

3. *Data extraction and image recovery:* After decrypting, divide the received image into blocks and separate the pixels in each block into S_0 and S_1 as did in data embedding. Then, for a decrypted block, let H_0 and H_1 be the new block obtained by flipping all active bits in S_0 and S_1, respectively. Finally, apply the fluctuation function defined in (1) to determine which one of H_0 and H_1 is the original image block and to extract the embedded data in the same way as in Zhang's algorithm.

Here, p is the only new parameter. One can get more active bits by increasing this parameter. Particulary, the improved algorithm includes Zhang's original one as a special case if taking $p = 1$.

We now explain why the improved algorithm can decrease the extraction error. Likewise, assume that H_0 is the original image block. When flipping all active bits of $p_{u,v}$, suppose that $p_{u,v}^L$ will changed to $\widetilde{p}_{u,v}^L$. Then we define

$$\widetilde{d}_{u,v}^L = \widetilde{p}_{u,v}^L - \frac{\widetilde{p}_{u-1,v}^L + \widetilde{p}_{u,v-1}^L + \widetilde{p}_{u+1,v}^L + \widetilde{p}_{u,v+1}^L}{4}. \tag{9}$$

Clearly, for the improved algorithm, the fluctuation function f_0 can also be formulated by (7), while f_1 is changed to

$$f_1 = \sum_{u=2}^{s-1} \sum_{v=2}^{s-1} |d_{u,v}^M + \widetilde{d}_{u,v}^L|. \tag{10}$$

As we have mentioned, the probability of $d_{u,v}^M = 0$ will increase when increasing l. However, in contrast to Zhang's algorithm, since $\widetilde{d}_{u,v}^L$ is likely not equal to $d_{u,v}^L$, according to (7) and (10), the case that $d_{u,v}^M = 0$ for all (u,v) will not necessarily lead to $f_0 = f_1$. Furthermore, $d_{u,v}^L$ and $\widetilde{d}_{u,v}^L$ can be regarded as the differences of the l LSB of natural image and modified image, respectively. So, in the above case, due to the correlation of natural image, $|d_{u,v}^L|$ is generally smaller than $|\widetilde{d}_{u,v}^L|$, accordingly, f_0 is also generally smaller than f_1, which can be shown in Table 2. Thus, the improved algorithm can effectively reduce the extraction error when the probability of $d_{u,v}^M = 0$ is high. Finally, we remark that, compared with Zhang's algorithm, the improved algorithm can increase

Table 3. The PSNR (in dB) of decrypted marked image, for different parameter p and flipped LSB number l. Notice that the case of $p = 1.0$ corresponds Zhang's algorithm.

	$p = 1.0$	$p = 0.9$	$p = 0.8$	$p = 0.7$	$p = 0.6$	$p = 0.5$	$p = 0.4$	$p = 0.3$	$p = 0.2$	$p = 0.1$
$l = 3$	37.9	38.8	38.9	39.5	40.1	40.9	41.9	43.1	44.9	47.9
$l = 4$	31.8	32.3	32.8	33.4	34.1	34.9	35.8	37.1	38.8	41.8
$l = 5$	25.8	26.3	26.8	27.4	28.0	28.8	29.8	31.0	32.8	35.8

the PSNR of decrypted marked image since only active bits are flipped. In fact, the expected value of the mean square error (MSE) between decrypted marked image and original image is

$$\frac{p}{2} \sum_{k=1}^{l} (2^{k-1})^2 = \frac{p}{6}(4^l - 1). \tag{11}$$

So, the PSNR of decrypted marked image is clearly

$$\text{PSNR} = 10 \cdot \log_{10} \frac{6 \cdot 255^2}{p(4^l - 1)}. \tag{12}$$

As shown in Table 3, the smaller the parameter p is, the larger the PSNR is, which means that the improved algorithm has a better PSNR than Zhang's algorithm where $p = 1.0$.

4   Experimental Results

A test image set containing 1200 images is formed by randomly selecting 400 images from each of Corel, NJIT, and NRCS databases[2]. Before testing, each selected image is cropped to 512×512 pixels.

To evaluate the proposed improved algorithm, the average error-rate of data extraction is computed for the flowing cases: the block size parameter $s \in \{4, 8, 16, 32\}$, the probability $p \in \{0.1, 0.2, 0.3, 0.4, 0.5, 0.6, 0.7, 0.8, 0.9, 1.0\}$ and the flipped LSB number $l \in \{1, 2, 3, 4, 5, 6, 7, 8\}$. Recall again that Zhang's algorithm is a special case of the proposed algorithm by taking $p = 1.0$.

First, Zhang's algorithm and the proposed algorithm are compared mainly on the variation of the average error-rate with the increase of the flipped LSB number l. As shown in Fig. 1 (for clarity, only a part of our experimental results are presented in Figs. 1 and 2), for the proposed algorithm of which p is set to be 0.7, the error-rate almost decreases monotonically when increasing l, which is greatly different from Zhang's algorithm. Fig.1 also shows that, the proposed algorithm can provide a much smaller error-rate than that of Zhang's.

---

[2] Corel database is available from CorelDraw version 10.0 software, NRCS database is available at http://photogallery.nrcs.usda.gov/, and NJIT database is set up by Prof. Shi-Yun Qing of New Jersey Institute of Technology, USA.

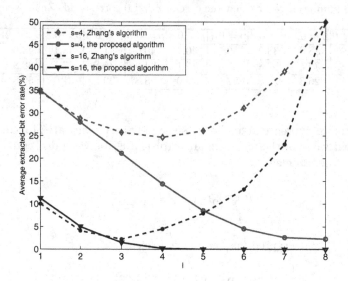

Fig. 1. Comparison of Zhang's algorithm [1] and the proposed algorithm on the variation of the average error-rate with the increase of the flipped LSB number l

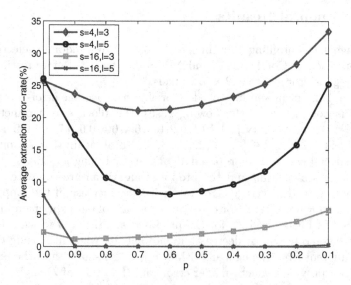

Fig. 2. Average extraction error-rate with respect to the parameter p

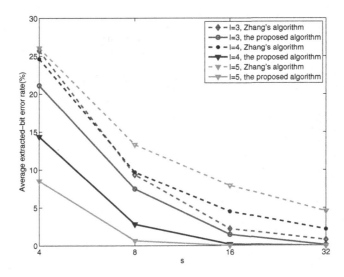

Fig. 3. Comparison of Zhang's algorithm [1] and the proposed algorithm and in the conditions that the flipped LSB number l takes 3, 4 and 5, respectively

Then, we study the influence of p on the proposed algorithm. Referring to Fig. 2, we see that with the decrease of p, the error-rate decreases first and then increases. Although the error-rate achieves its minimum at different p in different cases, its variation with the decrease of p is smooth and regular. In addition, we point out that, by our experience, the proposed algorithm works well in most cases when p takes around 0.7.

Considering the trade-off of the visual quality and the error-rate, we finally compare the proposed algorithm with Zhang's algorithm in the conditions that the flipped LSB number l takes 3, 4 and 5, respectively. For the proposed algorithm, p is set to be 0.7 in this and the following experiments. Fig. 3 shows that the proposed algorithm can provide a smaller error-rate than that of Zhang's. Especially, the superiority of the proposed algorithm over Zhang's algorithm is obvious when s is small while l is large. Furthermore, as mentioned above, the quality of the decrypted marked image of the proposed algorithm is also better than that of Zhang's algorithm when the parameters s and l are the same for the both algorithms. It should be pointed out that the average extraction error-rates of the proposed algorithm will further decrease if p is not fixed, but is adaptively set for different s and l.

Finally, it is worth to mention that, our method is a general idea and it can further improve Zhang's algorithm by employing a more sophisticated fluctuation function. Notice that, in Hong et al.'s algorithm [15], the authors proposed to replace the fluctuation function (1) by calculating the summation of differences between adjacent pixels in both vertical and horizontal directions (see (7) of [15]), and the usage of this new fluctuation function may effectively decrease the

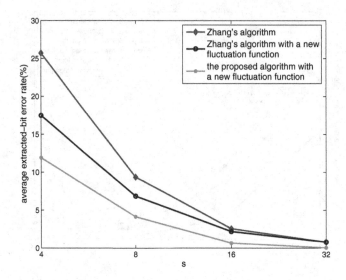

Fig. 4. Comparison of Zhang's algorithm [1], Zhang's algorithm with a new fluctuation function and the proposed algorithm with a new fluctuation function in the conditions that the flipped LSB number l takes 3 and the parameter p takes 0.7

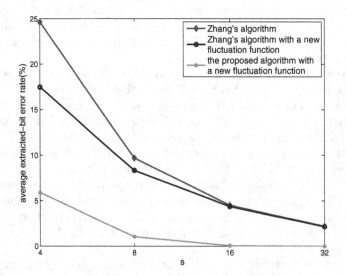

Fig. 5. Comparison of Zhang's algorithm [1], Zhang's algorithm with a new fluctuation function and the proposed algorithm with a new fluctuation function in the conditions that the flipped LSB number l takes 4 and the parameter p takes 0.7

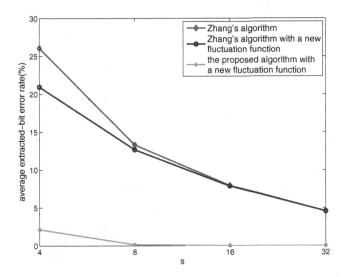

Fig. 6. Comparison of Zhang's algorithm [1], Zhang's algorithm with a new fluctuation function and the proposed algorithm with a new fluctuation function in the conditions that the flipped LSB number l takes 5 and the parameter p takes 0.7

error-rate of Zhang's algorithm. Actually, since the MSBs of adjacent pixels are expected to be close enough, our theoretical analysis is also applicable to this new fluctuation function. In this light, it is not surprised that a more smaller error-rate can be archived if applying this new fluctuation function in our method. Let us now see the Figs. 4, 5 and 6. It is clearly that with the new fluctuation function, the error rate is decreased, but it is further decreased when applying our algorithm. And the improvement is significant when l takes larger value.

5   Conclusion

In this paper, based on Zhang's work in [1], we proposed an improved algorithm for reversible data hiding in encrypted image. Zhang's algorithm can successfully implement privacy-preserving data embedding, but it has a certain error in data extraction, accordingly, the original image cannot be completely recovered. We found that the strong correlation of MSB of natural image likely causes the fluctuation function proposed in [1] to make mistakes in data extraction. The improved algorithm was proposed mainly to reduce such mistakes in data extraction. Our experimental results and analysis have shown the superiority of the improved algorithm over Zhang's algorithm in the accuracy of data extraction and the quality of decrypted marked image.

Acknowledgments. This work has been supported in part by NSFC under Grants No. 61003297, No. U1135001, and No. 61202415, in part by the 863 Program under Grant No. 2011AA010503.

References

1. Zhang, X.: Reversible Data Hiding in Encrypted Image. IEEE Signal Process. Lett. 18(4), 255–258 (2011)
2. Memon, N., Wong, P.W.: A Buyer-seller Watermarking Protocol. IEEE Trans. Image Process. 10(4), 643–649 (2001)
3. Lei, C.L., Yu, P.L., Tsai, P.L., Chan, M.H.: An Efficient and Anonymous Buyer-seller Watermarking Protocol. IEEE Trans. Image Process. 13(12), 1618–1626 (2004)
4. Zhao, B., Kou, W., Li, H., Dang, L., Zhang, J.: Effective Watermarking Scheme in The Encrypted Domain for Buyer-seller Watermarking Protocol. Information Sciences 180(23), 4672–4684 (2010)
5. Zhao, B., Delp, E.J.: Secret Sharing in The Encrypted Domain. In: Proc. IEEE ICC (2011)
6. Bianchi, T., Piva, A., Barni, M.: On The Implementation of The Discrete Fourier Transform in The Encrypted Domain. IEEE Trans. Inf. Forens. Security 4(4), 86–97 (2009)
7. Bianchi, T., Veugen, T., Piva, A., Barni, M.: Processing in The Encrypted Domain Using a Composite Signal Representation: Pros and Cons. In: Proc. IEEE WIFS, pp. 176–180 (2009)
8. Zheng, P., Huang, J.: Implementation of The Discrete Wavelet Transform and Multiresolution Analysis in The Encrypted Domain. In: Proc. of the 19th ACM International Conference on Multimedia, pp. 413–422 (2011)
9. Lu, W., Swaminathan, A., Varna, A.L., Wu, M.: Enabling Search Over Encrypted Multimedia Databases. In: Media Forensics and Security. SPIE, vol. 7254, p. 725418 (2009)
10. Schonberg, D., Draper, S.C., Yeo, C., Ramchandran, K.: Toward Compression of Encrypted Images and Video Sequences. IEEE Trans. Inf. Forens. Security 3(4), 749–762 (2008)
11. Liu, W., Zeng, W., Dong, L., Yao, Q.: Efficient Compression of Encrypted Grayscale Images. IEEE Trans. Image Process. 19(4), 1097–1102 (2010)
12. Hsu, C.Y., Lu, C.S., Pei, S.C.: Homomorphic Encryption-based Secure SIFT for Privacy-preserving Feature Extraction. In: Media Watermarking, Security, and Forensics III. SPIE, vol. 7880, p. 788005 (2011)
13. Puech, W., Chaumont, M., Strauss, O.: A Reversible Data Hiding Method for Encrypted Images. In: Security, Forensics, Steganography, and Watermarking of Multimedia Contents X. SPIE, vol. 6819, p. 68191E (2008)
14. Zhang, X.: Separable Reversible Datahiding in Encrypted Image. IEEE Trans. Inf. Forens. Security 7(2), 826–832 (2012)
15. Hong, W., Chen, T.S., Wu, H.Y.: An Improved Reversible Data Hiding in Encrypted Images Using Side Match. IEEE Signal Process. Lett. 19(4), 199–202 (2012)

Reversible Watermarking for Audio Authentication Based on Integer DCT and Expansion Embedding

Quan Chen[1,2] and Shijun Xiang [2,*], Xinrong Luo[2]

[1] School of Information Engineering, Guangdong Medical College,
Dongguan, Guangdong, China
[2] School of Information Science and Technology, Jinan University,
Guangzhou, Guangdong, China
xiangshijun@gmail.com

Abstract. Reversible watermarking which can restore the original media after the watermark is extracted, is a potential technique for integrity verification and tamper detecting. In this paper we proposed a reversible fragile watermarking scheme for audio authentication by using Integer Discrete Cosine Transform (intDCT) and expansion embedding. The main contribution consists of: 1) we observe that an audio frame would be distorted after undergoing the intDCT, amplitude expansion (AE) embedding and inverse intDCT operations. The distortion is analyzed in detail and the corresponding solution is proposed for; 2) In the integer DCT domain, two reversible audio watermarking algorithms based on difference expansion (DE) and prediction-error expansion (PE) are designed for the distortion and audio authentication. Experimental results show that the proposed reversible watermarking approaches can be used for integrity verification and tampering location while achieving better fidelity than the AE scheme for the same embedding payload.

Keywords: audio, reversible watermarking, integer DCT, Authentication, expansion embedding.

1 Introduction

Digital watermarking is a technique embedding the useful information into digital media in an imperceptible way for the applications including copyright protection, copy control, broadcast monitoring, content authentication and secret communication. Though the distortion of digital carrier because of watermark embedding is not easy to be perceived, even a little distortion is not accepted in some areas, e.g. military, law, medicine. This led to reversible watermarking (also called lossless data hiding) technique, which not only can extract watermark but also can restore the original data.

In the literature, most of reversible watermarking algorithms focused on image. Difference expansion (DE) proposed by Tian [1] is a high-capacity lossless data embedding strategy by grouping two adjacent pixels to compute an integer average and

---

[*] Corresponding author.

Y.Q. Shi, H.J. Kim, and F. Pérez-González (Eds.): IWDW 2012, LNCS 7809, pp. 395–409, 2013.

a difference for expansion embedding of the auxiliary information and payload. The capacity of the DE scheme is close to 0.5 bpp (bit per pixel). By extending the DE to a generalized integer transform, the auxiliary information can be reduced with groups of three or four pixels [2]. Another important improvement was proposed by Thodi et al. by using histogram shifting technique instead of a location map [3]. Sachnev et al. proposed a surprised improvement to the DE in [4] by dividing an image into two sets for double embedding. Since a pixel in a set was predicted by flooring the average of four immediate pixels in the other set, the improved DE method can significantly reduce the embedding distortion and achieve the capacity of 1 bpp. In this direction, Thodi et al. proposed a productive expansion embedding strategy by using a predictor but a difference operator. The differences to be expanded are the prediction errors, called by prediction error expansion (PE) embedding strategy [3]. The capacity of the PE scheme is bound to 1 bpp since each prediction error can be used for expansion embedding in theory. Lee [5] proposed a reversible image watermarking scheme based on integer to integer wavelet transform, where the watermark is embedded in high-frequency coefficients and adaptive embedding technology is employed for the reduction of the embedding distortion. Instead of embedding information in spatial domain, a reversible watermarking scheme based on integer DCT and expansion technique was proposed by Yang [6]. Recently, expansion embedding-based reversible watermarking is a fruitful research direction.

Reversible watermarking algorithms have also been proposed for digital audio [7-12]. In [7], Veen et al. proposed a novel reversible audio watermarking approach by first compressing the dynamic range of the original signal to render a number of unused bits. These unused bits are used to embed data including payload and information relevant to the bit-exact reconstruction of the original audio file. This method can achieve a satisfactory embedding capacity but suffer from an undesirable distortion due to quantization error and loudness change in the compression-expansion embedding phase. By introducing DE embedding technique for audio, Bradley et al. addressed two DE-based reversible watermarking methods: dyad-based (two samples as a group) and triad-based (three samples as a group) [8]. The dyad-based method can achieve at best 0.5 bits per sample (bps) while the triad-based one providing the maximal capacity of 2 bits in a group of three neighboring samples. The PE embedding technique [3] has also been introduced for digital audio in [9] in a way that the current sample is a linear combination of three past samples (in which each sample is corresponding to an integer weight coefficient). Steinebach et al. [10] reported a digital audio authentication scheme by combining fragile invertible watermarking and digital signature techniques. In [11], Huang proposed an excellent reversible watermarking scheme for acoustic steganography and integrity verification by using amplitude expansion (AE) in the intDCT domain. This scheme can not only reconstruct the original audio data, but also implement integrity verification and tampering location, the embedding capacity of which is bound to 0.5 bps. However, the AE operation in this scheme may cause much distortion .

This paper presents a reversible watermarking algorithm for audio authentication. We introduce DE and PE embedding strategies in integer DCT domain for reversible audio watermarking. Comparing with the AE-based scheme [11], the proposed schemes (using DE and PE in the intDCT domain) can effectively reduce the embedding distortion and improve the embedding capacity. Our watermarking scheme is fragile to any modification because the hash code extracted from an audio frame is chosen as part of the payload in the high-frequency component of the frame. Experimental result showed that our algorithm can obtain better fidelity and capacity, also has a satisfactory performance for integrity identification and tampering location.

The outline of this paper is as follows. We first observe and analyze the existing distortion problem in Huang's embedding scheme, and propose a corresponding solution for this problem. Next, a detail description of new embedding strategies in intDCT domain is followed. Then we address the proposed reversible watermarking scheme and test the scheme's performance.

2   Distortion Problem in Huang's Scheme

2.1   Distortion Appearance

In [11], Huang has proposed a reversible watermarking scheme in the intDCT domain for audio authentication. Firstly, the signal was transformed to intDCT domain. The frame feature (the hash code) is embedded in the high-frequency component, where the coefficients were marked by using AE, which doubles amplitude of a coefficient, and then the least significant bit (LSB) is replaced by a watermark bit. In this paper, we

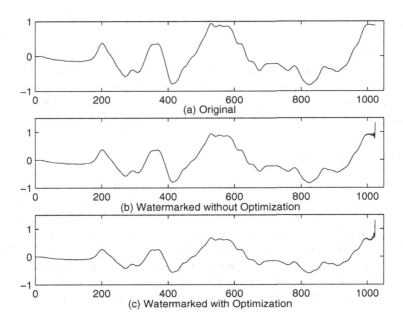

Fig. 1. Waveform of the 4th frame: (a) original, (b) watermarked without amplitude optimization and (c) watermarked with amplitude optimization

observe that the AE-based scheme may cause a severe distortion. More seriously, some frames in the watermarked signal have suffered from overflow problem even if these frames have undergone an amplitude optimization processing operation (which is a measure against overflow in Huang's scheme).

Take a drum music (denoted by '*drum.wav*') as example clip. Fig.1 shows the waveform of the 4th frame (frame size: N=1024). Fig.1 (a) is the original waveform, Fig.1 (b) is the watermarked one which has undergone AE embedding but no amplitude optimization (SHA-1 code is embedded in the highest frequency 160 bits of embedding area whose size is 512). Fig.1 (c) is the version resulted from Fig.1 (b) by using amplitude optimization. From Fig.1 (b), we can see the distortion at the end of frame waveform (sometimes the distortion occurs in the begging of the frame) and the distorted sample in amplitude is over 1 (indicating overflow problem). The type of distortion also exists in the other frames. The same distortion phenomenon is in Fig.1 (c) after using amplitude optimization. That is to say, the amplitude optimization in [11] cannot avoid the overflow problem due to watermark embedding.

To scientifically measure the performance of waveform in Fig.1 (b) and Fig.1 (c), we made the samples of marked signal normalized using

$$s' = s \cdot \frac{\sum_{t=1}^{N} |x_t|}{\sum_{t=1}^{N} |s_t|}, \tag{1}$$

where x is the original signal, s is the marked signal and s' is the normalized marked signal. Then the SNR value of normalized signal in Fig.1 (b) is 29.3403 and the one in Fig.1 (c) is 22.3338.

From the examples above we can see that Huang's scheme could make undesired distortion due to the watermark embedding in the intDCT domain by using AE and the type of distortion cannot be entirely avoided by using amplitude optimization proposed by Huang [11].

2.2   Distortion Analysis

In the reversible watermarking scheme [11], intDCT and AE are two important embedding operations. Since intDCT is a variation of DCT. In order to better analyze the reason of the distortion, we have applied DCT instead of intDCT for the same testing. Experimental results show that the distortion is similar, such as the distortion in the 4th frame as shown in Fig.2, where the frame in length is 1024 and the last 512 DCT coefficients are marked. We also choose different frame lengths for the testing, the distortion is similar. This indicates that DCT (or intDCT) and AE operations have an important impact on the distortion. The analysis in detail is described as follows.

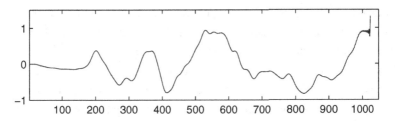

Fig. 2. Waveform of the 4th frame after DCT, AE embedding & inverse DCT

Denote $x = \{x(t) \mid t = 1,2,\cdots,N\}$ as an audio frame with the length of N. Take C_N^{IV} (the Type-IV DCT matrix [12]) for the DCT transform to generate the DCT coefficients $X = C_N^{IV} \times x$, where

$$C_N^{IV} = \sqrt{\frac{2}{N}} \cos\frac{\pi(2t-1)(2i-1)}{4N}, \quad i,t = 1,2,\cdots,N. \tag{2}$$

Suppose the length of the watermark is L and generally set $L \leq \dfrac{N}{2}$ for controlling the distortion. The L highest frequency coefficients are adopted for AE embedding:

$$S(L_1:N) = X(L_1:N) \times 2 \text{ and } S(1:L_1-1) = X(1:L_1-1), \tag{3}$$

where $L_1 = N - L + 1$. Perform the inverse DCT transform to generate the marked frame $s = \{s(t) \mid t = 1,2,\cdots,N\}$. Since C_N^{IV} is an orthogonal matrix, $x = C_N^{IV} \times X$ is with

$$x(t) = C_N^{IV}(t,1)X(1) + C_N^{IV}(t,2)X(2) + \cdots + C_N^{IV}(t,N)X(N). \tag{4}$$

Also, from $s = C_N^{IV} \times S$ and Equation (3), we have

$$
\begin{aligned}
s(t) &= C_N^{IV}(t,1)S(1) + C_N^{IV}(t,2)S(2) + \cdots + C_N^{IV}(t,L_1-1)S(L_1-1) \\
&\quad + C_N^{IV}(t,L_1)S(L_1) + \cdots + C_N^{IV}(t,N)S(N) \\
&= C_N^{IV}(t,1)X(1) + C_N^{IV}(t,2)X(2) + \cdots + C_N^{IV}(t,L_1-1)X(L_1-1) \\
&\quad + 2C_N^{IV}(t,L_1)X(L_1) + \cdots + 2C_N^{IV}(t,N)X(N).
\end{aligned} \tag{5}
$$

The difference between an original sample and a marked one is

$$
\begin{aligned}
s(t) - x(t) &= C_N^{IV}(t,L_1)X(L_1) + C_N^{IV}(t,L_1+1)X(L_1+1) + \\
&\quad \cdots + C_N^{IV}(t,N)X(N)
\end{aligned} \tag{6}
$$

From Equation (6) we can see that the difference $s(t) - x(t)$ in amplitude is determined by the sample values since the transform matrix keeps unchanged in the embedding process. When the coefficients $X(L_1), X(L_1 + 1), \cdots, X(N)$ have larger amplitude and have the same sign (positive or negative) as the transform matrix coefficients, there is going be a big difference between $s(t)$ and $x(t)$. As a result, the distortion even the overflow problem will occur. This explains why some frames in Huang's AE-based method have undesirable distortion due to the embedding.

Take the 4th frame of the drum music as an example. The corresponding 512 high-frequency DCT coefficients are

$$X(513:1024) = \{900, -902, 898, -896, 897, -895, \cdots, 636, -640, 641, -638\}, \quad (7)$$

where are taking bigger amplitude values. This explains the distortion due to the AE embedding, as shown in Fig. 1 and Fig. 2. We can see that the coefficients $X(513:1024)$ in the 4th frame are in the alternate arrangement of positive and negative, and the neighbor coefficients in odd or even positions are close. For most of the other frames, we have the same observation.

From the above analysis, we can see that the DCT and AE operations will cause the distortion. The basic reason is that the AE operation doubles the selected coefficients, resulting the difference between $s(t)$ and $x(t)$ being large. In order to avoid this kind of distortion, the best way is that in the embedding the DCT coefficients should be modified as small as possible.

2.3   Our Countermeasure

Based on the observations and analysis, we propose to use DE and PE embedding techniques in the intDCT domain to deal with the kind of distortion. In the embedding, since we expand the difference among adjacent coefficients instead of the current coefficient own, the modified amplitude on the current coefficient is significantly reduced. As a result, the distortion and the overflow problem can be effectively avoided. Another advantage, more importantly, is that the PE-based scheme can significantly enhance the embedding payload capacity for the same distortion. This is beneficial to improving the reversible watermarking-based authentication system.

3   Integer DCT and Expansion Embedding

For such a distortion problem in [11], in this paper we introduce DE and PE embedding strategies in the intDCT domain for reversible fragile watermarking of digital audio.

3.1   DE Embedding in the intDCT Domain

In the encoder, an audio is first segmented as frames in length of N. Then intDCT operation is performed on each frame respectively and the result is the sequence of N

DCT coefficients. We suppose the length of the watermark information for a frame is L. For the DE embedding, we choose the $2 \times L$ highest frequency coefficients to compute L differences for expansion embedding.

In Section 2, we have observed from the high-frequency component of most frames that two neighboring coefficients in odd (or even) positions are closer than two adjacent coefficients (one is in odd position; the other is in even position). So, our pairing approach is different from that in [8]. In order to reduce the prediction errors, we divide the $2L$ highest frequency coefficients into two sets: odd set (S_1) and even set (S_2). The grouping strategy is only done in the same set. For example, in a sequence $\{a,b,c,d,e,f,g,h\}$, the coefficients a and c forms the 1st pair, b and d is the 2nd pair, e and g is 3rd pair, f and h is the 4th pair.

The average l and difference h are calculated by

$$l = \left\lfloor \frac{X(i) + X(i+2)}{2} \right\rfloor, h = X(i) - X(i+2), \tag{8}$$

where $X(i)$ is the ith high frequency coefficient, $i \in \{N-2 \times L+1, N-2\}$. N is the length of the frame.

The difference h is expanded and a watermark bit b is embedded by

$$h_w = 2h + b. \tag{9}$$

The watermarked DCT coefficients are calculated by

$$S(i) = l + \left\lfloor \frac{h_w + 1}{2} \right\rfloor, S(i+2) = l - \left\lfloor \frac{h_w}{2} \right\rfloor. \tag{10}$$

Once the watermark information bits are completely embedded, the inverse transform is performed to generate the watermarked samples in the frame. One by one, all the frames are marked to reconstruct the marked audio signal.

In the decoder, the same segmenting and intDCT operation are implemented on the marked audio signal at first. For a pair of two coefficients, the average l and watermarked difference h_w are calculated by

$$l = \left\lfloor \frac{S(i) + S(i+2)}{2} \right\rfloor, h_w = S(i) - S(i+2). \tag{11}$$

The watermark bit b is extracted and the original difference h is restored by

$$h = \lfloor h_w/2 \rfloor, b = h_w - 2h. \tag{12}$$

The original DCT coefficients in embedding area are restored by

$$X(i) = l + \left\lfloor \frac{h+1}{2} \right\rfloor, X(i+2) = l - \left\lfloor \frac{h}{2} \right\rfloor. \tag{13}$$

Overall, all original DCT coefficients in a frame are restored. Then inverse intDCT is perform to restore the audio frame. Perform the same operation on the other frames to restore the original audio signal.

3.2   PE Embedding in the intDCT Domain

PE is a productive embedding technique, which can embed more payload with less distortion than DE because the predictor is more effective than difference operator and each predictor error can be used for embedding a watermark bit.

In the encoder, the segmenting and intDCT operation are implemented on the audio signal first. For a frame, we have N DCT coefficients and choose the $L+4$ highest frequency coefficients for the watermark bits in length of L. The first 4 coefficients are applied only for the prediction and keep unchanged in the embedding.

From the last highest frequency coefficient, in reverse order, the DCT coefficients are operated one by one as follows:

Consider the similarity between two neighboring coefficients in odd/even positions (as described in Section 2), the prediction value $\hat{X}(i)$ of the ith coefficient and prediction-error p are calculated by difference coding:

$$\hat{X}(i) = fix\left(\frac{X(i-2) + X(i-4)}{2}\right), p = X(i) - \hat{X}(i), \qquad (14)$$

where i is in the range $[N, N\text{-}1, \dots, N\text{-}L+1]$. $fix(.)$ is a function to strip off the fractional part of its argument, and returns the integer part. The function does not perform any form of rounding or scaling, e.g., $fix(-3.4)=-3$ and $fix(3.4)=3$.

The prediction-error p is expanded and a watermark bit b is embedded by

$$p_w = 2 \times p + b. \qquad (15)$$

The watermarked DCT coefficients are

$$S(i) = \hat{X}(i) + p_w. \qquad (16)$$

In the decoder, the same segmenting and intDCT operation are implemented on the marked audio signal. In the non-expanded area, $X(i) = S(i)$, $i = [1, 2, \dots, N\text{-}L]$. In the expanded area, from the first coefficient, sequentially, the DCT coefficients are operated one by one as follows:

The prediction value $\hat{X}(i)$ and prediction-error p_w are calculated by

$$\hat{X}(i) = fix\left(\frac{X(i-2) + X(i-4)}{2}\right), p_w = S(i) - \hat{X}(i), \qquad (17)$$

where $i = [N\text{-}L+1, \dots, N\text{-}1, N]$.

The watermark bit b is extracted and the original prediction-error p is restored by

$$p = \lfloor p_w/2 \rfloor, b = p_w - 2 \times p. \tag{18}$$

The original DCT coefficients in embedding area are restored by

$$X(i) = \hat{X}(i) + p. \tag{19}$$

Once the original DCT coefficients are restored, we can perform the inverse transform to restore the original frame in time domain. Once all the frames are recovered, we can reconstruct the original audio signal.

4   Reversible Fragile Watermarking for Authentication

The proposed reversible watermarking algorithm is designed for authentication. The method is very fragile to any small modification on the audio signal since we embed the hash bits of a frame into the high frequency component of the frame. The hostile tampering on a frame can be located by comparing the hash with the extracted watermark information. There are several important steps for the proposed authentication scheme:

- *Segmenting:* The frame in length is designed as $N = 2^p$, where p is a positive integer. In our testing, N is 1024 by making a tradeoff between the location precision and the embedding distortion. For the same watermark bits (L), N should be bigger than L. The bigger N, the less embedding distortion, the less embedding payload, the lower location precision is. The smaller N, the more embedding distortion, the more embedding payload, the higher location precision is.
- *Watermark:* For a frame, we compute the hash value (128 bits) by using MD5 standard, which is saved as part of the payload for integrity verification. Denote the hash by H. Part of the payload could be used for the auxiliary information and another purposes.
- *intDCT:* Perform the intDCT on the frame, choose the high frequency coefficients to compute the differences between adjacent coefficients for DE and PE embedding.
- *Embedding Region:* Since the human ears are less sensitive to the high-frequency component, the watermark bits are designed to embed in the highest frequency coefficients of intDCT domain and the number of the marked coefficients is not more than $N/2 = 512$.
- *Watermark extraction:* The watermark extraction is the inverse process of the watermark embedding. The same segmenting and transforming operations are performed on the audio signal. According to the embedding strategy, the watermark information including the hash feature (H) is extracted and saved.
- *Reconstruction of audio frames:* Since the watermarking algorithm is invertible, the original audio frame could be recovered if there is no any attack. Compute the hash from the restored frame (denote by H_1) and compare H_1 and H to judge if there is a tampering attack.

- **Integrity verification:** If $H_1 = H$, it means that the frame is authentic; Otherwise, we can claim that it is tampered. One by one, we can find those unauthentic frames and indicate the tampering locations.

5   Experimental Evaluation

We choose some different types of audio clips as test data. The 4 typical music clips[13], '*light.wav*' (20 seconds), '*drum.wav*' (25 seconds), '*pop.wav*' (40 seconds) and '*piano.wav*' (40 seconds), are adopted to report the experimental results. They are all single-channel, 44.1 kHz sampling, 16-bit quantization and PCM format.

5.1   Verifiability

The DE and PE based embedding strategies in the DCT domain are respectively employed to the 4 test audio clips to generate 8 watermarked audio clips. When these 8 audio clips are modified by using the following two attack methods, the proposed authentication scheme can identify the modification and locate the position.

Attack 1. The watermarked audio clip is tampered in single or several positions. Take the marked drum music for example, we modified 2 samples in different frames with HxD Hex Editor, substituting the original value 0.2784 to ZERO for the 5000th sample and -0.0287 to ZERO for the 600000th sample. Since the header information of '*drum.wav*' is in the position 00H~2BH bytes, the range of the data is begun from 2CH bytes. The 5000th sample is in the position of 273AH~273BH bytes which belong to the 5th frame (202CH~282BH bytes) and the 600000th sample is in 124FAAH~124FABH bytes which belong to the 586th frame (12482CH~12502BH bytes). The proposed scheme can identify that the 5th frame and the 586th frame had been modified, as shown in Fig.3.

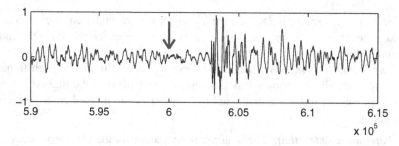

Fig. 3. Tamper the 600000th sample (*Attack 1*)

Attack 2. The watermarked audio clip is suffered cropping attacks. We cut the 600001st to 605000th samples in the watermarked drum clip, and the algorithm identified from the 586th to 590th frames which are all tampered. The example is shown in Fig.4.

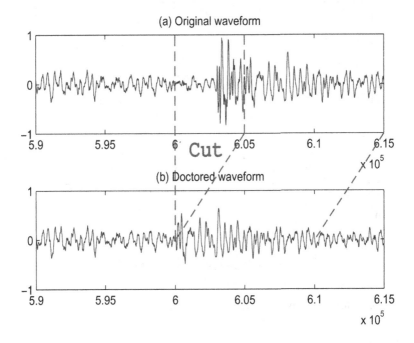

Fig. 4. Cut part of the samples (*Attack 2*)

5.2 Reversibility Testing

The fact that the difference between the original signal and restored signal is zero indicates our algorithm is reversible perfectly. For the drum music, Fig.5 shows the difference between the 4th frame and the restored frame by using DE-based embedding strategy in the DCT domain are zero.

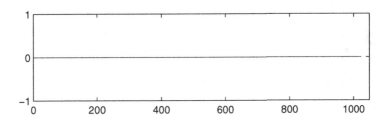

Fig. 5. Difference between the original and restored frame

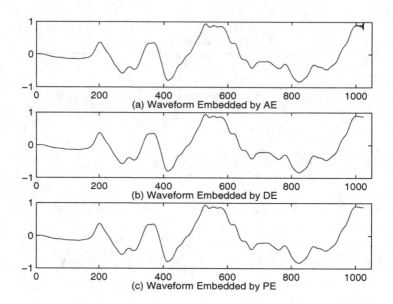

Fig. 6. Comparison between waveforms embedded by AE, DE and PE strategies

5.3   Fidelity versus Capacity

We have implemented three expansion embedding strategies (AE, DE and PE) based reversible watermarking for all four audio clips. The AE-based scheme was proposed by Huang in [11]. The DE and PE based schemes are proposed in this paper for solving the distortion problem in Section 2 and improving the embedding payload capacity.

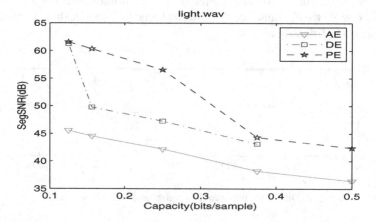

Fig. 7. Performance of the three algorithms with the 4 test clip. The AE scheme for clip 'drum' has the overflow problem.

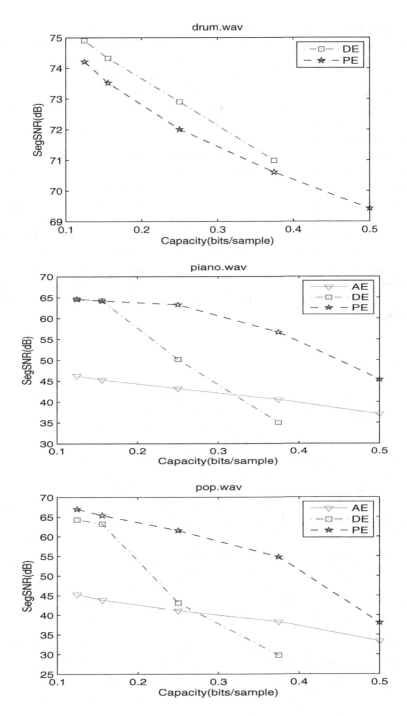

Fig. 7. (*Continued*)

For the four test clips, we have 12 marked signals by using AE, DE and PE embedding approaches. Listening testing results show that the watermarked clips by DE and PE are perceptibly similar to the original clips, but little and scattered noise could be heard in the marked clips by AE. Fig.6 is an example in the 4th frame of drum music. The waveforms of the 4th frame marked by AE, DE and PE strategies in the DCT domain are respectively shown in Fig.6 (a), (b) and (c), while their SNR values are 51.2397, 81.5309 and 81.6135 respectively. We can see from the waveform marked by AE is distorting so much at the end of the frame.

We have compared the AE, DE and PE embedding strategies by inserting different lengths of the watermark information. Five different hash codes, including MD5 (128-bit), SHA-1 (160-bit), SHA-256 (256-bit), SHA-384 (384-bit) and SHA-512 (512-bit), have different length respectively, but they can all serve for authentication. These five different hash codes are chosen to compute the hash as the watermark.

For four test clips, experimental results are respectively shown in Fig.7. From the drum music, the AE-based embedding strategy may cause the overflow problem in some frames. When the embedding capacity of the DE strategy is 0.375 bps, the size of the marked coefficients exceeds $N/2=512$. For all test clips, the PE-based scheme can provide the best embedding performance (the largest SegSNR values for the same embedding payload).

6   Conclusions

In this paper, we have investigated the overflow distortion problem by using AE in the DCT domain in [11] and proposed two solutions, that is, to use the DE or PE to substitute the AE to reduce the coefficient distortion. Since the watermark (the hash of a frame) is designed to embed into the high frequency component in a lossless way, the proposed DE and PE schemes are fragile to any modifications. Experimental results have shown that the DE and PE based schemes can effectively avoid the overflow distortion. Comparing with the AE scheme, the DE scheme is better, and the PE scheme can provide the best performance (with the lowest embedding distortion for the same embedding payload). Also, we have shown in experimental way that the fragile reversible watermarking can find even a single sample of modification on the audio, and can locate the position of the cropping attack.

In the future research, how to use the non-integer PE embedding [14] in the intDCT domain for the reduction of the embedding distortion is one consideration. Also, how for fault-tolerant application [15] of reversible watermarking an important issue, such as restoring the cropped samples by embedding them in other places.

Acknowledgments. This work was supported in part by the NSFC (No. 60903177, 61272414), in part supported by the Science and Technology Project of Guangzhou of China (No. 2012J4100108) and the National Training Programs of Innovation and Entrepreneurship for Undergraduates in Jinan University (No. 50421292).

References

[1] Tian, J.: Reversible Data Embedding Using a Difference Expansion. IEEE Trans. Circuits and Systems for Video Technology 13(8), 890–896 (2003)

[2] Alattar, A.M.: Reversible Watermark Using the Difference Expansion of a Generalized Integer Transform. IEEE Trans. Image Process. 13(8), 1147–1156 (2004)

[3] Thodi, D.M., Rodriguez, J.J.: Expansion Embedding Techniques for Reversible Watermarking. IEEE Trans. Image Processing 16(3), 721–730 (2007)

[4] Sachnev, V., Kim, H.J., Nam, J., Suresh, S., Shi, Y.: Reversible Watermarking Algorithm Using Sorting and Prediction. IEEE Trans. Circuits Syst. Video Technol. 19(7), 989–999 (2009)

[5] Lee, S., Yoo, C.D., Kalker, T.: Reversible Image Watermarking Based on Integer-to-Integer Wavelet Transform. IEEE Trans. Information Forensics and Security 2(3), 321–330 (2007)

[6] Yang, B., Schmucker, M., Funk, W., et al.: Integer DCT-based Reversible Watermarking for Images Using Companding Technique. In: Proc. SPIE Security, Steganography, and Watermarking of Multimedia Contents VI, vol. 5306, pp. 405–415 (2004)

[7] van der Veen, M., Bruekers, F., van Leest, A., Cavin, S.: High Capacity Reversible Watermarking for Audio. In: Proc. SPIE Security and Watermarking of Multimedia Contents V, vol. 5020, pp. 1–11 (2003)

[8] Bradley, B., Alattar, A.M.: High-Capacity, Invertible, Data-Hiding Algorithm for Digital Audio. In: Proc. SPIE Security and Watermarking of Multimedia Contents VII, vol. 5681, pp. 789–800 (2005)

[9] Yan, D., Wang, R.: Reversible Data Hiding for Audio Based on Prediction Error Expansion. In: IEEE International Conference on Intelligent Information Hiding and Multimedia Signal Processing, pp. 249–252 (2008)

[10] Steinebach, M., Dittmann, J.: Watermarking-Based Digital Audio Data Authentication. EURASIP Journal on Applied Signal Processing, 1001–1015 (2003)

[11] Huang, X., Nishimura, A., Echizen, I.: A Reversible Acoustic Steganography for Integrity Verification. In: Kim, H.-J., Shi, Y., Barni, M. (eds.) IWDW 2010. LNCS, vol. 6526, pp. 305–316. Springer, Heidelberg (2011)

[12] Huang, H., Rahardja, S., Yu, R.: A Fast Algorithm of Integer MDCT for Lossless Audio Coding. In: IEEE ICASSP 2004, pp. IV177–IV180 (2004)

[13] Xiang, S., Huang, J.: Histogram-Based Audio Watermarking against Time-Scale Modification and Cropping Attacks. IEEE Trans. on Multimedia 9(7), 1357–11372 (2007)

[14] Xiang, S.: Non-Integer Expansion Embedding for Prediction-Based Reversible Watermarking. In: Kirchner, M., Ghosal, D. (eds.) IH 2012. LNCS, vol. 7692, pp. 224–239. Springer, Heidelberg (2013)

[15] Weng, S., Zhao, Y., Pan, J.-S.: Reversible Watermarking Resistant to Cropping Attack. IET Information Security 1(2), 91–95 (2007)

Automatic Anonymous Fingerprinting of Text Posted on Social Networking Services

Hoang-Quoc Nguyen-Son[1], Minh-Triet Tran[2], Dung Tran Tien[3], Hiroshi Yoshiura[4], Noboru Sonehara[5], and Isao Echizen[5]

[1] The Graduate University for Advanced Studies (Sokendai), Japan
nshquoc@nii.ac.jp
[2] University of Science, Ho Chi Minh City, Vietnam
tmtriet@fit.hcmus.edu.vn
[3] Mica Institute, Ha Noi City, Vietnam
tien-dung.tran@mica.edu.vn
[4] University of Electro-Communications, Tokyo, Japan
yoshiura@hc.uec.ac.jp
[5] National Institue of Informatics, Tokyo, Japan
{sonehara,iechizen}@nii.ac.jp

Abstract. Social networking services (SNSs) support communication among people via the Internet. However, sensitive information about a user can be disclosed by the user's SNS friends. This makes it unsafe for a user to share information with friends in different groups. Moreover, a friend who has disclosed a user's information is difficult to identify. One approach to overcoming this problem is to anonymize the sensitive information in text to be posted by generalization, but most methods proposed for this approach are for information in a database. Another approach is to create different fingerprints for certain sensitive information by using various synonyms. However, the methods proposed for doing this do not anonymize the information. We have developed an algorithm for automatically creating enough anonymous fingerprints to cover most cases of SNSs containing sensitive phrases. The fingerprints are created using both generalization and synonymization. A different fingerprinted version of sensitive information is created for each friend that will receive the posted text. The fingerprints not only anonymize a user's sensitive information but also can be used to identify a person who has disclosed sensitive information about the user. Fingerprints are quantified using a modified discernability metric to ensure that an appropriate level of privacy is used for each group to receive the posted text. The use of synonyms ensures that an appropriate level of privacy is used for each group to receive the posted text. Moreover, a fingerprint cannot be converted by an attacker into one that causes the algorithm to incorrectly identify a person who has revealed sensitive information. The algorithm was demonstrated by using it in an application for controlling the disclosure of information on Facebook.

Keywords: Text anonymous fingerprinting, Social networking service, Generalization, Synonym.

Y.Q. Shi, H.J. Kim, and F. Pérez-González (Eds.): IWDW 2012, LNCS 7809, pp. 410–424, 2013.
© Springer-Verlag Berlin Heidelberg 2013

1 Introduction

Social networking services (SNSs) (such as Facebook, Twitter, and Google+) have become a worldwide phenomenon because they enable users to easily share information. However, sensitive information about a user can be inadvertently disclosed [5]. Although a number of rules have been created to prevent sensitive information from being disclosed to third parties [4], sensitive information can still be disclosed not only by the user but also by the user's SNS friends [3]. Therefore, it is necessary to anonymize the sensitive information. Moreover, if sensitive information is disclosed, the discloser should be identified. Because most of the data posted on an SNS is text (blogs, comments, status updates, etc.), we focus on text in this paper.

Most previous research on anonymizing information in text and detecting its disclosure has focused on databases [10,9] because they contain structured data. Research on detecting disclosure has focused on using fingerprints created using synonyms [15]. However, these approaches do not anonymize sensitive information. In contrast, we have developed an algorithm that uses both generalization and synonymization to both anonymize information and enable identification of a person who has revealed sensitive information. Information about a user in SNS text is generally conveyed in sensitive phrases, and methods for detecting sensitive phrases in SNS text were explored in the DCNL (Disclosure Control of Natural Language Information) Project [6]. The DCNL Project explored not only the detection of direct sensitive phrases but also discovering indirect sensitive phrases.

Our proposed algorithm automatically generalizes sensitive phrases to create anonymized ones. It then creates synonyms for the generalized phrases for use in detecting disclosure of sensitive information. After detecting a disclosure, the user could move the disclosing friend to a group with an appropriate level of privacy or unfriend the person.

Seven main property types (e.g., hometown, education, work, interests) in Facebook [12] with over 300 sensitive phrases are supported by the algorithm. Statistical evaluation showed that the algorithm can create a sufficient number of fingerprints to cover all of a user's friends in all groups for almost all cases. Fingerprints are quantified using the modified discernability metric [14] using data obtained directly from Wikipedia [13] to ensure that an appropriate level of information anonymity is used for each group of friends to receive the posted text. Synonyms are used to ensure that the friends in each group receive the same level of anonymization.

The strength of the algorithm is that it can detect information disclosure simply on the basis of sensitive phrases. It can therefore correctly identify a person who has revealed sensitive information even if he or she changed any of the non-sensitive phrases. Moreover, it can still work even if the attacker converted the fingerprint by generalizing any of the sensitive phrases.

An application using this algorithm was implemented on Facebook. It automatically detects the user's data profile after the user logs in and then controls the posting of information by creating a different version of the text for each of the user's friends and identifies anyone who discloses any of the sensitive information.

Section 2 describes the benefits and privacy issues of SNSs. Related work is described in Section 3. Our proposed algorithm is presented in Section 4. Section 5 discusses our evaluation of the algorithm. Section 6 presents our application of the algorithm, and Section 7 summarizes the key points and mentions future work.

2 Social Networking Services

2.1 Benefits

SNSs have become an important part of modern life, and many people use one or more SNSs every day. The most popular one, Facebook, had about 955 million users by the beginning of February 2012 [12]. Users can find a lot of information about other users and can easily and rapidly share information about their friends and/or other people.

2.2 Privacy Issues

However, there are privacy issues, and many laws have been created to protect user information. For example, EU law [4] requires that third parties be unable to access personal data. This means that an SNS cannot disclose user information to third parties.

Although many such laws protect user information, information on an SNS is often disclosed, both intentionally and unintentionally [5]. Most of it is revealed by either the user or one of the user's SNS friends. For example, Gross and Acquisti [3] analyzed the Facebook accounts of more than 4,000 students at Carnegie Mellon University and recovered the user's real name for 89% of them, the birthday for 88%, and the current residence for 51%.

A decade or so ago, SNS users rarely changed their default settings. For example, Gross and Acquisti [3] reported in 2005 that most users did not change their default settings. Furthermore, a survey by Ellison et al. [2] in 2007 showed that only 13% of the Facebook users in the Michigan State University network had limited their information sharing to "friends only." The situation has changed, however; SNS users are now more aware of these settings, and many now change them. In a report by the Pew Internet & American Life Project in 2010 [7], 71% of SNS users between the ages of 18 and 29 changed their SNS privacy settings. This trend towards protecting one's privacy on an SNS means that there is a stronger demand for automatic privacy protection.

Users often group their SNS friends on the basis of certain characteristics (e.g., relative, schoolmate, location), and there can be many friends in each group. By anonymizing sensitive user information in text to be posted differently for each group, a friend who has disclosed personal information can be identified.

3   Related Work

3.1   Anonymizing Text Information

There are two basic approaches to anonymizing information: use of generalization and use of suppression [9]. Generalization involves replacing a value with a less specific but semantically consistent value. Suppression involves not releasing a value at all [9].

Most previous research on anonymous text information has focused on databases because the data have a clear meaning within each item [9,10]. Moreover, anonymized text in sentences is very difficult to handle because of its semantic dimensions. In an SNS, however, most of the information about a user is conveyed by sensitive text phrases. We propose anonymizing this information by generalizing the sensitive phrases.

3.2   Detecting Disclosure of Sensitive Texts

There are two strategies to detecting disclosure in text: watermarking and fingerprinting. With watermarking (such as of an image, audio track, or text file), information is transparently embedded into the carrier signal [1]. For text, watermarking generally affects the structure of the text (font, color, size, word spacing, etc.) while fingerprinting creates a completely disjointed interpretation [1]. One approach to fingerprinting uses synonyms to create a fingerprint in the text [15]. However, this approach does not anonymize the information. We have extended this idea: we anonymize the sensitive phrases in SNS text by generalizing them, as described in section 3.1, and then use synonyms of the generalized sensitive phrases to detect disclosure.

3.3   Metrics to Quantify Privacy of Disclosed Information

Various metrics have been proposed for quantifying the loss of information due to generalization. The higher the level of generalization, the greater the loss and the greater the value of the metric.

To illustrate how we use generalization to anonymize information, we consider two quasi-identifiers, "university" and "prefecture," and two instances, "Massachusetts Institute of Technology," and "Tokyo." The corresponding generalization schemas are automatically created using the WordNet lexical database [8], as illustrated in Fig. 1.

Samarati Metric. The Samarati metric (Sam) [9] is calculated by adding the levels of generalization l_i :

$$\text{Sam} = \sum_{i=0}^{N-1} l_i$$

For example, the Samarati metric for "United States" is 4 and for "Asia" is 3. Therefore, the metric for {United States, Asia} is 7. This metric can be

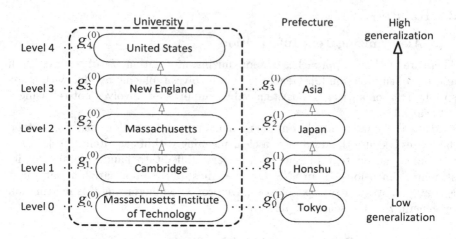

Fig. 1. Generalization schemas for two quasi-identifiers

automatically calculated from the structure of the generalization schemas. However, it does not take into account the number of possible generalization levels of the quasi-identifiers. For example, although "New England" and "Asia" are at the same level, "New England" can be further generalized to "United States."

Precision Metric. This disadvantage of the Samarati metric can be overcome by using the precision metric (Pre) [9] because it takes into account both the number of levels generalized l_i and the number of possible generalization levels of the quasi-identifiers L_i:

$$\text{Pre} = \sum_{i=0}^{N-1} \frac{l_i}{L_i}$$

Both the precision metric and Samarati metric simply take into account the structure of the generalization. They do not reflect the actual data. For example, the metric values for "Massachusetts Institute of Technology" and "Tokyo" are the same. However, only around 11,000 students are enrolled at MIT while over 13 million people live in Tokyo [13].

Modified Discernability Metric. We propose automatically collecting [13] to quantify generalizations made using the modified discernability metric (DM*) [14] previously used for databases. The the number of elements of the i-th class for the current generalization is denoted as n_i, and the number of elements of the i-th class for the lowest generalization is denoted as m_i:

$$\text{DM*} = \sum_{i=0}^{N-1} n_i^2 - \sum_{i=0}^{N-1} m_i^2$$

4   Proposed Algorithm

Our proposed algorithm has two processes, fingerprint creation and fingerprint extraction, as illustrated in Fig. 2.

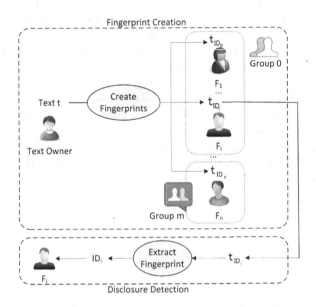

Fig. 2. Processes in proposed algorithm

In the fingerprint creation process, the input is user text t (e.g., blog entry, comment, status update). From t, the system automatically creates many fingerprints: $t_{ID_0}, t_{ID_1}, ...t_{ID_n}$. A different fingerprint is used for each friend in each group that will receive the text.

In the disclosure detection process, any sensitive information about the user disclosed by another user is analyzed, and the identifying fingerprint is extracted. Using this identifier, the system pinpoints the person who disclosed the information.

4.1   Fingerprint Creation

The fingerprint creation process has five steps.

Step 1 Detect sensitive phrases in input text (SNS text).
Step 2 Define generalization schemas for sensitive phrases.
Step 3 Quantify all possible generalizations.
Step 4 Create all possible synonym phrases of generalizations.
Step 5 Create and assign fingerprints for each person in the group of SNS friends who will see the text.

The following is a step-by-step description of this process using a blog entry for t: "*After graduating high school, I studied at the Massachusetts Institute of Technology. I was born in Tokyo and like udon noodles very much.*"

Detect Sensitive Phrases (Step 1). In the first step, from an idea proposed in the DCNL Project [6], the direct and indirect sensitive phrases in t are detected using function θ in Eq. 1 below on the basis of the relationship between phrases in t and the set of attributes in the user's data profile A using the Google distance metric. In the example used here, two sensitive phrases, p_0 = "Massachusetts Institute of Technology" and p_1 = "Tokyo," comprise set P of detected sensitive phrases. Table 1 shows the data used to detect them. The first sensitive phrase, "Massachusetts Institute of Technology," is directly detected from the "University" entry in the profile ("MIT"). Then, depending on the Google distance metric, the second sensitive phrase, "Tokyo," is indirectly detected from the entry for prefecture ("2-1-2 Hitotsubashi (NII)") because the address is only one of many locations in Tokyo.

$$P = \theta(A, t) = \{p_i\} = \{\text{Massachusetts Institute of Technology, Tokyo}\} \quad (1)$$

Table 1. Sensitive phrase detection

User's profile		Input phrases
First name	a_0 ={Adam}	Many
Last name	a_1 ={Ebert}	computer
Favorite	a_2 ={Football}	...
University	a_3 ={**MIT**}	**Massachusetts Institute of Technology**
Nickname	...	...
Prefecture	a_5 ={**2-1-2 Hitotsubashi(NII)**}	**Tokyo**
...	...	...

Define Generalization Schemas (Step 2). Generalization schemas $G^{(i)}$ are then defined automatically using function η in Eq. 2 for the sensitive phrases in P by using the WordNet lexical database [8]. The generalization schemas defined for "Massachusetts Institute of Technology" and "Tokyo" ($G^{(0)}$ and $G^{(1)}$) are shown in Fig. 1.

$$G^{(i)} = \eta(p_i) = \{g_j^{(i)}\} \quad (2)$$

Quantify Generalizations (Step 3). Next, holonym schemas for the sensitive phrases in P are automatically created using the Wordnet lexical database [8]. The number of people associated with each node is then automatically obtained from Wikipedia [13]. The data collected are shown in Figs. 3 and 4.

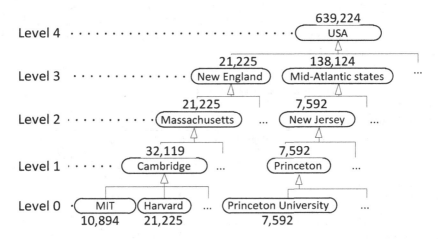

Fig. 3. Holonym schema for "University"

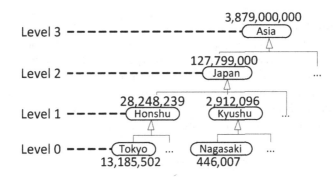

Fig. 4. Holonym schema for "Prefecture"

Possible generalizations for the sensitive phrases are then identified, as shown in the first column of Table 2. They can be then automatically quantified using the Samarati (Sam) metric, the precision metric (Pre), and modified discernability metric (DM*). In this paper, DM* [14] is used. For example, the DM* for generalization $\{g_0^{(0)}, g_1^{(1)}\}$ {Massarati Institute of Technology, Honshu} is calculated as follows:

1. Sum the squares of all node values for the same generalization level with the current generalization "Massachusetts Institute of Technology" and "Honshu."

2. Subtract the sum of the square of all node values for same generalization level with the lowest generalization "Massachusetts Institute of Technology" and "Tokyo."

The higher the metric value, the higher the level of privacy. Sorting the rows in the table by the DM* value results in the level of privacy increasing from top to bottom, as shown in the fourth column of Table 2. A generalization with an appropriate level of privacy is then used for each group to receive the posted text, as shown in the last column.

Table 2. Quantify possible generalizations

Generalization	Sam	Pre	DM*	Group
{Massachusetts Institute of Technology,Tokyo}	0	0.00	0.000000E+00	Family
{Cambridge,Tokyo}	1	0.25	1.200930E+09	Best Friends
{Massachusetts Institute of Technology,Honshu}	1	0.33	5.967829E+14	Teachers
{Cambridge,Honshu}	2	0.58	5.967841E+14	Students
{Massachusetts Institute of Technology,Japan}	2	0.50	1.117850E+15	Friends
{Cambridge,Japan}	3	0.75	1.117851E+15	Public
...		...	...	...	...

Create Synonym Phrases (Step 4). In the first three steps, generalizations are created for each group. For example, the generalization $\{g_0^{(0)}, g_2^{(1)}\}$ {Massachusetts Institute of Technology, Japan} is defined for the "Friends" group. In step 4, all possible synonyms of each generalization are automatically created by using YAGO [11], a huge semantic knowledge base derived from Wikipedia, WordNet, and GeoNames, and defined by function δ in Eq. 3, as shown in Fig. 5 for $\{g_0^{(0)}, g_2^{(1)}\}$ {Massachusetts Institute of Technology, Japan}.

$$S^{(i,j)} = \delta(g_j^{(i)}) = \{s_k^{(i,j)}\} \tag{3}$$

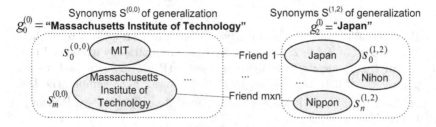

Fig. 5. Synonyms for generalization {Massachusetts Institute of Technology, Japan}

Create and Assign Fingerprints (Step 5). Using the synonym phrases created in step 4, the system creates fingerprints by replacing the sensitive phrases in the input text with appropriate synonym phrases. A different fingerprint is used for each friend who will see the text. For example, the following blog entry is seen by "Friend 1" in the "Friends" group.

*"After graduating high school, I studied at **MIT**. I was born at **Japan** and like udon noodles very much."*

4.2   Disclosure Detection

A user who discloses information about another user is identified using a two-step process.

Detect Sensitive Phrases (Step 1). First, sensitive phrases in disclosed text t' are detected in a manner similar to the fingerprint creation process on the basis of the attributes in the user's data profile using function θ in Eq. 4. In the example above, the set of detected sensitive phrases P' is composed of $p'_0 =$ "MIT" and $p'_1 =$ "Japan."

$$P' = \theta(A, t') = \{p'_i\} = \{\text{MIT}, \text{Japan}\} \tag{4}$$

Identify Disclosing Person (Step 2). Second, the person who disclosed the information is identified on the basis of the set of sensitive phrases detected in step 1. In this example, "Friend 1" disclosed the information.

5   Evaluation

5.1   Number of Possible Groups

The number of possible groups G that can receive a generalized version of the text depends on the number of sensitive phrases N and the number of levels of the i-th sensitive phrase $|G_i|$:

$$T = \prod_{i=0}^{N-1} |G_i|$$

To evaluate the practicality of the algorithm, we collected over 300 different sensitive phrases (such as "Tokyo," "Massachusetts Institute of Technology," and "researcher") for the seven main property types in Facebook: hometown, education, work, religion, political, sports, and interests. The average number of possible groups by property is shown in Table 3. The first column shows the number of different sensitive phrases (SPs) calculated, and the last one shows the average number of possible groups for all properties.

If none of the sensitive phrases is detected, the algorithm discloses the same input text to all groups because the text does not reveal any sensitive information about the user. If at least one sensitive phrase is detected, the average number of

Table 3. Average number of possible groups that can receive a generalized version of the text

SPs	Home	Education	Work	Religion	Political	Sports	Interests	Average
1	4.70	6.41	8.94	9.13	8.09	10.91	8.52	8.10
2	22.05	41.09	79.80	83.39	65.36	118.88	68.97	72.20
3	103.49	262.90	712.09	761.13	527.25	1294.93	608.38	610.03
4	485.42	1680.01	6349.58	6944.85	4246.72	14108.30	5097.05	5558.85

possible groups is greater than eight. Therefore, the algorithm can create enough fingerprints to cover most cases of SNSs containing sensitive phrases.

5.2   Number of Possible Friends

The number of possible friends F that can receive a fingerprint depends on the number of synonyms for the i-th generalized phrase $|S^{j0,\text{index}_{i,j}}|$ of the j-th generalization, where $\text{index}_{i,j}$ is the generalized level for the i-th group of the j-th sensitive phrase:

$$F = \sum_{i=0}^{T-1} \prod_{j=0}^{N-1} |S^{j,\text{index}_{i,j}}|$$

The average number of possible friends is shown in Table 4.

5.3   Performance

The algorithm was tested using about 10,000 tweets obtained from Infochimps[1] (an average of 15 words per tweet). The algorithm was executed for seven typical user attributes. It took 16 s on average to create fingerprints for all the user's friends for each tweet.

Table 4. Average number of possible friends that can receive a fingerprint

SPs	Home	Education	Work	Religion	Political	Sports	Interests	Average
1	1.4E+02	6.8E+02	3.9E+01	8.3E+01	1.0E+02	1.2E+02	8.3E+01	1.8E+02
2	2.0E+04	4.3E+05	1.5E+03	6.8E+03	1.1E+04	1.4E+04	6.7E+03	7.0E+04
3	2.9E+06	2.4E+08	5.8E+04	5.6E+05	1.0E+06	1.7E+06	5.4E+05	3.5E+07
4	4.3E+08	2.7E+10	2.2E+06	4.6E+07	9.6E+07	2.0E+08	4.2E+07	4.0E+09

5.4   Fingerprint Conversion

The algorithm detects fingerprints only on the basis of the sensitive phrases. It can therefore detect a disclosed message even if a receiver changed any of the non-sensitive phrases.

---

[1] http://www.infochimps.com

A sensitive phrase cannot be converted into a lower level one. In the example blog entry above, a receiver can convert "Tokyo" into "Honshu" or "Japan" but cannot convert "USA" into "Massachusetts Institute of Technology."

The algorithm uses the Google distance metric to detect exactly both direct and indirect sensitive phrases even if a sensitive phrase in the text has been changed.

6   Implementation

We implemented a secured social networking service as a web application using the proposed algorithm. The application controls the process of posting text on Facebook through the use of two main functions: fingerprint creation and disclosure detection.

Fig. 6. Fingerprinted blog entry

6.1   Fingerprint Creation

A user uses the application with an existing Facebook account. When the user composes a text to be posted, the application automatically creates fingerprints on the basis of the composed text for friends who will receive the text. An example for user Adam Ebert and the example blog entry above is shown in Fig. 6. The automatically created fingerprints are shown in red.

Each friend receiving the entry sees a different version. For example, the version Bob Smith sees is fingerprinted with "Massachusetts Institute of Technology-Honshu," as shown in Fig. 7, while that for Ellen Anderson is fingerprinted with "USA-Tokyo," as shown in Fig. 8,

Fig. 7. Facebook page of "Bob Smith"

6.2   Disclosure Detection

The algorithm detects disclosure even if the discloser has modified the entry by changing one or more non-sensitive phrases, the generalization of one or more sensitive phrases, or the position of one or more sensitive phrases. For example, Bob Smith might change the entry to *"I was born in **Japan** and lived there for long time. I like udon noodles very much. In my childhood, I became very interested in a number of wonderful computer applications. Therefore, I am learning computer science at the **Massachusetts Institute of Technology**."*

The algorithm would automatically detect the sensitive phrases and identify Bob Smith as the discloser as he was the only one who received the version containing "Massachusetts Institute of Technology."

Fig. 8. Facebook page of "Ellen Anderson"

7 Conclusion

With our proposed algorithm for fingerprinting text to be posted on social networking services, sensitive user information can be anonymized differently for each friend who will see the text. Moreover, a user can detect if the user's information has been disclosed and identify the disclosing person. The basic idea of this algorithm is to use generalizations of sensitive phrases to anonymize information and then to use synonyms for the generalized phrases to create a unique fingerprint for each person who will see the text. By using these fingerprints, users can identify a discloser even if that person converted the fingerprint by generalizing any of the sensitive phrases. The algorithm creates enough fingerprints for a unique one to be assigned to each of the friends receiving the text. The fingerprints are quantified using a precision metric so that an appropriate level of privacy is used for each group to receive the posted text. The algorithm was demonstrated by using it in an application for controlling the disclosure of information on Facebook.

Future work includes improving the semantics of the fingerprints.

References

1. Arnold, M., Schmucker, M., Wolthusen, S.: Techniques and applications of digital watermarking and content protection. Artech House Publishers (2003)
2. Ellison, N., Steinfield, C., Lampe, C.: The benefits of Facebook "friends": Social capital and college students' use of online social network sites. Journal of Computer-Mediated Communication 12(4), 1143–1168 (2007)
3. Gross, R., Acquisti, A.: Information revelation and privacy in online social networks. In: Proceedings of the 2005 ACM Workshop on Privacy in the Electronic Society, pp. 71–80. ACM Press (2005)

4. Hansen, M., Schwartz, A., Cooper, A.: Privacy and identity management. IEEE Security and Privacy Magazine 6(2), 38–45 (2008)
5. Joshi, P., Kuo, C.C.: Security and privacy in online social networks: A survey. In: Proceedings of the IEEE International Conference on Multimedia and Expo (2011)
6. Kataoka, H., Utsumi, A., Hirose, Y., Yoshiura, H.: Disclosure control of natural language information to enable secure and enjoyable communication over the internet. In: Christianson, B., Crispo, B., Malcolm, J.A., Roe, M. (eds.) Security Protocols 2007. LNCS, vol. 5964, pp. 178–188. Springer, Heidelberg (2010)
7. Madden, M., Smith, A.: Reputation Management and Social Media (2010), http://pewinternet.org/~/media//Files/Reports/2010/ PIP_Reputation_Management.pdf
8. Miller, G., et al.: Wordnet: a lexical database for english. Communications of the ACM 38(11), 39–41 (1995)
9. Samarati, P., Sweeney, L.: Generalizing data to provide anonymity when disclosing information. In: Proceedings of the 17th ACM SIGACT-SIGMOD-SIGART Symposium on Principles of Database Systems, vol. 17, pp. 188–188. ACM (1998)
10. Schrittwieser, S., Kieseberg, P., Echizen, I., Wohlgemuth, S., Sonehara, N., Weippl, E.: An algorithm for k-anonymity-based fingerprinting. In: Shi, Y.Q., Kim, H.-J., Perez-Gonzalez, F. (eds.) IWDW 2011. LNCS, vol. 7128, pp. 439–452. Springer, Heidelberg (2012)
11. Suchanek, F., Kasneci, G., Weikum, G.: YAGO: a core of semantic knowledge. In: Proceedings of the 16th International Conference on World Wide Web (WWW), pp. 697–706. ACM Press (2007)
12. Ullyot, T.: Facebook Current Report, Form 8-K, Filing Date July 26, 2012 (2012), http://pdf.secdatabase.com/700/0001193125-12-316895.pdf
13. Vokel, M., Krotzsch, M., Vrandecic, D., Haller, H., Studer, R.: Semantic Wikipedia. In: Proceedings of the 15th International Conference on World Wide Web (2006)
14. Xu, J., Wang, W., Pei, J., Wang, X., Shi, B., Fu, A.: Utility-based anonymization using local recoding. In: Proceedings of the 12th ACM SIGKDD International Conference on Knowledge Discovery and Data Mining, pp. 785–790. ACM (2006)
15. Zheng, X., Huang, L., Chen, Z., Yu, Z., Yang, W.: Hiding information by context-based synonym substitution. In: Ho, A.T.S., Shi, Y.Q., Kim, H.J., Barni, M. (eds.) IWDW 2009. LNCS, vol. 5703, pp. 162–169. Springer, Heidelberg (2009)

Memoryless Hash-Based Perceptual Image Authentication

Fang Liu, Qi-Kai Fu, and Lee-Ming Cheng

Department of Electronic Engineering, City University of Hong Kong, Hong Kong
{fangliu2,qikaifu2}@student.cityu.edu.hk, itlcheng@cityu.edu.hk

Abstract. It is well known that the rapid development of multimedia technologies has led to a huge growth of image editing tools. The popularity of image editing tools has further resulted in the growth of image illegal utilization. Unlike the traditional information authentication, perceptual image hashing approaches are recently proposed for content-based image authentication, which can distinguish maliciously altered images from the perceptually identical ones. However, these approaches need some other information to achieve the authentication, such as the hash codes of original images. Semi-fragile watermarking is also presented to deal with content-based authentication; however this approach focuses more on some specific aspect of robustness, for example JEPG compression. Hence, to avoid extra information storage and simultaneously achieve a global robustness against common image processing manipulations, this paper presents a memoryless hash-based perceptual image authentication algorithm using joint image hashing and watermarking method upon wave atom transform. Experimental results have demonstrated that the proposed algorithm possesses great robustness against common non-malicious manipulations and still keeps high sensitivity to malicious attacks. It can also provide perceptual image authentication successfully without any other information, even the hash codes of original images.

Keywords: image hashing, perceptual image authentication, wave atom transform, watermarking.

1 Introduction

With the rapid development and widespread utilization of multimedia technologies, digital images have been widely transmitted and manipulated. Perceptual image authentication technologies thus become more and more important which can prevent image forgery and unauthorized utilization. Recently, many perceptual image hashing schemes have been proposed [1-10] for perceptual image authentication. The main idea is to construct a hash by extracting image characteristics of human perception, then use the generated hash to authenticate an image without considering the various variables or formats of this image. These image hashing schemes are based on the content of images upon human perception, thus possess great robustness against common image

Y.Q. Shi, H.J. Kim, and F. Pérez-González (Eds.): IWDW 2012, LNCS 7809, pp. 425–434, 2013.

processing manipulations, such as JPEG compression and low-pass filtering. Moreover they also own great fragility against malicious manipulations, for example cut-and-paste and adding object operations. However, these approaches need other side information to authenticate images, such as the original images or at least the hashes of original images. Fortunately, semi-fragile watermarking schemes [11-17] can also provide content-based image authentication even without side information by imperceptibly embedding secret information into host images. By extracting the secret digital data, the authenticity of images can be protected. However, these approaches usually focus more on some specific aspect of robustness when applied to perceptual image authentication, for example the robustness against JPEG compression. The robustness of some other common content-preserving image processing manipulations, such as filtering, scaling and contrast adjustment, is not considered or tested [11-17]. Thus, these approaches could not always satisfy the robustness requirements of different content-preserving manipulations simultaneously.

In order to avoid extra information storage and simultaneously achieve a global robustness against common image processing manipulations, this paper presents a memoryless hash-based perceptual image authentication algorithm using joint hashing and watermarking method based on wave atom transform [18]. According to previous research [19], compared with some traditional transforms such as DWT and DCT, wave atom transform is adopted for the generation of image hash owing to its sparser expansion and better characteristics of texture feature extraction, which can show better performance in both robustness and fragility and achieve a higher perceptual image authentication accuracy. A public signature or logo of verified organizations can then be masked by the unique hash code extracted from each image itself and finally embedded into the image. In addition, to increase the perceptual authentication accuracy, BCH (15, 5) error-correcting code is also applied to the masked logo. Moreover, Rényi chaotic map is employed, combining with wave atom transform to ensure the security of proposed algorithm. The experimental results have demonstrated that the proposed scheme has shown great performance in perceptual image authentication without side information. It is robust against common content-preserving manipulations and also has the ability to detect the malicious tampering. Moreover, the image cannot be forged since each image has a unique watermark which is masked by its own hash adaptively.

The rest of paper is organized as follows. Section 2 gives a brief introduction about wave atom transform and the proposed algorithm is explained in Section 3. Experimental results are shown in Section 4, whereas the conclusion is given in Section 5.

2   Wave Atom Transform

Let $\psi_{m,n}^j(x)$ represent a 1D wave packet, where $j, m \geq 0$, and $n \in Z$, centered around $x_{j,n} = 2^{-j}n$ in space and $\pm w_{j,m} = \pm \pi 2^j m$ in frequency, with $C_1 2^j \leq m \leq C_2 2^j$, where C_1 and C_2 are two positive constants. The basis function can be defined as the following, when combining dyadic scaled and translated versions of $\hat{\psi}_m^0$ in frequency domain:

$$\psi_{m,n}^j(x) = \psi_m^j(x - 2^{-j}n) = 2^{j/2}\psi_m^0(2^j x - n) \tag{1}$$

where

$$\psi_m^0(w) = e^{-iw/2}[e^{i\alpha_m}g(\epsilon_m(w - \pi(m + 1/2)) + e^{-i\alpha_m}g(\epsilon_{m+1}(w + \pi(m + 1/2))) \tag{2}$$

with $\alpha_m = \pi/2\,(m + 1/2)$, $\epsilon_m = (-1)^m$ and g a real-value compactly-support C^∞ bump function such that $\sum_m |\psi_m^0(w)|^2 = 1$.

For each wave $w_{j,m}$ at scale 2^{-j}, the coefficient $c_{j,m,n}$ is treated as a decimated convolution,

$$c_{j,m,n} = \int \psi_m^j(x - 2^{-j}n)u(x)dx = \frac{1}{2\pi}\int e^{i2^{-j}nw}\overline{\psi_m^j(w)}\hat{u}(w)dw \tag{3}$$

By discretizing the sample u at $x_k = kh, h = 1/N, k = 1, \cdots N$, the discrete coefficients $c_{j,m,n}^D$ are calculated by utilizing a reduced inverse FFT inside an interval of size $2^{j+1}\pi$, centered around the origin:

$$c_{j,m,n}^D = \Sigma_{k=2\pi(-2^j/2+1:1:2^j/2)}\, e^{i2^{-j}nk} \times \Sigma_{p\in 2\pi z}\,\overline{\hat{\psi}_m^j(k + 2^j p)}\,\hat{u}(k + 2^j p) \tag{4}$$

By individually utilizing products of 1D wave packets, 2D orthonormal basis functions with four bumps are formed in frequency plane. 2D wave atoms are indexed using $\mu = (j, \boldsymbol{m}, \boldsymbol{n}) = (j, m_1, m_2, n_1, n_2)$ and the basis function is modified as

$$\varphi_\mu^+(x_1, x_2) = \psi_{m_1}^j(x_1 - 2^{-j}n_1)\psi_{m_2}^j(x_2 - 2^{-j}n_2) \tag{5}$$

A dual orthonormal basis can be established from Hilbert-transformed wavelet packets as

$$\varphi_\mu^-(x_1, x_2) = H\psi_{m_1}^j(x_1 - 2^{-j}n_1)H\psi_{m_2}^j(x_2 - 2^{-j}n_2) \tag{6}$$

By combining Equation (5) and Equation (6), basis functions with two bumps are provided in frequency domain, and directional wave packets oscillate in one single direction:

$$\varphi_u^{(1)} = (\varphi_\mu^+ + \varphi_\mu^-)/2, \quad \varphi_u^{(2)} = (\varphi_\mu^+ - \varphi_\mu^-)/2 \tag{7}$$

$\varphi_u^{(1)}$ and $\varphi_u^{(2)}$ are jointly denoted as φ_u and form the wave atoms frame. The wave atoms algorithm is based on the apparent generalization of the one dimension wrapping strategy to two dimensions.

3   Proposed Algorithm

In this paper, an image hashing scheme is proposed to generate image hash codes which are employed to mask the public signature or logo of verified organizations. To increase the accuracy of perceptual image authentication, BCH (15, 5) error-correcting code is employed to encode the masked logo and generate a new watermark. The watermark is then embedded into the original image using a proposed watermarking algorithm. Consequently, the processed images can be perceptually authenticated without side information. Fig.1 shows the basic flow diagram of the proposed algorithm. The detailed procedures are described below.

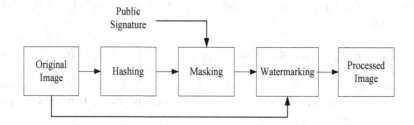

Fig. 1. Basic flow diagram of the proposed algorithm

3.1   Image Hashing

Fig.2 shows the procedure of hash generation. The original image is decomposed into five scale bands after wave atom transform, and coefficients in the third scale band are used to generate the hash code according to our previous work [19], which cannot be altered significantly unless the image is changed visually.

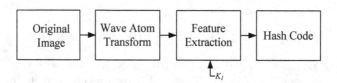

Fig. 2. Hash generation procedure

Let $C(j, \boldsymbol{m}, \boldsymbol{n})$ represent the coefficients, where j is the scale, and $\boldsymbol{m} = (m_1, m_2), \boldsymbol{n} = (n_1, n_2)$ indicate the phase. Assign an index i for each block of phase $\boldsymbol{m}$ in the third scale band and denote SUM_i as the summation of the i-th block. For all non-empty blocks, SUM_i is computed as follows:

$$SUM_i = \sum_{k=(1,1)}^{(l_1, l_2)} C(j, \boldsymbol{m}_i, \boldsymbol{n}_k) \tag{8}$$

where l_1 and l_2 is the length and width of the block respectively. To make sure the hash code cannot reveal the information of the original mutual relationship of wave atom blocks, a randomization governed by secret key K_1 is applied to SUM_i based on Rényi chaotic map [20] to generate a new sequence SUM_i'. Denote the total number of non-empty blocks as t. The new summation difference between each two blocks is used to generate one hash bit. The i-th bit of the hash is expressed by

$$h^{(i)} = \begin{cases} 1, if \ SUM_i' > SUM_{i+1}' \\ 0, Otherwise \end{cases} \tag{9}$$

where $i \in [1, \cdots, t-1]$.

3.2   Masking

The masked logo is generated by XORing corresponding hash with the public logo. Here, to increase the accuracy of the propose algorithm and protect the masked logo, BCH (15, 5) error correction code [21] is employed to encode the masked logo and generate a new watermark w_c. BCH codes have the ability to correct some error bits which might be introduced by image processing manipulations, hence ensure the robustness of the proposed algorithm.

3.3   Image Watermarking

In this paper, a wave atom based watermarking scheme is proposed and described as follows.

1. Divide the original image I of size $N \times N$ to four descriptions, I_1, I_2, I_3 and I_4 as follows:

$$I_1(p,q) = I(p, 2q - 1)$$

$$I_2(p,q) = I(p, 2q)$$

$$I_3(p,q) = I(N/2 + p, 2q - 1)$$

$$I_4(p,q) = I(N/2 + p, 2q)$$

where $p = 1, 2, \ldots, N/2$ and $q = 1, 2, \ldots, N/2$.

2. Apply wave atom transform to each description, and four coefficient sets S_1, S_2, S_3 and S_4 can be obtained respectively. The fourth scale band is employed to embed the watermark.

3. For sets S_1, S_2, S_3 and S_4, the fourth scale band coefficients C_u whose absolute values are smaller than a threshold r are selected to be modified, where $u = (j, m, n)$ of integer-valued quantities indexes a point (x_u, ω_u) in phase space and r is used to determine the number of coefficients for embedded the watermark.

4. S_1 and S_2 are used to embed the first half of watermark which contains $p/2$ bits, while S_3 and S_4 are used to embed the other half. In the fourth scale band of wave atom tiling, each pair of the two corresponding blocks chosen from the odd description (S_1 or S_3) and even description (S_2 or S_4) is used to embed a one bit value, where the phase of these two blocks is the same. If the bit value of w_c is one, certain

coefficients within the selected block in the odd description will be increased by the parameters α_a and α_b, while the corresponding ones in the even description will be decreased by α_c and α_d. In contrast, if the bit value is zero, certain coefficients within the selected block in the odd description will be decreased by α_c and α_d, while the ones in the even description will be increased by the parameters α_a and α_b. The coefficients are modified as follows:

For all non-empty blocks in S_1 and S_2,

For $i=1: p/2$

IF $w_i = bit\ 1$

In S_1,

IF $abs(C_u) > \delta$

$C_u = C_u \times \alpha_a$

ELSE

$C_u = C_u \times \alpha_b$

In S_2,

IF $abs(C_u) > \delta$

$C_u = C_u \times \alpha_c$

ELSE

$C_u = C_u \times \alpha_d$

ELSE

In S_2,

IF $abs(C_u) > \delta$

$C_u = C_u \times \alpha_a$

ELSE

$C_u = C_u \times \alpha_b$

In S_1,

IF $abs(C_u) > \delta$

$C_u = C_u \times \alpha_c$

ELSE

$C_u = C_u \times \alpha_d$

where $abs(.)$ is the absolute value of $(.)$, $u = (j, m, n)$ of integer-valued quantities, α_a, α_b, α_c and α_d are strength factors and δ is the embedding threshold which are introduced to control robustness and image quality.

Similarly, coefficients in S_3 and S_4 are modified in the same way. For this case, S_1 and S_2 are replaced by S_3 and S_4 respectively. Thus, the altered wave atom coefficient sets S_1', S_2', S_3' and S_4' are obtained.

6. Apply inverse wave atom transform to the modified coefficient sets S_1', S_2', S_3' and S_4' and construct the four new descriptions.

7. Recover the watermarked image I' by these descriptions.

Thus the watermark can be easily extracted by comparing the mean values of these blocks between the odd and even descriptions at the relative position. If the mean value is larger in the block of odd description instead of the even description, the extracted watermark bit will be chosen as "1", otherwise it will be as "0".

4   Experimental Results

In order to test the performance of proposed algorithm, 100 original images of size 512×512 are tested. The proposed algorithm is implemented in MATLAB on a PC with an Intel (R) Core (TM) i7 (2.80GHz) CPU (4G RAM).

Using the method described in Section 3 based on the same secret key and the same system parameters, the watermark and corresponding hash code can be extracted from received image. After XOR the watermark with the hash code, recovered logo can be obtained. By comparing it with the public logo in terms of normalized hamming distance (NHD), perceptual image authentication can be completed. Suppose that L denotes the length of the logo, NHD between the recovered logo s' and the public logo s is calculated as follows:

$$d(H, H') = 1/L \sum_{t=1}^{L} |s'(t) - s(t)| \qquad (10)$$

Consequently, NHD is supposed to approach zero for authentic images and 0.5 for perceptually different images. Here a discriminative threshold θ is defined to authenticate the received image. If d is larger than θ, the received image cannot be authenticated. Otherwise the received image will be authenticated.

In this section, some common non-malicious image processing manipulations with different parameters, which do not change the images perceptually, and some malicious attacks which do change the images are applied. The averaged NHD are computed using the extracted logos and the public logo based on 100 original images in Table 1.

Since the extracted logos depend both on the extracted watermarks and extracted hashes, the imperception of watermarking scheme and the stability of proposed hash scheme are both important. In this paper, the values of parameters α_a, α_b, α_c, α_d, r and δ are tested and chosen as 1.6, 2.1, 0.8, 0.6, 60 and 19 respectively for the best performance of watermarked images. Fig.3 shows two examples of the original images and their corresponding watermarked ones, which can demonstrate that the proposed watermarking method has little impact on the original images and is highly imperceptible. The hashing method is also expected to be robust against non-malicious manipulations, and at the meantime, be fragile enough to detect malicious tampering. Here the averaged NHD between hashes extracted from original images and the processed images are calculated to show the performance of proposed hash scheme in Table 1.

From Table 1, it can be observed that the values of NHD under different content-preserving manipulations based on hash method only are small for all cases, while the NHD is much larger under malicious attacks. It is also evident that NHD between the public logo and the logo recovered from non-maliciously processed images are relatively small, while the distances between the public logo and the logo recovered from maliciously processed images are quite high for all cases.

These indicate that the proposed scheme possesses high global robustness against all these common non-maliciously content-preserved manipulations described in Table 1, and is also fragile enough to detect the malicious attacks. It is also expected the NHDs based on logo are a little larger than NHD based on hash. Since the extracted logo is also influenced by the proposed watermarking scheme. Choosing the threshold as 0.1, the proposed scheme can distinguish malicious attacks from non-malicious attacks without any other information, and the accuracy of proposed perceptual image authentication scheme is up to 92%, which indicates that the proposed scheme can provide perceptual image authentication successfully without other information.

Table 1. Results against different manipulations based on Averaged Normalized Hamming Distance(NHD) of 100 images

Attacks	System Parameter	NHD based on Hash	NHD based on Logo
JPEG (quality factor)	25	0.0163	0.0953
	50	0.0099	0.0393
	85	0.0054	0.0140
Gaussian Noise (variance)	5	0.0241	0.0331
	10	0.0449	0.0651
Salt and Pepper Noises Addition (density)	0.01	0.0517	0.0871
	0.03	0.0663	0.0961
Gaussian Low Pass Filter (standard variance, window)	0.5,1	0.0040	0.0087
	1.5,1	0.0117	0.0163
	0.5,3	0.0117	0.0163
	0.5,5	0.0277	0.0400
Contrast Change	10%	0.0167	0.0243
	20%	0.0044	0.0093
	-10%	0.0043	0.0090
	-20%	0.0040	0.0087
Laplacian Sharpening (operator)	0.1	0.0073	0.0117
	0.3	0.0074	0.0120
	0.6	0.0074	0.0120
Cropping	10%	0.0101	0.0176
Histogram Equalization		0.0904	0.0927
Malicious Cut-and-Paste Attack	4%	0.182	0.1863
Malicious Adding Object Attack		0.1800	0.1800

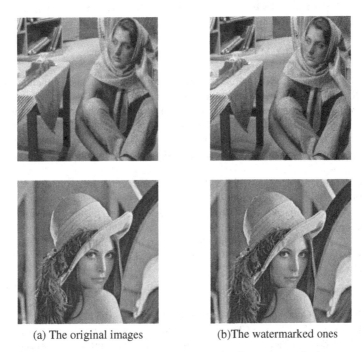

(a) The original images   (b)The watermarked ones

Fig. 3. Examples of original images and the corresponding watermarked ones

5   Conclusion

In this paper, a novel memoryless hash-based perceptual image authentication algorithm is proposed using joint image hashing and watermarking method, which needs none side information to authenticate images. Experimental results have also demonstrated that the proposed algorithm possesses a global robustness against common non-malicious manipulations compared with semi-fragile watermarking schemes, and also avoids extra information storage in comparison with common image hashing schemes.

References

1. Schneider, M., Chang, S.F.: A robust content-based digital signature for image authentication. In: Proc. IEEE Int. Conf. Image Processing, Lausanne, Switzerland, vol. 3, pp. 227–230 (1996)
2. Venkatesan, R., Koon, S.M., Jakubowski, M.H., Moulin, P.: Robust image hashing. In: Proc. IEEE Int. Conf. Image Processing, Vancouver, BC, Canada, vol. 3, pp. 664–666 (2000)
3. Kailasanathan, C., Naini, R.S., Ogunbona, P.: Image authentication surviving acceptable modifications. In: Proc. IEEE-EURASIP Workshop on Nonlinear Signal Image Processing, Baltimore, MD (2001)

4. Lin, C.Y., Chang, S.F.: A robust image authentication system distinguishing JPEG compression from malicious manipulation. IEEE Trans. on Circuits and Systems for Video Technology 11, 153–168 (2001)
5. Lu, C.S., Liao, H.Y.M.: Structural digital signature for image authentication. IEEE Trans. Multimedia 5, 161–173 (2003)
6. Bhattacharjee, S., Kutter, M.: Compression tolerant image authentication. In: Proc. International Conference on Image Processing, Chicago, USA, vol. 4, pp. 435–438 (1998)
7. Monga, V., Evans, B.L.: Perceptual image hashing via feature points: Performance evaluation and tradeoffs. IEEE Trans. Image Process. 15, 3452–3465 (2006)
8. Fridrich, J., Goljan, M.: Robust hash functions for digital watermarking. In: Proc. IEEE Int. Conf. Information Technology: Coding and Computing, Las Vegas, NV, USA, pp. 178–183 (2000)
9. Swaminathan, A., Mao, Y., Wu, M.: Robust and secure image hashing. IEEE Trans. Inf. Forens. Sec. 1, 215–230 (2006)
10. Monga, V., Mihcak, M.K.: Robust and secure image hashing via non-negative matrix factorizations. IEEE Trans. Inf. Forens. Sec. 2, 376–390 (2007)
11. Lin, C.Y., Chang, S.F.: Semi-fragile watermarking for authenticating JPEG visual content. In: Proc. SPIE, Security and Watermarking of Multimedia Contents, San Jose, CA, USA, pp. 140–151 (2000)
12. Lin, E.T., Podilchuk, C.I., Delp, E.J.: Detection of image alterations using semi-fragile watermarks. In: Proc. SPIE International Conference on Security and Watermarking of Multimedia Contents II, San Jose, CA, USA, pp. 152–163 (2000)
13. Maeno, K., Sun, Q.B., Chang, S.F., Suto, M.: New semi-fragile image authentication watermarking techniques using random bias and nonuniform quantization. IEEE Trans. Multimedia 8, 32–45 (2006)
14. Zhang, D.X., Pan, Z.G., Li, H.H.: A Contour-based Semifragile Image Watermarking Algorithm in DWT Domain. In: Second International Workshop on Education Technology and Computer Science, Wuhan, pp. 228–231 (2010)
15. Yu, G., Lu, C., Liao, H.: Mean quantization-based fragile watermarking for image authentication. Opt. Eng. 40, 1396–1408 (2001)
16. Zhu, Y., Li, C., Zhao, H.: Structural digital signature and semi-fragile fingerprinting for image authentication in wavelet domain. In: Proc. IAS, Manchester, pp. 478–483 (2007)
17. Cruz, C., Reyes, R., Nakano, M., Perez, H.: Image content authentication system based on semi-fragile watermarking. In: Proc. the 51st Midwest Symposium on Circuits and Systems, Knoxville, TN, pp. 306–309 (2008)
18. Demanet, L., Ying, L.: Wave atoms and sparsity of oscillatory patterns. Appl. Comput. Harmon. Anal. 23(3), 368–387 (2007)
19. Liu, F., Cheng, L.M.: A Novel Image Hashing Scheme Base on Wave Atoms. In: Proc. IEEE International Conference on IIH-MSP, Dalian, pp. 125–128 (2011)
20. Addabbo, T., Alioto, M., Fort, A., Pasini, A., Rocchi, S., Vignoli, V.: A Class of Maximum-Period Nonlinear Congruential Generators Derived From the Rényi Chaotic Map. IEEE Trans. Circuits Syst. I, Reg. Papers 54(4), 816–828 (2007)
21. Lin, S., Costello, D.J.: Error Control Coding, 2nd edn. Prentice Hall, Inc., Upper Saddle River (2004)

Visual Cryptography Based Watermarking: Definition and Meaning

Stelvio Cimato[1], James Ching-Nung Yang[2], and Chih-Cheng Wu[2]

[1] Department of Computer Science
Università degli Studi di Milano, Italy
stelvio.cimato@unimi.it
[2] CSIE Department - National Dong Hwa University, Taiwan
cnyang@mail.ndhu.edu.tw

Abstract. The proliferation of digital data, and their distribution over different kinds of communication channels are making the copyright protection a very important issue in the digital world. Watermarking techniques and visual cryptographic schemes have been recently used in different approaches for the copyright protection of digital images. Watermarking is generally used to embed "secret" information into an original image, with different purposes and different features, usually as a means to assess the ownership of the modified image. Visual cryptography refers to a way to decompose a secret image into shares and distribute them to a number of participants, so that only legitimate subsets of participants can reconstruct the original image by combining their shares.

The combination of both techniques can provide some important solutions for tampering verification and the resolution of disputes on the ownership of a given image, as provided by several proposals appeared in literature. In this work we try to provide a general model for the watermarking schemes obtained from the combination with visual cryptography. Furthermore we discuss some possible extensions of the combined approach taking into account different visual cryptographic schemes where multiple participants are involved and their possible applications in new scenarios.

1 Introduction

Copyright protection is a very important issue in our digital society, where a very large amount of multimedia data are daily generated and distributed using different kinds of consumer electronic devices and very popular communication channels, such as the Web and the social networks. The ever more and more growing integration of computer and communication technologies is posing new challenges to security and copyright management for digital materials, that can be transmitted and exchanged in a very easy way, exploiting an enormous set of platforms and devices.

From one side, the increased facilities for the production of digital information have lowered the costs and made image processing and distribution possible for all users. On the other side, there are enormous difficulties to protect the

Y.Q. Shi, H.J. Kim, and F. Pérez-González (Eds.): IWDW 2012, LNCS 7809, pp. 435–448, 2013.
© Springer-Verlag Berlin Heidelberg 2013

intellectual property rights and to control the diffusion of source multimedia data. This is due to the nature of digital information, which is very easy to duplicate in an indistinguishable way from the original, or to tamper modifying the data and producing a new "original" product.

A solution to some of the problems related to the copyright protection and tampering verification of multimedia data can be provided by the adoption of a *digital watermarking* technique. Commonly, a digital watermark contains some extra information that can be inserted into the original data in usually a imperceptible, to avoid distortion of the image, and robust, to contrast removal attempts, way. An illegitimate copy can be recognized by testing the presence of a valid watermark and a dispute on the ownership of the image resolved. Different kinds of watermarking techniques, providing different features and characteristics have been presented in literature [7].

The cryptographic technique for the visual sharing of secret images, denoted as *visual cryptography* (VC) or *Visual Secret Sharing* (VSS) has been firstly proposed by Naor and Shamir in 1994 [14]. Visual cryptography enables distributing sensitive visual materials to involved participants to the scheme, through public communication channels, as the produced random looking shares do not reveal any information if they are not combined as prescribed. Indeed, only qualified sets of participants are able to reconstruct the image by simply stacking together the shares they own. The attractiveness of this paradigm consists in the fact that the reconstruction phase does not require any computation, but it is performed directly by the human visual system.

Deviating a little bit from the main goal of the original schemes, visual cryptography has been exploited in many applications as a means to protect a secret image. Considering a $(2, 2)$ VC scheme, where the original image is shared into two random looking shares, it is possible to freely distribute one of the shares, while the other can be used as a key, that is necessary to reconstruct the original image and can be provided only to a legitimate user. More in general, in a (n, n) VC scheme, where all the shares are needed to reconstruct the original image, it is possible to hide one share from the other participants in order to protect the visually shared secret. In this sense, the hidden share can be seen as a key for the "decryption" of the protected image. Under this perspective, VC has been considered as a natural way to achieve the protection of the watermark in combined schemes, where one of the share is needed to correctly reconstruct the embedded watermark, and in this case resolve any dispute on the image ownership.

In literature different schemes combining watermarking techniques with visual cryptography schemes have been presented. Usually, in such schemes, a visual cryptography scheme is used to process the watermark and obtain one or multiple shares; the shares are then merged with the host image in order to produce a watermarked image that can be freely distributed. The presented schemes consider both black & white images and color images, and can be classified on the basis of the watermarking technique used to encode the original image and of the visual cryptographic scheme needed to process the watermark.

In this paper we try to provide a general model in which most of the proposed watermarking systems based on the combination with visual cryptographic schemes can be classified. Furthermore, we show how it is possible to extend the proposed model to consider other forms of visual cryptographic scheme, including larger number of participants. For $(2, n)$ and (k, n) VC schemes we devise a possible utilization and new application scenarios. In the next section we briefly introduce the basic notions related to watermarking and visual cryptography. In section 3 we describe the general model we propose for the description of watermarking scheme based on visual cryptography, and its extension discussing some possible novel application scenarios. Some final considerations are contained in section 5.

2   Basic Notions

In this section we survey the main features of watermarking techniques and VC schemes with the aim to provide an introductory explanation of both techniques. The survey is not intended to provide a complete description of all the features of these two research fields, since a large number of books (see for example [22,5]) and several hundreds of papers have been published in the recent years. Interested readers can look to some interesting surveys appeared on those topics [3,7].

2.1   Visual Cryptography

Visual cryptography schemes allow the encoding of a secret image, consisting of black or white pixels, into n shares which are distributed to a set of n participants. The secret pixels are shared with techniques based on the intelligent subdivision of each secret pixel into a certain number subpixels. Each share is then composed of black and white subpixels, which are printed in close proximity to each other, so that the human visual system averages their individual black/white contributions. White color means transparent, so that the superposition of white pixels, let the color of the pixel contained in the other shares pass through.

The shares are such that only qualified subsets of participants can "visually" recover the secret image, but other subsets of participants, called forbidden sets, cannot gain any information about the secret image by examining their shares. The shares can be conveniently represented with an $n \times m$ matrix S where each row represents one share, i.e., m subpixels, and each element is either 0, for a white subpixel, or 1 for a black subpixel. A matrix representing the shares is called *distribution matrix*.

To reconstruct the secret image a group of participants stacks together their shares. The grey level of the combined share, obtained by stacking the transparencies $i_1, \ldots, i_s$, is proportional to the Hamming weight $w(V)$ of the m-vector $V = OR(r_{i_1}, \ldots, r_{i_s})$, where $r_{i_1}, \ldots, r_{i_s}$ are the rows of S associated with the transparencies we stack. This grey level is interpreted by the visual system of the users as black or as white in according with some rule of contrast. Since each secret pixel is represented by m pixels in the shares, the reconstructed image will be bigger than the original (depending on m and on the actual positions of the pixels, the image can also be distorted; a perfect square is a good choice for m because it avoids distortion).

Two parameters are very important for visual cryptography schemes: The *pixel expansion*, corresponding to the number of subpixels contained in each share (transparency) and the *contrast*, which measures the "difference" between a black and a white pixel in the reconstructed image. In general, a scheme is characterized by other parameters: the number of participants n, the threshold k that determines whether a set of participants is qualified to reconstruct the image, the contrast thresholds ℓ and h, which determine whether a reconstructed pixel is considered white or black.

This cryptographic paradigm was introduced by Naor and Shamir [14]. They analyzed the case of (k, n)-threshold visual cryptography schemes, in which a black and white secret image is visible if and only if at least k transparencies among n are stacked together. The model by Naor and Shamir has been extended in [2] to general access structures (an access structure is a specification of all qualified and forbidden subsets of participants), where general techniques to construct visual cryptography schemes for any access structure have been proposed.

In order to provide shares to the participants the dealer chooses uniformly at random a distribution matrix from a collection of matrices C_1, if the secret pixel is black, or from a collection of matrices C_0, if the secret pixel is white. Let report here the formal definition of a deterministic VCS:

Let $(\Gamma_{\mathsf{Qual}}, \Gamma_{\mathsf{Forb}})$ be an access structure on a set of n participants. Two collections (multisets) of $n \times m$ boolean matrices $\mathcal{C}_i$ and $\mathcal{C}_\infty$ constitute a *visual cryptography scheme* $(\Gamma_{\mathsf{Qual}}, \Gamma_{\mathsf{Forb}}, m)$-*VCS* if there exist the integers ℓ and h, $\ell < h$, such that:

1. Any (qualified) set $Q = \{i_1, i_2, \ldots, i_p\} \in \Gamma_{\mathsf{Qual}}$ can recover the shared image by stacking their transparencies. Formally, for any $S \in \mathcal{C}_i$, the "or" V of rows $i_1, i_2, \ldots, i_p$ satisfies $w(V) \leq \ell$; whereas, for any $S \in \mathcal{C}_\infty$ it results that $w(V) \geq h$.

2. Any (forbidden) set $X = \{i_1, i_2, \ldots, i_p\} \in \Gamma_{\mathsf{Forb}}$ has no information on the shared image. Formally, the two collections of $p \times m$ matrices $\mathcal{D}_t$, with $t \in \{0, 1\}$, obtained by restricting each $n \times m$ matrix in $\mathcal{C}_X$ to rows $i_1, i_2, \ldots, i_p$ are indistinguishable in the sense that they contain the same matrices with the same frequencies.

In many schemes, the collection $\mathcal{C}_0$ (resp. $\mathcal{C}_1$) consists of all the matrices that can be obtained by permuting all the columns of a matrix M_0 (resp. M_1). For such schemes, the matrices M_0 and M_1 are called the *base matrices* of the scheme. Base matrices constitute an efficient representation of the scheme. Indeed, the dealer has to store only the base matrices and in order to randomly choose a matrix from $\mathcal{C}_X$ he has to randomly choose a permutation of the columns of the basis matrix M_X.

The basis matrices M_0 and M_1 in the $(2,2)$-VC scheme are:

$$M^0 = \begin{bmatrix} 0 & 1 \\ 0 & 1 \end{bmatrix} \quad M^1 = \begin{bmatrix} 1 & 0 \\ 0 & 1 \end{bmatrix}.$$

Naor and Shamir's Basic (2,2) VC Scheme. The basic idea of $(2,2)$ Naor and Shamir's encoding scheme is depicted in figure 1. The scheme encodes each single pixel p of a binary image into two shares S_1 and S_2. If p is white, the dealer randomly can choose one of the first two rows of the table in Figure 1 to build S_1 and S_2. If p is black, the dealer randomly chooses one of the last two rows of the table. The probabilities of the two encoding cases are the same, independently of whether the original pixel is black or white. Thus, an adversary looking at a single share has no information about the original value of p. When the two shares are stacked together, if p is black, two black sub-pixels will appear, while, if p is white, one black sub-pixel and one white sub-pixel will appear as reported in the rightmost column of the table. The human visual system will distinguish whether p is black or white. due to the contrast between the two reconstructed pixels, even if instead of a really white color, the color of the merged subpixel wil be gray.

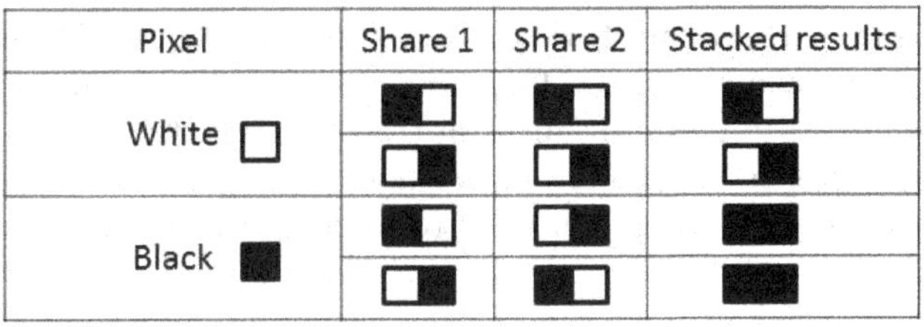

Pixel	Share 1	Share 2	Stacked results
White			
Black			

Fig. 1. Basic (2,2) VC scheme with 2 subpixels

As already discussed and showed in the table, for each pixel, two pixels will be associated in the reconstruction, i.e. the pixel expansion of the scheme is 2. This can cause a stretching of the original image and cause a distortion. To maintain the aspect ratio of the original secret image a larger pixel expansion can be selected, associating to each pixel of the secret image a block composed of $4(= 2 \times 2)$ subpixels, as reported in Figure 2. The encoding and decoding procedure are the same as considered in the case before. More correctly, considering the base matrices M_0 and M_1 reported at the end of the previous section, it is possible to note that the collections C_0 and C_1 will be composed of all the permutations of the columns of those base matrices.

As can be noted in the columns of the table, reporting the stacked result, the reconstructed pixel $r = S_1 \oplus S_2$ may contain two white and two black sub-pixels if p is white, or all four black sub-pixels when p is black. When all pixels in p are encoded in this way, and each time an independent selection is made for encoding each pixel p, the encoded shares S_1 and S_2 are indeed random

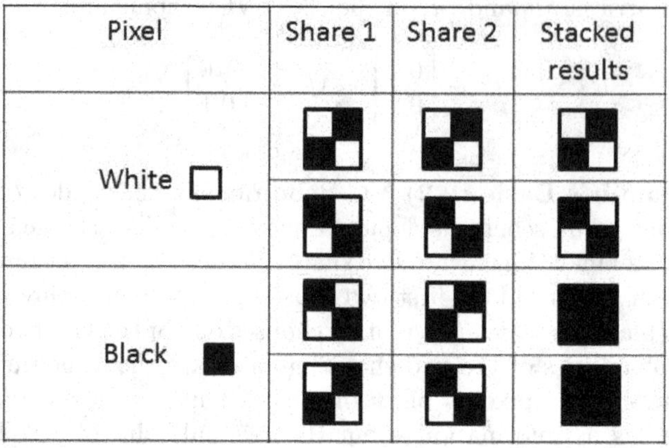

Fig. 2. Basic (2,2) VC scheme with four subpixels

pictures, containing no information on the original image. When S_1 and S_2 are superimposed, all of the four sub-pixels are black in the reconstructed blocks corresponding to each black pixel p, while two sub-pixels are white and the other two are black corresponding to each white pixel. Based on the contrast obtained, the human visual system can distinguish between white and black pixels in p from $S_1 \oplus S_2$. In some cases, the OR operation is substituted with the XOR operation obtaining some improvement in the reconstruction of the image. The price paid is that the reconstruction is no more performed by the human visual system, but some computation is needed to perform the XOR of the shares.

2.2   Watermarking

Digital watermarks are typically used as a method for the protection of intellectual property rights (IPR). Watermarks are digital codes embedded in the original data usually containing different kinds of information about the owner or the creator and/or the destination of the data. In the most simple case, a watermark is composed of another image or logo which can be directly related to the owner of the image; the relationship between the watermark and the owner can be assessed by storing the watermark at a Trusted Authority (TA) which can intervene in case of dispute.

To prevent attacks, the marks should be robust enough to avoid the intentional or accidental removal and should not introduce disturbing effect on the original data. On the other side in many cases only the selected receiver should be enabled to detect and manipulate the embedded watermark. So the usual application of watermarks is to detect copyright infringements and to be used as a proof in case of dispute between the owner or the legitimate destination and the malicious user. If a suspected image is examined and the embedded watermark detected, then a follow-up action can be started against the illegitimate use of the image. A typical scenario, is the one where the image creator makes its own images on-line available, but to avoid misuse or false ownership attribution, he embeds inside the images a watermark; in this case everyone can download the image, but in case of dispute, only the owner will be able to show the presence of the watermark inside the disputed image and claim its ownership.

Watermarking techniques have also been used for other goals, such as data authentication, data monitoring and tracking. In the first case a fragile watermark is embedded into the original data, so that any manipulation occurred during the data transmission can be detected; indeed a fragile watermark has the characteristic of being very sensible to slight modification of the embedding image. In the second case, watermarks are used by monitoring systems to automatically detect the owners of broadcast data and pay the due royalties to them.

Indeed watermarking techniques include several trade-off and conflicting requirements. As an example, security of the watermark is related to the imperceptibility of the embedding procedure but at the same time they should be robust enough in order to be detected by the detection algorithm and resist to several kinds of attacks, ranging from geometric manipulation till compression and distortions.

Requirements. Digital watermarking schemes are typically based on two phases, the embedding phase where the data of the watermark are merged with the data of the original image, and the extracting phase, where a watermarked image is examined and the inverse procedure is applied to retrieve the watermark. These are the basic requirements that a watermarking scheme should have:

1. Imperceptibility or Transparency. The watermark should be perceptually invisible and when embedded should not introduce too much distortion into the original image.
2. Robustness. The embedded watermark should be extractable and identifiable after that various intentional or occasional attacks are performed. These include both common signal processing operations and geometric distortions, such as blurring, JPEG compression, noising, sharpening, scaling, rotation, cropping, and so on. The watermark should resist against intentional attacks to remove it as well as occasionally introduced noise.
3. Security. Only the legitimate owner should be able to extract and modify the embedded watermark. The security should depend only on keeping the key secret, while the watermarking algorithm should be public.
4. Blindness. The original image is not needed to verify the existence and/or extract the watermark in the test image. In this case, the copyright owner is not required to utilize extra disk space to store original images. The blindness property is very useful in practical schemes.
5. Multiple watermarking. Sometimes the possibility of inserting multiple watermarks inside the original data is requested in order to trace the distribution of digital images. However, the possibility of crossing a latter watermark over a front watermark should be avoided and in general multiple watermarking schemes are complex and try to overcome this weakness.

6. Unambiguity. The embedded watermark should be verifiable without ambiguity and the ownership of the image correctly and unambiguously determined. The problem of confusing the ownership by simply appending an illegal watermark to the watermarked image, and the consequent possibility to have multiple claims of ownership (also called the deadlock problem, counterfeit attack, or invertibility attack) has been analyzed in [6].

To evaluate the robustness of the watermarks usually some very well known attack libraries are used as benchmarks: StirMark, unZign and Checkmark[16,15,1]. The Stirmark library [16] includes several attacks, such as compression, geometric transformations, processing for signal enhancement, and noise addition. The unZign benchmark [1] introduces local pixel jittering and is very efficient in attacking spatial domain watermarking techniques including estimation based attacks by considering prior information about the watermark. Checkmark benchmark library [15] includes new removal attacks, such as, maximum likelihood estimation attacks, maximum a posteriori (MAP) based attack, de-noising assuming low pass watermark, and other new geometric attacks. Generally, watermarking schemes are considered robust if they can survive attacks contained in the library.

3   Watermarking and Visual Cryptography

In watermarking schemes, usually the produced watermark is directly embedded into the image to be protected, in order to prevent abuses and illegitimate distribution of the image. When a visual cryptographic scheme is used in combination, usually the watermark is given as input to the VC scheme, obtaining a number of shares. One of the share is then used as watermark and given in input to the embedding phase of the watermarking algorithm, while the other ones will be stored and protected.

The typical scenario considered in combined watermarking VC based scheme includes a number of actors:

- the owner of the image who wants to mark its own image and prevent non authorized use of the image;
- a trusted authority (TA) who participates to the scheme and whose intervention can be requested to arbitrate the ownership of the image if a dispute occurs;
- finally, the adversary who wants to alter the image and/or its watermark and use it, cheating about the ownership of a stolen image.

3.1   Watermarking with (2,2) VC Scheme

Most of the schemes combining watermarking with visual cryptography are based on the use of a $(2,2)$ VC scheme. As mentioned in [14], such VC schemes can be thought of as a private key cryptosystem. Indeed, the secret printed message is encoded into two random looking shares: one of the two shares can be freely distributed and used as a cipher-text, whereas the other share serves as the

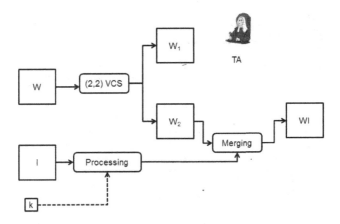

Fig. 3. Embedding phase for watermarking combined with a $(2,2)$ VC scheme

secret key. The original image is reconstructed by stacking together the two transparencies. This system recalls the one-time pad, as each page of ciphertext is decoded by using a different transparency. In combined watermarking schemes, the input image to the VC scheme is the watermark.

In figures 3 and 4 the embedding and the extraction phases of such kind of combined watermarking techniques are depicted. The owner of the image I, gives in input the watermark W to one of the variants of the $(2,2)$ VC scheme previously described in order to obtain two watermarks W_1 and W_2, which appear as random images. One of the shares, W_1 is then used as a key such that only the legitimate extractor can reconstruct the watermark and show it to a third party; in some cases W_1 is registered to a TA who can then resolve a dispute on the ownership of a claimed image. The second share, W_2, is then embedded into the original image, performing a merging operation that depends on the particular kind of watermark technique considered. Indeed, the original image I undergoes a processing phase, where some decomposition or some kind of feature extraction is used. For such phase, some schemes require the knowledge of a secret key K, needed for example to select the locations or the values of the original image which will contain the watermark bits. At the end of the process, the watermarked image WI can be published or distributed for any legitimate use.

In the extraction phase, depicted in figure 4, the process above is inverted. The owner of the image, wanting to claim the ownership on a suspected image during a controversy with an adversary, can use the secret key to extract the needed information from the image WI in order to obtain one the share of the watermark. At the same time she can use the second share W_1, possibly involving the TA where the share has been stored, to reconstruct the original watermark. If the image was belonging to the claiming owner, the watermark W' is equal or similar to the original watermark W and the dispute is resolved.

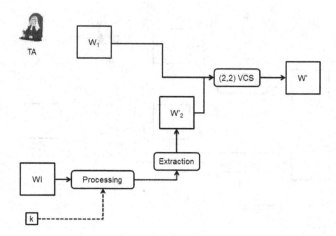

Fig. 4. Extraction phase for watermarking combined with a $(2,2)$ VC scheme

Several schemes respecting the structure above described have been proposed in literature, each one introducing some variations in the way the VC scheme is used to generate the shares, or the way that the image is processed and the watermark embedded into the original image.

3.2 Watermarking with (2,n)-VC Scheme

A possible extension of the previous schemes can be done by considering different kinds of VC schemes. As depicted in figure 5, by including a $(2, n)$ VC scheme it is possible to split the watermark in multiple shares. During the embedding phase, one of the share will be stored by by the image owner. The other shares will be deposited to different trusted authorities. During the extraction phase, the owner, in case of dispute will contact one of the involved TA and will run the extraction phase as previously described in the $(2, 2)$ case.

The advantage of such a solution is that multiple TA can be involved, enhancing the robustness of the whole scheme and extending the application scenarios. Indeed, it is possible to observe that the $(2, n)$ scheme can overcome the failure of a TA, due for example to unreachability reasons or corruption. Furthermore, such schemes could be easily applied in situations where multiple platform owners act, possibly not collaborating each with the other. Take for example the case of different social networks operators, usually in competition and not wanting to share collaborative services. Each social network could expose the watermark deposit service, so that the user will be able to prevent the unauthorized use of the image at the different social platforms. This however can require that the user contacts and deposits the generated shares of the watermark to each copyright protection service.

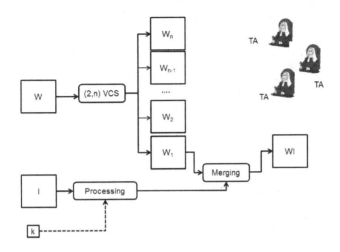

Fig. 5. Embedding phase with a $(2, n)$ VC scheme

3.3 Watermarking with (k,n)-VC Scheme and General Access Structure

VC schemes can be constructed requiring that at least a number of k shares are combined together to reconstruct the original image. In some cases, it is possible to modify the generation algorithm of the shares, in order to construct different shares and distribute them to the participants, so that only some particular subset of the participants to the scheme will be enabled to reconstruct the secret image. In this latter case, qualified subset of participants are organized in access structures. In both cases, the combined schemes can be easily extended, by building on the previous proposed model, modifying just the included VC scheme.

The application scenario for these schemes includes different possibilities. Considering (k, n) schemes, then at least k actors will be required to collaborate in order to successfully terminate a dispute resolution procedure. This can amount to involve k TAs where the generated shares have been deposited during the embedding phase. Again, in this case, the failure of 1 or more TA can be overcame by the fact at least k active TA should collaborate during the extraction phase.

Consider an image reselling web site, where users can buy professionally produced image for their scope. In such case the shares can be generated such that the reselling site, the buyer, and one or more of the TA are involved in the extraction phase. In case of dispute, the user will need the collaboration of the image reselling site and of the requested number of TAs in order to successfully complete the extraction phase. In this application scenario, it is the reselling site which generates the shares and acquire more control on the distribution and usage of the sold images.

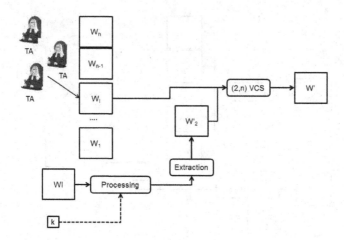

Fig. 6. Extracting phase with a $(2, n)$ VC scheme

4   Related Works

In literature, many papers combining visual cryptography and watermarking schemes have been presented. Most of them are instantiation of the model we presented in the previous section. The papers may differ on the particular technique used for watermarking or on the processing phase used to extract features from the image. One of the first attempt to combine visual cryptography and watermarking embedding procedure has been proposed in [9], where the original image is processed and some pixels are turned to gray color (with value 247) to avoid distortion when the watermark is embedded. In [11] the computed share is embedded choosing some random locations that are selected using a shared secret key as seed for a random generator. A simple variation of the above method has been presented in [8], where the VC scheme is not directly used, and W_2 is obtained by the application of the XOR operation. Some schemes, such as [13,4], use a watermark technique based on discrete wavelet transform. The scheme presented in [10], considers a statistics based method to extract some features from the image during the embedding phase. In [23], the original image goes through a processing phase where a numerical analysis technique, i.e. singular value decomposition (SVD), is used to determine some invariant values in the image, the singular values which will be included in the master share, The processing phase for the original image in [21] is based on the gain-shape vector quantization technique (GSVQ).

Many other papers have been presented, based on simple variations of the above presented schemes, sometimes giving not enough details about the functionalities of the scheme (see [20,19,18]). In general the question of security of the proposed watermarking schemes is not always sufficiently addressed. Indeed many works limit themselves to a simple demonstration of the application of the scheme on a sample image, without a formal discussion of the security properties.

5   Conclusion

The combination of watermarking techniques and visual cryptography provides some interesting solutions to the need of copyright protection for multimedia data. Usually, the use of VC allows the splitting of the watermark into two or more shares, one used as a secret symmetric key, and the other ones embedded in the original image. The schemes provide different solutions according to the particular watermarking technique used and the particular VC scheme adopted. In this paper a general model, useful to capture most of the proposed watermarking techniques based on visual cryptography, has been provided. Furthermore the extension of the model by including different kinds of VC schemes (other than $(2,2)$ VC scheme), useful for different application scenarios has been proposed. To our knowledge, no watermarking scheme combined with a VC scheme based on (k,n) or general access structure has been presented yet.

Future research directions in these topics involve the study of combined schemes under a more formal perspective which can be focused on the study of the security properties of the proposed model, well defining the threat model and the security requirements as done for example in [17,12]. Following this research line, it will be possible to move the first steps towards the definition of standard metrics against with both the robustness, the efficiency and the security of the watermarking schemes could be evaluated.

References

1. Unzign watermark removal software, http://www.altern.org/watermark/
2. Ateniese, G., Blundo, C., De Santis, A., Stinson, D.R.: Visual cryptography for general access structures. Information and Computation 129(2), 86–106 (1996)
3. Ateniese, G., Blundo, C., De Santis, A., Stinson, D.R.: Constructions and bounds for visual cryptography. In: Meyer auf der Heide, F., Monien, B. (eds.) ICALP 1996. LNCS, vol. 1099, pp. 416–428. Springer, Heidelberg (1996)
4. Chen, T.-H., Chang, C.-C., Wu, C.-S., Lou, D.-C.: On the security of a copyright protection scheme based on visual cryptography. Computer Standards & Interfaces 31(1), 1–5 (2009)
5. Cimato, S., Yang, C.N.: Visual Cryptography and Secret Image Sharing. Digital Imaging and Computer Vision Series. Taylor & Francis (2011)
6. Craver, S., Yeo, B.-L., Yeung, M.: Technical trials and legal tribulations. Commun. ACM 41, 45–54 (1998)
7. Hartung, F., Kutter, M.: Multimedia watermarking techniques. Proceedings of the IEEE 87(7), 1079–1107 (1999)
8. Hassan, M.A., Khalili, M.A.: Self watermarking based on visual cryptography. In: Proceedings of World Academy of Science, Engineering and Technology, vol. 8, pp. 159–162 (2005)
9. Hou, Y.-C., Chen, P.-M.: An asymmetric watermarking scheme based on visual cryptography. In: 5th International Conference on Signal Processing Proceedings, WCCC-ICSP 2000, vol. 2, pp. 992–995 (2000)
10. Hsu, C.-S., Hou, Y.-C.: A visual cryptography and statistics based method for ownership identification of digital images. In: Proceedings of World Academy of Science, Engineering and Technology, vol. 2, pp. 172–175 (2005)

11. Hwang, R.: A digital image copyright protection scheme based on visual cryptography. Tambang Journal of science and Engineering 3(2), 97–106 (2000)
12. Li, Q., Sencar, H.T., Memon, N.D.: Security issues in watermarking applications. In: ACM Workshop on Multimedia Content Protection and Security (2006)
13. Lou, D.-C., Tso, H.-K., Liu, J.-L.: A copyright protection scheme for digital images using visual cryptography technique. Computer Standards & Interfaces 29(1), 125–131 (2007)
14. Naor, M., Shamir, A.: Visual cryptography. In: De Santis, A. (ed.) EUROCRYPT 1994. LNCS, vol. 950, pp. 1–12. Springer, Heidelberg (1995)
15. Pereira, S., Voloshynovskiy, S., Madueno, M., Marchand-Maillet, S., Pun, T.: Second generation benchmarking and application oriented evaluation. In: Moskowitz, I.S. (ed.) IH 2001. LNCS, vol. 2137, pp. 340–353. Springer, Heidelberg (2001)
16. Petitcolas, F.A.P., Anderson, R.J., Kuhn, M.G.: Attacks on copyright marking systems. In: Aucsmith, D. (ed.) IH 1998. LNCS, vol. 1525, pp. 218–238. Springer, Heidelberg (1998)
17. Sencar, H.T., Memon, N.D.: Watermarking and ownership problem: a revisit. In: Digital Rights Management Workshop, pp. 93–101 (2005)
18. Singh, R., Gupta, R.: Digital watermarking with visual cryptography in spatial domain. In: International Conference on Advanced Computing, Communication and Networks 2011, pp. 948–951 (2011)
19. Surekha, B., Swamy, G.N.: A spatial domain public image watermarking. International Journal of Security and Its Applications 5(1), 1–12 (2011)
20. Tai, G.-C., Chang, L.-W.: Visual cryptography for digital watermarking in still images. In: Aizawa, K., Nakamura, Y., Satoh, S. (eds.) PCM 2004. LNCS, vol. 3332, pp. 50–57. Springer, Heidelberg (2004)
21. Wang, F.-H., Pan, J.-S., Jain, L.C.: Watermarking with visual cryptography and gain-shape VQ. In: Wang, F.-H., Pan, J.-S., Jain, L.C. (eds.) Innovations in Dig. Watermark. Tech. SCI, vol. 232, pp. 163–172. Springer, Heidelberg (2009)
22. Wang, F.-H., Pan, J.-S., Jain, L.C.: Innovations in Dig. Watermark. Tech. SCI, vol. 232. Springer, Heidelberg (2009)
23. Wang, M.-S., Chen, W.-C.: Digital image copyright protection scheme based on visual cryptography and singular value decomposition. Pattern Recognition 46(6), 1530–1541 (2007)

Region-in-Region Incrementing
Visual Cryptography Scheme

Ching-Nung Yang, Yi-Chin Lin, and Chih-Cheng Wu

Department of Computer Science and Information Engineering,
National Dong Hwa University, Taiwan
cnyang@mail.ndhu.edu.tw

Abstract. Recently, some region incrementing VCSs (RIVCSs) were proposed, which can gradually reconstruct secrets in a single image. In RIVCS, the secret image is subdivided into multiple secrecy level regions, in such a way that more shadows can be used to reveal the more secrecy level regions. The incrementing region property provides an attractive feature, which enables progressive decoding. However, the secret level regions of all previous RIVCSs are disjointed, which any two secrecy level regions do not have the same overlapping areas. In this paper, we discuss a (k, n) region-in-region incrementing VCS (RiRIVCS). Our (k, n)-RiRIVCS has $(n-k+1)$ secrecy level regions, which the next secrecy level region is in the preceding secrecy level region. Such region allocations in our RiRIVCS have more areas to hide the secret than the non-overlapping regions in the previous RIVCS.

Keywords: Secret sharing, Visual cryptography, Region incrementing visual cryptography.

1 Introduction

Visual cryptography scheme (VCS) copes with the visual version of secret sharing scheme. A (k, n)-VCS, where $k \leq n$, divides a secret image into n shadow images (referred to as shadows). One can reconstruct the secret image with any k or more shadows; but, one cannot obtain any information of the secret image from fewer than k shadows. The appealing property of VCS is the ease of decoding. In VCS, any k participants may photocopy their shadows on transparencies and stack them on an overhead projector to visually decode the secret.

The first (k, n)-VCS, invented by Naor and Shamir [1], encrypted a black-and-white secret by expanding a secret pixel into a collection of m (referred to as the pixel expansion) subpixels in each of the n shadows. The sizes of the pixel and the subpixel are equal. Hence, the shadow size is m times expanded. Since the visual quality of a reconstructed image is degraded by a large pixel expansion, most research papers on VCS had been published to enhance the visual quality and reduce the pixel expansion. Some of them even have no pixel expansion ($m=1$) which are known as the probabilistic VCS [2-5]. VCSs with specific features, such as sharing multiple secrets, cheating prevention, solving misalignment problem, achieving ideal contrast, sharing

Y.Q. Shi, H.J. Kim, and F. Pérez-González (Eds.): IWDW 2012, LNCS 7809, pp. 449–463, 2013.

color image, were proposed [6-14]. Although VCS cannot recover the original image without distortion, the simplicity of VCS provides new applications, e.g., visual authentication, steganography, and image encryption. More applications of VCS can be found in Chapter 12 "Applications of Visual Cryptography" in the book [15].

Recently, some region incrementing VCSs (RIVCSs) were proposed [16-18], which can gradually reconstruct secrets in a single image. In RIVCS, the secret image is subdivided into multiple secrecy level regions, in such a way more shadows can be used to reveal the more secrecy level regions. The incrementing region property provides an attractive feature, the progressive decoding, in VCS's applications. In [16], Wang proposed a (2, n)-RIVCS, which the i-th secrecy level region R_i, $1 \leq i \leq (n-1)$, can be decoded when stacking $(i+1)$ shadows. For example, in (2, 4)-RIVCS, the secret image is divided into three regions R_1, R_2, and R_3. When stacking two, three, and four shadows, we can decode the 1st, 2nd, and 3rd secrecy level regions, respectively. However, in Wang's (2, n)-RIVCS basis matrices of (2, n)-RIVCSs with n= 3, 4, 5, were directly given, but no construction had been studied. Shyu and Jiang [17] developed a novel and efficient construction for (2, n)-RIVCS using linear programming to reduce the pixel expansion and enhance the contrast. However, both Wang's scheme and Shyu and Jiang's scheme suffers from the incorrect-color problem, which the colors of reconstructed images may be reversed (i.e., the black and white are reversed). If the color of text is also the secret information, the incorrect-color problem will compromise the secret. In [18], Yang et al. solved the incorrect-color problem, and also extended the (2, n)-RIVCS to (k, n)-RIVCS, where k and n can be any integers. The formal contrast and security conditions of (k, n)-RIVCS were also formally defined in [18]. Meantime, Yang et al.'s (k, n)-RIVCS design the basis matrices, which is easier to generate shadows than Shyu and Jiang's algorithm.

However, the secret level regions of all previous RIVCSs [16-18] are disjointed, which any two secrecy level regions do not have the same overlapping areas. In this paper, we discuss a (k, n) region-in-region incrementing VCS (RiRIVCS). Our (k, n)-RiRIVCS has ($n-k+1$) regions which $R_i \supset R_{i+1}$, $1 \leq i \leq (n-k+1)$. Since the next region (R_{i+1}) is in the preceding region (R_i), we may have more areas to hide the secret than the non-overlapping regions in the previous RIVCSs.

2   Related Work

In this paper, we design the (k, n)-RiRIVCS based on Yang et al.'s (k, n)-RIVCS; as a result, we describe the (k, n)-VCS and briefly review Yang et al.'s (k, n)-RIVCS.

2.1   Naor and Shamir's (k, n)-VCS

Naor and Shamir (k, n)-VCS [1] encrypted a secret image by expanding a secret pixel into a collection of m subpixels in each of the n shadows. The whiteness is used to distinguish the black color from the white color, i.e., "$m-h$"B"h"W (respectively, "$m-l$"B"l"W) represents a white (respectively, black) secret pixel, where h and l are the whiteness of the white color and black color, and $0 \leq l < h \leq m$.

The collection of subpixels can be represented by an $n \times m$ Boolean matrix $S = [s_{ij}]$, where the element s_{ij} represents the j-th subpixel in i-th shadow. Black and white subpixels s_{ij} are represented by a 0 and 1, respectively. Stacking t shadows together, the grey-level of each secret pixel (m subpixels) of the stacked result is proportional to the $H(\text{OR}(i_1, \cdots, i_t))$, where $\text{OR}(\cdot)$ is an OR-ed ("OR" operation) m-tuples of any t rows $(i_1, \cdots, i_t)$ of S associated with the shadows we stack, and $H(\cdot)$ is the Hamming weight (the number of 1's in the m-tuples) function.

A (k, n)-VCS consists of two collections of $n \times m$ Boolean matrices $B_0^{(k,n)}$ and $B_1^{(k,n)}$. To share a white (respectively black) pixel, the dealer randomly chooses m subpixels in one row of a matrix in the collection $C_0^{(k,n)}$ (respectively, $C_1^{(k,n)}$). The collection $C_i^{(k,n)}$ can be obtained by permuting the columns of $B_i^{(k,n)}$ in all possible ways. Each collection has $m!$ matrices. The (k, n)-VCS is considered valid if matrices B_0 and B_1 satisfy the *contrast* condition (V-1) and the *security* condition (V-2).

$$
\begin{cases}
\text{(V-1) } H\left(\text{OR}\left(B_1^{(k,n)} \mid t\right)\right) \geq (m-l) \text{ and } H\left(\text{OR}\left(B_0^{(k,n)} \mid t\right)\right) \leq (m-h) \text{ for } t = k, \\
\text{where } 0 \leq l < h \leq m. \\
\text{(V-2) } H\left(\text{OR}\left(B_1^{(k,n)} \mid t\right)\right) = H\left(\text{OR}\left(B_0^{(k,n)} \mid t\right)\right) \text{ for } t \leq (k-1).
\end{cases}
$$

2.2   Yang et al.'s (k, n)-RIVCS

In Yang's (k, n)-RiRIVCS, when stacking $(i+k-1)$ shadows, one can decode the i-th secrecy level region, where $i=1, 2, \ldots, (n-k+1)$. Let LK_i^0 (respectively, LK_i^1), $1 \leq i \leq (n-k+1)$, be the matrix encoding a white (respectively, black) pixel for the i-th secrecy level region, and $|LK_i^0|$ and $|LK_i^1|$ be the number of columns. In [18], Yang et al. presented a systematic way to construct two types of (k, n)-RIVCSs: the proposed (k, n)-RIVCS (solving the incorrect-color problem) and the modified (k, n)-RIVCS (reducing the pixel expansion and enhancing the contrast). The matrices LK_i^0 and LK_i^1, $1 \leq i \leq (n-k+1)$, should satisfy the following conditions.

$$
\begin{cases}
\text{(R-1) } |LK_i^0| = |LK_i^1| \text{ for } 1 \leq i \leq n-k+1, \\
\text{(R-2) } \begin{cases} H\left(\text{OR}\left(LK_i^1 \mid t\right)\right) > H\left(\text{OR}\left(LK_i^0 \mid t\right)\right) \text{ for } t = i+k-1 \text{ (proposed scheme)}, \\ H\left(\text{OR}\left(LK_i^1 \mid t\right)\right) \neq H\left(\text{OR}\left(LK_i^0 \mid t\right)\right) \text{ for } t = i+k-1 \text{ (modified scheme)}, \end{cases} \\
\text{(R-3) } H\left(\text{OR}\left(LK_i^1 \mid t\right)\right) = H\left(\text{OR}\left(LK_i^0 \mid t\right)\right) \text{ for } t \leq i+k-2, \\
\text{(R-4) } LK_1^0 = LK_2^0 = \cdots = LK_{n-k+1}^0.
\end{cases}
$$

In condition (R-1), the matrices have the same number of columns in order to arrange subpixels of all regions in a shadow. Conditions (R-2) and (R-3) are the contrast and security conditions. When stacking $(i+k-1)$ shadows, one can reveal the i-th secrecy level region, and cannot decode any secret information for staking less than $(i+k-1)$ shadows. The areas where no secret is revealed are noise-like due to condition (R-4). The proposed scheme has the contrast condition $H\left(\text{OR}\left(LK_i^1 \mid t\right)\right) > H\left(\text{OR}\left(LK_i^0 \mid t\right)\right)$, so that it can reveal correct colors for all regions. Suppose that the secret image is a bi-level image and the color of image is not a secret. The secret information will not be compromised even though the black and white colors are reversed. Without the requirement of revealing correct color, the contrast condition (R-2) can be modified as $H\left(\text{OR}\left(LK_i^1 \mid t\right)\right) \neq H\left(\text{OR}\left(LK_i^0 \mid t\right)\right)$ to reduce the pixel expansion and enhances the contrast. Construction method for the proposed scheme is shown in Construction 1 (one can refer the construction method of the modified scheme in [18]). Moreover, Yang et al. also further enhance the modified scheme to improve the contrast of the first secrecy level region for $k=2$.

Construction 1. The white matrices are $LK_i^0 = \left[B_0^{(k,n)} \cup B_0^{(k+1,n)} \cup \cdots \cup B_0^{(n,n)} \right]$, and the black matrix is $LK_i^1 = \left[B_1^{(i+k-1,n)} \mid LK_i^0 - B_0^{(i+k-1,n)} \right]$, where $1 \leq i \leq (n-k+1)$.

Example 1. Construct Yang et al.'s (2, 4)-RIVCS by using Construction 1.
The basis matrices of Naor and Shamir's (2, 4)-VCS, (3, 4)-VCS, and (4, 4)-VCS used for constructing (2, 4)-RIVCS, $1 \leq i \leq 3$, are shown below.

$$
\left\{
\begin{aligned}
B_1^{(2,4)} &= \begin{bmatrix} 1&0&0&0 \\ 0&1&0&0 \\ 0&0&1&0 \\ 0&0&0&1 \end{bmatrix} \quad
B_1^{(3,4)} = \begin{bmatrix} 1&0&0&0&1&1 \\ 0&1&0&0&1&1 \\ 0&0&1&0&1&1 \\ 0&0&0&1&1&1 \end{bmatrix} \quad
B_1^{(4,4)} = \begin{bmatrix} 1&0&0&0&1&1&1&0 \\ 0&1&0&0&1&1&0&1 \\ 0&0&1&0&1&0&1&1 \\ 0&0&0&1&0&1&1&1 \end{bmatrix} \\
B_0^{(2,4)} &= \begin{bmatrix} 1&0&0&0 \\ 1&0&0&0 \\ 1&0&0&0 \\ 1&0&0&0 \end{bmatrix} \quad
B_0^{(3,4)} = \begin{bmatrix} 0&1&1&1&0&0 \\ 1&0&1&1&0&0 \\ 1&1&0&1&0&0 \\ 1&1&1&0&0&0 \end{bmatrix} \quad
B_0^{(4,4)} = \begin{bmatrix} 0&1&1&1&0&0&0&1 \\ 0&1&0&0&1&1&0&1 \\ 0&0&1&0&1&0&1&1 \\ 0&0&0&1&0&1&1&1 \end{bmatrix}
\end{aligned}
\right.
\tag{1}
$$

By using Construction 1, we can derive LK_i^0 and LK_i^1, $1 \leq i \leq 3$, of the proposed (2, 4)-RIVCS with $m=14$, as shown in Eq. (2).

$$
\left\{
\begin{aligned}
LK_1^0 = LK_2^0 = LK_3^0 &= \left[B_0^{(2,4)} \cup B_0^{(3,4)} \cup B_0^{(4,4)} \right] = \begin{bmatrix} 1&0&0&0&0&1&1&1&1&1&1&0&0&0 \\ 1&0&0&0&1&0&1&1&1&0&0&1&1&0 \\ 1&0&0&0&1&1&0&1&0&1&0&1&0&1 \\ 1&0&0&0&1&1&1&0&0&0&1&0&1&1 \end{bmatrix}, \\
LK_1^1 &= \left[B_1^{(2,4)} \mid LK_1^0 - B_0^{(2,4)} \right] = \begin{bmatrix} 1&0&0&0 \mid 0&1&1&1&1&1&1&0&0&0 \\ 0&1&0&0 \mid 1&0&1&1&1&0&0&1&1&0 \\ 0&0&1&0 \mid 1&1&0&1&0&1&0&1&0&1 \\ 0&0&0&1 \mid 1&1&1&0&0&0&1&0&1&1 \end{bmatrix}, \\
LK_2^1 &= \left[B_1^{(3,4)} \mid LK_2^0 - B_0^{(3,4)} \right] = \begin{bmatrix} 1&0&0&0&1&1 \mid 1&0&1&1&1&0&0&0 \\ 0&1&0&0&1&1 \mid 1&0&1&0&0&1&1&0 \\ 0&0&1&0&1&1 \mid 1&0&0&1&0&1&0&1 \\ 0&0&0&1&1&1 \mid 1&0&0&0&1&0&1&1 \end{bmatrix}, \\
LK_3^1 &= \left[B_1^{(4,4)} \mid LK_3^0 - B_0^{(4,4)} \right] = \begin{bmatrix} 1&0&0&0&1&1&1&0 \mid 0&0&0&1&1&1 \\ 0&1&0&0&1&1&0&1 \mid 0&0&1&0&1&1 \\ 0&0&1&0&1&0&1&1 \mid 0&0&1&1&0&1 \\ 0&0&0&1&0&1&1&1 \mid 0&0&1&1&1&0 \end{bmatrix}.
\end{aligned}
\right.
\tag{2}
$$

Obviously, all matrices have 14 columns and $LK_1^0 = LK_2^0 = LK_3^0$. Thus, conditions (R-1) and (R-4) are satisfied. Every row in all matrices has 7B7W subpixels, and thus all three shadows are noise-like. When stacking any two shadows, we have 10B4W in LK_1^0 and 11B3W in LK_1^1 for the 1st secrecy level region. Meantime, we have 10B4W in LK_2^1 and LK_3^1 for the 2nd and 3rd secrecy level region. Thus, only 1st secret is recovered and its contrast is 1/14 when stacking two shadows. When stacking three shadows, we have 11B3W in LK_2^1 and 12B2W in LK_2^0 and thus the contrast is 1/14 for 2nd secrecy level region for stacking three shadows. At this time, the contrast for 1st secrecy level region is enhanced to 1/7 (13B1W in LK_1^1 and 11B3W in LK_1^0 for stacking three shadows). When stacking all four shadows we have 12B2W in LK_3^1 and 11B3W in LK_3^0, so the contrasts of 3rd secrecy level region is 1/14. The contrasts of 1st and 2nd secrecy level regions are further improved to 3/14 and 1/7, respectively (14B0W in LK_1^1, 11B3W in LK_1^0, and 13B1W in LK_2^1, 11B3W in LK_2^0 for stacking four shadows). On the other hand, the modified (2, 4)-RIVCS only needs the pixel expansion $m=10$, and the contrast is enhanced (see TABLE 1 in [18]).

3   Motivation

The secret level regions of all RIVCSs [16-18] had the disjointed property, which any two secrecy level regions do not have the same overlapping areas, i.e., $R_i \cap R_j = \varnothing$ for $i \neq j$. In addition, the whole region R is the union of all sub regions, i.e., $R = R_1 \cup R_2 \cup \cdots \cup R_{n-1}$ for (2, n)-RIVCSs in [16, 17], and $R = R_1 \cup R_2 \cup \cdots \cup R_{n-k+1}$ for (k, n)-RIVCS in [18]. In this paper, we discuss a (k, n)-RiRIVCS with the ($n-k+1$) secrecy level regions which $R_i \supset R_{i+1}$, $1 \leq i \leq (n-k+1)$, and $R \supseteq R_1$. Since one secrecy level region is in another secrecy level region, we may have more areas to reveal the secret than the non-overlapping regions in the previous RIVCSs.

Let the secret in R_i be S_i. By stacking ($i+k-1$) shadows, one can sequentially reveal the secret S_i, $1 \leq i \leq (n-k+1)$, in R_i. After revealing S_i, suppose that the black and white areas of R_i are R_i^b and R_i^w, respectively, where $R_i = R_i^b \cup R_i^w$. To allocate the secrecy level region R_{i+1} in the secrecy level region R_i for our (k, n)-RiRIVCS, there are three possible ways arranging R_{i+1} in R_i: (i) the region R_{i+1} is located in R_i^b, (ii) the region R_{i+1} is located in R_i^w, and (iii) the region R_{i+1} is located in R_i. However, if R_{i+1} is located in R_i, the revealed secret S_{i+1} may be shown across the black and white areas in R_i. This will compromise the preceding reconstructed secret S_i. Therefore, in the proposed (k, n)-RiRIVCS, we only consider the first two allocations. Since these two allocations are non-overlapped and independent, we can use R_{i+1}-in-R_i^b and R_{i+1}-in-R_i^w simultaneously to enhance the areas to hide the secret.

Fig. 1(a) is the arrangement of three secrecy level regions of (2, 4)-RIVCS. The region allocations of the proposed (2, 4)-RiRIVCS using R_{i+1}-in-R_i^b and R_{i+1}-in-R_i^w are shown in Fig. 1(b). Since $R \supseteq R_1$, we herein use $R_1 = R$ for our (2, 4)-RiRIVCS.

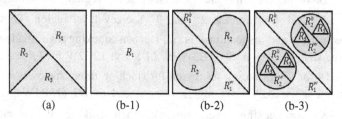

| (a) | (b-1) | (b-2) | (b-3) |

Fig. 1. Partition of three secrecy level regions: (a) (2, 4)-RIVCS (b) (2, 4)-RiRIVCS

4   The Proposed *(k, n)*-RiRIVCS

The secrecy level regions in RIVCS are non-overlapping. In this paper, we construct a (k, n)-RiRIVCS, which the secrets can be revealed in the preceding secrecy level regions. Two types of (k, n)-RiRIVCS are proposed. One is using the region allocation of R_{i+1}-in-R_i^b, and the other is using R_{i+1}-in-R_i^w.

4.1   *(k, n)*-RiRIVCS Using R_{i+1}-in-R_i^b

When using the allocation R_{i+1}-in-R_i^b, the (i+1)-th secrecy level region R_{i+1} is located within the region R_i^b. The black area in R_i is the background color for the secret S_{i+1} (note: the secret image is a bi-level image and the background is a white color). So, we use $LK_{i+1}^0 = LK_i^1$, $1 \leq i \leq (n-k-1)$. Therefore, the conditions of our (k, n)-RiRIVCS based on the allocation R_{i+1}-in-R_i^b are same as the conditions of Yang et al.'s except that condition (R-4) is modified as (R-4').

$$\begin{cases} \text{(R-1')}: \text{(R-1)}, \\ \text{(R-2')}: \text{(R-2)}, \\ \text{(R-3')}: \text{(R-3)}, \\ \text{(R-4')} \ LK_i^0 = LK_{i-1}^1, \ 2 \leq i \leq (n-k+1). \end{cases}$$

The proposed (k, n)-RiRIVCS is based on the (t, n)-VCSs, $k \leq t \leq n$. Let $B_1^{(t,n)}$ and $B_0^{(t,n)}$ be the black and white basis matrices of a (t, n)-VCS. In the proposed (k, n)-RiRIVCS using R_{i+1}-in-R_i^b, one can reveal the secret S_{i+1} in the region R_i^b by stacking (k+i) shadows. Thus, we need to use the black color of the preceding secret S_i (i.e., R_i^b) as the white color (background color) of the secret S_{i+1}.

Design concept is described as follows. We unite all white matrices of these (t, n)-VCSs, $k \leq t \leq n$, to construct LK_1^0. The white matrix of i-th secrecy level is the black matrix of $(i-1)$-th secrecy level. In designing the matrix LK_i^1 for the i-th security level region, we use $B_1^{(i+k-1,n)}$ in LK_i^1 to replace $B_0^{(i+k-1,n)}$ in LK_i^0. The proposed (k, n)-RiRIVCS, with LK_i^0 and LK_i^1 where $1 \le i \le (n-k+1)$, is formally described in Construction 2.

Construction 2. The white matrix is $LK_i^0 = LK_{i-1}^1$, and the black matrix is $LK_i^1 = \left[B_1^{(i+k-1,n)} \mid LK_i^0 - B_0^{(i+k-1,n)} \right]$ for $1 \le i \le (n-k+1)$, where the initial matrix LK_0^1 is $LK_0^1 = \left[B_0^{(k,n)} \mid B_0^{(k+1,n)} \mid \cdots \mid B_0^{(n,n)} \right]$.

Theorem 1. The proposed (k, n)-RiRIVCS using R_{i+1}-in-R_i^b from Construction 2 satisfies conditions (R-1′), (R-2′), (R-3′) and (R-4′).

Proof. Since black and white matrices have the same column size, i.e., $\mid B_1^{(i+k-1,n)} \mid = \mid B_0^{(i+k-1,n)} \mid$, we have $\mid LK_i^1 \mid = \left[B_1^{(i+k-1,n)} \mid LK_i^0 - B_0^{(i+k-1,n)} \right] = \mid B_1^{(i+k-1,n)} \mid + \mid LK_i^0 \mid - \mid B_0^{(i+k-1,n)} \mid = \mid LK_i^0 \mid$ for $1 \le i \le n-k+1$. Thus, condition (R-1′) is satisfied. From the construction, it is obvious that (R-4′) is satisfied.

By the definition of $LK_i^1 = \left[B_1^{(i+k-1,n)} \mid LK_i^0 - B_0^{(i+k-1,n)} \right]$, we have

$$\begin{cases} H\left(OR\left(LK_i^1 \mid t\right)\right) = H\left(OR\left(B_1^{(i+k-1,n)} \mid t\right)\right) + \\ H\left(OR\left(LK_i^0 \mid t\right)\right) - H\left(OR\left(B_0^{(i+k-1,n)} \mid t\right)\right). \end{cases} \tag{3}$$

Eq. (3) is true when the premise that LK_i^0 includes $B_0^{(i+k-1,n)}$ is true. As we know $LK_1^0 = LK_0^1 = \left[B_0^{(k,n)} \mid B_0^{(k+1,n)} \mid \cdots \mid B_0^{(n,n)} \right]$, so the premise is true for $i=1$. Since $LK_2^0 = LK_1^1 = \left[B_1^{(k,n)} \mid LK_1^0 - B_0^{(k,n)} \right] = \left[B_1^{(k,n)} \mid B_0^{(k+1,n)} \mid \cdots \mid B_0^{(n,n)} \right]$, it is observed that LK_2^0 includes $B_0^{(k+1,n)}$. By the similar induction, it can be easily verified that LK_i^0 includes $B_0^{(i+k-1,n)}$ for $1 \le i \le (n-k+1)$.

From Eq. (3), we have

$$\begin{cases} H\left(OR\left(LK_i^1 \mid t\right)\right) - H\left(OR\left(LK_i^0 \mid t\right)\right) = \\ H\left(OR\left(B_1^{(i+k-1,n)} \mid t\right)\right) - H\left(OR\left(B_0^{(i+k-1,n)} \mid t\right)\right). \end{cases} \tag{4}$$

Since $H\left(OR\left(B_1^{(k,n)} \mid t\right)\right) > H\left(OR\left(B_0^{(k,n)} \mid t\right)\right)$ for $t=(i+k-1)$ and $H\left(OR\left(B_1^{(k,n)} \mid t\right)\right) = H\left(OR\left(B_0^{(k,n)} \mid t\right)\right)$ for $t \le (i+k-2)$, we can derive that the proposed (k, n)-RiRIVCS satisfies conditions (R-2′) and (R-3′). $\square$

Example 2. Construct the (2, 4)-RiRIVCS using R_{i+1}-in-R_i^b .

By Construction 2, we can derive the basis matrices LK_i^0 and LK_i^1, $1 \leq i \leq 3$, of (2, 4)-RiRIVCS with $m=18$, as shown in Eq. (5).

$$
\begin{cases}
LK_1^0 = \left[B_0^{(2,4)} \mid B_0^{(3,4)} \mid B_0^{(4,4)} \right] = \begin{bmatrix} 1 & 0 & 0 & 0 & 0 & 1 & 1 & 1 & 0 & 0 & 0 & 1 & 1 & 1 & 0 & 0 & 0 & 1 \\ 1 & 0 & 0 & 0 & 1 & 0 & 1 & 1 & 0 & 0 & 0 & 1 & 0 & 0 & 1 & 1 & 0 & 1 \\ 1 & 0 & 0 & 0 & 1 & 1 & 0 & 1 & 0 & 0 & 0 & 0 & 1 & 0 & 1 & 0 & 1 & 1 \\ 1 & 0 & 0 & 0 & 1 & 1 & 1 & 0 & 0 & 0 & 0 & 0 & 0 & 1 & 0 & 1 & 1 & 1 \end{bmatrix}, \\[2em]
LK_1^1 = LK_2^0 = \left[B_1^{(2,4)} \mid LK_1^0 - B_0^{(2,4)} \right] = \begin{bmatrix} 1 & 0 & 0 & 0 & 0 & 1 & 1 & 1 & 0 & 0 & 0 & 1 & 1 & 1 & 0 & 0 & 0 & 1 \\ 0 & 1 & 0 & 0 & 1 & 0 & 1 & 1 & 0 & 0 & 0 & 1 & 0 & 0 & 1 & 1 & 0 & 1 \\ 0 & 0 & 1 & 0 & 1 & 1 & 0 & 1 & 0 & 0 & 0 & 0 & 1 & 0 & 1 & 0 & 1 & 1 \\ 0 & 0 & 0 & 1 & 1 & 1 & 1 & 0 & 0 & 0 & 0 & 0 & 0 & 1 & 0 & 1 & 1 & 1 \end{bmatrix}, & (5) \\[2em]
LK_2^1 = LK_3^0 = \left[B_1^{(3,4)} \mid LK_2^0 - B_0^{(3,4)} \right] = \begin{bmatrix} 1 & 0 & 0 & 0 & 1 & 1 & 1 & 0 & 0 & 0 & 0 & 1 & 1 & 1 & 0 & 0 & 0 & 1 \\ 0 & 1 & 0 & 0 & 1 & 1 & 0 & 1 & 0 & 0 & 0 & 1 & 0 & 0 & 1 & 1 & 0 & 1 \\ 0 & 0 & 1 & 0 & 1 & 1 & 0 & 0 & 1 & 0 & 0 & 0 & 1 & 0 & 1 & 0 & 1 & 1 \\ 0 & 0 & 0 & 1 & 1 & 1 & 0 & 0 & 0 & 1 & 0 & 0 & 0 & 1 & 0 & 1 & 1 & 1 \end{bmatrix}, \\[2em]
LK_3^1 = \left[B_1^{(4,4)} \mid LK_3^0 - B_0^{(4,4)} \right] = \begin{bmatrix} 1 & 0 & 0 & 0 & 1 & 1 & 1 & 0 & 1 & 0 & 0 & 0 & 1 & 1 & 0 & 0 & 0 & 1 \\ 0 & 1 & 0 & 0 & 1 & 1 & 0 & 1 & 1 & 0 & 1 & 0 & 0 & 1 & 0 & 1 & 0 & 1 \\ 0 & 0 & 1 & 0 & 1 & 0 & 1 & 1 & 0 & 1 & 0 & 1 & 0 & 0 & 1 & 0 & 1 \\ 0 & 0 & 0 & 1 & 0 & 1 & 1 & 1 & 0 & 0 & 1 & 1 & 0 & 0 & 0 & 1 & 1 \end{bmatrix}.
\end{cases}
$$

4.2   (k, n)-RiRIVCS Using R_{i+1}-in-R_i^w

The next secret can also be revealed on the preceding white area. Here, we show the construction of (k, n)-RiRIVS using the region allocation R_{i+1}-in-R_i^w . At this time, condition (R-4′) is modified from $LK_i^0 = LK_{i-1}^1$ to $LK_i^0 = LK_{i-1}^0$, $2 \leq i \leq (n-k+1)$. It is easily to derive $LK_1^0 = LK_2^0 = \cdots = LK_{n-k+1}^0$, which is the same as condition (R-4) in the (k, n)-RIVCS. Therefore, the (k, n)-RiRIVCS using R_{i+1}-in-R_i^w are just the (k, n)-RIVCS. They are exactly the same.

4.3   (k, n)-RiRIVCS Interlacing R_{i+1}-in-R_i^b and R_{i+1}-in-R_i^w

In fact, we can interlace R_{i+1}-in-R_i^b and R_{i+1}-in-R_i^w in a single region allocation. As shown in Fig. 2, we first use R_2-in-R_1^b in the second secrecy level and then R_3-in-R_2^w in the third secrecy level. On the other hand, Fig. 3 shows the other interlaced type for the (2, 4)-RiRIVCS. We use R_2-in-R_1^w in the second secrecy level and then R_3-in-R_2^b in the third secrecy level.

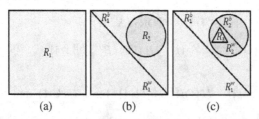

(a)   (b)   (c)

Fig. 2. Partition of three secrecy level regions in our (2, 4)-RiRIVCS: (a) 1st secrecy level region (b) 2nd secrecy level region R_2-in-R_1^b (c) 3rd secrecy level region R_3-in-R_2^w

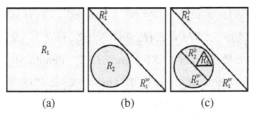

Fig. 3. Partition of three secrecy level regions in our (2, 4)-RiRIVCS: (a) 1st secrecy level region (b) 2nd secrecy level region R_2-in-R_1^w (c) 3rd secrecy level region R_3-in-R_2^b

Example 3. Construct the (2, 4)-RiRIVCS using R_2-in-R_1^b and then R_3-in-R_2^w.

LK_1^0, LK_1^1, LK_2^0, and LK_2^1 are just the same as those in Example 2. Since the third secrecy level region is R_3-in-R_2^w, we have $LK_3^0 = LK_2^0$. Then, the matrix LK_3^1 is obtained in the following equation.

$$\begin{cases} LK_3^1 = \left[B_1^{(4,4)} \mid LK_3^0 - B_0^{(4,4)} \right] = \left[B_1^{(4,4)} \mid LK_2^0 - B_0^{(4,4)} \right] \\ = \begin{bmatrix} 1\,0\,0\,0\,1\,1\,1\,0 & 1\,0\,0\,0\,0\,1\,1\,1\,0\,0 \\ 0\,1\,0\,0\,1\,1\,0\,1 & 0\,1\,0\,0\,1\,0\,1\,0\,1\,1\,0\,0 \\ 0\,0\,1\,0\,1\,0\,1\,1 & 0\,0\,1\,0\,1\,1\,0\,1\,0\,0 \\ 0\,0\,0\,1\,0\,1\,1\,1 & 0\,0\,0\,1\,1\,1\,1\,0\,0\,0 \end{bmatrix}. \end{cases} \tag{6}$$

Example 4. Construct the (2, 4)-RiRIVCS using R_2-in-R_1^w and then R_3-in-R_2^b.

LK_1^0 and LK_1^1 are just the same as those in Example 2. Since the second secrecy level region is R_2-in-R_1^w, we have $LK_2^0 = LK_1^0$. By using R_3-in-R_2^b for the third secrecy level region, we can derive other basis matrices in the following equation.

$$\begin{cases} LK_2^1 = LK_3^0 = \left[B_1^{(3,4)} \mid LK_2^0 - B_0^{(3,4)} \right] = \left[B_1^{(3,4)} \mid LK_1^0 - B_0^{(3,4)} \right] \\ = \begin{bmatrix} 1\,0\,0\,0\,1\,1 & 1\,0\,0\,0\,0\,1\,1\,1\,0\,0\,0\,1 \\ 0\,1\,0\,0\,1\,1 & 1\,0\,0\,0\,0\,1\,0\,0\,1\,1\,0\,1 \\ 0\,0\,1\,0\,1\,1 & 1\,0\,0\,0\,0\,0\,1\,0\,1\,0\,1\,1 \\ 0\,0\,0\,1\,1\,1 & 1\,0\,0\,0\,0\,0\,1\,0\,1\,1\,1 \end{bmatrix}, \\ LK_3^1 = \left[B_1^{(4,4)} \mid LK_3^0 - B_0^{(4,4)} \right] \\ = \begin{bmatrix} 1\,0\,0\,0\,1\,1\,1\,0 & 1\,0\,0\,0\,1\,1\,1\,0\,0\,0 \\ 0\,1\,0\,0\,1\,1\,0\,1 & 0\,1\,0\,0\,1\,1\,1\,0\,0\,0 \\ 0\,0\,1\,0\,1\,0\,1\,1 & 0\,0\,1\,0\,1\,1\,1\,0\,0\,0 \\ 0\,0\,0\,1\,0\,1\,1\,1 & 0\,0\,0\,1\,1\,1\,1\,0\,0\,0 \end{bmatrix}. \end{cases} \tag{7}$$

4.4 (k, n)-RiRIVCS Using R_{i+1}-in-R_i^b and R_{i+1}-in-R_i^w Simultaneously

We can simultaneously use these two allocations (R_{i+1}-in-R_i^b and R_{i+1}-in-R_i^w) to enhance the areas to hide the secret. As shown in Fig. 1(b-3), R_2-in-R_1^b and R_2-in-R_1^w are simultaneously used for the second secrecy level region, and that R_3-in-R_2^b and R_3-in-R_2^w are simultaneously used for the third secrecy level region.

Example 5. Construct the (2, 4)-RiRIVCS using R_{i+1}-in-R_i^b and R_{i+1}-in-R_i^w simultaneously.

Let the 2nd secrecy level region R_2 be composed of two sub-regions $R_{2,1}$ and $R_{2,2}$, where $R_2 = R_{2,1} \cup R_{2,2}$. We use $(R_{2,1}\text{-in-}R_1^b) \| (R_{2,2}\text{-in-}R_1^w)$, $(R_3\text{-in-}R_{2,1}^b) \| (R_3\text{-in-}R_{2,1}^w)$, and $(R_3\text{-in-}R_{2,2}^b) \| (R_3\text{-in-}R_{2,2}^w)$. Let $LK_{2,i}^1$ and $LK_{2,i}^0$ denote the black and white matrices for the sub-region $R_{2,i}$, $i=1, 2$. Since $(R_{2,1}\text{-in-}R_1^b) \| (R_{2,2}\text{-in-}R_1^w)$, we have $LK_{2,1}^0 = LK_1^1$ and $LK_{2,2}^0 = LK_1^0$. Then, we can derive $LK_{2,1}^1$ and $LK_{2,2}^1$ in the following equation.

$$\begin{cases} LK_{2,1}^1 = \left[B_1^{(3,4)} \mid LK_{2,1}^0 - B_0^{(3,4)} \right] = \left[B_1^{(3,4)} \mid LK_1^1 - B_0^{(3,4)} \right] \\ = \begin{bmatrix} 1 & 0 & 0 & 0 & 1 & 1 & 1 & 0 & 0 & 0 & 0 & 1 & 1 & 1 & 0 & 0 & 0 & 1 \\ 0 & 1 & 0 & 0 & 1 & 1 & 0 & 1 & 0 & 0 & 0 & 1 & 0 & 0 & 1 & 1 & 0 & 1 \\ 0 & 0 & 1 & 0 & 1 & 1 & 0 & 0 & 1 & 0 & 0 & 0 & 1 & 0 & 1 & 0 & 1 & 1 \\ 0 & 0 & 0 & 1 & 1 & 1 & 0 & 0 & 0 & 1 & 0 & 0 & 0 & 1 & 0 & 1 & 1 & 1 \end{bmatrix}, \\ LK_{2,2}^1 = \left[B_1^{(3,4)} \mid LK_{2,2}^0 - B_0^{(3,4)} \right] = \left[B_1^{(3,4)} \mid LK_1^0 - B_0^{(3,4)} \right] \\ = \begin{bmatrix} 1 & 0 & 0 & 0 & 1 & 1 & 1 & 0 & 0 & 0 & 0 & 1 & 1 & 1 & 0 & 0 & 0 & 1 \\ 0 & 1 & 0 & 0 & 1 & 1 & 1 & 0 & 0 & 0 & 0 & 1 & 0 & 0 & 1 & 1 & 0 & 1 \\ 0 & 0 & 1 & 0 & 1 & 1 & 1 & 0 & 0 & 0 & 0 & 0 & 1 & 0 & 1 & 0 & 1 & 1 \\ 0 & 0 & 0 & 1 & 1 & 1 & 1 & 0 & 0 & 0 & 0 & 0 & 0 & 1 & 0 & 1 & 1 & 1 \end{bmatrix}. \end{cases} \tag{8}$$

Let the matrices $LK_{3,i}^1$ and $LK_{3,i}^0$ denote the black and white matrices of the sub-region $R_{3,i}$, $1 \le i \le 4$, where $R_{3,1}$ is the sub-region of R_3 in $R_{2,1}^b$, $R_{3,2}$ is the sub-region of R_3 in $R_{2,1}^w$, $R_{3,3}$ is the sub-region of R_3 in $R_{2,2}^b$, $R_{3,4}$ is the sub-region of R_3 in $R_{2,2}^w$, and $R_3 = R_{3,1} \cup R_{3,2} \cup R_{3,3} \cup R_{3,4}$. Since $(R_3\text{-in-}R_{2,1}^b) \| (R_3\text{-in-}R_{2,1}^w)$ and $(R_3\text{-in-}R_{2,2}^b) \| (R_3\text{-in-}R_{2,2}^w)$, we have $LK_{3,1}^0 = LK_{2,1}^1$, $LK_{3,2}^0 = LK_{2,1}^0$, $LK_{3,3}^0 = LK_{2,2}^1$, and $LK_{3,4}^0 = LK_{2,2}^0$. Then, we can derive $LK_{3,1}^1$, $LK_{3,2}^1$, $LK_{3,3}^1$, and $LK_{3,4}^1$ in the following equation.

$$\begin{cases} LK_{3,1}^1 = \left[B_1^{(4,4)} \mid LK_{3,1}^0 - B_0^{(4,4)} \right] = \left[B_1^{(4,4)} \mid LK_{2,1}^1 - B_0^{(4,4)} \right] \\ = \begin{bmatrix} 1 & 0 & 0 & 0 & 1 & 1 & 1 & 0 & 1 & 0 & 0 & 0 & 1 & 1 & 1 & 0 & 0 & 0 \\ 0 & 1 & 0 & 0 & 1 & 1 & 0 & 1 & 1 & 0 & 1 & 0 & 0 & 1 & 1 & 0 & 1 & 0 & 0 \\ 0 & 0 & 1 & 0 & 1 & 0 & 1 & 1 & 1 & 0 & 0 & 1 & 0 & 1 & 1 & 0 & 0 & 1 & 0 \\ 0 & 0 & 0 & 1 & 0 & 1 & 1 & 1 & 0 & 0 & 0 & 1 & 1 & 1 & 0 & 0 & 0 & 1 \end{bmatrix}, \\ LK_{3,2}^1 = \left[B_1^{(4,4)} \mid LK_{3,2}^0 - B_0^{(4,4)} \right] = \left[B_1^{(4,4)} \mid LK_{2,1}^0 - B_0^{(4,4)} \right] = \left[B_1^{(4,4)} \mid LK_1^1 - B_0^{(4,4)} \right] \\ = \begin{bmatrix} 1 & 0 & 0 & 0 & 1 & 1 & 1 & 0 & 1 & 0 & 0 & 0 & 0 & 1 & 1 & 1 & 0 & 0 \\ 0 & 1 & 0 & 0 & 1 & 1 & 0 & 1 & 1 & 0 & 1 & 0 & 0 & 1 & 0 & 1 & 1 & 0 & 0 \\ 0 & 0 & 1 & 0 & 1 & 0 & 1 & 1 & 1 & 0 & 0 & 1 & 0 & 1 & 1 & 0 & 1 & 0 & 0 \\ 0 & 0 & 0 & 1 & 0 & 1 & 1 & 1 & 0 & 0 & 0 & 1 & 1 & 1 & 1 & 0 & 0 & 0 \end{bmatrix}, \\ LK_{3,3}^1 = \left[B_1^{(4,4)} \mid LK_{3,3}^0 - B_0^{(4,4)} \right] = \left[B_1^{(4,4)} \mid LK_{2,2}^1 - B_0^{(4,4)} \right] \\ = \begin{bmatrix} 1 & 0 & 0 & 0 & 1 & 1 & 1 & 0 & 1 & 0 & 0 & 0 & 1 & 1 & 0 & 0 & 0 \\ 0 & 1 & 0 & 0 & 1 & 1 & 0 & 1 & 1 & 0 & 1 & 0 & 0 & 1 & 1 & 1 & 0 & 0 & 0 \\ 0 & 0 & 1 & 0 & 1 & 0 & 1 & 1 & 1 & 0 & 0 & 1 & 0 & 1 & 1 & 1 & 0 & 0 & 0 \\ 0 & 0 & 0 & 1 & 0 & 1 & 1 & 1 & 0 & 0 & 0 & 1 & 1 & 1 & 1 & 0 & 0 & 0 \end{bmatrix}, \\ LK_{3,4}^1 = \left[B_1^{(4,4)} \mid LK_{3,4}^0 - B_0^{(4,4)} \right] = \left[B_1^{(4,4)} \mid LK_{2,2}^0 - B_0^{(4,4)} \right] = \left[B_1^{(4,4)} \mid LK_1^0 - B_0^{(4,4)} \right] \\ = \begin{bmatrix} 1 & 0 & 0 & 0 & 1 & 1 & 1 & 0 & 1 & 0 & 0 & 0 & 0 & 1 & 1 & 1 & 0 & 0 \\ 0 & 1 & 0 & 0 & 1 & 1 & 0 & 1 & 1 & 0 & 0 & 0 & 1 & 0 & 1 & 1 & 0 & 0 \\ 0 & 0 & 1 & 0 & 1 & 0 & 1 & 1 & 1 & 0 & 0 & 1 & 1 & 0 & 1 & 0 & 0 \\ 0 & 0 & 0 & 1 & 0 & 1 & 1 & 1 & 0 & 0 & 0 & 1 & 1 & 1 & 1 & 0 & 0 & 0 \end{bmatrix}. \end{cases} \tag{9}$$

5   Experiment and Discussion

We design four experiments A–D on (2, 4)-RiRIVCS: (A) using R_{i+1}-in-R_i^b (B) using R_2-in-R_1^b and R_3-in-R_2^w (the interlaced type) (C) using R_2-in-R_1^w and R_3-in-R_2^b (the interlaced type) (D) using R_{i+1}-in-R_i^b and R_{i+1}-in-R_i^w simultaneously, to demonstrate the effectiveness of our RiRIVCS. The secret images used in these experiments are black-and-white simple geometric shapes. The firs secret shape is a circle ●, the second secret is a square ■, and the third secret is a triangle ▲.

Experiment A. Construct (2, 4)-RiRIVCS using the matrices in Example 2.

Every row in all matrices LK_i^0 and LK_i^1, $1 \leq i \leq 3$, has 8B10W subpixels, and thus all shadows are noise-like. When stacking any two shadows, we have 11B7W in LK_1^0 and 12B6W in LK_1^1 for the 1st secrecy level region, and the contrast is 1/18. When stacking three shadows we have 15B3W in LK_2^1 and 14B4W in LK_2^0, thus the contrast is 1/18 for 2nd secrecy level region. Since $LK_2^0 = LK_1^1$, so the 2nd secret will be revealed in the black area of R_1. At this time, the contrast for 1st secrecy level region is enhanced to 1/9 (12B6W LK_1^1 and 14B4W in LK_1^0). When stacking all four shadows, we have 18B0W in LK_3^1 and 17B1W in LK_3^0, and the contrast of 3rd secrecy level region is 1/18. The contrasts for the 1st and 2nd regions are further improved to 1/6 (15B3W in LK_1^1 and 12B6W in LK_1^0) and 1/9 (17B1W in LK_2^1 and 15B3W in LK_2^0). Reconstructed images are shown in Fig. 4.

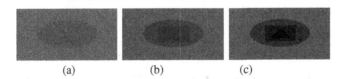

(a)   (b)   (c)

Fig. 4. Reconstructed images of the proposed (2, 4)-RiRIVCS using R_{i+1}-in-R_i^b by stacking: (a) two shadows (b) three shadows (c) four shadows

Experiment B. Construct (2, 4)-RiRIVCS using the matrices in Example 3.

Since Experiment B has the same LK_1^0, LK_1^1, LK_2^0, and LK_2^1 as Experiment A, Figs. 5(a) and (b) are the same as Figs. 4(a) and (b). We intentionally let the size of rectangle in Fig. 5(b) be smaller than Fig. 4(b), because we want to have more space in R_2^w area to demonstrate the 3rd secret ▲. Therefore the contrasts for 1st secrecy level region are 1/18, 1/9, and 1/6 for stacking 2, 3, and 4 shadows, respectively. The contrasts for 2nd secrecy level region are 1/18, 1/9 for stacking 3 and 4 shadows. When stacking all four shadows we have 16B2W in LK_3^1 and 15B3W in LK_3^0, so the contrasts for the 3rd secrecy level region is 1/18. Reconstructed images of the proposed (2, 4)-RiRIVCS interlacing R_2-in-R_1^b and R_3-in-R_2^w are shown in Fig. 5.

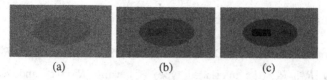

Fig. 5. Reconstructed images of the proposed (2, 4)-RiRIVCS using R_2-in-R_1^b and R_3-in-R_2^w by stacking: (a) two shadows (b) three shadows (c) four shadows

Experiment C. Construct (2, 4)-RiRIVCS using the matrices in Example 4.

Since Experiment C has the same LK_1^0 and LK_1^1 as Experiment A and Experiment B, Fig. 6(a) is the same to Fig. 4(a) and Fig. 5(a). Note: we intentionally let the size of circle in Fig. 6(a) be smaller than Fig. 4(a) and Fig. 5(a), because we want to have more space in R_1^w area to demonstrate the 2nd secret ■. The contrasts for 1st secrecy level region are 1/18, 1/9, and 1/6 for stacking 2, 3, and 4 shadows, respectively. The contrasts for 2nd secrecy level region are 1/18 (13B5W in LK_2^1 and 12B6W in LK_2^0) and 1/9 (14B4W in LK_2^1 and 12B6W in LK_2^0) for stacking 3 and 4 shadows. When stacking all four shadows we have 15B3W in LK_3^1 and 14B4W in LK_3^0, so the contrasts for the 3rd secrecy level region is 1/18. Reconstructed images of the proposed (2, 4)-RiRIVCS using R_{i+1}-in-R_i^b and R_{i+1}-in-R_i^w simultaneously are shown in Fig. 6.

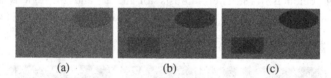

Fig. 6. Reconstructed images of the proposed (2, 4)-RiRIVCS using R_2-in-R_1^w and R_3-in-R_2^b by stacking: (a) two shadows (b) three shadows (c) four shadows

Experiment D. Construct (2, 4)-RiRIVCS using the matrices in Example 5.

Experiment D has the same LK_1^0 and LK_1^1 as Experiments C. The revealed 1st secret is same to other experiments. The contrasts for 1st secrecy level region are still 1/18, 1/9, and 1/6 for stacking 2, 3, and 4 shadows, respectively. For the 2nd secrecy level region, there are two areas demonstrating the 2nd secret ■, one is in $R_{2,1}$ (in the circle) and the other is in $R_{2,2}$ (in the background) (see Fig. 7(b)). The contrasts for 2nd secrecy level region are 1/18 in $R_{2,1}$ (15B3W in $LK_{2,1}^1$ and 14B4W in $LK_{2,1}^0$) and $R_{2,2}$ (13B5W in $LK_{2,2}^1$ and 12B6W in $LK_{2,2}^0$). When stacking four shadows, the contrasts for 2nd secrecy level region are enhanced to 1/9 in $R_{2,1}$ (17B1W in $LK_{2,1}^1$ and 15B3W in $LK_{2,1}^0$) and $R_{2,2}$ (14B4W in $LK_{2,2}^1$ and 12B6W in $LK_{2,2}^0$) for stacking four shadows. Consider stacking four shadows to get the 3rd secrecy level region, we have 1/18 for all four sub regions: $R_{3,1}$ (18B0W in $LK_{3,1}^1$ and 17B1W in

$LK^0_{3,1}$), $R_{3,2}$ (16B2W in $LK^1_{3,2}$ and 15B3W in $LK^0_{3,2}$), , $R_{3,3}$ (15B3W in $LK^1_{3,3}$ and 14B4W in $LK^0_{3,3}$) and $R_{3,4}$ (13B5W in $LK^1_{3,4}$ and 12B6W in $LK^0_{3,4}$). Reconstructed images of the proposed (2, 4)-RiRIVCS using the interlaced R_i-in-R^b_{i+1} and R_i-in-R^w_{i+1} simultaneously are shown in Fig. 7.

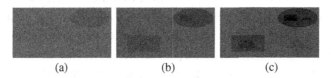

(a)   (b)   (c)

Fig. 7. Reconstructed images of the proposed (2, 4)-RiRIVCS using R_{i+1}-in-R^b_i and R_{i+1}-in-R^w_i simultaneously by stacking: (a) two shadows (b) three shadows (c) four shadows

Our pixel expansion is larger than Yang et al.'s (k, n)-RIVCS and Yang et al.'s modified (k, n)-RIVCS, which both adopt the union of matrices in their construction methods [18]. The union may reduce the pixel expansion, if there are some intersected columns. However, in our construction, LK^0_i needs including $B^{(i+k-1,n)}_0$ (see the proof of Theorem 1). To assure meeting this requirement, we just can use *concatenation* operation in our (k, n)-RiRIVCS rather than *union* operation in Yang et al.'s (k, n)-RIVCS. The pixel expansion, the contrast, and the number of region allocations of our (k, n)-RIVCS, where $2 \le k \le 4$ and $3 \le n \le 5$, are illustrated in Table 1. Note: the contrasts are calculated for using R_{i+1}-in-R^b_i.

Table 1. Contrast and pixel expansion of (k, n)-RiRIVCS using R_{i+1}-in-R^b_i

(k, n)-RiRIVCS		secrecy level	stacking 2 shadows	stacking 3 shadows	stacking 4 shadows	stacking 5 shadows
k =2	n =3 m =7	1st	1/7	2/7	–	–
		2nd	–	1/7	–	–
	n =4 m =18	1st	1/18	1/9	1/6	–
		2nd	–	1/18	1/9	–
		3rd	–	–	1/18	–
	n =5 m =44	1st	1/44	1/44	1/44	1/44
		2nd	–	1/44	1/22	3/44
		3rd	–	–	1/11	3/44
		4th	–	–	–	1/44
k =3	n =4 m =14	1st	–	1/14	1/7	–
		2nd	–	–	1/14	–
	n =5 m =39	1st	–	1/39	2/39	4/39
		2nd	–	–	1/39	1/39
		3rd	–	–	–	2/39
k =4	n =5 m =31	1st	–	–	1/31	3/31
		2nd	–	–	–	1/31

Examples 2–5 show some region allocations of (2, 4)-RiRIVC. There are two sub-regions ($R_{2,1}$ and $R_{2,2}$) for the 2nd level region and four sub-regions ($R_{3,1}$, $R_{3,2}$, $R_{3,3}$ and $R_{3,4}$) for the 3rd level region. Except no choosing, we have three possible choices of allocating sub-regions for the 2nd secrecy level region: (i) $R_{2,1}$-in-R_1^b , (ii) $R_{2,2}$-in-R_1^w , and (iii) $(R_{2,1}$-in-$R_1^b) \| (R_{2,2}$-in-$R_1^w)$. For the same reason, we have 15 possible choices of allocating sub-regions for the 3rd secrecy level region. Thus, the total number of region allocations is 3×15=45. However, there are some duplicated region allocations, when choosing $R_{2,1}$-in-R_1^b (or $R_{2,1}$-in-R_1^w) only. For example, when only choosing $R_{2,1}$-in-R_1^b , we do not choose $R_{2,1}$-in-R_1^w . This implies $R_{2,1}^b = R_{2,1}^w = R_1^w$, so that we have R_3-in-$R_{2,1}^b = R_3$-in-R_1^w , R_3-in-$R_{2,1}^w = R_3$-in-R_1^w , and $(R_3$-in-$R_{2,1}^b) \| (R_3$-in-$R_{2,1}^w)$ = $(R_3$-in-$R_1^w) \| (R_3$-in-$R_1^w)$. Therefore, there are three duplicated region allocations for choosing $R_{2,1}$-in-R_1^b only. This is also true for choosing $R_{2,1}$-in-R_1^w only. Finally, we have 39(=45–6) region allocations for the (2, 4)-RiRIVCS.

6   Conclusion

In this paper, we propose a (k, n)-RiRIVCS, which the next secrecy level region is in the preceding secrecy level region. Our (k, n)-RiRIVCS has more areas to reveal the secrets than the non-overlapping regions in the previous RIVCS. Also, we theoretically prove that our (k, n)-RiRIVCS satisfy security and contrast conditions.

References

1. Naor, M., Shamir, A.: Visual cryptography. In: De Santis, A. (ed.) EUROCRYPT 1994. LNCS, vol. 950, pp. 1–12. Springer, Heidelberg (1995)
2. Ito, R., Kuwakado, H., Tanaka, H.: Image size invariant visual cryptography. IEICE Trans. on Fund. of Elect. Comm. and Comp. Sci. E82-A, 2172–2177 (1999)
3. Yang, C.N.: New visual secret sharing schemes using probabilistic method. Pattern Recognition Letters 25, 481–494 (2004)
4. Cimato, S., De Prisco, R., De Santis, A.: Probabilistic visual cryptography schemes. The Computer Journal 49, 97–107 (2006)
5. Wang, D., Yi, F., Li, X.: Probabilistic visual secret sharing schemes for grey-scale images and color images. Information Sciences 181, 2189–2208 (2011)
6. Shyu, S.J., Huang, S.Y., Lee, Y.K., Wang, R.Z., Chen, K.: Sharing multiple secrets in visual cryptography. Pattern Recognition 40, 3633–3651 (2007)
7. Feng, J.B., Wu, H.C., Tsai, C.S., Chang, Y.F., Chu, Y.P.: Visual Secret sharing for multiple secrets. Pattern Recognition 41, 3572–3581 (2008)
8. Yang, C.N., Chung, T.H.: A general multi-secret visual cryptography scheme. Optics Communications 283, 4949–4962 (2010)
9. Tsai, D.S., Chen, T.H., Horng, G.: A cheating prevention scheme for binary visual cryptography with homogeneous secret images. Pattern Recognition 40, 2356–2366 (2007)

10. Yang, C.N., Peng, A.G., Chen, T.S.: MTVSS (M)isalignment (T)olerant (V)isual (S)ecret (S)haring on resolving alignment difficulty. Signal Processing 89, 1602–1624 (2009)
11. Liu, F., Wu, C.K., Lin, X.J.: The alignment problem of visual cryptography schemes. Designs, Codes and Cryptography 50, 215–227 (2009)
12. Cimato, S., De Santis, A., Ferrara, A.L., Masucci, B.: Ideal contrast visual cryptography schemes withreversing. Information Processing Letters 93, 199–206 (2005)
13. Verheul, E.R., Van Tilborg, H.C.A.: Constructions and properties of k out of n visual secret sharing scheme. Designs, Codes and Cryptography 1, 179–196 (1997)
14. Yang, C.N., Chen, T.S.: Colored visual cryptography scheme based on additive color mixing. Pattern Recognition 41, 3114–3129 (2008)
15. Cimato, S., Yang, C.N.: Visual cryptography and secret image sharing. CRC Press, Taylor & Francis (2011)
16. Wang, R.Z.: Region incrementing visual cryptography. IEEE Signal Processing Letters 16, 659–662 (2009)
17. Shyu, S.J., Jiang, H.W.: Efficient Construction for Region Incrementing Visual Cryptography. IEEE Transactions on Circuits and Systems for Video Technology 22, 769–777 (2012)
18. Yang, C.N., Shih, H.W., Wu, C.C., Harn, L.: k out of n Region Incrementing Scheme in Visual Cryptography. IEEE Transactions on Circuits and Systems for Video Technology 22, 799–810 (2012)

A Secret Enriched Visual Cryptography

Feng Liu[1], Wei Q. Yan[2], Peng Li[3], and Chuankun Wu[1]

[1] State Key Laboratory of Information Security, Institute of Information Engineering
Chinese Academy of Sciences, Beijing 100093, China
[2] School of Computing and Mathematical Sciences,
Auckland University of Technology, 1142, New Zealand
[3] Department of Mathematics and Physics,
North China Electric Power University, Baoding, Hebei, 071003 China

Abstract. Visual Cryptography (VC) is a powerful technique that combines the notions of perfect ciphers and secret sharing in cryptography with that of raster graphics. A binary image can be divided into shares that are able to be stacked together so as to approximately recover the original image. VC is a unique technique in the sense that the encrypted message can be decrypted directly by the Human Visual System (HVS). The distinguishing characteristic of VC is the ability of secret restoration without the use of computation. However because of restrictions of the HVS, pixel expansion and alignment problems, a VC scheme perhaps can only be applied to share a small size of secret image. In this paper, we propose a general method to let the VC shares carry more secrets, the technique is to use cypher output of private-key systems as the input random numbers of VC scheme, meanwhile the encryption key could be shared, the shared keys could be associated with the VC shares. After this operation, VC scheme and secret sharing scheme are merged with the private-key system. Under this design, we implement a (k, t, n)-VC scheme. Compared to those existing schemes, our approach could greatly enhance the ability of current VC schemes and could cope with pretty rich secrets.

Keywords: Secret Sharing, Visual Cryptography, Covert Data, Subchannel.

1 Introduction

Visual Cryptography Scheme (VCS) was firstly introduced by Naor and Shamir [1], which shares a secret image into $n \in Z$ pieces (printed on transparencies). The merit of VCS is that the decoding process is computation-free. The original image is able to be recovered by stacking any $k \leq n$ shares transparently. The underlying operation of the stacking is the logic *OR*. Lots of research focused on the novel applications of VCS [2–5]. Recently, some books covered an extensive range of topics related to VCS [6][7].

In traditional VCS, the amount of secret is severely constrained: pixel expansion of the shares implies that the size of secret image cannot be too big,

Y.Q. Shi, H.J. Kim, and F. Pérez-González (Eds.): IWDM 2012, LNCS 7809, pp. 464–484, 2013.

because a big transparency is inconvenient for the shares alignment; human eyes can only identify patterns of secret image when the contrast is good enough, i.e. the lines and dots in the patterns should be a block of pixels rather than a single pixel; Because of the alignment problem [8, 9], pixels within the shares cannot be too small. Many studies tried to increase the secret volume of VC shares, such as sharing a plural number of secret images in one VCS [10, 11], using rotated shares [12] or using color VC scheme [13–15]. However, these methods could not increase the capability too much if the ratio $R = \frac{t}{m}$ is taken into consideration, where t is the number of secret bits that are shared by every m sub-pixels. For the color VC scheme, it usually degrades quality of the revealed secret image severely. In this paper, we measure the capability of VC scheme by using the secret bits that will be shared.

The main contribution of this paper is that, the random inputs of VC scheme could be applied to carry covert data, the ciphertext of those private-key system based encryption algorithms could be considered as random inputs of a VC scheme, hence it increases the amount of secret shared by VCS. By using Shamir's secret sharing scheme [16], the encryption key is able to be shared into n sub-keys that could be associated with the corresponding shares. We call this scheme as the Enriched Secret Sharing VC Scheme (ESSVCS), or 3-in-1 VCS. The scheme articulately combined the two secret sharing schemes and private-key encryption scheme together. The secret shared by the ESSVCS includes two parts: Secret and Covert Data. Figure 1 and Figure 2 illustrate the encryption and decryption procedures.

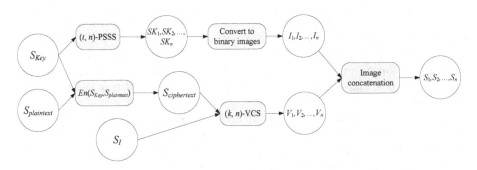

Fig. 1. The encryption process of the (k, t, n)-ESSVCS

In order to share the covert data, we need employ computational devices. By utilizing a (k, t, n)-ESSVCS ($k \leq t$), the VC scheme that carries additional covert data where any k out of n participants can visually recover the secret by stacking the shares, any t out of n participants can restore the additional covert data by computation. There are two computer aided VCS's schemes [17, 18], one is called 2-in-1 Image Secret Sharing Scheme (TiOISSS) [17, 18], which is able to reveal a secret image by stacking the shares and restore a much finer gray image by computation. The comparisons between our ESSVCS and the TiOISSS will

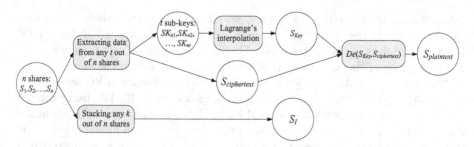

Fig. 2. The decryption process of the (k, t, n)-ESSVCS

be given in Section 4. Yang et al. [5, 19] also tried to make use of the pseudo-random inputs to carry confidential data. Unfortunately, the scheme is only for (2,2) access structure.

The proposed (k, t, n)-ESSVCS in this paper is a multi-threshold secret sharing scheme. k out of n members can share one secret, whereas a majority of participants $t \leqslant n$ can access the additional secret. By comparing our ESSVCS and any 2D encoding methods, we find that decoding a secret totally relies on a computing device by using any 2D encoding methods. If participants are in the scenario where there is no such computing devices, they cannot extract any information. But with our ESSVCS scheme, the participants could stack the shares and get part of the secret. Hence, our proposed ESSVCS scheme will have much wider application.

In this paper, we propose a specific construction of general (k, t, n)-ESSVCS by taking the VCS proposed in [11] and secret sharing scheme [16] into consideration. We investigate some relevant issues of ESSVCS scheme such as pseudo-random numbers as the input of VCS scheme, sufficient conditions to uniquely determine a share, and secret capacity of the proposed ESSVCS scheme; we also proposed an efficient decoding algorithm, comparisons to other schemes will be presented at last.

This paper is organized as follows. In section 2, we will give some preliminary results. In section 3, we will propose a general construction of the ESSVCS based on the construction of VC scheme in [11] and point out some relevant issues of ESSVCS. In section 4, we will compare the proposed scheme with the TiOISSS scheme. Finally, we will draw our conclusion in section 5.

2   Preliminaries

In this section, we will present some definitions about VC scheme, introduce the Droste's construction of (k, n)-VC Scheme [11] and Shamir's secret sharing scheme, namely Polynomial-based Secret Sharing Scheme (PSSS) [16], they are the start point of our proposed scheme.

2.1   VCS

We restrict ourselves to the images only consisting of black and white pixels, where we denote by '1' for a black pixel and '0' for a white pixel. In this paper, we only take the threshold (k, n)-VCS into consideration. For a vector $v \in GF^m(2)$, we denote by $w(v)$ as Hamming weight of the vector v. A (k, n)-VCS, denoted by (C_0, C_1), consists of two sets (pairwise different collection) of $n \times m$ Boolean matrices C_0 and C_1. To encrypt a white (*resp.* black) pixel, a dealer (the one who sets up the system) randomly chooses one of the share matrices (in the practical sense, the dealer can only choose the share matrices pseudo-randomly) from C_0 (*resp.* C_1) and distributes its rows (shares) to the n participants. More precisely, we present a formal definition of the (k, n) - VC scheme as follows:

Definition 1. *Let k, n, m, l and h be non-negative integers satisfying $2 \leq k \leq n$ and $0 \leq l < h \leq m$. The two sets of $n \times m$ Boolean matrices (C_0, C_1) constitute a (k, n)-VCS if the following properties are satisfied:*

1. *(**Contrast**) For any $s \in C_0$, the OR of any k out of the n rows of s, is a vector v that, satisfies $w(v) \leq l$.*
2. *(**Contrast**) For any $s \in C_1$, the OR of any k out of the n rows of s, is a vector v that, satisfies $w(v) \geq h$.*
3. *(**Security**) For any $i_1 < i_2 < \cdots < i_t$ in $\{1, 2, \cdots, n\}$ with $t < k$, the two collections of $t \times m$ matrices F_j for $j \in \{0, 1\}$, obtained by restricting each $n \times m$ matrix in C_j to rows $i_1, i_2, \cdots i_t$, are indistinguishable in the sense that they contain the same matrices with the same frequencies.*

In the above definition, m is called pixel expansion of the shares. A pixel of the original secret image is represented by m sub-pixels in the recovered secret image. In general, we are interested in schemes with m being as small as possible.

In Definition 1, the first two properties ensure that any k participants will be able to distinguish the black and white pixels, and the third property ensures security of the scheme that any $k-1$ or fewer participants can gain no information about content of the secret.

In order to share a complete image, the scheme has to be applied to all the pixels in the image. In the traditional VCS, sharing is applied to the secret pixels one at each time. However, we extend this method to share q secret pixels at each time, and call this scheme as the *q-pixel encryption model*. The traditional model is the *1-pixel encryption model*. The difference between the *1-pixel encryption model* and the *q-pixel encryption model* is that: in the *1-pixel encryption model*, the dealer generates one pseudo-random number which guides the choice of a share matrix at each time. However, in the *q-pixel encryption model*, the dealer generates one pseudo-random number which guides the choice of q share matrices at each time.

Now let's take VCS into consideration, the C_0 and C_1 are constructed from a pair of $n \times m$ matrices M_0 and M_1, which are called *basis matrices*. The set C_i ($i = 0, 1$) consists of the matrices obtained by permuting all the columns of M_i. This approach of VCS construction will have small memory requirements (it only keeps the basis matrices) and high efficiency (to choose a matrix in C_0 (*resp.* C_1) as it only needs to generate a permutation of the basis matrix). When the set of a VCS C_0 (*resp.* C_1) can be generated by the basis matrix, we call such VCS as the *basis matrix VCS*. Many studies in the literatures proposed to construct the *basis matrix VCS*, such as [11, 20, 21].

Recall that, by definition, the share matrices in C_0 (*resp.* C_1) are pairwise differently. Denote the different columns in the basis matrix M_i as $c_1, c_2, \cdots, c_e$ and the multiplicities of these columns are $a_1, a_2, \cdots, a_e$, we have that the number of share matrices in C_i is $|C_i| = \frac{(\sum_{i=1}^{e} a_i)!}{\prod_{i=1}^{e} a_i!}$, for $i \in \{0, 1\}$ (these share matrices are pairwise different). In order to choose a share matrix in C_i pseudo-randomly, length of the pseudo-random input for one secret pixel should be at least $\log_2 |C_i|$ bits.

2.2　Droste's Construction of (k, n)-VCS

In this paper, we take the construction of Droste [11] as our building block, and we recall his construction as follows:

Construction of (k, n)-VCS proposed in [11]:

Setup Let M_0 and M_1 be two empty matrices, where the basis matrices M_0 and M_1 are considered as the collections of their columns;

step 1 For all even $p \in \{0, 1, \ldots, k\}$, call **ADD**($p, M_0$);

step 2 For all odd $p \in \{0, 1, \ldots, k\}$, call **ADD**($p, M_1$);

step 3 Define P_0 (resp. P_1) be the collection consisting of all columns of every restriction of k rows of M_0 (resp. M_1), and define S_0 (resp. S_1) be the set consisting of all k-length boolean columns with an even (resp. odd) number of 1's. Define the remaining of M_0 (resp. M_1) be $P_0 \backslash S_0$ (resp. $P_1 \backslash S_1$), and define the *rest* of M_0 (resp. M_1) be the columns in the remaining of M_0 (resp. M_1), but not in the remaining of M_1 (resp. M_0), i.e. the *rest* of M_0 is $\{P_0 \backslash S_0\} \backslash \{P_1 \backslash S_1\}$ and the *rest* of M_1 is $\{P_1 \backslash S_1\} \backslash \{P_0 \backslash S_0\}$. If the *rests* are not empty:

(a) If p is an even number, add to M_0 all columns adjusting the *rest* of M_1 by calling **ADD**(p, M_0), where p is the number of 1's in column $l \in \{P_1 \backslash S_1\} \backslash \{P_0 \backslash S_0\}$.

(b) If p is an odd number, add to M_1 all columns adjusting the *rest* of M_0 by calling **ADD**(p, M_1), where p is the number of 1's in column $l \in \{P_0 \backslash S_0\} \backslash \{P_1 \backslash S_1\}$.

where the subroutine ADD is: **ADD**(p, M)

1 If $p \leq k - p$, add every column with $q = p$ (1's to M).

2 If $p > k - p$, add every column with $q = p + n - k$ (1's to M).

2.3　PSSS

Shamir[16] introduced the (t, n)-PSSS ($t \leq n$) to share the secret data into n shares. Any t shares can be used to reconstruct the secret, but any $t - 1$ or less shares get no information about the secret. To share the secret, it randomly generates a $(t-1)$-degree polynomial using modular arithmetic:

$$f(x) = (a_0 + a_1 x + \ldots + a_{t-1} x^{t-1}) \mod p \tag{1}$$

where a_0 is replaced by the secret data, p is a prime number greater than a_0 and n. The coefficients $a_1, a_2, \ldots, a_{t-1}$ are randomly chosen from a uniform distribution over the integers in $[1, p)$. Then we could generate n shares $(x_i, f(x_i)), i = 1, 2, \ldots, n$. Later, with any t out of the n shares, we can evaluate all the coefficients, particularly coefficient a_0 of the polynomial $f(x)$ by Lagrange's interpolation. However, any $t-1$ or fewer shares cannot get any information about the secret.

3   ESSVCS

In this section, we first propose a construction of the ESSVCS scheme by taking the pseudo-random inputs as a sub-channel, and then study some relevant issues of the ESSVCS: 1) The pseudo-randomness that the input of VCS requires; 2) The sufficient conditions to uniquely determine a share matrix in the set C_i for $i = 0, 1$; 3) The bandwidth of the sub-channel; 4) The method to decode the ciphertext of ESSVCS scheme.

3.1   Construction of ESSVCS

The main idea of this proposed scheme is to treat the private-key encryption algorithm as the pseudo-random generator of VCS. Thus the VCS can naturally carry the additional covert data encrypted by the private-key algorithm. In this paper, we take the VCS proposed in [11] as the building block. In practical, the encryption algorithm can be the AES or Twofish, etc. The cipher block chaining (CBC) [22] encryption mode is employed. The encryption key S_{Key} in ESSVCS is shared by (t, n)-PSSS into n sub-keys $SK_1, SK_2, \ldots, SK_n$. Therefore, any t or more sub-keys could be used to reveal the secret key, while any $t-1$ or less sub-keys together could restore the secret key.

   Before showing the construction, we need present the assumption that participants know the access structure they belong to, i.e. the i-th participant knows by himself/herself that (s)he is the i-th participant. Usually, the access structure of a VCS is not one part of secret, therefore this assumption is reasonable.

Construction 1
Encryption process:
Input: *The secret image S_I, covert data $S_{Plaintext}$ and the secret key S_{Key}.*
Output: *n shares.*
Step 1: *Encrypt the covert data $S_{Plaintext}$ by using the key S_{Key}, $S_{Ciphertext} = En(S_{Key}, S_{Plaintext})$;*
Step 2: *Share the secret image S_I into n shares $V_1, V_2, \ldots, V_n$ by using the (k, n)-VCS, where the encrypted data from the Step 1 is employed as the pseudo-random input of the (k, n)-VCS;*

Step 3: *Share S_{Key} into n sub-keys $SK_1, SK_2, \ldots, SK_n$ by using (t, n)-PSSS, then convert these sub-keys into binary images $I_1, I_2, \ldots, I_n$, and concatenate I_i $(i = 1, 2, \ldots, n)$ with share V_i to get the final share S_i.*

Decryption process:

Input: *Any t shares where $k \le t$.*

Output: *The secret image S_I and the covert data $S_{Plaintext}$.*

Step 1: *Stack any k shares to get the recovered secret image S_I;*

Step 2: *Determine the share matrices which are used to encrypt the secret image for each pixel by t shares, and hence get the ciphertext $S_{Ciphertext}$;*

Step 3: *Extract t sub-keys from t shares, then reconstruct the secret key S_{Key} by Lagrange's interpolation.*

Step 4: *Decrypt the ciphertext.*

    $S_{Ciphertext}$ by using the S_{Key}, $S_{Plaintext} = De(S_{Key}, S_{Ciphertext})$.

Remarks:

In practical, key length of the AES or Twofish scheme, usually, is 128 bits. Therefore, each sub-key is generated and converted into a 128 bits binary image which only takes a small area in the share.

For the (k, t, n)-ESSVCS, by stacking k shares we can reconstruct the secret image S_I. If one obtains t rows, (s)he can uniquely determine a share matrix and hence obtain the ciphertext, where "can uniquely determine a share matrix" means that there only exists one share matrix in C_i $(i = 0, 1)$ that contains these t rows (and "cannot uniquely determine" means there exist more than one share matrices that contain these t rows, hence we cannot determine which one is chosen by the dealer when encrypting the secret pixel). In another word, in order to get the ciphertext one needs t shares.

Security of the (k, t, n)-ESSVCS is based on the security of the encryption algorithm and that of VCS and PSSS scheme. Particularly, if an hacker wants to know the secret image, (s)he needs at least k shares; if (s)he wants to know the covert data encrypted by the encryption algorithm, (s)he needs at least t shares to extract the ciphertext and the secret key.

The VCS requires pseudo-random number inputs to guide the choice of VC share matrices. Denote the share matrices in C_i as $S_0^i, \cdots, S_{|C_i|-1}^i$ and $P(S_j^i)$ for $i = 0, 1$ and $j = 0, 1, \cdots, |C_i| - 1$ as the probability choosing the share matrix S_j^i. Hence inputs of the pseudo-random numbers should guarantee that

$$P(S_0^i) = P(S_1^i) = \cdots = P(S_{|C_i|-1}^i) \tag{2}$$

In order to choose a share matrix pseudo-randomly in C_i, the dealer needs at least $\log_2 |C_i|$ bits pseudo-random numbers (we will take the case that $\log_2 |C_i|$ is not an integer into consideration). Denote $B(j)$ as the binary representation of integer j with length $\log_2 |C_i|$, i.e. $B(j)$ is the binary string that represents j. Without loss of generality, we assume that when the pseudo-random number input is $B(j)$, the dealer chooses the share matrix S_j^i to encrypt the secret pixel i. Denote $P(B(j))$ as the probability of generating the binary string $B(j)$. According to the equation (2), we have:

$$P(B(0)) = P(B(1)) = \cdots = P(B(|C_i| - 1)) \tag{3}$$

In fact, ciphertext of AES or Twofish satisfies the equation (3), because they have passed the serial test [23]. Therefore, we can take AES or Twofish as the pseudo-random generator. This also is the ground truth why we do not use the covert data directly to guide the generation of shares.

To make things simple and clear, we give the following example for $(2, 2, 2)$-ESSVCS:

Example 1. The sets of share matrices of $(2, 2, 2)$-ESSVCS are as follows:

$$C_0 = \left\{ \begin{bmatrix} 10 \\ 10 \end{bmatrix}, \begin{bmatrix} 01 \\ 01 \end{bmatrix} \right\} \text{ and } C_1 = \left\{ \begin{bmatrix} 10 \\ 01 \end{bmatrix}, \begin{bmatrix} 01 \\ 10 \end{bmatrix} \right\}$$

The principle of choosing share matrix is that: if the pseudo-random input is 0, we choose the first share matrix in C_0 or C_1; if the pseudo-random input is 1, we choose the second option. Figure 3 presents an illustration for the procedure of the $(2, 2, 2)$-ESSVCS.

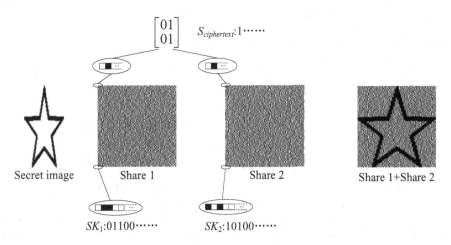

Fig. 3. The procedure of the $(2, 2, 2)$-ESSVCS

A secret image having 64×128 pixels is encoded into Share 1 and Share 2. Size of the shares and the recovered secret image is 129×128. Since the length of each sub-key is 128 bits, it only takes one line at the bottom of each share to attach the sub-key. Length of the ciphertext $S_{Ciphertext}$ encrypted in the shares is 2^{13} bits, i.e. the sub-channel can be used to carry extra 2^{13} bits of covert data. In the first step of the reconstruction, the secret image can be visually decoded by stacking two shares. In the second step, two sub-keys are extracted from the last row of two shares, and then we reveal the secret key S_{Key} by Lagrange's interpolation. With further observation, the ciphertext can be obtained by the uniquely determined share matric by share blocks. For example, the first block of share 1 is constituted by two sub-pixels '0' and '1', and the first block of share 2 is also constituted by two sub-pixels '0' and '1'. Therefore, we can determine the share matrix, which is the second share matrix C_0 and the recovered ciphertext is '1'. Finally, we get the covert data $S_{Plaintext}$ by decrypting the ciphertext $S_{Ciphertext}$. $\qquad\square$

3.2 Uniquely Determine a Share Matrix

For the (n, n)-VCS, if one has all the n shares, (s)he can uniquely determine the share matrices used when sharing the secret image S_I and hence to know the ciphertext.

We then focus our discussion on the (k, n)-VCS with $k < n$: we find that, for the VCS in section 2, $n - 1$ rows can uniquely determine a share matrix in the set C_0 (resp. C_1). The following theorem shows this result:

Theorem 1. *Denote M_0 and M_1 be the basis matrices constructed by (k, n)-VCS in [11], and denote C_0 and C_1 be the sets of share matrices generated from M_0 and M_1, respectively. If every t rows of a share matrix in C_i $(i = 0, 1)$ can uniquely determine a share matrix in C_i, then $t \geq n - 1$.*

Proof: *First*, for the case of $t = n$, it obviously can uniquely determine an n-row matrix from its all n rows.

Second, we show any $n - 1$ rows can uniquely determine a share matrix. According to the construction in [11], number of the 1's of each column in the basis matrix M_0 is from the set $T_0 = \{a | 0 \leq a \leq \lfloor \frac{k}{2} \rfloor, a \mod 2 = 0\} \bigcup \{a + n - k | \lfloor \frac{k}{2} \rfloor < a \leq k, a \mod 2 = 0\}$, and number of 1's of each column in the basis matrix M_1 is from the set $T_1 = \{a | 0 \leq a \leq \lfloor \frac{k}{2} \rfloor, a \mod 2 = 1\} \bigcup \{a + n - k | \lfloor \frac{k}{2} \rfloor < a \leq k, a \mod 2 = 1\}$. Hereafter, $\lfloor x \rfloor$ is the largest integer that is no greater than x and $\lceil x \rceil$ is the smallest integer no less than x.

Because $k < n$, when one has $n - 1$ rows of a share matrix M, he can stack k shares and hence knows the secret pixel. Without loss of generality, suppose the secret pixel is black. We determine last row of the share matrix M as follows: for the column p_i of M, where $i \in \{1, \cdots m\}$, denote number of 1's of the $n - 1$ rows in column p_i as h, then we have the entry of the last rows of column p_i be 0 if $h \in T_1$ and be 1 if $h + 1 \in T_1$. Hence, the last row can be uniquely determined by the $n - 1$ rows, because the participants know the access structure they belong to, the share matrix will be uniquely determined.

Third, we prove any $n - 2$ rows cannot uniquely determine a share matrix. Consider the construction in [11], we have that the basis matrix M_1 contains all the columns with Hamming weight are equal to 1. Let A be a share matrix in C_1. Without loss of generality, there exist two different columns c_1 and c_2 in A, whose Hamming weights are equaled to 1. Denote the position of 1 in column c_1 (resp. c_2) be p_1 (resp. p_2), we have $p_1 \neq p_2$. Let $X = \{1, 2, \ldots, n\} \backslash \{p_1, p_2\}$, then, by restricting all the rows of columns c_1 and c_2 in X, we get two same sub-columns. Suppose B is a matrix generated by exchanging positions of columns c_1 and c_2 in A, then B is also a share matrix in C_1. Therefore, by restricting all the rows of A and B in X, we are able to get two same sub-matrices. Namely, the $n - 2$ rows of share matrix A (the rows restricted in X) cannot uniquely determine a share matrix. Obviously, it also cannot uniquely determine a share matrix from less than $n - 2$ rows. □

Theorem 1 presents an explicit method to uniquely determine a share matrix in C_i $(i = 0, 1)$, and in light of the above discussion, we have the following theorem:

Theorem 2. *Let* $t = n - 1$, *then Construction 1 generates a* $(k, n - 1, n)$-*ESSVCS.* □

For general basis matrix visual cryptography (C_0, C_1), denote C_i^{All} as a set of all the possible columns that appear in the share matrices of C_i $(i = 0, 1)$. For any set of participants $X \subseteq P$, denote M' as a sub-matrix which is generated by restricting to the rows in X of a share matrix in C_i. First, we have the following lemma:

Lemma 1. *For every column* c' *of* M', *if there exists only one column* $c \in C_i^{All}$ *such that* $c[X] = c'$, *then the sub-matrix* M' *can uniquely determine a share matrix in* C_i, *where* $c[X]$ *is the sub-column generated by restricting to the rows in* X *of* c.

Proof: (Reduction to absurdity) Suppose M' cannot uniquely determine a share matrix in C_i, i.e. there exist two different share matrices, denoted by M_a and M_b, such that $M_a[X] = M_b[X] = M'$, where $M_a[X]$ is the sub-matrix generated by restricting to the rows in X of M_a. Since M_a and M_b are different share matrices, there exists at least one column that is different for M_a and M_b. Denote this column in M_a is c_a and that in M_b is c_b, i.e. $c_a \neq c_b$. Because of $M_a[X] = M_b[X]$, we have $c_a[X] = c_b[X]$, which is contradict to the assumption that there exists only one column $c \in C_i^{All}$ such that $c[X] = c'$. Hence, M' can uniquely determine a share matrix in C_i. □

According to Lemma 1, we present a general discussion for basis matrix (k, n)-VCS, denote $c_p, c_q \in C_i^{All}$ as two different columns, and denote $X_{pq}^i (\subset P)$ as the set of the participants such that for each $x \in X_{pq}^i$ satisfying $c_p[x] = c_q[x]$, where $c_p[x]$ is the x-th entry of c_p. Then we have the following theorem:

Lemma 2. *Let* $t = max\{|X_{pq}^i| + 1\}$ *for* $p \neq q$, $1 \leq p, q \leq m$ *and* $i = 0, 1$, *then a sub-matrix of* t *rows of a share matrix in* C_i *can uniquely determine a share matrix in* C_i.

Proof: Let c' be a column of the sub-matrix M' which is generated by restricting t rows of a share matrix in C_i ($i = 0, 1$). Denote a set of the participants of these t rows as X, i.e. $|X| = t$, where $t = max\{|X_{pq}| + 1\}$. We prove that there only exists one column c of M such that $c[X] = c'$.

(Reduction to absurdity): Suppose there exist two columns c_a and c_b such that $c_a[X] = c_b[X] = c'$. We have that c_a and c_b have t entries with the same values, i.e. $t = |X_{ab}|$, which is impossible because $t = max\{|X_{pq}| + 1\}$ which implies $t > |X_{ab}|$.

According to Lemma 1, we have that a sub-matrix M' with t rows can uniquely determine a share matrix in C_i.   □

According to Lemma 2, and let's recall that we have assumed $t \geq k$. (another reason that we assume $t \geq k$ is that, if $t < k$, then t participants cannot decide the sub-matrix of their t shares is from C_0 or C_1, and hence it may not get the ciphertext either) we hence get the following theorem immediately:

For a (k, n)-VCS, any $k - 1$ or less shares cannot get any information of the secret image. In another word, any $t(t < k)$ shares cannot decide the t-row sub-matrix is from C_0 or C_1, and hence we can not uniquely determine the share matrix. Therefore, it is reasonable to assume $t \geq k$. Further with Lemma 2, we get the following theorem:

Theorem 3. *For a basis matrix (k, n)-VCS, there exists a (k, t, n)-ESSVCS where $t = max\{k, |X_{pq}^i| + 1\}$, $p \neq q$, $1 \leq p, q \leq m$ and $i = 0, 1$.*   □

According to Theorem 3, we also examined other two known constructions of (k, n)-VCS in [21, 24], and found that the two constructions both have $t = n - 1$ too (the same as the results in Theorem 1). Because they both take the canonical matrices as building block, where the canonical matrices mean the matrices that all the columns of a given weight occur with the same frequency. And for the canonical matrices that have a column c_i with x 1's and $n - x$ 0's where $0 < x < n$, there exists a column c_j such that only two entries are different from c_i, which implies $|X_{ij}| = n - 2$, and hence $t = n - 1$.

3.3   Bandwidth of ESSVCS Scheme

We define bandwidth of the ESSVCS as the maximum amount of covert data it carries through its sub-channel. Denote columns in the basis matrix M_i as $c_1, \cdots, c_e$ and multiplicities of these columns are $a_1, \cdots, a_e$, let's recall that we have the number of share matrix in C_i being $|C_i| = \frac{(\sum_{i=1}^{e} a_i)!}{\prod_{i=1}^{e} a_i!}$ for $i \in \{0, 1\}$. To choose a share matrix in C_i, one needs at least $\log_2 |C_i|$ pseudo-random bits theoretically. By determining the share matrix which is chosen when encrypting the secret image in C_i, one can determine at most $\log_2 |C_i|$ bits information theoretically. Hence, the amount of the additional covert data that can be carried by the secret pixel i is at most $\log_2 |C_i|$ bits theoretically. We list the number of the share matrices $|C_i|$ of the VCS constructed [11] in the Table 1 and Table 2 as follows:

Table 1. The number of share matrices in C_0

k \ n	2	3	4	5	6	7	8	9	10
2	2	3	4	5	6	7	8	9	10
3		$4!$	$\frac{6!}{2!}$	$\frac{8!}{3!}$	$\frac{10!}{4!}$	$\frac{12!}{5!}$	$\frac{14!}{6!}$	$\frac{16!}{7!}$	$\frac{18!}{8!}$
4			$8!$	$\frac{15!}{3!2!}$	$\frac{24!}{6!3!}$	$\frac{35!}{10!4!}$	$\frac{48!}{15!5!}$	$\frac{63!}{21!6!}$	$\frac{80!}{28!7!}$
5				$16!$	$\frac{30!}{3!(2!)^6}$	$\frac{48!}{6!(3!)^7}$	$\frac{70!}{10!(4!)^8}$	$\frac{96!}{15!(5!)^9}$	$\frac{126!}{21!(6!)^{10}}$
6					$32!$	$\frac{70!}{4!(2!)^{21}3!}$	$\frac{128!}{10!(3!)^{28}6!}$	$\frac{210!}{20!(4!)^{36}10!}$	$\frac{320!}{35!(5!)^{45}15!}$
7						$64!$	$\frac{140!}{4!(2!)^{28}(3!)^8}$	$\frac{256!}{10!(3!)^{36}(6!)^9}$	$\frac{420!}{20!(4!)^{45}(10!)^{10}}$
8							$128!$	$\frac{315!}{5!(3!)^{36}(2!)^{36}4!}$	$\frac{640!}{15!(6!)^{45}(3!)^{45}10!}$
9								$256!$	$\frac{630!}{5!(3!)^{45}(2!)^{120}(4!)^{10}}$
10									$512!$

Actually, in practical, a pseudo-random number generator can only generate integer number of pseudo-random bits, and ciphertexts are also represented by integer number of bits. However, the values of $\log_2|C_i|$ are rarely integers, which means that some share matrices cannot be chosen by integer number of the pseudo-random bits, and it is hard to determine all the $\log_2|C_i|$ ciphertext bits, hence results in wasting of the pseudo-random resources. So from the practical viewpoint, the amount of the covert data carried by the ESSVCS is impossible to reach the theoretical value.

In fact, if the secret pixels are encrypted only one at each time, in order to choose a share matrix pseudo-randomly in C_i, one needs at least $\lceil \log_2|C_i| \rceil$ pseudo-random bits, and its length of the ciphertext can be at most $\lfloor \log_2|C_i| \rfloor$ bits. To fully make use of the pseudo-random resources, we propose to encrypt q secret pixels at a time, i.e. the q-*pixel encryption model*. Let $q = a_0 + a_1$, where denote a_0 as the number of white pixels and a_1 as the number of black pixels, the effectiveness of using q-*pixel encryption model* rather than 1-*pixel encryption model* is as follows:

First: the number of pseudo-random bits required to choose the share matrices when the q-*pixel encryption model* is $\lceil a_0 \log_2|C_0| + a_1 \log_2|C_1| \rceil$, and it satisfies:

$$\lceil a_0 \log_2|C_0| + a_1 \log_2|C_1| \rceil \leq a_0 \lceil \log_2|C_0| \rceil + a_1 \lceil \log_2|C_1| \rceil \tag{4}$$

which implies less pseudo-random bits are required by using the q-*pixel encryption model* than the 1-*pixel encryption model*.

Second: the number of pseudo-random bits determined by the share matrices when encrypting q secret pixels at each time is $\lfloor a_0 \log_2|C_0| + a_1 \log_2|C_1| \rfloor$, and it satisfies:

$$\lfloor a_0 \log_2|C_0| + a_1 \log_2|C_1| \rfloor \geq a_0 \lfloor \log_2|C_0| \rfloor + a_1 \lfloor \log_2|C_1| \rfloor \tag{5}$$

which implies more pseudo-random bits can be determined by using the q-*pixel encryption model* than the 1-*pixel encryption model*.

Table 2. The number of share matrices in C_1

k \ n	2	3	4	5	6	7	8	9	10
2	2!	3!	4!	5!	6!	7!	8!	9!	10!
3		4!	$\frac{6!}{2!}$	$\frac{8!}{3!}$	$\frac{10!}{4!}$	$\frac{12!}{5!}$	$\frac{14!}{6!}$	$\frac{16!}{7!}$	$\frac{18!}{8!}$
4			8!	$\frac{15!}{(2!)^5}$	$\frac{24!}{(3!)^6}$	$\frac{35!}{(4!)^7}$	$\frac{48!}{(5!)^8}$	$\frac{63!}{(6!)^9}$	$\frac{80!}{(7!)^{10}}$
5				16!	$\frac{30!}{3!(2!)^6}$	$\frac{48!}{6!(3!)^7}$	$\frac{70!}{10!(4!)^8}$	$\frac{96!}{15!(5!)^9}$	$\frac{126!}{21!(6!)^{10}}$
6					32!	$\frac{70!}{(3!)^7(2!)^7}$	$\frac{128!}{(6!)^8(3!)^8}$	$\frac{210!}{(10!)^9(4!)^9}$	$\frac{320!}{(15!)^{10}(5!)^{10}}$
7						64!	$\frac{140!}{4!(2!)^{28}(3!)^8}$	$\frac{256!}{10!(3!)^{36}(6!)^9}$	$\frac{420!}{20!(4!)^{45}(10!)^{10}}$
8							128!	$\frac{315!}{(4!)^9(2!)^{84}(3!)^9}$	$\frac{640!}{(10!)^{10}(3!)^{120}(6!)^{10}}$
9								256!	$\frac{630!}{5!(3!)^{45}(2!)^{120}(4!)^{10}}$
10									512!

A problem for the *q-pixel encryption model* is that, when encrypting more secret pixels at a time, the encryption scheme becomes more complex. So there exists a trade-off for the value of q.

To make things clear, we present the following example for a (2, 2, 3)-ESSVCS:

Example 2. For the sets

$$C_0 = \left\{ \begin{bmatrix} 100 \\ 100 \\ 100 \end{bmatrix}, \begin{bmatrix} 010 \\ 010 \\ 010 \end{bmatrix}, \begin{bmatrix} 001 \\ 001 \\ 001 \end{bmatrix} \right\} \tag{6}$$

$$C_1 = \left\{ \begin{bmatrix} 100 \\ 010 \\ 001 \end{bmatrix}, \begin{bmatrix} 100 \\ 001 \\ 010 \end{bmatrix}, \begin{bmatrix} 010 \\ 100 \\ 001 \end{bmatrix}, \begin{bmatrix} 010 \\ 001 \\ 100 \end{bmatrix}, \begin{bmatrix} 001 \\ 100 \\ 010 \end{bmatrix}, \begin{bmatrix} 001 \\ 010 \\ 100 \end{bmatrix} \right\} \tag{7}$$

We have that, from theoretic point of view, the amount of information bits that can be carried by a white secret pixel is $\log_2 |C_0| = \log_2 3$ and by a black secret pixel is $\log_2 |C_1| = \log_2 6$. And for 10 secret pixels with 5 white secret pixels and 5 black secret pixels the value will be $5 \log_2 3 + 5 \log_2 6 \approx 20.85$.

However, in practical, the 10-*pixel encryption model*, where take $a_0 = 5$ and $a_1 = 5$ as example, we have the amount of information that can be carried is $\lfloor \log_2 3^5 + \log_2 6^5 \rfloor = 20$, which is more than 1-*pixel encryption model*, where the corresponding value is $5 \lfloor \log_2 3 \rfloor + 5 \lfloor \log_2 6 \rfloor = 15$.   □

At this point, we can calculate the bandwidth of the ESSVCS as follows:

Theorem 4. *For a secret image S_I which consists of n_w white pixels and n_b black pixels, the bandwidth W of the ESSVCS is $W = \lfloor n_w \log_2 |C_0| + n_b \log_2 |C_1| \rfloor$, and it is achieved when using the q_a-pixel encryption model where $q_a = n_w + n_b$.*

Proof: For the q_a-*pixel encryption model* where $q_a = n_w + n_b$, which implies encrypt all the secret pixels in the secret image at each time. And it is clear that the amount of covert data carried by such ESSVCS is $W = \lfloor n_w \log_2 |C_0| + n_b \log_2 |C_1| \rfloor$. We only need to prove that W reaches its maximum when using the q_a-*pixel encryption model*, i.e. if one divides all the pixels in the secret image into several parts, and encrypts these parts respectively, the amount of covert data carried is less than the q_a-*pixel encryption model*.

Without loss of generality, let $q_a = q_1 + q_2$ (i.e. divide into two parts) and suppose encryption of the secret image S_I is realized by using q_1-*pixel encryption model* and q_2-*pixel encryption model*, and let $q_1 = a_0 + a_1$, $q_2 = b_0 + b_1$, where a_0, b_0 are the number of white pixels and a_1, b_1 are the number of black pixels. We have that the total number of pseudo-random bits can be determined is $\lfloor a_0 \log_2 |C_0| + a_1 \log_2 |C_1| \rfloor + \lfloor b_0 \log_2 |C_0| + b_1 \log_2 |C_1| \rfloor$, which is not greater than $\lfloor (a_0 + b_0) \log_2 |C_0| + (a_1 + b_1) \log_2 |C_1| \rfloor = \lfloor n_w \log_2 |C_0| + n_b \log_2 |C_1| \rfloor$. Hence, the theorem is true.   □

3.4   On Decoding the Ciphertext

For ESSVCS, in order to encrypt the secret pixels and decode the ciphertext, one needs to set a bijection between the set of pseudo-random numbers (ciphertext) and the set of share matrices. A simple way to realize that is to generate a table which contains all the share matrices and their corresponding random numbers. When the dealer generates the shares, (s)he needs to generate a pseudo-random number and find the corresponding share matrix by table-lookup, then (s)he can encrypt the shares by using the share matrix. When decoding the ciphertext, the participants get the share matrices according to the Theorem 1, and find the corresponding numbers by table-lookup, hence, they get the ciphertext. Disadvantage of this decoding method is that, the table requires us store all the share matrices in sets C_0 and C_1, and hence it has large memory requirements. In this subsection, we propose a decoding method which is more efficient than the above mentioned method.

The proposed decoding method contains two subroutines: the first is $MTN(S)$, which takes a share matrix in C_i ($i = 0, 1$) as its input and generates a number between 1 and $m!$, the second is $NTM(N)$, which takes a number between 1 and $m!$ as its input and generates a share matrix S. The subroutines $MTN(S)$ and $NTM(N)$ form a bijection between the set of the share matrices and the set of numbers between 1 and $m!$.

By using $MTN(S)$ and $NTM(N)$, when the dealer encrypts a secret pixel p, (s)he first generates a pseudo-random number between 1 and $m!$, and then consults the subroutine $NTM(N)$ to generate a share matrix in C_i ($i = 0, 1$), and encrypts the secret pixel p by using the share matrix. When the participants decode the ciphertext, they first generate the share matrix according to Theorem 1, and consult the subroutine $MTN(S)$ to get the ciphertext.

Denote the columns of the basis matrix as $c_1, \cdots, c_m$, first we take the case that $c_1, \cdots, c_m$ are pairwise different into consideration. In this part, we treat a matrix as a set of columns. The subroutine $MTN(S)$ which outputs a number between 1 and $m!$ given a share matrix S as its input is:

Subroutine: MTN(S)

> For $i = 1$ to $m - 1$
>> Find c_i in S, assume that c_i is the J_i-th column of S
>> Delete c_i from S
>
> Output $N = 1 + \sum_{i=1}^{m-1} ((m-i)!)(J_i - 1)$

The subroutine $NTM(N)$ which outputs a share matrix S given a number between 1 and $m!$ as its input is:

Subroutine: NTM(N)

> Initial S as an empty matrix
> $N_0 \leftarrow N - 1$
> For $i = 1$ to $m - 1$
>> $J_i \leftarrow \lfloor \frac{N_{i-1}}{(m-i)!} \rfloor + 1$
>> $N_i \leftarrow N_{i-1} - (J_i - 1)((m-i)!)$
> Insert c_m to S as its 1-st column
> For $i = m - 1$ to 1
>> Insert column c_i into S as its J_i-th column
> Output S

According to the subroutines $MTN(S)$ and $NTM(N)$ above, we have the following theorem:

Theorem 5. *The subroutines $MTN(S)$ and $NTM(N)$ form a bijection between the set of share matrices in C_i ($i = 0, 1$) and the set of numbers between 1 and $m!$.*

Proof: Because in subroutines $MTN(S)$ and $NTM(N)$, we represent the share matrices by the positions of its columns $(J_1, J_2, \cdots, J_{m-1})$ where $1 \leq J_i \leq m + 1 - i$ for $i = 1, 2, \cdots, m - 1$, we only need to prove that $MTN(S)$ and $NTM(N)$ form a bijection between the sets $X = \{(J_1, J_2, \cdots, J_{m-1}) | 1 \leq J_i \leq m + 1 - i \text{ for } i = 1, 2, \cdots, m - 1\}$ and $Y = \{1, 2, \cdots, m!\}$. Denote $f : X \to Y$ as a map from X to Y, we prove that f is a bijection.

First, given a number in Y, according to $NTM(N)$, there exists a $(J_1, J_2 \cdots, J_{m-1})$, hence f is a surjection.

Second, for any two different elements in X, $J = (J_1, J_2, \cdots, J_{m-1})$ and $J' = (J'_1, J'_2, \cdots, J'_{m-1})$ such that $J \neq J'$, we prove that their corresponding numbers $f(J)$ and $f(J')$ are different.

According to $MTN(S)$, we have $f(J) = 1 + \sum_{i=1}^{m-1} ((m-i)!)(J_i - 1)$ and $f(J') = 1 + \sum_{i=1}^{m-1} ((m-i)!)(J'_i - 1)$. Denote i^* as the smallest number that $J_{i^*} \neq J'_{i^*}$, without loss of generality, we suppose $J_{i^*} > J'_{i^*}$, i.e. $J_{i^*} - J'_{i^*} \geq 1$. Thus, we have:

$$f(J) - f(J') = \sum_{i=1}^{m-1} ((m-i)!)(J_i - J'_i)$$

$$= (m-i^*)!(J_{i^*} - J'_{i^*}) + \sum_{i=i^*+1}^{m-1} ((m-i)!)(J_i - J'_i)$$

$$\geq (m-i^*)! + \sum_{i=i^*+1}^{m-1} ((m-i)!)(J_i - J'_i)$$

Because $1 \leq J_i, J'_i \leq m+1-i$, we have $-(m-i) \leq J_i - J'_i \leq m-i$, hence

$$f(J) - f(J') \geq (m-i^*)! - \sum_{i=i^*+1}^{m-1} ((m-i)!)(m-i)$$

$$= (m-i^*)! - ((m-i^*)! - 1)$$

$$= 1$$

Therefore, $f(J) - f(J') \neq 0$, we have f is an injection. Hence, f is a bijection and the theorem follows. □

For the case that there are identical columns in the basis matrix, which means that there are identical share matrices in the $m!$ permutations of the basis matrix. Suppose there are e different columns in the basis matrix, and the multiplicities of these columns are $a_1, a_2, \cdots, a_e$. Denote N_d as the number of the different share matrices in C_i, then we have $N_d = \frac{(\sum_{i=1}^{e} a_i)!}{\prod_{i=1}^{e} a_i!}$, for $i \in \{0, 1\}$. Each share matrix appears $\frac{m!}{N_d}$ times in the $m!$ permutations.

Furthermore, according to the subroutine $MTN(S)$, each permutation corresponds to a number between 1 and $m!$, we can divide these $m!$ numbers into N_d groups, where each group contains $\frac{m!}{N_d}$ numbers, and the numbers in one group correspond to an identical share matrix. We hence can form an array of length N_d by choosing the smallest number of each group. Denote this array as A, and denote $S_1^i, S_2^i \cdots, S_{N_d}^i$ as all the different share matrices in the set C_i, the following subroutine generates A:

Subroutine: MC

> Initial an empty array A
> For $j = 1$ to N_d
> > For $q = 1$ to m
> > > Find the first c_q in S_j^i from left to right, assume that c_q is the J_q-th column of S_j^i
> > > Delete c_q from S_j^i
> > $A[j] \leftarrow 1 + \sum_{q=1}^{m-1} ((m-q)!)(J_q - 1)$

To differentiate the two cases whether there exist and do not exist identical columns, we denote MTN-d(S) and NTM-d(N) as the corresponding subroutines for the case that there exist identical columns:

Subroutine: MTN-d(S)

$A \leftarrow MC$

For $q = 1$ to m

Find the first c_q in S_j^i from left to the right, assume that c_q is the J_q-th column
of S_j^i

Delete c_q from S_j^i

$N' \leftarrow 1 + \sum\limits_{q=1}^{m-1} ((m-q)!)(J_q - 1)$

For $r = 1$ to N_d

if $A[r] = N'$

Output r

Subroutine: NTM-d(N)

$A \leftarrow MC$

$N' \leftarrow A[N]$

$S \leftarrow NTM(N')$

Output S

According to the Theorem 5, we have that, each group only has one smallest number. Hence the array A is a bijection from the set $\{1, 2, \cdots, N_d\}$ and the set of the smallest numbers in each group. Furthermore, because each group corresponds to a different share matrix we have that the MTN-d(S) and NTM-d(N) form a bijection between the set $\{1, 2, \cdots, N_d\}$ and the set of share matrices $\{S_1^i, S_2^i \cdots, S_{N_d}^i\}$. We summarize this result as the following theorem:

Theorem 6. *The subroutines MTN-d(S) and NTM-d(N) form a bijection between the set of share matrices in C_i ($i = 0, 1$) and the set of numbers between 1 and N_d.* □

The above subroutines are more efficient than the simple table-lookup method. Particularly, for the case that the columns $c_1, c_2, \cdots, c_m$ are pairwise different, the subroutines $MTN(S)$ and $NTM(N)$ are efficient, because they only need fixed memory requirements. For the case that there are identical columns in $c_1, c_2, \cdots, c_m$, the memory requirement of the subroutines $MTN - d(S)$ and $NTM - d(N)$ relates to the value of m. Because they only need to store the indexes of the share matrices $A[1], A[2], \cdots, A[N_d]$, they are more efficient than the simple table-lookup method. Furthermore, the table (the array A in Subroutine MC) can be previously generated and reusable.

4   Comparisons of ESSVCS and TiOISSS

From the viewpoint of carrying amount of the secret, both the ESSVCS and the TiOISSS are computer aided and carry two types of secrets, one is a secret image that can be revealed by stacking the shares, and the other is covert data which is revealed by computation. The two TiOISSS schemes [17, 18] can be also treated as (k, k, n)-TiOISSS, which means a vague secret image is revealed by stacking any k out of n shares, and further a much finer gray-scale secret image (i.e. the covert data) is revealed by computation with these k shares.

Taking the information carrying capability into consideration, we compare the amount of covert data carried by the ESSVCS and two TiOISSSs [17, 18].

First, the covert data carried by the ESSVCS is greater than that in Lin et al.'s TiOISSS [17]. Bandwidth of the proposed ESSVCS has been discussed in Theorem 4, and it can be evaluated from Table 1 and Table 2. Lin et al.'s TiOISSS [17] groups the share matrices into different types to carry covert data according to the first row. Let m be pixel expansion of the basis matrix, where each row contains b '1' and w '0' and $m=b+w$. There are $\binom{m}{w}$ different types of share matrix, and each secret pixel in VCS carriesy $\log_2 \binom{m}{w}$ bits. We list the number of share matrices generated by Droste [11] with different types in Table 3.

Note that in order to satisfy the security, we can only choose the type of one row and the remaining $(n-1)$ rows are then determined according to the type of share matrix. Therefore, only $1/n$ part of each share can be used to carry $\log_2 \binom{m}{w}$ bits. Since the covert data of each share is taken from the shadow image generated by polynomial-based secret sharing scheme, the total secret information carried by VCS is $k|S_I| \log_2 \binom{m}{w} /n$ bits, where S_I is the binary secret image of VCS.

Table 3. The number of share matrices with different types in Lin et al.'s TiOISSS

k \ n	2	3	4	5	6	7	8	9	10
2	2	3	4	5	6	7	8	9	10
3		$\frac{4!}{2!2!}$	$\frac{6!}{3!3!}$	$\frac{8!}{4!4!}$	$\frac{10!}{5!5!}$	$\frac{12!}{6!6!}$	$\frac{14!}{7!7!}$	$\frac{16!}{8!8!}$	$\frac{18!}{9!9!}$
4			$\frac{8!}{4!4!}$	$\frac{15!}{9!6!}$	$\frac{24!}{16!8!}$	$\frac{35!}{25!10!}$	$\frac{48!}{36!12!}$	$\frac{63!}{49!14!}$	$\frac{80!}{64!16!}$
5				$\frac{16!}{8!8!}$	$\frac{30!}{15!15!}$	$\frac{48!}{24!24!}$	$\frac{70!}{35!35!}$	$\frac{96!}{48!48!}$	$\frac{126!}{63!63!}$
6					$\frac{32!}{16!16!}$	$\frac{70!}{40!30!}$	$\frac{128!}{80!48!}$	$\frac{210!}{140!70!}$	$\frac{320!}{224!96!}$
7						$\frac{64!}{32!32!}$	$\frac{140!}{70!70!}$	$\frac{256!}{128!128!}$	$\frac{420!}{210!210!}$
8							$\frac{128!}{64!64!}$	$\frac{315!}{175!140!}$	$\frac{640!}{384!256!}$
9								$\frac{256!}{128!128!}$	$\frac{630!}{315!315!}$
10									$\frac{512!}{256!256!}$

Second, there is no fixed relationship between the amount of covert data carried by the ESSVCS and that of Yang et al.'s TiOISSS [18]. The TiOISSS [18] replaces the black pixels in the shares with gray pixels generated by polynomial-based secret sharing scheme. Therefore, each row of share matrix carries $8b$ bits, and the total amount of covert data are $8kb|S_I|$ bits, where b is the number of '1' in each row of share matrix. In most cases, especially when n is a small number, the covert data carried by Yang et al.'s TiOISSS [18] is more than that in the ESSVCS.

However, in some cases, the ESSVCS can carry more data. For example, for a (2,10)-VCS constructed by Droste [11], we have $\log_2|C_0| = 3.32$, $\log_2|C_1| = 21.79$, and $b = 1, k = 2$. In the ESSVCS, each white secret pixel carries 3.32 bits and each black secret pixel carries 21.79 bits, while in Yang et al.'s TiOISSS [18], sharing one secret pixel carries 16 bits. With proper proportion of the numbers of white secret pixels to black secret pixels, the ESSVCS can carry more covert data than Yang et al.'s TiOISSS [18].

From viewpoint of visual quality, both ESSVCS and TiOISSS can visually recover the secret image by stacking shares. The ESSVCS and Lin et al.'s TiOISSS [17] used traditional VCS as the building block, hence the recovered secret image is as same as that of the traditional VCS. In Yang et al.'s TiOISSS [18], the black pixels of shares are replaced by gray pixels, and the contrast of VCS is diminished. Therefore, visual quality of the recovered secret image by stacking shares is deteriorated in Yang et al.'s TiOISSS [18], which is a disadvantage of their scheme.

Besides, another disadvantage of Yang et al.'s TiOISSS scheme [18] is that, to reconstruct the covert data the participants have to obtain the greyness of each sub-pixel precisely, which is impractical if the shares are printed on transparencies. Occasional scrub may change the greyness of sub-pixels in the transparencies, which will be impossible to reconstruct the covert data.

Both the ESSVCS and Lin et al.'s TiOISSS [17] carry covert data by choosing different share matrices, hence there is a bijection between the set of pseudo-random numbers (ciphertext) and the set of share matrices. In Lin et al.'s TiOISSS [17], it employs a lookup table to map the different types of share matrices to the set of pseudo-random numbers. The disadvantage of their scheme is that, the table needs to store all the types of share matrices, which has large memory requirements. However, in the ESSVCS, an efficient algorithm is introduced to make the mapping more convenient.

5   Conclusions

In this paper, we proposed a construction of the (k, t, n)-ESSVCS scheme, which can carry additional covert data compared to the traditional (k, n)-VCS scheme by treating the pseudo-random inputs as a sub-channel. We analyzed some issues related to ESSVCS scheme such as the pseudo-randomness that the input of VCS requires, sufficient conditions to uniquely determine a share in the set C_i ($i = 0, 1$), and bandwidth of the proposed ESSVCS scheme. We also presented an efficient algorithm to decode ESSVCS secret. At last, comparisons of some relevant VCS schemes are given such as the TiOISSS scheme [17, 18].

The proposed (k, t, n)-ESSVCS scheme is especially useful for the case $(n - 1, n - 1, n)$-ESSVCS and the case (n, n, n)-ESSVCS, because in these cases, the qualified participants could get secret and covert data simultaneously. The constructions of $(k, n-1, n)$-ESSVCS and (k, n, n)-ESSVCS can be easily implemented by the proposed scheme. For general value of $k < t < n-1$, we left it as an open problem for future study.

Acknowledgements. This work was supported by NSFC grant No. 60903210, the "Strategic Priority Research Program" of the Chinese Academy of Sciences No. XDA06010701 and the IIEs Cryptography Research Project No. Y3Z001B102. Thanks for the anonymous reviewers' invaluable constructive comments and suggestions.

References

[1] Naor, M., Shamir, A.: Visual cryptography. In: De Santis, A. (ed.) EUROCRYPT 1994. LNCS, vol. 950, pp. 1–12. Springer, Heidelberg (1995)

[2] Surekha, B., Swamy, G., Rao, K.S.: A multiple watermarking technique for images based on visual cryptography. Computer Applications 1, 77–81 (2010)

[3] Monoth, T., Babu, A.P.: Tamperproof transmission of fingerprints using visual cryptography schemes. Procedia. Computer Science 2, 143–148 (2010)

[4] Weir, J., Yan, W.: Resolution variant visual cryptography for street view of google maps. In: Proceedings of the ISCAS, pp. 1695–1698 (2010)

[5] Yang, C.N., Chen, T.S., Ching, M.H.: Embed additional private information into two-dimensional bar codes by the visual secret sharing scheme. Integrated Computer-Aided Engineering 13(2), 189–199 (2006)

[6] Weir, J., Yan, W.: A comprehensive study of visual cryptography. In: Shi, Y.Q. (ed.) Transactions on DHMS V. LNCS, vol. 6010, pp. 70–105. Springer, Heidelberg (2010)

[7] Cimato, S., Yang, C.N.: Visual cryptography and secret image sharing. CRC Press, Taylor & Francis (2011)

[8] Liu, F., Wu, C.K., Lin, X.J.: The alignment problem of visual cryptography schemes. Designs, Codes and Cryptography 50, 215–227 (2009)

[9] Yan, W.Q., Jin, D., Kankanhalli, M.S.: Visual cryptography for print and scan applications. In: Proceedings of the 2004 International Symposium on Circuits and Systems, vol. 5, pp. 572–575 (2004)

[10] Iwamoto, M., Yamamoto, H.: A construction method of visual secret sharing schemes for plural secret images. IEICE Transactions on Fundamentals E86-A(10), 2577–2588 (2003)

[11] Droste, S.: New results on visual cryptography. In: Koblitz, N. (ed.) CRYPTO 1996. LNCS, vol. 1109, pp. 401–415. Springer, Heidelberg (1996)

[12] Iwamoto, M., Lei, W., Yoneyama, K., Kunihiro, N., Ohta, K.: Visual secret sharing schemes for multiple secret images allowing the rotation of shares. IEICE Transactions on Fundamentals E89-A(5), 1382–1395 (2006)

[13] Yang, C.N., Laih, C.S.: New colored visual secret sharing schemes. Designs, Codes and Cryptography 20, 325–335 (2000)

[14] Jin, D., Yan, W.Q., Kankanhalli, M.S.: Progressive color visual cryptography. Journal of Electronic Imaging 14(3), 033019 (2005)

[15] Shyu, S.J.: Efficient visual secret sharing scheme for color images. Pattern Recognition 39, 866–880 (2006)

[16] Shamir, A.: How to share a secret. Communications of the ACM 22(11), 612–613 (1979)

[17] Lin, S.J., Lin, J.C.: VCPSS a two in one two decoding options image sharing method combining visual cryptography (VC) and polynomial style sharing PSS approaches. Pattern Recognition 40, 3652–3666 (2007)

[18] Yang, C.N., Ciou, C.B.: Image secret sharing method with two-decoding-options: Lossless recovery and previewing capability. Image and Vision Computing 28, 1600–1610 (2010)

[19] Fang, W.P., Lin, J.C.: Visual cryptography with extra ability of hiding confidential data. Journal of Electronic Imaging 15(2), 023020 (2006)

[20] Blundo, C., De Santis, A., Stinson, D.R.: On the contrast in visual cryptography schemes. Journal of Cryptology 12(4), 261–289 (1999)

[21] Koga, H.: A general formula of the (t,n)-threshold visual secret sharing scheme. In: Zheng, Y. (ed.) ASIACRYPT 2002. LNCS, vol. 2501, pp. 328–345. Springer, Heidelberg (2002)

[22] Ehrsam, W.F., Meyer, C.H.W., Smith, J.L., Tuchman, W.L.: Message verification and transmission error detection by block chaining (1976)

[23] Soto, J., Bassham, L.: Randomness testing of the advanced encryption standard finalist candidates. In: Proceedings AES3, New York (2001), http://csrc.nist.gov/publications/nistir/ir6483.pdf

[24] Blundo, C., De Bonis, A., De Santis, A.: Improved schemes for visual cryptography. Designs, Codes and Cryptography 24, 255–278 (2001)

On the Security of Multi-secret Visual Cryptography Scheme with Ring Shares

Zheng-xin Fu and Bin Yu

Zhengzhou Information Science and Technology Institute, P.R. China, 450004
{fzx2515,byu2009}@163.com

Abstract. With visual cryptography in mind, the security property of a new scheme is always one of main concerns. However, the ideal security is not taken into account in some visual cryptography schemes sharing multiple secrets. In this paper, the security of a multi-secret visual cryptography scheme proposed by Feng et al. is analyzed. We show that the security of their scheme is not ideal. Precisely, it is insecure since some information of the secret images can be inferred by block attacking the second share alone. The main weak design is proved and shown by means of giving theoretical analysis and conducting some counter experiments.

Keywords: Visual cryptography, Security, Multiple secret sharing, Ring share.

1   Introduction

Visual cryptography scheme (VCS) was introduced by Naor and Shamir in Eurocrypt'94 [1]. The difference between visual cryptography and the traditional secret sharing schemes [2,3] is the decryption process. Most secret sharing schemes are mainly realized by the computer, while visual cryptography schemes can decrypt secrets only with human eyes. Due to the ease of decoding, VCS provides some new and secure imaging applications, e.g., visual authentication, steganography, and image encryption. In recent years, the studies of VCS focus on the general access structure [4], the optimization of the pixel expansion and the relative difference [5-8], and the grey and color images [9-12], etc.

Most VCSs can only encrypt one secret image, which reduces the work efficiency and limits its possible applications. A so-called multi-secret VCS (MVCS) was then proposed to encrypt multiple secret images simultaneously. Chen et al. [13] designed (2, 2, 2)-MVCS to encode two secret images S_1 and S_2 into two square shares A and B. S_1 was decoded by stacking share A and B directly. S_2 could be decrypted by overlapping shares A and the rotated share B with 90°, 180°or 270°. In order to overcome the angle restriction, the shares were devised to be circles in literatures [14,15]. Although the rotation angles were unlimited, the shapes of decrypted images were distorted from square to circular and the recovery images had less contrast.

Different from the square and circle shares, Hsu et al. [16] proposed a scheme to hide two images in two ring shares with arbitrary rotating angles and undistorted

Y.Q. Shi, H.J. Kim, and F. Pérez-González (Eds.): IWDW 2012, LNCS 7809, pp. 485–494, 2013.
© Springer-Verlag Berlin Heidelberg 2013

shapes. Although there was no restriction of angles in Hsu's scheme, only two secret images could be encrypted. In order to share more secret images, Feng et al. [17] designed a new (2, 2, *m*)-MVCS with ring shares based on four different visual patterns. The scheme could share *Y* secret images at most, where *Y* was the width of the secret images. The pixel expansion of Feng's scheme was 3*m*, where *m* denoted the number of secret images.

In the above schemes, one share is always used as a mask, while the other one is decided by the secret images and the mask. Therefore, the security of the secret images relies on the second share. Taking Feng's scheme for example, we analyze the relationship between the visual patterns which are the basic units of the shares. It is discovered that some information about the secret images can be inferred by computing the second share alone. This method is called block attacking. The weaknesses of (2, 2, 3)-MVCS and (2, 2, *m*)-MVCS are computed and discussed in detail, which threaten the schemes' security.

The rest of this paper is organized as follows. Section 2 briefly reviews the scheme in literature [17]. As the main part of this paper, Section 3 analyzes the security of the multi-secret visual cryptography scheme with ring shares. Section 4 concludes the paper.

2   Related Studies

To overcome the number restriction of secret images and the shape distortions, Feng et al. proposed a scheme to hide multiple secret images into two ring shares. Assume that the secret images $S_1, S_2, \cdots, S_m$ are all sized $X \times Y$, where X is the height and Y is the width of images. Their scheme rolls up the shares to rings so that it is possible to recover many secrets at some setting angles as shown in Figure 1.

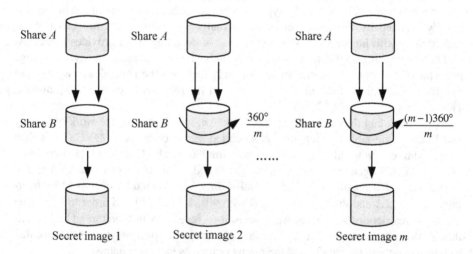

Fig. 1. The decryption model of Feng et al.'s scheme

Since each row of the secret images is independent with others, the scheme encrypts one row at a time. The basic unit in shares is block, corresponding to one pixel of every secret image. Collect m blocks with interval $360°/m$ to form a set. Therefore, all shares blocks on a row can be separated to Y/m sets. $a_i^P(b_i^P)$ denotes the i-th block in the p-th set of a certain row in the share A (B), where $1 \le i \le m$ and $1 \le p \le Y/m$. The relationship between the blocks and the secret images is illustrated in Figure 2.

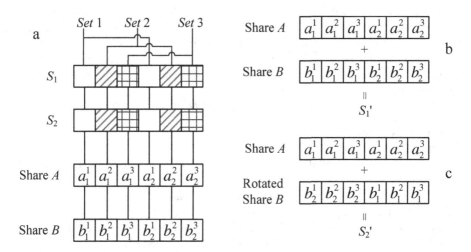

Fig. 2. The relationship between the blocks and the secret images: (a) The constructions of the shares. (b) The recovery of S_1. (c) The recovery of S_2.

In the scheme, each share block is filled with m visual patterns. $a_{i,j}^P(b_{i,j}^P)$ denotes the j-th pattern of $a_i^P(b_i^P)$. There are four visual patterns $P_E=\{1,0,1\}$, $P_I=\{1,1,0\}$, $P_W=\{1,0,1\}$, and $P_B=\{0,1,1\}$, which are used to produce some special features. The effective visual pattern P_E will reveal meaningful stacking results patterns P_W and P_B, while the ineffective pattern P_I will always cause black blocks. Table 1 shows the relations between the visual patterns.

Table 1. Necessary relations between visual patterns

Stacking operations	Block of results
$P_E + P_W = \{1,0,1\}$	White
$P_E + P_B = \{1,1,1\}$	Black
$P_I + P_W = \{1,1,1\}$	Black
$P_I + P_B = \{1,1,1\}$	Black

For the p-th process on the r-th row, $a_i^P(b_i^P)$ are generated according to the following equations, where $1 \le j \le m$.

$$a_{i,j}^{p} = \begin{cases} P_E & i = j \\ P_I & i \neq j \end{cases} \tag{1}$$

$$b_{i,j}^{p} = \begin{cases} P_W & S_{1+(i-j)\bmod m}\left(r, p+(j-1)Y/m\right) = 0 \\ P_B & else \end{cases} \tag{2}$$

The last part is using random permutation for every block to break up the regular pixel distribution. Then the pixel positions in a single share image are no longer related to the secrets. In other words, the security of the scheme is relied on the random permutation. Meanwhile, $a_1^P, a_2^P, ..., a_m^P$ and $b_1^P, b_2^P, ..., b_m^P$ are applied with the same random permutation, and therefore the secrets can still be decrypted by stacking the share images.

The complete encryption algorithm for $(2, 2, m)$-MVCS is as follows [16].

Input: Secret images $S_1, S_2, ... , S_m$
Output: Two share A, B
Step1: Adjust the size of all secret images to $X \times Y$ that the X must be a multiple of m.
Step 2: Initialize the processing row $r = 1$ of the images.
Step 3: Start the p-th process of the proposed scheme with $p = 1$.
Step 4: Select the 1, $m+1$, $2m+1$, $\cdots$, $X-m+1$ secret pixels to generate the blocks $a_1^P, a_2^P, ..., a_m^P$ and $b_1^P, b_2^P, ..., b_m^P$ according to Eqs. (1) and (2).
Step 5: Perform permutation on the generated blocks $a_1^P, a_2^P, ..., a_m^P$ and $b_1^P, b_2^P, ..., b_m^P$.
Step 6: Fill the blocks in the share images. a_i^P is the block on the r-th row and $(p + X(i-1)/m)$-th column of share A, and b_i^P is the block on the r-th row and $(p + X(i-1)/m)$-th column of share B.
Step 7: If $p<X/m$, return to Step 4 for the next process $p := p+1$.
Step 8: If $r <Y$, return to Step 3 for the next row $r:=r+1$.
Step 9: Out put the two shares A and B.

3   Security Analysis of MVCS

The security of visual cryptography schemes is as same as "one time pad" [1]. The attackers can't get any information on secret images from the forbidden set of participants. For the $(2, 2, m)$-MVCS, a single share should not leak any information on the m secret images. However, the scheme proposed by Feng et. al doesn't satisfy the ideal security. The main reason is that share B leaks the correlation of the secret pixels.

3.1   Block Attacking

The basic units of share A are P_E and P_I, which are independent with the secret images. Therefore, Share A is just like a mask used for effecting and ineffecting the blocks of share B. The attackers can't get anything information of secret images from share A.

On the contrary, the basic units of share B are P_B and P_W, which are decided by the secret images. The weakness of share B will threaten the security of the visual cryptography scheme.

Firstly, the characteristics of P_B and P_W are analyzed. Since $P_W =\{1,0,1\}$ and $P_B =\{0,1,1\}$, we can get $P_W \oplus P_W =\{0,0,0\}$, $P_W \oplus P_B =\{1,1,0\}$, $P_B \oplus P_B =\{0,0,0\}$, where $\oplus$ is XOR operator. Obviously, the XOR result reflects whether the two blocks are same.

Next taking the random permutation into consideration, let P_i and P_j $(i, j \in \{B, W\})$ denote two patterns. P_i' and P_j' denote the same random permutation of P_i and P_j. $H(P)$ denotes the '1's number of the pattern P. It is obvious that $H(P_i' \oplus P_j') = H(P_i \oplus P_j) = 0$ or 2.

Although we can not guess the color of the secret pixel encoded by P_i (P_j), the equality relation between P_i and P_j can be deduced. If $H(P_i' \oplus P_j')=0$, we can get $P_i \oplus P_j =\{0,0,0\}$, that means the secret pixels encoded by P_i and P_j are the same. Otherwise, if $H(P_i' \oplus P_j')=2$, we can get $P_i \oplus P_j =\{1,1,0\}$ or $\{1,0,1\}$ or $\{0,1,1\}$, that means the secret pixels are different.

Based on the relation between P_B and P_W, we can compute the different number in the m pixels encoded by b_i^P and b_j^P, which are consist of P_B and P_W.

The procedure of Block Attacking is as follows.

Input: $\hat{b}_i^P$ and $\hat{b}_j^P$, the i-th and j-th blocks in the p-set of the share B

Output: The correlation between the m secret pixels encoded in b_i^P and the m secret pixels encoded in b_j^P

Step1: Compute $\hat{b}_i^P \oplus \hat{b}_j^P$. $\hat{b}_i^P$ ($\hat{b}_j^P$) means the random permutation of block b_i^P (b_j^P), and the random permutations for b_i^P and b_j^P are the same.

Step2: Let d denotes the number of '1' in $b_i^P \oplus b_j^P$. d is equal to the number of '1' in $\hat{b}_i^P \oplus \hat{b}_j^P$.

Step3: According to characteristics of P_B and P_W, we can make sure that there are $d/2$ different pixels between the m secret pixels encoded in b_i^P and b_j^P.

Step4: Output $d/2$.

Although the attackers known nothing about the random permutation, they can get the correlations between the secret pixels. The results of the Block Attacking leak the information about the secret images.

3.2   Attacking to (2, 2, 3)-MVCS

In the section, a simple (2, 2, 3)-MVCS is analyzed firstly. Based on the Block Attacking, the security of general (2, 2, 3)-MVCS is discuss in detail.

Let $S_1 = [0\ 1\ 1]$, $S_2 = [1\ 0\ 0]$, and $S_3 = [0\ 1\ 0]$, which are three secret images with $X=1$ and $Y=3$. There is only one process needed with $r=X=1$ and $p=Y/3=1$. According to Eqs. (1) and (2), $a_1^1 =[P_E\ P_I\ P_I]^T$, $a_2^1 =[P_I\ P_E\ P_I]^T$, $a_3^1 =[P_I\ P_I\ P_E]^T$, $b_1^1 =[P_W\ P_B\ P_W]^T$, $b_2^1 =[P_B\ P_B\ P_W]^T$, $b_3^1 =[P_W\ P_W\ P_B]^T$. The secret images can be recovered by overlaying share A and B at three angles. The shares without random permutation are shown in Figure 3.

In order to break up the regular pixel distribution, let a random permutation $Permu$ $=(2,5,1,7,3,0,6,4,8)$ be applied to the blocks a_1^1, a_2^1, a_3^1, b_1^1, b_2^1, b_3^1. The attackers can't guess the secret pixels from the permutated blocks $\hat{a}_1^1, \hat{a}_2^1, \hat{a}_3^1, \hat{b}_1^1, \hat{b}_2^1, \hat{b}_3^1$. Meanwhile, the secret images can also be recovered by overlaying the share A' and B' at $0°$, $120°$, $240°$. The permutated shares and the recovery images are illustrated in Figure 4.

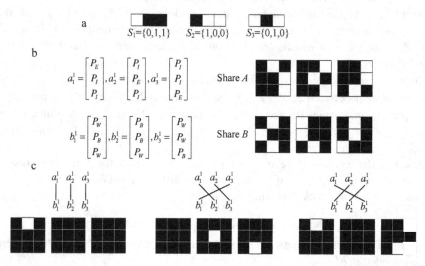

Fig. 3. An example of the (2, 2, 3)-MVCS: (a) Three secret images. (b) The generated share images. (c) The stacking secret image at $0°$, $120°$, $240°$.

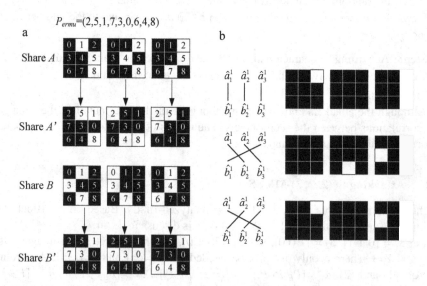

Fig. 4. The (2, 2, 3)-MVCS with permutation: (a) Permutation on share blocks. (b) The stacking secret image at $0°$, $120°$, $240°$

According to Figure 3 and Figure 4, the correlations between $b_1{}^1$ and $b_2{}^1$ are analyzed using the Block Attacking.

Step1: $\hat{b}_1^1 \oplus \hat{b}_2^1 = [110001111] \oplus [111000111] = [001001000]$.

Step2: There are 2 '1' in $\hat{b}_1^1 \oplus \hat{b}_2^1$. We can get the number of '1' in $b_1{}^1 \oplus b_2{}^1$, which is $d=2$. (Figure 5 shows that the numbers of '1' in $b_1{}^1 \oplus b_2{}^1$ and $\hat{b}_1^1 \oplus \hat{b}_2^1$ are equal as expectation.)

Step3: There are $d/2=1$ different pixels between the 3 secret pixels encoded into $b_1{}^1$ and $b_2{}^1$.

Step4: Output $d/2=1$.

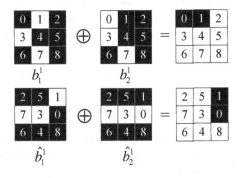

Fig. 5. b11⊕b21and $\hat{b}_1^1 \oplus \hat{b}_2^1$

According to the conclusion of the Block Attacking, the all combinations of secret pixels encrypted into $b_1{}^1$ and $b_2{}^1$ are enumerated in the Table 2.

Table 2. The combinations of secret pixels encrypted into $b_1{}^1$ and $b_2{}^1$

The possible combinations of 3 secret pixels encrypted into $b_1{}^1$	000	001	010	011	100	101	110	111
The corresponding combinations of 3 secret pixels encrypted into $b_2{}^1$	100	101	110	111	000	001	010	011
	010	011	000	001	110	111	100	101
	001	000	011	010	101	100	111	110

From Table 2, there are only 8×3=24 possible combinations for 6 secret pixels. However, if the (2, 2, 3)-MVCS is ideal secure, there should be $2^6=64$ combinations for 6 secret pixels. Although the attackers can't guess the exact secret pixels encoded into $b_1{}^1$ and $b_2{}^1$, the 6 secret pixels' space is reduced from 64 to 24. Actually, the secret pixels in $b_1{}^1$ are [010], and the secret pixels in $b_2{}^1$ are [110]. [010] and [110] are exist in Table 2. Therefore, the Block Attacking is effective.

The correlations between $b_2{}^1$ and $b_3{}^1$ can also be analyzed by the Block Attacking.

Step1: $\hat{b}_2^1 \oplus \hat{b}_3^1 = [111000111] \oplus [110111001] = [001111110]$.

Step2: There are 6 '1' in $\hat{b}_2^1 \oplus \hat{b}_3^1$, and $d=6$.

Step3: There are $d/2=3$ different pixels between the 3 secret pixels encoded into $b_2{}^1$ and $b_3{}^1$.

Step4: Output $d/2=3$.

The result means that the 3 secret pixels encoded into $b_2{}^1$ are all different from $b_3{}^1$. Taking the relation between $b_1{}^1$, $b_2{}^1$ and $b_3{}^1$ into consideration, there are only $8\times3\times1=24$ possible combinations for all 9 secret pixels. The 9 secret pixels' space is reduced from ideal $2^9=512$ to 24 by analyzing the share B alone. The weakness threatens the example of (2, 2, 3)-MVCS severely, which is ignored in Feng et al.'s scheme.

Using the Block Attacking to the general (2, 2, 3)-MVCS, let the sizes of the secret images are all $X\times Y$. There are $Y/3$ sets in every row, so the share B has $XY/3$ sets totally. The p-set contains 3 blocks $\hat{b}_1^p, \hat{b}_2^p$ and $\hat{b}_3^p$, and every 3 secret pixels are encoded into one block. There are 4 statuses of d, the number of '1' in $\hat{b}_i^p \oplus \hat{b}_j^p$ ($1 \le i \ne j \le 3$, $1 \le p \le XY/3$), which are shown in Table 3.

Table 3. The statuses of '1's in $\hat{b}_i^p \oplus \hat{b}_j^p$

d, the number of '1' in $\hat{b}_i^p \oplus \hat{b}_j^p$	The number of the different secret pixels	The possible combinations of the secret pixels encoded into b_i^P and b_j^P
0	0	$2^3 \times C(3, 0)= 8$
2	1	$2^3 \times C(3, 1)= 24$
4	2	$2^3 \times C(3, 2)= 24$
6	3	$2^3 \times C(3, 3)= 8$

The best situation for attackers is $d=0$ or 6 for every pair of the 3 blocks in every set. Then, the attacking difficulty of one set declines from 2^9 to 2^3. Furthermore, the attacking difficulty of the secret images decreases from 2^{3XY} to 2^{XY}.

The worst situation for attackers is $d=2$ or 4 for the blocks in every set. Then, the attacking difficulty of one set declines from 2^9 to $2^3 \times 3 \times 3 = 9 \times 2^3$. Furthermore, the attacking difficulty of the secret images decreases from 2^{3XY} to $2^{XY} \times 3 \times 3 \approx 2^{XY+3.2}$.

3.3   Attacking to (2, 2, m)-MVCS

Using the Block Attacking to the (2, 2, m)-MVCS, let the sizes of the secret images are all $X\times Y$. There are Y/m sets in every row, so the share B has XY/m sets totally. p-set contains m blocks $\hat{b}_1^p, \hat{b}_2^p, \ldots, \hat{b}_m^p$, and every m secret pixels are encoded into one block. There are $m+1$ statuses of d, the number of '1' in $\hat{b}_i^p \oplus \hat{b}_j^p$ ($1 \le i \ne j \le m$, $1 \le p \le XY/m$), which are shown in Table 4.

Table 4. m +1 statuses of '1's in $\hat{b}_i^p \oplus \hat{b}_j^p$

d, the number of '1' in $\hat{b}_i^p \oplus \hat{b}_j^p$	The number of the different secret pixels	The possible combinations of the secret pixels encoded into b_i^P and b_j^P
0	0	$2^m \times C(m, 0)$
2	1	$2^m \times C(m, 1)$
......	......	......
$2i$	i	$2^m \times C(m, i)$
......	......	......
$2m$	m	$2^m \times C(m, m)$

The best situation for attackers is $d=0$ or $2m$ for every pair of the m blocks in every set. Then, the attacking difficulty of one set declines from 2^{mm} to 2^m. Furthermore, the attacking difficulty of the secret images decreases from 2^{mXY} to 2^{XY}.

The worst situation for attackers is $d=\lceil m/2 \rceil$ or $\lfloor m/2 \rfloor$ for every pair of the m blocks in every set. Then, the attacking difficulty of one set declines from 2^{mm} to $2^m \times C(m, \lfloor m/2 \rfloor)^{m-1}$. Furthermore, the attacking difficulty of the secret images decreases from 2^{mXY} to $2^{XY} \times C(m, \lfloor m/2 \rfloor)^{m-1}$.

4   Conclusion

Although Feng et al.'s scheme can share many secret images without any distortion, the weakness of P_B and P_W threatens the security of the (2, 2, m)-MVCS seriously. Theoretical analysis and experimental results prove this argument. Furthermore, it is difficult to modify the scheme. If we use different random permutations for the m blocks in one set, the ideal security can be guaranteed, but the secret images can't be decrypted. Therefore, how to design the ideal secure (2, 2, m)-MVCS with a different method is our future work.

Acknowledgment. This work was supported by the National Natural Science Foundation of the People's Republic of China under Grant No. 61070086. The authors would like to thank the anonymous reviewers for their valuable comments.

References

1. Naor, M., Shamir, A.: Visual cryptography. In: De Santis, A. (ed.) EUROCRYPT 1994. LNCS, vol. 950, pp. 1–12. Springer, Heidelberg (1995)
2. Shamir, A.: How to share a secret. Communications of the ACM 22, 612–613 (1979)
3. Blakley, G.R.: Safeguarding cryptographic keys. In: Merwin, R.E., Zanca, J.T., Smith, M. (eds.) National Computer Conference, vol. 48, pp. 242–268. IEEE Press, New York (1979)

4. Ateniese, G., Blundo, C., Santis, A., De, S.D.R.: Visual cryptography for general access structures. Information and Computation 129, 86–106 (1996)
5. Hsu, C.-S., Tu, S.-F., Hou, Y.-C.: An optimization model for visual cryptography schemes with unexpanded shares. In: Esposito, F., Raś, Z.W., Malerba, D., Semeraro, G. (eds.) ISMIS 2006. LNCS (LNAI), vol. 4203, pp. 58–67. Springer, Heidelberg (2006)
6. Liu, F., Wu, C., Lin, X.: Step construction of visual cryptography schemes. IEEE T. Inf. Foren. Sec. 5, 27–38 (2010)
7. Shyu, S.J., Chen, M.C.: Optimum pixel expansions for threshold visual secret sharing schemes. IEEE T. Inf. Foren. Sec. 6, 960–969 (2011)
8. Yang, C.N., Wang, C.C., Chen, T.S.: Visual cryptography schemes with reversing. The Computer Journal. bxm118, 1–13 (2008)
9. Lin, C.C., Tai, W.H.: Visual cryptography for gray-level images by dithering techniques. Pattern Recognition Letters 24, 349–358 (2003)
10. Cimato, S., De Prisco, R., De Santis, A.: Optimal colored threshold visual cryptography schemes. Designs, Codes and Cryptography 35, 311–335 (2005)
11. Yang, C.N., Chen, T.S.: Colored visual cryptography scheme based on additive color mixing. Pattern Recognition 41, 3114–3129 (2008)
12. Ng, F.Y., Wong, D.S.: On the security of a visual cryptography scheme for color images. Pattern Recognition 42, 929–940 (2009)
13. Chen, L.H., Wu, C.C.: A study on visual cryptography. Master Thesis, National Chiao Tung University, Taiwan (1998)
14. Wu, H.C., Chang, C.C.: Sharing visual multi-secrets using circle shares. Computer Standards & Interfaces 28, 123–135 (2005)
15. Shyong, J.S., Huang, S.Y., Lee, Y.K., Wang, R.Z.: Sharing multiple secrets in visual cryptography. Pattern Recognition 40, 3633–3651 (2007)
16. Hsu, H.C., Chen, T.S., Lin, Y.H.: The ring shadow image technology of visual cryptography by applying diverse rotating angles to hide the secret sharing. In: Proceedings of the 2004 IEEE International Conference on Networking, Sensing & Control, pp. 996–1001. IEEE Press, New York (2004)
17. Feng, J.B., Wub, H.C., Tsaic, C.S., Chud, Y.P.: Visual secret sharing for multiple secrets. Pattern Recognition 41, 3572–3581 (2008)

An Image Super-Resolution Scheme Based on Compressive Sensing with PCA Sparse Representation

Aixin Zhang[1], Chao Guan[1], Haomiao Jiang[2], and Jianhua Li[1]

[1] School of Information Security Engineering,
Shanghai Jiao Tong University, Shanghai, P.R. China
[2] Department of Electrical Engineering,
Stanford University, CA, 94305, USA
{axzhang,gc_forever,lijh888}@sjtu.edu.cn, hjiang36@stanford.edu

Abstract. Image super-resolution (SR) reconstruction has been an important research fields due to its wide applications. Although many SR methods have been proposed, there are still some problems remain to be solved, and the quality of the reconstructed high-resolution (HR) image needs to be improved. To solve these problems, in this paper we propose an image super-resolution scheme based on compressive sensing theory with PCA sparse representation. We focus on the measurement matrix design of the CS process and the implementation of the sparse representation function for the PCA transformation. The measurement matrix design is based on the relation between the low-resolution (LR) image and the reconstructed high-resolution (HR) image. While the implementation of the PCA sparse representation function is based on the PCA transformation process. According to whether the covariance matrix of the HR image is known or not, two kinds of SR models are given. Finally the experiments comparing the proposed scheme with the traditional interpolation methods and CS scheme with DCT sparse representation are conducted. The experiment results both on the smooth image and the image with complex textures show that the proposed scheme in this paper is effective.

Keywords: Super Resolution Reconstruction, Compressive Sensing (CS), Primary Component Analysis (PCA).

1 Introduction

There is an increasing demand on the images with high pixel density, especially in the fields of military monitoring, public security controlling and medical diagnosis, etc. But sometimes the high-resolution images are difficult to get due to the inherent resolution limitations of low-cost imaging sensors. Therefore the technique of super-resolution (SR) reconstruction has been an active area of research. Nowadays various image SR schemes have been developed, which can be roughly divided into three classes: interpolation-based method, reconstruction-based method and machine-learning based method.

Y.Q. Shi, H.J. Kim, and F. Pérez-González (Eds.): IWDW 2012, LNCS 7809, pp. 495–506, 2013.

As a traditional SR approach, the interpolation-based SR is to map the LR image to the target HR image, and then to apply the non-uniform interpolation to get each pixel of HR image. Common image interpolation methods include zero-order interpolation, bilinear interpolation, bicubic interpolation [2] and so on. The shortcoming of these methods is that the generated HR images tend to be blurred with jagged edges. The reconstruction-based SR schemes normally recover the original HR image by fusing a set of LR images of the same scene. Each of the LR images imposes some linear constraints on the unknown high resolution intensity values. Thus the HR image can be reconstructed by adopting this kind of observation model. Generally speaking, the reconstruction-based SR method is a severely ill-posed problem, which means the solution from these reconstruction constraints is not unique because of the insufficient number of low resolution images. Besides the performance of this type of SR algorithms degrades rapidly when the desired magnification factor is large or the number of available input LR images is small. The third class of SR approach is based on machine learning techniques. This work is first conducted by Freeman et al. In [3] they first apply Markov network to establish the corresponding relations between the LR patches and the HR patches, and then find the optimized solution via Bayesian belief propagation. But this method is time-costing since it needs hundreds of thousands of Markov Networks. In [4] a mixed pattern combining the global parameter model with the local non-parameter model is proposed for the SR of face image.

More recently, the idea of compressed sensing (CS) is applied into SR applications. In [5] the low-resolution (LR) image is viewed as a down-sampled version of the high-resolution (HR) image, and each patch of LR image is assumed to have a sparse representation with respect to an over-complete dictionary of signal atoms. According to CS theory, the HR image can be correctly recovered from the sparse representation of LR image under some mild conditions. The experiment results demonstrate that it is effective to take the sparsity as prior knowledge for regularizing the ill-posed super-resolution problem. The works, such as [6], [7] and [8], take the similar idea of SR reconstruction. As it has been pointed out in [5] there are two questions need to be solved, one is how to decide the number of raw sample patches required to generate a dictionary satisfying the sparse representation prior, the other is how to effectively build the dictionaries that contain multiple types of textures or multiple object categories. This is mainly because of the non-adaptive characters of CS. Then several adaptive SR schemes based on CS have been proposed. The concept of examples-aided redundant dictionary learning are introduced into the single-image SR reconstruction in [9], and the compact redundant dictionaries are learned from samples classified by K-means clustering in order to provide each sample an appropriate dictionary. This scheme needs huge computation, so the multi-task learning for the redundant dictionary learning and sparse representation is adopted. [10] proposes an image de-blurring and super-resolution method with adaptive sparse domain selection and adaptive regularization. In this scheme, to represent the underlying image better with a proper sparse domain, various sets of bases are learned from a pre-collected dataset of example image patches, and one set of bases are adaptively selected to characterize the local sparse domain for a given patch to be processed. A texture constrained sparse representation for single image super resolution is given in [11]. This method requires some texture databases be prepared in advance. First, the low resolution image is segmented into different texture regions which are classified into different texture categories using the designed texture classifier. Then the high resolution segments are reconstructed by sparse representation with relevant texture dictionaries. It is obviously that all of these adaptive SR schemes are computationally intensive. In this paper we try to look for a simpler approach for the CS based super-resolution reconstruction without degrading the quality of the recovered HR image.

It is well known that the CS framework consists of three parts: sparse representation, sampling procedure and reconstruction. The sparse representation is to represent the natural signal on a certain transform basis or a tight frame to get its sparse form. During the sampling procedure, by choosing a sampling matrix, we can get the measurements of the original signal with a much lower dimension but contain the most important information. The reconstruction is a process of recovering the original signal from its measurements as accurately as possible. The common CS process is non-adaptive. One of the reasons is that the sparse representation methods adopted are non-adaptive. Although the dictionary-learning based approach has been applied in the sparse transformation stage, it also brings the problems of large computation and extra memory cost. As a typical adaptive data analysis method, the principal component analysis (PCA) transformation can reserve more texture and detail of an image compared with the fixed basis transformation, and the computation of PCA transformation is much less than the dictionary based representation. So in this paper we choose the PCA domain for sparse representation in the CS process. There are three steps during the PCA analysis, which are the feature matrix computation by the covariance matrix of signal, the transformation matrix design through the feature matrix and the restoration of the signal. It is obvious that the covariance matrix of signal plays an important role in the PCA analysis. Whether the covariance matrix can be predicted or not depends on different practical applications. Thus two SR models based on the CS taking PCA as sparse basis are discussed according to the facts that covariance matrix of the signal is known or not. The experiment results demonstrate that the proposed schemes perform better compared with the SR based on normal CS and the traditional interpolation-based SR method.

The rest of the paper is organized as follows. In Section 2, the theory of PCA and CS are introduced briefly. Section 3 illustrates the proposed SR mode in detail. The simulation results are discussed in section 4. Finally, the conclusion is considered in section 5.

2   Brief Overview of PCA and CS

Since the SR scheme we proposed here is based on the CS theory adopting PCA sparse representation, so in this section we first review the PCA foundation and the CS procedure briefly.

2.1   The PCA Foundation

Principle Component Analysis (PCA) is a widely used signal processing algorithm, which can be used to largely reduce the correlation between the sampled signals. It is also a self-adapting algorithm due to the fact that different transformation matrix are used in accordance with the signal during the PCA analysis procedure. Meanwhile, the PCA is of lower complexity and less calculation.

For the signal $X=(x_1, x_2, \ldots, x_m)^T$, $x_i \in R^n$, the PCA process can be briefly introduced as follows.

First X can be denoted by

$$X = \begin{bmatrix} x_1^1 & x_1^2 & \cdots & x_1^n \\ x_2^1 & x_2^2 & \cdots & x_2^n \\ \vdots & \vdots & \vdots & \vdots \\ x_m^1 & x_m^2 & \cdots & x_m^n \end{bmatrix} \tag{1}$$

Denote the i-th row of X as $X_i = [\, x_i^1 \; x_i^2 \; \ldots \; x_i^n \,]$, then the mean value of X_i can be calculated as

$$u_i = \frac{1}{n}\sum_{j=1}^{n} x_i^j \tag{2}$$

So X_i can be centralized as

$$\overline{X}_i = X_i - u_i = [\, \overline{x_i^1} \; \overline{x_i^2} \; \ldots \; \overline{x_i^n} \,] \tag{3}$$

where $\overline{x_i^j} = x_i^j - u_i$. Accordingly, the centralized matrix of X is

$$\overline{X} = [\overline{X}_1^T \; \overline{X}_2^T \; \ldots \; \overline{X}_m^T]^T \tag{4}$$

Then compute the covariance matrix Ω of $\overline{X}$ as

$$\Omega = \frac{1}{n}\overline{X}\overline{X}^T \tag{5}$$

Since Ω is symmetrical, it can be written as:

$$\Omega = \Theta \Lambda \Theta^T \tag{6}$$

where $\Theta = [\, \theta_1 \; \theta_2 \; \ldots \; \theta_m \,]$ is the m×m orthonormal eigenvector matrix and $\Lambda = \mathrm{diag}\{\lambda_1, \lambda_2, \ldots, \lambda_m\}$ is the diagonal eigenvalue matrix with $\lambda_1 \geq \lambda_2 \geq \ldots \geq \lambda_m$.

The goal of PCA is to find an orthonormal transformation matrix P to de-rrelate $\overline{X}$.

By setting

$$P = \Theta^T$$
(7)

We can finally get

$$\overline{Y} = P \overline{X}$$
(8)

$$\Lambda = \frac{1}{n} \overline{Y} \, \overline{Y}^T$$
(9)

And the inverse PCA transformation can be performed as:

$$\overline{X} = P^T \overline{Y}$$
(10)

2.2   The CS Theory

Compressive sensing theory [12] suggests that it is possible to perfectly recover a signal from significantly fewer samples or measurements, given that the signal can be represented by a small number of non-zero coefficients in some basis. Considering the fact that image super-resolution is a kind of typical inverse problems, which tries to obtain a high resolution image from its low resolution version, CS offers a theoretical framework for the SR problem. The procedure of CS contains three steps: sparse representation, sampling and sparse recovery.

The sparse representation is to transform the signal $x \in \mathbb{R}^N$ onto a basis $\Psi \in \mathbb{R}^{N \times N}$ to get a k-sparse representation $S \in \mathbb{R}^N$. That is,

$$x = \Psi S$$
(11)

where S can be well approximated using only $k \ll N$ non-zero entries.

Secondly, design the sampling matrix Φ with size of M×N ($M \ll N$) which is incoherent to Ψ. By analyzing the structure of the sampling device, the sampled measurements y can be as :

$$y = \Phi x$$
(12)

where y is an M×1 measurement vector.

Thirdly, recover the original signal x from its measurement y. If the measurement matrix Φ satisfies the Restricted Isometry Property (RIP), The signal can be reconstructed by solving the following optimization problem:

$$\min \|S\|_1 \quad \text{s.t. } y = \Phi \Psi S$$
(13)

As far as the CS scheme proposed in this paper, the sparse representation is achieved via PCA transformation.

3   The SR Model Based on CS Adopting PCA Sparse Representation

In the view of the theory of CS, the SR reconstruction problem can be defined as:

$$\min\|S\|_1 \quad \text{s.t. } y = \Phi \Psi S \tag{14}$$

where $\mathbf{Y}$ is the measured LR image, Φ represents the sampling matrix and $\Psi \mathbf{S}$ is the HR image in the PCA sparse representation form. Thus the main points of the SR model proposed in this paper lie on the design of sampling matrix and the sparse representation model. In this section, we will give a detailed description of the SR model based on CS adopting PCA sparse representation.

3.1   The Sampling Matrix Design

It is obviously that we can get the LR image $\mathbf{Y}$ from the corresponding HR image $\mathbf{X}$ after being sampled by matrix Φ. Thus the design of Φ is an importatnt component of the proposed SR scheme. For simplicity, we just assume that the length and the height of the HR image $\mathbf{X}$ is as twice as that of the LR image $\mathbf{Y}$ respectively. Suppose $\mathbf{X} \in R^{N^2 \times 1}$, $\mathbf{Y} \in R^{(N/2)^2 \times 1}$ and the sampling matrix $\Phi = [\varphi_1 \ \varphi_2 \ ... \ \varphi_N]$, φ_i is the column vector of Φ and $\varphi_i = [\phi_i^1 \ \phi_i^2 \ ... \ \phi_i^N]^T$. A direct way of getting $\mathbf{Y}$ from $\mathbf{X}$ is to set the value of each pixel in $\mathbf{Y}$ as the average value of the four pixels at the corresponding position in $\mathbf{X}$. Thus the samping matrix of the SR scheme proposed here can be defined as:

$$\phi_i^j = \begin{cases} 1/4, & j = \lceil i/2 \rceil \bmod (N^2/4) \\ 0, & \text{otherwise} \end{cases} \tag{15}$$

Next, we will discuss the sparse representation problem in detail.

3.2   The PCA Sparse Representation Model

The design of the sparse representation model is equal to the design of the sparse transformation basis Ψ.

$$\Psi : S \rightarrow X \tag{16}$$

Here we try to give the PCA sparse representation function. From section 2.1, we can see the PCA analyze process is to find an orthonormal transformation matrix $\mathbf{P}$, and the computation of $\mathbf{P}$ depends on the covariance matrix of the signal under analyzed. But in some certain situations, the covariance matrix cannot be known beforehand. So we will discuss two cases according to the covariance matrix is known or not.

3.2.1   The Sparse Representation Model When Covariance Matrix Is Known

In some applications, it is possible to known the covariance matrix beforehand. For example the covariance matrix can be predicted dynamically in the Wireless Sensor Networks (WSN). In such cases when the covariance matrix is known, the sparse representation function works as Fig.1. Considering the cost of computation and memory, we apply the block-PCA implementation in the SR scheme.

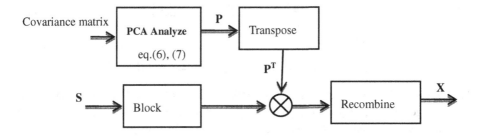

Fig. 1. The function of sparse representation Ψ when the covariance matrix is known

As can be seen from Fig.1, for the input S, the function of Ψ is to treat S with inverse PCA transformation using the block algorithm.

Besides, according to CS theory, the inverse transformation Ψ^{-1} is needed to solve (16). It can be infered easily that Ψ^{-1} is actually a block PCA transformation, which is showed in Fig.2.

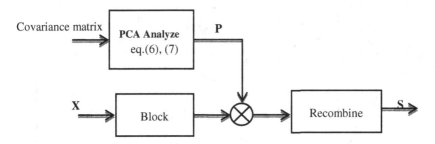

Fig. 2. The inverse transformation function Ψ^{-1} when the covariance matrix is known

It should be pointed out that different sizes of blocks perform differently in the proposed SR schem, which will be showed in section 4.

3.2.2   The Sparse Representation Model When Covariance Matrix Is Unknown

In the situation when the covariance matrix is not available, we should get the covariance matrix using eq.(2)-(5) firstly, and then to perform the PCA transform adopting eq.(6)-(7). In this section we will straightforwardly establish the sparse representation model for the SR problem.

For an image I with the size of $2N \times 2N$,

$$I = \{I_{ij}\}_{i,j=1}^{2N} \tag{17}$$

We can divide I into four sub-images I'_1, I'_2, I'_3 and I'_4 as follows

$$I_{ij} \in I'_p, \quad p = 4 - (i \bmod 2) - 2 \times (j \bmod 2) \tag{18}$$

From above we can see

$$U_{p=1}^4 I'_p = I, \quad I'_i \cap I'_j = \emptyset \; (i \neq j; i,j = 1,2,3 \text{ or } 4) \tag{19}$$

and each sub-image is of the same size as that of the LR image. Furthermore all of the sub-images and the LR image have the similar structure and texture. So the PCA transformation of the LR image approximate to the PCA transformation of one of the sub-images.

Therefore the function of sparse representation Ψ can be got as Fig.3 shows.

Similarly, the inverse transformation Ψ^{-1} can be defined as Fig.4.

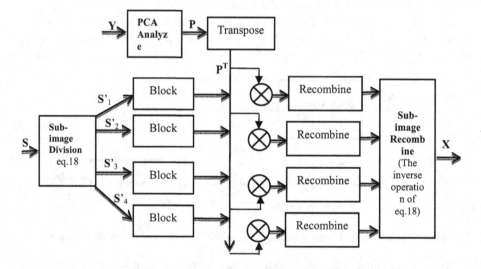

Fig. 3. The function of sparse representation Ψ when the covariance matrix is unknown

Similarly, the inverse transformation Ψ^{-1} can be defined as Fig.4.

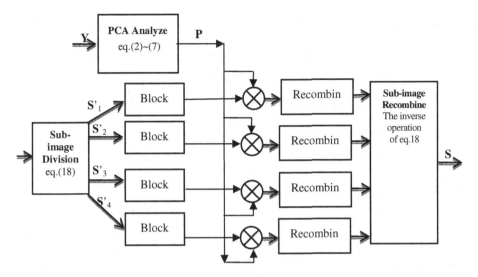

Fig. 4. The inverse transformation function Ψ^{-1} when the covariance matrix is unknown

4   Experimental Results

In this section, we will demonstrate the effects of the proposed SR scheme both on the smooth image and the image with complicated textures. The experiments are conducted on two kinds of situations (the covariance matrix is known or not) respectively. And also we will compare the proposed SR method with the traditional Bicubic algorithm and the CS based SR scheme using DCT sparse transformation.

4.1   The Experiments on Smooth Image

We choose the picture "boat" for experiment. The size of the HR image and the LR image is 256*256 and 128*128, respectively. Here we attempt to recover the HR image from the LR image.

a. HR image of "boat"   b. LR image of "boat"

Fig. 5. The HR and LR image of "boat"

The results are showed in Table.1.

Table 1. The experiment results on smooth image

	The Proposed Scheme				
	Covariance Matrix is Known			Covariance Matrix is Unknown	
	Block No	Block 16*16	Block 64*64	Block 16*16	Block 64*64
PSNR	27.18	30.52	28.98	26.85	28.52
	CS With DCT Transformation			The Interpolation Models		
	Block No	Block 16*16	Block 64*64	Nei-ghbor	linear	Bi-cubic
PSNR	29.98	26.52	27.15	27.54	29.25	29.78

From Table 1 we can see that the proposed SR scheme with known covariance matrix performs the best when the block size is 16×16. As for the proposed SR model with known covariance matrix, the smaller PCA block is, the better result will be. While for the proposed SR model when the covariance matrix is unknown, the bigger the block is, the better SR result will be obtained. For the SR scheme adopting the CS with DCT sparse re[resentation, however, the method without blocking the image get the highest PSNR value. We can also find that the Bicubic SR method performs best among the interpolation models. Some reconstructed HR images are listed in Fig.6.

a. The proposed SR with known covariance matrix
16*16 blocks

b. The proposed SR with unknown covariance matrix
64*64 blocks

c. Bicubic method

d. The SR adopting CS with DCT sparse representation

Fig. 6. The experiments on smooth image "boat"

4.2   The Experiments on the Image with Complex Textures

The texture picture "Barbara" are selected for experiments. The size of the HR image and LR image is 512*512 and 256*256 respectively.

a. HR image of "Barbara"   b. LR image of "Barbara"

Fig. 7. The HR and LR image of "Barbara"

The SR experiments results are showed in Table 2.

From above we can draw the similar conclusions as that in section 4.1. Some reconstructed HR images are listed in Fig.8.

Table 2. The experiment results on texture image

		The Proposed Scheme				
		Covariance Matrix is Known			Covariance Matrix is Unknown	
		Block No	Block 16*16	Block 64*64	Block 16*16	Block 64*64
PSNR		24.31	26.70	26.00	23.32	25.56
		CS With DCT Transformation			The Interpolation Models	
		Block No	Block 16*16	Block 64*64	Nei-ghbor	linear	Bi-cubic
PSNR		23.52	22.46	22.48	24.99	24.84	24.80

a. The proposed SR with known covariance matrix   b. The proposed SR with unknown covariance matrix
16*16 blocks   64*64 blocks

c. Bicubic method   d. The SR adopting CS with DCT sparse representation

Fig. 8. The experiments on texture image "Barbara"

5   Conclusion

The image super-resolution scheme based on the CS theory adopting the PCA sparse representation is proposed in this paper. The main points of the proposed scheme are the design of the measurement matrix and the sparse transformation function during the CS process. According to whether the covariance matrix is known or not, two kinds of SR models are proposed. The experiments on the smooth image and texture image have proved that the proposed scheme is effective. Thus it is feasible to apply the CS with PCA sparse representation on the image super-resolution. We can also infer that the CS and PCA can be adopted in many other image process fields, such as the forensics, the retrieval and digital rights management of images and videos.

Acknowledgements. This work is supported by the National Basic Research Program of China (2010CB731403, 2010CB731406), the National Science Foundation of China (61071081, 61071152 and 61171173), the National "Twelfith Five-Year Plan" for Science & Technology Support (2012BAH38B04) and the Opening Project of Key Lab of Information Network Security of Ministry of Public Security (C12608).

References

1. Tsai, R.Y., Huang, T.S.: Multiple frame image restoration and registration. In: Advances in Computer Vision and Image Processing, pp. 317–339. JAI Press, Greenwich (1984)
2. Hou, H.S., Andrews, H.C.: Cubic spline for image interpolation and digital filtering. IEEE Trans. Signal Process. 26(6), 508–517 (1978)
3. Freeman, W.T., Pasztor, E.C., Carmichael, O.T.: Learning low-level vision. IJCV, 1182–1189 (2000)
4. Liu, C., Shum, H.Y., Zhang, C.S.: Two-step approach to hallucinating faces: global parametric model and local nonparametric model. In: CVPR (2001)
5. Yang, J., Wright, J.: Image super-resolution as sparse representation of raw image patches. In: CVPR (2008)
6. Yang, J., Wright, J., Huang, T., Ma, Y.: Image Super-Resolution via Sparse Representation. IEEE Transaction on Image Processing 19(11), 2861–2873 (2010)
7. Sun, G., Qin, C.: Single Image Super-Resolution via Sparse Representation in Gradient Domain. In: Third International Conference on Multimedia Information Networking and Security (MINES), pp. 24–28 (2011)
8. Jing, G., Shi, Y., Lu, B.: Single-Image Super-Resolution Based on Decomposition and Sparse Representation. In: International Conference on Multimedia Communications (Mediacom), pp. 127–130 (2010)
9. Yang, S., Liu, Z., Wang, M., Sun, F., Jiao, L.: Multitask dictionary learning and sparse representation based single-image super-resolution reconstruction. Neurocomputing 74, 3193–3203 (2011)
10. Dong, W., Zhang, L., Shi, G., Wu, X.: Image deblurring and super-resolution by adaptive sparse domain selection and adaptive regularization. IEEE Transactions on Image Processing 20(7), 1838–1856 (2011)
11. Yin, H., Li, S., Hu, J.: Single Image Super Resolution via Texture Constrained Sparse Representation. In: ICIP 2011, 1161–1164 (2011)
12. Donoho, D.L.: Compressed Sensing. IEEE Transactions on Information Theory 52(4), 1289–1306 (2006)

A Novel JFE Scheme for Social Multimedia Distribution in Compressed Domain Using SVD and CA

Conghuan Ye[1,2], Hefei Ling[1], Fuhao Zou[1], Zhengding Lu[1],
Zenggang Xiong[2], and Kaibing Zhang[2]

[1] College of Computer Science, Huazhong University of Science & Technology, Wuhan, China
[2] College of Computer and Information Science, Hubei Engineering University, Xiaogan, China
p2pgrid@gmail.com

Abstract. The advent of social networks has made social media sharing in social network easier. However, it can also cause serious security and privacy problems, secure media sharing and traitor tracing issues have become critical and urgent. In this paper, a joint fingerprinting and encryption (JFE) scheme based on Game of Life (GF) and singular value decomposition (SVD) with the purpose of protecting content distribution in social networks. Firstly, the fingerprint code is produced using social network analysis. Secondly, fingerprints are embedded into the LL, HL and LH subbands. At last, GF and SVD are used to for confusion and diffusion respectively. The proposed method, to the best of our knowledge, is the first JFE method using GF and SVD in the compressed domain for security and privacy. The use of fingerprinting along with encryption can provide a double-layer of protection to media sharing in social network environment. Theory analysis and experimental results show the effectiveness of the proposed JFE scheme.

Keywords: fingerprinting, encryption, social media sharing, SVD, cellular automata, social network.

1 Introduction

Social media distribution offer distinctive challenges for social network such as privacy and security issues. Multimedia encryption and digital watermarking are two typical ones for content protect [1]. Encryption is one way which may ensure the content security and prevent an unauthorized access [2]. However, the well known RSA, AES, and DES seem not desirable to be applied to multimedia encryption and do not meet the real-time constraint of social media sharing in social networks [3]. But multimedia encryption algorithms based on chaos may often be "lightweight" in order to accommodate computational complexity restrictions [3]. In recent years, there is an increasing trend of designing multimedia content encryption algorithms based on chaotic maps [4, 5]. The desired security disappears after the data are decrypted into clear text [6, 7]. Once the ciphered data is deciphered by the authorized user, it is unprotected, and it is still possible for a legal user to deliver decrypted data to an unauthorized user for some purposes. In this case, extra protection schemes should be

Y.Q. Shi, H.J. Kim, and F. Pérez-González (Eds.): IWDW 2012, LNCS 7809, pp. 507–519, 2013.
© Springer-Verlag Berlin Heidelberg 2013

adopted to deter content redistribution. In fact, watermarking [1] is another technology which enables the owner to embed some information in the contents to protect copyright further.

Since none of encryption and watermarking alone can provide the protection. D. Bouslimi et al. proposed a joint encryption/watermarking algorithm for medical images [8], in this model, the malicious staff member can be tracked by a watermarked clue. An interactive buyer-seller watermarking protocol for invisible watermarking was proposed in [9]. But watermarking can't trace somebody who redistributed the copies. Fingerprinting, which was first introduced by Wagner [10] in 1983, can do that. Digital fingerprinting is an emerging technology to embed the information related to a buyer into a given multimedia content through the process of robust digital watermarking [7]. Embedding of unique customer identification as a watermark into data is called fingerprinting which is used to identify adversary who leak copies of the content, represents the ID of a user [11, 12]. In this case, fingerprinting can be regarded as another cryptologic mechanism for the copyright protection of digital data. Although the approach of embedding and extracting fingerprints is similar to that of watermarking. Basically, watermarks embedded into multimedia data for enforcing copyrights [13] must uniquely identify the data, but fingerprinting is aimed at traitor tracing [14].

There are some related works about joint fingerprinting and encryption for multimedia content protection. Kundur et al.[3] proposed a novel architecture for joint fingerprinting and decryption that holds promise for a better compromise between practicality and security. In [7], the authors investigated the secure multicast of anti-collusion fingerprinted video in streaming applications. In [15], the proposed scheme was a combination of a broadcast encryption scheme, a fingerprinting scheme and an encryption scheme inspired by the Chameleon cipher, the protection scheme could provide confidentiality, traceability and renewability in the context of broadcast encryption. In [16], a scheme integrating anti-collusion code and Home Page PKC was described. In [17], a new genetic fingerprinting scheme was proposed for copyright protection of multicast video. In the scheme, multimedia contents are scrambled based on genetic algorithms. The encrypted content is decrypted and immediately fingerprinted with a distinct mark at the receiver. Lian SG et al.[18, 19] proposed schemes, which include fingerprinting, encryption, and encoding, to distribute multimedia content. A joint fingerprinting and decryption (JFD) scheme based on vector quantization is proposed with the purpose of protecting media distribution [14].

However, all the above schemes didn't be applied to security and privacy for social network. How to use social network analysis to embed fingerprint information in encrypted contents and how to make the content sharing system robust against attacks is not deeply considered. Undoubtedly, safeguarding privacy and security of personal information in social network is still in its infancy.

CA (Cellular automata) is capable of developing chaotic behavior using simple operations or rules offering the benefit of high speed computation, which makes CA an interesting platform for digital image scrambling [20]. Fast computation helps in achieving this capability. SVD performs an optimal matrix decomposition in a least-square domain for matrices in real number domain. Moreover, it uses non-fixed orthogonal bases in contrast to some other unitary transformations which adopt fixed orthogonal bases.

To encrypt the important data only, transform domain algorithm can improve the encryption speed, but the encryption effect is weaker obviously. In practice, permutation and diffusion are often combined in order to get high computational security. A novel JFE algorithm based on GF and SVD in DWT domains is proposed. According to our best knowledge, there has been no report yet on the implantation of JFE scheme based on GF and SVD for secure content sharing in social network environment. Basic theory is introduced in section 2. In section 3, we discuss the proposed methods and show the performance of the scheme. In Section 4, we present its security. We conclude our paper and provide suggestions for future work in Section 5.

2   Basic Theory of the Proposed Scheme

2.1   SVD

SVD [21] is a very useful tool in linear algebra, which   is a factorization and approximation technique. From the perspective of image processing, an image can be viewed as a matrix with non negative scalar entries. Mathematically, SVD of a rectangular matrix A is expressed as

$$A = USV^T \qquad (1)$$

where S is also known as singular value matrix in SVD domain, U and V are the unitary matrices. Both of U and V components are composed of eigenvectors of matrix A,   and T represents the conjugate transpose operation. U and V are also orthogonal matrices. Therefore, the following conditions are always satisfied

$$I_N = U^T U = U U^T \qquad (2)$$

$$I_M = V^T V = V V^T \qquad (3)$$

where I_N and I_M are identity matrices with size $N \times N$ and $M \times M$, respectively.

2.2   Chaotic Maps

1D Logistic map is an example chaotic map, it is described as $x_{n+1} = u x_n (1 - x_n)$ where $u \in$ [0,4], $x_n \in$ (0,1), n=0,1,2,... the research result shows that the system is in a chaotic state under the condition that $3.56994 < u \leq 4$.

The PWLCM can be described in Eq. (4):

$$y_{n+1} = F(y_n, \eta) = \begin{cases} y_n / \eta, & 0 \le y_n < \eta \\ (y_n - \eta)/(0.5 - \eta), & \eta \le y_n < 0.5 \\ 0, & y_n = 0.5 \\ F(1 - y_n, \eta), & 0.5 \le y_n < 1 \end{cases} \qquad (4)$$

where $y_n \in (0,1)$, n=0,1,2,..., when control parameter $\eta \in (0, 0.5)$, Eq. (4) evolves into a chaotic state, η can be served as a secret key.

2.3   Cellular Automata

CA [20] are dynamical complex space and time discrete systems. The (2-D) CA called the GF, which consists of an $[M \times N]$ matrix of cells, where each cell may take only two states: alive and dead (respectively represented by one and zero). At every time step, all the cells update their states synchronously by applying rules (transition function). Each cell has eight neighbors which are the cells that are horizontally, vertically, or diagonally adjacent. Each cell computes its new state by applying the following transition rules.

   (1) Any live cell with fewer than two live neighbors dies
   (2) Any live cell with two or three live neighbors lives on to the next generation.
   (3) Any live cell with more than three live neighbors dies, as if by overcrowding.
   (4) Any dead cell with exactly three live neighbors becomes a live cell, as if by reproduction.

3   The Proposed JFE Scheme

3.1   Encoding Using Social Network Analysis

A graph $G = (V, E)$, to model social networks, can be completely described by giving the adjacency matrix A , whose entry a_{ij} (i, j=1, ..., |V|) is equal to 1 when the link l_{ij} exists, and zero otherwise. Given a graph $G=(V,E)$ with |V| nodes, the objective of classical algorithms for identifying community in a social network is finding a partition $P = \{S_1, S_2, ..., S_c\}$, c is the number of communities shown in Fig.1. Given a social network, we first decompose the set of users into hierarchical and overlapping communities. Fingerprint code design plays an important role in resist collusion attacks which is a cost-efficient attack for fingerprinting schemes, where illegal users compare several copies with the same content but different fingerprints for the purpose of attenuating or removing the fingerprints. The dendrogram of social network can provide a good concatenated fingerprinting code design by the tree-based fingerprint scheme to reduce the length of code. In this design, users are grouped into a dendrogram structure. At last, users who are likely to collude are in the same community and own the same community code segment which is regarded as multilevel outer code.

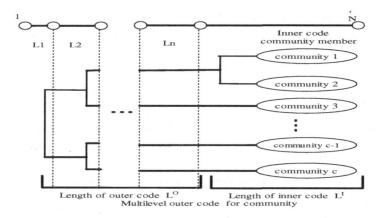

Fig. 1. Encoding using social network analysis

3.2   DWT

In DWT transform, an image is split into one approximation (also called LL sub-band) and three details in horizontal, vertical, and diagonal directions which are named (or coefficients in LH subband), (coefficients in HL subband), and (coefficients in HH subband). The LL subband is then itself split into a second-level approximation and details, and the process is repeated.

3.3   The JFE Scheme

Generally, two properties of secure content sharing in social network need to be protected, i.e., confidentiality and redistribution tracing. Cryptography techniques transform content into an enciphered, unintelligible form for secure sharing among users [3] ;   while the redistribution tracing is often protected by digital fingerprinting. Most of the time, they have been researched independently since their fundamental roles are quite distinct. However, an untrustworthy user may distribute the decrypted contents to the third side without permission of owner. In this case, the privacy of owner may be infringed.   Protecting contents from illegal use is imperative in the whole distribution process since digital social media contents are easy to be manipulated by copying and redistributing without quality distortion[16]. The convergence of the two technologies is now facilitating privacy and security studies. In [8], encryption and fingerprinting are considered together to trace content during its distribution. From this stand point, encryption, rather appear as an "a priori" protection mechanism; watermarking is an "a posteriori" control mechanism.

Now, we focus on how to integrate them for building a secure content sharing mechanism in social network. The highest-level approximation in DWT domain, which is used to embed the inner code part of fingerprints, is called the base content, and the other coefficients used to embed the community code, are represented as supplementary contents. First, fingerprints are embedded into the coefficients. Second, the fingerprinted contents are encrypted totally via CA permutation process and SVD diffusion process.

3.3.1   Fingerprint Embedding and Traitor Tracing

In order to embed fingerprinting information in the contents, a watermarking technique should be applied. In this paper, we focus on blind watermarking to embed fingerprints because the watermark is detected without reference to the original once a pirated image was found. Considering the robustness against attacks, the fingerprint should be embedded in the DWT domain. For watermarking techniques, a QIM method [22] is useful as a fingerprint can be embedded when the coefficients are quantized. In order to preserve the perceptual quality of the fingerprinted image, each coefficient to be embedded into fingerprint is quantized adaptively by a specially customized quantization step size.

Suppose N_u is a set of users. We choose the robust coefficients in all LH- level and LH- level subbands to combine a vector, $X^O = (x_1, x_2, ..., x_{L^O})$, as host signals to imbed community fingerprint code, and choose another robust coefficients sequence in LL subband to combine vector, $X^I = (x_1, x_2, ..., x_{L^I})$, where L^O and L^I is the length of outer codeword and inner codeword respectively, so the length of fingerprint code is $L = L^O + L^I$ the outer codeword hiding scheme are described in Eq. (5), the inner codeword embedding scheme is similar to that of the outer codeword.

$$Y_k = Q_\Delta(X_k^O + W_k + d_k) - W_k - d_k, k = 1, 2, ..., N_u \tag{5}$$

where $Q_\Delta(\bullet)$ is the quantization function with step size Δ, W_k is the fingerprint information for user k, d_k, a dither sequence denoted as of length L^O follows a uniformly distribution over ($-\Delta/2$, $\Delta/2$).

In our implementation, we apply minimum-distance detector from Eq.(6) to trace the traitor who leaked information. The L robust coefficients extracted from all LH-level and LH- level subbands, and LL subband compose a long vector Z with size L. By deducting, the difference is as follow:

$$\hat{m} = \arg\min_{k=1,2,...N_u} \|Z - Y_k\|^2 \tag{6}$$

with the above detector, the $\hat{m}$ th user is declared as a traitor.

3.3.2   Encryption and Decryption Algorithm

Social media encryption should be not only secure against cryptographic attacks but also secure in human perception [1]. To limit the unauthorized viewing of images and videos, the more degraded their visual quality is, the higher the security is [16].

Well-known traditional encryption algorithms, such as DES ,AES, RSA, ElGamal, PKC are considered computationally infeasible for high volumes of multimedia content [3]. In this paper, a smaller subset of the important content in the DWT domain is encrypted to lower computation and delay while integrating the fingerprinting with encryption. CA is capable of developing chaotic behavior for image scrambling using simple rules offering the benefit of high speed computation [20]. SVD performs an optimal matrix decomposition in a least-square domain for matrices in real number domain. To overcome the drawbacks of conventional permutation-only type image cipher, a novel image encryption based on CA and SVD in DWT domain is proposed in Fig. 2. The encryption process is composed of substitution with GF and diffusion based on SVD of random matrix in DWT domain. The proposed encryption algorithm can be divided into the following steps:

Step 1: We calculate the one-level DWT coefficient matrix of the compressed image I. Then we can get four sub-bands: the approximation coefficients LL, and the detailed coefficients HL, LH, HH. The low-frequency LL subband of the one-level DWT is a down-sampled image of the origin image. Perform two-level DWT decomposition on the LL subband;

Step 2: Use logistic map to generate sequences ($x_1 x_2 \cdots x_{M/4 \times N/4}$) respectively, where x_0 and u are given in advance as keys. Then we create a two-dimensional grids of cells G^0, as the seeds of GF by the sequences, the rule is that if the value of x_i is bigger than the mean value of the sequence, the corresponding cell is alive, else dead. Where G^0 is used to permute the DWT transformed coefficient matrixes; An $M \times N$ GF automaton is set up with an initial random configuration A_0, and is set to run for k generations, thus obtaining $\{A_1, A_2, ..., A_k\}$ matrices, at each step in time, the proposed permuted algorithm can be described as follows:

(1) Let I_G denote the matrix grid, then getting the patches set of $\{Pl_1, Pl_2, ..., Pl_k\}$ in the original matrix. For every Pl_r in the patches set (for $r = 1, ..., m$). Let Pl_r denote the input patch; Cp_r denotes the output permuted patches and A_1 is the first generation produced by the GF. Set row=1, col=1.

(2) For all (i, j) such that $A_1(i, j) = 1$, take the value of element P_e (row, col), put it in $Cp_r(i, j)$, and increment (row, col) with row-first order to point to the next element in the input matrix. For $p = 2, ..., k$, for all i, j such that $A_p(i, j) = 1$ and $A_n(i, j) = 0$ (for $n = 1, ..., p-1$), take the value of element P_e (row, col), put it in $Cp_r(i, j)$, and increment (row, col) to point to the next pixel.

Step 3: When producing the k th generation G^k by the rules of GF, the corresponding plain coefficients are put to the scrambling matrix one by one.

Step 4: After R rounds iteration, we stop and put the rest of the value into the scrambling coeffcient matrix;

Step 5: To protect content further, diffusion processes with the PWLCM map and SVD can enhance the resistance to attack. Using the PWLCM map to generate chaotic sequences $FP_{M \times N}^{J^K} = \{ fp_1^{J^K}, fp_2^{J^K}, ..., fp_{M \times N}^{J^K} \}$, then we can get the sequences $CP_{M \times N}^{J^K} = \{ cp_1^{J^K}, cp_2^{J^K}, ..., cp_{M \times N}^{J^K} \}$, cp_i =ceiling(fp_i), which is one-to-one correspondent with the coefficient sequence in DWT domain; where J denotes decomposition level, $k = \{LL\}$.

Step 6: The obtained chaotic sequence $CP_{M \times N}^{J^K}$ is arranged in the form of a matrix of dimension $M \times N$, which is denoted by CPK , as a random matrix. Perform SVD on CPK ,   we get $CPK = U_{CPK} V_{CPK} V_{CPK}^T$

Step 7: Deform all coefficients of each subband using orthonormal matrices U_{CPK} and V_{CPK}^T , as

$$I_K^E = \begin{cases} U_{CPK} I_K V_{CPK}^T, M \leq N \\ V_{CPK} I_K U_{CPK}^T, M > N \end{cases}$$

Step 8: After fingerprints are embedded, perform two-level IDWT reconstruction with the encrypted wavelet transform coefficients. We can get the scrambled and finger-printed image I^{JFE} .

Image decryption algorithm is as follows:

Step 1: Perform two-level DWT decomposition on the image I^{JFE} . We can get the scrambled and fingerprinted image $\hat{I}_K^{JFE}$;

Step 2: Perform inverse deformation on coefficients of every subband, as follows

$$\tilde{I}_K^{JFE} = \begin{cases} U_{CPK}^T \hat{I}_K^{JFE} V_{CPK}, M \leq N \\ V_{CPK}^T \hat{I}_K^{JFE} U_{CPK}, M > N \end{cases}$$

Step 3: Use Step 2, Step 3, and Step 4 in encryption process to reverse the permutation of the DWT transformed coefficient matrixes;

Step 4: Perform two-level IDWT reconstruction with the decrypted wavelet transform coefficients matrixes. We can get the fingerprinted image I^F .

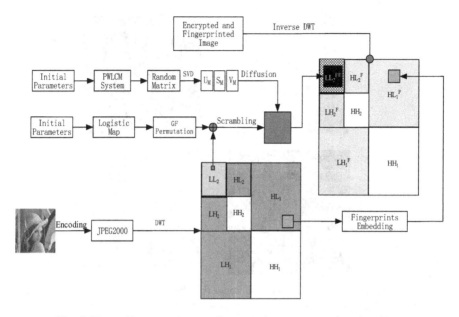

Fig. 2. The architecture of image fingerprinting and encryption algorithm

4   Experiment Results and Security Analysis

We set parameters x_0 =0.987636945231, u =3.99857324256, y_0 = 0.457641243242, η =0.459677893132. Fig. 3(a) shows the original image, the encrypted image is shown in Fig. 3(b). Fig. 3(c), (d) show the decrypted image under the wrong secret key and the correct key, respectively. From the result of our experiment, we can see it is difficult to recognize the original image from Fig. 3(b), Fig. 3(c) shows that we can not recover the image with the wrong secret key. It is obvious that our algorithm achieves good encryption.

4.1   Perceptual Security

Generally, the encrypted image should be unintelligible for confidentiality. In the proposed scheme, the LL coefficients in DWT domain are encrypted by permutation via GF firstly. Then the scrambled values of coefficients are changed using SVD. The visual impact of the proposed encryption scheme is demonstrated in Fig.3 (b). It is clear that all the encrypted images become noise-like images and are all actually unintelligible. Therefore, the proposed scheme indeed possessed high perceptual security.

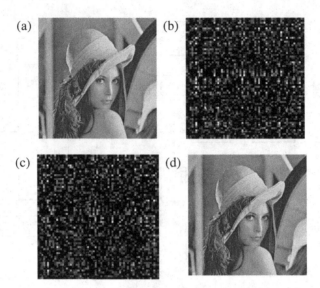

Fig. 3. Experimental result: (a) The original image (b) The encrypted image (c) The decrypted image with a different initial value (d) The decrypted fingerprinted image with correct keys.

4.2   Imperceptibility of the Fingerprint

The fingerprint is embedded in the image during the decryption process. In order to preserve visual quality, the fingerprint in the fingerprinted copy should be imperceptible and perceptually undetectable. Fig. 3(d) shows some experimental results of decrypted fingerprinted images. It can be observed that the quality of the fingerprinted image doesn't have any change observably.

4.3   Ability of Resisting Exhaustive Attack

The total key space includes two processes of confusion and diffusion. Our encryption algorithm actually does have some of the following secret keys: (1) Initial values x_0 (Logistic map), y_0 (PWLCM system); (2) Parameters u (Logistic map), η (PWLCM system), k; (3) The iteration times R. The sensitivity to x_0, y_0, u and η is considered as 10^{-16} [23], The total key space is about $10^{16 \times 4} = 10^{64}$. This key space is large enough to resist the brute-force attack.

4.4   Resistance to Statistical Attack

The correlation analysis says that a good encryption technique must break the correlation among the adjacent image pixels. We randomly select 2000 pairs (horizontal, vertical and diagonal) of adjacent pixels from the original image and the encrypted image. Fig. 4(a), (b) show the correlation of two adjacent pixels in the original *lena* image and its encrypted image. Fig. 4(b) shows that the correlations of adjacent pixels in the encrypted image are greatly reduced.

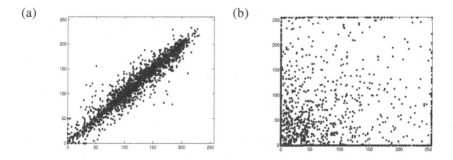

Fig. 4. Correlation of two adjacent pixels

4.5   Discussion of the Encryption Process

We knew that the permutation process only enhances the unintelligibility of the encrypted image. Therefore, if confidentiality is in high demand, the proposed method with diffusion can be applied. On the other hand, even if the chaotic map used in GF is cracked, the hacker still cannot decrypt the image since the random matrix key of diffusion in SVD encryption process remains secret.

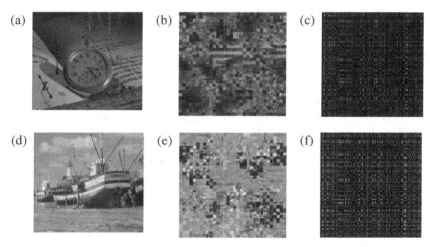

Fig. 5. Evaluation of the encryption process. (a) and (d), original images, (b) and (e), 4 × 4 blocks in the 2-level LL subband permutation via GF, (c) and (f) image encryption with permutation on 2-level LL subband via GF and diffusion using SVD distortion.

5   Conclusion

The traditional JFE methods don't consider the relationship between users, therefore then cannot be applied to secure media sharing for social network because of the tremendous scale of social network. In this paper, the first JFE method based on CA and SVD in the DWT transform domain for social network to deal with the issues of media sharing and traitor tracing is proposed. The proposed JFE method offers one main contribution: a discussion of how to use social network analysis, CA and SVD to realize secure content sharing in social networks.

The experiment results and algorithm analyses show that the new algorithm possesses a large key space and can resist brute-force, and statistical attacks. Our methods does not require a great deal of computation time in comparison with full encryption because the proposed algorithm only encrypts the important data in DWT domain. Therefore, the encryption efficiency is desirable, our algorithm is meant to be a good candidate to ensure the security of multimedia distribution. The fundamental goal of our research has been to provide a useful synthesis of social network analysis for the field of secure multimedia distribution for social network. The limitation of the proposed method is dynamical property of social network. For the future work, we will analyze the security of this JFE scheme theoretically according to the change of social network.

Acknowledgment. This work is supported by NSF of China Grants 61272409, 60873226, 60803112 , National 863 Hi-Tech Grant 2009AA01Z411, the Fundamental Research Funds for the Central Universities and Wuhan Youth Science and Technology Chenguang Program, Natural Science Foundation of Hubei Province of China (No.2011CDC029), Key project in Hubei Provincial Department of Education (No.D20122606).

References

1. Lian, S., Chen, X.: Secure and traceable multimedia distribution for convergent Mobile TV services. Computer Communications 33, 1664–1673 (2010)
2. Cheng, H., Li, X.: Partial encryption of compressed images and videos. IEEE Transactions on Signal Processing 48, 2439–2451 (2000)
3. Kundur, D., Karthik, K.: Video fingerprinting and encryption principles for digital rights management. Proceedings of the IEEE 92, 918–932 (2004)
4. Chen, J., Zhou, J., Wong, K.W.: A modified chaos-based joint compression and encryption scheme. IEEE Transactions on Circuits and Systems II: Express Briefs 58, 110–114 (2011)
5. Kanso, A., Smaoui, N.: Logistic chaotic maps for binary numbers generations. Chaos, Solitons & Fractals 40, 2557–2568 (2009)
6. Cox, I.J., Kilian, J., Leighton, F.T., Shamoon, T.: Secure spread spectrum watermarking for multimedia. IEEE Transactions on Image Processing 6, 1673–1687 (1997)
7. Zhao, H.V., Liu, K.J.R.: Fingerprint multicast in secure video streaming. IEEE Transactions on Image Processing 15, 12–29 (2006)
8. Bouslimi, D., Coatrieux, G., Roux, C.: A joint encryption/watermarking algorithm for verifying the reliability of medical images: Application to echographic images. Computer Methods and Programs in Biomedicine 106, 47–54 (2012)
9. Memon, N., Wong, P.W.: A buyer-seller watermarking protocol. IEEE Transactions on Image Processing 10, 643–649 (2001)
10. Wagner, N.R.: Mathematical Sciences Department Philadelphia, Pennsylvania 19104 (1983)

11. Dittmann, J., Schmitt, P., Saar, E., Ueberberg, J.: Combining digital watermarks and collusion secure fingerprints for digital images. J. Electron. Imaging 9, 456–467 (2000)
12. Trappe, W., Wu, M., Wang, Z.J., Liu, K.J.R.: Anti-collusion fingerprinting for multimedia. IEEE Transactions on Signal Processing 51, 1069–1087 (2003)
13. Thomas, T., Emmanuel, S., Subramanyam, A., Kankanhalli, M.S.: Joint watermarking scheme for multiparty multilevel DRM architecture. IEEE Transactions on Information Forensics and Security 4, 758–767 (2009)
14. Lin, C.Y., Prangjarote, P., Kang, L.W., Huang, W.L., Chen, T.H.: Joint fingerprinting and decryption with noise-resistant for vector quantization images. Signal Processing (2012)
15. Adelsbach, A., Huber, U., Sadeghi, A.R.: Fingercasting–Joint Fingerprinting and Decryption of Broadcast Messages. Transactions on Data Hiding and Multimedia Security II, 1–34 (2007)
16. Hou, S., Uehara, T., Satoh, T., Morimura, Y., Minoh, M.: Integrating fingerprint with cryptosystem for internet-based live pay-TV system. Security and Communication Networks 1, 461–472 (2008)
17. Huang, H.C., Chen, Y.H.: Genetic fingerprinting for copyright protection of multicast media. Soft Computing-A Fusion of Foundations, Methodologies and Applications 13, 383–391 (2009)
18. Lian, S., Wang, Z.: Collusion-traceable secure multimedia distribution based on controllable modulation. IEEE Transactions on Circuits and Systems for Video Technology 18, 1462–1467 (2008)
19. Lian, S., Chen, X.: Traceable content protection based on chaos and neural networks. Applied Soft Computing 11, 4293–4301 (2011)
20. Wolfram, S., Gad-el-Hak, M.: A new kind of science. Applied Mechanics Reviews 56, B18 (2003)
21. Golub, G.H., Van Loan, C.F.: Matrix computations. Johns Hopkins Univ. Pr. (1996)
22. Cheng, G., Ling, H., Zou, F., Li, P.: An improved QIM based anti-collusion fingerprinting scheme. In: 2010 IEEE 10th International Conference on Signal Processing (ICSP), pp. 1865–1868. IEEE Press (2010)
23. Khan, M.K., Zhang, J., Alghathbar, K.: Challenge-response-based biometric image scrambling for secure personal identification. Future Generation Computer Systems 27, 411–418 (2011)

A Robust Image Classification Scheme with Sparse Coding and Multiple Kernel Learning

Dongyang Cheng[1], Tanfeng Sun[1,2,3], and Xinghao Jiang[1,2,*]

[1] School of Information Security Engineering Shanghai Jiao Tong University,
Shanghai 200240, China
{dycheng,tfsun,xhjiang}@sjtu.edu.cn
[2] National Engineering Lab on Information Content Analysis Techniques, GT036001,
Shanghai 200240, China
[3] Department of Electrical and Computer Engineering, New Jersey Institute of Technology,
Newark 07102, USA

Abstract. In recent researches, image classification of objects and scenes has attracted much attention, but the accuracy of some schemes may drop when dealing with complicated datasets. In this paper, we propose an image classification scheme based on image sparse representation and multiple kernel learning (MKL) for the sake of better classification performance. As the fundamental part of our scheme, sparse coding method is adopted to generate precise representation of images. Besides, feature fusion is utilized and a new MKL method is proposed to fit the multi-feature case. Experiments demonstrate that our scheme remarkably improves the classification accuracy, leading to state-of-art performance on several benchmarks, including some rather complicated datasets such as Caltech-101 and Caltech-256.

Keywords: Sparse coding, MKL, Feature fusion.

1 Introduction

Nowadays, image classification has captured a lot of interest in computer vision. The common classification schemes mainly consist of two parts: image representation and classification.

With regard to image representation models, Bag of Words (BoW) model with following three modules has been widely used and shows good performance: (i) Region selection and representation; (ii) Codebook generation and feature quantization; (iii) Frequency histogram based image representation. Specifically, the codebook consisting of entries of visual words is used to reconstruct the input local features. The process to generate the codebook and quantize features governs the quality of image representation. But the frequently used k-means method may lead to severe information loss since it assigns each feature to only one visual word in the codebook.

---

* Corresponding author.

Y.Q. Shi, H.J. Kim, and F. Pérez-González (Eds.): IWDW 2012, LNCS 7809, pp. 520–529, 2013.
© Springer-Verlag Berlin Heidelberg 2013

After the image is represented as a histogram of visual words, a classifier will be required to make the decision that which category the histogram belongs to. Kernel based classifiers such as support vector machine (SVM) are now widely used by many researchers for their wonderful performance. For SVM, the input histograms are mapped to a higher dimensional space by kernel function, in which they can be easily classified in a linear way. However, the sensitiveness of kernel function to categories will increase the fluctuation in accuracy, resulting in a relatively unsatisfying overall performance.

Many works have been done to improve the classification performance. Yang *et al.* [1] applied sparse coding instead of k-means since it can learn the optimal codebook and reduce the information loss. Zhang *et al.* [2] proposed a framework by leveraging an improved sparse coding method, low-rank and sparse matrix decomposition techniques. Linear SVM classifier is used for classification. Gao *et al.* [3] proposed a robust Laplacian sparse coding algorithm for feature quantization which generated more discriminative sparse codes. Naveen *et al.* [4] presented a new framework which was built upon a way of feature extraction that generates largely affine-invariant features and an AdaBoost based classifier. From the perspective of classifier, multiple kernel learning (MKL) can increase the stability of overall performance by learning a linear combination of a series of kernel functions. Bosch *et al.* [5] combined different features by using a weighted linear combination of kernels, where the weights were learnt on a validation set. Lampert *et al.* [6] proposed a method to combine the efficiency of single class localization with a subsequent decision process that worked jointly for all given object classes.

In this paper, we devise a novel image classification scheme by adopting sparse coding and multi-feature MKL, which can ameliorate the image representation and classification phase respectively. The improved multi-feature MKL is proposed based on original MKL, in order to adapt to multi-feature case. Specifically, SIFT and SURF descriptors are extracted and then converted into sparse vectors precisely by the trained dictionaries. The images can be represented by these vectors using max-pooling method which is proved to be more robust than others. After that, the two descriptors are combined into a single vector. Finally, multi-feature MKL approach is implemented to train and test those histograms, generating stable results due to the auto adjustment of the linear combination of kernel functions for each feature.

2   Proposed Scheme

As two main parts in image classification scheme, image representation and classification can substantially affect the classification performance. On one hand, a good kernel method for classification is necessary, for it provides an intuitive and principled tool for learning from high-dimensional vectors that represent images. On the other hand, the performance of kernel method strongly depends on the data representation of images, which means an accurate image representation algorithm is indispensable. Our paper is to enhance the image classification accuracy through the amelioration of both parts.

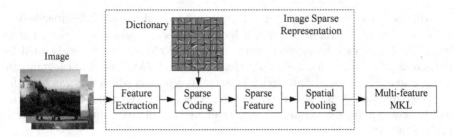

Fig. 1. Framework of proposed scheme (ScMMKL)

Fig. 1 is the framework of the proposed scheme which mainly consists of sparse coding and multi-feature MKL (ScMMKL). The extended multi-feature MKL is defined theoretically for feature fusion method.

The process of our algorithm is as follows:

1. 128-dimentional D-SIFT and 64-dimensional D-SURF descriptors are extracted from the images.

2. Dictionaries are learned based on those features using sparse coding method. This step is of most importance in image sparse representation phase because a better dictionary yields more accurate image representation.

3. Each feature point is denoted as a sparse vector based on the dictionaries trained previously.

4. Represent the image as a single vector using spatial pooling method. Thus an image can be represented as a 128-dimensional (SIFT) or 64-dimentional (SURF) vector after the pooling. Then the two vectors are combined together.

5. The last step of our algorithm is the multi-feature MKL. Kernel combinations are determined for each feature and the final decision can be generated.

2.1   Implementation of Sparse Representation

Comparing with k-means, sparse coding method represents images more precisely, for it describes each feature as a linear combination of basic vectors with minor

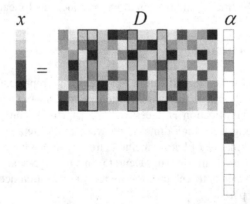

Fig. 2. Visually explanation of sparse representation

quantization loss. Besides, the high dimensional space used to represent features can lead to an easier classification. Fig. 2 is the visually explanation of this procedure.

There are two main steps to apply sparse coding to image representation: dictionary learning and sparse representation. These two steps are similar to codebook generation and vector quantization in traditional BoW model using k-means.

In the phase of dictionary learning, a small set of images should be selected from the whole image dataset randomly. For each image, D-SIFT and D-SURF features are extracted. Then the set of SIFT or SURF descriptors $X = [x_1, x_2, ..., x_k]$ is used to optimize an empirical cost function to train the dictionary:

$$f_k(D) = \frac{1}{k} \sum_{i=1}^{k} \ell(x_i, D)$$

(1)

Where $D \in \mathbb{R}^{m \times n}$ is a dictionary and $\ell(x, D)$ is a loss function of which smaller values yield better dictionaries. The loss function can be defined as the optimal value of the ℓ_1 sparse coding problem:

$$\ell(x, D) = \min_{\alpha \in \mathbb{R}^n} \frac{1}{2} \|x - D\alpha\|_2^2 + \lambda \|\alpha\|_1$$

(2)

Where λ is a regularization parameter. Here, we base our algorithm on [7] which is one of the most efficient dictionary learning algorithms.

Given the trained dictionary, the image can be denoted by the pooling of all descriptors which are sparsely represented. In detail, every descriptor can be represented as a sparse vector using:

$$x_i \approx D\alpha_i$$

(3)

Where $D \in \mathbb{R}^{m \times n}$ is the dictionary, and $\alpha_i \in \mathbb{R}^n$ is the sparse representation of descriptor x_i. Least Angle Regression (LARS) algorithm [8] is used to solve this problem.

In order to represent an image with a single vector P, a pooling method needs to be applied. Among the commonly used pooling methods such as average pooling, max pooling and square root pooling, the max pooling procedure is well established by biophysical evidence in visual cortex [9] and is empirically justified by many algorithms applied to image categorization. So in our case, we also use max pooling denoted as follows:

$$p_j = \max\{| \alpha_{1j} |, | \alpha_{2j} |, ..., | \alpha_{kj} |\}$$

(4)

Where p_j is the j-th element in vector P and α_{ij} is the j-th element in the i-th descriptor α_i. Thus, vector P is the sparse representation of the image.

2.2   Multi-feature MKL

As a typical kernel method, the performance of SVM is sensitive to feature type and kernel parameters, while MKL could generate the optimal result through combination of different kernels. In our scheme, two features are involved and a new MKL method (multi-feature MKL) should be developed to achieve multi-feature classification.

For the original MKL, the objective is to optimize jointly over a linear combination of kernels:

$$k^* = \sum_{m=1}^{F} \beta_m k_m(x,x') \tag{5}$$

Where F is the number of kernels and $\beta_m > 0$, $\sum_{m=1}^{F} \beta_m = 1$. The objective function can be denoted as follows [10]:

$$\min_{\alpha,\beta,b} \left(\frac{1}{2} \sum_{m=1}^{F} \beta_m \alpha^T K_m \alpha + C \sum_{i=1}^{N} L(y_i, b + \sum_{m=1}^{F} \beta_m K_m(x)^T \alpha) \right) \tag{6}$$

Where $L(y,t) = \max(0, 1 - yt)$ denotes the Hinge loss, C is the misclassification penalty, parameters $\alpha \in R^N$ and $b \in R$ are of an SVM. The decision function is like this:

$$F_{MKL}(x) = \text{sign}\left(\sum_{m=1}^{F} \beta_m (K_m(x)^T \alpha + b) \right) \tag{7}$$

Where $K_m(x)$ is the kernel response of the m-th kernel for a given sample x and $K_m(x)^T$ is the transposition of the vector $K_m(x)$.

However, the original MKL could only be used in single feature classification. For our scheme, different kernel combinations will be learned for each feature and:

$$k_{MF} = \sum_{i=1}^{n} c_i k_i^* \tag{8}$$

Where k_{MF} is the kernel combination for multiple features, n is the number of features, c_i is the coefficient for each kernel combination and k_i^* is the kernel combination for feature i. The multi-feature MKL function can be defined based on (5):

$$k_{MF} = \sum_{i=1}^{n} \left(c_i \sum_{j=1}^{m_i} \beta_{ij} k_{ij}(x_i, x_i') \right) \tag{9}$$

Where m_i is the number of kernels combined for feature i, k_{ij} is the j-th kernel in feature i and β_{ij} is the coefficient for k_{ij}. In order to obtain the best performance, we need to consider the weight of both features and kernels. So the constraint for kernel coefficients should be changed to $\sum_{i=1}^{n} c_i \sum_{j=1}^{m_i} \beta_{ij} = 1$. Take (9) into (7) and we can get the final MKL decision function for our algorithm:

$$F_{MKL} = \text{sign}\left(\sum_{i=1}^{n} c_i \left(\sum_{j=1}^{m_i} \left(\beta_{ij} (K_{ij}(x_i)^T \alpha + b) \right) \right) \right) \tag{10}$$

Through the above definition, this extended multi-feature MKL can be directly used for any multi-feature problem.

3   Experimental Result

3.1   Experimental Setup

We evaluate the proposed approach ScMMKL on three public dataset: Scene-15, Caltech-101 and Caltech-256. In the phase of sparse coding, the dictionaries trained for SIFT and SURF are $R^{128 \times 500}$ and $R^{64 \times 300}$ respectively. The outputs of sparse coding are a series of sparse codes, each representing one image.

For multi-feature MKL, we base our algorithm on SimpleMKL [10] and extended original MKL to a multi-feature one. Certain parts of sparse codes are combined with labels (1 for positive and -1 for negative) to generate the training matrix and some other sparse codes without labels are used for testing. For detailed parameters, ref. [11] proposed that high values of C in (6) turned out to work better and C = 100 is found to perform the best in our case. Moreover, some iteration processes with corresponding stop criterion should be utilized to gain optimal parameters. Through experiments with small sample size, the duality gap with parameter of 0.01 is more suitable for our scheme.

3.2   Kernel Selection Experiment

The following experiment is designed to determine which kernel combination works best for our scheme. As Gaussian and polynomial kernels are most commonly used, seven kernel combinations are taken into consideration: 3P, 5G, 10G, 5G+1P, 5G+2P, 5G+3P and 10G+3P, where G and P denote Gaussian and polynomial kernel respectively.

Fig. 3 shows the result for SIFT and SURF features on Scene-15 and Caltech-101. It can be seen that after eliminating polynomial kernels, the accuracy becomes slightly better for Scene-15, while the performance for Caltach-101 is extremely poor. Take SIFT feature for instance, the results for Scene-15 and Caltech-101 are 88.1% and

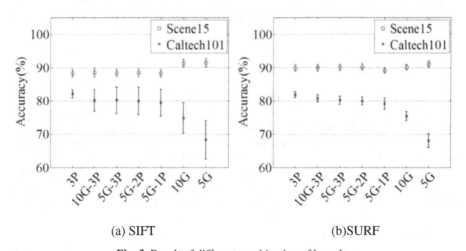

(a) SIFT   (b)SURF

Fig. 3. Result of different combination of kernels

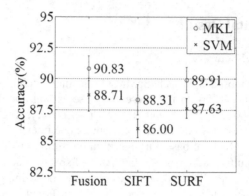

Fig. 4. Classification accuracy on Scene-15 dataset

Mountain (98.2%)   Forest (97.6%)

Industrial (78.4%)   Highway (73.8%)

Fig. 5. Sample images in Scene-15 dataset

82.1% using 3 polynomial kernels. With only Gaussian kernels, though the accuracy rises up to 91.5% for Scene-15, the data for Caltech-101 are unacceptable with 68.3% accuracy and 5.75% standard deviation. This happens to SURF feature as well. In consideration of stronger practicability, the combination of 3 polynomial kernels is selected for both features.

3.3   Scene-15 Dataset

The Scene-15 dataset has 4,485 images in 15 categories. Experimental process is repeated for 10 times with randomly selecting training and testing images to obtain reliable results. Each category is treated as the test database in turn, and one versus rest scheme is employed. According to common practice, both of the chosen training set and testing set include 100 images. The final results are reported by the mean and standard deviation of classification rates per category which are recorded in each run.

Fig. 4 is the result of single vs. multi feature and SVM vs. MKL comparison on Scene-15. It's obvious that feature fusion and multi-feature MKL are better design choices.

Fig. 5 shows some sample images from classes with highest and lowest classification accuracies in Scene-15 dataset. Our scheme performs better for categories like mountain and coast because the meaningful part takes a large percentage of the whole image, while the complicated background objects in industrial and highway may lead to misjudgments.

Table 1 gives the performance comparison of our approach and some other methods proposed in [1] [2] [3] [12]. The first 3 algorithms are based on sparse coding and SVM with the same experimental parameters comparing with ours. Ref. [12] is an improved BoW model using k-means and SVM.

As can be seen from the table, our scheme with sparse coding and multi-feature MKL generates a satisfying performance in image classification. The ascendency of sparse coding to k-means is apparent comparing with [12], because it can represent images more precisely with less quantization loss. Besides, our scheme outperforms [1] by 10% due to the superiority of multi-feature MKL with combinations of kernels. Though the accuracies in [2] [3] are fairly high, our scheme still achieves 1% improvement.

Table 1. Comparison on Scene-15 dataset

Method	Accuracy
ScSPM[1]	80.28±0.93
LScSPM[3]	89.75±0.50
LR-Sc+SPM[2]	90.03±0.70
Improved BoW[12]	79.0
ScMMKL	**90.83±1.01**

3.4   Caltech-101 Dataset

The Caltech-101 dataset contains 102 classes with high intra-class appearance and shape variability. In this dataset, we randomly choose 15/30 images per category for training, another 15 and up to 30 images for testing.

Table 2 gives the performance comparison of the method proposed in this paper and some other literatures [1] [2] [4]. [4] adopted an improved sparse coding method and an AdaBoost based classifier. As is shown in the table, our scheme outperforms the LR-Sc+SPM [2] by more than 11.5% for 15 training and 10% for 30 training. The superiority over [1] and [2] is reasonable because the accuracies in [1] and [2] fluctuate due to the large volume of categories in Caltech-101 and the sensitiveness of single kernel function to categories, while the kernel combination in MKL can stabilize the performance since it can adjust the weight of each kernel automatically to gain the optimal result. Our scheme also achieves a 3%-4% improvement compared with [4] whose classifier performs better than SVM.

Table 2. Comparison on Caltech-101 dataset

Method	15 training	30 training
ScSPM[1]	67.00±0.45	73.20±0.54
LR-Sc+SPM[2]	69.58±0.97	75.68±0.89
Naveen *et al.*[4]	78.38	83.28
ScMMKL	**82.93±1.42**	**86.32±0.88**

3.5   Caltech-256 Dataset

The Caltech-256 dataset has 29,780 images of 257 classes. The intra-class variance including object location is much bigger than Caltech 101 and makes it a very challenging dataset so far for object recognition. The image number for training and testing are set to 15, 30 and 45 as usual practice, and the experiment is repeated for 5 times under each allocation.

Table 3 gives the comparison results with [1] [2] [3] [4]. Significant improvement with 30%-40% gap can be seen from the table. With more categories in this complicated dataset, the ascendency of MKL with strong adaptability is more pronounced.

There is another reason for this advantage compared with [1] [2] [3] which use SPM kernel. It's notable that the linear SPM kernel takes spatial information into consideration, but the high intra class variability and object location variability in Caltech-256 result in the totally different backgrounds of objects. The image is divided into several patches by SPM, but some patches may have no correlation with target objects. Therefore, the consideration of background by SPM kernel may lead to misclassification and drag final accuracy down.

It's noteworthy that as the category number increases, the performance of our approach has a small fluctuation, providing a scheme with strong stability and practicability.

Table 3. Comparison on Caltech-256 dataset

Method	15 training	30 training	45 training
ScSPM[1]	27.73±0.51	34.02±0.35	37.46±0.55
LScSPM[3]	30.00±0.14	35.74±0.10	38.54±0.36
LR-Sc+SPM[2]	35.31±0.70	N/A	N/A
Naveen *et al.*[4]	39.42	45.83	49.3
ScMMKL	**71.47±1.32**	**74.44±0.63**	**78.26±0.76**

4   Conclusion

In this paper, we proposed an image classification scheme with sparse coding and multi-feature MKL techniques, which improves the image representation and classification phases simultaneously. Furthermore, feature fusion scheme is used and the original MKL is redefined to adapt to multiple feature case, providing theoretical and experimental support to the extension of MKL. Experimental result shows that ScMMKL has a state-of-art performance on several public datasets with strong adaptability and stability.

Acknowledgment. The work of this paper is sponsored by the National Natural Science Foundation of China (No. 61071153, No. 61272249), the National New Century Excellent Talents Support Plan of Ministry of Education, China (No. NECT-10-0569). It is also under the Project of International Cooperation and Exchanges supported by Shanghai Committee of Science and Technology (No. 12510708500).

References

1. Yang, J., Yu, K., Gong, Y., Huang, T.: Linear spatial pyramid matching using sparse coding for image classification. In: CVPR, pp. 1794–1801. IEEE, Miami Beach (2009)
2. Zhang, C., Liu, J., Tian, Q.: Image classification by non-negative sparse coding, low-rank and sparse decomposition. In: CVPR, pp. 1673–1680. IEEE, Colorado Springs (2011)
3. Gao, S., Tsang, I., Chia, L., Zhao, P.: Local features are not lonely-Laplacian sparse coding for image classification. In: CVPR, pp. 3555–3561. IEEE, San Francisco (2010)
4. Naveen, K., Li, B.: Discriminative Affine Sparse Codes for Image Classification. In: CVPR, pp. 1609–1616. IEEE, Colorado Springs (2011)
5. Bosch, A., Zisserman, A., Munoz, X.: Image classification using rois and multiple kernel learning. Intl. J. Computer Vision (2008)
6. Lampert, C., Blaschko, M.: A multiple kernel learning approach to joint multi-class object detection. In: Proceedings of the 30th DAGM Symposium on Pattern Recognition, pp. 31–40 (2008)
7. Mairal, J., Bach, F., Ponce, J., Sapiro, G.: Online Learning for Matrix Factorization and Sparse Coding. Journal of Machine Learning Research 11, 19–60 (2010)
8. Efron, B., Hastie, T., Johnstone, I., Tibshirani, R.: Least angle regression. Annals of Statistics 32(2), 407–499 (2004)
9. Serre, T., Wolf, L., Poggio, T.: Object recognition with features inspired by visual cortex. In: CVPR, pp. 994–1000. IEEE, San Diego (2005)
10. Rakotomamonjy, A., Bach, F., Canu, S., Grandvalet, Y.: More efficiency in multiple kernel learning. In: ICML, pp. 775–782. ACM, Corvalis (2007)
11. Gehler, P.V., Nowozin, S.: On feature combination for multiclass object classification. In: ICCV, pp. 221–228. IEEE, Kyoto (2009)
12. Hao, J., Jie, X.: Improved Bags-of-Words Algorithm for Scene Recognition. In: ICSPS, pp. 279–282. IEEE, Dalian (2010)

Author Index